THE ACADIAN REFUGEES IN FRANCE

1758-1785

Jean-François Mouhot

Translated by Russell Desmond

THE ACADIAN REFUGEES IN FRANCE

1758-1785

The Impossible Reintegration?

2018
University of Louisiana at Lafayette Press

© 2018 by University of Louisiana at Lafayette Press
All rights reserved
ISBN 13 (paper): 978-1-935754-75-6

http://ulpress.org
University of Louisiana at Lafayette Press
P.O. Box 43558
Lafayette, LA 70504-3558

Printed on acid-free paper in the United States
Library of Congress Cataloging-in-Publication Data

Names: Mouhot, Jean-François, author. | Desmond, Russell, translator.
Title: The Acadian refugees in France 1758-1785 / Jean-François Mouhot ;
 translated by Russell Desmond.
Other titles: Réfugiés Acadiens en France 1758-1785. English
Description: English edition. | Lafayette, LA : University of Louisiana at
 Lafayette Press, 2017. | Includes bibliographical references and index.
Identifiers: LCCN 2017004061 | ISBN 9781935754756 (alk. paper)
Subjects: LCSH: Acadians--France--History--18th century. |
 Acadians--Relocation--History--18th century.
Classification: LCC F1038 .M87813 2017 | DDC 944/.034--dc23
LC record available at https://lccn.loc.gov/2017004061

To Claire, Anna, Paul, and Hugo

There are in today's world an increasing number of refugees of a kind unknown to the contemporaries of the Grand Dérangement. Refugees chased not directly by the hand of man but by the scarcity of food, by hurricanes, the erosion of the soil, drought, the rising level of the oceans, or floods. According to some estimates, these environmental or climate refugees are now totaling nearly twenty-five million worldwide, more than the number of traditional refugees. During the course of the twenty-first century this figure may be multiplied ten times over.

The refugees whose story is told in the following pages were able to maintain, during the course of their tribulations, the hope of returning one day to their beloved Acadia, and a certain number of them actually were able to make it back to Nova Scotia. Some descendants of these Acadians are today living in territory in the delta of the Mississippi at the mercy of rising waters and hurricanes. Many suffered a cruel experience in 2005 thanks to hurricanes Katrina and Rita. Like the inhabitants of the Netherlands, the Maldives, or Bangladesh, whose territories are also threatened by flooding, the Cajuns will not even be able to maintain the hope of returning to their lands if they are swallowed by the ocean; they will have to return to the path of exile.

It is not too late to prevent such an exile. The causes of climate change are well established. The remedy is as well: lowering the consumption of fossil fuels. Let the history of the Acadians serve to remind us of the sorrows of exile. Let the knowledge of the past help us to act in the present, and for the future.

Table of Contents

Maps, Figures, and Tables IX

Abbreviations XI

Acknowledgments XIII

Preface To The English Edition XV

Preamble XIX

Introduction 1

Part One
To Assemble or Disperse?
The Plans for Settlement

Chapter I
"An Attachment Bordering on Fanaticism for France":
Causes for the Arrival in France 23

Chapter II
The French Administration And The Acadian Groups 31

Chapter III
The Plans for Settlement:
to populate the Empire (c. 1760-c. 1765) 43

Chapter IV
The Plans For Settlement:
Clearing Land In France (1763-1772) 57

Chapter V
The Plans For Settlement:
Establishing The Acadians In France (1772-1785) 67

Part Two
The Subsidies And Economic Problems

Chapter VI
The Subsidies: Spoiled Children of the Ancien Régime? 87

Chapter VII
Details Of The Assistance 101

Chapter VIII
"Work, Take The Trouble"..115

Chapter IX
A Sufficient Supplement:
A Factor In The Integration?...135

Chapter X
Impressions Of The Acadians:
The View Of The Administrators..153

Chapter XI
A Group Apart?..169

Chapter XII
The Opinion of the Popular Classes and Matrimonial Intermingling.......185

Epilogue and Conclusion..203

Appendices

Glossary..227

Biographical References..233

Map of Correspondence Between Acadians..239

Bibliography and Sources...241

Endnotes..255

Index...349

Maps, Figures, and Tables

Map 1
Acadia after the Treaty of Utrecht (1713). From *L'Acadie par les cartes* (http://www2.umoncton.ca/cfdocs/cea/documts/c/vhtml/htm.cm?cle=c0015)

Map 2
Acadia or Nova Scotia in 1755. From *L'Acadie par les cartes*

Figure 1
Outline of the administration responsible for the Acadians before 1773

Figure 2
Outline of the administration responsible for the Acadians (Saint-Malo region)

Map 3
Places of residence of the Acadians in the Saint-Malo region from 1758 to 1785

Figure 3
Evolution of the number of Acadian and mixed marriages at Cherbourg

Table 1
Professions claimed by the Acadians at the time of the embarkation for Louisiana or on "L'État des Acadiens qui restent en France" (1785)

Table 2
Trades claimed by the Acadians to the priests coinciding with a family event in the Nantes region, between 1775 and 1785

Table 3
Acadians implicated in cases of tobacco fraud in the Saint-Malo region (1766-1768)

Figure 4
Number of documents in which at least one mention of the phrase "national body" or the term "nation" occurs designating the Acadians

Figure 5
Frequency of use of the terms "nation" or "national body" in the documents transcribed in the data base

Figure 6
Cumulative proportion of documents using the word "nation" to designate the Acadians (percentage of documents) excluding baptism, marriage, and burial acts

FIGURE 7
Analysis of geographic distribution of marriage acts

TABLE 4
Estimates of the rates of endogamous and exogamous marriages in the Acadian population in France between 1758-1785 and differences by gender

FIGURE 8
Distribution of marriages between Acadians and mixed marriages.

FIGURE 9
Number of marriage acts in which at least one of the parties is Acadian (Cherbourg, Le Havre, Saint-Malo, and Nantes)

FIGURE 10
Chronological evolution of the number of endogamous or mixed marriages at Le Havre, Cherbourg, Saint-Malo, and Nantes

FIGURE 11
Proportion of Acadian marriages within the total and average curve

FIGURE 12
Marriages in the Saint-Malo region

FIGURE 13
Marriages in Nantes

FIGURE 14
Distribution of Acadian and mixed marriages (types A and B) according to place of residence

MAP 4
Correspondence between Acadians during the period of exile (1757-1785)

Abbreviations

Note: All of the internet sites were verified in August 2012. On some rare occasions, for more extensive information, we refer the reader to the integral text of the thesis from which this work originated, as well as to the appendices (volume II) of the same thesis, available in Acrobat Reader/PDF version on the internet sites: www.septentrion.qc.ca/acadiens and http://jfmouhot.free.fr.

- 1773-04-271: reference date referring to the documentary database (www.septentrion.qc.ca/acadiens). See note 19, p. *257* as well as the presentation of the database on the site.
- AD: Archives départementales; AD Ile-et-Vil.: Archives départmentales d'Ille-et-Vilaine
- AGI: Archivo General de Indias (Seville, Spain)
- AHN: Archivo Historico Nacional (Madrid, Spain)
- AN: Archives Nationals de France; ANC: of Canada; AN Col.: Colonies (Aix-en-Provence)
- Arch.: Archives
- BM: Bibliothèque nationale
- CEA: Centre d'études acadiennes
- Comm.: commissaire
- *Dict. Acad.: Dictionnaire de l'Académie française, 1762*
- *Dictionnaire biographique du Canada*, 14 vols., available at http://www.biographi.ca
- Dép.: depot
- Fo: folio(s)
- Li.: liasse (folder)
- MAE: Ministry of Foreign Affairs
- Martin: Ernest Martin, *Les Exilés acadiens en France*, 1936
- Mem. & doc.: Memoirs and documents (MAE), Paris
- Mi.: microfilms
- Ms.: manuscript
- Orig.: original(s)
- PPC: Papeles Procedentes de Cuba (Archivo General de Indias)
- PF: Sacred Congregation "de Propaganda Fide" or of the Propaganda (Vatican)
- *RAPC: Rapport sur les archives canadiennes (RAPC 1905-1 = year 1905, volume 1)*
- Pol. Corresp.: Political correspondence (in the MAE)
- Reg.: register(s)
- Roy, *Rapport*: Jean-Edmond Roy, *Rapport sur les archives de France relatives à l'histoire du Canada*, Ottawa, 1911
- S.: *sous*
- SEM: Secretary of State for the Navy (Sécrétaire d'État à la Marine)
- SHM: Historical Service of the Navy (Marine)
- Sup.: supplement
- Transc.: transcriptions
- *Trévoux: Dictionnaire universel français et latin vulgairement appelé dictionnaire de Trévoux*, Trévoux, 1771

Acknowledgments

VERY MANY PEOPLE HELPED ME during the course of my research. I would first of all like to thank my thesis director, Laurence Fontaine, as well as the members of the jury who examined my doctorate, Sylvie Dépatie, Anthony Molho, and Daniel Roche, who honored me by accepting to read the manuscript that served as the origin of this book.

Many researchers agreed to complete research that I was unable to conduct myself. I would particularly like to thank Gérard-Marc Braud for his constant availability and for the data that he willingly shared with me allowing me to calculate the ratios of the Acadian marriages. My gratitude also goes to Alain Roman, historian of Saint-Malo, for complementary research in the municipal archives of his city. With constant kindness and enthusiasm, Jean-René Lassonde, conservator of the Division of Monographies in the *Bibliothèque nationale* of Québec, provided especially valuable support and facilitated my access to various documents that I had been unable to procure elsewhere. Ronnie-Gilles LeBlanc, formerly responsible for the archives of the *Centre d'études acadiennes* (CEA) of the University of Moncton, also kindly supported me (even if he did not always agree with me) in much of my research and allowed me to benefit from his vast knowledge of the sources of the CEA and the history of Acadia. A great thanks goes also to John Johnston, historian at Canada Parks, for the various articles he sent me and for his frequent advice. Naomi Griffiths also guided me many times at the start of my research and generously sent me a great number of articles and books. Yves Landry, director of the *Programme de recherché sur l'émigration des Français en Nouvelle-France* (PREFEN), and Robert Larin, author of a thesis on a connected theme, advised me and supported me in my study of the Canadians in France. Michèle Godret generously sent me photocopies of all of the files of dispensations of consanguinity she discovered in the diocesan archives of Coutances. Damien Rouet gladly answered my questions, and Jacques Nerrou sent me many facts concerning Rochefort and La Rochelle. Finally, my brother allowed me to benefit from his computer expertise and oversaw placing the documentary database online; my mother and Maurice Gueneau read a large part of this work. I thank them all. *Last but certainly not least*, my wife Claire read, commented on, and improved every part of this work and supported me through the duration of the many years of research. Without her constant support, her patience, and the sacrifice of her time, this book would not exist.

I also benefited from the friendship and advice of the following people (alphabetically): Bernard Allaire; Gérard Ardon-Boudreau, chairman of the association *Les cousins du Poitou*; Pauline Arsenault, conservator of patrimony in the departmental archives of Charente-Maritime; Maurice Basque, director of Acadian studies at the University of Moncton (and, more generally, all of the staff there); Hélène de Bellaigue, conservator of patrimonial sources for the municipal library of Bordeaux; Gérard Bouchard, professor at the University of Québec at Chicoutimi; Pierre Boulle, professor emeritus at McGill University; Daniel Brandily; Stéphane Charbonneau and Phaedra Royle; Luca Codignola, professor of Canadian history at the University of Gênes and chairman of the International Association of Acadian Studies; the Abbé Couppey, conservator of the diocesan archives of Coutances; Jean-Pierre Dedieu, director of research at the *Centre national de la recherché scientifique* (CNRS); Denys Delâge, professor at Laval University (Québec); Bernard Desjardins, director of the program of research in historical demography (University of Montréal); Jean-François Dubost, professor at Paris University XII; Daphné Ducharme, Francesca Dello Strologo; Guillaume Eckendorff; Gilles Foucqueron, author of *Saint-Malo, 2000 ans d'histoire*; Marcel Fournier, chairman of the Canadian-French Genealogy Society; Dominique Guillemet, professor at the University of Poitiers (unfortunately now deceased); Bruno Haffreingue; Fernard Harvey, researcher at the *Institut national de la recherché scientifique* (INRS); Tamar Herzog, professor at Stanford University; Christophe Horguelin, doctoral student at the University of Toronto; Ollivier Hubert, professor at the University of Montréal; Bruno Isbled, conservator of patrimony in the departmental archives of Ille-et-Vilaine; Sébastien Jahan, assistant professor at the University of Poitiers; Megan Metters, doctoral student at the *Institut universitaire européen*; Raymonde Litalien, former director of the Service of Documentation of the *Centre culturel canadien de Paris*; André Magord, director of the *Centre d'études acadiennes et québécoises* of the University of Poitiers; Silvia Marzagalli, assistant professor at the University of Bordeaux III; Peter N. Moogk, professor at the University of British Columbia; R. Darrell Meadows; Marguerite Onraet, genealogist of Saint-Servan; Igor Perez Tostado, doctor in history; Hélène and Jean-Claude Trottier; F. R. Perron, vice-president of *Amitiés acadiennes*; Mrs. Reydellet, conservator in the departmental archives of Ille-et-Vilaine; François Roux; Peter Sahlins, professor at the University of California (Berkeley); Gérard Scavennec, chairman of *Racines et Rameaux français d'Acadie*; James Turpin; P. Gérard Vieira, conservator of the General Archives of the Congregation of the Holy Spirit; Patrick Weil, director of research at the CNRS; and Thomas Wien, professor at the University of Montréal. My sincere thanks go to all of these individuals as well as to those whom I may not have mentioned. Many others are also mentioned at various places in the work, having supplied me with information on a relevant subject.

This book could not have come about without a research grant from the *Institut universitaire européen*, from the Vasco de Gama chair of the history of European expansion, and from the French Ministry of Foreign Affairs. I also benefited from the timely support of the *Bibliothèque national du Québec* (a research grant for foreign researchers) and from the *Association internationale des etudes québécois* (a grant for participation in the colloquium of the French Colonial Historical Society in Washington, D.C., in May 2004).

I would like to thank the two anonymous evaluators of the *Aid to Scholarly Publications Program* (now Awards to Scholarly Publications Program) of the Canadian Federation of Human Sciences, for their attentive reading of the manuscript and their numerous suggestions and critiques, as well as Septentrion Editions and, in particular, Denis Vaugeois, founder of the press.

Finally, I would like to thank Michael S. Martin, Director, Center for Louisiana Studies and Director of UL Press, for offering to translate this book and make this American edition happen. Thanks also for the translator, Russell Desmond, for his fine job at translating my prose.

Preface to the English Edition

THE FIRST EDITION OF THIS BOOK (itself a revised version my doctoral thesis presented in 2006 at the Institut Universitaire Européen) appeared in Canada in 2009 published by Septentrion Editions (Québec). As this first edition quickly went out of print and was practically not distributed in France at all, I could only be pleased at the decision of the Presses Universitaires de Rennes to republish it in 2012. I was even more delighted when the UL Press offered to translate the book into English.

Who, then, were these Acadians, whose history is so often unknown outside of some regions of Louisiana and eastern Canada? Readers will find a general presentation of Acadia in the introduction. Here I will limit myself to recalling that Acadia is the name that was given to a region corresponding to the present Nova Scotia, south of the Gulf of Saint Lawrence, in the Maritime Provinces of eastern Canada (see maps on pp. xx and 5)."[1] Acadia, colonized by the French in 1604, became a site of rivalry with the United Kingdom because of its strategic position and the constant conflict between the two European powers. A large part of the territory passed to the English crown in 1713. The Neutral French, so-called for they had promised to remain neutral in case of conflict with France, prospered until 1755. Suspected of not truly abiding by this neutrality, they were deported in that year to the North American colonies—from New England to Georgia—and to France (a portion also fled to what would later become Québec and to Louisiana). For the Acadians, this was the start of lengthy peregrinations. Dispersed along the whole North American Atlantic coast during the course of what has been called the "*Grand Dérangement*" (Great Upheaval), from Canada to Louisiana, but also in France, England, Saint-Domingue (the future Haiti), and even to Guyana, some were assimilated, while others successfully founded communities that maintained a memory of this tragic event.

As this book will show, a portion of the Acadians, particularly a large group that passed in transit to France, managed to go to Louisiana in 1785. There they found other refugees who had reached the former French colony, ceded in the meantime to Spain before it became, following its sale by Napoleon in 1803, a territory of the new United States. These Acadians were the foundation of the community of "*Cadiens*" or "Cajuns." In the course of time, they intermingled with the francophone population already present in Louisiana—as well as with other French exiles, such as refugees from Saint-Domingue. For over 250 years, the now-"Cajun" community has kept a kind of collective memory and continued to speak a French dialect.

At the end of the eighteenth century, other descendants of the Acadians who had been deported in 1755 returned closer to historic Acadia. As a result, today the largest number of descendants of the victims of the *Grand Dérangement* are found in the province of New Brunswick, Canada.[2] There, the Acadians have mostly resisted assimilation, despite the absence of a representative political body (as there is no Canadian province named Acadia).

Today they consist of about a third of the population (as compared to 5 percent in the other maritime provinces of Nova Scotia and Prince Edward Island), or around 250,000 to 300,000 people of a population of 750,000 inhabitants of the province in 2011. In 1884, at the Acadian national convention in Miscouche, the Acadians of the Maritime Provinces of Canada chose as national emblems the French tricolor flag embellished with a star, in homage to Mary, the patron of the Acadians, and the hymn *Ave Maris Stella*, indicating their continued attachment to the Catholic religion. Likewise, the French language, spoken by a majority of the Acadians of New Brunswick, continues to be a major factor of identity for many.

As Benedetto Croce famously wrote, "*All history is contemporary history.*" In other words, any historical analysis avoids the concerns of the moment with difficulty. This is particularly true for understanding the Canadian historical literature on the Acadians. In fact, the francophone Acadians had to battle a double geographic and linguistic isolation: isolation from France, obviously, but also isolation with regard to the francophone nucleus of Québec. While the population of Québec was able to enact laws protecting its culture and language, the Acadians, minorities even in the heart of the province of New Brunswick, had to be content with bilingualism. Franco-Canadian historians—among them Acadian academics—therefore sought to defend their cultural and linguistic identity against the aggressions (perceived, real, willful, or involuntary) of the Anglophone majority of the Maritimes, Canada, and North America.[3] This desire to maintain a sense of Acadian belonging for the francophone minority of New Brunswick is entirely admirable but, in my view, leads some to seek the origin of a mythic Acadian "identity" well beyond what the sources might allow.

So, it is not by chance if the numerous reviews of this book in the media or in specialized journals—until now quite friendly and constructive—have practically all mentioned my remarks on the subject of the Acadian "identity" (whether to praise or criticize).[4] This is not surprising. I expected that my approach, different from that of so many books published on the question, would be debated. It should be noted that the Canadians have a real desire to debate the question of identity that might be surprising in other countries. One of the principal university texts for Canadian studies is called *A Passion for Identity*. Thus, a journalist from Québec, concluding a review of my book, objected, "[a]s the Canadians of the eighteenth century, ancestors of the people of Québec, the Acadians of the same period already had a consciousness of belonging to the New World. France was no longer their country, Europe was no longer their continent. Which history will continually confirm."[5]

However, perhaps because I did not explain it clearly enough, many critics misunderstood that my approach on the question of the Acadian identity preceding the deportation of 1755 was not that of a denialist but, rather, that of an agnostic. What I simply tried to say is that the historical sources do not allow us to definitively establish what the Acadians themselves thought, nor to know if they considered themselves as primarily French, as "Acadians," as a combination of the two, or as something else. A Jean de La Fontaine fable, "*La Chauve-souris et les Deux Belettes* [The Bat and the Two Weasels]" summarizes in an admirable and poetic manner the situation in which the Acadians found themselves. It tells the story of a bat who falls by accident into the nest of a weasel. The latter, taking the small mammal for its cousin without wings—a *souris* is a mouse—prepares to devour him when the bat, to save his skin, tricks him: "*Me*, a mouse! Hateful you are, to say such a thing./ Thanks to the creator of the universe/I am a bird: see my wings./Long live those who ply the skies!" The weasel is convinced and allows the bat to leave. Alas, "Two days later, our hapless hero/Blindly thrusts himself/Into the home of another weasel," this one being an enemy of birds. One can easily see what follows. The bat, playing on his double identity, this time presents the other side of his nature: "Who is a bird? It's just plumage./I am a mouse: long live the rats!/Jupiter confound the cats!" And La Fontaine concludes: "By this adept repartee/He saved his life twice./Many are those who, turning their coats/So, too, have laughed at danger/According to some, the wise man says both/ "Long live the King!" and "Long live the [anti-king] League!"[6]

Placed in a comparable situation to that of the bat in the fable, threatened by a hostile Anglo-American administration and a French power that they defied and/or which they sought to placate, the Acadians often intelligently adopted the strategy of the bat. Depending on the interlocutors and the circumstances, they adapted their dialogue and claimed their attachment, turn by turn, to France or to Great Britain. Clever would be the one who could say if, from the elements of the fable of La Fontaine, the bat really felt himself to be a mouse, a bird, or a bat. We are confronted with the same question in the case of the Acadians, and on the basis of the documents available, it does not seem possible to me to conclude in one sense or the other.[7] In some cases, when one can not conclude but the results are not that essential, one should dare to say that one does not know. Moreover, even if the feeling of belonging to an Acadian nation only dates from, for example, the nineteenth century, this surely in no way lessens the legitimacy of their present claims to maintaining the Acadian language and identity today.

It is also true that the affirmation of an early Acadian "identity" allows us to give more meaning to the turpitudes of the refugees in France. Historian William Cronon has shown that all of the stories (*histoires*) are needed in any account.[8] Starting with the study of many works on the Dust Bowl in the United States, he thus shows how it is possible to write entirely different accounts, and to arrive at diametrically opposed conclusions about the causes and consequences of that ecological disaster. Some authors thus present a positive vision of history as a march towards constant progress, in which the episode of the Dust Bowl is only a stumble along the way. Other authors have, on the contrary, a declension interpretation and describe the progressive degradation of nature and the ecosystem of the Great Plains into a more and more hostile environment because of the activity of mankind. Even if these strategies are inevitable in producing a meaningful account that interests the reader, from the facts most of the "stories" are not linear and do not go in a single direction, which is also the case with the Acadian refugees in France. If the task of the historian is to reestablish order and to untangle knots, we must beware of imposing an order that only exists in our imagination. The rhetorical procedure that for a long time has consisted of introducing into Acadian history a linear guideline, a narrative—that the Acadians, after the original cataclysm of the deportation, survived adversity and resisted assimilation thanks to their feeling of belonging to a nation—does not withstand examination. We must accept that the Acadian refugees in France were divided, that they aspired to different things, some opposing the others, and that many were transported here and there against their will. And we must especially accept that the departure of the Acadians from France in 1785 was not inevitable, that another *dénouement* might have been possible. The departure to Louisiana was also the result of happenstance (a word that the historians do not like very much), or, if it was not that, at least of factors whose ultimate causes we do not know.

But the identity question, though having kept the attention of the critics until now, is but a (small) part of my work, and it is not necessarily the question that may most interest my readers. I hope they will find as much interest in the chapters concerning the problems of integration and the assistance for the refugees.

A single regret regarding the reception of this work: the fact that there has been so little mention of the online documentary database that accompanies it. The relative "invisibility" of this database is perhaps due to the fact that it was presented in too short a manner in the first edition.[9] I therefore invite the reader to visit the virtual appendices to this work on the internet.[10] These include, first, a database containing the transcription of more than 1,500 documents related to the theme of the book, which, to my knowledge, makes it the first of its kind in the world. It allows any reader to consult the text *in extenso* of all of the documents cited in the notes to the work. The context in which each document was written can thus be examined. It also allows researching the text of all of the documents, for example, by proper name or by site name.

Moreover, on the same site as that of the database, readers will find numerous documents complementing the text of this book, principally:
- various unpublished texts found during the research done for the writing of this book;
- a comparative study of the treatment of the refugees who came from the Saint Lawrence River valley during the same period;
- various tables, maps, and biographical lists complementing the biographies presented on pages 233-37 of the book;
- expansion of subjects only mentioned in the work (the lodging of the Acadians or the destinations to which they wanted to subsequently emigrate);
- a bibliography and repository of sources consulted.

I hope that these supplements, and, more generally, this book, may contribute to making the exciting and tragic history of the Acadians better known.

Jean-François Mouhot
Les Courmettes, France, December 2016

Preamble

On May 10, 1785, the *Bon Papa*, a modest, three-masted ship of 280 tons, hoisted sails at Paimboeuf, near Nantes, making the cape to the west. Aboard were thirty-six families that the owner of the ship had promised to bring to a good port. The ship's charter, approved by the consul of Spain, had been signed four days before and ordered "conduct of the passengers to the port of New Orleans in Louisiana."[1]

The vessel, arriving at its destination on July 29, 1785, after eighty days of crossing was but the first of seven ships that, during the same period, carried nearly 1,600 Acadians to the Mississippi Valley. This emigration is considered by the Cajun community in Louisiana as one of its founding moments.[2] Nevertheless, it remains largely unknown by the Canadian and European public.

Thirty years almost to the day before the arrival of the *Bon Papa* in New Orleans, seven or eight times as many Acadians prepared to embark in ships departing from Nova Scotia, at the southeastern extremity of Canada. Between July 28 and July 31, 1755, the English governor of this colony, Charles Lawrence, as a prelude to the Seven Years War, had made the decision to exile all the inhabitants of French origin under his jurisdiction, in order to spread them among the thirteen English colonies.

Joseph LeBlanc, then aged twenty-five, originally from the Minas Basin, was among those transported to Virginia, and from there to England.[3] Repatriated to Morlaix in Brittany in 1763 (after the signing of the peace agreement between France and England), and provisionally settled on a patch of land at Belle-Île-en-Mer with some compatriots, then going to Poitou in 1773, and then on to Nantes, he, with his wife, Anne Hébert and their two children, was among those aboard the *Bon Papa*.[4] Many other individuals who had been exiled in the summer of 1755 and followed parallel routes were aboard the same ship. Did Joseph LeBlanc and his companions think about the circumstances of their first departure, thirty years earlier, on leaving the Brittany coast? Why did he leave France? To form an idea of why, let us go back some years previously.

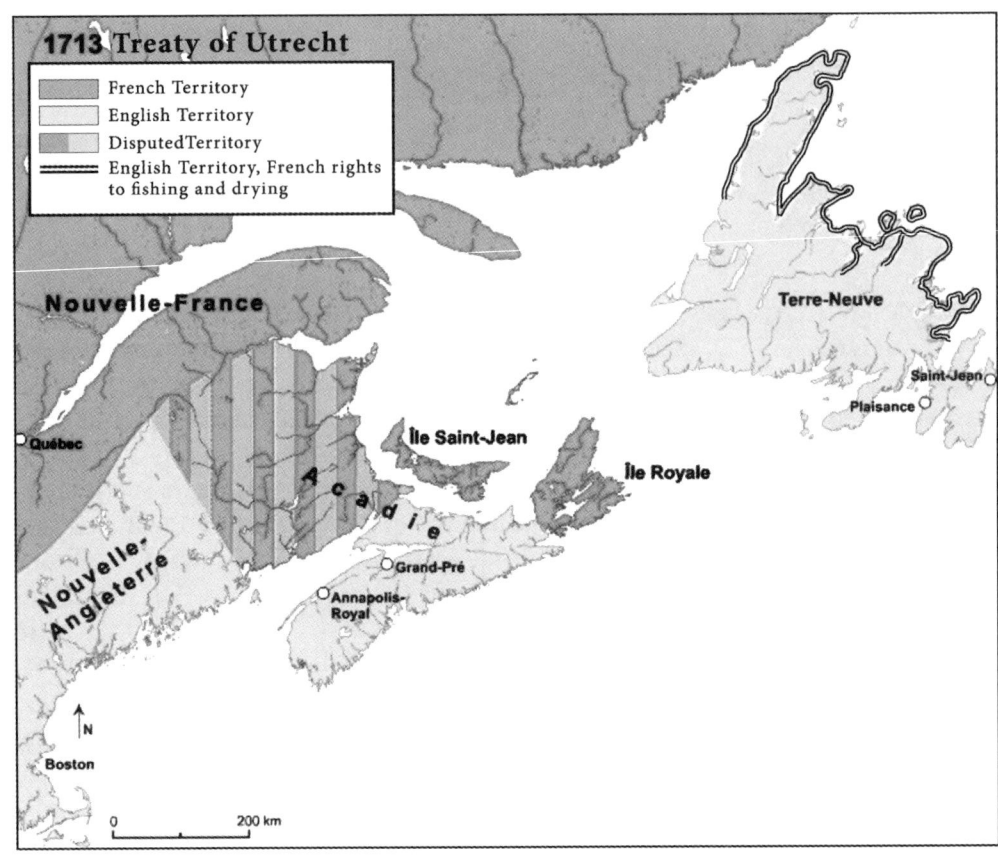

MAP 1
Acadia after the Treaty of Utrecht (1713). From *L'Acadie par les cartes*
(http://www2.umoncton.ca/cfdocs/cea/documts/c/vhtml/htm.cfm?cle= c0015)
Centre d'études acadiennes Anselme-Chiasson (CEAAC)

The War of the Spanish Succession (1701 to 1714) between France and Spain (with its allies England, Austria, Bohemia, Holland, and Hungary) profoundly influenced the balance of power in Acadia and New France. Trying to put an end to this costly war, France agreed to the terms of the Treaty of Utrecht (1713). According to this treaty, France agreed to cede Acadia, Newfoundland, and the Hudson Bay territories to England. She also recognized the authority of England over the Iroquois territories. On the other hand, she kept Île Saint-Jean, Cape Breton, and New France as well as the fishing and drying rights for the northern coast of Newfoundland. However, as many passages of the text of this treaty were ambiguous, the borders of Acadia, among other places, were contested by one side or the other for almost fifty years.

Introduction

History, Census, Definitions

ALMOST EXACTLY TWO HUNDRED years before the mass arrival in France of almost a million *Pieds-Noirs* forced to leave Algeria, the French administration had already encountered a first wave of repatriated colonists. Between six and eight thousand refugees came, about half from what was then called Canada (that is to say the St. Lawrence River valley), and the other half from Acadia, arriving in various French ports on the Atlantic and the department of Manche.[1] Apart from the case of the Canadians, who, for the most part, chose to leave freely after the conquest of their country in 1759-1760, it is appropriate to here briefly discuss the source and circumstances of the arrival of the Acadians.[2]

Historical Summary

The Beginnings of Colonization until 1755

In 1604 the first attempt at French colonization occurred on the island of Sainte-Croix (now Duchot Island off the mouth of the St. Croix River in Maine), opposite the territory known for nearly two centuries afterward by the name of Acadia.[3] However, the colonists who attempted this adventure, mistakenly seduced by the relatively southern latitude, had not anticipated the wintertime conditions that they encountered. Imprisoned by ice on an island cut off from the continent and its food sources and decimated by scurvy, a large number of the colonists did not survive the winter, and most of those who escaped re-embarked for France once spring had come. Nonetheless, a small number of French merchants stayed in the area in the following years and had manpower, in the form of indentured servants, shipped over to them. The implantation of an agricultural society in Acadia, named in memory of the Greek *Arcadia*, only really began in 1632, twenty-four years after the founding of Québec by Samuel de Champlain, one of the survivors of the expedition of 1604. The colony developed more slowly than did the French settlements of the St. Lawrence River valley to the north, which profited from Europe's taste for beaver fur and perhaps from a stronger interest on the part of the French authorities. Acadia remained on the margin of the New France of which it theoretically formed a part. However, Acadia also constituted a geo-strategic position, and that was to be its misfortune. It was in fact along the route of the ships making the journey between London and the Anglo-American settlements, including Massachusetts (Boston having been founded in 1630), and in the proximity of the cod fishing banks south of Newfoundland.

Acadia therefore quickly became the source of rivalry between England and France. The territory frequently changed its allegiance during the eighteenth century, until, in 1713, by the Treaty of Utrecht,[4] the United Kingdom definitively obtained sovereignty of the peninsula, which it had called *Nova Scotia* (New Scotland) since 1621. By the same treaty, however, France kept Île-Royale and Île Saint-Jean (today's Cape Breton and Prince Edward Island) as well as, *de facto*, the western part of the isthmus of Chignectou, in the present New Brunswick, including the mouth of the St. John River, in the present region of Saint John. The precise borders of Acadia, ceded by the Treaty of Utrecht "in its old borders," were never well defined. Because of the mistrust of one side or the other, France and England could never settle the "question of borders" of the former Acadia, and the zone of the isthmus of Chignectou (the region around the present town of Amherst) was bitterly disputed by the two enemies. During this period, France built the fortress of Louisbourg on Île-Royale.

The change of sovereignty in Nova Scotia did not, however, lead to great changes from a demographic point of view: most of the Acadians chose to remain, and in the years following the Treaty of Utrecht, the British government did not try to populate the colony with its own subjects. The structure of the population, the majority of which traced its origin to the west of France, changed little, and the colonists kept their French language and customs, as well as their Catholic religion (immigration of members of the "supposedly reformed religion" was theoretically forbidden in New France). The Treaty of Utrecht guaranteed the inhabitants of the colony freedom of religion if they chose to remain:

> Article 14: In all said places and colonies granted by the Very Christian King [Louis XIV], the subjects of the King will have the freedom to go elsewhere with all of their moveable property within the space of a year's time. Those who nonetheless want to remain and live under the domination of Great Britain must enjoy the free exercise of their religion, in conformity with the usage of the Roman church, as much as the laws of Great Britain allow.[5]

Furthermore, the colony was administered from afar and in a relaxed-enough manner by the British. The Acadians could organize and elect delegates charged with representing them before the English authorities. In addition, some Acadian villages had a Catholic priest in residence from France.

Certainly, the British authorities distrusted these French and Catholic inhabitants. Was there not the risk that, during the recurrent conflicts with Québec, they might add manpower to the Franco-Canadian militias from the St. Lawrence River valley and defeat the English soldiers? The period was hardly one of religious tolerance, and the British feared the fanaticism of these "papists." Therefore, many times after 1713 the authorities asked the colonists to swear an oath of allegiance to the British crown. These oaths and their various formulations were the object of varied interpretations on the part of the protagonists.[6] In 1730, the Acadians swore a conditional oath to the governor of the colony, Richard Philipps, who nevertheless does not seem to have informed London of its exact conditions. By 1745, most of them had therefore only sworn a partial allegiance in the eyes of the authorities of Nova Scotia. With the fear of reprisals that might arise from one side or the other, the Acadians wanted at all costs to remain neutral in case of a new Franco-English war. They thus came to be known as the "Neutral French."

In fact, the period following Utrecht was one of peace and prosperity for the Acadians, "the happiest population of America," according to the Abbé Raynal.[7] The population rapidly grew to around fourteen thousand individuals by 1755. The inhabitants lived principally from fishing and agriculture. The exploitation of the land was based especially on the technique of *aboiteaux*, imported from France but adapted locally. This system of dikes facilitated drying out very fertile marshes or partially submerged lands and nourishing a sizeable livestock. The building and maintenance of these dikes was done collectively.

The Acadians primarily lived in small hamlets close to one another—usually in family groups of parents and their direct descendants. The houses were most often constructed of wood with a thatched roof and sometimes with stone foundations. The colonists did not live in isolation but exchanged their produce, furs, grains, cattle, and wood, for arms, powder, tools, textiles, spices, and rum, either with Massachusetts to the south, with the French settlements to the north, or with the Micmac Indians.

A new war in Europe, the War of the Austrian Succession, put an end to these decades of peaceful existence. Louis XV, who had never renounced his claims to Nova Scotia, launched three expeditions to re-conquer the former colony. The last, in 1746, was a notable fiasco. The logistical aid brought by some Acadian inhabitants to this expedition revived the mistrust of the British authorities for the French in their care.

This was exacerbated by the activities of French agents sent to the colony, in particular one Abbé Le Loutre, a missionary among the Amerindians of the peninsula. Operating for the French government in a meddlesome manner, he wrote to the Minister of the Navy in 1749:

> As we cannot openly oppose the undertakings of the English, I think that we cannot do better than to stir up the savages to continue making war on the English. My aim is to get the savages to tell the English that they will not allow them to put in new settlements in Acadia, that they want it to remain the way it was before the war, and that if the English persist in their design, the savages will never ally with them and will declare eternal war on them. . . . There, *Monseigneur*, is the part I will play for the good of the State and the religion, and I will do everything possible to have the English believe that this aim comes from the savages themselves and that I have nothing to do with it.[8]

In fact, Le Loutre tried to raise the tribe of the Micmacs against the English by enticing them with monetary compensation. A witness recounts that, in August 1753, the Micmacs "reported eighteen scalps that they had taken from the English in the different paths that they had made on their settlements during the last month, and Mr. Le Loutre was obliged to pay them 1,800 *livres* in money from Acadia," a sum that French authorities reimbursed.[9]

Moreover, Le Loutre tried to convince the neutrals to return to the portions of Acadia still controlled by the French. To force them to emigrate, he threatened the recalcitrant with reprisals by the Micmacs and even suggested that he would withhold the sacraments. The departure of a substantial portion of these Frenchmen around 1750 (about a thousand Acadians migrated to the islands north of the peninsula or to present New Brunswick) contributed to further anxiety for the British governor of Halifax.[10]

Deportation from Nova Scotia

The situation was tense at the start of the 1750s, and the return of hostilities between French Canada and the British colonies in 1755, preceding the European Seven Years War (1756-1763) only made matters worse. In June 1755, the English seized Fort Beauséjour, a frontier post within Nova Scotia and the zone that had remained under French control. They discovered there a large number of armed Acadians, who were thus in violation of their oath of neutrality.[11] At the end of July, they gathered together the principal representatives of the Acadian villages and renewed the injunction that they swear an unconditional oath to the British crown. But the delegates once again refused. The council of Nova Scotia then decided to undertake the systematic deportation of the Acadians so as to avoid all risk of uprising by the colony in case of a Franco-Canadian attack.[12]

In order to seize the element of surprise, the plan was put into effect almost immediately. By August 11, 1755, the first Acadians were rounded up. The order of deportation provided by Lieutenant-Colonel John Winslow stipulated that, "All of your lands and inhabitances, cattle and livestock of any kind are confiscated by the Crown, as well as all of your other goods, except your money and moveable property, and you must yourselves be removed from this Province that belongs to it."[13] In other places the deportation would begin some weeks later.

The embarkation of the families was often made in disorder, as one of the banished later reported: "the haste and confusion with which we were embarked contributed to increasing our misfortune…. For many families were separated, parents from their children, and children from their parents."[14] The troops confiscated cattle and burned houses as a measure of retaliation and as a way to ensure that those exiled would not return. Many Acadians nonetheless managed to escape to French territories, like Québec and Île-Royale and Île Saint-Jean. If the large majority of the Acadians were deported in the autumn of 1755, a certain number of inhabitants, having succeeded in hiding, were exiled later, as they were captured or surrendered themselves. The deportation only ended in 1762. In all, more than ten thousand individuals were forcibly embarked.

The choice of destination for the Acadians in 1755 appeared to be the British North American colonies, the future Thirteen Colonies. In addition to ease of access, deporting the Neutral French to the American colonies allowed the British authorities to rid Nova Scotia of potentially dangerous inhabitants and simultaneously to populate the American colonies with Europeans destined sooner or later to assimilate into the Anglo-Saxon and Protestant melting pot, while prohibiting them from increasing the enemy ranks. "A great and noble scheme": that is how the *Pennsylvania Gazette* described the deportation of the Acadians in September 1755.[15]

The plan was simple, but the procedures were only beginning. The British were committed to dispersing the Acadians in order to prevent any dangerous reassembly. Numerous families were thus separated from one another by many hundreds of miles.

About 1,100 people had been deported to Virginia, then sent on to England by 1756 as Richmond refused to take on, at its own expense, colonists imposed upon it without its consent. These Acadians spent many years in various English ports, and around eight hundred of them went to France in 1763.[16] This, in brief, was the route of a portion of the Acadians first deported, but who would be the last to arrive in France. A greater number of Acadians were deported directly to France in 1758.

Deportation from Île Saint-Jean and Île-Royale

A portion of the Acadians escaped deportation in 1755 and fled to Québec or to Île Saint-Jean, which remained under French sovereignty. But, in 1758, after the taking of the fortress of Louisbourg, the capital of Île-Royale, the English became masters of the rest of

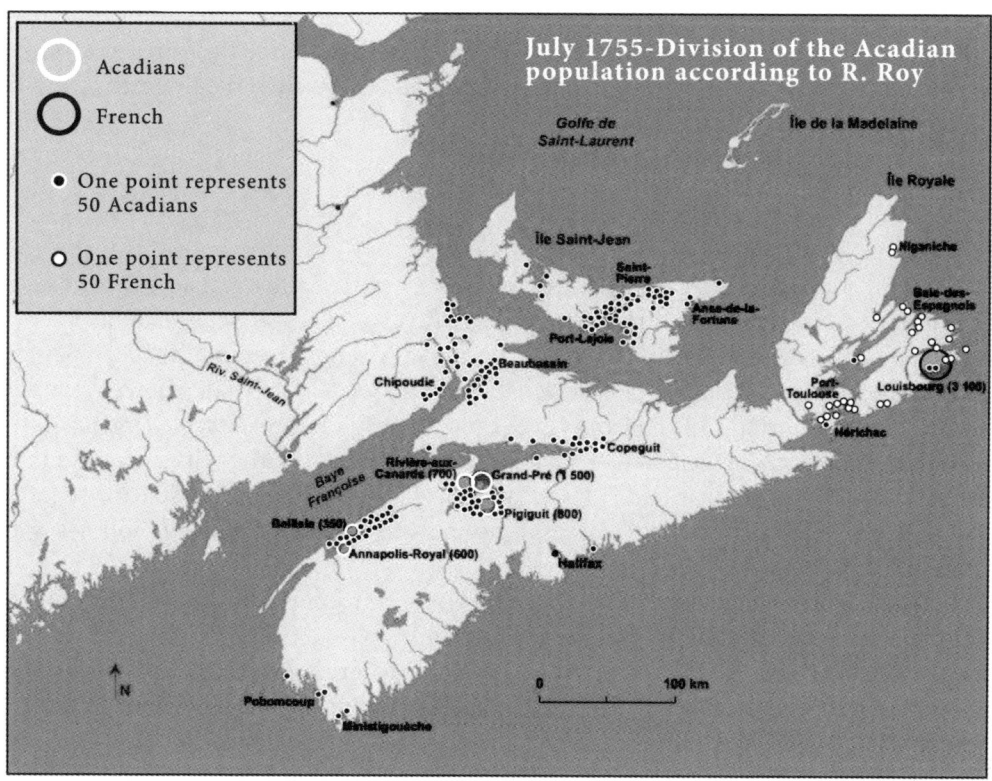

MAP 2

Acadia in 1755. From *L'Acadie par les cartes*. Centre d'études acadiennes Anselme-Chiasson (CEAAC)

The years preceding the deportations were marked by unusual migrations to the Acadians' territory. English colonists began to arrive in large numbers in the colony, little by little imposing on areas until then occupied by the Acadians. Furthermore, the latter had to register with the British authorities, who increasingly demanded their unconditional allegiance to the king of England.

Many Acadian families therefore decided to leave their lands to move to the regions claimed by France, namely Île Saint-Jean, Île-Royale, and the territory to the north of the Missagouèche River (the present New Brunswick).

Populations as illustrated are based on information obtained by Raymond Roy in his study of the demographic growth of Acadia from 1671 to 1763 (as interpreted by the designer of the map).

French Acadia and deported these inhabitants. Most were therefore former colonists of English Acadia who had left their settlements to go to the islands under French dominance either in the 1720s or, more likely, at the beginning of the 1750s.[17] However, since there was some question of whether these Acadians were officially subjects of the king of France, and also because the American colonists did not want to receive any more Acadian refugees, these almost 3,500 people found themselves transported to France, where they arrived beginning in mid-September 1758. The ex-inhabitants of Louisbourg disembarked first at Rochefort and La Rochelle, while the unfortunate colonists of Île Saint-Jean were largely left on the coasts of Manche, notably at Saint-Malo, Cherbourg, Le Havre, and Boulogne. The conditions of their voyage were most frequently dreadful. A large proportion of the exiles died during the crossing: many ships sank with no survivors and an epidemic of small-pox raged among the others.

Arrivals in France

The first Acadians who arrived in France therefore were not, in fact, those deported directly from Acadia in 1755, but the inhabitants from Île Saint-Jean and Île-Royal, along with some persons displaced from the St. Jean River and Cape Sable Island, later made prisoners or again deported from Gaspé.[18] The arrivals were spaced out between September 1758 and the spring of 1759.[19] The last sizeable contingent to arrive in France included the 1,500 Acadians deported in 1755 from the Grand-Pré region, sent first to Virginia and then to the United Kingdom. Dispersed to various places in England, they disembarked in many groups at Morlaix or Saint-Malo.[20] Finally, some families, having passed through Saint-Pierre and Miquelon or the Magdalen Islands, arrived sporadically in the following years, particularly 1767-1768.[21]

We should note that, according to population concepts of the time, the inhabitants of Nova Scotia were considered by the government of Great Britain to be British.[22] It was inconceivable to consider returning this population to France, which would thus amount to reinforcing the enemy. For this reason, the authorization to go to France or to Louis XV's other colonies, like Saint-Domingue, was refused to those deported to New England, at least originally. Until the end of the war, the British feared that the Acadians would lend manpower to the colony of the St. Lawrence River valley. On the other hand, the populations occupying French Acadia, Île Saint-Jean and Île-Royal, and the present New Brunswick, were logically transported directly to France since, in this case, they incontestably "belonged" to the king of France. It was for this reason that the victims of the second deportation in 1758 arrived directly on the European continent before those of the first deportation of 1755.

What happened to the Acadians in France between 1758 and 1785 is the principal subject of this book. Between 2,000 and 2,500 of those repatriated arrived in France starting in September 1758. The king had aid distributed to them and became involved with their reinstallation. In 1763, after its defeat in the Seven Years War, France ceded Canada and Louisiana to Great Britain and Spain: the Acadians who had been deported to England were then able to go to France. In all, their former homeland thus received about 3,000 Acadians. In the first years of their stay, the Acadians were threatened with having to populate the Southern Colonies that remained French, notably Guyana, the Antilles, and the Malouines (the present Falklands). Facing reluctance from most of them, the government attempted to settle 350 refugees on Belle-Île-en-Mer in 1764. In the following years, the ministry contented itself with studying proposals by various individuals for settlement on lands that needed clearing. None of these plans saw the light of day. Many Acadians then made frequent trips to Saint-Pierre and Miquelon (Newfoundland), while others, fairly numerous, provisionally settled on the archipelago or in other French colonies. In the summer of 1772, following a request by the refugees to rejoin their compatriots who had been taken from the Anglo-American colonies to Louisiana,[23] the king's council accepted the offer of the marquis de Pérusse d'Escars to settle them on his lands. The Commissioner of the Navy,

Antoine-Philippe Lemoyne, then made a tour of the ports to take a census of the Acadians and urge them to accept the offers of the government. The large majority then went to Poitou, but, for various reasons explained below, the Acadians very soon asked to leave the settlement, and nearly all of them returned to Nantes in 1775. It was from there that most of them then departed for Louisiana in 1785.

The Other Exiles

As for those Acadians dispersed across the whole North American Atlantic coast—from Québec to Georgia, (excluding the present maritime provinces of Canada where some Acadians were successfully able to remain)—it soon became clear that they could not easily integrate into the Protestant population, mainly because of the hostile reception they received.[24] In 1763, therefore, after the peace treaty, many Acadians were authorized to leave. A majority went to French territory, notably Saint-Pierre and Miquelon, and to areas along the St. Lawrence. Many others settled in the present province of New Brunswick, south of the Gaspésie. It is there that, today, one finds the greatest number of their descendants. Most did not return to Nova Scotia, as official authorization to resettle there was only given later, in 1764.

Some also opted for Louisiana, which had become Spanish. The refugees flocked to this colony starting in 1763-1764, after having passed through Saint Domingue (the present Haiti), where they were not especially well-received by the French authorities. In 1785 they were rejoined by their 1,500 compatriots who arrived from France, having obtained authorization to emigrate and reunite with part of their families. Along the bayous of the Mississippi Valley they were able to establish a new "little Acadia."

Census Taking in France

Let us return to the Acadian exiles while they were in France. It is difficult to ascertain their exact population between 1758 and 1785: this number fluctuated depending on the successive arrivals and departures, and the Acadians continually moving within France as well as beyond its borders. In 1762 there were 1,126 at Saint-Malo and Saint-Servan.[25] In 1772-1773, a large number, averaging 2,500, were supplied by the commissioner of the Navy, Lemoyne, who was specially charged with counting them.[26] The variations demonstrate the difficulty that administrators had keeping track of the groups of refugees from North America and among the regular departures of the Acadians to Saint-Pierre and Miquelon, or to Acadia (whose quantity is not known). As for those returning to North America (except for Saint-Pierre and Miquelon), they are yet more difficult to estimate because of the clandestine nature of these departures. However, some firm numbers surface on occasion, notably when the government was concerned with desertions.[27] As a final marker, there were the nearly 1,600 people who embarked for Louisiana in 1785.[28]

Ultimately, it is difficult to form an exact idea of the true number of returnees, unless we make detailed calculations based on civil records scattered across almost all ports on the Atlantic seaboard, and we therefore have to rest content with the numbers given by the various censuses made of the Acadians in France by the ministry of the Navy. However, even these numbers only provide a rough estimate. It is in fact difficult to know exactly who was included in these censuses, for they often only aimed at counting those who received, or asked to receive, "sustenance."

We have noted how the number of Acadians coming from Nova Scotia, or "historic Acadia," was relatively small. Even if it is difficult to establish proportions, those coming from the Minas Basin, by way of Virginia and England, and from Cape Sable Island amount to only 800 to 1,000 people of the above-mentioned total of around 2,500 to 3,000 Acadians—a third, in other words. Most came from Île Saint-Jean and the rest of French Acadia.

How Would One Be Considered an Acadian?

In this text, the ethnic term "Acadians" will be used in a general way to designate the population of French origin living in the part of Acadia that was ceded to England in 1713 by the Treaty of Utrecht, which then took the name of Nova Scotia. But it also designates the population who inhabited Île Saint-Jean and the part of Acadia that remained French after Utrecht, to the west of a poorly defined line passing through the isthmus of Chignecto, that is to say, *gross modo,* the present New Brunswick and the south of Gaspé, and some Acadian families from Île-Royale.[29] This population principally consisted of refugees who fled English Acadia and, for the large part, were already receiving assistance from the French government as of 1751.[30] Most of the time the inhabitants of all of these areas were designated under the generic term of Acadians upon their arrival in France.

Before their arrival there, the term "Acadian" was little used. In the eighteenth century it was sometimes used by visitors of the colony[31] or by French and English administrators, but, to my knowledge, one finds no reference to it by inhabitants of Nova Scotia or the islands remaining under French control before 1755.[32] Before this date, the terms most frequently used in the texts are simply those of "inhabitants of the Minas Basin," of Copequit, etc. The inhabitants of the colony were designated as "neutral," the term being most often joined to "French," and, more rarely, to "inhabitants" or "Acadians" (whether translated into English or not). The French government took exception to this usage for diplomatic reasons during the negotiations with England at the time of the signing of the peace treaty of 1763.[33] Except for some documents recalling the previous use of the term, the refugees were no longer designated as "neutral" when they were in France, but as Acadians, and sometimes "inhabitants of North America" or "Canadians." For their part, after having for a long time emphasized their neutrality by designating themselves as "neutral French," the refugees also began to call themselves "Acadians" upon their arrival in France (including those who came, for instance, from Île Saint-Jean).[34]

These are therefore the people designated explicitly as Acadians who provide the subject of this study. This choice includes a somewhat arbitrary aspect that should be emphasized: the terminology of the period was far from exact. For the French administration, to be an Acadian was most often to be someone inscribed on numerous lists (called registers) meant to identify persons in need. Certainly, the registers were exclusive and not everyone could be inscribed on them: one had to have disembarked from a ship duly identified or in possession of a certificate if one came from another port; one also had to be recognized by the other deportees. The verifications were lengthy and fastidious.[35] However, it is inevitable that mistakes and abuses slipped into these lists, all the more so as it represented the key to receiving aid from the king for whomever was so inscribed on these "*matricules.*"

It is therefore possible that some individuals designated as Acadians were, at the most, emigrants born in France who, for example, went to St. Jean or to Louisbourg after 1745 to perform various activities. In the end, reflecting on who should be considered as an Acadian is to perform a kind of categorization that was also undertaken by the French administration itself upon the arrival of the Acadians in France, essentially for the practical reasons of the distribution of assistance.[36] But, nothing proves that the people themselves ever had or wanted to define themselves as "Acadians" before their arrival in France. The term was probably accepted without complaint by most of the refugees, but it was perhaps imposed on others. It is difficult to know to what degree it was freely chosen by those individuals so designated.

The most difficult problem of definition concerns the former inhabitants of Louisbourg, the fortified capital of Île-Royale. In fact, the population of this town was composed of a sizeable minority of Acadians, but also fishermen, soldiers, and civil and military officers newly arrived from France. All of these individuals were most often designated as "from Île-Royale," "from Louisbourg," or from "North America." In this group, we should distinguish, when possible, the individuals known to be former inhabitants of Acadia and Île Saint-Jean or bearing explicitly Acadian surnames, from others having come more recently from France.[37]

But, in a general manner, only the descendants of the colonists who had settled for at least one or two generations in Acadia have been designated as Acadians. Additionally, after a long period of delays, the administration distinguished the Acadians from the former inhabitants of Île-Royale and of Canada, to whom the government also distributed assistance for a certain time, but who were then treated differently.

To summarize, the individuals considered in this work are thus:
- those whose origin or birth in Acadia is clearly indicated;
- those whose origin or birth is not mentioned and do not necessarily have an explicitly Acadian surname, but to whose name the notation "Acadian" has been added;
- in certain cases, the inhabitants of Louisbourg, amalgamated and identified with the Acadians or bearing an Acadian surname.

Nonetheless, the goal is not to establish a rigorous distinction between the Acadians and the "non-Acadians," but to study the interactions of the refugees designated as Acadians as a group with the French authorities. In the end, the precise delimitation of who is Acadian and who is not depends on the question posed. For the parts of this work concerned with the distribution of assistance or even with the representations of these refugees, these questions are secondary. On the other hand, when we examine the desire to be integrated among members of a group, it is important to know whom we are considering. We must especially distinguish between those families implanted in Acadia for many generations and those individuals who had more recently immigrated to America.

The Acadians in Historical Writing

Even if the studies dedicated to the history of France in the eighteenth century are silent about the Acadian refugees there, publications bearing on them directly are not at all lacking.[38] Indeed, they could easily fill many shelves of a library. Genealogy certainly occupies a place of priority: the old registers of some towns and regions have been explored in a practically exhaustive manner by researchers searching through the piles of baptismal, marriage, and burial acts, or the lists of disembarkations and embarkations, and very many transcriptions of them have been published for over a century now. The subject has even made appearance in fiction.[39]

Among the historical work, local studies, limited to the examination of the stay of the Acadians in a particular region or town, are numerous. Studies of the whole group are rarer, but we can still count three monographs on the question,[40] as well as many chapters included in works about Acadia or about Louisiana, prompting us to summarize the current state of knowledge.

All of the studies on the refugees from the deportations of 1755 and 1758 question the reasons for the departure of the Acadians to Louisiana in 1785. But no author has analyzed in an in-depth manner the attitude of the French government and that of the Acadians. Rather, more frequently opinions are offered, though rarely supported and often subordinated to the conclusion the author was seeking to make.

The first to outline the great stages of the Acadians' sojourn in Europe was the Frenchman Rameau de Saint-Père, who, in 1889,[41] was able to benefit from the final oral testimony of direct descendants of actual Acadians who had been deported.[42] Another Frenchman, Émile Lauvrière, dedicated many chapters to the Acadian presence in France in a book published in 1922.[43] In his work, the founder of the *Comité France-Acadie* sought, above all, to defend the reputation of his country, accused of having abandoned Canada, by insisting on the "constant zeal" for the homeland among the refugees. For Rameau, as for Lauvrière, the departure of the Acadians to Louisiana in 1785 posed no real problem, as the Acadians did not consider permanently settling in France.

The work of a third Frenchman, Ernest Martin, published in 1936, has remained until now the basic reference about the Acadians' time in France.[44] Like Lauvrière, the object of the author, beyond a narration of the odyssey of the Acadian exiles, was to answer the accusations then brought against the administration of Louis XV by Canadian opinion.[45] This questionable aim forms the main thread of his work. Martin explicitly questions the motives for the departure of the Acadians in 1785 and partially blames the refugees. In his view, during the course of their stay in France, the Acadians progressively transformed themselves into "spoiled children" who refused the offers that were proposed to them and abused public funds. He also proposes a series of specific explanations for the failure of the settlements, notably the weak quality of the available French lands compared to those in Acadia,[46] the high seigniorial dues, or the legal tangles involved with private property that rendered any settlement extremely complicated. Nonetheless, Martin's ultimate interpretation consists of introducing the theme of a certain cultural incompatibility: "Even less than the hard work of clearing the lands, the Acadians were not prepared to share the political and social conditions of the French peasants at the end of the *Ancien Régime*. From their previous life in English or French Acadia, they brought habits of independence that could not fit within the conditions prepared for them, despite all sorts of exemptions and privileges."[47] But, for Martin, insisting on the cultural incompatibility of the Acadians is also a way of exculpating the State from its responsibility for the departure of 1785. Therefore, he, like Lauvrière, concludes that the government worked to help and keep the Acadians, but that they ultimately lacked the desire to insert themselves into French society.

American Oscar Winzerling's *Acadian Odyssey*, which appeared in 1955,[48] was also mainly dedicated to the sojourn of the Acadians in France. This work, weakened by many inaccuracies,[49] marks a turning point in the interpretation of the Acadian's experience in France. He introduces the notion of "Acadian survival" in a hostile and neglectful milieu that sought to "absorb" them. Winzerling introduces the term "Acadian nation," and he affirms that the Acadians felt themselves different from the French and that they were considered by the latter as inferiors.[50] Here, for the first time, one sees a glimpse of the question of identity. This directional shift would become particularly noticeable in the later writings of the Anglo-Canadian historian Naomi Griffiths.

Griffiths, in her 1969 thesis and many later writings, was concerned with the Acadians in France.[51] She, in turn, questioned the survival of Acadian "nationalism." In a work published in 1992, after having described the emergence of an "Acadian identity" before the deportation, she dedicates pages to the group deported to France.[52] She specifically examines the causes for the departure to Louisiana in 1785 and concludes:

> At first, this departure might be surprising. After all, the Acadians had already known exile in the English territory. As they were Catholic French speakers, one might conclude from this that they shared the interests of France, and all the more as they had benefited from considerable assistance from the French government. Moreover, one proposed to settle them in regions where their ancestors had originated. Everything leads one to suppose easy assimilation. However, despite their French ties, the Acadians were also North Americans. During their stay of twenty years in France, defined especially by an identity forged in "Acadia or Nova Scotia," they proved little inclined to the influence of the country of their ancestors.

For Griffiths, then, factors of identity played a determinative role in explaining the departure of 1785. The same themes were repeated by a Louisiana historian, Carl Brasseaux. In a work dedicated to the populating of Louisiana by the Acadians after the deportation, he, too, devoted a chapter to the Acadians' stay in France and repeated many of the above-mentioned theories to explain their departure from France.[53] According to Brasseaux, the Acadians, apart from considering their deplorable material conditions, dreaded the prospect of being absorbed into the French population.[54] Not surprising, then, in this context, they sought to leave at any cost.[55] Brasseaux finds the failure to implant the Acadians in France as inevitable.[56]

This brief state of the field would not be complete without mentioning two recent works. The first, Jean-Marie Fonteneau's *Les Acadiens citoyens de l'Atlantique*, appeared in 1996.[57] Meant for the general public, it summarizes the works mentioned above, apart from a large section about Belle-Île that is based on new research. The work does not present a new interpretation. The second is a recent synthesis of the history of the deportation, *A Great and Noble Scheme*. This work, written for both the general public and for those with more knowledge of the subject by an historian from Yale University, John Mack Faragher, is the most well known in North America.[58] The book contains some short pages on the stay of the Acadians in France.[59] Faragher, there again, offers no new interpretation of the reasons for the departure to Louisiana. Moreover, he does not consider issues of identity, preferring to speak of the poor conditions offered to the Acadians in France.[60]

Concluding this summary of the historiography, we can say that, except for Faragher, who only touches on the subject, for all of the authors since Ernest Martin, the question of the survival of the Acadian culture and identity is what explains the departure of the Acadians from France in 1785.[61] We can also say that all of the authors seem nearly unanimous in agreeing on two things: first, the "natural" aim of the government was, "evidently," to keep the Acadians in France; and, moreover, that the Acadians themselves never really wanted to assimilate into the French society, because of their "identity" or cultural distinctiveness.

But did the Acadians truly never want to settle in France? And did France truly ever want to integrate them into herself? If yes, how, and if no, why not? These questions have never been clearly asked, for historians have implicitly answered them in advance. They have most often presented the departure by the Acadians to Louisiana as the failure of the policy of integration of the French government. But can one speak of a precise policy or even desire for integration on the part of the government? Lacking this, can one speak of any such substantive and continuous desire at all? The ideas of the ministry on the integration or the assimilation[62] of the Acadians evolved considerably between 1758 and 1785. They can certainly not be summed up, as one would believe from reading certain authors, in the distribution of assistance and the succession of plans for settlement that were to fail in their relatively advanced stages.

The Problem of Acadian Identity Before 1755

Let us return to our first problem: did the deportees truly ever want to be permanently settled in France? For some observers, the question need not even be asked, so widespread is the idea that the Acadians arrived in France strongly detached from the mother country, autonomous and conscious of forming a unique and thus inassimilable people. This preexisting Acadian "identity"[63] is presented by these historians as the main explanatory element behind the reluctance of the Acadians to integrate. Some even imply that the Acadians formed a different ethnicity from the French.[64] But if one considers the contemporary definition of this term,[65] anachronistic for the period, nothing proves that this was the case. Their language was most often the same as that of the inhabitants of the places where they took refuge. Their religion was the same as that of the majority of the French. And, as for their "culture,"[66] it remains difficult to grasp, for lack of documentation.

In order to examine the desire of the Acadians for integration, we must first of all examine their state of mind upon their arrival in France. As we have seen, most historians insist on the presence of strong feelings of identity among the Canadians and the Acadians before the events of the Seven Years War, essentially founded on the differences between the Canadians and the French as mentioned by the administrators of the period. The affirmation of this identity has become commonplace in the history of both Canada and that of Acadia.[67]

It would be too long and tedious for the reader to discuss here in detail the question of the Acadian identity before 1755. Let us simply say that, like some other specialists of Acadia, for many reasons I am far from convinced by those who promote "identity" as the main explanatory element of Acadian history in the eighteenth century.[68] First of all, many documents that I have examined, nearly all related to the period previous to the hypothetic maturity of this feeling of identity, only very rarely refer to themes that one might qualify as cultural or having to do with identity. Moreover, these references were always anecdotal. On the other hand, the Acadians constantly make reference to their allegiance to the king of France, to the (French) "fatherland," and to the Catholic religion. Certainly, one might reasonably object that, as the documents consulted were almost always written either by or for the French administration, the Acadians were not speaking freely. But one does not find claims of sentiments of belonging to an "Acadian-ity" so to speak, in the private correspondence of the exiled, only allusions to religious sentiments or to the desire for family reunion. One might respond that the documents do make reference to the Acadian "nation" many times. But we will see that this was a relatively late invention, that the term was not used in the first ten years after the arrival of the Acadians in France, and that its sense was quite different from what it signifies today. One may justly argue that it is pointless to search the documents for an explicit way of affirming this "identity" as expressed in the way of life and behavior. The words of Jean-Claude Ruano-Borbalan, according to whom "identity only exists in acts,"[69] actually seem quite pertinent to me and his method more reliable than a simple analysis of statements to judge the feelings of the Acadians. If, as some authors affirm, this community or national feeling of identity was important enough to be the principal characteristic element of the Acadians, then this would have shown itself in their activities. The departure for Louisiana cannot be explained by a desire for the "survival" of Acadian "nationalism."

Besides, the word identity is used in a very ambiguous manner, and often includes very different meanings.[70] For example, according to the dictionary *Le Petit Robert*, cultural identity is: a) a "group of cultural traits proper to an ethnic group (language, religion, art, etc.) that confers on it its individuality" and b) the "feeling of an individual of belonging to a group."[71] As one sees, the term combines two completely different meanings, and a transition from the one to the other is not necessarily made. The fact that external observers recognize an identity (sense "a") in the manner of living of the Acadians before 1755 does not necessarily mean that the Acadians themselves were conscious of their similarities, nor that they positively claimed a sentiment of belonging (sense "b") to the Acadian "group." It might be somewhat hasty to affirm that a manner of living different from those of France necessarily modified the colonists' value system.

Besides, even when authors use the term "identity" in the sense of a feeling of belonging, they often still do so with two different meanings implied. In one case, the authors insist on a strong and fundamental sense of the identity, and, in the other, on a weak notion of its meaning. In the first instance, the members of a group sharing an identity are strongly bound and homogenous; their feeling of belonging to the group is exclusive or predominant; the members of the group are clearly differentiated from non-members; and a clear barrier exists between the interior and the exterior of the group. In the second instance, the identity is understood as weakly constructed and fluid, and identities may be multiple. As Brubaker and Cooper have remarked, the problem is that these two meanings are employed without being sufficiently defined beforehand:

> A specific form of affectively charged auto-comprehension which one often designates as "identity" [is] the feeling of belonging to a specific and limited group, implying both that one experiences a solidarity and a total accord with the companions who make up the group and that one feels different, that is to say one holds an antipathy towards those outside of it. The problem is that the term "identity" is employed to designate *both* this kind of group auto-comprehension, exclusive

and affectively charged *and* much broader and more open forms of auto-comprehension, which imply a certain feeling of affinity or affiliation, of community or alliance with other specific individuals, but deprived of the feeling of total agreement with regard to a constitutive "other." These two types of auto-comprehension (exclusive feeling of belonging to a closed group or more lax feeling of affinity—as well as the intermediary forms between these two extremes—are important in the same way, but inform the personal experience and condition the social and political action in a clearly distinct manner.

If it is the first sense of identity that is meant by the authors when speaking of Acadian identity, how do we explain the strong divisions among the Acadians staying in France, the assimilation of a large number of them, or their indecision about the choice of a new destination?[72] If it is the second sense that is understood, then why use the term "identity," which, as we have seen, is strongly subjective, when one may find less problematic wording, such as a "feeling of affinity or of affiliation, of community or of alliance." Moreover, if identity is understood in the weaker sense and only played a minimal role in the individual choices of the Acadians, the usefulness of the concept, for a historian seeking to explain the history of the Acadians, is limited. "To rank under the concept 'of identity' all kind of affinity and affiliation, all kind of belonging, all feeling of community, of alliance or of cohesion, all kind of auto-comprehension and of auto-identification, is to attach oneself to an indifferent, weakened and vapid terminology."[73]

It is regrettable that the authors postulating the existence of an Acadian "identity" never make the effort to define what they really mean by this term. The most recent work by Naomi Griffiths, *From Migrant to Acadians*, in which "identity" plays a preponderant role, is symptomatic in this regard. The author uses the term more than a hundred times in the work, but without ever defining it. She characterizes this word most often by attaching it to the word Acadian ("Acadian identity"), but also, in turn, she gives it to a sense of local, community, political, social, cultural, and even national identity, which are all relatively distinguishable.[74] The existence of a feeling of "national" Acadian identity is particularly problematic to the degree that there is a large consensus among the historians recognizing the birth—rather the construction or invention—of these strong national feelings, or of nationalism, at the end of the eighteenth century.[75] But Griffiths situates the birth of this national feeling in Acadia well before, at the end of the seventeenth century.[76] "Acadia is, on the contrary, . . . the creation, the invention of a social movement that was designed in the middle of the nineteenth century and which, on the debris of former French Acadia and the mythic elaboration of a people, would literally create the Acadian identity," adds Joseph-Yvon Thériault.[77]

The fact is that the Acadian inhabitants and merchants themselves left almost no testimony of their values or of their feelings of belonging before deportation. Consequently, the discussion by historians about Acadian identity tends to repeat only the words of the colonial elites of the eighteenth and nineteenth centuries. This somewhat simplistic reading has been denounced by many historians.[78] I now would like to briefly take two concrete cases of fruitless attempts to demonstrate the existence of an Acadian "national identity" before deportation.

First of all, let us take the example of a work of popular history frequently cited in the bibliographies on Acadia, *L'Histoire des Acadiens*, by Bona Arsenault. This work argues that there existed in the former Acadia a manner of living relatively distinguishable from that of

INTRODUCTION 15

France, which would have led to an early identification by the inhabitants with the place in which they lived. In a passage on "the idea of the Acadian homeland," the author quotes long excerpts from the writings of Rameau de Saint-Père.[79] Curiously, the extracts copied show the Acadians closeness to France. Rameau insists on the strength of religious sentiment and on "the old songs of France" and speaks of those "rough men" who "were not exempt from those faults of the French race which one finds everywhere it has settled." After this long quotation, Arsenault describes the Acadian means of transportation, typically bark canoes and snow shoes. He then speaks of the "works of the fields and woods," then of the popular culture, "the old songs of another time," the "rustic dances," and "the French hospitality." The conclusion of this section, in which Arsenault describes no Acadian in particular, follows:

> It is thus that the idea of the Acadian homeland was specified, among the sons and grandsons of the first French colonists who had arrived in Acadia. Two or three generations, sometimes four, had already contributed to the formation of a distinct people, possessing customs and traditions of their own. The feeling of the Acadian homeland had penetrated their soul. The love of the Acadian soil had entered their hearts. They had become Acadians.[80]

This example, in some respects a caricature, is, moreover, symptomatic of many authors who confuse the delineation of different manners of living with the formation of a feeling of belonging to a particular "homeland."

Griffiths, in *L'Acadie de 1686 à 1784: contexte d'une histoire*, also maintains the existence of a strong Acadian identity prior to the deportation. This short work particularly concerns the deportation of 1755 and the question of the birth of a distinct culture before the *Grand Dérangement*.[81] In it, every Acadian particularity is evoked and counterbalanced with arguments opposing or barely compatible with each other, leading her to use the term "identity" sometimes in a strong sense, and at others in a weaker one.[82] Elsewhere, as we have seen, Griffiths would have us believe that factors of identity played a determinative role in explaining the departure of 1785. She does this based on a single document that theoretically supports her proof, which she introduces thus:

> In a letter written in 1759 by a lawyer of Dinan to the Naval Commissioner of Saint-Malo, requesting assistance for the twenty-two Acadians whom he had settled on his own farm, one finds the reasons for this indifference: "Firstly, these people were raised in a country of abundance, of lands at will, consequently less difficult to cultivate . . . furthermore, many men . . . already felt urges that no longer stir us, they used their hatchets to build lodgings and primitively enough in their hands, what one can only call a 'hacker of wood,' while the women sewed a bit of stockings." According to this same witness, the Acadians required much bread, wanted milk and butter, but refused cider; and they preferred North-American food to French nourishment.[83]

The argument would seem to be convincing. The problem is that here Griffiths provides erroneous information. The author was not a lawyer and the date and the place are inaccurate.[84] Above all, the extract itself is considerably deformed and the summary that Griffiths makes of the end of this letter leads the reader to a distortion of its meaning when compared to the original text, which reads thus:

> These people seem to live well, and I doubt that they eat more than two pounds of bread per person; I bought them ten bushels of wheat for 5 *pounds*, 3 *sous* per bushel, which supplied more than 70 pounds of bread; they can only get it currently for 5 *l* 10*s* a bushel, and rye is rare in this canton; these people accustomed to milking cattle are obliged to pay 4*s* for a pot of milk and 8 to 9*s* for a pound of butter, meaning that it is impossible for them to afford their livelihood without the King's payment. I have advised them to purchase cider to supplement the milk and butter.[85]

If it is true that the Acadians, according to this observer, were used to having milk and butter and that he advised them to purchase cider to replace the too-costly dairy goods, what are the "North American foods" mentioned by Griffiths?[86] But this document is the only one (at least in the French context) to support her thesis, according to which the Acadians left in 1785 because they were already strongly distinguished from the "Frenchmen of France" and did not want to assimilate to the population of France.[87]

What to conclude, then, about the existence of the Acadian "identity" at the time of their arrival in France? The assertion that the Acadians considered themselves from the end of the seventeenth century "firstly and above all Acadians rather than members of any other group"[88] is insufficiently supported. Such an affirmation reflects a teleological reading of Acadian history. The argument is based on fragmentary documentation, insufficiently and uncritically assessed and often misinterpreted. Moreover, the idea of national "identity" has been justly criticized by different authors and is largely anachronistic for the eighteenth century. It is nonetheless possible to retain the notion of a feeling or alliance of affinity or affiliation that was reinforced *a posteriori* by the common experience of the deportation. It is therefore not a question of denying that such a sentiment might have developed in Acadia before the deportation. Nor is it a question of affirming that no ties existed that might have bound the Acadians to each other, nor of making them feel like they were part of the same group, having in common ways of life, history, and traditions. But this was not specific to the Acadians: the provinces of France also had their own particularities and loudly and proudly claimed their privileges.

It is true that a large number of Acadians felt strongly tied to France because of their former ties with the home country and the other neighboring French colonies, as well as their religion, which had considerably more importance to them than a dubious feeling of national identity. The fact that many of them chose to leave English Acadia to go to Île Saint-Jean before the deportation shows that they were influenced by the patriotic discourses of the Abbé Le Loutre and illustrates, at a minimum, the multiplicity of Acadian sentiments of belonging.[89]

Finally, regarding the existence of feelings of belonging to the group of Acadian inhabitants of Nova Scotia, beyond the question of the importance of this feeling and its alliance to the feeling of affiliation to the totality of "France," is it also a question of its existence, properly speaking? For Acadia before 1755, we should observe in what circumstances and to whom the Acadians presented themselves as "neutral French," "Acadians," or "Frenchmen." The same Acadian could present himself as "French" to the Abbé Le Loutre and as "neutral" to the English administration, depending on his intentions.

In the absence of documents that might settle the question, we must therefore examine the actions of the Acadians. These show that their allegiance to the French crown and to their view of themselves as subjects of the king of France, their Catholic religion, their family relations, and their material conditions of survival after the deportation held much more significance to them than their feeling of belonging to an Acadian group. This feeling certainly did not constitute the principal or determinative element explaining their departure in 1785. However, the feeling of affinity for the group still constitutes one not insignificant explanatory element in understanding the history of the Acadians in France.

The Integration and Assimilation of the Refugees

The principal objective of this study is to explain how the "integration" or the "assimilation" of the Acadians in France actually took place. These terms are here understood by their respective contemporary definitions of "entering into a group so as to become an integral part" and of "becoming similar to the citizens of a country: adapting, melding, inserting, integrating."[90]

Inquiring about the integration of "foreign" populations in the eighteenth century poses a problem in and of itself. First of all, the use of the word "integrate" with regard to individuals only dates from the twentieth century and does not figure in the old dictionaries.[91] In the century of the Enlightenment, it was solely a term of mathematics. The verb and its derivatives therefore never surface in our documents. Nor does one find "assimilate" in the texts—a term that existed, however, already in the eighteenth century in the sense of "making similar"[92]—nor does "insert" or "insertion," "adapt" or "adaptation" (except for one occurrence).[93] Thus, in order for an assimilation or an integration to be able to occur, we must accept the following postulate, that the Acadians were not "similar" to the "Frenchmen," therefore not "assimilated," or, to return to the definition of integration, outside of the "whole" constituted of all of the French. Moreover, in order for the policies of integration to exist, we must admit that the government perceived the differences between the Acadians and the rest of the French population, and that it endeavored to reduce these differences.

But these two postulates are debatable. The basis of the first has been criticized above. Besides, rather than the supposed "differences" of the Acadians, what struck the French administrators more were their "true French feelings": the fact that they spoke the same language as the French, which was rare at the time among "the common people," as well as the fact that they were all Catholic. As for the second postulate, which is quite debatable, it is to theorize the integration of "foreign bodies" into a hypothetical "French nation," which was itself still composed of nearly as many diverse "peoples"[94] as there were provinces. The "Bretons," the "Poitevins," the "Provençaux" all spoke different dialects, with dissimilar customs and costumes, and their principle point in common was probably their allegiance to the same king. Peter Sahlins summarized the problem well in a recent work: "Officially, until the French Revolution, there was no 'nation' to which foreigners were expected to assimilate."[95]

Is the idea of "integration" or of "assimilation" into the "French nation" thus anachronistic and inconceivable before the French Revolution? No. First of all, it is not necessary for a problem to have been clearly formulated in a given period for historians to have the right to be interested in it. Moreover, we must distinguish between two different realities: the economic and social aspect, and the "cultural" aspect. We specify, except for notice to the contrary, that "integration" in this text evokes essentially or exclusively the economic and social aspect; while "assimilation" is to be understood in more of the cultural sense.[96] The "integration" aspect is present throughout the length of the period. From the beginning, in fact, it was clear to everyone that the Acadians were not integrated into the economic and social fabric of their welcoming regions. Without necessarily being expressed in a contemporary manner, then, the problem of the integration of the Acadians was very evident, and it appears in nearly all of the texts consulted. We notably find there several times the verbs "getting used" to, "becoming accustomed" to, and "attaching oneself" to the land.

As for the second aspect, it does not appear to be anachronistic as of the middle of the 1770s. "Blend" employed in an entirely similar sense to "assimilate" was used repeatedly. In fact, if the concept of "nation" was ambiguous before the Revolution, we should still assert that a certain idea of the French "nation" already existed. "The terminology employed by the agents [to take census of the foreigners] shows . . . that the notion of 'foreign peoples' existed as opposed to others defined by common belonging to a 'French nation,'" notes Sahlins.[97] And, indeed, it is about the assimilation of a foreign "body" into the heart of the "French nation" that the Controller-General Jacques Necker spoke in a letter to the minister, Antoine de Sartine, written in 1778 about the Acadians:

> One has therefore thought to divide [the Acadians] and to blend them, so to speak, into the society, in order that each of them might become a sailor, a soldier, a craftsman, a merchant, a laborer, following their talents and dispositions, without clinging more to a particular body of nation the idea of which it is impossible to allow to subsist within the breast of the French nation itself.[98]

Not only does this extract from a letter by the principle minister of the kingdom clearly show that the idea of the French nation very well existed in one form or another in 1778, but one even considered it important to "blend" the Acadians thereto. We must therefore admit the existence of an outline of a policy concerning the integration of the Acadians. We therefore can inquire about the strategies for integration and assimilation of the various parties, while keeping in mind the limits posed above.

With these necessary introductions and definitions made, we can now consider the study itself. The principal question that historians who have worked on this group of refugees before now have tried to answer, namely, the reasons for the departure of a majority of the Acadians from France to Louisiana in 1785, still forms the underlying thread of this book. Nevertheless, the question will be approached from a new angle. Three main approaches that renew and deepen the previous examinations of the integration and assimilation will be examined: the attitude of the French government, the attitude of the Acadians, and the "reality" of the integration. In other words, we will consider the following questions: Did the French government want to integrate or assimilate the Acadians, or both? Did the Acadians want to assimilate? If yes, why? If no, what could have been the cause of their reluctance? And, what was the reality of this integration-assimilation from an economic, social, and cultural point of view? We will successively study the physical integration; the integration by means of assistance; and finally the economic, social, "cultural," and political integration. As assimilation can occur without an explicit desire for it, we must be content to observe the existence of resistance to the assimilation, or the lack thereof, rather than a positive desire to blend into the population, which is more difficult to discern.

In the pages below, we will show that the French government did not attempt to assimilate the Acadians to the populations of the provinces in which they found refuge, for the refugees were above all meant to return to the colonies and not to settle in France. Once plans for settlement in the Antilles or in Guyana were abandoned, the government only barely concerned itself with the refugees. The few commissioners or large landowners who were then charged with helping them had a more positive image of them than did the common Breton or Poitevin people, who, in any case, did not want their assimilation either. On the whole, then, France did not seek to "assimilate" the Acadians in the modern sense of the word. The Acadians, for their part and for reasons that are easily understandable, were mainly motivated by material concerns: their extremely precarious conditions of existence, their dispersion and the interrelated problems of mutual communication, their lack of unity and internal divisions, all prevented them from considering a collective strategy to escape the difficulties into which they were immersed. It was not, therefore, "identity" or "culture" that mainly motivated them, even if these elements might sometimes have played a secondary role. The departure to Louisiana was a fortuitous event, sought by a determined, if barely scrupulous, Frenchman who forced the hand of many undecided Acadians, some of whom were, in the meantime, relatively well integrated into their new locales. It was in no way inevitable, as we will see.

Part One

**TO ASSEMBLE OR DISPERSE?
THE PLANS FOR SETTLEMENT**

Chapter I

"An attachment bordering on fanaticism for France": Causes for the Arrival in France

If one were to believe the French naval commissioner Antoine-Philippe Lemoyne, the ties binding the Acadians and their former homeland could be summed up as "an attachment bordering on fanaticism for France."[1] Lemoyne's opinion was far from negligible; it as much reflects the many Acadian petitions that constantly affirmed such an attachment as it does the opinion of the majority of administrators of all ranks who were involved with the refugees, in both France and the American colonies.[2] But, beyond these preemptory affirmations, do the actions of the Acadians confirm or diminish this view? Did not some Acadians provide testimony of their feelings on voluntarily leaving English Acadia or, later, France? A study of the circumstances and exact causes of the departures will allow us to have a more exact idea of the desire of the Acadians to go to France. To what degree was it their choice of destination? The answer will inform one of our principal questions: before asking if the Acadians resisted being assimilated into France, it is appropriate to ask if they indeed desired to go there. To answer this, we must distinguish three sorts of instances or cases: the circumstances of the departure from English Acadia, the question of the Acadians exiled in England, and, finally, the case of the Acadians deported from the islands north of Nova Scotia, Île Saint-Jean and Île-Royale (the current Prince Edward and Cape Breton Islands).

The Forced Departures from Nova Scotia

In the first case, and, after the brief account of the deportation described above, it may be useful to inquire about the causes of the departure of the Acadians. It was undoubtedly a forced departure. Acadian petitions sent to the French administration at the end of the eighteenth century sometimes present a very different version, however, lending credit to the thesis that their departure from Acadia was more or less voluntary, "thanks to their faithfulness to France and to the King."[3] The Entremont family wrote thus in an eloquent petition (one example among many others):

> Owners . . . of an immense plot of land whereon were found all of the needs and charms of a quiet life in abundance, [the Entremonts] abandoned it to the English, their conquerors, and did not hesitate in removing themselves to France to prove their faithfulness to their king and their attachment to the religion of their fathers. Despite the generous offers of the victor, honors and riches, nothing could disrupt their determination.[4]

Many other requests were founded on the same argument. To read these requests filled with references to the patriotic attachment of the "neutral French," one might get the impression that the Acadians voluntarily chose exile. However, they certainly had not anticipated the *Grand Dérangement*. Even if the rumors of deportation were already being heard by 1720, the inhabitants of Nova Scotia probably hoped that the equivocations of the English authorities regarding the unconditional oath of allegiance would continue. From 1713, the British had demanded this oath without ever having taken extreme measures to obtain it.[5] If the Acadians had been confronted with the clear choice of being deported to France or taking the oath, it is not certain that they would have chosen to go to France.[6] Undoubtedly, they hoped to preserve their neutrality and not have to take up arms against France, which is understandable in and of itself, without having to prove their pro-French patriotism. The colonists would have claimed faithfulness to France if they had had to choose between remaining on their lands and taking an oath to England or being deported, but they never had to make this choice. The only ones who actually did choose France were those who voluntarily left the peninsula to reassemble in other regions under French administration, particularly Beaubassin and Île Saint-Jean.

The argument of a more or less voluntarily exile in faithfulness to France seems to have been accepted without criticism back in the homeland. None within the administration seemed to question the basic Acadian rhetoric. On the contrary, many historical reports drawn up by various Frenchmen emphasized the Acadians' sacrifice for their religion, king, and country, such as the report that Lemoyne made of events of the summer of 1755. The same thread and often the same words are found in numerous other similar accounts:

> Under the pretext of confirming and ratifying their privileges, [the Acadians] of Beauséjour were ordered to go to the fort that General Moncton commanded and those in Beaubassin, to Port Royal, those in Minas Basin and other areas were ordered to go to Halifax, where Admiral Boscawen commanded. As soon as the Acadians were assembled in these forts, the commanders informed them that they had to take an oath of fidelity to the King of England and to take up arms for the English. Admiral Boscowen overdid the procedures. At the notice he made of this order, all of the Acadians had to kneel, and, after a very short prayer, the older people stood up and, speaking for all, said: "We have taken the oath of fidelity, we are ready to renew it, but we want to keep the privilege of neutrality and we will never take up arms against France." At this, the admiral, furious, drew his sword and cried: "What insolence! I don't know what keeps me from putting my sword through you." At this threat, one of the old men uncovered his breast and told him: "Strike if you dare; you can kill my body, but you have no power over my soul and you will never take from my heart my attachment to my religion nor my fidelity to my first and legitimate sovereign, Louis."[7]

According to this primary source version, then, based on the account of the refugees themselves, the deportation occurred because the Acadians refused to take up arms against France.[8] It is difficult to evaluate to what degree this interpretation has a basis in reality.[9] Certainly, the English demanded an "unconditional" oath of fidelity from the Acadians in 1755, which would have perhaps led them, in some circumstances, to take up arms against France, but probably only in the actual case of a French attack.

Over time, the reasons for the deportation surreptitiously transformed themselves, ending up in rewritings more susceptible to critical analysis: "We were expelled from Acadia and lost our property for having taken up arms for the King of France against the English,"[10] wrote the Acadians from Nantes in 1783. With such statements, the Acadians surely sought to bring their patriotism to the fore. However, apart from the three hundred Acadians who took up arms in the fort of Beauséjour and who, it seems, were compelled to fight for the French,[11] the great majority of the population of Nova Scotia does not seem to have fought the "English." With memories blurring themselves and becoming incapable of clearly drawing the distinction between places and circumstances, an old Acadian woman who was (she said)[12] nine years old at the time of the deportation, interviewed in 1822, affirmed that the Acadians were deported because they did not want to abandon their religion.[13] In this case it is clearly an alteration of the reality, since it had never been a question on the part of the English of having the Catholics under their administration in Nova Scotia deny their faith.

Beyond the reality of the rhetoric aimed at flattering the French administration in order to obtain its favor, it is quite difficult to deduce the true feelings that motivated the Acadians from this initial examination of the sources. Attachment to the Catholic religion surely allied them to France, while the fervent desire to remain neutral may be interpreted in many ways. It is likely that the colonists were motivated as much by the desire to remain far from fatal conflicts as by their repugnance at fighting "former compatriots" and fellow church members.[14]

The Acadians in England

The question of the fidelity and patriotism of the Acadians who were deported first to Virginia, and then sent to England in 1756, is no less complicated.[15] Were they any more masters of their own destiny than their compatriots exiled elsewhere? Could they choose among many options? All else aside, what can we deduce about their patriotism and their desire to go to France?

At the time of the peace discussions in 1762-1763, a report by the French ambassador in London, the duc de Nivernais, and his emissary, La Rochette,[16] suggests that practically all of the Acadians wanted to take refuge in the realm of His Very Christian Majesty. According to this same source, the English attempted to entice the detained by urging them to return to Acadia. The text provides numerous details about these initiatives: a commissioner of Liverpool recruited an Irish priest to try to convince the Acadians, and various members of the English nobility "lowered themselves" to doing the same. La Rochette conceded that a portion of the Acadians—"nearly all of whom were elderly"—did go to Liverpool because of these proposals, while in other locations they were divided. But it was not a question of errant travelers. Once La Rochette appeared (if we are to believe the French emissary) the doubts of the Acadians softened and their French sentiments returned.

It is interesting to compare this partisan piece with other sources. Indeed, if we would believe an English report and the information reported by Naomi Griffiths, the Acadians were invited by the British commissioners to express their own preferences about what they wanted to do after the peace. Their answer, which clearly demonstrates that they wanted to return to Acadia, contradicts Nivernais's version.[17]

This text only mentions the reply of one of the four groups of Acadian prisoners[18] in England, the one in Bristol. However, we have information about the desires of the other

Acadian groups. As at Bristol, those at Southampton and Liverpool wanted to return to Acadia. The English commissioners noted that some of these Acadians sought "transfer to being under the French government,"[19] however, those at Penryn asked for time in order to send their response.

Griffiths justly criticizes the position taken in the report of Nivernais. While it insists on the patriotic attachment of the Acadians to France,[20] Griffiths takes the opposite position, describing the exiles as being rather well-integrated into England,[21] though wanting to return to Acadia, and little interested in repatriation to France. She notes no inquiry in the report of Nivernais about the Acadians' feelings of belonging and how the French agents seemed incapable of imagining that the Acadians might prefer a destination other than France. She thus appropriately emphasizes the existence of a report sent by some Acadians in Liverpool seeking their return to Nova Scotia and the fact that a request for repatriation in France came from a French pilot who was a prisoner and was brought to London by an Irishman rather than by the Acadians themselves. La Rochette himself was received in Southampton with a lack of enthusiasm. The report recognizes that they (the Acadians at Falmouth near Penryn) had "contracted inclinations that were hardly French" and mentions a general defiance by the Acadians of a plan to send them to France.[22] Griffiths concludes her analysis by affirming that the Acadians wanted to return to Acadia and in no way wanted to go to France.[23]

Her argument, however, presents two problems. In the first place, Griffiths does not explain why the Acadians in fact finally did go to France if, by her reasoning, the large majority of the exiles wanted to return to Acadia. Furthermore, Nivernais's report and at least two other documents affirm that the British tried to convince the Acadians to return to Nova Scotia, proving, at the very least, that England was not opposed to such an emigration.[24] Griffith's silence on this point is probably explained by the absence of sources: we do not know if the Acadians really had the choice of returning to their country. After all, as she herself writes, the expatriates could be considered as British subjects and therefore "did not belong" to France. Additionally, England also sought to populate its own colonies and, shortly after the peace, would authorize the normalization of the Acadians in Nova Scotia.[25] In sum, nothing proves that the unfortunate Acadians did not receive authorization to go to Acadia and that they did not then voluntarily choose France instead.

It is nonetheless possible that the Acadians had no other choice than to go to France. To be certain, we would have to know the final decision taken by the United Kingdom. But we can only glimpse the English opinion through French diplomatic correspondence. In fact, the fate of the Acadians was the subject of close negotiations between the rival powers. The first reference to these dealings, in December 1762, leads us to believe that the English had at that time taken no position:

> Mr. George Greenville . . . First Commissioner of the Admiralty . . . over the last few days gave me a long and embarrassed discussion about the Acadians who, during the present war, were dispersed in the English colonies or brought to England for having refused to take the oath of obedience to [England]. He told me that they were still embarrassed by those who still were living in England . . . . He asked me what would be the fate of these people and what I thought one could do with them. . . . As I am sure that he only made this overture to me in order to [delay the peace negotiations] I did not consider it appropriate to answer him anything other than that I had no documents or instructions on the subject.[26]

Except for speculating that this discussion was only a pretext for delaying the peace negotiations (as did Nivernais), it would seem that the government in London had not decided what path to pursue. Subsequently, and many times, the deported were alluded to many times in the negotiations, but we do not have the answers to the French suggestions. In January 1763, the English attempted to exclude the "neutral Acadians" from a general amnesty then under discussion.[27] The duke Etienne-François de Choiseul intervened so that the Acadians would not be excluded and specified, furthermore:

> The King [Louis XV] proposes sending them all to France in letting them sell their property. There is more: as these Acadians lived in Canada, they must have full liberty either to remain there, or to return to France after having sold their property in conformity with article 2 of the preliminaries that stipulates that "the French inhabitants or others who were subjects of the most Christian King in Canada can withdraw, etc."[28]

Thus France in this period had arrived at the point of wanting the "Neutral French" to return to Canada. But we do not know what the response of the British was to these suggestions; we can only guess that it was probably negative. It is perhaps because the Acadians then were refused the right to return to Acadia that, sometime afterwards, the duc de Nivernais referred to the "Canadian prisoners" asking to go to "Miquelon island."[29] Who were these "Canadian prisoners?" We have seen how the vocabulary of this period often considers the terms Acadians and Canadians as synonyms. But a later letter by the duc de Choiseul—probably referring to the same people—specifies that it was "the inhabitants of the Gulf of Saint Lawrence, the Canadians, the fishermen of Île Saint-Jean, those from Louisbourg, etc. who wanted to be sent to Miquelon Island."[30] The fate of these candidates for emigration to the islands of Saint-Pierre and Miquelon is not known, but what is certain is that shortly after this letter, perhaps after being informed of Nivernais's report of February 1763, Choiseul again tried to strongly convince the Acadians to come to France:

> The advantage you will bring the State by engaging [the Acadian families] to go into the Kingdom is that much more agreeable to His Majesty as he has considered them for a long time for a new colony in the case that they want to accept his intentions, but even if they determine to remain in the Kingdom, this population is too precious to not be received with pleasure.[31]

At this date, it is probable that Nivernais was already aware of the English intentions, but he says nothing of them. We can nonetheless state that the process of repatriation of the Acadians to France was then begun.

So the issue is not settled. If, as Griffiths suggests, the Acadians actually did want to return to Acadia, why was their plan not accomplished? Was it the refusal of the government of Great Britain to let them return? That is the most plausible hypothesis. After all, the English undoubtedly still mistrusted the Acadians, and this option would have been more costly than to let the exiles go to France. Adding up the debts contracted by the Acadians in England, according to a document of March 1763, amounts to around 15,000 French *livres*, and the refugees were in no condition to pay for the voyage themselves.[32] If the Acadians did not want to return to France, how can we explain that some of them solicited France to return there?[33] Did they leave voluntarily, while they apparently had a free choice?[34] How to explain the letters sent by the Acadians in England to their compatriots dispersed in the North American colonies asking them to go to France themselves in order to join them there?[35] How to explain the many subsequent petitions by the Acadians in the American colonies all asking to go to France or to Saint-Domingue?[36] How to explain, also, that the Acadians then strongly claimed to have chosen to go to France?[37] And, finally, how to explain that those Acadians deported to the Thirteen Colonies rejoined the French colonies rather than returning to Acadia, even though the English government gave them authorization to return to Acadia on July 11, 1764?[38]

We have seen that the Acadians dispersed in North America were indeed told of the passage of some of their compatriots in England to France. The duc de Nivernais seemed convinced that the first of them would easily and voluntarily return to France. In his report, in fact, he wrote:

> Supposing the king cannot deliver all of these dispersed Acadians, neither by reclaiming them as subjects nor by ransoming them as captives, it is certain that one could always have the majority return by secretly agreeing to safeguard all of those wanting to escape the treatment given the Acadians in Europe today.

If Nivernais forced the hand of the Acadians in England, he was less confident in his ability to attract those in the Thirteen Colonies. In fact, it seems that the Acadians in North America, perhaps more convinced of the impossibility of returning to Acadia or still experiencing more precarious living conditions, more readily sought out passage to France. Nor did they reject going to one of the French colonies, as many letters attest.[39] Thus one group of Acadians wrote: "Since the English took us from our lands we have always desired to go to France or to one of the French colonies . . . [in order that] we might have the pleasure of enjoying all of the freedoms of our religion."[40] As for the "neutral inhabitants of Acadia" staying in Maryland, they only sought "the means of joining the number of faithful subjects of the glorious monarchy of his Very Christian Majesty the King of France and of Navarre," and they forwarded a list of all the Acadians who wanted to go to France.[41] We could continue supplying examples. However, it should be noted that very few of these Acadians actually went to France or to the French colonies. Most of them ended up in Louisiana, New Brunswick, or Quebec.

The second weak point in Griffith's argument is that if she justly criticizes Nivernais's report, she is less attentive to the answers—however nuanced—that were supplied by the Acadians to the English commissioners. Surely, the refugees asked to return to their lands and their homes, which is easily understandable. But they also immediately asked that the free exercise of their religion be again assured. Furthermore, they specified that they wanted missionaries to be sent to them in France.[42] Moreover, it is not inconceivable that the Acadians, mistrusting the English, ardently wanted to go to France, but that they did not dare express this frankly to the British commissioners for fear of possible reprisals. After all, according to Griffiths, the British noted that an anonymous petition by the Acadians in Liverpool asked to again be placed "under the French government," and it is plausible that La Rochette's report reflected the feelings of at least some of the Acadians. It is indeed evident that the statements of the Acadians demonstrated self-censorship and varied depending on the authorities to which they were addressed. Thus the refugees asked to return to Acadia when they addressed the British, while they said that they wanted to return to France when they addressed Nivernais.

What might we conclude? First of all, one cannot give blind credence either to the report of Nivernais or to the affirmations of Martin, according to which the Acadians wanted very much to be repatriated to France from England. However, we can hardly draw a definitive conclusion about the attachment of the Acadians to France. It is unlikely that the exiles were entirely opposed to the idea of going back to France. Moreover, perhaps we should not consider the Acadians in England as being one united group: the wishes of the refugees in Liverpool seem far removed from those of Penryn. Finally, it is clear that the Acadians all shared a desire to return to Acadia and a desire to preserve their religion.[43] But they were reluctant about the idea of returning to Nova Scotia under a regime that they mistrusted. As for going to France, this would indicate a renunciation of their now-English native country. Is it possible that the various promises made by Nivernais to the Acadians tipped the balance in favor of their going to France?[44]

The question of whether the Acadians truly had a choice of returning to Acadia when they were in England in 1763 can not be resolved. It will only be answered if deeper research eventually uncovers what the true intentions of the English government were regarding them. The motives for the transferal of the Acadians from England to France in 1763 are not known in a definite manner. If the official reason familiar in France throughout the period of our study—namely, their fidelity to France and refusal to abandon their religion and their sovereign—should only be accepted with caution, it cannot be discarded, either.

The Inhabitants of Île Saint-Jean and Île-Royale

The group that we have just examined was the first to have been deported, in 1755. We have seen, however, that the largest contingent of deportees who reached French soil in the 1760s consisted of the deportees from Île Saint-Jean, along with some families from Île-Royale. As with the preceding group, it may seem pointless to inquire about the causes for their departure, since they were similarly deported only three years after their unfortunate compatriots. We should not forget that the majority of these refugees were Acadians who voluntarily rejoined the French colonies before 1755.[45] Some, then, were individuals whose attachment to France was perhaps paradoxically less questionable than that of the inhabitants of Acadia. Nonetheless, in truth, the emigration of the Acadians to Île Saint-Jean or to Île-Royale was not necessarily due to an attachment to France, but rather the result of great anxieties, as the Acadians feared for their safety.[46] The French government, here employing the carrot, and there the stick, encouraged this emigration in various ways. The French missionary Le Loutre forcefully (sometimes physically) encouraged the families to leave their homes to go to the French possessions of Acadia, notably Île Saint-Jean.[47] Thus it is unrealistic to hope to determine to what degree the Acadians went to Île Saint-Jean in good or bad faith, or to conclude that those who went there had a stronger attachment to France than did their compatriots who remained on the peninsula of Nova Scotia.

Lastly, a portion of the inhabitants of Île Saint-Jean was similarly composed of families sent there after the deportation of the summer of 1755. It is difficult to estimate their exact number, probably over five hundred people.[48] The Abbé Le Guerne wrote a moving account of the wanderings of some of these Acadian families who ended up going to the island under French rule.[49] Jean-Baptiste Robichaux, whose life story is told in the *Dictionnaire biographique du Canada*, supplies another example. As the Acadians naturally sought to flee deportation, the fact of taking refuge on Île Saint-Jean does not constitute proof of their attachment to France.

Despite these reservations, the deported Acadians of Île Saint-Jean legitimately seem to have shown more attachment to "the religion and to France" than those who remained in Acadia. Though, curiously, while the refugees of Île Saint-Jean were more numerous in France than those from Acadia proper, the Acadian petitions and the historical reports drawn up by the French administration never give precedence to this second deportation. The reason for this is probably that the government had never promised anything to the deportees from Île Saint-Jean and Louisbourg, whereas, to the contrary, the Acadian refugees had in the interim gone to England. The strategy of the refugees of Île Saint-Jean was therefore to build their ties with those repatriated in England rather than to explain their specific situation.

Conclusion

What may we conclude, then, from this examination of the circumstances of the repatriation? According to some patriotic texts from the period 1755-1785, the Acadians surely suffered from the deportation but were consoled by the possibility of being rejoined to France and to a king and a religion that they cherished more than they did their native country. This rhetoric was partially repeated by the historiography, although some historians try to show that the Acadians felt almost completely detached from France. A careful examination of the situations of the departure subtly but seriously distinguishes these two antagonistic positions. Contrary to what they later affirmed, the choice was never proposed to the Acadians from Nova Scotia between accepting the unconditional oath of allegiance or being deported to France. The exile was submitted to, not chosen. As for those who were made prisoners in England, if we should be wary of partisan affirmations like those of the Nivernais's report that present the Acadians as strongly wanting to be repatriated in France, the contrary thesis is not proven, either. It is difficult to believe that all of the deported unanimously wanted to return to Acadia. The Acadians seem to have already been especially strongly divided over what they wanted to do. Finally, if the Acadians who emigrated to Île Saint-Jean and Île-Royale before 1755 were perhaps those who most showed a desire to "remain French," it is difficult to judge to what degree their choice may have been made under duress. On their arrival in France, then, if the refugees were happy to find a refuge, to live under a friendly government and with the assurance of being able to practice their religion, a large number of them were undoubtedly less enthusiastic than Nivernais would lead us to believe. The greatest number must still have greatly missed Acadia, and the choice of France was surely only one of default. No doubt they were not excessively enthusiastic about the idea of being assimilated into the home country population. At best, the settlements promised by Nivernais probably seemed to them to be a last resort.

Chapter II

The French Administration and the Acadian Groups

The Bureaucratic Organization:
The Navy, the Colonies, and the Contrôle Général in Charge of the Acadians

Upon their arrival in France, the Acadians were taken into the care of the French administration, which involved itself with distributing emergency assistance to them and, later, with relocating them. Before studying these activities in detail, it is appropriate to briefly outline the government's branches responsible for the refugees.

In the colonies overseen by the Secretary of State of the Navy, the personnel of this ministry received the refugees upon their arrival in the ports.[1] Since the time of Jean-Baptiste Colbert, the Navy had advanced from an administrative point of view, thanks to a remarkably centralized system and agents who were "truly functionaries in the modern sense of the term."[2] On the coast, the Navy was represented by an intendant or a general commissioner who supervised the work of subordinates such as the ordinary commissioners responsible for the various sectors of activity. Locally, the Acadians most often depended on the administration of the "divisions," an inheritance from the military service (which was obligatory only for the sailors). Thus, at Saint-Malo, it was a "commissioner of divisions," one Isarn, who officiated with regard to the Acadians; at Morlaix, it was the corresponding agent, Quétier, who supervised the refugees, and the same at Cherbourg.[3] It is probable that the general commissioners and the intendants, unlike the commissioners of divisions, only had indirect contact with the Acadians: thus, at Saint-Malo, it was not Guillot himself who directly supervised the distribution of assistance. He was the one, however, in correspondence with the Paris offices. An initial transference of orders and information therefore occurred even within the local offices, but as it was most often done orally, this transmission was not documented. This point is important to remember for the analysis of the texts. It is hardly likely, for instance, that Guillot himself ever conversed with the Acadians for very long. The commissioner—very likely a noble as were most of the personnel of his rank—surely rarely frequented the company of the Acadians, an assembly of people of "lower status."

At the central level, the ministry of the Navy, directed by a Secretary of State, was then split into eight bureaus.[4] The Acadians depended on the Bureau of the Colonies, created in 1710. Each bureau was directed by a "first principal agent," or "first commissioner." Plucked from the thread of the texts, we find amid these bureaus the names of individuals who were charged with coordinating the administration of the Acadians: Accaron, "counselor and first agent of the Navy," in 1763-1764; and La Roque, also first agent, specifically charged with Acadian affairs in July 1772.[5] It was these agents who were truly in charge of the files, and it was probably they who rendered accounts to the minister and prepared most of the decisions that were signed by the Secretary of State. These agents managed the actuarial services, along with their appointed clerks.[6] Here, as elsewhere, it is difficult to know to what degree the ministers themselves decided on the broad directions of the policy to be followed, and what was their personal involvement. Often we suspect that this participation was minimal for some ministers, the Acadians being only one among their many preoccupations. On many occasions, however, the administrators or the missionaries said that they had personally met with the minister on site to discuss the situation of the Acadians.[7] Whatever the case, all of the Secretaries of State of the second half of the eighteenth century had some familiarity with the Acadian file at one time or another.

Other institutions were actively involved with the Acadians. The States of Brittany also played a brief, but important role, at the time of the settlement of the Acadians on Belle-Île. Moreover, many municipal councils took urgent initiatives and similarly intervened in the management of affairs involving the refugees. In some towns, the councils organized lodging for the Acadians upon their arrival. At Nantes, the municipal council supported a request from one Acadian, Basile Henry, in 1782.

Various individuals were also officially and successively charged with acting for the refugees, in parallel with the organization described above. First, there were members of the clergy. The Abbé de l'Isle-Dieu, vicar general of the bishopric of Québec, was the first to whom the care of the exiles was entrusted, in 1760.[8] His role was not clearly delineated, but he did act as an intermediary between the Acadians and the minister. In 1763 came the turn of the Abbé Le Loutre to be responsible (in connection with de l'Isle-Dieu, who had retired) for the settlement of the Acadian families at Belle-Île-en-Mer.[9] In fact, the former missionary to the Micmacs remained the intermediary between the Acadians and the ministry until his death on September 30, 1772. Entrusting the care of the refugees to missionaries brought some advantages. The Abbé Le Loutre knew the refugees personally, and he was a dynamic and effective manager. The relative success of the settlement of Belle-Île-en-Mer surely owes much to him. Moreover, these priests seem to have been relatively well received by the ministry and by the Acadians, more than would be the later commissioner-general, Lemoyne. However, even if their mission was official, they always had to act as intermediaries with regard to the ministries, which especially delayed operations. There was no true delegation of power, and the Abbé Le Loutre had a narrow space in which to maneuver. In any event, the ministry seemed satisfied with the mediation of the Church, and, upon the death of Le Loutre, the Abbé de Grandclos Mêlé, "theological and canon archdeacon" of the cathedral of Saint-Malo, was soon presented to "replace the Abbé with regard to the Acadians." Grandclos, who knew the exiles domiciled in his diocese well, nonetheless refused this "unprofitable task" proposed to him.[10]

This role of intermediary between the Acadians and the minister was then held by a commissioner of the Navy delegated to the ministry, Antoine-Philippe Lemoyne. Following the refusal of Grandclos, and at the request of Lemoyne himself, the Abbé de l'Isle-Dieu recommended the commissioner of Rochefort to fill the role of protector of the Acadians.[11] Lemoyne had been called some time before to Versailles to present various projects that he had conceived relating to the Acadians.[12] It seems that his proposition was accepted and that Lemoyne was then orally charged with taking over care of the Acadians towards the beginning of 1773. He remained responsible for them until the end of 1774. In fact, Lemoyne essentially guaranteed the role of liaison in the new arrangement that was put into place in 1773. In truth, in 1772, according to many sources, the king had personally intervened to request that land be given to the Acadians. It subsequently was decided that the Acadians would no longer depend on the Navy but theoretically on the Contrôle Général, beginning on July 1, 1773. In practice, the change took much longer, and Lemoyne, for better or worse, oversaw the transition. On the local level, from that time on, the Acadians did not depend on the naval administration, but on the intendants, and, more specifically, on the sub-delegates.[13] On the central level, the general ministry of Finances was organized in a manner similar to that of the Navy; various agents were specifically charged with Acadian affairs.[14]

Beyond the missionaries, the Navy administration, and the Contrôle Général, a number of other officials were involved with the Acadians. Among these were diplomatic personnel of the French embassy in London, and, more generally, agents of the ministry of Foreign Affairs, at the time of the negotiation of the peace agreements in 1763. The most active was La Rochette, already mentioned, who arranged the contacts with the refugees, took charge of the repatriation of the Acadians in the United Kingdom, and regularly sent accounts of his activities to the duc de Nivernais.[15] The second individual involved with the moving of the exiles was one Moreau, Director-General of Garden Nurseries, who, five years before Lemoyne, made a first tour of the ports to take census of the Acadians for the purpose of undertaking land clearings.[16] His name nonetheless does not appear until after 1767. Other individuals participated in the management of the "Acadian file," though we do not have much information about them. Thus we find one Mr. Parent, "bureau chief for Mr. Bertin," and one Mr. de Rozière, "bureau chief of court funds."[17] The marquis de Pérusse d'Escars, finally, also played a great role, since he coordinated the settlement of the Acadians in Poitou and was further charged with the distribution of aid to the Acadians during the time that the "colony" was stationed in Poitou (he nonetheless shared this responsibility with the intendant of the site, a certain Blossac).

The Acadian group, having drawn the sympathy and compassion of many important people of the State, also solicited from its protectors intervention on its behalf from the king or from his ministers. At the moment of Necker's arrival in power, according to an undoubtedly exaggerated report: "Every three months two or three fathers of families arrive who come in the name of all of them to seek the justice and goodness of the King. All of the individuals of the royal family have received and recommended their reports."[18] One finds in the texts many references to people who intervened in favor of the Acadians.[19] These individuals sometimes interfered with the official orders, soliciting privileges or exemptions for the Acadians.

We can thus try to reconstitute an organizational chart of the administration of the Acadians from the documentation that remains. For the period previous to 1773, which is to say when the Acadians were still the responsibility of the Navy, the diagram is hierarchically simple enough (Figure 1).

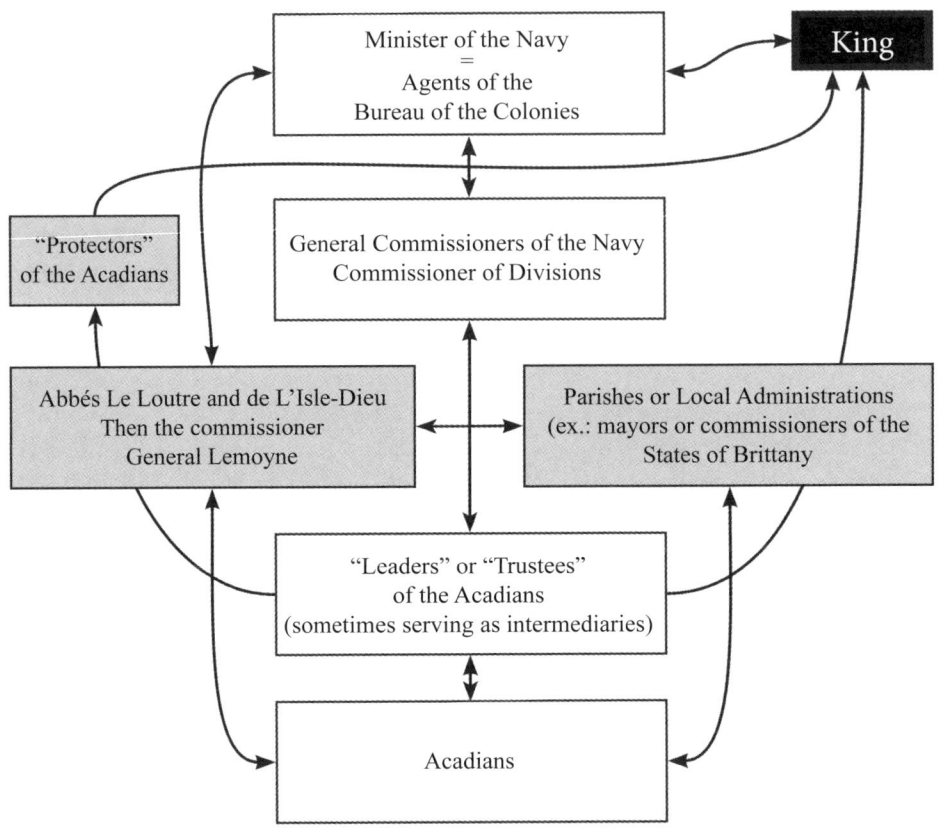

FIGURE 1
Organizational chart of the administration responsible for the Acadians before 1773

For the period after the change of ministry in guardianship, the situation becomes more complicated, with a number of more or less informal intermediaries (Fig. 2). Lemoyne, in particular, rendered account of his activities to three ministers at once: the Controller-General, to whom he was officially attached by his mission, the Secretary of State of the Navy, and, finally, the Minister of Agriculture, Bertin, who very closely followed the land clearing project of the marquis de Pérusse. We can only imagine that the coordination of activities was not thus made any easier.

Functioning of the Administration

This diagram of the whole set does not reveal if this form of governance was effective. The administration of France's *Ancien Régime* is too often judged by "the measure of our contemporary criteria, individualistic and democratic, and by a degree of prosperity unimaginable in that period."[20] Taking account of the limited means of the period, the bureaucracy actually functioned rather well, especially allowing that the agents had to face numerous constraints. The path of the affairs involving the Acadians was chaotic and led

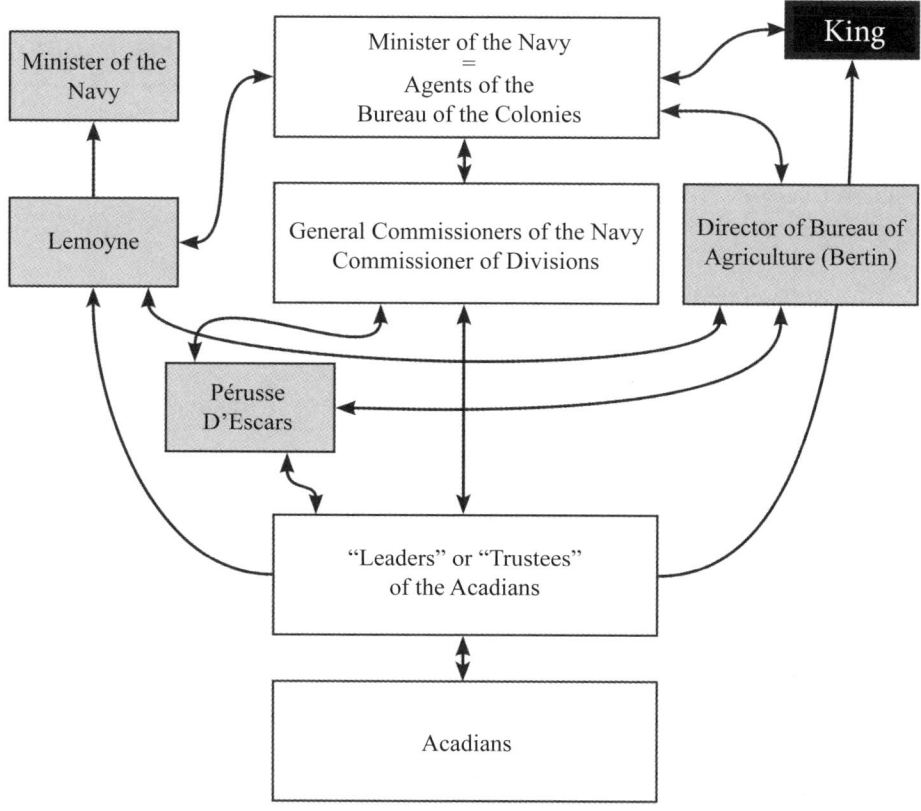

FIGURE 2
Organizational chart of the administration responsible for the Acadians after 1773

to considerable delays, even from the arrival of the very first refugees. This was notably the case with the distribution of aid, for instance.

The "Delays"

The lack of punctuality in the outlay of assistance and in making decisions in general, though largely overlooked by Ernest Martin, is nonetheless constantly mentioned by the documents originating either from the Acadians themselves or from the administration from the very beginning of the distributions. Aid was not immediately disseminated, despite the urgency. Thus the mayor of Saint-Malo wrote some days after the first Acadians arriving in the "city of corsairs," that, "Mr. Guillot told [me] that he paid 6s a day to these inhabitants but had not counted them."[21]

Unfortunately for the Acadians this was only the start of a long series of complaints on the subject. In January 1760, Ranché, naval intendant at Le Havre, communicated to the minister the impossibility of the situation in which he found himself, lacking funds to pay the "inhabitants of Île-Royale and Île Saint-Jean." In May 1760, came further indications that the treasuries of the colonies had not provided the funds meant to be distributed in eight months.[22] Curiously, while delays were the same in all of France, in nearly the same period, those in Saint-Malo were only delayed for two or three months.[23] If we examine the best-documented cases, like that of the port of Cherbourg, during the whole duration of the period studied, delays of six months, nine months, or a year were common. In May 1773, a climax was reached: payment was urgently ordered of back payment due to the Acadians for a year and a half.[24] In 1785, shortly before the departure of the Acadians for Louisiana, the Spanish ambassador, Pedro Pablo Abarca de Bolea, count de Aranda, could write in all calmness to the minister of Foreign Affairs, Charles Gravier, comte de Vergennes, that his country would take charge of the assistance for the Acadians by January 1785: they had evidently still not been paid.[25]

The Acadians very soon began to complain about the delays, and this theme recurs like a leitmotif in many petitions. In May 1759, in Rochefort, a former inhabitant of Île-Royale dared address the Minister of the Navy about the protests over the delay of assistance that the king had promised the poor families of Île Saint-Jean who were in La Rochelle.[26] Some months later, new recriminations were expressed, but, after an investigation, the minister was "very pleased to learn that [the families of Île-Royale] had no part in the complaints that had been brought [to him] and that a sergeant of the ground troops who had married a *créole* [an Acadian woman] was the sole author of the reports addressed [to him]."[27] The tempestuous minister was worn out by these complaints, and, rather than try to prevent the causes of extra delays, he simply regretted that the intendant had not prevailed.[28] It is possible that this notification by Nicolas-René Berryer, comte de la Ferrière, the Minister of Navy, stopped the number of complaints on the subject. Indeed, in the following years, one finds hardly any more recriminations on the subject by those involved, despite the changing of the minister. We learn in an indirect manner, however, that the Acadians suffered from the situation. Thus, those who were deported to England affirmed to La Rochette at the time of his turn in office that "they feared experiencing the same fate on arriving in the kingdom" as those of "their brothers who were transported to France at the beginning of the war [and] remained many months without receiving any aid." They had received their information directly from the Acadians who were "in France, Boulogne, Saint-Malo and Rochefort" and who had corresponded with them.[29]

If, for some time, the Acadians no longer dared to complain directly to the minister, many administrators or clergy charged with their affairs described the difficulties engendered by these delays. Some years later, Mistral begged the minister "to provide orders . . . to ensure that these unfortunate people would no longer have to wait for payment of a balance whose set denomination proves that [it] should be being paid daily."[30] However, in November, 1771, an entire "delegation" of Acadians went to Versailles or Compiègne, according to a report of June 1778, to "solicit payment of the balance."[31] Other petitions were still sent regularly, as one in 1775 from Poitou requesting payment for aid not received for many months.[32]

Cause of the Delays

How to explain the delays? The difficulties were of different kinds. First of all, the naval commissioner took the initiative to provide the urgent aid.[33] At Saint-Malo, the commissioner first allowed municipal generosity to be offered. Before a regular payment of subsidies could occur (the first general directives only date from January 1759), the administrators had to solicit the view of the minister.[34] The latter then most often requested regular lists of the Acadians, which were then often sent with delays, because of the difficulty in compiling a census of the refugees.[35] The problems with payment were also recurrent because of the colossal debt of the State in the eighteenth century. The problem affected not just the refugees: the intendants themselves often had problems getting paid.[36] Moreover, a portion of the funds intended to help the Acadians sometimes ended up diverted. In many letters, the agents are reproached for "speculating" and "intrigue" involving ration notes."[37] Berryer sharply reprimanded the intendant of the Navy at Rochefort on this subject.[38] The Acadians also complained of withdrawals from their balance.[39] Pérusse sent calculations to Blossac meant to prove that a third of the sums distributed for the Acadians had been diverted.[40]

Finally, the general process of decision making could not go any faster than the stage coaches, which, in the eighteenth century, still took five days to go from Paris to Lyon, nine to Marseille, and at the most fifteen days for the other large provincial towns.[41] In 1758, letters only reached the naval commissioner at Saint-Malo six days after having been signed by the minister.[42] But the slowness and difficulties in communication only partially explained the delays. These were most often engendered by the succession of orders and baffling counter-orders. This negligence probably reflects more disinterest on the part of the minister than a true disorganization. In April 1772, Pierre-Etienne Bourgeois de Boynes admitted to Lemoyne that he had mislaid his reports![43] The same commissioner often had no answers to his missives and frequently complained that the Acadian question was not a priority.[44] De Boynes sent Guillot erroneous instructions thanks to a misreading of a previous letter.[45]

Even when bad faith did not disrupt the equation, mistakes were frequent. Pages supposed to be attached to folds in the documents often fell missing.[46] Moreover, when decisions were made, they were rarely communicated at the same time in all places.[47] Thus, a directive by the minister from December 1772 ordering the cessation of payments of sustenance to the families from America on April 1, 1774, "not having arrived in the various places where these families were in residence, the Acadian families continued to be paid until July 1, even until the 15th,"[48] deplored Lemoyne, who from then on had to repeat the instructions and repair the confusion. But sometimes we need not take these criticisms too literally. In certain cases, critiques of the absence or poor quality of instructions were a convenient excuse for the correspondents to explain their own inadequacies.

Conclusion

Thus the management of the Acadian affairs was successively dependent on the Ministry of the Navy until 1773, then the Contrôle Général of Finances until the end of the period. To the traditional hierarchical scheme were added many intermediary officials and others who, on the margins of the administration proper, tried to coordinate or support the actions undertaken to benefit the refugees, though conveniently not forgetting their own interests. The role of the religious should not be surprising at a time when the Catholic Church played an official role in the State. The administration knew how to demonstrate remarkable organization in cases of need, despite the difficulties of the period, but the Acadian question was, from all evidence, not a priority for the successive governments. This is the main reason for the delays in distribution of assistance, which weighed heavily on the Acadians. It would, of course, be absurd to entirely blame the administration for its inadequacies; nonetheless, Martin's theory of a "good welcome" acknowledges too few of these deficiencies, which partially explain the lassitude and discouragement of the Acadians confronting an administration that acted in such a chaotic manner. Undoubtedly, we may already find in this dysfunction one of the causes for the ultimate defection of the Acadians in 1785.

Organization of the Acadians

After this preliminary examination of the administration, we should now explain the bottom tier of the two organizational charts presented above, that is to say, the internal organization of the Acadian group itself.

The Spontaneous Regroupings

The successive arrivals of the Acadians in France in a dispersed fashion has been noted above. The largest number were left at Saint-Malo, but other ships landed at Rochefort, La Rochelle, Brest, Cherbourg, Le Havre, and Boulogne.[49] The first impulses among organization of the Acadians were spatial: we find the main regroupings around Saint-Malo.[50] Thus, while the number of refugees disembarked in this city in 1759 rose to around 850,[51] this figure did not stop rising until the departure to Poitou in 1773, when it was around 1,800 people.[52] This increase cannot be explained by new births or by later arrivals, but rather indicates familial regroupings. In fact, from the first disembarkations passports were granted to a large number of people in order to allow them to rejoin kin in another town.[53]

A reassembling of the Acadians in places they lived was shown in many locations. At Morlaix, at Le Havre, and at Boulogne, the Acadians were grouped around the same parish, as they were later at Nantes.[54]

These concentrations of Acadians were, at first, closely connected to the desire of members of the same family to join together, for many extended and even nuclear families had been separated at the time of the deportation. This phenomenon, easily understandable, was similarly shown among the Acadians deported to the North American colonies.[55] Thus, a young man solicits authorization to marry without the agreement of his parents, explaining that they were in Philadelphia for four years and that he had no news from them for two years, "without knowing if they are living or are dead."[56] We do not know why the families were separated. In this case, perhaps the son emigrated later to Île Saint-Jean while his parents remained in Acadia. The many letters exchanged between the exiles evoke in a recurring manner the theme of "rediscoveries," if we judge by just the examples that have come down to our time.[57] An Acadian woman at Cherbourg expressed her desire to see her family again and her firm intention of working to achieve that goal:

> I do not know how to express to you the desire that I have to see you as well as all of your family, and knowing nothing and hardly seeing any evidence that we might see each other again very soon. . . . I beg you to remain calm until we know what our fate will be . . . and I hope that you will do as much as you possibly can so that we may be reunited.

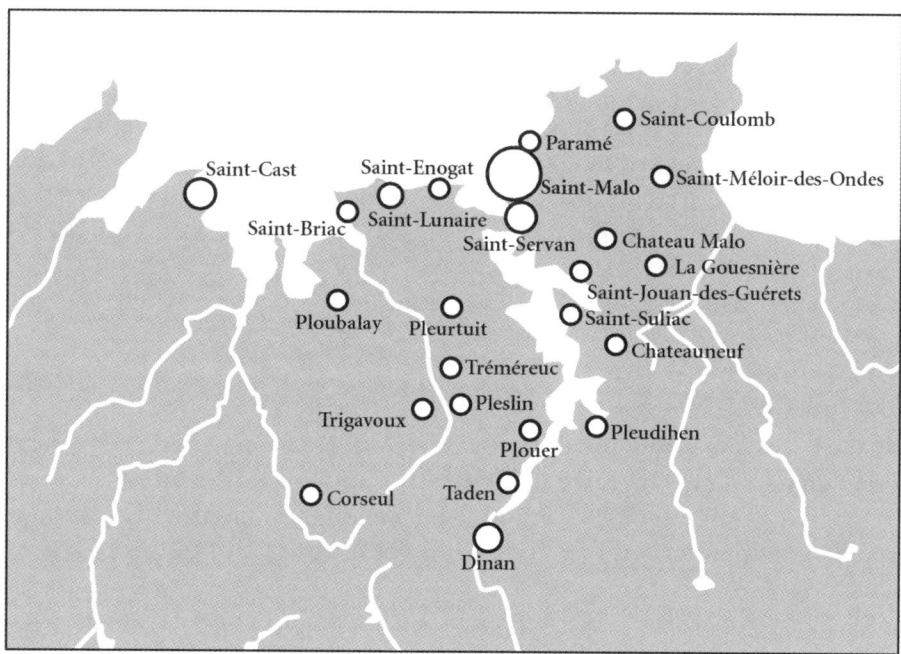

MAP 3
Places of residence of the Acadians in the Saint-Malo region from 1758 to 1785.
From a map made by François Roux.

Some ten years later, her desire to rejoin her family had not diminished, nor her feeling of powerlessness.[58] Her nephew expressed the same feelings of resignation and also courage. "God has separated us," he wrote, "[but He can] rejoin us and return our property as in the past."[59] When they solicited authorization to leave the kingdom of France, the Acadians frequently justified their petitions with their desire to reunite with their families—asking, for example, to go to Boston for this reason in 1784.[60] In any event, even if they could not reassemble, the Acadians exchanged an intense correspondence, whether within the interior of France, or across the Manche department and the Atlantic, to their compatriots spread through England and North America. Many sources indicate that the letters exchanged were more plentiful than the few that remain. The Acadians were not content with giving family news, they also exchanged information about the aid that they were given, their living conditions, the welcome that they received, and even the latest happenings in the kingdom.[61]

These regroupings and exchanges of information served the goal of mutual survival. After all, the dispersion of the Acadians had been conceived by the English to prevent the formation of a dangerous group in the Thirteen Colonies, as well as to assimilate the deported among Anglo-American populations.[62] This strategy was explicitly described in a missive by the governor of New York in 1756 and was equally applied in England, since the Acadians were found there divided between four cities, Bristol, Liverpool, Southampton, and Falmouth. In reaction, the Acadians seem to have sought to reform a numerically higher nucleus once their departure was planned from England, or, if nothing else, to remain in close written correspondence.⁶³ A letter written in Great Britain by four exiles to their "brothers" dispersed in the American colonies in March 1763, is explicit on the subject: "On our part, we are all for going to France. We all pray to God to see you there with us."⁶⁴ Moreover, the Acadians in Liverpool expressly asked to rejoin their compatriots at Boulogne, which they were allowed to do.⁶⁵ It is probable that, at the beginning, the hope of the Acadians was to form a "New Acadia" in France, that is to say, a single and large family. This is what the Abbé de l'Isle-Dieu eloquently expressed to Cardinal Castelli in 1767.⁶⁶ Little by little, the victims of the *Grand Dérangement* became aware that, by regrouping, they would be stronger when it came to protecting their mutual interests.

Political Organization

So it was that the Acadians came to progressively present themselves as a "body of a nation," beginning in the early 1770s. The meaning of this expression is not easy to understand.⁶⁷ Let us summarily say that this phrase implies the idea of a community, the existence of a common leader, of a combining "of interests and feelings," and even of a collective experience.

The Acadians organized themselves in an informal-enough manner. They chose some delegates—returning to a custom dating from before the *Grand Dérangement*—to perform specific tasks, such as visiting lands or carrying a petition to Versailles.⁶⁸ The first such *syndics* were selected starting in 1774.⁶⁹ With time, the work of this advocate could be active and diverse—as shown, for instance, by the note acknowledging the tasks accomplished by the *syndic* Augustin Doucet—or it could be a role as a representative or counselor.⁷⁰ A formal council was put into place among the Acadians by December 1774 in Poitou, in conjunction with the selecting of agents. Pérusse spoke of this council of six people who would decide "if they will or will not execute the orders provided" or suspend this "little republican administration." Nonetheless, some delegates were not recognized by the whole community, others were only supposed to represent some families, and many debated the idea of the best strategy to adopt when confronting a recalcitrant or inactive administration.⁷¹

One portion of the Acadians seems to have progressively arrived at the conclusion that it was only by remaining in groups that they would be able to obtain from the government fulfillment of its promises of land made in 1763 or, at least, the authorization to emigrate. The problem was that the Acadian groups in France, despite their regular contact through correspondence, were themselves extremely divided over what they should request from the government, whether to emigrate again or to find a settlement in France. But many leaders, despite these disagreements, wanted at all costs to avoid an implosion of the main group, that which was formed at Saint-Malo and then migrated together to Poitou and finally to Nantes. This is what explains the tensions within the "body of nation" every time that there was a question of moving. Thus, when Lemoyne went to Saint-Malo, the majority seemed to rally to delegate Jean-Jacques LeBlanc's view of not emigrating to Poitou, while a minority seemed much more open to Lemoyne's proposals. The commissioner benefited from the internal dissensions of the group to convince the entirety to emigrate.⁷² He was successful, since a certain number of Acadians were talked into attempting the experiment proposed by the marquis de Pérusse. But it was a

Pyrrhic victory. In fact, Jean-Jacques LeBlanc and other Acadian delegates he had won to his cause decided to follow the rest of the "nation" from Saint-Malo to Poitou so as to not break up the Saint-Malo group. They had to stop denigrating the proposed settlement and convince the Acadians to collectively leave where they were at the time.[73] This time they were able to achieve their goal, even if occasionally using physical intimidation of those who wanted to try their chances on the lands of Archigny and Monthoiron. Pérusse d'Escars understood the strategy of LeBlanc and his consorts very well, and he forcefully denounced it. According to him, the Acadian delegates were persuaded "that being joined in the body of one nation, it would be easier for them to obtain the absurd permission that they were seeking to go to Louisiana."[74]

This desire to regroup into a "body of a nation" and this awareness that unity provides strength and that, grouped together, the Acadians would have a better chance to obtain what they sought nonetheless does not seem to have been shared by all the refugees. First of all, the reassembling at Saint-Malo was only partial: most of the Acadians remained in the ports where they had arrived or migrated to other areas for reasons that are unclear. The family regroupings were not systematic, either, probably because it was not materially possible for the families to move. Direct requests by the Acadians themselves to be reassembled were rare.[75] Some even deliberately chose to separate from the group by remaining at Saint-Malo and in various other port towns, while the large majority emigrated to Poitou or decided to take advantage of the lands offered by Pérusse when the Acadians collectively departed for Nantes. In 1778, most of the Acadians did not resist the prohibition to disperse, apart from Jean-Jacques LeBlanc and some families that persisted in their idea of departing to Louisiana.[76] A sizeable minority, somewhere between 30 and 40 percent of the families, would remain in France in 1785.

Conclusion

Amongst the Acadians of the diaspora, we find a clear desire to reassemble and the establishment of a vast resource of the exchange of information when physical proximity was not possible (corresponding to observations made by Faragher about the Acadians in North America). But, beyond the family regroupings that are quite understandable after the trials of separation, some Acadians became aware that it was only by organizing themselves politically that they would be able to have their voices heard by the government. They organized as they had in Acadia, electing delegates, but had difficulty finding a unifying leader capable of directing the whole group. Indeed, the dissensions within the interior of the core of the Acadian population seem to have been paralyzing and were probably behind the delay in obtaining a decision from the government, whatever it might have been. And it was ultimately a Frenchman, Peyroux de la Coudrenière, who was able to negotiate *in fine* the emigration to Louisiana and to convince a large number of the Acadians to go there, despite their divergence of views. Despite his perseverance and his intelligence, (recognized and feared by many observers),[77] the delegate Jean-Jacques LeBlanc did not succeed in being recognized by all as their representative; he did not succeed in incarnating the hope of the other Acadians, perhaps because the destination that he proposed was not very attractive for his compatriots. A good number seemed to truly fear the heat of the Mississippi[78] and preferred living in the utopian hope that the

French government would finally assign them lands of quality or the authorization to return to Acadia, or in a similarly moderate climate, like that of Saint-Pierre and Miquelon. In the end, this desire to remain together certainly prohibited their integration, but it also allowed the survival of the group, which nevertheless had difficulty deciding on a common direction.

Chapter III

The Plans for Settlement:
to populate the Empire (c. 1760-c. 1765)

In the preceding chapters, we have considered the state of mind of the Acadians upon their disembarking in France, and, more specifically, their willful selection of France and, consequently, their resistance to integration and assimilation. We then studied the organization of the administration and described the management of the Navy as having been fairly passive, little concerned with the problem of reclassifying the refugees. We also considered the manner in which the Acadians tried to organize themselves politically, by reassembling around a nucleus in the region of Saint-Malo and then maintaining this compact and united group. Finally, we saw how, for Émile Lauvrière or Ernest Martin, there was no doubt that the French government wanted to integrate-assimilate the Acadians into France as best it might.

As this last assertion does not seem to me to be entirely accurate, it is appropriate now to examine the attitude of the government more thoroughly by confirming the government's desire to integrate the Acadians, and the Acadians' desire to be integrated, before examining why those efforts failed. In fact, we can detect a clear evolution between 1760 and 1785. At the start, it is difficult to speak of any real governmental policy. Certainly, the distribution of aid (discussed in a later chapter) might be considered as a sort of policy of integration. But, more than a real policy, it was rather a series of temporary measures, barely prearranged, and adopted step-by-step. What is more, during and just after the Seven Years War, the government did not want to integrate the Acadians, because, on the contrary, it intended to send them back to the colonies. After this first period, came a second phase during which the various ministers only wanted to bind the Acadians to the lands of the kingdom and not necessarily to assimilate them among the French. Only a little later do we see a concern for integration and assimilation on the part of the administration and the government. This chapter will show that the theory that the government always sought to integrate and assimilate the Acadians should be more nuanced and that the emergence of such a policy must be placed in its proper context.

As stated earlier, reflections on the question of integration and assimilation of the Acadians was limited to arranging the spatial organization of the refugees on the map. For the majority of administrators, the solution offered to the Acadian problem crystallized around the question of knowing if they should be left grouped together or dispersed. Any interest in the question of the Acadians' integration soon leads to examining the discussions and deals involving this theme. We may consider two or three phases. Discussion by the government evolved from a refusal to integrate the Acadians into a gradual desire to assimilate them. This desire can, in its turn, be divided into two intermediary phases: the early one, with a minimalist policy of assimilation, the goal of which was to clear land in France by leaving the Acadians grouped in a "little Acadia"; and the later one, with a plan to settle the Acadians in France that was never put into effect.

If we want to accurately examine the resources applied to the task of integrating the Acadians, it is important to not restrict ourselves to the discussions by those who gave the orders, but also to consider the voices of those who executed them and the opinions of the Acadians, those involved with the measures, and, at least to a minimum degree, those of the local native populations.

The Plans for Return to the Colonies (1758-1765, then sporadically)

In order to properly grasp the slowness with which governmental action in favor of the Acadians was put into effect over the long term, we must fully understand that, upon their arrival in France, no one seriously imagined that they would remain. In 1759 Berryer wrote expressing the general sentiment: "Their stay is only momentary; they are destined to return to America."[1] This opinion persisted for many years and was even reinforced with the signing of the peace in 1763. The principal concern of Choiseul at that time was to divert attention from the French decline by developing a new empire, and the Acadians were always the first to be considered as participating in populating the colonies envisaged. "French" volunteers were hardly anxious to go[2] but, even when they were, Choiseul harkened to the older principle of Colbert: "the intention of the king [is] not to populate his colonies at the expense of the population of his provinces." [3]

The peace had not yet been signed—nor the Acadians repatriated from England—when the minister wrote to various intendants the precise means of passage to the colonies:[4]

> [the Acadian families] who want . . . to go to Cayenne, Martinique, Saint-Lucie, Guadeloupe, or to Saint-Domingue, will continue to enjoy the same graces that his majesty granted them in France [six *sous* per day] and one will find for them foodstuff at the same prices apart from the slight assistance and individual protection that I will have granted them; . . . His Majesty will additionally grant them 50 *livres* in silver per family composed of a father, a mother, and child, which gratuity will be increased by 10 *livres* with each new extra child arriving, in order to put them in a position to purchase the small amenities in France that might be necessary before their departure. You will also inform them that they will have their passage and nourishment on board ship for free, and on arrival in the colony they will be lodged and nourished there for a month at his majesty's expense, without any deduction from the six *sols* granted them, in order to give them time to arrange themselves in the sites indicated by the governor, who will take care to find work for them to enable them to live most comfortably. His Majesty hopes that, by providing this instruction on the first of April, you will be able to convince these families to accept the offers made for them on your part.[5]

French Guyana

Even if, in the letter above, Choiseul mentions many colonies of the Antilles, his idea was mainly to colonize Guyana. Moreover, the Acadians were not the only "foreigners" considered for this destination: Choiseul also solicited German, Maltese, and Alsatian families.[6] To increase the chances of convincing these families, the minister similarly worried about "preventing [their] melancholy!"[7]

> This colony being denuded of all objects of frivolity and these families having been dispersed and on their own, especially in the moments when they are not occupied, it seems to me to be necessary, to prevent the melancholy that they might be subject to following hard work and *their reflections on their being far from their native country, which might bring much discomfort to these new inhabitants*, to find them some small-drum players who would have no other job than to divert them in the moments when they would want to make use of them.[8]

History does not tell us if the colonists who left to colonize Guyana and who, for the most part, spent the rest of their lives there were accompanied by these small-drum players. Whatever the case, for the period 1762-1765, many documents mention the passage of the Acadians to various parts of the empire. One of the destinations that most attracted the Acadians was unquestionably Saint-Pierre and Miquelon, but the lack of available land on those islands obliged the government to limit the number of those who could go there. Some Acadians were also involved in another of Choiseul's projects (also doomed to failure): the colonization of the Malouine (Falkland) Islands. The expedition going there, under the direction of the soon-to-be-famous Louis-Antoine de Bougainville, included many Acadian families who would later mostly return to France.[9] Choiseul especially tried to get the families to go to the Antilles and Guyana. They sometimes left voluntarily,[10] sometimes reluctantly,[11] but the large majority refused, concerned that the climate would not suit them.[12] The Guyana project was a disaster: nearly two thirds of some ten thousand colonists who were sent there (mostly Germans and Alsatians) died during the course of the voyage or upon arrival in the colony, where nothing had been prepared for them.

The fear of suffering from the very high temperatures, chiefly invoked in refusals to go to Guyana, was without a doubt the main reason for the Acadians' reluctance to embark for this colony.[13] This very understandable concern was not a passing whim: some refugees were still worried about the heat when it later became a question of going to Louisiana.[14] The concern was also mentioned by many observers who theorized about the degenerative effects of the climate.[15] Nonetheless, it is also entirely possible to interpret the resistance of the Acadians to go to the warmer French colonies at the government's instigation as another sign of their desire to remain assembled together, and of their fear of being dispersed all across the surface of the globe.

Forced and Constrained?

Choiseul had promised not to force the Acadians in England to go to the colonies if they did not want to do so. He only partially kept his promises, and the correspondence to various commissioners in the ports reveals this ambivalence. On the one hand, he declared to the *ordonnateur* of Le Havre that the Acadians must not be obliged to go to Cayenne;[16] on the other, many letters show that he encouraged coercive means to enlist the Acadians. Thus, on April 14, 1764, he encouraged Mistral, commissioner of the Navy at Le Havre, to no longer pay the "subsistence" to the Acadians who should go to Guyana but were refusing to do so.[17] Some weeks later, he expressed his frustration at the resistance of the Acadians in Boulogne:

> I rendered an account to the King of the repugnance that the Acadians in your department express for going to Cayenne. His Majesty was very surprised to learn that they persevered in so obstinate a refusal, despite his offering to feed and clothe them for two years, and supply them with tools and implements needed for the cultivation of the land to be granted to them as property in proportion to what they are able to farm. His Majesty asks you to make them understand how he, for his part, feels how this obstinacy is misplaced since, on the one hand, the country where they are being sent is excellent, and their fellow citizens of Cherbourg, Le Havre and Morlaix had no problem accepting such advantageous offers,[18] and, on the other hand, there is no way to place them elsewhere, and it will be impossible to continue providing them subsistence if they persist in doing nothing about it and not taking part. His Majesty hopes that, after having reflected on these matters, they will decide to give him new proof of their obedience on this point and he expects a more satisfying answer from them.[19]

The affirmation by Choiseul that "there is no way to place them elsewhere" reveals that it was not at all his intention—at least at this time—to settle the Acadians in France. But, following the Acadian resistance and the disastrous failure of the colonization of Guyana, the minister gradually abandoned his plan to send them to populate the colonies. Nonetheless, this idea resurfaced sporadically following international incidents, notably during the American War of Independence. Nevertheless, these projects explain the lack of other plans for the integration or assimilation of the Acadians by the ministry in the earlier phase (with the exception of the project for Belle-Île-en-Mer).

In any case, it is very difficult to estimate the number of refugees who accepted the various proposals of Choiseul. An anonymous document from April 1764 estimates at five hundred the number of refugees who left France for Saint-Domingue, Martinique, and Saint-Pierre and Miquelon. A hundred others were preparing to leave for Cayenne.[20] Another letter written a year later by a French merchant of Cap-Français[21] estimates at three thousand the number of Acadians then present at Saint-Domingue.[22] Yet most of these Acadians did not come from France, but left the Anglo-American colonies for the large island in the Caribbean.[23] Most would soon also cross over to Louisiana. Other Acadians would emigrate to the French colonies sporadically during the period from 1763 and 1785.[24]

Consequences of the Plans for Settlement in the Empire

Choiseul's plans to send the Acadians throughout the Empire and the absence of a desire to integrate the refugees into France led to many consequences, particularly the regrouping of the Acadians around Saint-Malo, as well as a sizeable amount of intermarriages.

Other inconvenient consequences engendered by this situation will be examined further on, notably the impossibility for the Acadians to plan projects for the long term, *e.g.*, to build a house or to seek stable work.

The Regrouping of the Acadians Around Saint-Malo

We have seen how the refugees were disembarked in various ports of the country in 1758-1759, and how a reassembly of the Acadians in France was noticeable. Many references by the minister of the Navy allow us to understand how these scattered arrivals had not been foreseen and that orders stipulating disembarking at Saint-Malo or La Rochelle had been provided.[25] It would therefore seem that, initially, the minister wanted a reassembly of the refugees at La Rochelle or at Saint-Malo.

This desire of the government to concentrate the Acadians in those two towns posed some clear logistical problems of lodging and food supply on the local level. This is surely what officially justified the desire of the Secretary of State of the Navy, Berryer, to "spread out" the Acadians around the ports, as well as to lessen the expenses that they generated:

> It would be suitable for you to be rid [of the inhabitants of Île Saint-Jean], who could start working somewhere as soon as possible. . . . You could address Mr. d'Invault, intendant of Amiens, to . . . assist you in placing these families in areas of the generality where they might most usefully work, whether in manufacturing in the provinces, or in the cultivation of land.[26]

Such considerations probably also led the intendant of Brittany to order the mayor of Saint-Malo to disperse the Acadians near the town.[27] The magistrate nevertheless soon felt the echo of their resistance. In January 1759, Le Fer de Chanteloup wrote to the intendant that he had received his letter "on the subject of the inhabitants of Louisbourg and Île Saint-Jean, having arrived in this town a few days before, that you will consider it expedient to expel from this country."[28] Some days later, the inhabitants were reviewed and reported on:

> I asked them if they wanted to withdraw further into the terrain [?] or spread around the area of Saint-Malo. Only twenty-two[29] agreed to go to the locations indicated to them, some others answered that they could only leave this town or its suburbs after the settling of those of their families for whom they were responsible. . . . I can assure you that they are very inclined to remain in the environment of this town, and that the transportation I promised them with the three *livres* of gratuity per person to enable them to go to the locations indicated was not a sufficient allure for them to transplant themselves elsewhere.

If the mayor made no mention of the reasons why the Acadians wanted to remain together, we may easily imagine why these refugees, wounded and weakened after the trials of the deportation and many weeks at sea, did not want to separate. Some weeks afterwards, the Acadians seem to have obtained a compromise: if they spread through the parishes along the estuary of the Rance, they would all still remain in the environs of Saint-Malo, sufficiently close to communicate with one another and to occasionally re-assemble without too much difficulty.[30] Furthermore, as we have seen, they were joined by a certain number of their compatriots coming from other ports.

Therefore it would seem that, in the first phase, there was a certain convergence between the spontaneous assembly of the Acadians and the intentions of the government, since, to facilitate sending the refugees overseas at the time of the peace, it was better that they remained relatively grouped together. We should also certainly consider that, for the ministry, the regroupings facilitated the distribution of aid, taking of censuses, and general supervision. The government did authorize the inhabitants to move from one town to another and ordered that their payment be distributed to them wherever they might go. The Secretary of State only recommended that they not take on "the habit of a wandering life" and that they not receive double payments.[31] The government did not have to worry too much about this, because the refugees themselves were convinced that they would soon leave France and, at that time, they did not consider separating.

Some years later, at the time of the repatriation of the Acadians who had initially been deported to England in 1763, the Minister of the Navy still seemed convinced of the benefit of concentrating the Acadians within a very limited area. Even if the reasons for the selection of Saint-Malo and Morlaix for the disembarking of some seven to eight hundred[32] of the repatriated are not known for certain,[33] it is likely that the recommendations of Nivernais's report were followed by the government. Among other things, the duke specified that the Acadians had requested to remain together[34] and proposed three regions capable of welcoming them in good conditions—especially Boulogne, because of the depopulation it had suffered during the war and "the proximity there of their brethren."[35] It is thus likely that the choice of Saint-Malo was conditioned by the desire to keep the Acadians together, as they had requested, and by the belief that the province could supply them with work. Certainly the participation in the activities of repatriation by the Commissioner-General of the Navy at Saint-Malo, Guillot (who went to England on the orders of Choiseul) must have also played a large role.[36]

In sum, if some intendants, probably for practical reasons, wanted to disperse the Acadians about the territory of their oversight or in the villages around the great ports like Saint-Malo, it seems that, in a general manner, the intention of the government was to keep the Acadians relatively grouped together, in part to satisfy the refugees, but especially because this suited the objectives of the Secretary of State to send the Acadians to the colonies. So Choiseul wrote Nivernais: "It would be appropriate to try to keep [the Acadians] assembled within the same port, in order to . . . have them go . . . to Miquelon and Saint-Pierre."[37] On the whole, in fact, the strong concentration of Acadians around Saint-Malo did not appear to pose any particular problems for the government or the local administrators. Berryer, for instance, was in no way bothered by it, and Choiseul encouraged it. So there is no indication that the State had anticipated problems that such an assembly as was made at Saint-Malo might create.[38] Nonetheless, this "policy" remained but partial, as, during the first phase, there was no re-assembling of all the Acadians dispersed in the various ports into one single place. For their part, the Acadians beyond the region of Saint-Malo did not seek to re-gather in a very tangible manner, even if they corresponded a great deal among themselves. In any case, material possibilities for reassembling remained limited for them, since they were dependent on assistance from the king and on the good will of the parishes in which they were refugees. Now and again the government was concerned with the economic integration of the Acadians in wanting them to find them work, but the plans for their departure negated this effort by preventing them from making long term plans. We should especially note that in no way did the administration encourage the assimilation of the Acadians into the local communities during this period.

The Encouragement of Endogamous Marriages

The plan to send the Acadians back to the colonies brought other consequences. The government still encouraged reassembly of the Acadians by urging them to marry amongst themselves, notably by supporting young people who needed a dispensation in order to contract consanguine marriages. Once again, during this period, the needs of the government coincided with the desires of the exiles themselves.

This wish to remain "amongst themselves," perhaps simply a continuity of the Acadian familial patterns from the beginnings of the colony, is clearly expressed in the requests for dispensations from the "prevention of consanguinity" made by numerous exiles spread throughout the French territory.[39] The earliest requests were made very shortly after the arrival of the first Acadians and reached the Minister of the Navy through the intermediary of the Abbé de l'Isle-Dieu, vicar-general for the bishop of Québec in Paris. The minister, answering the intercession of this Abbé, wrote on December 15, 1759:

> It would undoubtedly be desirable for these inhabitants [Acadians] to marry [in order] . . . to increase the French inhabitants [in the colonies]. But, as those from Acadia are today reduced to a small number, it would be difficult to make contracts amongst themselves if we have them hold to the letter of the law of degrees of relation prohibited by the rules of the Church. What is more, these inhabitants should not be regarded as being native to France;[40] they are only here in passing. If they were in Acadia in the small numbers to which they are reduced, there would be no difficulty in granting them the dispensations that they might need. It is with this in view that they should be considered. Their stay is presently only temporary; they are meant to return to America. If they are refused the contracts that they propose to make, this would be in effect to commit them to making others with other inhabitants and perhaps dissuade them of the idea of returning to their own country. It is of interest to be warned of this problem. I think, therefore, that it would be suitable in all respects to facilitate their marriages as much as this might be done without abusing the rules.[41]

On February 22, 1760, Berryer (probably again at the request of the Abbé de l'Isle-Dieu) wrote the king's ambassador to the Vatican asking that the Acadians be exempted from the various fees attached to these requests.[42] The main problem of the Acadians in obtaining the requested dispensations was financial. The Abbé l'Isle-Dieu evidently solicited Berryer to obtain his support on this exact point, not on the idea itself of allowing the Acadians to "ally with one another."

Following the intervention of Berryer, the first general dispensations were granted by the bishop of Saint-Malo in April or May. These dispensations were granted not only to the former inhabitants of Île-Royale, but also to those of Île Saint-Jean, which constituted the majority of the group.[43] New "faculties" or dispensations were granted by the bishops of Vannes and Saint-Malo on September 16, 1767, (with the author of the dispatch specifying that, if the Acadians changed diocese, they could obtain new dispensations by informing

Rome),[44] and finally, by that of La Rochelle in July 1769.[45] It is difficult to know exactly how useful these general dispensations were, since individual exemptions were granted easily enough (for instance, to the Acadian families of Cherbourg).[46] Perhaps they were intended to avoid the lengthy procedures[47] and especially the costs connected to them, which was the main purpose of the letter reproduced above from February 22, 1760. This theme is repeated in all of the files from Coutances.[48]

The motivations underlying request for these indulgences explicitly manifested the desire of the Acadians to not mix with those "of French origin."[49] It is thus worthwhile to examine a bit more thoroughly the dispensations from consanguinity prevention, which are, in fact, among the most revelatory documents about the state of mind of the Acadians and greatly clarify the reasons that brought them to marry amongst themselves.

In the individual proceedings preserved at Coutances involving the Acadians of Cherbourg,[50] the documents almost always mention the same motives. The written statements were made following a codified formula: first a general declaration summarized the problem of consanguinity or affinity and presented the genealogy of the applicants with blood ties to the third or fourth generation.[51] There followed the testimony of the petitioners, the future spouses and four witnesses (generally two parents and two non-parents), that particularly expressed the reasons why the plaintiffs wanted to marry.

The reasons invoked by the Acadians should surely be read with much caution, since they are in the position of petitioners, and it is not possible to know with what good faith they expressed their arguments. It is especially clear that the witnesses repeated themselves, and the proceedings and proposals were somewhat altered, standardized, and interpreted. The formulation of the petitions undoubtedly also came from the Acadians themselves, who were probably instructed about some of the arguments in advance. The Acadians, however, clearly kept another portion for themselves, for improvisation; for the arguments advanced remain in the realm of the credible and in the "realm of expectation" of the ecclesiastical tribunal. Even if what is expressed did not always exactly conform to the feelings of the petitioner, the argument had to at least be plausible and informative about the Acadians' feelings in general.

The Acadians domiciled in Cherbourg had to argue on two fronts. They had to justify their actions, showing the impossibility of their seeking the dispensation from consanguinity from the Vatican[52] which makes them dependent on the local bishop, and they had to explain the reasons for which they requested authorization to marry within degrees prohibited by the Church. The rhetoric involved with this second point went through several stages. The first—described below, as it touches directly on the problem of mixed marriages—consisted of showing that the Acadians could not easily marry the French.[53] This problem resulted from two principal causes: their foreseen imminent departure and the consequential suspension of the king's payment.

As for the second stage, it focused on showing (once a local partner was established) that, among the Acadians the partner being considered was the only one suitable. Most often, this second part of the petition is based on the fact that the claimant is in any event related to all of the other Acadians in the town, and, as for other potential partners among the Acadians, they are rejected for various reasons including being of the age required by the petitioners.

In the first phase, then, the Acadians sought to justify their preferred selection of an Acadian partner. Their main argument consisted of expressing their fear, in the hypothetical case where they might marry someone from Cherbourg, of the problems that would arise at the time of their departure to return to America. The double affirmation of an obligatory, sometimes imminent foreign voyage, and of the reluctance of the French spouses to go there is presented in all petitions but three.[54] Sometimes, only the voyage to America is noted, without mention of the reluctance of the French that would prevent them finding a partner.[55] Examples of this rhetoric are frequent, but that of Joseph Lapierre is especially eloquent:

> With the intent of the petitioner to return to the islands of Canada after peace is made, as experience has shown at the time of the last war, he has reason to fear, in this one, that a girl taken as his wife at Cherbourg or the neighboring area would not want to follow him on his return, as many girls of the area married at Cherbourg have already refused to do. (file 2)

The files of dispensations of parental consent, consanguinity, and affinity of the Acadians of the Cherbourg region point to two difficulties that particularly disheartened the French facing the prospect of leaving the country: the exhaustion of the voyage and the difficult adjustment to the new country. Thus one witness declared that girls from France were "in no condition to support the difficulty of the ocean voyage nor even to accustom themselves to the air of a foreign country." (file 3)[56] Another "fears that in marrying a girl from the country [Cherbourg], she would have no desire to follow him there, nor enough temperament to support the ocean voyage and to then acclimate herself to the country." Like Joseph Lapierre, many mention the similar experience during the war, and an empirical familiarity with the problem: "as experience has shown, a wife taken in this country will perhaps not be inclined, to follow her husband." (file 3) One adds "that one has even been obliged to force many of his acquaintance [non-Acadian women who did not want to follow their husbands] by aid of the military in order to have them embark" (file 3, p. 11). Furthermore, one needed only to open one's ears, as certain women of Cherbourg, "announced as of today" (file 2) that they would not return with their husbands to the American continent. Another witness explained:

> If the petitioner were to marry a girl from Cherbourg or from the neighboring area, he would have grounds to fear that this girl, on becoming his wife, would not want to follow him on his return to the islands of Canada after the peace is made, as has already happened when many girls from Cherbourg married to Acadians loudly declared that they would not follow their husband at the time of their embarking to be transported to their former country (file 3, p. 13).

Again and again, mention is made of the fact that the inhabitants of France were not seeking Acadian men or women to marry unless special motives were involved: this seems to be a statement of the general rule. One Acadian witness thus declared: "if [the woman petitioner] does not marry another Acadian it is very probable that a young man of this country would not want her" (file 10, p. 9). Another future wife declared "that the men of this country are not quick to pair up with Canadians" (file 11). At no time, however, did they insinuate that this reticence to marry Acadians might be a form of discrimination.[57]

Reflecting the attitude of the times, the problem of departure was not considered in the same way by the men and as it was by the women. While the Acadian men feared that their potential French wives would not want to follow them to their new home, for their part, the women originally from Cap de Sable feared that their husbands might keep them in France. Men and women both especially expressed the problems foreseen by the husbands, but one Acadian woman declared, however, "that she could not marry a person from Cherbourg who would keep her there despite her desire to return to the islands after the peace is made" (file 5).

This evocation of the departure, omnipresent in the declarations, which is a testimony of the hopes and fears of the Acadians, is, however, rarely explicit. Thus the destination considered was never clearly specified. The subject most often repeated in the files is "island" (singular or plural), often with no further details, which does not allow us to know if the term means returning to the "islands of Canada," that is, Saint-Jean, Royale, Saint-Pierre and Miquelon islands, or to the southern islands.[58] The first files, from January 1761, are the most explicit, referring to the "islands of Canada," to "Acadia," or to "Louisbourg," undoubtedly expressing the hope of a return after the peace. The subsequent files, dated from June 1761 to July 1763 (and April 1772), do not mention more than departure toward "the islands," and, in fact, the Acadians even specify, "that, besides, they do not know to which foreign islands in America that the king will have them transported." The following file, from August 1771, does not even mention the departure, but that of June 1773 is the only one that refers to a return of the Acadians "to their country."

In the same way, the imminence of departure is not felt either, depending on the period. Thus, the first files all mention departure "once peace is made." In the files from March to July 1763, peace is felt to be very near and allusions to it become more frequent:

> She [the petitioner] would be exposed to the risk of not finding a suitable party . . . considering the little time that she apparently has to remain here, since they are only waiting for the order for all of the Acadians to return to different islands, where the petitioner would possibly be separated from the one who might suit her. (file 6)

One petitioner even specifies that the Acadians "day by day are only waiting for the order [to leave], considering that many of them have already received it." But the departure being still delayed, the last files, if they still refer to it (except for number 9), more prudently no longer specify the date.

Finally, the initial desire to leave gradually evolved into a resignation or, rather (according to some documents), into a form of passive resistance. Thus, all of the first files express the will, hopes, and desires of the Acadians. But starting in March 1763, mention is only made of waiting for orders and of the renowned "good pleasure" of the king: "one only awaits the order for the Acadians to return to the different islands" (file 6). This passivity is no doubt explained by their anticipation of where the final destination might be, depending on the orders of the king. We clearly see that the desire of the first phase involved returning to Acadia, while the resignation of the second phase involved a passage to the islands which were no longer those of Canada—the Acadians seem to have given up hope of returning there.

This recurrent mention of an approaching departure in the petitions of the Acadians reveals their profound uncertainty concerning their future. According to their statements, this uncertainty about their situation was the main reason for their difficulty in finding a partner outside of the group.⁵⁹ It is interesting to note here that the reluctance to marry outside of their community affected the Acadians as much as it did the people of Cherbourg.

The analysis of this first series of arguments does not, then, allow a definitive settling of the question considered or a positive conclusion that the Acadians did not want to marry the French. But the second argument employed in rejecting the choice of a non-Acadian partner is less ambiguous. Even if there were no problem of a hypothetical departure, many Acadians did not want to marry French women because they then risked losing the payment from the king for their spouse. Eustache Parré thus declared that, if he married a Cherbourg girl, "he would lose the king's payment for his new spouse as happened to a man named L'Anglois, originally from Île Saint-Jean."⁶⁰ This argument was, however, only used in four of the ten files,⁶¹ which perhaps suggests that the feeling was less legitimate than the fear of departure and that it was only partially true.⁶²

Starting with these allegations, it is therefore very difficult to determine the real interest of the Acadians in Cherbourg in marrying persons from there, and yet more difficult to determine if one of the two communities sought to ostracize the other. We must not exclude the possibility of a real desire of the Acadians to marry Cherbourg residents—and of a refusal by the latter to answer their advances—but it seems that, beyond the interest shown in keeping their payments, "the inclination" of the Acadians often tilted towards members of their own group, shown by a certain will to keep unto themselves.

In fact, another recurrent argument in all of the files except one⁶³ is that of an "inclination," of a previous friendship, or "love" for the partner, which often goes back many years to neighborhood relationships in Acadia. This previous companionship was important in the eyes of the claimants, who saw therein the guarantee of a solid marriage thanks to previous familiarity with the character of the future partner. Thus Marie-Rose Daigle declared "that she would do herself harm by marrying a person whose mind and disposition she did not know, although from the same country [of Acadia]" (file 5). Another writer, very sure of himself, mentions that the other Acadians are too young for him and that:

> Besides, he would fear that a young girl with little intelligence and little inclination to raise his children would only disturb the peace of his home and that he would prefer to not get married and expose himself to this danger, which he does not risk in the case of the foresaid Mélanson, whom he knows to be wise, sweet and prudent and of a mature age. (file 3, p. 3)

So the marriages among the Acadians can also be explained by the network of closer relations within the group than outside of it.

For the period covered by the files of the dispensations of consanguinity that have been found, the majority of Acadians present in France did not live in Cherbourg, but in the Saint-Malo region. Was the case of Cherbourg representative, or was it the exception? If we compare the statistics concerning Acadian marriages in these two towns,⁶⁴ we find 25 percent mixed marriages as compared to 75 percent Acadian marriages, almost to the same proportion, following the sequence shown below (Figure 3). It is thus probable that the case of Cherbourg was not an exception and, since general dispensations were being granted by the bishop of Saint-Malo by 1760, we may judge that the problem of consanguinity occurred there in the same manner and that the case of Cherbourg is very representative of the national level.

FIGURE 3
Evolution of the number of Acadian and mixed marriages at Cherbourg

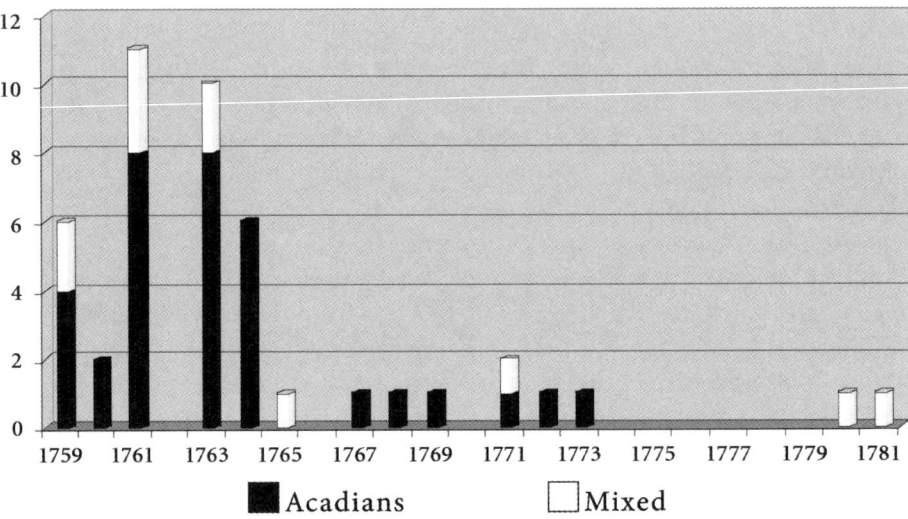

These dispensations, which were always granted, only explain how the rates of endogamous marriages, relatively exceptional for a small community, were legally feasible.[65] They also clarify the feelings of the Acadians. But it is very possible that these exemptions measure more a degree of rejection by French society than the desire of assimilation of the Acadians. The motives for such rejection could be very specific from place to place, as shown by a letter by the intendant of Caen to Jacques Necker, in 1781:

> The plan of a settlement for Miss d'Entremont probably can never be achieved. Her attachment to her parents, whose care becomes daily more necessary, will not allow them to be separated. The delicacy of her feelings makes it difficult for her to choose a man with whom to be united. Moreover, few people are likely to step forward to marry a *mademoiselle*, in truth of fine nobleness, but who brings as a dowry only her only misery as well as that of her parents.[66]

It is difficult to know if the support of the government for the endogamous marriages—shown by Berryer's letter above and the refusal to pay the balance of payments to the French partners of the Acadians—survived beyond the period during which the refugees were urged to return to the colonies. We find no references later than those mentioned above. At the most, we may note that, still in 1767, the Controller-General, in order to not have to pay from public funds, encouraged a young Acadian woman to marry an Acadian rather than enter a convent.[67] We have tried to estimate the apportionment and chronological evolution of the marriages, mixed or among Acadians, during the refugees' stay in France, to try thereby to detect a possible change in their situation. This question is addressed in the final chapter.

Conclusion

In sum, we can state that in the years immediately following the arrival of the refugees in France the government in no manner sought to assimilate them. The goal of the ministers in office at that time was rather to send these colonists to populate the colonies that they then wanted to develop. This brought on many consequences. First of all, they allowed the exiles to assemble at their convenience, which was shown on the geographic level as well as by their encouragement of endogamous marriages. The Acadians justified their reluctance to marry outside their community by the fact that, in case of a departure, they would have difficulty convincing their "French" partner to follow them; the women feared having to separate from the group, the men feared not being able to bring their spouses. In this first period, the restraint with which the Acadians wove ties in France is more the fault of the governmental goal (of which they were well aware) of sending them to the colonies than of a pronounced self-identity reflex. Indeed, if the refugees showed a desire to not disperse, they did not show a desire to unite in the same location. The question of the reassembling or of the dispersion of the Acadians would progressively crystallize during the planning of the settlement at Belle-Île-en-Mer, and would finally become a question of primary concern at the point when Necker became Controller-General.

Chapter IV

The Plans For Settlement:
Clearing Land In France (1763-1772)

Even before the repatriation of the Acadians from England, Choiseul knew that many of them did not want to go to the Southern Colonies—Cayenne (French Guyana), Martinique, Saint-Lucie, Guadeloupe, or Saint-Domingue. Some of the families asked to return to Canada or to be settled in France. Pursuing the Colbert-inspired populating strategies mentioned above, Choiseul wrote to the Controller-General by April 4, 1763, to request lands within the Kingdom for those of the Acadians who did not want to leave:

> The North American families who came to France after the taking of Île-Royale, Île St. Jean and Canada have been supported until now from colonizing funds at the rate of 6s per day in subsistence.... The intention of the king immediately after the peace was to have these families go to Cayenne ..., but they generally refused to take this route and ... for this reason asked, in preference, to be placed in the provinces of the Kingdom, or be free to return to Acadia and Canada. As it is important for the State not to lose this population that may include some 4,000 people ... and as these families could be usefully employed either in the cultivation of land or in manufacturing, I beg of you to indicate to me if you have some means of placing them either in the provinces that they now inhabit or in having them go into the interior. The duc de Nivernais proposes to employ others who should be coming steadily from England on the island of Bouin that belongs to him. They even have requested it. It is very much desirable that we place the rest in areas that we intend on clearing within the interior of the Kingdom.... In all respects it is very important to keep these families in the Kingdom and to not allow them to be in a position to request returning to North America. We would lose this population that could increase as much as might the English; you as well as I can imagine the consequences.[1]

Though many later commentators affirm that the Acadians were "abandoned" during this period (1763-1772), that is not entirely the case, because, on many occasions after the above-cited letter, Choiseul solicited various individuals for the benefit of the Acadians.[2] The Controller-General, Henri Léonard Jean Baptiste Bertin, relayed Choiseul's request to numerous intendants.[3] An investigation conducted in different regions[4] concluded resettling the Acadians would be impossible. Nearly all of the sub-delegates answered with the same *leitmotiv*: that there were already "more workers than one could employ" in Normandy, as one wrote.[5] "I do not think, thank God, that the population is lacking by our count, or that we have need of new inhabitants. The country is having a very hard time feeding those it has," wrote another.[6] In the district of Périgueux, the rich landowners showed no hurry to welcome the refugees, either, because they had no lands to be cleared, or because they feared the expense "for which they would not be reimbursed by the work of the Canadians."[7] In a polling of Avranches, there was neither "commerce nor manufacturing" that might employ the Acadians.[8] François-Jean Orceau de Fontette, the intendant of Caen, summarized the general opinion of his sub-delegates by explaining to Choiseul that, across the entire western front, there exited a problem of unemployment as much in manufacturing as in day labor and that, consequently, the settlement of the Acadians was not possible in his jurisdiction.[9] Pierre Le Fer de Chanteloup, the mayor of Saint-Malo, was practically the only one to propose concrete measures for settling the Acadians, or at least to find them work. He suggested that they be given tools and be authorized to clear lands of the royal domain.[10] He, too, was the first to mention the fee-farm granting on Belle-Île-en-Mer and to suggest installing the Acadians there.[11]

Belle-Île-en-Mer

It is difficult to know if Chanteloup's letter initiated the settlement of seventy-eight Acadian families, or 363 people, at Belle-Île-en-Mer. The government only participated in an indirect manner in this project, which was proposed by the States of Brittany in July 1763 at the moment of the arrival of the Acadians from England. It was, in fact, only these who were considered in the first phase for colonizing the island, and the great majority of the fee-farm grantees of Belle-Île were indeed those repatriated from the United Kingdom. Whatever the case, it was on the occasion of this settlement that the issue of the assimilation of the Acadians into the local populations of the islands was presented for the first time.

The proposal was to settle on the island seventy-seven families who had been sent from England. This was no gift to the Acadians, since the idea was to repopulate the island to fortify it against new attacks by the English Royal Navy. The plan implied the displacement of the islanders and the redistribution of lands. While the reorganization of the island was under negotiation, the refugees benefited by asking to be regrouped into a single parish, "to facilitate the reunion of our families which were divided by our enemies over eight years ago."[12] Their proposals opened a debate on the best way of assimilating the Acadians within local populations. It was the first time that they expressed their desire to be reunited in such a direct and explicit manner.

The Abbé Le Loutre, who supervised the settlement of the families, on many occasions also became the interpreter of the Acadians' desire to remain together. In a letter to Richard de Warren, the governor of the island, Le Loutre maintained that the Acadians wanted to be "placed all together" and wanted to live "as they had lived, still neighbors and within a proximity of one another, and to not be mingled with the Belle-Île residents."[13] Le Loutre did not disguise his personal interest in this reassembly: "I cannot hide from you, Monsieur, that I would prefer the Acadians [to be together] so that I could be amidst them, animate them, and encourage them to work," he wrote on April 14, 1764.[14]

If it was on the occasion of the settlement of Belle-Île that we find for the first time the desire expressed by the Acadians to live in close proximity to one another, it was also on this occasion that the first resistance appeared. It did not, however, come from the government itself. The reasons advanced might seem curious: the texts actually express the possibility of "regenerating" the local populations by blending them with a pure and new people who had come from the Americas. In fact, most of the then-residents of the island were considered by one Isambert, inspector of domains at Belle-Île-en-Mer, as being "extremely lazy." Isambert therefore specified "that it would be suitable to inspire a love of work in the other colonists . . . to place in these various villages more laborious people." He added that, "The States have approved and do so approve this view."[15] Warren shared the analysis of Isambert and expressed it in a completely straightforward manner: "[the Acadians] would provide models to the natives of the country who are very lazy and not industrious," he wrote to the naval intendant at Brest.[16]

Other reasons were invoked to justify the dispersal of the Acadians. First, chronologically, was the difficulty of placing them all side by side. Indeed, in this case the previous residents would have to leave their lands to make room for the newcomers. Le Loutre's plan of regrouping his faithful within a single parish at the center of the island brought yet more expropriations than the concurrent plan that consisted of spreading them on free land in each village, that is to say, dispersing them. But the emotion was strong among those whose land would be expropriated. The rector of Bangor explained how his parishioners "all came to tell [him] that their women and children cried out strongly and would not agree to leave in order to make room for the Acadians."[17] It was certainly not a question of flat out expropriation, properly speaking, since the States of Brittany proposed to the Belle-Île residents a general reimbursement. The islanders, who up until then were not owners of their lands, would become so at the end of the process but only by continuing to pay high rents. The government tried to prove to the islanders that they would not lose in this transformation,[18] but without great success. Le Loutre suffered insults and invectives from some Belle-Île residents, many of whom continued to sow their former lands with seed though they were now meant for the Acadians. This created "a pile of difficulties. It seems that they are enjoying it, it drags everything out longer, nothing is completed. . . ."[19] Some months later, on October 14, 1765, he wrote that "the former colonists presume that everything is theirs. They do not want to allow the Acadians to work, and they have gone so far as to prohibit them from cutting the hay. . . ."[20] This patent hostility towards the newcomers was evidently akin to a kind of proto-racism. To limit the resistance of the inhabitants, many local administrators therefore opposed the plan of reassembling the Acadians in a single parish preferred by Le Loutre. This opinion was expressed at the start by one of the reporters of the commission established by the States of Brittany:

> The reunion of all of these families into one parish seems to us to be as difficult as it is impracticable, not only with regard to the division of lands, but again because one would have to expel from their holdings the former colonists among whom are found good, active and laborious cultivators who deserve concern and who would be offended by their expulsion from their former holdings.[21]

Warren noted the perceived hostility of the local populations, and he, too, advocated dispersing the Acadians in order to prevent it. But he pushed his reflection further and was the first to advance the idea that the Acadians, in this manner, would do better to mingle with the locals. Warren envisaged no further latent cultural or identity problems, even if the two populations did not speak the same language, since he expected this method to allow the formulation on the island of "one single mind and one people."[22] Le Loutre seemed more dubious about the capacities for assimilation of the local population and about the desire of the Acadians to let their group be dissolved. Facing the opposition presented to his plan for regrouping, the Abbé pleaded for a compromise. If he was ready to grant the universal sharing of land, he still hoped to be able to avoid the assimilation envisioned by Warren:

> You should have the kindness, if we are dispersed into the four parishes, to at least allow our Acadians to be near one another, in order that they may assist each other in their work, and not be mingled with the Belle-Île residents who do not regard them fondly and whose language they do not understand.[23]

The plan of fee-farm (*afféagement*) granting of Belle-Île was mainly conducted by four local intervening parties and brought an intense correspondence between the States of Brittany, the governor of the island, Warren, the previous colonists, the *gourdiecs*,[24] the four rectors (priests) of the island, and lastly, the Abbé Le Loutre and the Acadians. The government also often intervened. Choiseul enthusiastically approved the project.[25] Though the minister's intervention was subsequently limited to material or logistical assistance, in December 1763 he engaged the Abbé Le Loutre to urge the Acadian families (initially reluctant) to settle on the island.[26] In June 1764, he solicited the Controller-General of Finances for the payment of a sum of 56,000 *livres* required by the States, for supplies of material for the settlement and payment of the price of transportation of the Acadians.[27]

More importantly, Choiseul, taking the side of Le Loutre against Warren, encouraged him in his project of reassembling the Acadians. He thus wrote to the duc d'Aiguillon, governor of Brittany, to leave the management of the operations of fee-farm leasing of Belle-Île to Le Loutre and to "reunite these [Acadian] families in a single village. They are all related, they will help each other."[28] This injunction of Choiseul aimed at regrouping the Acadians within the same parish strongly contrasts with the later views of his successor, Necker. In each case, this problem of the regrouping and/or dispersion of the Acadians occupies a large place in the correspondence relative to the settlement. I do not know why the principal minister of the kingdom urged the Acadians to be regrouped, but we may consider the hypothesis that Choiseul, observing affairs from afar, was more sensitive to the desires of the repatriated and of the Abbé Le Loutre himself than to the practical problems eventually posed by this regrouping of Acadians in the largest of the Breton islands.

The resistance to reassembling the Acadians in Belle-Île therefore seems to have come entirely from the local level. Despite the support of Choiseul, Le Loutre and the Acadians did not win their cause. Indeed, if the States advocated placing the newcomers at the extremity of the three parishes, "starting with where they are reunited step by step," they added a clause nullifying the effects of this, since they prohibited "forcing the previous inhabitants from their homes, at least if they did not consent to it individually."[29] On the land, the local resistance was very strong, with the inhabitants not wanting to give up their fields and residences.[30] Resistance by the islanders did not weaken, and a revolt against the plan of the Abbé was formed at the instigation of one of the rectors on the island, to such a point that Le Loutre had to capitulate. After September 1765, he made no further reference to the problems of the regrouping or the dispersion of the Acadians. They had to yield and, in the end, were spread throughout the island.

In all, therefore, the settlement of Belle-Île constituted the first attempt at an assimilation of the Acadians into a local population (less "French" than the former, since they spoke Breton). While the refugees claimed to have authorization to remain bound together as a community, the island authorities, on the contrary, strongly encouraged intermingling of the populations.[31] The government supported the desire of the refugees, but the impossibility of putting the decision into effect with regard to the local populations led to *de facto* intermingling.

The concern for integrating the Acadians on site was also felt in the reestablishment of their civil status, which was lost at the time of deportation. In 1767, the States of Brittany ordered an oral enquiry among the Acadians of the island to establish the genealogies and parental ties among all the refugees. The verifying of these genealogies had, as its aim, a return to normal life, the verification of marriages, and rendering legally "vouchable" these people who until then could be considered as, in effect, vagrants.[32] All of the family leaders present on the island were therefore questioned and had to indicate their affiliations back to their ancestors who had come from France. This procedure certainly implied a desire to insert the Acadians into the civil society of Belle-Île.[33] No similar procedure was undertaken anywhere else in France.

The prospect of being intermingled with the island population undoubtedly contributed to limiting the number of Acadians who ultimately volunteered to colonize the island.[34] Relations between the islanders and the Acadians seem to have been relatively strained for some time after the arrival of the group at the end of September 1765. This led to the flare-ups between the Acadian Laurent Babin and many islanders.[35] The conflicts only subsided after the installation of the last families from America, but signs of quibbling continued until 1768 or 1769,[36] though this hostility, patent or latent, did not prevent a large number of mixed marriages from occurring.[37]

The question of whether the settlement of Belle-Île was a success or a failure has been greatly debated, most often summed up in a debate over the total number of Acadians who left the island. For instance, Dominique Guillemet estimates that two-thirds of the initial population was still present on the island in 1792.[38] But these figures—rarely detailed or explicit—are hardly significant. Concerning the numbers provided by Guillemet, it is clear that most of the "Acadians" present at Belle-Île in 1792 were born on the island and descended from mixed couples. If we take the list of the 235 Acadians living on the island in 1786, we can quickly count among the names mentioned at least 126 people born after 1765. Therefore only 109 of the 363 persons who came to the island were still present, or less than a third. Surely, many had died naturally, but it seems certain that a good proportion had left the island voluntarily. Most notably, 125 Acadians left Belle-Île to embark for Louisiana in 1785.[39]

The motives that prompted the Acadians to leave the island appear in fine print in many later documents. It mainly seems that the newcomers had many difficulties in developing their properties (among the worst on the island).[40] When a time of bad harvests arrived between 1769 and 1772,[41] the situation of the Acadians became extremely precarious. In September 1772, Warren alerted the Abbé Le Loutre of the consequences of the bad harvests and poor fishing that put most of the Acadians in peril. Warren castigated the greed of the stewards who were only concerned with claiming rents and did not want to even loan seeds for the season. The following month, Warren explained to Terray why he feared for the Acadian colony: according to him, the lands that were distributed to the newcomers were of a quality very inferior to that which was promised by the States of Brittany. And when the rents were increased, many Acadian families were inclined to leave. Warren asked the Controller-General for free seeds for the Acadians.[42] We do not know if he agreed to this request, but what is certain is that many fee-farm grantees left the island shortly after this letter was sent. De Boynes, the Minister of the Navy, actually wrote to Guillot at the end of December 1772 that he had received letters from the Acadians saying that "the land that had been granted to them being completely sterile, however hard they tried, they could not procure the means to subsist from it [and] they were obliged to abandon it and to depart to Saint-Malo." They again requested to receive payment like their compatriots in the Saint-Malo region. The minister, who thought that he had "fulfilled the promise that had been made to them" by giving them lands at Belle-Île, instructed Guillot to no longer "regard them as Acadians."[43]

Nine months later, the Commissioner Lemoyne, on passing through the region, adopted a more conciliatory tone. After an enquiry, he explained why so many Acadians had left the settlement, mentioning the poor lands, mediocre harvests, and excessive rents. He considered the risk that all of the Acadians might leave Belle-Île as long as conditions were so poor.[44] Some days later, he recommended a thorough inspection of the lands of all the Acadians present on the island. Those whose lands were poor could look forward to going to the settlement of Poitou, while the others should be considered as having already benefited from the graces of the king and should not, then, be authorized to go there.[45] A certain number of Acadians then finally left the island to be admitted to the Poitou colony. Some years later, another dispersion occurred at the time of the departure for Louisiana: we have noted above that nearly a hundred individuals then left Morbihan. And at least one Acadian later requested to leave the island to go to Saint-Pierre and Miquelon.[46]

In sum, beyond the disputes over the total numbers of Acadians who remained at Belle-Île-en-Mer, it seems that the grafting of the Acadians onto the local population only partially succeeded in adapting them to the island. We have noted how the partial failure is essentially explained by economic problems. The Acadians simply had too much trouble feeding themselves. Perhaps their allotments were less than those of the previous colonists; their mobility, however, is explained by their relations with the rest of the Acadian diaspora and the possibilities offered to them of rejoining their compatriots in Poitou or Louisiana. Did the cultural and linguistic factors, the group affinities, play a role in explaining these departures? It is pointless to debate this in the present state of research, as the sources make no direct mention of problems of this kind after the start of the process, but we can assume that these aspects did play a role in at least a portion of the departures. Estimates of the rate of mixed marriages indicate that the two communities intermingled quickly enough. The Acadians who remained were rapidly assimilated, even if memory of their roots had been revived recently, with the beginning of exchanges with Québec and Canada in general.[47]

Other Plans

We have seen how the settlement of Belle-Île only involved a modest number of Acadians. Before the apparent success of this endeavor, the State was concerned with settling the rest of the Acadians in France, still around three thousand individuals. Given the lack of resources, it remains very difficult to determine what exactly the actions of the government were, but they seem to have been very limited. In any event, in the few plans of which we possess details, the ministry did not adopt the point of view of the Belle-Île administrators who advocated dispersing the Acadians. Other indications suggest rather that the government wanted to settle the Acadians all together. Even if no reason is shown in the documents, we can imagine that the government wanted to settle the Acadians all together for practical purposes: a single settlement involved fewer procedural difficulties than would numerous ones.

In an eloquent August 1767 letter to the Vatican, the Abbé de l'Isle-Dieu wrote that one sought to "assemble" the Acadians in "one same and single province." The "reunion" of the families would form a "small new Acadia."[48] Le Loutre's hopes of reassembling the Acadians in a single place were supported by the ministry, which was, at that time, disposed to reuniting five to six hundred families (according to the Abbé's statements). Moreover, it was in order to preserve the "purity" of the Acadian people that the Abbé de l'Isle-Dieu sought to have them be reunited. The government then had no plan for the assimilation of the Acadians—very much the contrary, since the goal was rather to regenerate the local populations. One week before, Le Loutre mentioned what was undoubtedly the same plan in a letter to Governor Warren, elaborating a bit more on the reasons to keep the Acadians grouped together:

> The minister seems disposed to reunite them all in the same province and to just form one and the same settlement with distinct and separate parishes, without any intermingling of the parishes already formed by the previous inhabitants.[49]

This plan was surely made more urgent by the repatriation of a large number of Acadians settled initially in Saint-Pierre and Miquelon and by the cost engendered by the assistance distributed to them, "considering the excessive cost of bread and other subsistence."[50] Even if, for reasons of confidentiality, the location considered for the settlement in question was specified by neither l'Isle-Dieu nor Le Loutre, it was probably part of a "plan of settlement in the forests of Brix and Valognes"[51] proposed by the commissioner of Francy, regarding which César Gabriel de Choiseul, duc de Praslin, wrote to the Controller-General: "I believe that this deserves all of your attention and that it is truly an affair of State. . . . I beg you to inform me as soon as possible of the results of your reflections."[52] Despite this warm recommendation, the answer of the Controller-General was delayed and the plan—like many others that followed—was buried with no one knowing exactly why.[53] Nevertheless, it would seem that, with the later plans, the problems of rights regarding the lands and woods dependent on the royal domain engendered some latent complications.[54]

Still, over a year later, the desire of the government to settle the Acadians all together and the optimism of the missionaries remained intact, if we believe the testimony from Le Loutre to Warren. The latter affirmed candidly that he was "on the point of having a decision from the ministry about the settlement of the families that . . . still remain to settle in France [and that] they have finally resolved to place them all in the same canton, and it seems that there are only certain arrangements to be made . . . to complete . . . this business."[55] The plan being discussed was no longer that of Brix, but perhaps a new suggestion by the government to settle the Acadians on Corsica (as described in detail further below).[56]

The Initiatives of Individuals

Parallel to these governmental plans, Choiseul, and then Praslin, solicited individuals more, especially as they took into account the difficulty of establishing the Acadians on lands belonging to the royal domains. In fact, most of these plans were issued by large and small property owners.[57] Choiseul was not the only one to consider placing the Acadians on privately owned lands.[58] Commissioner Lemoyne was behind a certain number of plans and recruited landowners from among his friends. The Acadians were still considered as manpower at a good price, productive, patriotic, and attractive because of the amount of rent that they would be paying. The landowners were rarely hesitant because of scruples.[59] They smelled "good business." The Acadians were also thought of as a means to make the government more aware of the landowners. And, in fact, many individuals presented a plan that utilized the Acadians: from Irish entrepreneurs to a prince of the blood (comte de la Marche).[60] Some correspondents hoped or imagined that the "pure morals" of the Acadians might provide an example locally.

These plans shared the basic characteristic of only providing settlement for a few families at once. None of them claimed the advantage of settling all of the Acadians in the same locale. This is perhaps a reason why the plans to resettle the Acadians were not retained by the French administration. It is very likely that resistance to these "small" settlements, which would have led to a new dispersion of the Acadians, was expressed either by them directly or by the Abbés Le Loutre and de l'Isle-Dieu. Such resistance no doubt would have coincided with the desire of the Acadians while, at the same time, family regroupings were being pursued. Thus, in the same period, Joseph LeBlanc, called Le Maigre ["the thin man"] declined going to the North American colonies (namely Saint-Pierre and Miquelon), so that he could rejoin his older son at Belle-Île.[61]

One of the plans that came closest to fruition was that of placing the Acadians in Corsica. The reasons that the plan failed are known thanks to the account of a visit of the island by Le Loutre and five Acadians.[62] Again, the question of legalities involving the ownership of the land reemerged, as did the problem of placing the Acadians all together, as they seem to have requested. In fact, the Acadians did request to be reassembled, as the intendant of the island reported in 1769: "The Acadians request placing four hundred families on the east coast, . . . and, lacking the possibility to settle them all in this region, they request [other lands on the west coast].[63]

Most of the cases lack sources that might help us understand the absence of a response by the government, whether that was a refusal or an abandonment of the plans. Most often, however, it does not seem as if the abandonment of the plans was directly connected to the possibility of settling the Acadians all together. A certain number of individuals recanted after having become more fully informed. For instance, Nivernais himself was warned by his intendant that room was lacking for the Acadians on the island of Bouin.[64] In other cases, the administration judged that the conditions were not right for a suitable settlement. Thus, the naval intendant at Le Havre examined the proposals for settling the Acadians near Cherbourg and gravely concluded "that there was not the slightest solidity in this project."[65] It is perhaps for similar reasons that many ideas were buried, such as that of the comte de Chateaubriand, who proposed granting a portion of his lands at Combourg to be rented.[66]

Once again, lacking sufficient documentation, the attitude of the government in the majority of these plans is known only in a fragmentary manner or through deduction. How might we form an idea of the attitude of the ministry? The most probable hypothesis is that the government barely worked to favor the Acadians and was content with a passive attitude, only taking a position episodically, when petitions or proposals were addressed to it. When the plans were submitted, lacking a strong policy, the obstacles seemed so insurmountable that the initiatives were nipped in the bud. Undoubtedly the secret hope of Choiseul (then of Praslin, who succeeded him at the Navy) was that the Acadian problem would manage itself, and that the refugees would end up spontaneously "dispersing," finding work, or at least ceasing to trouble the ministry. And the government also undoubtedly left the initiative up to individuals for financial reasons. In fact, the government was coming to grips with many contradictory imperatives, such as the lack of liquidities to finance the entirety of the settlement itself and supply the lands, the desire to satisfy the Acadians, and the personal interests of the ministers who were tempted to satisfy their clientele, and as we have seen, sometimes personally involved in the affair.

We do not know if the Acadians were consulted about the various ideas for settlement. Most of the projects rarely arrived at a sufficiently advanced stage to be submitted to them (with some exceptions, as in the case of Corsica). But the refugees were not unaware of the intentions of the government, since the ministry and the commissioners on site constantly spoke to them about their departure. In fact, the exiles remained convinced that they would again emigrate.[67] Whether this would be to the colonies, to return to Canada, or to go elsewhere in France to clear lands that the government might provide to them, they expected to have to leave their place of residence sooner or later. Regardless of their feelings about renewed departure, pro or con, we can easily imagine that such a perspective did not encourage assimilation. The uncertainty also largely negated initiatives of economic integration by the Acadians, since such a prospect for the future could only prevent any plans for the long term. If, during this period, the Acadians seemed largely passive, content to await the proposals that were made to them, it was probably also because the refugees were extremely divided about what attitude to adopt and about what destination was appropriate to request from the government. There was no consensus among the Acadians about requesting to go to Louisiana. From all evidence, some of the refugees wanted to remain in France and accepted the offers that the government made to them. Others undoubtedly wanted to leave at all costs, most often to Acadia or to Saint-Pierre and Miquelon, and sometimes to Louisiana. All of these factors limited the scope of the Acadian petitions that went to the administration, requesting to go to either Saint-Pierre and Miquelon,[68] to return to Acadia,[69] to go to Louisiana,[70] or to be settled in France.[71]

Finally, after having maintained the hope during the war of sending the Acadian people to the Southern Colonies, the government gradually realized the impossibility of putting this program into effect. Choiseul then sought possibilities for their settlement in France, but without much conviction or much success. After the establishment of the Acadian colonists at Belle-Île, for the most part the Ministry of the Navy then lost interest in the situation of the exiles, content to relay the proposals made by various individuals. It was mainly to this end that the effort of integrating the Acadians by the ministry was limited between 1763 and 1772. For their part, the Acadians were strongly divided and largely passive. It was only in the later period that they organized themselves more actively and tried to have their voices heard, facing a government just recovering from the problem of their settlement.

Chapter V

The Plans For Settlement:
Establishing The Acadians In France (1772-1785)

Attaching the Acadians to the Soil

A CHANGE OCCURRED IN THE ATTITUDE of the government towards the middle of 1772, when the settling of the Acadians became the subject of a discussion before the Council of the King. It is difficult to determine the exact reasons for this return to the Acadian question, after the period of relative inactivity observed above. We may conjecture, however, that a crisis was in the works. Some weeks before this meeting of the Council, the naval commissioner at Saint-Malo had intercepted a letter from the Bailiwick of Jersey urging the Acadians to desert France and to return to the English colonies of North America.[1] The capture of this letter seems to have caused the failure of this plan, according to the opinion of the minister, but the government became preoccupied by the fear of a massive flight of the Acadians outside of France, which would amount to a shameful failure of French diplomacy and a consequent loss for the kingdom.[2]

Furthermore, some days after the interception of this letter, the Acadians sent a petition requesting that they be sent to Louisiana.[3] It was not the first time that the minister had received such a request, but it was probably the first petition directly addressed to him specifically in this way. It clearly showed him that the problem of their integration was not going to resolve itself. The idea of settling the Acadians in Corsica was, in fact, defunct. A year before, Le Loutre had gone to Compiègne on the way to the island of Beauté, accompanied by four Acadian leaders. He dined with de Boynes, but the plan was afterwards put aside because of its complexity.[4] Otherwise, plans previously submitted by Commissioner Lemoyne one after another proved impossible to achieve, from the sheer fact of the many complexities of the unwritten laws.[5] The administrative sluggishness on all levels ended up discouraging some noblemen of the province who were *a priori* disposed to welcome the Acadians. The comte de Closnard withdrew after learning that the refugees, protected by the government, put "no limits on their presumptions." He feared "that his tranquility would be constantly disturbed" by their frequent complaints.[6]

Different elements combined, then, to urge one or the other minister to propose to the Council that they allow the Acadians to leave for Louisiana, rather than letting them flee clandestinely to Acadia or to continue draining the budget at home for years. The chronological line of facts is vague and depends on a small number of documents that are somewhat contradictory.[7] Many historians believe that a delegation of Acadians went to Compiègne to plead directly to the king. In any event, the information of these historians should be accepted with caution.[8] The date, as well, is not certain.[9] Though all of the historians who have related the event place this meeting in July 1772 (clearly following the many later letters of the marquis de Pérusse d'Escars), according to Lemoyne, it happened in September of that year. The testimony of the commissioner is more credible than that of Pérusse, for his correspondence with Bertin only began in the middle of September 1772. It hardly seems possible that Lemoyne would have waited two months before writing to Bertin when, otherwise unoccupied in Paris, he was anxious to act.[10] Here is the account of the events as they are summarized in an anonymous report dating from June 1778:

> In 1772, after this fruitless initiative in Corsica, the ministry of Finances found the Acadians to be very burdensome and the Acadians themselves were distressed at being so long dependent on the State. They proposed that they be allowed to go to settle under the domination of the King of Spain, whether in Louisiana, or in Sierra Morena, where they were wanted and the minister of Finances who saw himself thus freed of 300,000 *livres* per year was favorable to this plan. He proposed it to the Council and concluded with its acceptance. Everyone's opinion followed his, but the King refused to follow through. He wanted to keep the Acadians in his kingdom and ordered that they be found settlements conforming to the promise that had been made them, and seemed to be dissatisfied that it had not happened in ten years. The intention of His Majesty was to [11]attach them to the soil; this is what they had been promised; it was to render them useful and happy by providing them with their primitive occupation, and it was also the only means of preserving the purity of morals of this excellent species of men.[12]

It is interesting to note "the intention of the king to attach them to the soil." It is possible that this same expression was employed by the king, for it is reported by practically all of those who wrote of the meeting in exactly the same terms, and the phrase appears in no previous document but one. Does the use of this new term embody a projected change in the governmental policy?

The soil was a "foundation of land to which the serfs were attached and which they would cultivate."[13] Did the king want to make the Acadians serfs? No document attests to this, and it is very improbable considering that, in 1779, Louis XV would suppress personal tenure and servitude in his domains and there were practically no longer any serfs in France during this period. Let us add—as we have seen above concerning the term *règnicole* ["native"]—that the legal vocabulary was not always properly used, and we should not seek exact precision in all of the statements that were apparently made by the king. What, then, could this phrase from the program indicate? Terray provides a first interpretation, writing to de Boynes: "You know . . . the desire that the king has expressed to procure for [the Acadians] settlements to attach them to the soil, to establish them and naturalize them in France in a manner useful both to themselves and to the State."[14] It is interesting to note here the use of the term "naturalize," which implies that the Acadians were in fact foreigners.[15] Evidently, here it was no longer simply an issue of the distribution of lands or the fulfillment of promises. The question of "national integration" was clearly implied in this discussion. The other important theme was that of "establishment." In this regard, a later report actually specifies that the desire of His Majesty "is that [the Acadians] form settlements [in Poitou] that, by attaching them to the soil, will forever establish their status among his other subjects."[16]

It is not certain, however, that the program defined by the king's words involved a real rupture with previous policy, except perhaps in the use of these terms that might have further disheartened the Acadians. Actually, theories about the necessary attachment of the Acadians were not new. We have already noted above how various documents recommended that the Acadians not become accustomed to a wandering lifestyle.[17] It was especially for this reason, and to assure the Acadians a civil status and respectability, that the government ordered at Belle-Île the oral inquest known as the "declaration of genealogy" of the Acadians. The problem of ties to the soil was intimately joined to that of naturalization. According to the *Dictionnaire de l'Académie*, "nationals are bound to others[18] that can help them; foreigners are bound to no one, it is fitting that they be bound to the soil." In other words, the foreigners must be attached to the soil in order to be naturalized, and this is exactly what the text above advocates. More prosaically and concretely, it was above all a question of providing land to the refugees, and this was to be done by putting into operation the plan presented by a private individual, the marquis de Pérusse d'Escars, who had previously submitted many proposals for settlements.

The Plan of Pérusse d'Escars

We do not know exactly why the plan of Pérusse found favor in the eyes of the ministry while so many others remained only in a state of outline. Without a doubt, the marquis enjoyed powerful support within the government; he also knew the Abbé Le Loutre and had often conversed with him; and he had even met the Acadians before having sent his first report.[19] Moreover, Pérusse had already welcomed onto his lands some German families. By 1763, he had solicited the Controller-General, Bertin, for financial assistance to welcome these foreigners onto his land at Poitou.[20] In a report, the marquis added that the Germans would undoubtedly like the place, for "the German Catholic likes the French well enough."[21] Therefore, in the 1760s Pérusse recruited a dozen German families who agreed to come clear his lands at Poitou.[22] In 1770, in a new report, Pérusse again advocated having more people come to work on his lands. Certainly he recognized that "these clearings could be done by able-bodied vagabonds and beggars." But, Pérusse, considering that "this type of man, accustomed to an idle kind of profession, is cowardly, lazy, without courage, without industriousness, and without emulation," thought that they might only be useful in the second or third generation. He was certain it would be much more advantageous to have foreign workers come: "Germany, Switzerland, Holland, Austrian Flanders, Scotland and Ireland could abundantly supply them."[23] It was probably while looking for these foreign families that Pérusse heard talk about the Acadians. No doubt he was familiar with the government's fears of seeing these refugees emigrate outside of France, since the first report he presented proposing his lands played precisely to this governmental apprehension and presented the geographic site of Poitou as a remedy for emigration:

> Besides, it seems very interesting to me in all events to remove these people from the seacoast. The more that they miss their home land and the other fine [?] colonies, the less they should be able to see the people coming from there daily which

can only bring them new regrets . . . ; the further they are from the border and the coast, the less they will think of another emigration that would be even more difficult for them.[24]

Pérusse's report of January 1772 was to the point. Bertin, then Director of the Bureau of Agriculture, had already dealt with this matter many times. The Acadians' request to go to Louisiana revived the anxiety of the government and instilled a sense of urgency. The other plans for settling on the lands of individual landowners had amounted to nothing, and the prospects of establishing the refugees on lands of the royal domain vanished as one became aware of the insurmountable legal difficulties. But the instant that the king seemed to become personally interested in the question, a solution to the settlement of the Acadians had to be found. "It was then at that time" explains a later report, "that the late king appeared discontent that one had yet to fulfill the promises he had allowed to be made in his name and to execute the orders that he had given in their favor; and, after the discontent he expressed to his ministers in 1773, they began the settlement that was being prepared for them in Poitou."[25]

As with the settlement of Belle-Île-en-Mer, we do not need to describe in detail here the installation of the Acadian families on the *Grand Ligne*, since this settlement is the main subject of the work of Ernest Martin and of the thesis of Damien Rouet—readers seeking more information may refer to them. Let it suffice for us to summarize the significant facts. As we have seen, the proposal of Pérusse d'Escars, dated January 1772, was probably debated in July or September of that year in the Council of the King. Then, in September, it was proposed that some Acadian delegates from Brittany—Alexandre Trahan, Pierre Henry, and Alexandre Bourg, accompanied by the Abbé Le Loutre—visit the lands of the marquis near Archigny and Monthoiron (the Abbé died en route). In early October 1772, the three delegates wrote to the marquis that the lands they had seen, "which only consist of heaths," "seemed very barren" to them, if not unhealthy because of stagnant water. They thus categorically refused his offer, so as "to avoid the just reproaches that our colleagues would make to us in that case, which would then pass down from one generation to another."[26]

In correspondence for the months following this first visit, one hardly sees Poitou mentioned. Lemoyne continued surveying, in search of a settlement that might be more suitable than the one proposed by the marquis. In particular, he tried to convince Bertin and the Acadians to accept the proposal of his relative, the Chevalier de la Borde, or of his friend Saint-Victour[27], to welcome some families onto their lands. Moreover, Lemoyne had still not abandoned the hope of placing the refugees on the royal domains, despite the extreme complexity of the law regulating those lands. However, one after another, all of these new plans failed. Was it the commissioner who finally re-launched the plan of the marquis? Perhaps. In early February 1773, Lemoyne visited the School of Architecture at Annel directed by Sarcey de Sutières,[28] the agronomist picked by Pérusse to supervise the development of the cultivation of his lands of Archigny.[29] After this journey, the commissioner seemed more convinced that the settlement was viable,[30] but he suggested modifications to the marquis' plan.[31] In the meantime, when negotiations were under way with the Ministry of the Navy and the comte de la Marche for settling eighty Acadian families in Corsica,[32] the Poitou plan was officially accepted by the Minister of Finances in May 1773. The latter wrote to his corresponding Navy minister: "I have not found a simpler and more suitable plan to fulfill the desires of his majesty than that [of Archigny],"[33] and so a "plan for the settlement of the Acadians that would reconcile the offers by Mr. le Marquis de Pérusse with the aims of the ministry" was drafted shortly afterwards by Destouches, secretary of the Controller-General.[34] The exact reasons for the selection of Pérusse were not explained. Terray only mentioned to the Abbé de l'Isle-Dieu the fact that the various plans of Lemoyne were too expensive as compared to that of Pérusse.[35] If it seems that the marquis' plan was adopted by default, we should note that the opinion of the Acadians concerning the quality of the lands, though quite clearly expressed, was absolutely not taken into account. Some days later, Lemoyne received instructions to make a tour of the ports of the kingdom where the Acadians were in refuge in order to encourage them to settle on the lands of the marquis and to make a general census of the faculties of all, that is to say to distinguish those who might be useful for the agricultural work from the rest.[36]

Lemoyne's Resistance

Lemoyne thus found himself once again charged with promoting the plan of Pérusse to the Acadians. But the commissioner undoubtedly was not the best choice to motivate them, as he himself was only half convinced by Pérusse's proposals. His distrust of the plan seems to have come in part from his own frustration at being unable to place the Acadians either on the lands of his relatives and friends or on the lands of the royal domain, despite months invested studying the feasibility of these projects. What is more, as if to emphasize his own incapacity at finding lands for the Acadians, Lemoyne was marginalized in this new program, since Pérusse was its principal instigator and knew very well how to manage the affairs, to the point of administering the payment of the balances himself, something that particularly irritated the commissioner. But the latter also seems to have been increasingly convinced that reassembling the Acadians in one given place was not a good thing in itself. Here it is interesting to follow Lemoyne, whose path prefigures that of the entire government. In his first reports about the best way to settle the Acadians, Lemoyne seemed to envisage placing all of the Acadians together. Even if he only stated this clearly in one document, he let it be understood in many others. Thus, in May 1772, he wrote that he had told Closnard (a landowner wanting to welcome some sixty Acadian families)[37] "that the allied families would follow one another because it would be suitable to place them as close together as possible."[38] Soon enough, however, Lemoyne began to express reservations on the subject. The exact reasons for this sudden change are not known, but Lemoyne had been informed of the measures taken to settle the Acadians at Belle-Île, and he had surely heard of the problems there. Moreover, it is also probable that Guillot had warned him of the dangers and difficulties inherent in a large regrouping of the Acadians. The two commissioners were close to each other in their views. But Guillot wrote to Pérusse in October 1772 deploring the fact that the refugees, numbering 1,800 in the Saint-Malo region, "began to form a body, which is a problem, for from this come committees and reflections, etc."[39] This missive, written shortly after the first visit to the marquis' lands by three Acadian leaders, reveals the slight irritation of the commissioner. It is the first time that the Acadians so categorically refused an offer that was made to them. Guillot soon saw the reassembling of the Acadians into a "body" as an affront to the marquis, while the reasons for the new resistance by the Acadians are perhaps to be found elsewhere.

Whatever the case, Lemoyne soon returned to the idea that to leave the Acadians assembled together risked arousing their resistance and would pose other problems. Shortly after Guillot's letter, Lemoyne began to advocate dispersing the refugees. First off, the commissioner defended the same positions that had been previously noted in the study of the settlement of Belle-Île-en-Mer. Thus, in a letter to Bertin, he suggested separating the Acadians so as to not create a concentration that might risk upsetting the local populations.[40] In another missive written to de Boynes on the same day, he advocated separating the Acadians to allow them to learn the techniques of cultivation in France by observing other, more experienced cultivators.[41] The idea that the Acadians were poor cultivators contrasts with the opinion of the States of Brittany and the governor of Belle-Île at the time of the settlement of the refugees in Morbihan.[42] Lemoyne's opinion on the subject of the inopportuneness of leaving the Acadians assembled was more clearly shown again some months later in his marginal comments about a very detailed new plan put together by Pérusse. While the marquis advocated authorizing the placing of 2,000 people on his land, Lemoyne warned the government: "Does it suit the government to maintain the theme of nationality for this people and maintain it together in one body?"[43] The ministry, however, took no account of Lemoyne's views and preferred to go forward with the plan proposed by Pérusse. Moreover, the instructions given to Lemoyne at the time of his departure for his summer 1773 tour of the ports of Brittany stipulated that he should enquire "what one might hope would be useful in the reunion [of the Acadians] in the settlements."[44]

It was while Lemoyne was at Saint-Malo and having difficulty convincing his subordinates to accept Pérusse's offers that the commissioner became most violently irritated against the reunion of the Acadians "in too large a number in one and the same place." The presumptions of the refugees in forming the "body of a nation" incited Lemoyne to openly advocate their dispersion, first to punish some of the delegates or leaders, and, more generally, because such regrouping seemed dangerous to him. To punish the recalcitrant, he suggested that the Controller-General "threaten to make the suspected mutinous families leave, and to repatriate them in different locations in the interior of the kingdom to support themselves as best they might."[45] This idea returned as a *leitmotif* in many of the later letters. On July 26, 1773, in a letter to an agent at Versailles, he again warned his superiors: "reunited, this people would become very dangerous. It is inconceivable how they could have changed, they have become very spoiled at Saint-Malo because they were in too great a number and they were always comforted no matter what foolishness that they performed."[46] In a letter to the Controller-General written the same day, Lemoyne went further in his analysis of the situation. He feared that, left together, "this nation would form . . . what would in effect be a foreign people in the center of Poitou." For the commissioner, there was no doubt that, once reassembled, the Acadians would not assimilate. In this same letter, Lemoyne also shed a little light on why the government favored regrouping the refugees, "the administration . . . might draw great benefits from the reunion in a single location [of the refugees]: its surveying of them so made easier; but, then, too, what disadvantage might it risk?" Lemoyne concluded by recalling that his marginal observations in February about the plan of Pérusse "only prove themselves true all too well today at Saint-Malo."[47]

Lemoyne's opposition to the regrouping of the refugees clearly implies the notion that the union of the Acadians would allow them to mutually support one another and form a common front. We do not need to pursue much further his desire to control the rebellion by dispersing the Acadians according to the ancient principle of "divide and conquer." However, Lemoyne also seems to have been sincerely convinced of the impossibility of assimilating the Acadians in Poitou while they remained grouped together. In this he reflected the opinions of Warren and the commissioners of the States of Brittany described above in the study of Belle-Île.

Despite his reservations about the regrouping of all of the Acadians at Archigny, and although he himself recognized that the lands were mediocre,[48] it seems that Lemoyne had made his decision to execute the orders of the Controller-General—and even to exceed them—in an authoritarian manner. Here we may recall that three Acadians had visited the lands of Pérusse in October 1772 and that they had refused, in the name of their compatriots, to settle there because of their poor quality. When he was at Saint-Malo charged with recruiting the manpower to settle on the marquis' lands, Lemoyne was confronted by massive opposition from the refugees.[49] Curiously, while neither the Controller-General nor Pérusse ever asked him to use coercive means to convince the Acadians go to Châtelleraudais,[50] Lemoyne openly threatened those who objected with various reprisals. He decided to organize a counter-estimate of the land, sending back one of the most malleable delegates and falsifying the results. During this second visit, the two delegates opposing the plan, Jean-Jacques LeBlanc and Simon Aucoin, were separated into two different groups, a strategy conceived by Lemoyne to avoid their mutually encouraging each other in denigrating the quality of the soil. The report concluded with the quality of the lands being good, but it was not at all objective because of the pressure put on Aucoin and LeBlanc.[51] Upon the return of the delegates to Saint-Malo, the refugees were hardly duped by the maneuver and persevered in their refusal, at least in the beginning. According to Lemoyne, the two delegates, Leblanc and Aucoin, said nothing bad about the lands, but when they were asked if they would go to Poitou, they answered, "Oh, my God, no!" Despite his threats,[52] which were in flagrant violation of the formal orders of the Controller-General to not treat the Acadians forcibly, Lemoyne laboriously recruited 150, and then 250 people.[53] He finally left Saint-Malo after this failure, but nevertheless sent the first volunteers to Archigny some weeks later; while other Acadians coming from Cherbourg and other ports reached Pérusse's lands some time later.

The Emigration to Poitou

Nonetheless, for undetermined reasons, a number of the Acadians in Saint-Malo decided to leave for Poitou in the following months. Because of the small number of people he had been able to recruit, Lemoyne at first authorized "widows of Acadians charged with families" to go to Monthoiron.[54] Pressed to fill his assigned quota of 1,500 people, Lemoyne seems to have recruited a certain number of older people or those in no condition to work. Still, it was only at the end of December 1773, that he announced to the Controller-General that many Acadians had changed their minds and that nearly nine hundred of the people domiciled at Saint-Malo were now ready to go to Poitou. Most of them went there the following spring.[55] By the end of July 1774, nearly 1,500 immigrants had gone to Poitou, if we believe a petition addressed to Queen Marie-Antoinette.[56] Though Lemoyne provides no indications for the causes of this change of heart, it is probable that a group reflex played a part. Faced with the prospect of losing three to four hundred compatriots, some of the opponents of the Pérusse plan probably considered that it was better to not risk dividing the group, and so then decided to move to Poitou collectively, dragging all of the undecided in their wake. In Châtelleraudais, they knew that they would find other Acadians who had previously been dispersed elsewhere in France; some undoubtedly hoped that, with the general disorganization soon resulting from the land clearings and construction of houses, that they would then be in a position of strength in making their request to leave the kingdom.[57] In fact, this is almost exactly what happened, but the authorization to leave France would still take another ten years to be granted.

The desire of the Acadians to remain near one another was incontestable. Though the documents consulted do not mention explicit requests in this regard,[58] this hope was evident. In fact, the plans for settlement of Pérusse clearly specify that the villages would be near one another, which leads us to think that this was the desire of the refugees. Moreover, the minutes from the second visit of the Acadian delegates to the lands of the marquis clearly indicate that the villages would not be separated by rivers or streams.[59] Furthermore, in many reports sent to the court promoting the plan, Pérusse strongly stressed that the settlement envisaged would allow the Acadians to remain together, as was their desire. "This will be a consolation for [the Acadians] to be together," he wrote in one of the first reports.[60] In a later letter to Nivernais he added:

> They generally want to be settled all together or at least within reach of one another, and I think that it would be very bad to disperse them, for, besides the fact that the reasons they are in the Kingdom should eliminate any fears of having them assembled here, it is certain that the good principles in which they were raised, from which their religion, morals, and fidelity derive, will be maintained if they remain together, and their good example might even have some effect on the neighbors around them; whereas, by dispersing them, they may find themselves instead drowned in the crowd of license and bad examples.... The isolated honest man must fear being led astray by bad example.[61]

For Pérusse then, the regrouping of the Acadians would not be dangerous, since the circumstances of their arrival in the kingdom proved their fidelity and their patriotism. It should be said that Pérusse was wholly convinced of the benefits of leaving the refugees grouped together, and this was one of the reasons for his clashes with Lemoyne. The marquis thus wrote the latter a letter that takes the exact opposite position of what Lemoyne had written previously, advocating giving the Acadians their own church, to thereby avoid a division of the population.[62]

Far from finding the Acadians' claim to form a "body of a nation" dangerous and rejecting it, we thus find Pérusse convinced that this was a good thing. This reflects the marquis' conviction that the Acadians formed an extremely virtuous people capable of regenerating the local population. This idealization of the Acadians surely comes from his discussions with the Abbé Le Loutre and the Abbé de l'Isle-Dieu, as well as from his reading many historical reports written about the Acadians that praise the patriotism of the refugees and, more generally, their zeal facing every trial.[63] Besides, reassembling the Acadians in one and the same place seemed to him to be an excellent antidote to their desire to emigrate—"a family will have more trouble leaving their relatives and compatriots and emigrating when it has no relatives or friends to hold it back"[64]—and it would also allow the refugees to be more of a solid body. The marquis de Pérusse thus wrote to Lemoyne that he wanted to keep the Acadians grouped together "in order to place them all equally well within range to help one another."[65]

These arguments in favor of regrouping the refugees were undoubtedly aimed at persuading the government as much as the Acadians themselves, and were sufficient to convince the latter, who only accepted going to Poitou after Lemoyne's various maneuvers.[66] But the prospect of being able to live assembled together was not enough to hold the refugees more than a few months in Poitou. While the first Acadians arrived on what would become the Acadian Line in the month of October 1773 (amounting to 1,461 on site in June 1774),[67] by the fall of 1775 and spring of 1776, almost all of them left the region to go to Nantes.[68] We will not expand further here on the causes for the failure of this settlement. In any event, the reason must remain incompletely known, due to our inability to tell exactly what the Acadians were thinking. Let us simply say, to summarize, that the barely conciliatory mindset of many of the Acadian leaders and delegates upon their arrival in the region of the Acadian Line did not bode well from the start. Furthermore, the arrival of the Acadians happened in a hurried manner, when the houses meant to welcome them had still not been constructed. On top of this, the incapacity of the government to quickly make a decision about the status of the lands granted to the Acadians led to their refusal to start clearing the land. And even those to whom lands were distributed were incapable of working them, for lack of oxen. In sum, nothing advanced, and the Acadians who had become accustomed to working in the ports decided to leave for the summer season of 1775 to find work in Saint-Malo. It was at this moment that Anne Robert Jacques Turgot—finally convinced by Pérusse that the surplus of people incapable of doing the agricultural work on the sites was ruining the advancement of the project—authorized the Acadians who wanted to leave the settlement to go to Nantes, on July 18, 1775.[69] But, while Turgot thought six hundred people would remain in the settlement, nearly all of the Acadians then went to Nantes.[70]

New Emigration to Nantes

This mass departure was not fortuitous, but rather a clear indication of the desire to maintain the integrity of the group, at least on the part of certain leaders. In numerous letters, Pérusse describes the many maneuvers of some leaders to ensure that all of the Acadians would follow each other. Thus, less than a month after the Controller-General had given the official authorization to those who wanted to leave the Acadian Line to go to Nantes, Pérusse mentions the pressure exerted on those who wanted to remain on their lands.[71] On August 12, Pérusse explained that a "mutiny on the part of the leaders becomes stronger every moment; they have resolved to prevent any Acadian from remaining in this country. All the laborers and good cultivators who want to remain here are led into town by threats in order to declare to Mr. Herault that they want to follow the others and return to the sea ports."[72] Some days later, Pérusse supplied a delegate with the names of the victims of this treatment.[73] If we are to believe the marquis, other methods were used to sabotage the settlement, as well, evidently with the aim of repulsing those who wanted to remain: wells were filled with construction materials and roofing tiles removed, for instance.[74] Pérusse then referred this to the Controller-General and expressed in an eloquent and perceptive manner the strategy of the Acadians. According to him, the desire of the delegates was to not be settled in any part of France, for in fact they wanted to be expatriated to Louisiana. In other respects, the delegates wanted to remain united:

> [The delegates Jean-Jacques LeBlanc and Basile Henry] are more anxious than everyone to leave the country, hoping . . . to plot so that there will be no Acadian left there, convinced as they are that, having reunited into the body of a nation, it will be easier to obtain from the court the absurd permission they have requested to go to Louisiana, a desire quite contrary to the general one of the Acadians, the large majority of whom are surely truly attached to France.[75]

Moreover, from this moment on, Pérusse vigorously denounced what he had advocated previously, namely, the reassembling of the Acadians.[76] If the marquis did not request that they be dispersed,[77] he denounced what he considered to be a subversive strategy to put pressure on the government. The denunciation of the Acadian "national body" reappeared in many later reports by Pérusse.[78] According to the marquis, as late as November 1775, LeBlanc and Henry, upon their departure, "demanded from all of the others a promise to not remain in this country."[79] In December, Pérusse complained that one of the delegates, Simon Aucoin, insulted the Acadians who wanted to remain in the settlement.[80] Once at Nantes, the refugees continued to strongly urge the few families remaining at Poitou to rejoin them. They sent many letters whose substance Pérusse repeated in much of his correspondence,[81] and which the intendant intercepted for some time,[82] in vain. In these letters, the Acadians explained how they were received in Nantes and the promises made to them, and they affirmed that they would soon obtain authorization to return to Acadia. They apparently even sent a certain Livoye to Poitou in February 1776 to try to convince the final reluctant few.[83] Of the small number remaining there, most then left to rejoin the Acadian group at Nantes. Between the end of 1779 and 1784, about 80 to 170 individuals who had remained then departed.[84]

As we have just seen, the gathering of the Acadians at Nantes was no longer the result of spontaneous assembly—for familial reasons or from affinity—but had evolved into an intentionally organized project. The constitution of a "national body" became tied at that moment with a very precise aim of obtaining objective results. The Acadians established themselves into a kind of organized union, whose individual members were asked to respect the will of the group. Some individuals separated, however, and left the community. Why? Damien Rouet notes that those who settled at Archigny had family ties and common geographic histories: indeed, most often they had not stayed at Saint-Malo before. Those who had not stayed in the Rance region before were therefore not, as one might say today, "communitized." We should also not forget the material advantages so acquired: the government gave the families who remained in Poitou a house and a plot of land. While the first Acadians who left were never able to occupy these houses, all of those who remained a bit longer were lodged in these newly built homes. These advantages, even though modest, surely counted for a lot in the decision to remain. Moreover, those who remained were assured of payment of the balance of assistance for some time still, while it was not promised to those who left for Nantes. On this subject Rouet notes that at the moment when payment stopped in Poitou many of the Acadians left for Nantes.[85] Finally, many Acadian women remained because they had married men from Poitou.⁸⁶ Most of the families seem to have been torn by the choice facing them and tensions must have been strong, as shown by the testimony of Benjamin Boudrot collected by Rameau de Saint-Père in 1860:

> [Benjamin Boudrot] vividly recalled the goodbyes that were said at his home when they left; one of their cousins named Ambroise... came one day with other young people to embrace them all; there was also one Sauvion; his father and brother still wanted to go with them, but his mother held them back.... Wandering up and down the line, the most determined and adventurous among the Acadians said, on coming to see the others: "So, for example, should we stay here just to eat heathier ?... No, we have to flee this country."⁸⁷

One of the brothers of Benjamin Boudrot wanted to leave with the other Acadians, but Boudrot tells that, "as one of my sisters had married the coachman of Pérusse, and as Mr. Pérusse likes us very much, he spoke so fondly to my father and mother that he convinced us to stay."⁸⁸

A Minimal Desire to Integrate

We have seen above how Lemoyne had gone from a rather conciliatory attitude towards the Acadians' desire to remain grouped together to seeking a way to break up the "national body," which, in his view, became a source of resistance to the orders with which he was bound. We have similarly seen how, at the start of the attempts to clear land in Poitou, Pérusse opposed Lemoyne on this subject and how he specifically arranged for the Acadians not to be separated. But if we find these two men clearly in strong disagreement on this point, the debate seemed to fall apart in the absence of the principal actor in the drama: the government. Lacking sources, we hardly know what the ministers in place thought of the question. None of them advocated dispersing the Acadians, but it is not certain that they encouraged the alternative, either. At that time the government does not seem to have been concerned with this question, but left it entirely to the marquis de Pérusse with his conviction that it would be better to leave the Acadians together. An anonymous report dated from October 1773 even affirmed that "the government did not [want] to intermingle other people with them."⁸⁹ We have seen above that the instructions to Lemoyne at the start of his tenure, signed by Terray, still spoke of reuniting the Acadians in the settlements,⁹⁰ and though Lemoyne quickly asked that many Acadians at Saint-Malo be banished from the town to remove them from the other refugees, no official instruction was ever issued to this effect. Lemoyne was even clearly disavowed by the Controller-General, in his letter of August 15 1773.⁹¹ Thus no initiative to disperse the Acadians was shown at that time. In fact, they came to Poitou and left grouped together, creating a new Acadian concentration that, though not as consequential as that of Saint-Malo, seemed to be increasingly better organized and capable of bringing together some of the Acadians isolated in small groups in the ports of Cherbourg and Le Havre.

If we analyze the actions of the government at the time of the attempted settlement of the Acadians in Poitou, we notice that the program "of attaching [the Acadians] to the soil" defined in 1772 did not constitute a great change in the governmental policy of integration. Indeed, the initiative in Poitou still corresponded to a minimalist vision of the integration-assimilation of the Acadians. For the government it was essentially a question of fulfilling a promise made in the name of the king by the duc de Nivernais at the time of the repatriation of the Acadians from England, of assuring the stability of the Acadians by preventing them from leaving the kingdom,[92] of allowing them to consider the possibility of leaving the fruit of the land clearings to their children, and in the short term, of bringing income to the cash boxes of the State, increasing its population and helping its finances by ending the distribution of assistance. The principal difference with the previous projects was how these took some steps towards being realized, which had never been the case at Belle-Île. On the other hand, the ideas of assimilation were very limited: the Acadians were consciously left together by specifically claiming that they could keep their customs, help one another, and be less tempted to leave. Such a minimalist program should not be surprising. We have already said that the France of the eighteenth century consisted of an extraordinary cultural mosaic that was only the object of limited attempts at uniformity on the part of the government. We have notably mentioned the case of the language, which, despite what the Ordinance of Villiers-Cotterêts would have one believe, was not homogenous at the end of the *Ancien Régime*. One could even say the same thing of what was immediately visible to an observer: the fashion. Nicole Pellegrin has emphasized the extreme diversity of the clothing in France before the Revolution: "It is in vain that the revolutionaries declared unconstitutional the diversity of clothing of the *Ancien Régime*, it is in vain that they wanted 'to hope that sooner or later the Revolution would lead to the benefit of a national costume, and that the traveler, passing from one department to another, would no longer think he had gone amongst different peoples.'"[93] Another reason for this lack of ideas of cultural assimilation is to be sought in the unflattering representation that the administrators and the landowners shared of the indigenous peasants and the local population in general.[94] Moreover, these peasants were considered by the landowners and administrators as being a potential danger to the "pure" Acadians, whether from the possible contagion of their bad morals or from the discouragement that they might stir among the protégés of the government. Pérusse held the peasants of the Archigny environs responsible for the deplorable opinion one had of the Acadians upon their first visit to his lands.[95] By comparison, the Acadians were initially perceived as being quite superior: they spoke the language of the educated elite, a distinctive sign valued at a time when two thirds of the French people spoke something other than French every day;[96] they were tall, of good morality, patriotic, when patriotism was considered as a particularly important virtue[97]; courageous, and able bodied. In brief, even the idea of mixing good elements with the bad did not then really exist, except in terms of the possible eventual emulation of the Acadians by the local peasants.

The Plans for Dispersal and for Assimilation: Necker and the Fusion of the National Body

Up until the years 1776 or 1777, therefore, at Versailles we find no sign of any real desire to assimilate the Acadians. How, then, did the government arrive at the idea of intermingling the Acadians, as advocated by Necker and mentioned above? We have seen that Turgot, in his orders of July 18, 1775,[98] had, in fact, organized a new reassembly of the Acadians at Nantes. During the following two years, the documentation slacks off considerably, and it is more difficult to know what in fact the government did. If, however, we believe the two later reports, nothing much happened during the two years when four Controllers-General followed each other in office. Apparently the intendant of Brittany proposed a new settlement "on the domains of Brittany,"[99] a plan that was abandoned because of its prohibitively high cost. The plan of settling the Acadians in Corsica also reemerged. No doubt the government again envisaged regrouping the Acadians, since the two reports mentioning this new plan considered sending all of the Acadians from France there.[100] But this plan, too, was finally abandoned, in part because of the cost, in part from the resistance of some Acadians, and finally because the American War of Independence offered the prospect of eventually regaining Canada, where the government might send back the Acadians. Finally, according to one report, the request of the refugees to go to Louisiana was again examined, and although Necker was apparently favorable to the idea, it was rejected.[101]

Pursuing other ideas, perhaps, and facing opposition by a portion of the Acadians, it seems that Necker became convinced that the organization of the Acadians into a "national body" posed a problem. The impact of the failed initiatives of settlement or integration by other means and that of the settlement of Poitou—attributed to the organization of this Acadian union—made its way through the mysterious corridors of the government. Necker came to believe that the refugees could never be left together without creating problems. In reaction to the progressive uniting of the Acadians into a "national body," Necker advocated defeating the resistance by "breaking the body," undoubtedly following the divide and conquer principle. In an apparent paradox, when the government indeed decided to integrate, it was by means of disassembling the national body. From this perspective, there was at least the outline of a policy of assimilation.

Soon after his arrival to the ministry Necker became aware of the problem, and it was towards the end of 1777 that, for the first time, he advocated dispersing the Acadians throughout the territory of France. Following a report presented to him in November,[102] he determined to disperse them. In December, he charged the intendant of Brittany to sound out the Acadians. The sub-delegate of Nantes, Ballays, rendered his account of this operation in a report dated January 4, 1778.[103] He told how he had the Acadians assembled to announce to them the necessity that they disperse, by choosing a location "under French domination." After a first inconclusive meeting, the report specifies that the Acadians were again assembled on January 2, 1778, and that all of them consented "without murmuring and without complaining" to the directives of the sub-delegate, apart from one "Jacques LeBlanc," an agitator, who wanted to go to Louisiana "where his relatives are, which he has requested now for twenty years." Some twenty families then joined him in supporting his request. According to the sub-delegate, all of the other Acadians accepted the proposal made to them, that is, to be freely transported to the place of their choosing and to receive payment of 3s per day per person for two years. According to Ballays, 450 people then wanted to remain at Nantes, 200 to go to Saint-Pierre and Miquelon, 160 to Saint-Malo, and 4 to Le Havre, while some families awaited the return of their husbands still at sea. Finally, 80 families wanted to go to the "Dianne" (in Guyana) and awaited news from a company that had made them generous proposals.[104]

However, it does not seem that this report was followed. In the subsequent months, Necker inquired about the exact conditions proposed by the Company of Guyana to the

Acadians. In April, the refugees answered the Controller-General that they had not received any news since January.[105] It was on this occasion that Necker contacted Antoine de Satine, Minister of the Navy and the Colonies, asking for more information about this company. Coincident with this request for information, he provided Sartine with a summary of the situation and of his policy regarding the Acadians. Necker explained to his colleague that he had decided to divide the Acadians because "in no province of the Kingdom is there territory available to keep them together and allow them to live off of their work." Necker especially judged that "as long as [the Acadians] live assembled together, they would do nothing for themselves nor for their government." He thus specified: "Therefore we have thought to divide them and have them mingle with society, so to speak; in order that each may become a sailor, soldier, craftsman, merchant, laborer, according to his faculties and his dispositions, without clinging any longer to a particular national body, the idea of which is impossible to allow to exist within the very heart of the French nation."[106] The aim was that the "nation would disperse . . . by imperceptible dissipation," according to the interpretation of a later report.[107]

Yet these measures never were translated into action. Why? Lacking sufficient documents from the period, we can only hypothesize. Undoubtedly the Acadian resistance provided the first and foremost explanation. This was shown, for instance, by an anonymous later report (already quoted above), that contradicted Ballays's report:

> One would like to think that this nation will thus dissipate following an imperceptible transpiration; but, on the one hand, no province has offered concrete means of welcoming them, and, on the other, the Acadians, who still maintain hope of having lands to cultivate, are entirely opposed to this dispersion. We have stopped insisting on it from the moment when the affairs of North America have taken a favorable turn, and now, with the return of peace, consider some combination that could send the Acadians to their former country or that might offer a nearly equivalent result. We have taken the position of being patient and provisionally paying for their pecuniary situation.[108]

That the Acadians were "entirely opposed to this dispersion" seems likely. We have seen that, according to Pérusse, some Acadians had thought of gathering together in order "to be stronger," any dispersion would therefore have appeared to these Acadian leaders as an attempt to weaken the community core, which risked putting the group in peril and ending the material advantages and having the new plan of emigration fail. We must not forget that the Acadians had powerful support, including from the duc de Nivernais and some members of the royal family. Many Acadians, angered by the many prior fruitless attempts, wanted a sure way to return to Acadia or go to Louisiana—in any event, to not remain in France. It is thus clear enough that the Acadians did not view this plan favorably. How, then, might we explain the Ballays's report? The Acadians probably truly were divided about what they wanted to do and, besides, it is possible that Ballays had presented the proposals of the government in an altered manner, or that he had put pressure on them, or, again, that he minimized the resistance of the Acadians in his report. It might also have been a strategy on the part of the Acadians, who preferred passive resistance to outright opposition, and who counted on the impact of inertia at Versailles, an inertia whose effects they had observed on numerous occasions since their arrival in

France. In brief, we may presume that these Acadians questioned by Ballays accepted the plan proposed to them against their wishes—and only nominally.

Otherwise, we should believe the above report, that "no province has offered concrete means to welcome them," which is credible since we have seen how plan after plan during the years 1760 to 1770 met no success. The legal and financial difficulties had not vanished in the interim either, and the problematic experiences of Belle-Île-en-Mer and Poitou, along with the weariness that must have undoubtedly affected a large number of the provincials who had been responsible for handling the Acadians for a number of years already, no doubt explain the lack of enthusiasm for new proposals to welcome the Acadians.

Another practical concern similarly prevented the dispersion of the Acadians: the weight of their debts. Indeed, the refugees could not leave Nantes without having paid what they owed, for the government had provided guarantees to their creditors.[109] But the Acadians most often said that they were incapable of reimbursing their credit. As for the government, the payment of debts without the explicit commitment of the Acadians was out of the question, if one believes the report cited above. Therefore Necker adopted a passive attitude, which hardly contrasted with that of his predecessors.

Furthermore, the American War for Independence, also mentioned in the note above, revived hopes for some Acadians of returning to their country, whether under the French or possibly American domination. If Nova Scotia had been conquered and held by the insurgents in 1776, it is quite likely that their desire to return to the peninsula would have been more favorably heard by Louis XVI. In this case, since the Americans were allies of France, it would have undoubtedly been easier for the French State to allow the Acadians to leave French territory.

Finally, the author of the report of June 1778 (from which the above passage is extracted) is hardly an advocate of dispersing the Acadians, since he reaffirms that this dispersal would not negate the legal obligation to supply them with a settlement.[110] This report, which was probably presented to Necker, perhaps contributed to his beginning to think that the dispersion of the Acadians would probably not settle the problem once and for all, as he had hoped.

With the departure of Necker, then the eventuality of peace with England, but with no return of Canada, the government decided to accept the "median" solution advocated by the Acadians, that is to say emigration to Louisiana. The departure of the Acadians was accepted as of 1783.

Conclusion

Failure of the Policy of Assimilation?

At the beginning of this section, the question was posed: can a conclusion be reached regarding the success or failure of the French government's policy of assimilation? Considering all that we have recounted, it would seem that we cannot arrive at this conclusion, because no policy of this kind was ever truly put into practice. In truth, to speak of the success or failure of the policy of the government requires distinguishing its method and deployment. We cannot judge Necker's assimilation model, since it was never put into effect. On the other hand, the entire activity of the government between the years 1760 and 1785 regarding the Acadians may very well be considered a bitter failure, with the departure for Louisiana its result. The State had not succeeded in "attaching to the soil" its former colonists, nor in integrating them economically and socially. If France was able to save appearances because the Acadians left the homeland for an allied kingdom, the State had, however, spent relatively sizeable sums on them for over nearly thirty years in vain.

Necker was not the only one in the eighteenth century to put into effect a policy advocating dispersal of populations instead of assimilating them. This policy was based on the idea that isolated individuals, once in a group, would end up assembling with the group and taking on its characteristics.[111] Thus, the idea of dispersing the Acadians in order to better assimilate them was put into action, many years before Necker, by the North American colonists of the Thirteen Colonies. The governor of New York, Charles Hardy, told how:

> Thursday, August 22 [1756], 78 neutral French [Acadians] ... were able to reach Long Island with the intention of returning to Nova Scotia. I thought it necessary to prevent them from putting this plan into execution and for this I had them dispersed into the most isolated parts of this colony and the most suitable for placing them in tutelage. At the same time I asked the magistrates to provide work for those capable of working, and to place the children in apprenticeships with people who could take good care of them. This is the surest method of making good subjects of them.[112]

Megan Metters, in her study comparing French and American approaches to immigration and integration, noted that the idea of assimilation already existed in the eighteenth-century United States. It therefore seems mistaken to see in the remarks of Necker a prefiguring of a "French model of assimilation," which is often contrasted with the "multi-culturalist" American or Canadian model.[113] If we can hardly speak of coherent or followed-through action regarding the Acadians on the part of the power in Versailles, we cannot say either that there was ever any reflection about a real policy of integration, though the idea of attaching the refugees to the soil seems itself to have been an outline of such a policy, as archaic and rudimentary as it may have been.

On the other hand, the "assimilation" plans defended by Necker probably indicated an evolution of ideas. While the *Ancien Régime* tolerated cultural diversity and was unconcerned with the existence of a significant linguistic and cultural diversity within the home territory, we know that the French revolutionaries violently opposed these regional differences. It is thus that, after having been forced to transmit the decrees and constitutional acts into the regional languages, in 1793, standard French was imposed everywhere.[114] Similarly, as we have seen, the revolutionaries wanted to promote a "national costume" that would be the same from the North to the South of France.

Finally, the departure to Louisiana may be interpreted as a later desire for reassembling, for reunification with the enlarged family. Thus the petitions of the refugees requesting passage to Louisiana insistently noted the desire to join friends and family. In a first request addressed to the Spanish authorities, the Acadians said that they could have their brothers in the American colonies come along,[115] assuredly a sign that they were in contact and that they wanted to be reunited with them. In another petition drafted in April 1784 to the French Minister of Foreign Affairs, the Acadians again evoked this motif: "We think that the most fortunate fate for us would be to rejoin our relatives and friends settled on the banks of the Mississippi."[116] Many other later documents confirm this impression.[117]

Part Two

THE SUBSIDIES AND ECONOMIC PROBLEMS

Chapter VI

The Subsidies: Spoiled Children of the Ancien Régime?

Reasons for the Assistance

In the preceding section, we have studied an initial facet of French governmental policy, namely the efforts made to procure lands for the Acadians. Now we will focus on another, complementary, aspect of the policy regarding the Acadians:[1] the distribution of assistance in the form of financial aid provided by the government. These distributions began with the arrival of the first Acadians in the ports in 1758 and were continued until well after the Revolution. In his work, Ernest Martin has insisted on the relatively large sums paid by the French government, as this reinforces his thesis of a very generous France. Though he notes measures of assistance continuing up until 1822 or 1823,[2] we could go even further, for subsidies were paid at least to descendants of the deported up until 1884.[3]

The distribution of subsidies to the Acadians constitutes probably the most solid and durable bond between the Acadians as a specific group and the French government. Consequently, and indubitably, this subject generated the most plentiful sources, and it is about this aspect of their stay in France that we are best informed. To give an idea of the immensity of the documentation, of about 1,600 documents re-transcribed in the database for the period previous to 1789, one out of two or three has as its main theme the distribution of assistance—or treats that subject in some depth.

From an archival point of view, the assistance to the refugees produced an abundant correspondence within the administration and various kinds of documents: requests for instructions or additions to the list of beneficiaries, orders for distribution, statements of accounts (issued generally every three months), payment of past due amounts, repeated instructions by ministers to lessen expenses, and numerous lists supplying various types of annotations.[4] For the Acadians, receiving the assistance represented an important aspect of their daily life and is mentioned in nearly all of the documents emanating from them. As much in their private correspondence and in requests for dispensations of consanguinity as in the registering of acts of tutelage for Acadian orphans this element is continually touched upon.[5] Petitions asking for payment of assistance are plentiful as well.

Despite the abundance of sources, the policy of distribution of assistance to the Acadians has not been fully analyzed. According to most authors, the policy of assistance seems to have been unquestioned. Lauvrière and Martin's studies, which describe the assistance in the most detail, do not investigate the reasons for these distributions other than in an implicit manner. For these two authors, pure compassion lay behind the assistance to the

Acadians. The problem, however, is that they only selectively use documents favorable to their theses, that of France being generous to the Acadians.

Before examining the mechanics of distribution of the assistance in detail, it is thus important to inquire about the reasons that brought successive French governments to distribute daily payments to the Acadians starting in 1758. Looking at this topic brings us back to asking if Versailles really wanted to integrate the Acadians and if the aid was part of this strategy. Did they have other goals? This protection granted the Acadians was justified by many reasons. Those who perceived the population as human capital that needed to be invested pushed to repopulate the territories as quickly as possible (while waiting for the signing of the peace and a plan for transporting them). The secular tradition of hospitality towards foreigners and humanitarian feelings were stirred by this onrush of an uprooted populace. Moreover, the desire to compensate the patriotism and fidelity of the repatriated was often mentioned in the correspondence. We should also not exclude from this motivation a desire for propaganda: the government wanted to be able to show itself as generous, and all the more so as it attempted to place itself morally above England, which had sullied itself by deporting the Acadians. The two powers rivaled each other in offering benevolence to the victims of the *Grand Dérangement*, with each side using the other's proposals to outbid the other. Finally, it does not seem as if the government felt a need to control a population potentially capable of fomenting trouble, though, on the other hand, on many occasions the assistance served as a coercive means of obliging the refugees to follow the government's instructions.

"This Precious Class of Individuals"
"This people is too precious to not be received with pleasure."[6]

The Context: Fear of the Depopulation of France

One of the main motives explaining the distribution of assistance in France may be traced to the belief in an ongoing depopulation of the Kingdom.[7] In this context, the Acadians were perceived as precious capital not to be wasted. To assist the Acadians was to maintain this capital by preventing it from losing too many members to hunger or illness. Similarly, it was to avert a desire to leave again, as well as to attempt to draw to France or to the French colonies all of the Acadians dispersed in North America. This vision was not new: at least since the Renaissance, men were considered as a form of wealth, which the kings could make use of according to their good wishes. Jean Bodin illustrates this idea well with his famous phrase, "There is no wealth like men," as does Jean-Baptiste Colbert in a letter to Jean Talon, first intendant of New France, regarding the latter's request to send colonists to develop and populate the still young colony: "It would not be prudent to depopulate [the] Kingdom . . . in order to populate Canada."[8]

For Colbert the population was like currency: as little should leave the Kingdom as possible. To supplement the weak emigration to Canada, the government tried to rely on mixed Franco-Amerindian marriages in the seventeenth century.[9] Y. Landry, seeking to understand the minimal encouragement of the monarchy to emigrate, notes that Jean-Baptiste Moheau denounced the fact that in the sixteenth century in "France expatriation was a national sickness." According to Landry, "this false impression came from the fact that there were many more Frenchmen overseas than foreigners in France." It explained how "The State itself, during the whole French regime—with rare exceptions—refused to send colonists directly [to New France]."[10] This belief in a depopulation of France, as false as it may have been, persisted during the whole century.[11]

This fear of seeing France depopulate itself found a corollary in the general hostility to the enterprises of colonization. This view was well summarized in the entry concerning the colonies in *L'Encyclopédie*:

> It would, however, be to go against the object of the colonies itself, to allow them to be settled by depopulating the dominant country of origin. Intelligent nations only send the superfluity of their men there little by little, or those for whom the society is responsible . . . . Circumstances could therefore arise where it would be useful to prevent citizens of the homeland from leaving at their will to inhabit the colonies in general, or some colony in particular.[12]

The hostility of the *philosophes* to the colonization enterprises also spread to the popular classes, but for different reasons. The unusual desire of the Acadians to return to the colonies is exactly what made them yet more valuable in the view of the administrators and justified taking charge of them by the administration, which counted on making use of these voluntary colonists at a later time. The Acadians, in particular, were kept close at hand in order to be able to repopulate Canada or Acadie, should the case arise.[13] Many plans for the re-conquest of Canada received the support of the government, and of Choiseul in particular, up through the years 1772-1773.[14] The Acadians were therefore potentially capable of being returned across the Atlantic to repopulate their respective countries. The payments, in this case, facilitated keeping the Acadians available.

The population obsession was in no way unique to France and was shared by many countries. "All of the European States have the fear of depopulation," wrote Jean Meyer.[15] This was evident in the English desire to assimilate the Acadians to the North-American population and to not send them to France, which they feared would strengthen her.

The Particular Case of the Acadians

If the fear of a demographic hemorrhaging of France becomes apparent to anyone who skims the texts written in the eighteenth century, one might also expect that some indifference might have eventually prevailed regarding the Acadians due to the small number of people involved. There was nothing of the kind, however, as to the fear of suffering a clear loss for France was added the fear of strengthening the enemy. Thus, Choiseul wrote to his colleague Bertin: "It is important for the State to not lose this population which may comprise the sum of 4,000 people. . . . We would lose this population that would thereby strengthen that of the English; you as well as I can imagine the consequences."[16] Another repeats: "It is very well thought by the government to retain the 4,000 Canadians [Acadians] and not let the benefit of them go to our greatest and too estimable enemies [the English]."[17] This populating obsession is repeated in many other documents involving the Acadians, particularly at the end of the Seven Years War. We must add that this main idea was most often tied to the conviction that this population could be a future source of wealth, either benefiting the State with the taxes that they would sooner or later pay, or by the land clearing that they might conduct on territory granted for fee-farming by a lord. This population was therefore valuable for the State, but also for the rich land owners who might succeed in appropriating them. The discussions about this plan and its implementation evolved over time. Thus, after the failure of the settlement at Poitou, the Controller-General seriously considered reviewing the policy of distribution of assistance. It seemed impossible to him to continue a useless expense, since there remained "no hope of seeing them incline to increase the population of the provinces at the Center of the Kingdom where they were meant to go, nor improve the agriculture of these same provinces."[18]

The sense that the Acadians were a valuable population was thus a recurrent theme in the documents consulted, and we have seen how it fits well with what the historiography has stated elsewhere. Nonetheless, fear of the depopulation of the kingdom, if it certainly motivated the distribution of subsidies, does not thereby imply a desire to integrate or assimilate the Acadians within the kingdom.[19] The Acadians were considered all the more valuable as they were meant to repopulate the colonies where the scarcity of "European" population was more glaring than in France. Moreover, if populating affirmations are omnipresent in the texts, it would be a stretch to insinuate that utilitarian considerations were the only ones motivating the government: other more altruistic considerations also played a large role.

From the Ancient Tradition of Welcome to International Law

Actually, the subsidies distributed to the Acadians also belonged to an ancient tradition of assistance for the poor and the expatriated. If the eradication of pauperism was most often incumbent upon the Church and the local parishes, in the eighteenth century, the State tried to organize systems of benevolence and to take them under its mantle. The idea of lay assistance was born at that time in opposition to the religious charity practiced in the past, expanding theories from the *Contrat social* (1762) of Rousseau.[20] Before Rousseau, Montesquieu was the champion, according to the phrase of Maxime Leroy, of a "socialism of a patriarchal State" which "owes to all the citizens a guaranteed subsistence . . . and a kind of life which would not interfere with health."[21] These theories would be explicitly formulated under the Revolution, with the slow maturation of the society, but they were already partially put into effect before 1789.[22] The eighteenth century nonetheless began to distance itself from this old tradition of welcome by moving towards more legally codified practices. If the Acadians, on arriving in France, were well placed under the protection of the king—in the traditional role of seekers of asylum[23]—the government could only not welcome the Acadians with great difficulty. "No nation can refuse, without good reason, providing habitation—even perpetual—for a man chased from his home," wrote Vattel.[24] All the more so as, for many years, "monarchial propaganda presented the kingdom of France as a welcoming land for refugees."[25] Shortly before the signing of the Treaty of Versailles, Vattel recommended, "never losing sight of the charity and commiseration that are owed to the unfortunate [exiles]."[26] Evidently, it would have been inconceivable to let the exiles die of hunger or from cold on French soil.

The themes of compassion and charity owed to the Acadians were present in a large number of the texts consulted. Moreover, the term itself, charity, was frequently used as a synonym for assistance by the French administrators.[27] It is also the term that the mayor of Saint-Malo uses to describe what motivated him to distribute emergency assistance to the Acadians:

> As the misery of these latter [persons disembarked from Île Saint-Jean] is extreme and the lack of foodstuff along with the scurvy has reduced them to a condition deserving compassion, I thought it necessary to order assistance in their favor despite the exhaustion of our finances. Charity and the fear that these miserable people might spread some epidemic illnesses in [the] town . . . compelled me to proceed with this action.[28]

The Christian nature of the charity with which the Acadians were welcomed is often emphasized: the assistance was frequently designated by the term "grace."[29] One also often finds in the texts the idea of "compassion" owed to them. Thus Gabriel Rousseau, sieur de Villejoint recommends the Acadians of Île Saint-Jean not because of their right to assistance, but in the name of "commiseration."[30] Besides, the exiles themselves constantly implored the "charitable" assistance of the government and frequently tried to receive a "compassionate view" of their situation.

We should add that this charity and compassion were sometimes a bit forced. Morally, the government had to assist the Acadians. With the first arrivals of the inhabitants of Île-Royale and Île Saint-Jean at Rochefort, in September 1758, the minister spoke of the arrangements to be made "regarding the assistance it will be *necessary* to procure for them."[31] Some years later, in a circular ordering continuation of the payments to the Acadians, the minister insisted on both the impossibility of the Acadians procuring what they needed to live and on the compassion of the king.[32] Moreover, one of the reasons given by Necker to justify the continuation of the distribution of subsidies at Nantes in 1778 (while they had been interrupted at Bordeaux and elsewhere), was that the people at Nantes were "assembled in large number" and there was not enough work for all of them.[33] Here again we find the problem of economic integration described at the start of this chapter that forms an underlying thread of these distributions of assistance.

Compensation for Patriotism and Indemnification for Damages

> *The king, touched by the proofs of fidelity and attachment that the Acadians have given him as their sole and unique master, as well as by the sacrifices and those feelings for his person made by them, since they have become refugees in France, has made assistance available to help them subsist.*[34]

A third reason repeatedly advanced to legitimize the distribution of the payments was the one most often presented, namely, just compensation for the fidelity of the repatriated colonists "to the king, to the country, and to the religion."[35] The Acadians therefore deserved the concern of the king from the fact of their faithfulness. This was among the most frequently mentioned motives in the documents, beginning with the mission of La Rochette to the Acadians who were being held in England in 1763, when he wrote: "They always maintain love of their king, their country and nothing can diminish their zeal for the true religion." On the arrival of the first Acadians in Louisiana, the acting French governor Charles Philippe Aubry wrote: "The Acadians are laborious, brave, religious, attached to their prince and to their country beyond all expression. I knew them in New England; they only spoke of going to mass and of the king."[36] This kind of discourse became a nearly systematic refrain by Le Loutre and Lemoyne.[37]

The distributions of assistance were thus increasingly perceived as an indemnity for the damages caused to the Acadians and suffered because of their faithfulness. The government soon advocated distinguishing between those who had lost little or nothing, like the Canadians,[38] and those who had lost everything, such as the Acadians. Lemoyne described this eloquently: "The subsistence that the king grants the Acadians is an indemnity for their abandonment of their properties in Acadia." He then suggested providing them with lands in exchange for those that they had abandoned.[39] On numerous other occasions, the fact that the Acadians had been well off before deportation was invoked to justify the assistance.[40]

Moreover, Lemoyne increasingly made the loss of their goods in Acadia the main justification for their assistance and for the settlements. This is what he recalled, in a long report that tried to rationalize the distributions made for the benefit of the Acadians:

> At the time of the taking of Louisbourg, the English took away all of the goods [of the inhabitants of this town and of Île-Royale] . . . and sent them back to Europe. . . . Only the Acadians had the right to financially administered assistance. One should only consider as Acadians those who had truly been settled in Acadia . . . or on Île St. Jean, a colony formed by the Acadians who were also removed from it. . . . The families from Canada [were able to keep] their goods.[41]

To say patriotism was a reason advanced by the administration is not to say that we should read these discourses uncritically, as some authors have done.[42] The administrators in charge of the Acadians never seemed to question their patriotic stances and seem to have believed them. La Rochette thus compared the comportment of the French soldiers or sailors imprisoned in England during the Seven Years War to the supposed patriotism of the Acadians favorably: "Many of our French prisoners let themselves be dazzled by the promises of the English, and in this, have shown much less faithfulness to France and less of a desire for vengeance than have the unfortunate Acadians."[43] These opinions confirm the thesis of Dziembowski, according to which, at the end of the Seven Years War, "many Frenchmen are convinced that the moral power of the enemy, source of a remarkable patriotic spirit, is the principle responsible for the surprising victories of England. To hope to retrieve the rank that should be hers, France must imperatively also be inspired by this virtue."[44] This explains the distributions of assistance as much as it does the largely positive view of the Acadians at the start of their stay in France.

This also applies to France's prestige in fully assisting the Acadians. It was a question of placing itself morally above the English, for France had to show that it would humanely repair the wrongs inflicted on the unfortunate poor by England. The naval commissioner, Lemoyne, emphasized the danger to "the honor of the government" if it did not react appropriately to the Acadian emigration to Jersey. If the government "appeared to pay scant attention to this event, it would seem thus to be authorizing it and to have abandoned its subjects who have merited too much by their attachment to the king, the country and the religion, for it not to keep them under its protection and not to help them," wrote the commissioner.[45] To not help the Acadians would be to break a tacit contract, which might bring a negative image of France abroad and be equally damaging in the colonies.[46] Lemoyne proposed a solution to prevent the reproaches that might be addressed to France regarding the treatment given the Acadians: everything that the king has done for them should be published "in the public papers" in order "to instruct France and Europe with the suitable details and emphasis in promoting the benevolence of the King to this people." Not without some contradiction, Lemoyne considered the assistance to be a "grace," while the Acadians also "deserved" this assistance by their "attachment" to the king and to the State.[47] In sum, the real or presumed patriotism of the Acadians was frequently invoked by the administration to justify the assistance that was distributed to them as a kind of natural compensation for the sacrifices that they have endured. This motif, as well, had no connection with any governmental desire to integrate or assimilate the Acadians.

A Tool for Pressure and Control?

In America, the Acadians had not paid most of the taxes to which the Third Estate of France was subjected. Moreover, they were in frequent contact with the "savages" so reputedly egalitarian and rebellious to authority as well as with the potentially corrosive British system. Thus I initially imagined finding in the writings of the administrators fears that the Acadians might stir up troubles or spread subversive ideas in the population of France. But this was not the case.[48] On the contrary, according to a somewhat enigmatic document, the French government not only did not fear trouble on the part of the Acadians, but it was so confident of their fidelity to the "King, to the Country, and to the Religion" that, at the time of the peasants' rebellion of Brittany, it even considered removing the rebels to replace them with the Acadians. An officer of a seneschal in Brittany, Châteauneuf du Faou,[49] reports having had the following conversation in April 1766:

> [The provost] told me that the . . . report of rebellion [following the sedition that occurred at Saint-Goazec when they wanted to begin fencing lands] made the king's council so frightened that such a [sedition] might cause an outbreak, that there were orders in case further rebellion were attempted, notably in the land of Saint-Goazec, to take as many of the King's troops as necessary to depopulate it, to send those arrested to the colonies and replace them with the Canadians [Acadians] who had just come to France.[50]

If we are to believe this text, the Council of the king did not fear revolt on the part of the Acadians and even thought that they could be placed into sensitive areas. This is confirmed by the fact that the Acadians were placed at Belle-Île-en-Mer, a location exposed to attacks by the English and open to the Atlantic. The distribution of subsidies therefore did not have controlling the Acadians as a goal. Nonetheless, by means of the distribution of subsidies, the State could be precisely informed of the number of Acadians and of their exact location. The subsidies allowed stopping any hint of troubles at the root, since, in case of rebellion, the Acadians would risk having their subsidies suppressed. The distribution of the payments also encouraged the concentration of the refugees in some specific locations, which also better facilitated controlling them.[51]

The assistance similarly served as a means of applying pressure to force the Acadians to behave themselves. The government often conducted extortion with the assistance. In 1759, Berryer ordered withdrawing payments from North American inhabitants who refused to embark on the corsairs of the king.[52] Later, Choiseul threatened many times to interrupt the payment of aid to the Acadians who did not agree with his views. On February 13, 1764, for example, he warned the refugees at Saint-Malo that, if they did not go to Cayenne, their subsistence would be taken from them.[53] The commissioner of Cherbourg, one de Francy, did not hide his methods for this: "I assembled . . . all of the Acadians that are here. By preaching to them I was able to get 121 to agree to go to Cayenne as much in good will as in fear of losing the king's benefits."[54] Two months later, he suppressed payments for all of the recalcitrant Acadians. The measure was nonetheless not very efficient, and the record notes specifically that it did not change the view of a man named François Daigle and his wife.[55] These suspending measures were approved by Choiseul.[56] Thus one finds at Cherbourg in 1764 a "list of families from North America who without good reasons do not want to go to the Island of Cayenne, although very suitable to populate and cultivate this new colony and who, if they were not granted passage to the islands of Saint-Pierre and Miquelon, preferred to remain in France and renounce the benefits of the King and the advantages that he could offer them elsewhere."[57] The payment at Cherbourg would be reestablished some months later,[58] encouraging the Acadians to think that the threatened suspension of payments would never be applied for very long.[59]

Some years later, Lemoyne used the same procedure to recruit Acadian colonists otherwise reluctant to be settled in Poitou. Although he had not received instructions to do so, he threatened the Acadians with suspension of their payment.[60] This time, however, the Controller-General clearly disapproved this extortion, though with some delay:

> Regarding [those who refuse the Poitou settlement], whatever may be the origin of their resistance, I do not consider it suitable to use rigorous means or to employ authority to force them. It is a question of assisting their settlement in France and in no way forcing them to accept the offer of Mr. de Pérusse.[61]

The Opinion of the Acadians: Assistance Deserved

We have mentioned above the reasons behind the distributions of assistance. But how did the Acadians regard the aid that was being distributed to them?

For the Acadians, the assistance was always first considered to be just compensation for their patriotism and the immense sacrifices they had made for France. A speech given by Jean-Jacques LeBlanc to Lemoyne in July 1773 was, in this regard, very telling. Lemoyne had just arrived at Saint-Malo, where he threatened the Acadians with suppressing payments if they refused to go to Poitou. Practically all of them had refused to go, though without providing very precise reasons. Lemoyne reports:

> Finally came the turn of Jean Jacques LeBlanc . . . . He told me that all of the Acadians were full of love for the King in awareness of all the benefits that he had

provided to them up to that time, and that these were the compensation for their fidelity and their attachment to his person and to France, fidelity and attachment that they had proven by the sacrifice that was well known that they had made of their goods and even of their bodies, that the Acadians had always been full of the same feelings that had decided their conduct after all the paternal tenderness that the King had always shown them.[62]

In their petitions the Acadians also often recalled the promises that had been made to them in England in 1763 in the king's name. These promises were made orally, and it is difficult to know exactly what was involved. Nonetheless, it seems to have initially been only a promise to settle the Acadians on lands in France.[63] In other respects, it is not certain that he had expressly promised them assistance,[64] even if the Acadians imagined that the government had promised to pay them assistance until they would be settled. The connection between the two aspects, settlement and assistance, is nearly always made in the documents. The reports towards the end of the period claiming that the duc de Nivernais had promised the Acadians a subsidy that, if not the exact letter of what he had promised, at least fulfilled the general spirit of his promises. Thus a report from June 1778 affirmed that the Acadians had a legal right to the assistance of six *sous* per day until their settlement because that is what the duc de Nivernais had promised in 1763: "Their stipend in England was for six *sols* per head. . . . They were assured that the stipend they would receive in France would be yet more advantageous." [65] A later report noted: "Originally, the Acadians were owed a balance or lands; such was the promise of the late king transmitted by the duc de Nivernais, then ambassador in England."[66] This promise made to the Acadians on its own justified the payment of aid for many charged with applying the directives of the government. At stake was the honor of the government, and word, once given, then had quasi-legal value.

Moreover, for the Acadians, it seems that there was a kind of tacit contract: if the government stopped providing them with aid without having settled them, then they would have to leave. Joseph Landry wrote to his cousin: "Our hope is that if [the king] no longer gives us anything we will be free." [67] Many other Acadian petitions used the same rhetoric: "Since the government has abandoned us, as it no longer thinks of finding us a settlement, then we ask to go to Saint-Pierre and Miquelon, Boston, or Louisiana."[68] This argument seemed entirely acceptable as much to Lemoyne as to the commissioner of divisions at Cherbourg, de Francy, who repeated it in a report addressed to the Controller-General.[69] Therefore, the distribution of aid, in the opinion of the Acadians, justified the prohibition that had been made to them to not leave the national territory. This prohibition on its own was directly tied to the populating and propagandizing ideas of the French State, which wanted to keep men on its soil and did not easily accept the idea—destabilizing to morality and patriotism—that former colonists, Catholics, French speakers, and subjects of the Very Christian King, might prefer returning to America rather than remaining in the mother country.

The Economic Obsession

Above, we examined the reasons that prompted the government to distribute assistance to the Acadians. But there are very many texts that also exist arguing in favor of ending the payment of aid to the Acadians, or at least for a more rigorous framework of the distributions. To what effect? Below we will undertake a small survey of the justifications advanced by various individuals.

The Payment of Balances: A Measure of Last Resort

From the very start, and on many occasions, various government officials tried to lessen the costs of the assistance by lowering either the total of sums distributed or the number of beneficiaries. Often they blamed the balance of payments and the duplication of work. Directives aimed at decreasing the cost of this assistance came concurrently with the start of the distributions. From the beginning, the orders of Berryer were clear. Among the inhabitants, four classes were distinguished: those who had no need of help, those who could be employed, those "who need only a permit to go to their families," and finally, those "without resources to whom one must provide a ration."[70] Note that only the impoverished were deemed capable of receiving the ration. The assistance, in the mind of the minister, was but a measure of last resort, and, additionally, was meant to remain temporary. Some days later he wrote to the intendant at Rochefort:

> With regard to the inhabitants and individuals of the populace, we must, as you suggest, have all of those who may be of use work in the ports in the service of the King while paying them the ordinary wages and ensuring them a means of subsistence without giving them the ration, and for those who are absolutely poor and in no condition to do anything, they must be given six *sols* per day per person until new orders.[71]

In this period, therefore, the desire of the ministry to decrease costs was clear and the argument was limited to economic considerations. We will see, however, that, in the matter of assistance, there was often a gap between the directives and their achievement. Nonetheless, the Acadians soon demonstrated their indigence, and the hunt for those committing fraud or at least assumed to be doing so began by 1758. Some administrators openly criticized the desire of the government to reduce expenses, sometimes with a surprisingly frank tone. In August 1760, an anonymous correspondent of Guillot, probably the commissioner of the divisions of Saint-Malo, Isarn, or the canton, Grandclos Mêlé, objected to the instructions from Berryer of August 12 of the same year requesting that they "cut off the subsistence [from the families] who are in a position to do without it"[72]—"does the minister believe in good faith that those poor colonists who work this season will earn enough to pay the debts they have contracted since he has not provided them with their 6s?"[73] Other examples of resistance exist, as well.[74] No doubt some administrators painted the situation of some beneficiaries of the aid as being bleak so as to not have to suppress their payments.

The Nefarious Effects

For some members of the government, the sums distributed to the Acadians were "a pure loss."[75] Worse, in their view, the aid had a nefarious effect on the Acadians. Very quickly then, the government tried to put into place measures to limit the negative effects of the distribution of aid.[76] The battle against secondary consequences consisted mainly of trying to prevent the onset of laziness and indolence among the Acadians. According to Choiseul: "The intention of the King [is not] to nourish lazy people who want to do nothing!"[77] Some years later, Praslin thus justified a reduction of the payment: "For a long time [the individuals that comprise the Acadian families in France] have been paid with no other result than to have them sustained in laziness."[78] That the distribution of aid allowed the Acadians to live without working was considered a great danger by the administrators. Even the anonymous author of the letter cited above—attacking Berryer's order, in 1760, to reduce the aid for the Acadians who could do without it—judges that many lazy individuals were content to take the assistance and do nothing with their days. Thus, on a "list of inhabitants from North America from whom it would appear that one could withdraw subsistence," he described the situation of Louis Gilbert:

> Louis Gilbert, his wife, five children. This is surely the family that is the best example to be struck from the lists of those receiving assistance. She is comfortable. The husband, who is a carpenter, does nothing but walk around, resting off the industriousness of his wife who keeps a busy boutique of second hand material. If we cut off the assistance that the King grants a person who works to provide for needs that six *sous* per day does not satisfy, we should with more cause cut off a man who lives in indolence while his family subsists with a profitable commerce.[79]

This argument presented nothing new. We find the same ideas in *Candide* (1759), where Voltaire proclaims that work removes three great evils: ennui, vice, and need.[80] These principles constitute the main impetus behind the creation of charitable workshops.[81] The battle against laziness and idleness was a fixed idea of the government. One of the nefarious effects of the assistance was indeed, according to one of the administrators in charge of the Acadians, to weaken their desire to work. Regarding a refugee, one administrator wrote: he "works and is very industrious; if we deprive [this person] of the subsistence it seems to me it would be appropriate to continue to employ the rest of the family [to] combat any threats to industriousness."[82]

While the problem of the integration of the Acadians was being settling, the Acadians became paupers in the eyes of those responsible for them. The Abbé Girard, former missionary in Acadia, refusing an offer by Pérusse that he become priest of the settlement at Poitou, justified himself with his doubts about the capacity of the Acadians to escape the vicious circle of what our day would describe as "welfare dependency."[83] Pérusse, in turn, made the "corruption" of the Acadians by the payments the key explanation of the failure of the attempt to implant the Acadians on his lands.[84] The solution to the Acadian problem, he wrote in a letter to his confident Blossac, was to suppress the payments:

> All of those people only want to perpetuate the payments that were assuredly necessary during the first moments of the their arrival in France, but whose duration for 18 years has made them lose the habit of working; the majority of the group rejects whatever settlement that is proposed. They will go wherever one leads them with the aim of continuing these payments; but as they see that the result of any settlement is to effectively stop them, they will do the same in Corsica, on France Island [Mauritius], in Brittany or elsewhere as they have done at Belle-Île-en-Mer or here, in Limousin, on the land of Mr. de Saint-Victor and in whatever place in

Brittany where one has already wanted to settle them. Many of those who would go to Corsica will perish and this would be a useless loss of men.[85]

In practice, if it was generally accepted that distributing aid was harmful in the long term, the government had great difficulty achieving its objectives, since the distribution of aid continued indefinitely. The various initiatives for settling the Acadians at Belle-Île-en-Mer and in Poitou similarly highlighted the same idea: the refugees should be made autonomous by placing them on lands where they could support themselves and no longer be dependent on public charity.

With the arrival of Necker to power, the talk against laziness was stiffened and made concrete, this time by general measures suspending the payments. The principles enunciated by Necker were relatively simple: "those who are in condition to work cannot ask for aid." In a letter written in 1778, he attacked the woeful effects of the assistance and payments that "were onerous and only maintained them in inactivity. . . . It is impossible to become accustomed to the idea of paying a subsidy to able-bodied men of age, for the sole reason that they are doing absolutely nothing although they can and should work."[86]

To summarize, if we are to believe the view of those in charge of the Acadians, economic aid would have been harmful to their economic integration. Their being paid to do nothing led them to indolence, and the fear of losing the aid from the government brought some of them to refuse employment. We have seen how some administrators opposed the ministry's desire to suppress the assistance. But the few voices that periodically arose from the group of naval commissioners in charge of the Acadians requested either renewal of payments interrupted for various reasons, or the necessity of these payments for the survival of some number of the poor deported, without justifying their requests with the arguments of economic integration. The only arguments expressed were humanitarian, and they were aimed at commiseration rather than defending the usefulness of the aid. In all, practically all of the documents consulted argued that the aid nullified the economic integration of the Acadians. As our aim here is not to evaluate the effects of the aid on the real integration of the Acadians, but only the discussions about the aid's utility, we will later return to what may be learned about the effects of the distribution of subsidies in a later chapter.

The Public Money

If, as we have just seen, one finds a clear escalation in the language starting with Necker, this minister was also the first to introduce a new idea to justify the restrictions imposed on the Acadians: that of the public money. He mentions the fact that "the King can only do something for one portion of his subjects at the expense of the others" and that the assistance is based on the "sweat of the French people among whom [the Acadians] have found an asylum."[87] Necker judges that, human necessities being limited, one must give each according to his rights. Answering a letter of Blossac that no doubt referred to the needs of the Acadians, Necker replied:

> It is not exactly [the] needs [of the Acadians] to which one will put a limit with difficulty, but it is their rights that must be managed, and, after having taken . . . the part of interpreting to their advantage [everything that one could], it is as necessary as it is just to hold to that. They must understand that, as the assistance

granted to them is the fruit of the contributions of their neighbors, the great majority of whom do not have the same resources as they do, it is indispensable to put a limit to it.[88]

Conclusion

The allocation of subsidies to the Acadians and Canadians somewhat belies the notion of a monarchy caring little for the poor or for refugees. At the same time, the reasons mentioned above explaining this assistance inscribed themselves within traditional reasoning: on the one hand, refuge and compensation for patriotism or fidelity to the king, on the other, the fear of depopulating the kingdom. But they came in a new framework, whether the centralization of power or the lay organization of the aid. These distributions of aid reflected only a little on the nationality of the refugees: foreign populations would undoubtedly have been welcomed with more or less the same good will.[89] And, it should be noted that the financial assistance given to the refugees, if it played a role—positive or negative—in the integration of the Acadians, was not conceived *a priori* as a tool of economic and social integration. While it was put into effect from the first days of the arrival in France of the refugees, the intention of integrating them came much later. Even if it is likely that the assistance was implicitly conceived by some functionaries as intended to fill this integrating role, most of the time, the subsidies—in the eyes of those responsible—poorly fulfilled it. Only those voices denouncing the counter-productive effects that the aid dispensed had on the economic integration of the Acadians were heard.

Chapter VII

Details Of The Assistance

After studying the reasons that prompted the aid, it is important to consider the manner in which it was distributed: when, to whom, and where. No exact chronology of the execution and evolution of the aid has ever been established. Ernest Martin describes rather briefly a situation that he over simplifies. Here we will show that local arrangements prevailed and that all of the Acadians did not receive six *sous* per day during the entire period of 1758-1785.

The Establishment of the Distributions

The first subsidies from the government to the Acadians did not date from their arrival in France. In fact, the documents attest that the first distributions of provisions were made in 1722 at Île-Royale and at the start of the 1750s at Île Saint-Jean.[1] Assistance was also distributed to some inhabitants of Île-Royale who returned to France after the first capture of Louisbourg, in 1745. The commissioner-general of the Navy at Saint-Malo, Guillot, wrote that he had distributed 1,200 *livres* to the "poorest of the inhabitants of Île-Royale." "They are all as destitute as rats and are all bare," he added. "Some have only been sustained during their stay in France by means of small hand-outs," while others were able to work as day laborers.[2] To alleviate the bareness of these miserable people, Guillot even ordered the distribution of pants (the surplus of a fruitless military operation conducted shortly beforehand).[3] In 1756, the first persons to arrive in France from Acadia, four missionaries, were immediately helped by the minister, who gave each of them five hundred *livres*.[4] As the missionaries of the Acadians were practically functionaries of the State, there was nothing abnormal in the minister offering them a gratuity or urgent assistance upon their return to France. It is possible that aid was then distributed to the inhabitants of Louisbourg starting in February 1757 (at least this is what refugees from the town assumed much later in 1792).[5]

In September 1758, the first reaction to the arrival of the boats loaded with inhabitants coming from Louisbourg came as a surprise. The minister was unaware of what had happened at Île-Royale.[6] While he inquired about the situation, the naval intendant had the first subsidies distributed:

> I have taken all possible care to procure lodgings in the town [for the people from Île-Royale] that have disembarked here. I have had a ration provided to the inhabitants and their families and prepared a place to receive the sick at the

foundries. . . .[7] Fortunately there are only very few of them until now. I hope that you will honor me with your orders on the subject of what conduct I should observe regarding these inhabitants.[8]

The initiative for assistance therefore first originated at the local level. It is clear that the intendant could not allow these travelers who had disembarked after a painful crossing to die of hunger.[9] Subsequently, the minister asked to identify among the families "those who can do well in France and who can procure their sustenance on their own, those who, having a profession, could continue practicing it in Rochefort or want to go to some other area of the Kingdom. Finally, those of the workers or fishermen who might be employed in the [naval] service."[10] Officers, functionaries, and soldiers were treated differently from the simple inhabitants; for the time being, their salary mostly continued being paid as usual. The missionaries also received different treatment. As for the rest, on October 9, the minister gave instructions that only "those who are absolutely in no condition to do anything and without any resources" be assisted.[11]

Therefore, in the beginning, the intendant had to provide work for those who were able and distribute rations to the others:[12]

> As for those of these inhabitants who seemed suitable to me for work in the arsenal . . . I have distributed them among the various workshops. In their regard, I have arranged that the heads of families who work in the arsenal will be provided nourishment for themselves, their wives and up to two children, and that if they have more than two children, they exceed the ration. If I have the ready cash I could give them 6-7*s* per head instead of paying the ration for commissary credit of 10*s*, everyone would be happy while I would thereby make great savings.[13]

This latter proposal by the intendant, meant to reduce costs, was quickly accepted. Soon only a lump sum of six *sous* per day was distributed.[14] Therefore, as of December 12, the minister ordered Guillot to have this sum distributed to all of the individuals, "in the case they are truly in poor condition."[15] After some attempts, this sum became the rule that the minister made official by a circular sent to the naval administrators in the different ports where the Acadians were refugees.[16] When these instructions arrived, it was already some months since the first Acadians had disembarked in the ports. The payment of aid was retroactive, however, at least for some, as shown, for instance, by a "list of inhabitants of Île-Royale, Île Saint-Jean, Gaspé, and other places to whom the King grants the subsistence counting from the day of their disembarking."[17]

While waiting, however, the disembarked travelers still had to be fed. If, at Rochefort, the naval administration had rations distributed from the first days, at Saint-Malo, in 1759, the Acadians had to count on the charity of the local inhabitants. The mayor of the city spent 400 *livres* to provide for the most urgent necessities.[18] In 1763, the same problem again arose for the Acadians who had been repatriated via England, but this time the mayor no longer had any money to distribute. However, orders had been given by Choiseul to the commissioner of divisions of Saint-Malo by April 7, 1763, for the Acadian families who were "unceasingly" arriving from England to receive "a subsistence of six *sols* per day, as do the former inhabitants of North America who are at Saint-Malo and the surrounding area."[19] The Acadians deported to England similarly received payment "equivalent to six *sous*" paid by the king of England.[20]

An account of the later decisions concerning assistance for the refugees gives us an idea of how a situation initially considered to be temporary progressively became entrenched. We must first note the multiple orders and counter-orders relative to the subject. Thus, with the pretext of the arrival of the "poor families from Canada" by way of England that the Navy had to assist, minister Berryer ordered by a circular in July 1761, "withdrawing [the aid] from those of the inhabitants of Île-Royale [and Île Saint-Jean] who, having received it for more than the two years they have been in France may be in a condition . . . to be employed to make a living."[21] However, following complaints by many municipalities, the minister specified that "the intention of the king is not do deprive those who are absolutely in need of the 6*s* per day that his majesty wanted to distribute to them since their arrival."[22] An annulment of this first missive was sent by Choiseul very shortly after Berryer left the ministry.[23]

A year later, Choiseul again sent a circular stipulating that the aid be recommenced "considering the harshness of the current season," "for the first quarter of the following year, beyond which time [it will stop]."[24] But, less than four months later, the minister annulled his own orders with a new circular ordering the continuation of assistance "until a new order."[25] At this time, then, the principle of the allocation of six *sous* per day for all individuals was well established, and thoughts of reforming it subsequently became more circumspect or rare. With some exceptions,[26] the deported who were in no condition to work[27] thus received the same sum until January 1, 1767, the date on which the allocation was reduced to three *sous* per day for children less than ten years of age, on the order of the new Minister of the Navy, Praslin.[28] The reason advanced by him for this was that, for a long time, the Acadians were paid "with no other benefit than that of having them maintained in idleness." The payments made by the naval ministry continued for some years still, even if it is impossible to affirm if all of the Acadians dispersed in the various ports received them without interruption. Thus, a petition by the Acadians in Morlaix in January 1774 thanks Lemoyne for the "reestablishment" of their payments (after his visit there in September 1773), leading us to assume that the payments had been interrupted at some point before 1774.[29] Moreover, it is not entirely certain that the instructions for the reduction of payment to three *sous* per day for children less than ten was applied. Thus Lemoyne counts the payment of 108 *livres* per year and per person for 2,370 people in 1772, meaning that all of the Acadians must have received payment.[30]

We have seen that the Controller-General was charged with finding a settlement for the Acadian families in France during the summer or early fall of 1772. By a letter of May 5, 1773, he informed the Minister of the Navy that he had found a location to settle the families and the ministry of Finances was charged with directly paying the assistance to the exiles starting on July 1, 1773.[31] At that time, only the families from Île-Royale and Canada were still being paid by the Navy. Lemoyne was charged with making a survey of the Acadians in the ports, a survey partially motivated, in fact, by making a distinction between the "truly Acadian" families and those from Canada and Louisbourg who should still be receiving aid from the Navy.[32] The situation was later further complicated, for, from that moment, the administration theoretically maintained a distinction between the Acadians who accepted going to Poitou and the rest.[33]

Thus, those Acadians who accepted the offer of the marquis de Pérusse still received their payment during their stay in the Châtelleraudais. A reconstitution of the chronology of the distribution of aid after the subsequent departure of the large majority of them from Poitou is more difficult. A letter written by the Controller-General at the end of August 1776[34] specifies that the aid to the Acadians would be paid until January 1, 1776, but that then a distinction would be made between the Acadians depending on their profession. To some, three *sous* would be paid, and to others, two *sous*, while to still others, nothing. The payment to all was supposed to end on June 30, 1776, yet those who continued clearing the lands of Pérusse received gradually decreasing sums until January 1, 1781.[35] In truth, it is doubtful that these instructions were applied: one document specifies that payment was still due from July 1, 1776, and January 1, 1778, to nearly all of the Acadians then counted by the administration in France;[36] and an Acadian orphan girl was paid in Nantes in September 1776.[37] Other documents, however, would suggest that the Acadians were not always being paid by even mid-1778.[38]

The documentation is therefore deficient and contradictory for this period. What seems certain is that the payments were reduced for all of the Acadians in Brittany from six *sols* to three *sols* per day as of January 1, 1778.[39] Necker had ordered that it only be paid for two years.[40] But, once again, it does not seem that his injunction was enacted, since we find different documents mentioning payments of aid to the Acadians in Brittany in 1782, 1784, and 1785.[41] It therefore seems to not have been interrupted between 1778 and 1785.

For those who decided not to go to Poitou, the situation was different, at least theoretically. According to the official instructions of Controller-General Terray to Lemoyne, it was specified that "the subsistence will be continued to all indiscriminately," that is to those who wanted to go to Poitou as well as to those who refused, at the rate of six *sols* per day per person until January 1774.[42] However, when Lemoyne had some difficulty in recruiting volunteers at Saint-Malo for the settlement of Poitou, he began to threaten the Acadians with suspending payments to pressure them to accept the project.[43] As we have seen, however, Terray refused to approve these threats and, on the contrary, gave Lemoyne opposing instructions.[44] Lemoyne—rightly or wrongly—interpreted the instructions from the Controller-General as an order to continue the aid to the Acadians until December 31, 1774. This is what is shown by the instructions he sent to Rochefort, La Rochelle,[45] and Cherbourg, for example.[46] The least we can say is that the intentions of the Controller-General were unclear. He himself later wrote to the intendant of Caen that "the surplus [of Acadians at Cherbourg who did not leave for Poitou] will remain in your generality and benefit from the payments until January 1, 1774,"[47] suggesting that it would then be suppressed. Yet this was not the case, since he later ordered to "continue it during the year 1774 to those who do not go to Poitou."[48] These contradictions clearly show the difficulty of rendering an exact account of the various ministerial instructions for each town.

In fact, the aid seems to have been paid in a different manner depending on the town of residence. Thus, if Lemoyne's instructions quoted above were indeed followed, the assistance was distributed until January 1, 1775 in Bordeaux as well as in Aunis.[49] It seems that these Acadians no longer received payments after this date. In Le Havre, a letter by Terray ordered payment of aid until January 1, 1776,[50] a year longer than in the other towns. No explanation is provided for this favorable treatment. As there was a deficit, Terray authorized the intendant to withdraw payments to Acadians who refused from "a spirit of mutiny or cabal to register to go to Poitou." At his discretion, the intendant could even "stop it entirely and manage the funds more easily to assist the infirm and the orphans."[51] In Brittany, the details of payment after this date are not known.

The aid paid to the Acadians after the departure of a large portion of them for Poitou is best documented at Cherbourg.[52] Let us recall that, according to the official instructions, the aid was to be paid to all of the Acadians until December 31, 1773. It was indeed paid until December 31, 1774,[53] but only part of the Acadians received the whole amount.[54] Subsequently, the intendant of Caen proposed relieving the government by having the payments made to the Acadians of his generality taken "from the free funds of the poll-tax."[55] Authorization for this was granted by the Controller-General for the years 1775 and 1776.[56]

The following August, the Acadians in Cherbourg addressed a petition to the intendant of Caen. They declared that "five families, amounting to 23 people, have not received one *sou* of payment from the king since the first of July, 1773,"[57] and thus asked for arrears. But this is surprising, as it is illogical that some families had seen their payment suppressed on July 1, 1773, since it was normally scheduled to continue until December 31 of that year. Some time later, "fifteen other families [residing in Cherbourg] numbering 63 people" similarly protested that they "had not been paid since January 1, 1777."[58] The subsequent instructions again seem contradictory: in January 1779, the intendant wrote his sub-delegate, de Valognes, that the payment would be continued to the Acadians for the year 1779.[59] But, some months later, Necker ordered that payment stopped being given to able men, in order to "train the orphans without resources in trades" and in order to "continue to take what was indispensable to pay from the free funds of the poll-tax."[60] In 1782, facing the sad condition of the families of Entremont and Bellefontaine, the intendant received authorization to again pay them a sum of six *sous* per day, per person.[61] Two years later, a new intendant in turn complained that it was not up to the province, from the funds of its poll-tax, to pay the Acadians, and asked the royal government to take charge of the payment.[62]

Subsequently, it becomes yet more difficult to follow the changes in the directives of the ministers among orders and counter-orders, though it seems that at Cherbourg no one received aid after 1777,[63] except, perhaps intermittently, the families of Mius d'Entremont and Bellefontaine, and some older people and children under fourteen. For the latter, it is probable that there were really not any precise criteria, and that the decision to help or not help them depended on the good will of the administrators.

This, then, is what can be said of the functioning of the distributions of assistance to the Acadians before 1785. The reconstruction above shows that the government measures were far from being as rational, generous, and thorough as Ernest Martin has suggested. Counter-orders succeeded orders, general rules were either late or nonexistent, and local arrangements predominated.

Other Kinds of Assistance

The aid distributed by the government was not just monetary in nature.[64] Other types of relief are mentioned many times in the texts, mainly at the time of the arrival of the Acadians in the ports. We note, for example, "conduct passes"[65] granted to various individuals to search for their families who disembarked in other locations.[66] Clothes were distributed to the exiles disembarked at Granville. Solicited by the town mayor in mid-January, Berryer approved the expense of 235 *livres* "despite the dearth of funds" to provide the poor Acadians "cover for the rigors of winter."[67] Varied other assistance of this kind was distributed. Thus Berryer approved an expense of 26 *livres* per month for the commissioner of divisions of Cherbourg to pay "those who supply tools to all of the inhabitants" of Île Saint-Jean at the hospital.[68] Indirect assistance could also take the form of support in the search for employment: many naval commissioners requested work for the Acadians, and sometimes supplied it themselves, as they were able. Nonetheless, it would seem that, apart from the exceptional case of Rochefort,—where the intendant recruited nearly all of the able men to work in the port—only a minority of Acadians were able to be so employed. On the contrary, in many ports those responsible for naval affairs wrote that they had no work to offer the Acadians. One particularly zealous commissioner at Cherbourg also struggled to gather three thousand *livres* to pay the dowry of an Acadian woman named Marguerite Bazer, who wanted to enter a convent (though there is no indication that this dowry was ever actually paid).[69]

After the departure of a large portion of the Acadians to Louisiana in 1785, one report made various proposals of the way to employ those who remained in France. At Morlaix, for example, it specified finding a trade for "a young [Acadian] man 21 years old who is reportedly a very good subject, who asks to be employed in the offices of the Navy." At Lorient, Paul Daigre, "father of a family of seven children," including a sick daughter, was recommended for "a position as guardian of Saint-Michel Island in the dry dock of Lorient [which] is constantly vacant and counts on the Navy."[70] We learn from a later report that the post was not granted.[71] At the same time, the Controller-General "sought what was most suitable for those [of the Acadians] who remained, either some lands, letters of mastery, or some subordinate employment."[72] Note that in each case these were only proposals, reflections on the part of the government that likely were not followed through with any action (with some exceptions). If some employment was distributed after this report, no trace of it remains in the documentation. The mayor of Cherbourg left no doubt about his inability to provide work to those at Cherbourg: "I have conferred with the gentlemen of the mayoral office about the method we might employ here to sustain the work [of the Acadians]. We have found none. . . . As for the subordinate jobs, I see none that can be given, all of those in public works being already filled, and, besides, I do not think that they were suitable to fill those posts."[73]

There was another kind of governmental aid: various exemptions or price reductions on some products often were requested by or for the Acadians. In particular, some of the Acadians benefited from reduced prices for salt and tobacco.[74] So, when the families went *en masse* to Poitou, Lemoyne asked that salt be offered "for the price of the lower salt tax" for the refugees. He specified that the Acadian families, "regularly in the sea ports since taking refuge in France, have had salt at a low price and [that] in Le Havre they paid the price of the lower salt tax for it."[75] Nonetheless, the letter does not tell us if the Acadians in the ports benefited from the special measures, as it was rather an allusion to the price of salt in the sea-side areas being lower than it was in the rest of France.[76]

In the same petition, Lemoyne also requested that tobacco be offered to the Acadians "for the same price as it is to the troops," at least for the working men. Tobacco was another heavily taxed product that the Acadians consumed in large enough quantities, if we are to believe various sources,[77] and that they sometimes obtained at advantageous rates. Thus, tobacco rations were granted at modest prices to the Acadians in Belle-Île-en-Mer on the orders of Choiseul starting in 1765.[78] These favorable rates were shown from 1766[79] until at least 1769,[80] and the free distributions of "Nicot's herb" were recommended on various occasions in the plans for the settlement of Poitou.[81]

The Acadians also requested various exemptions. Thus they addressed a report to Praslin in 1767 complaining "of being obliged to keep watch every night alternatively with the local inhabitants, which keeps them from being able to work to support their wives and children."[82] Praslin forwarded the claim to Choiseul and asked him to collectively relieve the Acadians of this responsibility. Choiseul only partially agreed to the request, since he rejected any collective exemption favoring the exiles,[83] except for "those who are usually occupied in cultivating the lands, navigation, working in the port, or wherever else."[84] This partial refusal did not prevent the former colonists living in the Saint-Malo region from requesting some years later to not be submitted to the formalities of justice in France, notably in the case of tutelage for minors.[85] This favor, also, was not granted.[86]

Among the other kinds of assistance for the Acadians, though undoubtedly very modest and irregular, were the various alms received from the local authorities, particularly at the time of their disembarking. These alms, which we briefly mentioned above, are notably attested to by various documents at Saint-Malo, La Rochelle, and Cherbourg, and it is probable that similar aid was distributed in other French ports. We noted above how the mayor of Rochefort made a contribution in September 1758 to lodge the Acadians. At La Rochelle, the municipality intervened to help in lodging the disembarked travelers, and the municipal officers of the town supplied the necessities to clean the clothes of the refugees from Île-Royale.[87] In 1763, the community of Morlaix also helped the Acadians who came from England find lodgings.

In the city of corsairs [Saint-Malo], the Acadians received subsidies from the municipality. The mayor of the town had 150 refugees brought to the main hospital and also took care of the rest of the inhabitants "spread through the town," often suffering with scurvy, by ordering assistance worth 400 *livres* to "procure shirts along with the most urgent other needs" for them. He also indicated that "the charities of our inhabitants have contributed much to the comfort of these miserable people who are lacking everything, and are found in a pitiful condition."[88] One week later, the mayor announced that a collection had been organized for the Acadians and that it resulted in distributions of "meat, bread and shirts, coming from the collection that was made to benefit these unfortunate people."[89] Moreover, in July 1759, the mayor made an advance of "three *livres*" and "20 *sols* for conduct" to each inhabitant, on the orders of the intendant.[90] The same problems again arose in 1763 at the time of the repatriation of the Acadians from England, but this time the mayor noted that "the two landings of the English on our coasts and the burning of nearly a hundred vessels in our port"[91] had weakened the finances of the city and that "we have already begun a collection for them, not being entirely convinced of the barrenness of alms in a town such as ours, which for a number of years has endured only losses and disgraces."[92]

In any case, another nongovernmental actor intervened: the local inhabitant. It was most likely the inhabitants who provided the primary assistance at the outset by gratuitously offering hospitality to many of the deported. It is also possible that this hospitality lasted for some time, if not many years; and it certainly also existed in other ports. Not that it was entirely disinterested, however. Thus, at Cherbourg, in 1763, a document indicates that the inhabitants of the town who, in charity for the Acadians, "advanced them food, clothing and the other most indispensable necessities of life began to refuse to give it to them for the king had decided that this subsistence should end the first of the next April."[93] The inhabitants were therefore counting on being reimbursed, undoubtedly with interest, as we will see further on.

Later testimony also shows the initial generosity of the inhabitants. The Abbé Le Loutre, for example, writes that, among the Acadians "who disembarked in the ports of France sick and dying, a very large number of them died despite the abundant aid that they received from the inhabitants."[94] The author of a memorandum adds that the Acadians were "beloved" for they were in a "position to stir sentiments."[95] These two accounts, by insisting that this aid had ended, suggest that the hospitality of the inhabitants did not last, or that it had become institutionalized.

Fortunate Beneficiaries

After this attempt at chronologically reconstituting the distribution of assistance, it is appropriate to examine more precisely those for whom it was intended. As with the previous discussion, we should not imagine that rigid and strict criteria were established. Lemoyne himself recognized this later on:

> One must agree that there was a bit of arbitrariness in the start of this administration, but also one cannot help but avow that it was nearly impossible for those responsible not to make mistakes; the orders to grant aid had as their only motivation the urgent need.[96]

If it was not easy for the administrators of the period to exactly understand whom the ministry wanted to benefit from this aid, it is all the more so difficult for us to know. Was the assistance assigned to all of the repatriated who were not official colonial personnel, or only to those who would most benefit from it? Who, then, judged their needs? We will try to provide the guidelines that emanate from the successive ministerial directives.

The Nobility

The Civil and Military Officers and the Missionaries

Upon the arrival in the ports, the administration immediately distinguished those arriving by their previous positions: thus the former colonial personnel and the missionaries were quickly treated separately.[97] The civil and military officers and their families[98] who came from Louisbourg, Canada, and to a lesser degree Île Saint-Jean, were the subject of special treatment, since they were still in the service of the king. Men in military service (including the troops) were regrouped in specific locations, for example at Rochefort. Most of them no longer having the right to fight because of the treaties of capitulation, they had to wait for the end of the war in order to be able to again take up active service.[99] They were subsequently reassigned in other locations, specifically, the colonies. As for the civil officers, they were more or less soon reassigned, also mostly overseas. Neither group received supplemental assistance, rather half-pay that was sometimes converted into a pension (notably for widows or orphans of officers killed in combat).

The French religious also came under a special rule. On their disembarking the minister Berryer ordered payments of twelve *sols* per day to nuns and 20 *sols* to missionaries.[100] Most of these missionaries then succeeded in obtaining benefits and pensions so as to finish their lives sheltered from want.[101] With the exception of the d'Entremont and Bellefontaine families, the civil and military officers and the missionaries were, with rare exceptions, not born in Acadia, and have thus been excluded from this study.

The Other Nobles

Only one Acadian family of refugees in France claimed nobility: the d'Entremont family.[102] Their case deserves to be outlined, because of its particularity.[103] This family is often associated with another family, the Bellefontaines, who, without being truly noble, deserved a separate status for services rendered in the militia in Acadia and for its "previous wealth."[104] These two families, allied and both deported to Cherbourg,[105] seemingly treated like ordinary Acadian families at first, asked for different treatment in June 1766, making the most of some of their "relatives residing in Rochefort," and receiving pensions of 200 to 300 *livres*, "instead of 6*s* and 12*s* per day for subsistence" that they evidently received in Cherbourg. It is therefore possible that they received 12 *sous* per day instead of six from the beginning—but this is not confirmed by other documents.[106] The two or three hundred *livres* no doubt refers to the pensions distributed to the families of the officers mentioned above.[107]

Starting in 1766, in any case, an abundant correspondence developed between the d'Entremonts and the Bellefontaines with the naval commissioner of divisions at Cherbourg, the intendant, and the minister. They first requested "aid proportionate to their status and situation."[108] In March 1767, de Francy, commissioner of divisions at Cherbourg, sent three lists of the Acadians residing in his town, the first of "Acadians of honest families . . . who have performed the functions of military officers," the second of those "of recognized noble extraction and their allies," and the third of the sick and the dying. For the first and second, de Francy proposed pensions from one hundred to four hundred *livres* with slightly higher pensions for the nobles, which is to say the family (enlarged to sixty-one people) of Mius d'Entremont.[109] It seems likely that these suggestions for pensions remained a dead letter despite the evident support and reiteration by the commissioner of divisions of Cherbourg and the intendant of Caen, and despite the renewed requests of the d'Entremont family.[110] In 1773, Lemoyne renewed the request for preferential treatment for the d'Entremonts and the Bellefontaines and recommended distributing them twelve *sous* per day.[111] Moreover, Lemoyne was not content proposing doubling the payments for the d'Entremonts. Shocked that individuals of this rank were being treated like workmen, he recommended providing them with a particular village for the settlement then planned at Poitou. But they refused.[112] The sub-delegate of Cherbourg supported Lemoyne's new request, but a clerk from Contrôle Général encouraged the sub-delegate to seek other solutions.[113] The doubling of payment was finally granted in January 1774, but by the intendant of Caen and not by the Controller-General.[114] This locally-made decision explains why, four years later, the new Controller-General requested that the letter containing the decision from the intendant at Caen be forwarded.[115]

This local decision had effects, for the record of payments indeed attests to supplementary distributions for the d'Entremonts.[116] Nonetheless, they were not exempted from the suspension of payments to all at the end of 1774. In October 1775, they sought the payment that they said they had not received since the previous January,[117] and in the following month one of the Bellefontaines stated that he had been "previously paid at the rate of five hundred *livres*."[118] In December of the same year, the intendant of Caen relayed these requests to the Controller-General of Finances,[119] who agreed to the "continuation" of aid to the Acadians of Cherbourg and a return to the payment of twelve *sous* per day to the d'Entremonts.[120] As before, many orders and counter orders succeeded each other. It seems that the payment was again suppressed in January 1777.[121] In 1782, an order was given to provide the d'Entremont and Bellefontaine families six *sous* per day, per person.[122] The payments are attested to episodically. In 1784, the intendant of Caen was on the point of distributing nearly 9,000 *livres* to 11 Acadians who were in no position to earn their living, of which 3,300 *livres* was meant for Charles d'Entremont and his wife alone.[123] Yet he added:

> I cannot allow you to ignore that the other Acadians who are in misery and in no shape to earn a living have seen with great pain that they have been forgotten. They say that in the other provinces everyone was paid without distinction between nobles and commoners.[124]

In fact, we can note requests coming from the d'Entremont family until shortly before the start of the Revolution. Thus, one still finds orders for payments to the family in 1788 and a request for aid coming from the intendant of Caen in February 1789.[125]

The "Inhabitants and Individuals of the People"

Let us now occupy ourselves with the group that more especially interests us, namely, the general group of Acadian "inhabitants."[126] Did all of the Acadians receive aid? What were the conditions under which they received it? As with the above chronological reconstitution, it is not easy to answer these questions, despite there being a very large number of dispatches on the subject.

Conditions for Income

In principle, only individuals "absolutely in no shape to do anything and without resources" or those "truly in terrible condition" should have been allowed to receive aid.[127] But the very repetition of these instructions by the successive ministers suggests that they were not being applied or were only applied poorly. Besides, there was undoubtedly no inhabitant capable of providing for his own needs except those to whom work had been supplied. We remain relatively blind in this area since we are much better informed about the orders that came down from the royal government than about the local responses, which might have explained why the orders were sometimes not applied.[128] The Acadians disembarked from afar, finding themselves without any local contacts. Even if they had been able to bring some goods along, this did not constitute an income. Some Acadians perhaps had families or acquaintances in France with whom they might lodge, but these must have been very few in number. Travel permits and travel expenses were provided to various individuals, but it seems that these passes most often served for them to rejoin the rest of their families disembarked in other ports. Furthermore, as the Acadians and the inhabitants of Louisbourg were frequently intermingled upon arrival, we do not know if some Acadians were actually excluded from the aid. And once the individuals were "employed," the administration had great difficulty stopping the aid, even for those who earned their living rather well.

Differences in Place of Origin

The second criterion necessary to be assigned aid was very clear: one had to be a former inhabitant of "North America."[129] Until April 1, 1773, there was no real distinction between places of origin in North America, at least for "those of the common people."[130] Thus, at the time of the first disembarkations, the instructions from Berryer were clear: though families that could provide for their own needs and those who needed aid were to be treated separately, there was no distinction between the place of origin of individuals from Île-Royale, Île Saint-Jean, Gaspé, and the other locations.[131] Nor was there any such distinction made in the lists of distributions of aid at Saint-Malo. What's more, the terms "Canadians" and "Acadians" were often used synonymously.

However, from the circumstances of the arrivals, a major portion of the inhabitants from Île-Royale, including Acadian families, were found to have disembarked at Rochefort and La Rochelle, while the inhabitants of Île Saint-Jean and Acadia proper were nearly all in the ports of Manche, from Morlaix to Boulogne, with a strong concentration also at Saint-Malo. From this resulted a certain differentiation between these two groups from the start, as Lemoyne noted in a report wherein he explained that the administration of the latter "was as distinct and separate from that of the families of Île-Royale as the different ports had no reciprocal correspondence in this regard."[132]

In a letter of February 1773, the minister de Boynes ordered clear distinctions between the families still receiving aid, those families from Île-Royale and Canada, on the one hand, and those from Acadia and from Île Saint-Jean, on the other. The minister wanted to decrease the "abuses" and suppress a certain number of families from the first category. The Acadians were treated separately since the government still was occupied "with finding them settlements in the Kingdom," and they alone would have the right to some land.[133] After April 1, 1773, the aid did not entirely cease for the most needy of the inhabitants of North America, but it was no longer automatic,[134] and a fixed fund of around fifty thousand *livres* was reserved for this purpose. It seems however that it was more liberally provided to the Acadians—at least for a while.

There was often confusion on the part of the naval commissioners over the difference between the two categories of individuals. Lemoyne's "review" had the aim of distinguishing as clearly as possible between these two groups, with the difficulties and the mistakes that we can imagine, it being obvious that many families could fit into both categories, and that, most of the time, all of the documents of civil or other status having been lost, the sorting was based on the testimony of a third party.[135] Not to mention that many administrators clearly were ignorant of the geography of the former North American colonies: often, starting in 1773 and when the decision was made to rigorously separate the two groups, Lemoyne was obliged to send lengthy instructions to the ports so that those charged with applying the decisions would pay careful attention to not mixing up the different populations.[136] Here again, the repetition of Lemoyne's instructions is a strong indication that they had not been followed or had been compromised. Lemoyne himself often doubted what he should do in some circumstances, and his requests for clarifications from the agents of the Bureau of Contrôle Général provided no solution.[137]

In any case, if we hold to the criteria of Lemoyne stated after April 1773, only individuals having proven residence in Acadia or in Île Saint-Jean could be included on the lists of Acadians.[138] Lemoyne thus resumed his instructions: "One should only consider as Acadians those who were truly settled in Acadia, who had possessions there, or at Île Saint-Jean, the colony formed by the Acadians who were expelled from there."[139]

Married Couples

Should the "Europeans" married to Acadians receive assistance?[140] The commissioners of the Navy requested instructions on this subject from the ministers on many occasions.[141] The refugees in Normandy feared that by marrying a person from Cherbourg their spouse would not receive the supplement: this argument is found in the majority of the files of petitions in the archdiocesan archives of Coutances.[142] It is possible that this rule was followed at Cherbourg, but we have not found any trace of an official directive of its kind. It is therefore likely that, once again, the situations were different depending on the place of residence.

At the time of the granting of fee farming at Belle-Îsle, it was decided to also grant aid to the non-Acadian spouses in order to assist with their settlement. So Choiseul ordered that a sergeant and a soldier from the troops of Louisbourg, married to two Acadian women, and "the woman named Marie Lecog de Saint-Servan married to an Acadian," who until then had not received the supplement, be included in the distributions.[143] It is possible that these instructions established "jurisprudence," because, in 1773, Lemoyne wrote:

> Since the European women who married Acadians whose Acadian husbands are living enjoy the same benefits as the Acadians, their husbands enabling them to share their classification [implying that this rule was generally respected before this date], I thought that the Acadian widows having by their marriage been identified with the nation, it would be just to maintain them in this category as long as they remain widows. This is why I ask you to request that Marguerite Viard, widow of Dominique Hébert, again receive subsistence, as would an Acadian woman.[144]

However, these generous arrangements were not always applied everywhere, as shown, for instance, by the reluctance of an executor in 1784 to distribute aid to a widow "originally from this town [Cherbourg]." "It is here that her [Acadian] husband married her and she was never in Acadia, and not long ago I was assured that women like her, born and married in France after the Acadians arrived, were never placed on the lists for payment of aid," he wrote the intendant.[145]

If the men could transfer their "classification" of being Acadian to their "European" wives, the inverse does not seem to have been possible.[146] Nonetheless the women did not clearly lose their status or payment in a mixed marriage, as Lemoyne indicates to the *ordonnateur* of Bordeaux:

> The Acadian women who married either Europeans or men from Île-Royale or from Canada will be treated specially because of their birth as Acadian women, and will generally enjoy the benefits granted to all of the Acadians, but their husbands and children will not. However, the children of widows of Acadians remarried to men who are not will receive it as does their mother because of their origin and they should be placed on the list of Acadians.[147]

If the measures aimed at excluding spouses from aid were effectively applied, this undoubtedly induced the Acadians to marry their compatriots rather than French women. If the government did not strongly encourage this secondary effect of the distribution of aid, it clearly recognized it, for reasons we have seen.

Variation in Sums for Individuals of "Lower Standing"

We have also seen above how the aid went from a ration of ten *sous* per day at the very beginning, to six *sous* per day, and finally to only three *sous* for children less than ten years old; and how military and colonial personnel were treated separately, as were, progressively, the inhabitants of North America. We have stated how sometimes the supplement was suppressed in many areas or for some individuals only. But did all of the Acadians of "lower standing" at a given place and time receive the same sum? Nothing is less clear.

In 1759, Charles Claude de Ruis-Embito de La Chesnardière had a ration and a half distributed to many ship pilots (who were probably previously employed by the king).[148] The minister dryly reminded the intendant that everyone should be on the same regime of six *sous* per day and then often repeated the same instructions.[149] However, in 1766, Lemoyne—then occupied with twelve Acadian families and almost 2,500 Germans—in a meddlesome memorandum affirmed that he distributed to these two groups six *sous* per day and "two *sous* for lodgings," totaling eight *sous* per day per person.[150] It is true that Choiseul was less strict on this subject than his predecessor, Berryer. If we again examine the situation at Saint-Malo, it would seem that, in 1763 and in 1765, all of the Acadians indiscriminately received six *sous* per day.[151] Yet in 1766 or 1767, changes came because of family situations, and the supplement was reduced for children.[152] The children did receive assistance from their birth, in conformity with the directions of Berryer who, in May 1759, approved payment of the aid "for the women of these inhabitants newly mothers" at Boulogne.[153] The refugees at Rochefort, however, were not lodged by the same standard, as Berryer ordered some months later for aid not to be paid for the children if there were more than two in a family. In this case, the aid paid was then only three *sous* per child.[154]

Did elderly people receive a supplemental income, as Ernest Martin states?[155] This generalization, for which Martin provides no references, is probably based on a document from November 1774 in which older Acadians received the same favorable treatment as they had received at Saint-Malo, eight or nine *sous*, which was withheld from them at Poitou.[156] At Cherbourg, it indeed seems that some older people received a bit more money, for some time at least, but nothing demonstrates that this was a general rule.[157] Finally, when older or ill individuals were incapable of attaining their needs, the government sometimes had them admitted to hospitals that were theoretically paid twelve or sixteen *sous* per day per person in compensation.[158] The administrators often affirmed that the Acadians did not want to go to these hospitals, even under the most extreme circumstances. In some cases, at the site of the hospital, it is possible that a supplement of six *sous* per day was also paid.

Conclusion

What may we conclude from this accumulation of partially incomplete and sometimes contradictory information? In the area of the distribution of aid, exemptions and privileges were themselves the rule throughout the whole period. The image depicted by Lauvrière and Martin of France being generous to the exiles, scrupulously distributing a daily payment of six *sous* per day to all of the refugees, though not entirely false, is exaggerated. The flexibility of the intendants and naval commissioners regarding the Acadians was relatively broad, at least to the extent that funds were available, which was rarely the case. Undoubtedly, the state's chronic deficits most often led to restrictive interpretations of orders that were often barely explicit or contradictory. But, in this regard, the lack of uniformity in aid for the Acadians was in complete conformity with the rest of the society of the *Ancien* Régime: equality of treatment between provinces was not the rule, and the impositions varied considerably from one region to the other, as we will find further along.

Chapter VIII

"Work, Take The Trouble"

The governmental assistance constituted only part of the income of the refugees. In fact, many Acadians could add to their assistance income from their employment, though not without overcoming some difficulties. We have seen that at some times the government prohibited and at others tolerated combining the six *sous* with work income. To continue evaluating the economic and social integration of the Acadians, it is appropriate to examine more closely the daily occupations of the refugees. Their employment was often strongly encouraged by the ministers who succeeded each other in the government, for it allowed the suppression of their aid payments and encouraged them not to be lazy.[1] According to Berryer, if the aid was so modest, it was precisely for this reason.[2] Ministers, intendants, and commissioners thus received explicit instructions to find occupations for the Acadians.[3] "All of the fishermen and seamen who can serve and all of the laborers or day workers who are in a condition to work must be employed in the service of the sea or in the ports," Berryer constantly insisted.[4] But, as it was not always possible to employ the Acadians in the ports, these ideas were apparently most often never put into effect.

Enquiries About the "Talents" of the Acadians

In order to employ the Acadians, one had to first find out what they were capable of doing. Hence, the intendants or the naval commissioners on many occasions sought to learn more definitely what the "talents" of the Acadians were. Sometimes, the information arrived unsolicited. Some months after the arrival of the first boats loaded with Acadians in the Saint-Malo region, a certain Ladvocat de La Crochais rendered an account of "the examination [that he] made of the talents of these people and of their faculties for gaining a living":

> First of all, these people were raised in a country of abundance, lands at one's disposal, and consequently less difficult to cultivate than those of the cantons here, and whose customs were different . . . . They handle a bit the axe, only making something too slowly and poorly in their way (which we can only refer to as hacking of wood). The women sew poorly enough, that is to say with very large thread and making few stockings. These are the only talents that I know that they have.[5]

This judgment, strongly tainted with ethnocentrism, insists on the supposed incapacities of the Acadians (who, furthermore, "seem exhausted") and was most suited for claiming the continuation of their payments. The author of the report, who was seeking this continuation, specified that to suppress it would be to expose them to poverty: "I would be quite angry to have to blame myself if an unfortunate man died at my door for lacking aid and if the payment of the king was suppressed, I would have such regret." Thus we should not take Ladvocat's sharp judgment of the abilities of the workers as being conclusive. Some years later, the commissioner charged with examining the Acadians' status and settling them—and who knew their general situation well enough—presented a more optimistic version of the competency of the refugee colonists: "The men are usually cultivators and some carpenters, that is to say, capable of handling an axe well enough to make the basic carpentry of a house." Others were "builders of fishing boats, able to make nets, many are fishermen, navigators," or dry-curers, and "there are good sailors, others can be woodworkers, blacksmiths, and capable of making farming tools, etc."[6]

The Work Proposed for the Acadians

How to benefit from these abilities? The minister suggested various ideas, giving preference to non-specialized, more risky work. For him, the essential thing was to reduce the cost of the assistance being provided to the refugees. He specified that the Commissioner of Divisions at Boulogne should hire the refugees "either in the manufacturing in the province or in the cultivation of the land."[7] Similar instructions were sent to all the places where the Acadians had disembarked. Calculations were made of the feasibility of using the talents of some of the Acadian women in the sewing trades, but as the hoped-for profits were too low and the costs of investment too high, this plan was abandoned.[8] It was then advocated that the Acadians be used in the port, working at Dunkirk, or working the land.[9] The inhabitants were urged to work in navigation: "nothing prevents these inhabitants from embarking on the corsairs or frigates of the king: they are not prisoners," specified Berryer. He even suggested to the commissioner of divisions at Boulogne: "As for the young men who are suitable to embark on armed corsairs or frigates at Dunkirk and who refuse to take on this role, we can only withdraw the aid that the king provides them."[10] Many intendants suggested employing them in the maintenance of the roads.[11] One of the intendants suggested that the refugee colonists be employed in fabricating nets, and Bertin even advocated sending them to work in the mines.[12] On this subject, however, Choiseul remarked that Bertin's proposal should "be rejected, for it would be cruel for those who are living comfortably and who have sacrificed everything for their zeal and attachment to France to have to endure such forfeit."[13]

The Trades of Preference

Trades for the Men

The proposals above were only ideas, and no evidence proves that the Acadians were actually employed in these various activities. On the other hand, through available documentation one finds mention of the trades the Acadians actually engaged.

A large portion of the Acadians simply performed day labor.[14] The precariousness of the living conditions of this category of laborers becomes evident in the testimony given by Anselme Boudereau, a day worker at Saint-Servan. Summoned by employees of the farm of Saint-Malo to justify his employment, which began on March 3, 1767, he declared that he "left Saint-Servan . . . at around 7 o'clock[15] [in the morning] to go to Saint-Malo in a boat, and from there [he] left to go and try to make a living working in the country."[16] The employment of many Acadians as simple day workers surely reflects the fact that they were convinced that they would only reside in this place of refuge temporarily, as we have seen above. This uncertainty did not help the economic and social integration of the refugees, who, before being able to find a stable job, sought to know their future situation. No doubt this was one of the reasons why such a large number settled for working from day to day. It is difficult to estimate the number of days that an Acadian might work each year, thus it is near impossible to extrapolate what might represent the salary they brought home. The Acadians were also employed in road maintenance at Boulogne.[17] This work was supplied by the commissioner of divisions, and, this time, the assistance was suspended during the time they worked and recommenced at the end of the contract. In the Saint-Malo region, many Acadians worked for many months "repairing the tide mill of la Minotais, in Plouër."[18]

Various occupations involving wood, with the common thread of maritime construction, also occupied a good number of Acadians. Many were simply designated as woodcutters or carpenters, while others were specifically employed in the construction of boats. Thus, in 1785, at Morlaix, there were fourteen naval carpenters. Among the rarer professions, though still involving wood, one finds at least one wooden shoe maker, apparently installed on his own account as he had to borrow two hundred *livres* for "materials suitable for his work with wooden shoes" from suppliers."[19]

Navigation

The other great occupation of the men was navigation, in all of its forms. A report from August 1760 mentions "[Acadian] boys from Pleudihen and Plouër who navigate in the boats."[20] Some, following ministerial orders, were employed on commercial or slave ships, like Aimable Henry, who claimed that he embarked on a corsair in Saint-Malo in 1759 and was captured by the British. Freed from his detention in England, he then embarked "for the coast of Guinea." On his return to France, in late 1764 or early 1765, he asked to receive payment from the king "for the time that he was in the prisons."[21] Alain Roman notes that one finds a fair number of Acadians so embarked: thus, the "lists of the naval corsairs" indicate five Acadians of a total of thirty sailors aboard *L'Hercule*.[22] Many other Acadians sailed aboard the commercial vessels: "some of them had the trade of sailor and earned a bit more, enough to prevent them from having to personally take assistance from the king," wrote the commissioner of divisions of Cherbourg.[23] At the end of the period, one even notes in Morlaix a "man 36 years old, captain for many years" and in Nantes a "good sailor who will receive the letters of a captain of vessel once he has again completed a voyage for the king."[24]

Fishing

Many other men took up to fishing, especially on the ships going to the fishing banks of Newfoundland. Some profited from this by clandestinely returning to Acadia, as was the case of Basile Boudrot, whose story is narrated through the course of many letters of the d'Entremont family. He left Cherbourg and went to Cape Sable Island, in the south of the present Nova Scotia, probably by way of Saint-Pierre and Miquelon. In 1761, Boudrot, aged about twenty and required as a witness in the inquiry of a dispensation of consanguinity, stated his profession as navigator, "being in Acadia and in Cherbourg with no opportunity to pursue it."[25] In a later document, he said that he was "navigator and merchant on his own account" with his father and that he "sometimes goes fishing for fresh fish." A number of refugees practiced coastal fishing, such as Jean and François Rambourg, "inhabitants of North America" and "very hard-working young men who go fishing every day, which undoubtedly procures them a reasonable subsistence."[26] It seems that in some cases the Acadians borrowed funds to allow them to purchase the tools needed for fishing. Thus, a certain Jean Le Chaux borrowed money from a merchant of Cherbourg for the purchase "of a boat, rigging and fishing materials."[27]

Some possibly used exotic techniques, like "fishing with Cormorant." In an indictment the following dialogue is reported between a custom-officer named Guegot and two Acadians keeping warm in a tavern five kilometers from Saint-Malo:

> Mister Guegot . . . entered the tavern, and asked two Acadians who were there where they came from. "From hunting cormorant," they answered. "Do you have guns?" Replied the employee. "We have two," they told him, "and we were five men in a boat which was in the inlet of the fields." "Where is your fishing permit?" continued the employee. "A strong wave," said the two Acadians, "took away the master's coat from where he had been standing."[28]

One might very well ask what this hunting cormorant entailed. It is possible that the Acadians actually did engage in it. What is certain in this case, however, is that it served them to cover up transporting "contraband tobacco" and guns.[29]

Fishing, a communal activity in Acadia, was thus practiced by many Acadians in France as amateurs, if we would believe a naval administrator who preferred that they would accept his offer to be settled on lands.[30] If we examine the professions performed by the witnesses in the procedures for dispensations of consanguinity of the Cherbourg region, we will notice that the activities declared most often involved the sea.[31] Although the sampling is by no means representative, it nonetheless provides some indications. Of the fifty-four men serving as witnesses in eleven cases, we count twenty-five fishermen selling their catch, as well as seven individuals who were navigators, mariners or sailors. It is interesting to note the evolution. In the files predating 1764, all (or nearly all) of the Acadians declared themselves to be fishermen selling their catch, which perhaps corresponds more closely with their professions in Acadia or on Île Saint-Jean than to their then-current situation. Diversification then followed: in the files dating from 1771 to 1773, one finds other professions: carpenter, caulker, barrel-maker, manual laborer, and day-worker.

Lemoyne noted that many Acadians were "blacksmiths, capable of making farming tools," but this profession is rarely mentioned in the records.[32] Similarly, if for a number of the administrators the Acadians were naturally cultivators, very few took up this activity except as day workers. It is difficult to know if this was because of lack of opportunities, or due to their discouragement on finding the relatively poor quality of the lands that were proposed to them and the burden of the taxes. It is likely that the latter point was particularly important for these country folk who were accustomed to cultivating lands exempt from all but nominal taxes. Injunctions contained in a letter by Jean-Baptiste Semer suggest this, mentioning Louisiana, where "there are neither duties nor taxes to pay."[33] This is further confirmed by the many Acadian petitions and inquiries about taxes that were systematically posed at the time of considering the plans for resettlement. In sum, the trade of countryman in France, "a way of life rather than a profession or a trade," under the *Ancien Régime*, hardly seemed to offer many real vocations for the Acadians for reasons analyzed in more detail further on.[34]

On the other hand, we find Acadians represented in yet another activity, common among the migrants and uprooted in France under the *Ancien Régime*: the army. But this is more difficult to decipher in the archives. Lemoyne noted that "there are many young Acadian men engaged in the troops of the king and all there have a fine reputation."[35] But this was clearly not always the case, as Le Loutre wrote in 1771 that he obtained pardon for an unfortunate man "perpetually condemned to the galleys for having deserted the regiment of Foix."[36]

One also finds mention of other exiles engaged in more diverse activities, though in a more anecdotal manner, like one named Saint-Paoul employed by a count to keep watch over his horses. This count wrote: "I have here an Acadian who arrived not long ago from England who proposed to be a stable man and I have tried this for eight days now. He is, furthermore, a very good marshal and shoes the horses well, without having to have a second person hold the horse's foot."[37] One Jacques Daigle, "native of Acadia, bishopric of Québec, aged 45 years, a surgeon as his profession," asked and obtained authority to be "admitted to the number of inhabitants and citizens of this town [Saint-Malo] to enjoy the same privileges as the other inhabitants enjoy and to have the same responsibilities."[38] In Morlaix, in 1786, we also find an Acadian "sub-corporal of farms," which is to say an employee of the general tax farm which, in the maritime regions, was mainly charged with controlling the entry of taxed merchandise, like tobacco or cloth. In Brest, another Acadian was an "assistant wig-maker."[39] Finally, in what seems to be an exceptional case, Jean Thibaudeau practiced the trade of tavern-keeper in Pleudihen.[40]

Still others, more fortunate, benefited from their stay in France by learning a qualified trade. At Cherbourg in 1767, Michel Bellefontaine, "[ex] officer in the militias [of the St. Jean River] and courier for the King in Canada ... aged 34, completed in this port his course of hydrography and navigates in the ships that go cod-fishing along the coast of the Petit Nord of Terre-Neuve"; the records also note one "Larent Paré ... aged 13, [who] goes to school and sometimes goes fishing with his father."[41] It is worth noting that these two individuals were sons of former militia officers, and it is possible that, by this right, they had the benefit of free instruction.

Among those who benefited from instruction, we should note the particular case of four young Acadians who, under the Abbé de l'Isle-Dieu, became priests as of 1766.[42] In 1766, the abbé, learning that the English government had decided to prohibit the entry into Canada of priests coming from Europe, "at least if they did not originally come from Canada or from some of the colonies composing the territory of his diocese," decided to encourage vocations of the priesthood of four young Acadians exiled in France. The Abbé de l'Isle-Dieu was clearly counting on their North American origins to allow them to then be readmitted into Canada after a solid education in France.[43] He had them instructed, at first in the colleges at Saint-Servan and at Saint-Méen, then in the Paris region at the Seminary of the Holy Spirit.[44] These Acadians followed the traditional course of study for the clergy: humanities and philosophy, then theology, and were financially helped throughout the length of their studies by the abbé (as the six *sous* per day distributed by the king were insufficient). Finally, in the spring of 1772, he sent the first two first to Canada, having completed their education:[45]

> I took a risk with the two young Acadians [Joseph Mathurin Bourg and Jean-Baptiste Brault] that I had in Paris at the seminary of the Holy Spirit and who had just finished their third year of theology based on the fact that, being of Acadian origin, they were thereby Canadian and free to reenter their country of origin and rejoin the rest of their families who remained, despite the treatment suffered by those who had been uprooted and deprived of everything that they possessed. . . . But for the others remaining to me, I was given to understand that there was no reason to risk them and that, if they were sent back [from Canada], this might bring harm to the first two who, though priests, might have to suffer a similar fate.[46]

The documentation concerning those of the priests who remained in France is then interrupted, but there is every reason to suppose that they probably continued to live there.

Professions for Women

And what of the women's professions? The principal activity of many—mothers of a family—was, not surprisingly, never specified as such. One does find in the files of dispensation of consanguinity some mentions of women occupied in domestic work, such as Madeleine Landry, "occupied daily at her home in the work of housekeeping."[47] Rarely enough, it is specified that a woman was "without profession."[48] Consequently, the allusions to trades performed by them are much fewer than those of their masculine compatriots. There was no doubt that many of the numerous housewives were unable to work outside their homes.

Nonetheless, often we find names of women in the documents. Many of them practiced the activities of small trading. We have already briefly mentioned above the case of the wife of one Gilbert, who, besides caring for their five children, "maintained a busy second-hand shop." In the same document, the wife of one Julien Le Lièvre "operates a shop." A certain Guyonne Poirier, then witness in a tobacco fraud case involving Anselm Boudereau, declared that she exercised the trade of a "retail merchant."[49] Husband and wife sometimes performed a trade together: thus "Philippe Nicolas d'Arme" and his wife "kept a reputable-enough inn and seem to conduct their business well." No mention is made in the documents from which we have extracted these cases of the source of the capital that allowed the purchase of material for and founding of this commerce.[50]

More commonly, women were relegated to a small number of what would have been considered lesser professions. According to Lemoyne, the "talents" of the Acadian women were fairly limited. "The women can be dressmakers, spinners on spindles or spinning wheels, or may just know how to sew,"[51] he wrote, although we have no way of knowing if this enumeration reflects observations he made on the spot or if, on the contrary, he only was only expressing his own relatively limited expectations about the capacities of the women "of the common people." The trade of dressmaker attracted a certain number of Acadian women, perhaps more from necessity than vocation. Thus

Lemoyne interceded in Le Havre for "two good dressmaker girls." Other dressmakers included Suzanne Richard[52] in Morlaix and Marie-Rose Daigle, "seamstress and stocking maker," in Cherbourg.[53] Some other women became nuns, like the "Carmelite sister" in Morlaix in 1785.[54] Many other women tried to gather the funds needed to be able to enter the convent.[55]

Chambermaid was another traditional activity for single women.[56] In 1774 Lemoyne received a visit from an Acadian woman who claimed this as her profession. We should also note an entirely exceptional case, that of Marie-Madeleine de Billy (born Buot).[57] Baptized in in Beaubassin, in Acadie, in 1734, she married a French officer in the garrison of Louisbourg. This officer, de Billy, had to resign from the army because the marriage was considered to be a misalliance by his superiors. By 1762, Marie-Madeleine de Billy, then a widow, was in France. She was assisted by her father-in-law, "the first agent of General-Control for the house of the king." Thanks to him, Marie-Madeleine obtained a pension of five hundred *livres* "in consideration of the services rendered by her husband both in Canada and Acadia." In particular, she occupied the position of chambermaid to the sister of the king, then to his daughter, and finally to the Dauphin. The daughter of Marie-Madeleine de Billy became the first chambermaid of Louis XVI. She notably accompanied him on his flight to Varennes.[58]

The above examples do not presume to be exhaustive nor even particularly representative. To have an exact idea of the trades performed by the Acadians, one would have to conduct a systematic examination of all of the registers, notarized acts of baptisms, marriages, and burials. Furthermore, the professions mentioned on these documents were not always mentioned, nor is the information there necessarily credible. Without a doubt, a certain number of Acadians tended to over-rank their profession. If, at the time of a marriage, they declared themselves to be hired laborers while they were in fact only day-workers, the embellishment would not necessarily be denounced by the priest officiating the ceremony, nor by the witnesses. The interpretation of these documents is difficult. Nonetheless, some amateur but enlightened investigators have made such estimations for specific places and periods, or from very specific, limited types of documents.

Thus, Guy Bugeon and Monique Hivert-Le Faucheux made an exhaustive examination of the embarkation registers of the Acadians to Louisiana in 1785, as well as some other supplementary lists and later research in the Saint-Malo region.[59] Following these examinations they made some very interesting estimates that it is appropriate to describe here.

Professions at the Embarkation for Louisiana

Here we will only summarize the results described in the introduction of Bugeon and Le Faucheux's *Les Acadiens parties en France en 1785 pour la Louisiane: listes d'embarquement*. It is they who made the calculations that I am only reproducing while adding some supplementary commentary and statistics. Without notice to the contrary, all of the citations in quotations below come from their work.

The estimates made involve two sites and two significant periods of the Acadian stay in France beginning with the region of Saint-Malo in the years following the disembarkations. At the time of the first census of the Acadians in Saint-Malo in 1758-1759, "The professions catalogued are relatively few: laborer, carpenter, sailor, shoemaker, and that is about all. Sometimes the competence declared is double: laborer and carpenter, for instance. Curiously, the women are credited with no trades." The results presented for Saint-Malo were not based on exhaustive examination,[60] but Le Faucheux observes an increase through the years in the number of sailors practicing three sorts of activity: coastal fishing, deep sea fishing (to the cod-rich banks of Newfoundland), or errand sailing. The Acadians specialized in trades offered by the port activities of Saint-Malo, to the detriment of those of the laborer, who had only limited options in that region. As for the women, when mentioned in the documents, they were spinners, weavers, knitters, servants, or midwives.

After Saint-Malo, Bugeon and Le Faucheux estimated the activities performed by the Acadians at Nantes until the departures of 1785, following the lists as exhaustively as possible. All of the men present in the lists declared their professions at that time, which is not to say, however, that they were all employed. The administration on many occasions noted the difficulties that the Acadians had finding work in the locations where they were staying; moreover, the Acadians often professed to be laborers or sailors without performing that activity at the precise moment when they professed it. Thus many Acadians professed to be sailors in Poitou![61] Certainly, some of the Acadians made return trips from Poitou to Saint-Malo to embark during the winter and thereby earn some money. But we can easily imagine that all of the Acadians who professed to be sailors in Poitou were not then active. Thus we should consider mention of a profession provided in the documents as being a trade practiced most recently by the declarer, who might actually have performed several trades or have been currently out of work.

Although documentation shows a great diversity of professions performed, the women's trades are rarely mentioned. Nonetheless, one finds among the Acadian women in Nantes in 1785 mention of domestic, chambermaid, day worker, spinner, linen-draper, dressmaker, tailor, and sail-maker,[62] or of women working "in Indians [fabrics]."[63]

The men's trades were systematically indicated in the embarkation lists. They were therefore much more numerous, with a total of forty-six professions reported. Here we reproduce the table presented by Bugeon and Le Faucheux, adding a column reflecting the respective proportion of each profession:

TABLE I

Professions claimed by the Acadians at the time of the embarkation for Louisiana or appearing in the "List of Acadians who remain in France" (1785)

Trades	Leaving from Nantes for Louisiana	Remaining in France	Total	%
Gunsmith[64]	1		1	0.2
Caulker[65] [W] [M[66]	11		11	2.4
Ship Captain [M]		1	1	0.2
Cable Worker[67] [M]	1	1	1	0.2
Carpenter[68] [M]	107	8	115	25.0
Surgeon		1	1	0.2
Colorist[69] [T]	1	1	2	0.4
Clerk	1		1	0.2
Ship Builder [W] [M]		2	2	0.4
Foreman	2		2	0.4
Rope-maker[70] [M]	5	1	6	1.3
Shoemaker[71]	7	2	9	2.0
Cook	1		1	0.2
Domestic	2	1	3	0.7
Employee	1		1	0.2
Contractor		1	1	0.2
Grocer		1	1	0.2
Handkerchief Maker [T]		1	1	0.2
Blacksmith		1	1	0.2
Baker's Assistant		1	1	0.2
Carver[72] [T]	3		3	0.7
Greyeur[73] [B]		4	4	0.9
Printer[74] [T]	11		11	2.4
Cotton Printer[75] [T]	1		1	0.2
Gardener		1	1	0.2
Day Worker	58	4	62	13.5
Laborer	43	4	47	10.2
Ship's Lieutenant [M]		1	1	0.2
Mason		3	3	0.7
Mason's Helper	3	4	7	1.5
Sailor [M]	81	28	109	23.7
Joiner [B]	10	5	15	3.3

Artisan	1		1	0.2
Pareteur[76] [B]	4		4	0.9
Faience Painter		1	1	0.2
Borer[77] [B]	2	2	4	0.9
Perreyeur[78]	1		1	0.2
Pulley Worker[79] [M]	2		2	0.4
Long Saw-man [B]	5		5	1.1
Tailor	2		2	0.4
Stone Mason		1	1	0.2
Tanner		1	1	0.2
Weaver [T]		1	1	0.2
Barrel-maker [B]	6	2	8	1.7
Faience Turner		1	1	0.2
Sail-maker[80] [M]		2	2	0.4
Wood trades [B]	145	23	168	36.5
Ocean trades [M]	99	36	135	29.3
Textile trades [T]	16	3	19	4.1
TOTAL	372	88	460	100
%	**80.9**	**19.1**	**100**	**100**

Source: Guy Bugeon and Monique Hivert-Le Faucheux, *Les Acadiens partis de France en 1785 pour la Louisiane: listes d'embarquement*, Poitiers-Rennes (typescript), 1988.

It is difficult to interpret this Table as the data that might allow us to explain it is incomplete. Bugeon and Le Faucheux inquire if the range of professions reflects "deliberate choices" by the Acadians or simply the work market available at Nantes. We have no way of knowing, but it is likely that, for the Acadians, the question did not pose itself in these terms at a time when, in the popular classes at least, our contemporary notion of work for individual fulfillment followed far behind the necessities of daily life.

The table allows an appreciation of the kinds of trade that the Acadians practiced around 1785 at Nantes. We find two areas of preference: wood related trades and those related to the sea, but with a strong interconnection between the two. The number of sometimes highly qualified textile workers is no doubt explained by the intense activity at Nantes in this area. Textiles served for the fabrication of ships' sails, and also for exchange currency for the purchase of slaves in the triangular slave commerce.

We can compare this table to the numeric data supplied by Gérard-Marc Braud in his study on the Acadians of the Nantes regions. These numbers do not come from the study of the embarkation lists for Louisiana or from the list of Acadians remaining in France, but result from of a body of around 1,300 baptismal, marriage, and funerary certificates. The notations of professions in these acts are likely more reputable than those that may be found in the lengthy embarkation lists or in the lists of aid distribution. In fact, in most cases, the priests who registered the civil acts knew the individuals, so the risks of mistakes or false declarations are less likely than in the lists elaborated by administrators, who were most often ignorant of the particular situation of each person.

It is in any case interesting to compare these two sources of data. To facilitate the comparison, I have transcribed the information in the form of a table:

TABLE 2

Trades professed by the Acadians to the priests on the occasion of a family event in the Nantes region, between 1775 and 1785.

Trades	Number Professed	Proportion
Ship Carpenters	72	33.33%
Sailors	68	31.48%
Day Workers	27	12.50%
Laborers	22	10.19%
Joiners	6	2.78%
Perreyeurs	5	2.31%
Long Saw Workers	5	2.31%
Shoemakers	6	2.78%
Artisans	5	2.32%
Cotton Printers	"some"	
Total[81]	216	100%

Source: Gérard-Marc Braud, *Les Acadiens en France, Nantes et Paimboeuf, 1775-1785, Approche généalogique*, Ouest Edition, 1999.

On the whole, we should not be surprised to find the results comparable to those of G. Bugeon and M. Le Faucheux. The wood-related trades, in the first table, occupy 36 percent of the individuals; here, exactly one third (33.3 percent) are designated as "ship carpenters." Ocean-going trades in the first table make up a little under 30 percent of the men; here just over 30 percent profess to be sailors. The same proportions of day workers are found almost exactly. Braud provides no quantitative indication of women's professions, though, in a later publication, he made the following list of activities mentioned in the baptismal, marriage, and funerary acts: domestic, day worker, chambermaid, spinner, dressmaker, washerwoman, tailor, knitter, weaver, servant, and sail-maker.[82]

Letters of Mastery

Finally, it is worth noting that, in the transcriptions of the lists made by Bugeon and Le Faucheux, the professions mentioned designate only the trade and field, and never the rank of hierarchy occupied within the group. We know that professional craftsmanship—a "distinctive privilege" of the Third Estate—was organized according to a very hierarchical structure. The essential body of the craftsman's trade was incorporated, that is, organized into a corps and, within this framework, aligned into three levels of professionals. At the top, the masters, titled with letters of mastery and proprietors of their businesses, dominated socially and economically. The associates, qualified workers of whom only a small minority would one day reach mastery, passed a sort of professional examination and received a certificate of apprenticeship. Then, the journeymen were "salaried workers [who] did not form part of the associates: having finished no apprenticeship, they were charged with the more tedious tasks, requiring little capability, and remained fixed in their condition, without even a theoretical possibility of achieving mastery." Finally, completing the portrait unofficially, we should add the apprentices, that is, young people in the course of being educated.[83]

It is probable, in the absence of indications on the lists, that the Acadians were practically all journeymen, practicing without letters of mastery or without having achieved the rank of associates, with the exception of Joseph Devau (to be examined further on).[84] Possession of letters of mastery would without a doubt have been mentioned if the individuals indeed had them: the status of being a master carpenter or companion carpenter would have been specified, for instance.[85] These letters of mastery were promised by the administration to many Acadian refugees and were requested by a number of those residing in France, but they were only rarely granted, however.

Upon their arrival in France, no Acadian had letters of mastery because these were not then in effect in the colonies. By this simple fact, the refugees were relegated to practice their professions in a lesser manner and only had the option of having jobs poorly paid by the day or by the task. As most of the refugees thought that their stay in France would be of short duration, it is likely that they did not try to remedy the situation right away.[86] It was only in 1773 that one sees surface the first requests to obtain letters of mastery for free (at that time it cost eight hundred *livres* for a certificate of master carpenter in Paris, for instance).[87]

The idea of proposing letters of mastery for the Acadians possibly came from Lemoyne. He had already stated the obstacles to economic integration engendered by the difficulty of obtaining such certificates for Germans for whom he also was responsible.[88] It seems that the idea of letters of mastery reflected an interpretation by Lemoyne of the instructions he had received for his term of 1773.[89] From the start of that year, Lemoyne solicited the intendant of the generality of Rouen for two dressmakers, "who are counting on [the] generosity [of the intendant] to obtain letters of mastery."[90] Lemoyne obtained a positive response for these women, since he wrote the following month: "I observe that at Le Havre there was no problem with the letters of mastery for those who stayed there," that is to say those who could not go to Poitou, because the "professions that they had adopted made them subject to membership in a guild. They were promised what was sufficient for them to practice." Note the slight nuance introduced into the passage by Lemoyne: it was no longer a question of letters of mastery, but of letters "sufficient to practice."[91] A month later, in another report, Lemoyne in fact only promises letters of mastery or "pardons having the same effect."[92] These were no longer authentic letters being promised, but "equivalent" documents and, from that moment, this was all that Lemoyne would commit to writing. Thus, in a summer 1773 account to the Controller-General at the end of his term, Lemoyne only speaks of "privileges" and of "protection," much more vague and less binding than authentic letters of mastery.[93]

In any case, the ministry subsequently endorsed Lemoyne's promise, since the Controller-General later wrote the intendant of Caen, Fontette: "the king authorizes me to gratuitously grant certificates of mastery to those who desire them and who need them to gain from their industry income to replace that which the burden of the State can no longer allow to continue."[94]

However, in the juridical and corporatist jungle of the *Ancien Régime*, things were not so simple. This promise, made without taking into account the very strong local resistance, was not kept. In the year afterward, one does find allusions to the government's desire to provide letters to the Acadians: thus the intendant of Caen reaffirms his determination to give certificates of mastery and, to do this, he asks his sub-delegate to draw up a list of Acadians remaining at Cherbourg who wanted them.[95] In March of the following year, Controller-General Terray again made a declaration of his intention to the intendant of Rouen.[96] However, in the following years, the only documents mentioning these letters of mastery were the petitions submitted by various Acadians.

The example of Joseph Devau is especially interesting. According to the various documents concerning him in a French National Archives file,[97] he was born around 1745 in French Acadia between the present villages of Shédiac and Bouctouche, facing Île Saint-Jean. These details are provided in a copy of his burial certificate from "the parish church of Saint-Sulpice in Paris."[98] He arrived at Rochefort (we know not how nor when), which he departed in 1763 to go to Paris "to visit," he writes, "the Abbé de l'Isle-Dieu, grand vicar of Québec, as well as the Abbé Le Loutre who know him personally and who are resident in the foreign missions, having taught him his religion when he was still very young and taught him the trade of carpenter which he continues today."[99] It is probable that the company of these two Abbés, themselves in relatively regular contact with the ministers, singularly facilitated Devau's relations with the administration. He benefited from a more advanced professional education than most of the Acadians, since he was the only refugee to be qualified as an associate carpenter.[100] In addition, Devau seems to have been "made a gentleman" by Louis XV. This, in any case, is what his wife assumed some years later without it being possible for us to verify.[101] Whether the assertion was true or false, it remained sufficiently plausible for Joseph Devau and his wife to brag about it, and it gives us an idea of the advantageous position that this carpenter held.

However, despite this strategic position within the network of supporters of the Acadians and his geographic proximity to the center of power, Joseph Devau had the greatest difficulty obtaining the letters of mastery that had been promised to him and that he requested starting in 1776. Indeed, Joseph claimed to have "dealt with the Controller-General" that year to establish his business. According to him, he was then to have been "granted the sum of 524 *livres* to purchase the tools needed for his trade" and was then promised "a letter of mastery *gratis*," which he never received. "I have always asked for my letter of mastery," he wrote, "although it has always been denied. I am presently asking that they have the generosity to grant me the sum of eight hundred *livres* which the mastery is worth in Paris, or the years' subsidies of 6*s* from 1776 to the present."[102] Three years later, Joseph renewed his request, repeating that he had received nothing since 1775 "despite being promised the mastery of his trade as carpenter." At the top of his letter, as a marginal inscription, is a hand written note signed by Pérusse: "I certify to have full knowledge of the promise that Mr. Turgot made to the named Joseph Devau, Acadian, to have him granted by the king letters of mastery of carpentry." This annotation again shows that Joseph Devau benefited from a network of significant relationships and from a certain reputation. It was only many months after he died, in October 1783,[103] after a year "of a lengthy, lingering illness," that his widow, Marie Michelle Théfruit (or Tefruit) obtained from the Controller-General the sum of 800 livres.[104]

After 1785: Solicitations for Letters of Mastery or for Subordinate Employment

The example of Joseph Devau, exceptional in many ways, provides an idea of the even greater difficulties that must have confronted the ordinary Acadians who sought to obtain letters of mastery. In fact, no proof exists that such letters were ever granted. And it is not because petitions for them were lacking. We find a fair number of them in the documentation, particularly after the departure of a large part of the Acadians to Louisiana, which suggests that the promises made to them had probably been renewed at that time. It is likely that, after the initial promises of Lemoyne, which, from all evidence, were not followed through, the government decided to again consider the question in 1785, with the aim of definitively settling the Acadian problem. It was in fact a question of seriously considering the situation of those who did not want to go to Louisiana, and especially of separating those who still should receive assistance from those who could live by their own means. However, to settle accounts with the latter, representatives of the government proposed to exchange letters of mastery or some regular income for a "renunciation of the balance of payment."[105] Declarations of intentions then followed each other: "I am seeking what would be most suitable for those who remain, whether some land or letters of mastery, or some subordinate employment,"[106] wrote, for instance, Charles-Alexandre de Calonne, the Controller-General, to the intendant of Caen. The following year, he raised the stakes: "I will try to procure for all of those who are capable either employment or letters of mastery, since it has been often demonstrated that we cannot procure land for them."[107]

Starting in 1785, therefore, we find the most documents relative to requests for certificates of mastery. In a long text recapitulating those who remained in Brittany after 1785, reference is often made to the Acadians requesting them. Thus, at Nantes, a list mentions fourteen individuals "to the aid of whom, following the offer of the minister, we could once and for all grant them letters of mastery for the trades they practice, and for which it is said they are very well trained." These fourteen individuals were in fact three Acadians and eleven "Frenchmen married to Acadian women." For the "Frenchmen" were needed "a mastery in bakery, in joinery, two in shoemaking, one as turner, one for surgery, one for weaving, one for dying fabrics, one for tannery, and, by means of these letters, their women will renounce their rights to payment." As for the three Acadians, there was a "good sailor who will have letters from a ship's captain once he will make another voyage for the king" and two joiners.

At Brest as well, one finds traces of a similar petition. The report specifies: "One [of] the Acadians [from Brest] has not received payment for a long time, because he wanders through the country as a wigmaker's assistant. He is asking for back pay and for letters of mastery as a wigmaker. The intendant thinks it would be suitable to grant him the latter favor, and that he could be denied the former."[108] Elsewhere, one finds "Eloi Thibaudeau, of Acadian nationality, 41 years old," who, in 1784, after twenty-two years of service "on the vessels of the king," requested a certificate of mastery of crew on the ships of the king or those of the Company of the Indies.[109] It seems that the intendant intervened in favor of this individual, for, on December 26, 1784, the naval commissioner at Lorient excused himself to the intendant for not having been able to employ Thibaudeau.[110] Eloi is again mentioned in 1786 in the previously cited report, in the part concerning Lorient: "a certificate of mastery of crew on the vessels of the king is needed for Eloi Thibaudeau. It seems that the intendant has requested it from the minister of the Navy."[111] This implies that Thibaudeau had evidently not yet received the certificate required by that date.

Sometimes it was not letters of mastery that were requested as such, but only authorization to legally practice an activity regulated by the guilds and corporations. A report by the sub-delegate of the intendancy of Morlaix dated August 1786, provides many details on the subject of three sisters—Margeurite Rosalie, Anne Suzanne, and Marie Esther Richard—who were tailors and seamstresses. In their regard, the report specifies: "As they are very busy, they do not request any aid payment. But, fearing that they will be stopped by the trade community of tailors, they request that they be granted complete authority to practice their profession."[112] In some cases, these letters were perhaps unnecessary, as affirmed by the mayor of Cherbourg, for instance: "There are no trade communities in our town, and everything is free here, therefore one does not have to think of providing them [the Acadians] with letters of mastery."[113]

In sum, since 1773, declarations of the intentions of the administrators and the ministers and the requests of the Acadians to obtain letters of mastery do not seem to have been followed through. The constant repetition of the requests emanating from the refugees and the example of Joseph Devau suggest that the letters were never distributed and that the promises of this kind were not fulfilled. Even if nothing confirms it, however, it is not inconceivable that, in some specific cases, the letters were obtained by some individuals after 1785, or that a financial compensation was paid, as was the case for Joseph Devau for example. Undoubtedly the obstacles to obtaining these certificates were many and, even when the letters were delivered to the refugees, there was no doubt still discontent, jealousy, or hostility felt on the part of the guilds or the local trade communities. Moreover, these letters probably did not have the same value as "true" certificates of mastery in the eyes of the local clients who must have been aware of their provenance.

Unemployment

We have described the professions declared by the Acadians and the manner in which they were regulated. Not all of the refugees were permanently employed, however, particularly at the start of their stay in France, for they disembarked in Brittany into a situation of endemic unemployment because of the war and the English blockade of the French coasts that had begun in January 1758,[114] which rendered the traditional maritime activities of fishing and trade extremely difficult.[115] This, at least, is what we learn from a jumble of varied but generally agreeing testimonies. As is usually the case, the less empowered elements of society suffered the most from unemployment. Ladvocat de La Crochais, reporting on the Saint-Malo region, under great stress after the English raid of Cancale and Paramé on June 18, 1758, noted that "the poor in the country have been without work for half of the year," which made him doubt that the Acadians would be able to find work either.[116] What was more concerning to La Crochais, having observed the Acadians working, was that he considered them little capable of it. Some time later, a document confirms that in the Saint-Malo region, "neither the time nor the place is suitable for them to earn [their living]."[117] The end of the war does not seem to have resolved the problem, or at least not immediately. Many months after the signing of the Treaty of Paris in February 1763, the mayor of Saint-Malo wrote that the Acadians "find no occupation, whether cultivating land, or in our ports, because the inhabitants of the country are frequently lacking such themselves, and our day workers only rarely find work either in the country or in town."[118]

In Normandy, the situation does not appear to have been any more favorable. The naval intendant at Le Havre explained that the Acadians "until now have only been able to work for the king, the trade being totally inactive here though it will nonetheless later return, but this will still not be a resource for them as the merchant who needs workers will only be interested in taking the best available." Note in this passage the underlying assumption of the poor quality of the work of the Acadians, who could not constitute a competitive manpower in the marketplace with the local workers. As for the situation at Dieppe and Cherbourg, it was worse than that of the great port at the mouth of the Seine. There was less "occasion still than at Le Havre to make use [of the Acadians] for jobs for which they would be suited."[119] At Cherbourg, according to the proceedings for dispensations of consanguinity, many Acadians simply declared that they "lived on the payment from the King."[120]

In 1763, a great inquest was launched by all of the intendants to try to find jobs for the Acadians.[121] Many of them shifted the responsibility to their sub-delegates.[122] The answers were all identical. The sub-delegate of Périgeux answered that there was no work in his district.[123] That of Saint-Lô wrote that "the reforming of the troops," that is, the disbanding of soldiers at the end of the war, "today provides this department with many workers that one cannot employ. The time is so bad that no one is working." The sub-delegate added that, according to him, "the sole means would be to employ them in working on the roads" and that it "would be suitable to grant them an exemption for 10 years from any tax which would help attach them to the country and forget about Canada."[124] Note, in passing, the expression "attach them to the country," which reveals a concern for integrating them through work that was scarce at the time. The sub-delegate of Vire gave practically the same answer.[125] At Avranches, as well, it was not possible to employ the "Canadians." If the specific problem of unemployment is not mentioned, the sub-delegate noted that there was neither any commerce nor any manufacturing that might employ them.[126] Finally, in the sub-delegation of Coutances, the intendant's representative could not arrive at any means of employing the refugees, either: "The general misery," he wrote, "brought by the surcharge of taxes and the cessation of commerce which has only slowly been reestablished . . . prevents one from employing the poor day workers and craftsmen that one finds begging in crowds in the towns and in the country. This is why the Canadians are not finding any occupation."[127] Some years later, Lemoyne would testify to the difficulties that the Acadians encountered in finding work in the years following their arrival in France. The commissioner affirmed that the Acadians very much wanted to work, and he blamed their situation on the endemic unemployment, along with their waiting to be settled as they had been promised, which prevented them from committing to activities of long duration. In his words, "the places where these families were deposited could barely furnish work to the people already in the area and the regular inhabitants."[128]

Nonetheless, it is possible that the situation improved subsequently in the regions where the Acadians were welcomed, for we only find rare mention of the problem later on in Brittany. Still, there were exceptions. For example, a report from the sub-delegate of Saint-Malo in July 1775, draws attention to the catastrophic situation of the refugees of the place, caused by, among other things, the lack of work: "These poor people . . . are finding nothing to earn in this season where there is no work in the port, and only little in the country to which one should add that, as wheat is expensive, the laborers are taking on almost no new workers."[129] Moreover, at the moment of the arrival of the Acadians, the sub-delegate at Poitiers advised against installing the Acadians in that town for, he wrote, "the fabrication of stockings and bonnets and linen work has been so scarce for some years that many poor people of the town itself are lacking this work, and for all the more reason so are the foreigners."[130] Some months later, actually, the Acadians who came to the area solicited work during the winter through Lemoyne, who wrote that they begged him "to procure occupation during the winter, six *sols* being too little on which their family could subsist and be maintained."[131] In short, this request shows that the refugees did not easily find work by themselves, and yet this appeal was the only one for work on the part of the Acadians found in the documents.

The Causes of Unemployment

We have seen that the problems of unemployment were not unique to the Acadians and affected other segments of the population. However, it is probable that the exiles were handicapped for the work market because they did not belong to the local community. Lemoyne judged that the Acadians had difficulty working because of the preference given "to naturals domiciled who in that respect would be preferred and in fact have been."[132] The "people of the region" and the "longtime regulars" were frequently opposed to the Acadians, as if to show that, if there were not enough work for the longtimers, there was even less for newcomers. Without necessarily speaking of discrimination (a word unknown before the end of the nineteenth century), it is likely that the Acadians had more trouble finding work than the locals because they were outside of the traditional networks of relationships. This "local preference" does not necessarily demonstrate hostility towards those who were often designated as "foreigners" in the community, but it does show an understandable tendency to first employ those whom one knows and with whom one is accustomed to working. Moreover, at the beginning—as the comments of Ladvocat de La Crochais cited above demonstrate—the Acadians were judged incompetent in many areas, because of prejudices and perhaps because their methods of working were different from those in France. And it is not impossible that the inverse phenomenon also occurred, namely, that some individuals—like the many intendants whom we have spoken of above—employed the Acadians by priority because they knew the distress of their situation. But, in this case, the Acadians perhaps aroused the jealousy of the other inhabitants, some of whom were undoubtedly hardly treated any more favorably.

It is nonetheless possible that ill will was also directed towards the Acadians from a feeling of injustice due to the favors that they received from the government. Elsewhere we will study the hostility of the populations to encountering the Acadians. More specifically, regarding their labor, a report written by Lemoyne indicates a significant problem that our contemporary epoch might describe as "social dumping":

> The people believe that [the Acadians] who are working are stealing their bread; they are convinced that they are being hired to work for less because of the support of assistance they receive. When they disembarked at Saint-Malo . . . the country was depopulated by the quantity of men, especially younger men, who either died during the war or who were still in the prisons, and there was infinitely more work available than men. Far from being a burden, they were useful. . . . As the country has been repopulated, they have become a burden.[133]

In sum, the locals accused the Acadians of accepting lower salaries—thanks to the supplemental income that they received from the Navy—and therefore of bringing unfair competition for labor. This testimony—coming from an exterior observer—is, however, sufficiently unusual that it should necessarily be taken with precaution. The only other tangible indication of such hostility on the subject of the Acadians' labor was a list of petitions by the latter, recopied and sent by Lemoyne to Blossac in November of the same year and already mentioned above. This list solicited jobs to complement the six *sols* payment. But not for any price: the Acadians were careful to request work "that takes nothing from the people of the country, if possible." "Jealousy is an obstacle that will only increase hatred if they are paid less than customary," added LeMoyne. "Have the good will to remark that the inhabitants of Châtellerault consider the Acadians . . . as additional manpower that renders their own much less valuable."[134]

In brief, the Acadians were probably found caught between two constraints difficult to reconcile: having to work in order to supplement their assistance, at the risk of passing for profiteers or work-thieves, or having to refuse the salaries proposed to them (perhaps lower than the usual pay), and thereby be considered idle lay-abouts. It is hardly surprising, in this context, that some took up a third way: contraband. In fact, the Acadians tried to accumulate all of the income, legal or illegal, that they could.

Income From the Work

How might we estimate the income the Acadians received from their work? The question is difficult to answer, or even to provide generalities about. The little information that we may glean from the texts provides few numeric indications or, where so, they are very imprecise, apart from that considered above in the discussion about the employment of day workers. We can make no use of the commentary, for instance, of the administrator who complained about "work that produces so little and that is so short in duration" and could not provide a living for the large Acadian families.[135] Mistral was not any more precise when he indicated, in 1767, that "some Acadians practice the trade of sailor and gain a bit more, and enough to exempt themselves personally from the king's assistance."[136]

Conclusion

Exploitation of the Acadians?

It is likely that some Acadians were victims of abuse by employers who may have exploited their vulnerability. Could the exiles really have been that particular about the salaries and employment proposed to them (as is presumed in some texts cited above)? We can only speculate on the subject, but from the fact of some cautionary moves by Lemoyne, it would seem that many individuals possibly did try to abuse the situation. Thus, on the arrival of the refugees in Poitou, Lemoyne assumed that certain locals had "proposed some spinning to the women but at a price that shows the abuse that one sought to make of their needs." He then asked the intendant if it were not be possible "to procure [spinning] for them at the same price as the manufacturers pay."[137] The same misadventures had already happened to the Germans whom the commissioner had been responsible for at Saint-Jean-d'Angély: "It did not take long for me to notice that the greed of the moment dictated the terms of employment and that, far from wanting to settle them [the Acadians], they only sought to receive their labor at a very low price, without assuring them a certain station."[138]

In the preceding pages, we have tried to closely examine the daily activities of the Acadians. Beyond the list of professions and some insights about their daily life, it is very difficult to evaluate what might have been the conditions of life and work of the refugees. To pursue this further, one would have to examine locally and in depth the documents produced by the guilds, for example. Working from the administrative archives, the social integration of the Acadians can only be understood indirectly. If we can state that the Acadians practiced various professions, it is more difficult to know what their exact station was within these professions. Nevertheless, it seems that, within the corps of the strongly regulated trades, the majority of the refugees occupied only temporary posts, of little potential and not very remunerative. The petitions to obtain letters of mastery eloquently demonstrate the difficulty that they had in being accepted by the local guilds, which did not facilitate their integration.

Chapter IX

A Sufficient Supplement: A Factor In The Integration?

The Cost of the Aid

WHAT BURDEN DID THE CUMULATIVE assistance provided the Acadians represent within the budget of the kingdom? It is difficult to estimate the precise impact of the assistance, at least until 1781, the date when Necker had the first official accounting of the receipts and expenses of France published. Martin estimates that "the sums paid by the Treasury in the name of 'Aid to the Acadians,' from 1763 to 1778, reached around 300,000 *livres* per year, which, for those fifteen years alone, amounts to a total of about 4,500,000 [*livres*]."[1]

These numbers join those that have been reconstituted from existing documents, allowing us to calculate an annual average of expenses of around 270,000 *livres*.[2] Evidently, the total cost was much higher, since we must add the salaries of the administrative personnel and the costs of the correspondence, which are clearly impossible to quantify and were in any case included in the overall expenses of governmental functions. We must add other expenses that are difficult to estimate, as well, like the sums paid to hospitals for sick or invalid Acadians, the particular treatment of the Bellefontaine and d'Entremont families, and various other assistance from the king that we have mentioned above, including the cost of the initiatives to settling in Belle-Île-en-Mer and in Poitou. Documents also exist that present more or less exact amounts of expenses made, whether for the supplements or for other costs like those of the settlement at Poitou; their credibility, however, is quite variable. The lists of accounts and the correspondence from the Controller General or the naval administration—where the money originated—are clearly much more credible than are the various letters like those of the Abbé de l'Isle-Dieu or of Pérusse, which sometimes indicate astronomical sums that clearly are exaggerated. These documents nonetheless roughly confirm the average amount mentioned above.

The expenses for the Acadians probably neared three hundred thousand *livres* per year.[3] If we add all of the expenses of the government over twenty-seven years, we arrive at an amount in the range of 10 million *livres tournois*.[4] The exact total was, however, probably less than this, since all of the Acadians did not always receive their payment and it was partially reduced starting in 1778. The effect of these distributions of aid on the budget of the State therefore remained modest.

Six Sous Per Day: A Consequential Sum?

In the previous section we described the methods of distribution of the assistance to the refugees and the total cost of this assistance to the State. We have seen how, in the best of cases, the Acadians received six *sous* per day per person. But what did this sum, equivalent to 108 *livres* per year, concretely represent?[5] Ernest Martin qualifies this sum as being generous and consequential.[6] But his desire to represent France in the best light leads him to bend the facts. First of all, we have seen above that, contrary to what he affirms, all of the Acadians did not always and at all times receive six *sous* per day—far from it. The situation was much more complicated.

To be able to effectively estimate what the sums distributed by the government amounted to, we must take into consideration many factors, including estimates of the sums that they may have received apart from this assistance and of the expenses that a typical household had to pay. An estimation of this kind is practically impossible.[7]

In the matter of the receipts received, we can mainly distinguish several aspects: the salaries paid to the Acadians who worked, the charitable aid other than that of the government, and finally the sums or goods brought or sent from Acadia. The expenses paid by the Acadians are more difficult to calculate. The most sizeable was undoubtedly that for bread, which deserves particular attention. But the Acadians did not consume only bread: they also had to be lodged and have heat, elements that are often mentioned in the documentation.

The Salary of a Day-Worker

Martin compares the six *sous* per person distributed by the government to the salary of a day-worker of Poitou that he fixes at "12 *sols*, plus nourishment," the day-worker then having to feed all of his family with his salary. But the day-workers were the most pitiful of the peasants, living in dire conditions.[8] Most could not feed a family with their salary alone and supplemented this, in the country, with other activities, a garden and the fruits of the work of their wives and children, who began contributing at a very young age. But it is very difficult to estimate the salaries in France in the eighteenth century.[9] The problems are many: the sources remain rare and many activities and sorts of work were remunerated in kind; what is more, the regional differences were great, and it is extremely complicated to outline national trends. G. Frêche notes the importance of local or regional deviations.[10] Frêche indicates that "within the proximity of Toulouse a wine grower in 1724 garnered between 24 to 30 *sous* per day; but only 15 to 16 in the diocese of Montauban, 9 in those of Rieux and Comminges. On the eve of the Revolution, a day-worker earned 30 *sous* per day at Bordeaux, 24 to 28 in Rochefort or in La Rochelle, 20 in the Bordeaux area or in Pau, 15 at Tarbes and in Limoges, 11 to 12 *sous* in the Aquitaine countryside."[11] Michel Morineau estimates the salary of a day-worker at the start of the century to be 112 *livres* per year, with 250 days of work, making for a wage of 9 *sous* per day.[12] Contrary to some accepted notions, there was not any equality in the salaries under the *Ancien Régime*: the differences were very large depending on levels of qualification. In 1746, a master carpenter earned 80 *sous* per day, but his workers only 25 to 26 *sous*.[13] The salary of 12 *sous* per day indicated by Martin is therefore hardly typical. The naval commissioner, Lemoyne, estimated the salary of the Acadians at Saint-Malo at 30 *sous* per day at the maximum, and from this sum holidays, sick days, and days of unemployment had to be deducted, reducing the salary to 14 or 15 *sols*. Lemoyne estimates this amount as insufficient to feed a family and added that many workers did not earn as much as this.[14]

LeMoyne's calculations seem to be realistic.[15] In any case, they do not appear to have convinced the Acadians that they were impracticable, though they were possibly counting on continuing to combine their salaried work with the assistance, despite the commissioner's threats.

The Problem of Combining Income

Another issue substantially affected the income of the Acadians. Was it possible for them to combine their supplement with their income from work? Here again, the question is relatively complex and the administration approached it in a contradictory manner.

At the start of the Acadians' sojourn in France, the instructions from Berryer were very clear: those who were hired to work could no longer receive assistance. For example, the inhabitants of Île Saint-Jean who went from Cherbourg to Le Havre to work there as day laborers in the port did not have the right to receive any assistance beyond the payment for their labor.[16] The same goes for those in Rochefort. This prohibition was repeated many times. Secondary effects of this policy were soon felt, however, when the administration became aware that this inflexibility did not encourage the Acadians to work, since the salary for their labor barely exceeded the amount of their assistance. At the same time, many Acadians sought to accumulate the aid and work on the side (no doubt working more or less at the whim of the administration). Many documents refer to the Acadians working and receiving the supplement at the same time.

At least once, because there was a lack of sailors and the government resorted to this measure as a solution, the ability to work and to receive the supplement at the same time was officially proposed to the Acadians by Choiseul.[17] Although the official prohibition made to the Acadians of not accumulating income along with the supplement from the king apparently was never lifted, it seems that local commissioners proved to be much more lax, and that, following the order of Choiseul, the practice became quite widespread. In 1766, a certain number of Acadians combined the income drawn from their work with their supplement, apparently without it troubling the *ordonnateur* of Le Havre: "they have assured me that they would prefer to remain in Le Havre with their subsistence, and with what they might earn as day workers, than to go and settle on the sea and sand," wrote Mistral after the refusal of the Acadians to settle on territory newly put into cultivation in Flanders.[18] Praslin found nothing to object to the practice, since he wrote to Choiseul in 1767: "The six *sous* per day that the king supplies these families [in Saint-Malo] not being nearly sufficient for them to subsist on, they are obliged to work to obtain the necessary surplus."[19] Other indications describe the combinations of incomes that occurred, such as a petition sent by four Acadians in their sixties who complained that they only received six *sous* per day "as do all of the young people who are capable of working to alleviate themselves."[20] In his turn, Lemoyne endorsed this practice and proposed that the supplement be held in reserve for the Acadians employed in the army until the time when they were discharged; he imagined that the little lump sum saved would serve them well in getting settled.[21] Some months later Lemoyne pleaded on behalf of a chambermaid whose payment had been suspended (he guessed accurately that it was not because she was working that it had been withdrawn).[22]

On his arrival in the ministry, Necker then prohibited the practice of combining incomes and refused payment to those who worked as well as to those only suspected of doing so.[23] Nonetheless, it is difficult to evaluate to what degree these measures were actually applied.

Contraband Tobacco

Before the prohibition of combining authorized work with the assistance from the State, and in order to cope with the problems of unemployment, the Acadians *en masse* fell back on other, less legal activities. A good dozen of them were arrested for dealing in contraband tobacco during just the years 1765 to 1769.[24]

It is difficult to estimate the amount of the fraud perpetrated by the refugees: a study of contraband tobacco in the eighteenth century in the region of Saint-Malo does not even mention the Acadians.[25] However, we have found at least nine cases implicating the refugees for the period from late December 1765 to June 1769, either for the crime itself, or for disturbing the peace or rebellion associated with such trafficking.[26] And these cases implicating the Acadians were undoubtedly just the tip of the iceberg.[27] The behavior of some exiles did indeed draw the attention of the employees of the income farms of the king, who suspected the Acadians of engaging in the crime massively and collectively. This is what was said, for example, in the account of events that occurred at an inn kept by Jean Thibaudeau and his wife at Pleudihen. The employees of the income farm of Saint-Malo wrote:

> Having been informed that *nearly all of the Acadian inhabitants of the parish of Pleudihen daily* made *armed* transports and dispersal of contraband tobacco and other prohibited merchandise, [we] went to said parish on March 8, 1767 where [we] laid in wait about fifty steps from the house of the man named Jean Thibaudeau, one of them, a cabaret-keeper.[28]

It is very likely that many Acadians were implicated, in varying degrees, in these fraudulent activities that must have involved a significant amount. What is also clear is that a portion of them maintained conflicting relationships with the customs officers, as various "rebellion" trial transcripts mentioning the Acadians demonstrate. Surely, these rebellions were not that exceptional: tobacco fraud was massive in the region of Saint-Malo and this trafficking was supported by "the great majority of inhabitants" who collaborated, actively or passively, notably by purchasing the contraband tobacco in great quantities.[29]

Word of the implication of the Acadians in the tobacco fraud went to the highest levels, on many occasions. Witness a letter from Choiseul dated 1767:

> I see where you have pointed out to me from the report that [the intendant of Caen] sent me . . . that there remained at Saint-Servan of the Acadian families only the most corrupt who only stay there from indolence, a desire for contraband and the guaranteed subsistence that they receive from the generosity of the king.[30]

The following year, Choiseul's cousin, Praslin, was in turn warned by informants of trafficking by certain Acadians. He intervened with more compassion, however, in favor of a refugee in an unfortunate position. The latter, Victor Forest, called "Mitouche," had been arrested on April 17, 1768, in the company of two of his compatriots, Pierre Le Blanc and Jacques Terriot, in possession of 52 pounds and 4 ounces of tobacco.[31] On May 21, 1768, appearing before the tribunal of commerce of Saint-Malo, each of the trio was condemned to pay 1,000 *livres* as penalty.[32] On July 29, 1768, following a standard procedure, the king's prosecutor granted the request of the prosecutor of the income farms of the king to convert the unpaid penalty of Victor Forest into punishment in the galleys.[33] In a letter addressed to the Controller-General, on November 11, 1768, Praslin asked for clemency for Forest:

> [Forest] was transferred to the prison of Rennes to await there being chained and brought to the galleys of Brest. This man belonged to an old family that, together with all of the Acadians, requested clemency for him; he is the father of seven children whom he supported by his work and his crime is a result not of a penchant for crime, but of the misery in which they all were reduced in the winter, having only 6*s* per day.[34]

Nothing indicates that clemency was actually granted to Victor Forest, but it is likely that the Controller-General did not oppose Praslin. Forest figures some years later in a list of indebted Acadians in the Saint-Malo region, but we cannot assume that he had not served his time in the interim. [35]

The Acadians probably became engaged in contraband for at least three reasons. First of all, the conditions of their daily life were especially precarious, and, as such, they likely all the more often were asked to transport prohibited merchandise.[36] Moreover, many witnesses described their sizeable personal consumption of tobacco, and they were not accustomed to paying taxes on this product.[37] And, finally, it is probable that their ability in matters of navigation, their knowledge of the English language (learned in Acadia or during their captivity in Great Britain between 1756 and 1763), and the ties that they maintained with some inhabitants of Jersey especially predisposed them to actively participate in the smuggling.[38] The Acadians also engaged in smuggling contraband products to the North American colonies, as shown, for example, by the trafficking witnessed between Saint-Pierre and Miquelon and Nova Scotia.[39]

How much income might the trafficking have brought the Acadians? It is probable that the trade in "false tobacco" was very profitable for the various Saint-Malo associates, despite the risks entailed. However, it is very difficult to estimate the payments that the participants may have received, particularly the Acadians. The only tangible indications that we have on the subject are those from the July 1768 interrogation of Honoré Caret and Pierre Landry. It is not certain that the two accused told the truth, as they likely sought to minimize the amounts they had received. But the information that they gave was plausible, all the same, and remains the only such available. Thus, Caret, "navigator by profession," declared that a cargo of tobacco seized "belonged properly to Gascon and Pierre," two accomplices who escaped, and "that he was only paid 30 *livres* in silver for his voyage and to command the boat, that he knew nothing of the price of tobacco or of his destination, but only that they would disembark at the port of Saint-Jean." As for Landry, he claimed to have received no wage, but only a certain quantity of tobacco. He declared "that he had been employed by said Gascon and Pierre to make the voyage from Jersey, that he had no wage but only a portion of a half a hundred of the tobacco in the boat, that he knew nothing of the price because said Gascon and Pierre had made the purchase, that they were to sell it for him and render him an account."[40] A hundred corresponded to a measure of a hundred pounds.[41] The portion going to Pierre Landry would thus have been fifty pounds of tobacco. According to the testimony of Anselme Boudereau, reported in a hearing brought by the customs officers, the tobacco was sold for around twenty-seven *sous* per pound (weight).[42] In all, then, the profit for Pierre Landry would have been about seventy *livres*. The sums that the intermediaries received seem to have always been relatively small. Some individuals thus transported small quantities of tobacco for modest sums: a woman was said to have received six *sols* for taking six pounds of tobacco from the town of Saint-Malo; another received a promise of three *livres* to pass the tobacco with the town.[43]

It should be noted that the quantities seized in the three cases implicating the Acadians Jean Thibaudeau and Étienne Terriot (484 pounds), Caret and Landry (1,637 pounds), and Joseph Aucoin and Pierre Boudiche (398 pounds and 6 ounces), were larger than average. Indeed, according to the calculation of Aubert, of the 282 sentences in which the weight of the tobacco seized was specified, 60 percent of the seizures were of less than ten pounds of tobacco; and seizures between ten and one hundred pounds and those higher than one hundred pounds were, respectively, 25 percent and 15 percent of the sentences. As for the Acadians, these were three seizures of the six that exceeded one hundred pounds, and the seizure from the boat piloted by Caret and Landry was even cited by Aubert as an example of a particularly good one.

In all, it is still very difficult to estimate the profit made by the Acadians from this tobacco trafficking. A puzzle remains: how were the Acadians supposed to pay the 1,000 *livres* to which they were condemned, considering their precarious level of existence? It is possible that their aforementioned associates paid at least a portion of the penalty. It is also possible that some Acadians were involved in transforming the tobacco into powder (its most popular form) for wages that it also remains difficult to estimate.[44]

Finally, the Acadians did not just transport "*faux tabac*" ["false" or bootleg tobacco] but also contraband codfish.[45] The prosecutors of the income farms of the king also asked that Boudereau be condemned to a penalty of 3,000 *livres* in "payment" for these codfish.

Prices and Penalties: Geographic and Temporal Variations

Although the sum of six *sous* per day would not have been insignificant in 1758 for a family budget, we must consider that the prices of consumption evolved considerably between 1758 and 1785. In fact, although the regional and geographic variations were great, there was a general rise in prices in France starting in 1730. This increase continued until at least 1778, the year when an agricultural recession took hold, affecting the whole end of the reign of Louis XVI.[46] Moreover, the prices varied enormously from one year to another, depending on the seasons and the product. During the stay of the Acadians in France, therefore, prices increased in a moderate but continual manner, with occasional surges. The "purchasing power" of the Acadians gradually declined. Starting in 1768, the circumstances worsened for the French population: bread became expensive and the recession culminated with crises of subsistence in 1770-1771 and 1775, and with the famine of 1788-1789.

Table 3

Acadians Implicated in Proceedings for Tobacco Fraud in the Saint-Malo Region (1766-1768)

Names of Acadians	Date of Incident	Court Date	Documents Found	Rebellion	Remarks	Tobacco Seized	Penalty
Pierre & Georges Haché	Dec. 31 1765	Aug. 23 1766	J[47]	No	The judgment states that Pierre and Georges Haché were Brothers and "of Acadian origin"	6 ozs.	Released[48]
Pierre Duon	Oct. 3 1766	Dec. 20 1766	J	No	"Pierre Duon, of Acadian origin"	1.5 lb.	1000*l*[49]
Jean Thibaudeau & Ètienne Terriot	March 8 1767	May 13 1768	CP	Yes	Criminal complaint for "armed rebellion against the employees of the farm and contraband in tobacco"	398 lbs., 6 ozs.	1000*l*.
Anselme Boudereau	March 3, 1767	May 16, 23 & 30 1767	R	No	Anselme Boudereau was accompanied by four other persons, at least two of whom were Acadians. Seizure of tobacco and three bales of codfish.	?	Released?[50]
"Many Acadians"	Nov. 5, 1767	–	PC	Yes	The principal accused, E. Zerby, was accompanied by women "either Acadians or living in the area."	–	–
Joseph Aucoin & Pierre Boudiche	Jan. 21, 1768	May 21, 1768	J	No	Were judged in the company of Yves Le Neuder, called la Fleur and Julien Saquet (not Acadians, *a priori*).	484 lbs.	1000*l*.
Pierre Le Blanc, Jacques Terriot, Victor Forest	April 17 1768	May 21 1768	PV	No	Victor Forest, called Mitouche, was condemned on July 29, 1768, to the galleys for default in paying his penalty.	52 lbs. 4 ozs.	1000*l*.
Honoré Caret & Pierre Landry	July 15 1768	Sept. 16 1768	PV		Were in the company of "Le Gros," Acadian, and two other persons.	1637 pounds	1000*l*.
"Many Acadians"	June 11 1769	–	PV	Yes	Many "individuals," "taken with wine," among whom the employees recognized "many Acadians," insulted and attacked the "tax gatherers."[51]	–	–

Differences Between Taxes and Prices

If wages and prices varied depending on the region, this was also very much the case for the taxes that strongly influenced purchasing power.[52] Thus, taking an extreme example, but one that gives an idea of the whole, the price of salt, with tax included, might vary between 1/2 *sous* and 12 *sous* per pound depending on the region.[53] From this perspective, the Acadians in Cherbourg—who on many occasions requested exemptions from the taxes on salt and tobacco—were less well fortunate than those living in Brittany, a region with a low rate of taxes and where there was no salt tax whatsoever.[54] This is what Necker pragmatically stated in his *Traité sur l'administration des finances* in 1785.[55]

Before the Revolution, food remained the primary budgetary concern of poor families: "The sole expense of bread for a family . . . normally took up almost half of the earnings, and took 80 to 90 percent in a famine, and sometimes more."[56] Men consumed nearly two and a half pounds of bread daily, women one and a half pounds, and a child of twelve one pound.[57] Are these quantities perhaps a little too high?[58] One observer was indeed surprised, regarding the Acadians—having just disembarked, weak and hungry from the deprivations of the transatlantic voyage: "These people seem very lively, and I doubt if they do not eat two pounds of bread per person."[59] According to one author, before 1750 bread was normally worth three to four *sous* per pound, though, after poor harvests, it could reach six to eight *sous*.[60] Such estimates are difficult to assess, at least regarding Cherbourg, since in one letter an Acadian is happy that the price of bread had fallen to a much lower level: "for a year bread has been at a better price than it has been before as seven years ago there was famine in France. Bread was worth four *sols* per pound and now it is worth no more than two *sols* a pound."[61] However, even at two *sous* per pound of bread a man working would consume five *sous* per day in bread alone. Other food was yet more expensive: "those accustomed to having milk are obliged to pay 4*s* for a pot of milk and 8-9*s* for a pound of butter," wrote the witness quoted above.[62] In fact, the daily sums dispensed for nourishment for vagabonds imprisoned in the poor houses rose, in 1767, to five *sous* per day per person, allowing the purchase of "a pound and a half of bread, four ounces of vegetables and two ounces of rice only with difficulty."[63] In sum, six *sous* did not go very far at all.

The "generosity" of the French government described by Martin takes on yet another aspect if we compare the sums distributed to the Acadians with other contemporary incomes. First of all, the Canadian officers or those who served in Canada and returned to France, nobles for the most part, received between three and six times more, that is to say between 300 and 600 *livres* per year.[64] These individuals certainly made use of other income and capital, as shown by the rich inventories found after their deaths in the departmental archives of Indre-en-Loire.[65] The English prisoners of war also received sums superior to those obtained by the Acadians, though it is possible that these sums were then reimbursed by England. In 1758, the Minister of the Navy, Berryer, recommended not giving more than "24*s* to the officers of the vessels of the king of England and 12*s* to the Navy guards."[66] Finally, in 1771, the minister de Boynes asked for a benefit of 3,000 *livres* for the Abbé Le Loutre.[67]

Contemporary Opinion

The documentation also often provides evaluations of the amounts of assistance. From this perspective, the correspondents are all in agreement: six *sous* per day was insufficient to live on. So, from the start, the administrators interceded with the government so that higher sums might be paid to the Acadians. The Minister of the Navy thus answered the intendant of Amiens that "the aid of six *sous* that I . . . have provided per day is all that I can do [for the Acadians] in the current circumstances."[68] Solicited again on the same subject, the minister explained himself very frankly: "the aid that has been arranged for these families being only temporary, it has been set at a moderate sum per day in order that they seek by their own employment to procure a more advantageous livelihood."[69] Some years later, the mayor of Morlaix did not hesitate to qualify the payment of six *sous* per day as "a small amount."[70] The Abbé de l'Isle-Dieu wrote regarding four young Acadians, "they are very poor as their only resource is the 6*s* per day of subsistence that the king provides them."[71] One year later, the commissioner of divisions of Cherbourg produced a touching portrayal of the misery of the Acadian families who were unfortunate enough to have only the supplement to count on for their subsistence:

> Their situation would surely affect you if you saw it . . . there are . . . women who, forced to remain in bed from their illnesses, do not have a pair of sheets to change, others only have one blouse, others have no clothes to keep them warm; and added to this is the high price of ordinary foodstuff, which increases day by day.[72]

The situation worsened when prices increased and yet more when the decision was made to reduce the supplement to three *sous* for the children. The Minister of the Navy himself was worried about it in 1768. It is impossible for the refugees, he wrote, "especially since the rise in price for bread, to maintain themselves with the subsistence . . . of 6*s* per man or woman and 3*s* for each of their children under 11 years. Work only affords them a feeble supplement."[73] In 1771, Le Loutre pleaded on behalf of the Acadians to the minister in similar terms, concluding that, "for three years we have seen them go for 7 to 8 months without receiving any of the subsistence that his majesty agreed to grant them, and during the winter of these three years there have been deaths from hunger and misery."[74] It is notable that this testimony by Le Loutre is the only document affirming that Acadians had died of hunger in France.[75] Some years later, Pérusse estimated that it was impossible for the refugees to hope to live in Poitou or at Saint-Malo without spending at least one to ten *sous* per day per person. It would be impossible to provide them with meat and wheat bread for the amount of their assistance.[76] Lemoyne remarked later that the cost of living in Châtellerault was much higher, as the inhabitants abused the situation and sold produce for higher than the usual amounts.[77]

The Acadians themselves also affirmed that the payment distributed to them was very meager to live on. Nonetheless, it seems to have been possible to survive on this sum, although in deplorable conditions, since Marguerite Landry wrote in 1773 to her brothers-in-law: "Since coming to France we have only received the supplement of six *sols* that the king has granted us. You must know from this that we are in a sad enough situation and are unable to earn anything on our own in this country."[78] Other Acadians complained, "the sustenance pension of 3*s* per day is not sufficient for the children considering the high price of foodstuff," and they requested back payment or, for those individuals who had not been included, to be added to a list to receive the assistance.[79] On the other hand, even if the Acadians often complained about their miserable condition, they never asked for more than the six *sous* that was distributed to them,[80] which was still described in a petition as a "very small pension."[81] In a later document[82]—addressed to the Spanish authorities, therefore more openly critical of France—Olivier Terriot, summing up the conditions of daily life of his compatriots in Nantes before their departure for Louisiana, judged that the supplement only allowed a "miserable" life: "they lived miserably until 1785 . . . . I say miserably for their advance [sic] which was for six *sous* per day for each, was soon reduced to three *sous*, awaiting, they were told, fulfillment of the promise that had been made to provide them with lands." Though testimony like that of Terriot is rare, it is plausible that unofficial or oral requests had been made to individuals locally responsible for distributing the assistance.

Should we then believe the documents about the insufficiency of the sums distributed? We should surely not go to the opposite extreme, like Martin. The local administrators had every interest in requesting supplementary assistance from the government for those in their care; it did not cost them much. At least one document indicates that the Acadians were able to put aside a portion of the aid distributed to them. Thus, in 1765, a document mentions the case of the Broussards (an Acadian sister and two brothers), who had been robbed "of a sum of 110*l*. saved from their subsistence." It is nonetheless quite possible that, in this case, the two brothers had worked and received the assistance as well, which, by combining the two wages and the three supplements, would have allowed them to live in relative comfort and to save the sum "which they had arranged in order to teach a trade to their sister," as the text specifies.[83] Many other documents lead us to believe that the Acadians were not all completely in misery.

For example, at Nantes, one finds in the municipal council's 1782 registers that a deliberation followed the request[84] for an exemption from "transporting the troops"[85] made by Basile Henry to the intendant and brought by the latter to the municipality for the council's advice. According to what we can reconstitute from the text, Henry had bought some cattle, and it is possible that his neighbors asked that he assist in the transportation of troops and lodging of soldiers, a double obligation to which individuals of a certain income level were subject. The members of the municipal council, sympathetic, took up for Basile: "Some people have taken as a sign of high income [and] of being well off the cattle that he [Basile] had bought just previously, but they are wrong. He made this purchase with money from a benefactor in the hopes that it would be a means to supply the needs of his family more completely," specified the "bureau."[86] Probably summing up Henry's own arguments, the councilors explained that the Acadian was able to feed his family only with much difficulty. They therefore advised that Henry be exempted from the obligation. Even if it is difficult to have an exact idea of the material status of Basile Henry from this text, the discussion about the difficulty he had feeding his family, which the municipality echoed, should be taken with caution. A pair of cattle at that time was worth about 300 *livres*, a consequential sum that certainly proves that Henry was not so miserable as he indicated.[87] Moreover, we also find at Nantes the case of an Acadian woman, a servant, with a dowry in 1790 of a sum—sizeable at the time—of 1,200 *livres*, the origin of which is unknown.[88] In sum, all of the Acadians were probably not completely miserable, speaking objectively, nor relatively—in comparison with the status of their neighbors.

Conclusion

Beyond these various discussions, it is very difficult to know exactly what the sums distributed meant to the Acadians. Were they sufficient to live on without working on the side? It seems that some Acadians, ill or in abject poverty, were only able to live from the supplement alone in a miserable manner. However, it is probable that they then received assistance of other kinds: lodging for free or at reduced rates, various charity from their neighbors, from the family or their compatriots. Surely six *sous* per day was not an insignificant sum. It undoubtedly represented a bit higher amount for the refugees of the Saint-Malo region than for those of Cherbourg, who were subject to heavy taxes. This sum was surely also more significant upon the arrival of the Acadians in France, when bread was still a relatively good buy, than at the time of their departure to Louisiana, when not only had the supplement been nominally reduced from six to three *sous*, but further by the depressed value of the money. Thus, contrary to the impression that is made from reading the text of Martin, this assistance—even at the start—was probably barely sufficient to live on, and then very modestly: it scarcely allowed a man to buy his daily bread in those years when the harvest was not too bad.

The question of whether or not France was generous to the Acadians is ultimately a simple matter of approximation: we can either say that she did the minimum necessary or that she did the maximum possible. And, besides, that is not the real question: especially from the perspective of our contemporary criteria, it is not a question of judging the still embryonic mechanics of assistance from the State. As often in these cases and at least in reconsidering the structures of the society of the *Ancien Régime*, the margin of budgetary maneuvering was slim. The sum was relatively generous for those who could find work on the side and thus receive the payment as a supplement. Though this arrangement was perhaps tolerated on the local level, it was nonetheless forbidden by the ministers, who only allowed the fathers of large families to combine work pay with the supplement for their children.[89] On numerous other occasions, the Secretary of State provided instructions that those Acadians who found work should be struck from the lists for assistance. Precisely because of this official prohibition to not combine assistance and employment, it is difficult to know if the Acadians worked as a group or not, at least at the beginning of their stay in France. After their departure from Poitou, there is no doubt that almost all of the Acadians worked or sought to work, since the payment was considerably reduced, the overdue payments were very large, and, consequently, the Acadians could no longer count on them to live on.

For those, on the other hand, who did not have the ability to work—the elderly or the extremely poor, especially—the supplement, when it was paid, was without a doubt just barely sufficient for them to not die of hunger. A great fragility thus characterizes the situation of the Acadians. The supplement made them comparable to salaried individuals and, like all salaried people of societies where inflation is not stabilized or where the prices of materials of primary necessity are greatly fluctuating, the Acadians were in a precarious position.[90] In total, if the six *sous* had been distributed at the proper time, it would have probably constituted a relatively high sum for those who could supplement it with remunerative activity, notably because of the rarity of currency in the society of the *Ancien Régime*. But the fact that the assistance was probably very irregularly paid, that it was decreased for children starting in 1768, then for all starting in 1778, obliged the Acadians to contract sizeable debts, which in turn led a large number of families into a bind of dependency and inextricable poverty.

The Assistance—A Factor of Integration for the Acadians?

To conclude, we must return to our initial inquiry. Did the assistance contribute to the economic integration of the Acadians? We have previously seen how the unanimous opinion of the administrators was that the assistance had rather nefarious economic effects in the short and the long term for the Acadians: the fear of losing their supplement made the Acadians lazy. However, it is difficult to know to what degree these accusations were not chiefly motivated by the primary objective of the administrators: to lessen expenses.

An Aid to the Integration

In reality, we should not let things be clouded by this first impression spread by the administrators. It very well does seem as if the economic integration of a good number of the Acadians was achieved, at least in part, thanks to the governmental assistance. The distributions of these few *sous* allowed the Acadians to survive and sometimes to purchase the basic tools necessary for their labor. But they form the silent mass that only rarely appears in the documentation, for they did not pose any problems. It is probable that the large majority of individuals who refused to go to Louisiana, or who opened small retail businesses, for example, were able to assemble the capital necessary for the startup of their activity thanks to the assistance of the supplement.

An Indirect Restraint

The complaints that the subsistence distributed by the State encouraged the indolence of the Acadians are also partially unjustified. Rather than the assistance itself, it was more the ministerial injunctions to remove from the supplement those Acadians who worked that ultimately waged a "war on industry," since the prohibition of combining employment and the supplements obliged the refugees to make an impossible choice. The aid in itself probably had no negative effect, since we have seen how the sum of six *sous* per day per person was surely just enough to live on in the good years. The refugees who could work certainly did not content themselves with the aid when they had the potential to earn more. Finally, other factors that the administrators do not mention may have contributed more to encouraging the Acadians not to work in order to sustain their payments. Expecting any moment to be sent wherever the government needed them to go, they undoubtedly hesitated to become employed in the areas where they resided, preferring to parcel out the aid from the king whose constancy seemed more assured.

Nonetheless, we should not wholeheartedly reject the complaints addressed about the distributions of aid by the administrators, for the nefarious effects that they described no doubt reflected a certain reality. Cases of Acadians having refused employment to maintain the aid from the government are entirely plausible, though it is impossible to estimate the extent of this phenomenon. It is clearly shown from a study of the files of the requests for dispensations of consanguinity in the bishopric of Coutances that the distribution of a daily supplement to the Acadians constituted a restraint on social integration, since the argument most utilized by the refugees requesting to be married to one of their compatriots was precisely tied to this question. They all said that they did not want to marry French men or women because they needed the supplement of their Acadian spouse to live on.[91]

Moreover, the distributions of aid seem to have generated a bad opinion and some rancor amongst the local populations toward the refugees. This, for example, was the opinion of the prosecutor of "the general adjudicator of income farms of the king with the monopoly of tobacco sales" in the Corsair City:

> No one is unaware in this town [Saint-Malo] of the license with which the Acadians abuse the benefits of the sovereign [that is to say, the supplement] to abandon themselves to the impudent practice of fraud [in tobacco]. It is time for the enlightened zeal of the public ministry to strike and eliminate this license.[92]

We will examine further on this question in more detail, but, if the facts are accurate, they probably did engender an additional difficulty to integrating socially.

The governmental assistance probably played an especially damaging role in the integration of the Acadians for yet another reason. We have seen that the promises of the government in financial matters often were realized only with much delay. But all of these delays brought serious consequences for the Acadians. They were often actually constrained to resorting to using credit in order to survive. This aspect—which surfaces in many documents, but that we will illustrate here with only a few examples—must surely be examined if we also want to understand how the Acadians could live on their six *sous*.

From the start, the Acadians undoubtedly had a very slim financial margin in which to maneuver. Even if some had brought with them some money and things of value,[93] most depended entirely on the aid that was distributed to them. But, as the aid arrived very late, the Acadians quickly resorted to credit. The administration did nothing to remedy this situation. It was even Berryer who originally suggested resorting to this means to alleviate the deficiencies of the Navy. "While waiting for the funds to come to you, it is necessary for you to engage the bakers to supply bread for them; they will not delay in being paid for it," he thus wrote to the intendant of Rochefort only three months after the arrival of the first of the repatriated.[94] Similar arrangements with the bakers were made at Saint-Malo in 1773.[95] In this port, as Guillot warned many families from North America about the bakers, the aid was even delayed beyond the prescribed date in order that the commissioner did not have to go back on his word.[96] The bakers were sometimes authorized to deduct the income of the Acadians prior to its disbursement in order to pay their bills. This, at least, was the instruction given by Lemoyne to one of his colleagues at La Rochelle.[97] It was not only at Saint-Malo and at Rochefort that the Acadians contracted debts, and the bakers were not the only creditors. At Cherbourg, the town inhabitants provided advances to the unfortunate exiles, from their generosity, according to the Commissioner of Divisions at Cherbourg. This generosity, however, quickly reached its limits. De Francy thus wrote that the delays in payment soon reached nine months.[98]

The matter of money is never mentioned in a sufficiently precise manner in the documents for us to be able to determine what rate of interest was ordinarily involved, dependent on the situations and the locales, but there is no doubt that the money was not normally loaned to the Acadians gratuitously. We know that Catholic Europe prohibited credit in theory, though in practice another reality was revealed. Not only was credit widely used in France, but, "legal rates, fluctuating at the will of the States, were imposed throughout Catholic Europe."[99]

The rates were probably rather high, if not usurious. Le Fer de Chanteloup, mayor of Saint-Malo, deplored the fact that the Acadians—because of the delays in payment of six to eight months—could only "buy things on credit, and consequently pay much more than if they paid at the end of every month."[100] Lemoyne made similar remarks on the subject of the Acadians who had gone to Poitou.[101] Some months later, the Acadians who remained in Morlaix complained about the delays of their supplement: "The detention of our supplement . . . is very aggravating to us, because it makes us contract debts even for the most essential things, where often one must pay at double the ration because the creditor often cannot defer and even loses if his money is delayed in being paid."[102] They added a note from their baker attesting to a debt of 1,200 *livres*![103]

The debts of the Acadians also kept them in a state of dependency *vis-à-vis* their creditors and the administration. This dependency also acted as a constant setback to the often-sought emigration of the Acadians—even in 1785, when the government agreed on the departure for Louisiana, until the last minute the ambassador of Spain in France requested the urgent payment of overdue supplements in order for the indebted Acadians to be able to embark.[104] In some cases, too many debts prevented their departure. This is what is discovered from reading a "list of Acadians who remain in France": "Anastasie Levron, the widow Lejeune [and six children]: note: spent the last six months of 1784 with those who went to Spain, but has not left because of her debts."[105] Olivier Terriot also referred to his personal problem of indebtedness at the time of the embarkation for Louisiana, as well as that of the collective debt of his compatriots.[106] Some days before departure, Terriot mentioned a special agreement between France and Spain that the Acadians only leave once their debts have been paid. But, according to Terriot, France still owed the refugees six months of supplements. "The Acadians, finding themselves squeezed so tightly between an unapproachable debtor and authorized creditors, all of the sudden took the position of not leaving" he wrote. After negotiations, the intendancy of Rennes agreed to pay the overdue amounts.[107] The refugees were thus kept until the end in a state of dependency on the good will of the administration.

This "bind of debt" certainly did not facilitate the integration of the Acadians since it forced them to undertake conflicting positions with their moneylenders. Even if this bind of dependency was only rarely mentioned directly by the Acadians, it still permeated a number of their petitions. Charles de Mius d'Entremont described the unfavorable situation in which he found himself and his difficulties with his creditors, and pleaded for the prompt payment of the aid that had been promised to him: "I am forced to buy on credit those things that I need and my creditors are tired of getting nothing back," he wrote. "It is hard for me to not be able to satisfy them and to be continually obliged to make new debts that the long illness of my wife and daughter has further multiplied."[108]

The extent of the debts contracted by the Acadians is difficult to estimate quantitatively, but we may nonetheless have some idea of it. Upon the death of a former inhabitant of Île Saint-Jean practicing the profession of cobbler at Saint-Malo, his compatriots sent a letter to the minister in which we learn that the deceased had in all nearly three hundred *livres* in debts, amounting to nearly three years' worth of the supplements.[109] Another document from 1778 reveals the extent of debts contracted by the Acadian families of the department of Saint-Malo and for whom a withdrawal from the aid distributed was authorized. This "list of debts of the Acadian families of the department of Saint-Malo until January 1, 1778" included a total of 391 families, the majority of the Acadian families of the region. The sums due often reached or exceeded eight hundred *livres*, like those owed by Victor Forest, the Acadian previously fined a thousand *livres* as a penalty for having engaged in tobacco trafficking, who owed 783 *livres*, or René Landry, whose debt rose to 830 *livres*. Nevertheless, per family, the average indebtedness was only 90 *livres*.

Conclusion

What balance sheet might be drawn up from these reflections on the financial assistance provided to the refugees? It seems that the ministers and intendants offered advice depending on what the circumstances, budgets, and petitions demanded and on what their analysis of the situation of the individuals involved may have been. Although the assistance was initiated at the top of the State, by the whims or changes of heart or the constraints of the ministers, the local arrangements once again seem to have prevailed, and we can barely detect any effort at uniformity in the distributions. While they foresaw a distribution of aid for only some months, they were ultimately renewed from year to year until the Revolution and even beyond.

Without a doubt, the distribution of aid seems to have thus been very helpful to the Acadians, who never knew in advance what was going to be given to them. The uncertainty on the subject of the sums they could count on considerably damaged their integration into the communities, since they were unable to make financial plans, if only for a short while. The subsidies undoubtedly did amount to a tool of economic integration that was especially effective in playing the role of micro-financing in the heart of a population frequently deprived of the minimum of currency needed to begin any activity. But the prohibition of combining incomes from work with the king's payments and the great difficulty in getting a French spouse to benefit from the aid played a negative role, while also possibly generating resentment among the local populations. The haphazard distributions and delays probably considerably limited the positive effects of the supplement for the Acadians, who were quickly absorbed in a spiral of indebtedness.

Part Three

The Game Of Identities

Chapter X

Impressions Of The Acadians: The View Of The Administrators

The Acadians in the View of the Administrators

As we are interested in the integration of the Acadians into French society, it is appropriate to inquire about the way in which they were perceived during their stay in France. The abundant documentation still available on the subject offers unique insight, yet despite this, and despite the profusion of studies of these refugees, no analysis of the image that the Acadians presented during their stay in France has ever been conducted. To fill this omission, we will analyze terms used to refer to the Acadians in the thousands of documents consulted. Perceptions by the French were not monolithic and reflected a number of viewpoints: that of the administrators, that of the Acadians themselves, that of the law, and that of the local populations.

This chapter will first examine the terms used by the elites to designate the Acadians and will show that very few cultural differences were actually remarked upon by the observers. It will examine the Acadians' particularities: indeed, "to blend" two groups together implies that they were initially distinct and that they did not amalgamate easily. But what was the nature of these differences? To answer this, it will also consider the point of view of the Acadians themselves and will remark on their tendency to increasingly present themselves as a group not far removed from French society. A later chapter will analyze the use of the term "non-native" to designate the Acadians, and their legal status, at various times. Finally, we will evaluate what the Acadians may have thought of the local populations, and we will analyze Acadian marriages in order to determine their desire to be integrated into France.[1]

Designation of the Acadians

How, then, were the Acadians perceived by the administrators or, more generally, by the elite who were in contact with them? Can we decipher patterns in their impressions? The documents make clear that the specific situation of the refugees was little known outside of the Naval Administration and the locations at which they arrived. Many of those who spoke about the Acadians had only an indirect or limited knowledge of them, based on a fairly large number of reports that circulated during the period, rather than on direct and personal observations. Some less well-informed individuals apparently knew nothing of who the Acadians were: this was especially the case of a correspondent of Lemoyne, named

La Borde.² A landowner to whom Lemoyne had proposed in an initial letter to have the Acadians come to clear his lands, La Borde did not know of whom the commissioner wrote to him about, and Lemoyne was obliged to explain in a second letter who the Acadians were and the circumstances of their deportation.³ Similarly, the preliminary clarifications at the start of very many missives seem to have had the specific aim of more precisely informing the correspondents of the Acadians situation. It is possible that, after 1770, the allusions made to the deportation of the Acadians in the works of Edmund Burke and the Abbé de Raynal contributed to making the situation of the deportees more widely known.⁴

The most frequent manner of designating the refugees in France was evidently the use of the nouns and adjectives, *"Acadiens"* (Acadian men) and *"Acadiennes"* (Acadian women), or related terms.⁵ Most often, the term, as an adjective, was associated with the nouns "individuals," "families," or "refugees" (this latter term figuring in over a hundred documents). But this was only one of many identifiers. It is worth noting that "Acadian" was only put into use extensively upon their disembarkations in the ports of France. At the time of their stay in England the Acadians were most often designated by the term "French neutrals." "French neutrals" is then only found after 1758 in documents that were all historical accounts.⁶ The expressions, "inhabitants of Île Saint-Jean, from Acadia," and the like were also common early in their existence in France. One also finds some rare occurrences of "expatriated." "Exiled" shows up very little. The inhabitants of Île Saint-Jean and Île-Royale were also sometimes designated by the term "islanders." Other appellations demonstrated the imprecision of the terms and the ignorance often involved: Berryer, Minister of the Navy, twice regretted being unable to do more for "many persons of this kind" who had just arrived at Boulogne.⁷

The administrators used different terms to designate the exiles with the hope of building sympathy among their correspondents in order to obtain assistance for the Acadians. A first group of adjectives evoked pity: "poor" and "unfortunate" were found in 180 and 150 documents, respectively. The paternalism of Lemoyne had him frequently use vocabulary like "purity," "childhood," or "innocence." Lemoyne, very much a paternalist like the majority of the administrators, regarded the "little people," the Acadians as "spoiled, grown up children."⁸ The commissioner frequently employed all of these terms and their derivatives. The Acadians found themselves assigned various qualities and especially various faults.⁹ If they were sometimes judged as "deserving," "exemplary," as "fine people" having "good morals," they were most often "lazy" or "insolent," and sometimes "hateful, odious, corrupt," "rebellious," "gone mad," or "acting like they were Lords."¹⁰

In the eyes of the administrators, the Acadians above all subjects held a status that was particular and yet not very well defined. The lexical terrain surrounding the colonies was plentiful. "Colonist" and "colony" were used many times. It also should be noted that, in the period, this term was used in two different senses that were frequently combined in the writing of the administrators. Indeed, "colonist" could designate both "he who cultivates a plot of land" or an "inhabitant of the colonies."¹¹ The term was used on many occasions, in particular in connection with the idea of making land-clearers of the exiles in France. Thus Lemoyne spoke of "subjects of the colonies," and another interlocutor of the "respectable colony" when speaking of the Acadians being settled at Belle-Île-en-Mer.¹² The term *peuplade* ["tribe, people"] also showed up on many occasions. This word was then used in its traditional sense of "multitude of inhabitants who go from a country to another in order to populate it," called otherwise and again, "colonists." Thus Choiseul wrote that the king "will receive with pleasure this new people in his kingdom."[13] The Acadians were again designated by Terray as "natives of the country [of Île-Royale]"[14] and many times as "creoles,"[15] then simply the "name that one gives to one of European origin who is born in America."[16]

In fact, the Acadians were above all considered as uprooted migrants. It is for this that the State sought on multiple occasions to "procure a settlement" for them in France or again to "attach them to the soil." We will see below that the Acadians were often opposed to the term "domiciled naturals."[17] They were also sometimes treated as "fugitives"[18] and were considered as being "in storage."[19] We know the importance of opinion in society at the time: to have someone who could answer for one was the basis for social alliances in the *Ancien Régime*. If the Acadians only rarely seem to have been considered as "vagrants" [literally "without someone to vouch for them"][20]—because they arrived grouped together and therefore always had priests, administrators or members of their family who could recognize them—the refugees still ran the risk of being considered as they were on leaving Poitou: "they will be ordered not to leave the place that they have chosen under penalty of being treated as vagabonds or vagrants."[21]

A Physical Portrait

The physicality of the Acadians is only rarely mentioned, perhaps because there were not many differences to notice. At the very most, their robustness and tallness is mentioned, probably due to a better diet in North America. This tallness of the Acadians was attested to, for example, by Pérusse: "As for their appearance, these people are as one would desire them to be: all of the men are in general strong, robust and perfectly well constituted; some are rather tall, but generally from five feet 3 to four inches.[22] . . . The women are nearly the same in strength and industriousness, they are in general all tall, robust, laborious and very fertile."[23] A much later witness confirms this impression: "The Acadians were nicknamed crabs or sea spiders because of the length of their arms and their legs. They were taller than the indigenous French; their descendants preserve this characteristic as well as that of having a bronzed tint."[24]

A Moral Portrait

The Manner of Working

The Acadians also were the subject of a series of value judgments. Two areas provoked a significant amount of commentary: their ability and ardor in working and more generally their "morals," the word most typically employed.

In a period when many held the opinion that France faced depopulation and when the Physiocratic theories had great success, the Acadians were perceived as a valuable group meant to repopulate France while stimulating its agriculture.[25] They were therefore essentially considered "colonists," that is to say, as we have seen, as persons meant to repopulate the colonies or to cultivate lands in France. They therefore saw themselves as being assigned an implicit mission, and it was within the framework of this mission that they were most often judged. Opinions about the work of the Acadians were quite divided. We find nearly the same number of accusations of idleness[26] as affirmations of the reverse,[27] preventing any conclusion. Often these peremptory affirmations seem directly tied to the contexts in which the opinions were expressed, but not always. They were sometimes based on direct observation of the Acadians on the job, but these cases are relatively rare and do not prevent previously held prejudices from influencing the judgments. Most of the time it was rather a question of gratuitous affirmations, founded on "hearsay" or on accounts so varied that they may as well have been imagined.

Most of the documents in which we can inventory references to the presumably poor quality of the work of the Acadians or to their difficulty in performing qualified jobs are documents wherein reference is made to a governmental effort to suppress the supplemental aid. In other words, these writers insisted on the fact that, because of their lack of skills, the Acadians had difficulty earning enough to live on, and that their food supplies thus should not be cut. These documents therefore sought less to reproach the Acadians than to assist them. This was the case, for instance, with the letter by Ladvocat de La Crochais mentioned above. The only two other letters directly questioning the quality of the work of the Acadians were written in answer to a circular by Berryer requesting that all of those capable of working be stricken from the list of the beneficiaries of the assistance.[28] The intendant of Le Havre thus excuses himself because commerce is slow and merchants only take "the best workers that he might have,"[29] therefore not the Acadians. Another mentions the "lack of skills" of the refugees "for the work that was in progress" in the country.[30] The only references to their lack of ability are therefore all concentrated at the start of our period of study and expressed only when the assistance risked being suppressed. Additionally, if the Acadians possibly did work differently than the native French upon their arrival in France, they had to adapt to the local manner of working quickly (which might also explain the aim of the references to their incapacity).

In other contexts, correspondents praised the labor capacities of the Acadians. The first to do so was the mayor of Saint-Malo, Le Fer de Chanteloup, who insisted on considering the refugees to be "nearly all good laborers or sailors." But here again the statement probably reflected some self-interest, since Chanteloup also affirmed that the "neighboring parishes as well as the Navy are lacking people,"[31] revealing his populating aims. Thus he had an interest in minimizing the costs of welcoming the refugees by insisting on their ability to soon be self-supporting. Another observer, who seems to have personally studied the Acadians, made a favorable judgment of their work. In two successive letters, he was enthusiastic about it: "these are people of all trades. . . . They have very good scythe workers,"[32] he affirmed first of all, adding that they were "very good cultivators, laborious, with much religion, and integrity in their reverence and total respect for the head of their family who was the judge of all of their differences."[33] Finally, many other testimonies about the capability of the work of the Acadians surfaced on the occasion of their settlement on Belle-Île. It was because of their ability that one recommended dispersing them, in order to encourage the emulation of their example by the islanders.[34] The inspector of the province of Belle-Île expressed the feeling of many locally when he wrote in 1763, "accustomed to exercising all kinds of trades, [the Acadians] only ask for tools and materials and they will make their lodging and what is needed to grow food. Witnesses such as *monsieur* the duc d'Aguillon and *monsieur* the duc de Nivernais, in letters I have seen, speak of their good will, intelligence and talent, assuring you what a fine acquisition you would make by having them."[35] Indeed, the work of the Acadians was always positively reported in the documents involving Belle-Île-en-Mer. As for Lemoyne, if he personally seemed doubtful of the talents of the Acadians, when seeking to place his charges he did not hesitate to depict the exiles in a more favorable light. Thus, trying to convince a high functionary to transfer the lands of the royal domain to the refugees, he did not hesitate to write, "The Acadians are all cultivators and very intelligent, they are very honest, have the best morals, and are vassals to be desired."[36]

Some other texts also mention the steadfastness of the Acadians. For example, in 1763, the intendant of Saint-Lucie wrote regarding workers from Louisbourg, that they "are very fine subjects, very disposed to cultivate the land, ready to do anything one commands and who, besides, all having large families, will be very good colonists."[37] The same year a sub-delegate judged that "it is claimed that these people are more active and more industrious than our own farm workers."[38] Finally, many documents relating to Belle-Île praised the Acadians' love of working.

If some observers considered the Acadians to be relatively able and arduous workers, many others documented their supposed idleness. Some administrators deplored the laziness of the refugees, we have seen, in order to prevent the Acadians from being stricken from the supplemental payment. It was in a similar letter that the commissioner of divisions at Saint-Malo, Isarn (in the letter already cited above), deplored "the innate indolence" of the Acadians.[39] Isarn was, however, the only one who implied that the Acadians were born lazy. Other commentators, to the contrary, generally insisted on the acquired nature of their idleness, which was nearly always blamed on the assistance that had been distributed to them. The first allusion to this is in the writings of an intendant of Saint-Domingue, Cluny, with whom the Acadians had conflicting relations.[40] Cluny reproaches the laziness of the Acadian, Canadian, and Alsatian families who "found it sweeter to be fed at the king's expense, doing nothing to seek to earn their living by working."[41] Some weeks later, Choiseul took his turn to judge the Acadians as "indolent."[42]

The Acadians subsequently often ended up accused of idleness, although baron de Warren tried in vain to refute this insult.[43] De Francy complained of the "laziness,"[44] of the Acadians, and Choiseul, some years later, was convinced of the "laziness" and the "debauchery" of those who were domiciled in Saint-Servan.[45] In the same letter, a reference to the trafficking in tobacco practiced by some Acadians perhaps explains why Choiseul, with this bias, had heard bad things about the Acadians.[46] Even later, Lemoyne remarked: "one has represented [the Acadian people to the Controller-General] as idle, and given as proof the little use that they made of the aid that the king granted them starting in 1758."[47] The financial assistance to the refugees provided the basis of the explanations advanced for this "nonchalance." Lemoyne tried to dismiss this reproach made about the supplement by showing that six *sols* in aid per day per head did not allow one to save any money and that the Acadians had never refused to work.[48] Nonetheless, Lemoyne does not seem to have convinced his correspondents, for allusions to the laziness of the Acadians continued in the following years. One finds them in the writings of Turgot and Pérusse, for instance, and implicit in that of Necker. It is nonetheless important to note, once again, that the indolence of the Acadians was practically always reproached when they refused to do something that they had been asked to do.

Morals

Many documents also show complaints about or condemned the Acadian "morals."[49] There again, the most predominant, trenchant judgments (rarely nuanced or supported by precise examples) were only a pretext for bringing good will to the Acadians or, on the other hand, for castigating their rebelliousness and resistance. The first reference to the subject is again found in the above-mentioned letter of Ladvocat de La Crochais, in which he praises "the simplicity of their morals" and their fairness.[50] Until the mid-1770s, one finds practically only praise for these morals, as much in England[51] as on their arrival in France,[52] or again, on the occasion of their settlement in Belle-Île-en-Mer and Poitou.[53] In the latter cases, we have seen how the supposed purity of the Acadian morals was emphasized with the aim of alternatively either preserving them as a group, or dispersing them.[54] Surely, Choiseul and some agents of the tobacco income farms of Saint-Malo deplored the debauchery of the Acadians towards the end of the 1760s, but the overall image that dominates is very much that of a population with pure morals. We rediscover this vision of an idyllic Acadia in the *Histoire des Deux Indes* by Raynal, whose first edition was printed in 1770. For Raynal, the Acadians, functionally patriots, lived off the land and were far from any source of corruption. The simplicity of their morals, the solidarity among them, made of the Acadians "the happiest population of America."[55] Though it is hardly likely that Raynal learned about the subject of the Acadians from the refugees themselves in France or from the administrators,[56] his discussion is entirely in line with the dominant tone of the administrators. It would be interesting to exactly retrace the origin of the idyllic image of Acadia and its inhabitants, which clearly antedated Raynal's account. These "pure morals" attributed to the Acadians actually contradicted the ideas conveyed in the philosophical writings of the eighteenth century: a work like *L'Ami des Hommes* by Mirabeau castigated the poor morals of the colonies in general.[57] The positive image of the Acadians in the opinion of the enlightened elite undoubtedly came from a host of factors: first of all, the populating ideas mentioned above cast them in a positive light, since they represented a potential richness for the State. Then, the galvanizing aspect of their patriotism was insisted upon. Finally, and especially, these discussions inarguably drew on Rousseau's theme that generous and inviolate nature could only engender simple and perfect peoples and, moreover, the climate of Acadia, considered extremely cold and healthy, was considered as a factor of improvement for the race.[58]

We note, however, a certain reversal in the years that followed. Many documents make allusions to rumors circulating on the subject of the Acadians towards 1772-1773. Thus, Lemoyne writes an historical report to the secretary of the Controller-General, whose aim was to "dissipate the prejudices that have been instilled in him against the Acadians." The Abbé de l'Isle-Dieu also informed the exiles that "unfavorable prejudices" had been made against them.[59] This negative reputation of the Acadians circulated to the highest levels of the State. The role of Lemoyne is rather ambiguous: he peddled the rumors at the same time as he tried to destroy them, with little conviction at some points. If there is practically no information about the origin of these rumors or those who repeated them, the subjects of the rumors were sometimes more detailed.

One document specifically notes insinuations that the Acadians must have had "deranged morals." More precisely, they were accused of being "opposed to procreation," or, that is to say, of having used contraceptive means to restrict births, a capital crime at the time. Lemoyne shows the falseness of these rumors by the number of children raised: "of 2,370 individuals . . . , there exist 1,215 children procreated since 1758 . . . . Does this procreation prove that these were people who withdrew from the duties of marriage and leisure? No!"[60]

The refugees were also accused of putting prices on the heads of Englishmen in Nova Scotia, before the deportation. Lemoyne again tried to demonstrate the falseness of the accusation, showing that, on the contrary, the Acadians saved many British from the hands of the Micmac warriors when they were in the colony.[61]

Pérusse became the principal defender of the purity of the Acadian morals around 1773-1774. Yet some years later, when his plans for clearing land brought him to the edge of ruin, Pérusse, too, began to denigrate the "corruption" that was, according to him, deeply rooted among the Acadians. However, this corruption of morals seemed to him to have been caused by their contact with French bad habits: "They brought from Acadia only their virtues and they would have cause today to reproach us for having allowed them to contract faults that may tarnish them, but that are neither considerable enough nor inveterate enough for one to be able to not destroy them once one wants to take up the means," he wrote.[62] Here he is only more or less returning to the already old argument of Lemoyne, according to which the Acadians were spoiled in France because of the excessive care that had been provided to them.[63] Pérusse, like Lemoyne before him, judged the Acadians by the measure of their docility: when they resisted, he described them as "spoiled children" or "foreigners." When, on the other hand, he wanted to "place" them with landowners, he presented them as being excellent subjects. Thus, there were many publicly aired perspectives, depending on the circumstances. As for the more personal opinion of the administrators, that is much harder to discern.[64]

Comparison with the Local Peasantry

Image of the Local Peasantry

It is interesting to compare the opinions and stereotypes disseminated on the subject of the Acadians to those that were circulated about the "people" in general. Studies of the perception of the people by the elites are numerous.[65] Certainly, people of the time made clear distinctions between "the inferior and devalued situation of the people with regard to the higher categories—the nobles, the clerks, the rich, the well-off, the scholars—that is to say, the line between dominant-dominated, popular-educated."[66] Even the word "work" in the *Ancien Régime* had a largely pejorative connotation, though a progressive valorization of manual labor occurred in the eighteenth century, and, consequently, the image of the "people" improved, as reflected by the article on the subject in the *Encyclopédie*, which describes (precisely in reaction to the deplorable image that remained the most widespread amongst the elites) the working classes in a very positive manner. The laborer and the worker "always form the most numerous and necessary portion of the nation" wrote the chevalier de Jaucourt, who criticized a maxim of the period advising that "such men must not be left at their ease, if one wants them to be industrious and obedient."[67] Nonetheless, texts in which the peasants are represented in a positive manner are rare even in the second half of the century. The populace in question in the documents that we have consulted were only those of the countryside. They inspire pity, but seem capable of reform, and were not to be confused with the "mob." These texts confirm the observations of modern historians about the extreme paternalism of the elites: "The people could only be children, with all of their characteristics, weakness, credulity, foolishness, fear," writes Daniel Roche.[68] Indeed, for Lemoyne, the "peasant has no deportment"[69] and is generally "spiteful."[70] The commissioner, who prided himself on knowing agronomy, was convinced that the poverty of the peasants reflected bad management of lands. He thought it good to provide advice in advance for three Acadian women he proposed sending to his friend Saint-Victour as farmers paying rent in kind, "good country managers, intelligent with the livestock, the care of wool-bearing animals and the milking of cows and goats": "the farmer should use milking with great circumspection from fear of starving the young animals; the greatest profit, to repeat, depends on such economizing." He then detailed the qualities of the local peasant, who is "very healthy and very vigorous in this canton."[71] Lemoyne could have written these lines by the Abbé Coyer: "the people ask themselves about their condition: are we just animals, then? People! This could be the case!"[72] Pérusse shared the same condescension for the farmers, "a living portrait of misery and laziness," according to him, and a possible source of corruption for the Acadians.[73]

Comparison with the Acadians

Compared to these French peasants who were very poorly regarded, the Acadians were considered superior, whether on the level of morals or that of their ability to work. If, in their respective studies of the Acadians, Oscar Winzerling and Naomi Griffiths affirm that they were regarded in France with disdain, the contrary is actually shown in the documents. With little exception, the Acadians were always presented as being superior to the local population (even if there evidently remained only a trace of the local populace in the sites assigned to them).[74] We have already mentioned this matter, showing that this rather positive vision of the Acadians did not encourage the government to assimilate the refugees into the mass of the local populations. For, on the contrary, the refugees were often urged to influence the locals that they were meant to regenerate. Thus, the commissioners of the States of Brittany wrote that they desired the settlement of the Acadians, as "their industry, their love of work, might inspire emulation amongst the established [inhabitants] of Belle-Île, who are naturally slow and lazy, and negligent of the cultivation of the large part of their lands in order . . . to go fishing for sardines."[75]

Every time that a member of the elite compared the Acadians with the people of a locale, the comparison flattered the former. Thus, regarding the refugees, Barbier Lescoët judged that "two of their men do more work than the three best of our cantons."[76] As for Pérusse, he immediately saw "how valuable they are to preserve: this is a sort of man very different from all who inhabit our provinces both physically and morally."[77] He would affirm their attachment to the monarch on the occasion of the death of Louis XV: in a report addressed to the new king, and asking for his protection, he made up a new catalogue of Acadian morals comparing them to those of the Poitou peasants:

> I dare to affirm to you that our peasants, although assuredly very faithful and very attached to their sovereign, are but automatons next to these people; who have,

moreover, more pure morals, much uprightness and probity, which is the fruit of a great depth of religion still very much existing amongst them and preserved until now from the alteration so common in this century. Such is the portrait of the real Acadians, regarding their morals. . . . As for the physicality of these people, it is very superior to the norm of our peasants; it is a very fine species of strong, robust, active and industrious men; their population is very numerous since of the 1500 individuals sent to this province to be settled here, around half of the children were born since they came to France and nearly all of the women arrived here pregnant.[78]

The purportedly high birth rate of the Acadians was obviously considered as a great asset. Lemoyne, despite his remarks about "the indocility" and the "rebelliousness" of the Acadians, made a very praiseworthy description of them, and always compared them favorably to the French people. He thus wrote that the Acadians "could do all differently and infinitely more than could our European peasants." This letter was, however, written in answer to a missive by Pérusse wherein the latter implicitly accused the commissioner of speaking poorly of the Acadians. Lemoyne thus defended himself from having criticized the Acadians, which perhaps led him to exaggerate his idyllic description of the Acadians—a kind of self-censorship.[79]

In sum, all of the correspondents who took the time to describe the Acadian morals and compare them to those of the local peasants were unanimous in finding the former superior to the latter. One finds, however, a letter addressed under a seal of confidence that breaks with the official consensus. The author of this letter, Guillot, charged with supervising the aid for the refugees of Saint-Malo, found that the Acadians did not withstand the comparison with the French farmers.

> Since you want me to explain myself completely regarding them, I believe that one should not judge them by comparison with our farmers in France, for this point of view would be too unfavorable to them. Perhaps they, too, could be as capable of a quick and prompt attack of the work, but I do not think that they would exert as much consistency, assiduity and multiple efforts as would our valiant farmers. I believe that they are not accustomed to the same frugality in nourishment, nor in the same modesty in clothing, as the peasants of our fields. I presume also that they know little or nothing of the different ways that one treats the land in France to conquer its sterility and to have it produce despite its ungratefulness, and, if one settles them on lands, the major portion of which only offer mediocre terrain, with some good veins and some bad, one would by necessity have to put a French farmer in charge of them who would have enough talent to direct their cultivations, to earn their confidence and sustain their ardor, at least for the first three or four years.[80]

For Guillot, the reasons for this inferiority of the refugees were to be sought in the more favorable conditions of cultivation in Nova Scotia, conditions that would not have accustomed the colonists to perseverance and effort. Yet Guillot prudently surrounded his remarks with other reflections on the health and purity of the morals of the "neutral French" before their arrival in France. It was perhaps not only a matter of public precautions: these praises of an already quasi-mythified Acadia rather demonstrate the profound penetration of a positive bias about the refugees within the heart of the administration. The administrators were unable to resolve the apparent contradiction between, on the one hand, what was said about them, and, on the other, what they observed at hand. The refugees before them did not appear to be the same as those whom they had heard about, "so praised" for their merits. It is nonetheless equally possible that the commissioner of Saint-Malo did not dare fully express his real feelings about the Acadians. In other words, it is possible that the remarks on the Acadians were more a translation of a sort of political rectitude or politically-correct notion before the fact, rather than a reflection of the actual opinion of the correspondents.

A Different "Culture"?

We have already mentioned elite perceptions of the Acadians' morals, as well as judgments about their attitude towards work. It is now appropriate to pause for a while on the perception, among these same elite, of other "cultural" traits,[81] supposedly more specifically Acadian or North American.

The Cultural Problems Ignored

If the Acadians were progressively presented as a group apart, as we will see below, it is rare that the correspondents considered what might actually differentiate the Acadians from the "Frenchmen" of France in their view. On the contrary, until very late, the administrators praised the attachment of the refugees to the king, to the Catholic religion, and to the French character of both. The common points with the Frenchmen were thus often emphasized. In reality, cultural aspects such as foodways, the manner of educating children, dress, or life style, little interested observers at the time, or at least only rarely brought precise, detailed descriptions. Once again, we should hardly be surprised by this: those supplying the most important sources, nearly all from the superior classes of society and nobles, showed much condescension towards these "men of the people and of low condition," but little real interest. We might expect to find more allusions to these issues in the files of the dispensations of consanguinity. But, the Acadians do not mention problems of this kind in justifying their desire to marry their "compatriots." A single passage in one of the files might lead us to judge that the cultural aspect was important. Marie Rose Daigle declared "that it would be difficult for her to marry someone whose spirit and disposition she did not know, even from the same country [of Acadia]" to justify her exclusive choice of the partner she considered marrying among her compatriots.[82] The other sources by the Acadians themselves do not further mention these issues. In sum, if the administrators thought that the Acadians were very different from the French, they did not say so; and if the Acadians felt different from the French, they did not claim so either.

Observers of the period did not discern what we would call today a profound "cultural shock" among the Acadians upon their arrival in France. Was it from a lack of sensitivity on the part of the elites? This is possible, but we should nonetheless recall that, at the time, there was no cultural homogeneity in the kingdom itself. The popular customs and traditions of the provinces, and even the languages, were most often quite distinct. The administrators were accustomed to maintaining their correspondence in French with their colleagues and communicating in the local languages with their charges.[83] This is to say that they were used to the "folkloric"[84] differences between the regions, and they found nothing really new in this; this undoubtedly explains the scarcity of testimony about the Acadian way of speaking or about their clothing.

The Language

Even the linguistic difficulties, which were quite real—in the case of the Acadian "regulars" of Morlaix, for instance—are completely ignored in the sources. The only occasion that this subject was approached was at the time of the plan for settling in Belle-Île-en-Mer. At least once in this instance the Acadians asked to "not be confused with the Belle islanders whose language is either unfamiliar or foreign to them."[85] This request was then retransferred by various individuals but was not taken into account, since the francophone Acadians were finally dispersed among the other inhabitants of the island, who spoke Breton.[86] To interpret the silence of the sources on this issue is difficult. It is likely that these problems were so common that perhaps the administrators barely paid attention to them. Most of them were bilingual and often served as intermediaries between their charges and the royal power—the priests, particularly, constantly played the same role. We do find some mention of the problems of comprehension between individuals of different languages in the sources,[87] but these components confirm in a convincing manner that "the language was hardly, between the sixteenth and the eighteenth century, considered an argument of identity or of territorial assignment. . . . Until the Revolution, no essential difference was registered between those who were native and those who were not."[88]

Difficulties in Adapting in France?

The problems of adaptation were not always where we might expect to find them. Contemporaries noticed more of a problem with the "climatic" adaptation of the Acadians in France. From the first weeks of the arrival of the deported, Ladvocat de La Crochais mentions their sensitivity to the first "hot weather."[89] This remark may bring a smirk, as the start of the month of May in the region of Saint-Malo is not particularly torrid. But the Ladvocat's remark is understandable due to the prevalence of an already well-rooted cliché according to which the Acadians came from a cold country. This remark is the only one of its kind concerning the supposedly difficult adaptation of the Acadians to the Breton climate. On the other hand, these former inhabitants of Northern countries were often judged unable to populate the Southern Colonies. This idea was already evident in the report of Nivernais of 1763,[90] and would be repeated on numerous occasions by the Acadians themselves. In 1763 the Acadian families "considered that, being born in a cold climate, they could not withstand the heat of Southern America."[91] On the other hand, on many occasions, the Acadians stressed the climatic aspect (in this case suiting their familiarity) when requesting passage to Saint-Pierre and Miquelon.[92]

These discussions about climate do not suggest that there was a significant problem with the "hot weather," though we should not underestimate its importance.[93] According to then-current assumptions, to change one's climate more or less mechanically induced an alteration in morals. Philosophers were convinced that hot climates brought on degeneracy in men, while cold climates, on the contrary, reinforced their morals.[94] No doubt the positive deductions that many observers of the time made concerning the refugees was reinforced by this belief, then widely in circulation.

Well-adapted to Canada and to the Easy Life

For the administrators of the period, then, the Acadians were perfectly adapted to the conditions of life in North America.[95] During the Seven Years War, when military missions were being considered in Canada, the familiarity of the refugees with the area and with American means of transport was immediately remarked as an asset. Thus, when loading a corvette to leave men at the mouth of the St. Jean River to bring messages to Montréal, Berryer immediately suggested recruiting Acadians and sending them "supplies of snow shoes, Indian footwear and sledges."[96]

The observers were also often in agreement in judging that the Acadians had "habits of life" particular to Canada. Thus, the mayor of Cherbourg wrote in 1785 that the Acadians wanted to go to Saint-Pierre and Miquelon because they were "accustomed to this climate and to the kind of life that one leads in these countries. One finds fishing and hunting there, and they are fishermen and hunters."[97] De Ruis very early mentioned, regarding the Acadians, that their "habits [and] their manner of being changed" upon their arrival in France, because of the fact that they had been chased from their lands and the losses that they had sustained.[98] Lemoyne, also, thought that—in the matter of the children's education—the Acadians "operated among themselves following the custom of their country."[99] We should nonetheless note that these references are exceptional and rarely come as generalizations.

For many observers, the Acadians were especially accustomed to an easy life in an American paradise where nature is generous and where one becomes rich without much effort, in comparison at least with Europe. The administrators evidently were immersed in an intellectual ambiance that exalted nature and the inhabitants on the fringe of society and thought civilization corrupting, and often spread such preconceptions of the period. From all evidence, the observers likened the *Arcadia*[100] of the Acadians in various degrees to the *"Nouvelle Cythère"* (Tahiti), extensively described by Bougainville and whose praises Diderot sang. The cliché was further reinforced by the remarks of certain administrators who found in the generous bounty of American nature an explanation for the supposed "laziness" of the Acadians.

The point of view of Guillot well illustrates these views. For him, the facilities of the *agriculture* in North America explained to a great degree the differences of the *culture* of the Acadians.

> We should . . . consider [the Acadians] as a people who come from a blessed land, as landowners who each had one, two, three or four leagues of fertile terrain. Their possessions were covered with woods, rich pastures and animals. A moderate working, a little labor and some manure would provide them with abundant harvests. The cleaning of the animals, done by their own hands, supplied them with clothes. Flax grows more abundantly on their land than on ours. Hunting, fishing, the fruit of their flocks, added as much pleasure to their life as abundance and variety on their table. Content with an honest subsistence, that fulfilled all of their needs, they did not think to hoard. The thirst for gold never corrupted their hearts: they did not close their doors; the enthusiasm and the good conduct of the missionaries maintained them in the spirit of moderation, justice and disinter-

estedness. Nothing excited their emulation, nothing required a forced effort. The agriculture did not require a special industriousness or broad knowledge. They had no care to conduct research, which was pointless in their situation, although it is necessary to those on less fertile soil. Their agriculture was therefore just born, and the fecundity of their soil precluded them from having to perfect it. When it came time to marry their children, they built houses for them a short distance away. They brought provisions and led animals there. They granted their children a portion of their immense domains, and thus sent them on their way. They passed their evenings with one another. Some pipes of tobacco provided their relaxation and their delights. One could not impose on them the trouble of doing more work than was necessary: they are unaccustomed to it. Their morals were irreproachable. Their education and their lifestyle, although soft in comparison to that of our peasants, are not corrupting. They are the product of their situation. Their faithfulness to France has severed them from a state of comfort that they will no longer rediscover. France praises them, but it is the cause of their misery. Has one committed a crime in having brought to France the morals and customs that are a consequence of their education? If they are not as laborious, as consistent and as indefatigable in their work as those who have been forced to be accustomed to being so from birth, it is because they were raised in Canada and they were not born in France. Men are not formed in a day; they do not change customs and principles when they have nothing to be ashamed of, and especially when they have not had the occasion to feel that it is necessary to do so.[101]

Facing this inadaptability to the methods of cultivating the land in France, Guillot recommended "educating" the Acadians. It is also worth noting that on no occasion did the commissioner indicate that he took this lengthy description of the Acadian manner of life from the view of the Acadians themselves.

Although rare, the Acadians sometimes asked to maintain their particular customs. Nonetheless, here again, they hardly dwelled on the subject, and most of the time they were content asking not to be integrated with the people of the area. This is particularly true at Belle-Île, and we have already cited many documents to this effect. Some years later, the Acadians of Saint-Malo claimed the same autonomy that they enjoyed in America in the matter of tutelage of orphans:[102] "since their departure from Acadia, they have been considered in the midst of France as a nation apart, that one has allowed to govern itself by its own customs, without restricting them to weighty laws under which they were not born; and this in all the places where they have gone and stayed." They presumably fulfilled the spirit of the law and protected the minors, "doing all for no cost and equitably, as they had the custom to do in Acadia."[103] We have seen how the administration did not simply remain passive, imagining that the Acadians would act according to their customs. In the case of Belle-Île, some administrators thought it preferable for the cultural differences between the Acadians and the locals to disappear, so that, in the words of Warren, "all of the inhabitants would have the same spirit and be one and the same people."[104] Here we clearly are revisiting the problems of assembling versus dispersing the Acadians, discussed elsewhere in more detail.

Another theme emerges in many documents, which has become a predilection for the Canadian historiography, namely that of the imitation of the Native Americans by the Acadians.[105] This supposed imitation is rarely based on any other than an imaginary foundation, however. The first reference to this type of cultural transfer is found in a letter by La Rochette.

He remarked amusedly on the use that the Acadians made of the word "*butin:*" [booty, spoils] "this is the word that they use in imitation of the savages to designate their effects in general," he wrote.[106] But La Rochette, undoubtedly too infatuated with the accounts of exploration and perhaps for that reason seeking an exotic or savage word where there is none, was completely mistaken about the etymology of "*butin.*" This noun was perfectly well known in the dictionaries of the *Académie* and of *Trévoux* that provide no mention of an Amerindian origin of the term; it was rather a term of Germanic origin that appeared in French by the 1350s.[107]

The several other allusions to the subject remain quite rare and all come from Lemoyne. The reality of the imitation is often less tangible than the underlying rhetorical process. The use of tobacco "like the savages" also mentioned in another document thus deserves discussion.[108] Nothing demonstrates that the Acadians were any greater consumers of tobacco than the French population or that they particularly consumed it in imitation of the Native Americans. The same goes for the "Indian-like harangue" of Jean-Jacques LeBlanc: this expression was particularly used to castigate the trickery of the Acadian leader.[109] Finally, imitation of the Indians was at the root of a long tirade by Lemoyne:

> [The Acadians being] raised like the savages, with a thousand commodities indispensable to the Europeans being useless to them, I am even certain that two thirds of them would have been more flattered to have been placed into the field on their own lands with the means to settle themselves than to be given all of the luxuries that one might allow them to enjoy. How were our Europeans settled in Canada, on the Mississippi, if not in the hot countries? They did as they saw the savages do. Thrown onto a deserted riverbank in the middle of the woods with tools and foodstuff, they made use of everything that brute nature offered them, they were at first in the shelter of either leaves, or huts, formed of mud and grass and then worked to make it more solidly. Without taking it too literally, or making a cliché of the idea, but let us consider the analogous possibilities in France and one will judge the part one might take at the start and that surely would have provided them with a more rapid and advantageous success.[110]

In fact, here again, beyond repeating many clichés drawn from the travel accounts, this line of discussion had a specific aim: that of urging Pérusse to make the Acadians land owners as quickly as possible, in order that they might be free to conduct the work that they wanted to do in the way they wanted on their own lands. This way of describing the Acadians used to being autonomous and undertaking their own initiatives was a disguised attack against the precautionary delays of Pérusse. Moreover, Lemoyne does not seem to completely believe the words he professes. And, finally, his very general reflections on the influence of the Amerindians on the Acadians are not supported by direct observation and remain extremely marginal among the masses of documents perused.

"Gourmands" Accustomed to the "Good Life"

Documents that reference Acadian character traits differing from those of the "French of France" are very rare. We do possess some suggestions as to the culinary customs of the Acadians, however. Ladvocat de La Crochais notes that the Acadians, at the time of their disembarkation, consumed many milk products and much bread and were used to eating abundantly. By necessity, they were obliged to reduce the level of their consumption on arriving in France.[111] Some years later, Guillot judged that the Acadians "are not used to the same frugality with food . . . as are the peasants of our fields."[112] As for Pérusse, he spoke of the "singular gluttony" of certain Acadians.[113] A later witness notes that the Acadians were used to eating much meat in Nova Scotia, "more meat than bread."[114] In all, then, these references do not stress qualitative differences with France, but rather quantitative. One single document mentions a difference in the products consumed. In a report proposing settling the Acadians in Lorraine, a marshal of the court of King Stanislas (who probably never met any Acadians in his life) insisted on the fact that these "Canadians" were supposedly not used to eating wheat bread, that they would adapt better to a sterile country that produced only corn flour, a nourishment with which they were already quite accustomed.[115]

Excluding this one anecdotal document, the testimonies all agree on one point: that of the great quantity of food consumed by the Acadians. This aspect is also another facet of a similar character trait often remarked—and reproached—of the Acadians, their excessiveness. Thus, the remarks of Ladvocat de La Crochais included within his general appreciation of the Acadians: if they eat a lot, it is because they "seem to live life at large."[116] The same goes for Guillot, who judged that in Acadia the inhabitants were "content with an honest subsistence, that fulfilled all of their needs, [and] did not think to hoard. The thirst for gold had not corrupted their hearts: they did not close their doors; the enthusiasm and the good conduct of the missionaries maintained them in a spirit of moderation, justice, and disinterestedness."[117] In all, we should seek nothing behind these discussions other than the usual commonplace notion of the period regarding the ease with which nature nourishes man in more exotic and virgin countries.

A "Singular Attachment" to the Children

The manner of handling children, a theme often broached in the historiography relative to New France, brought only one comment, that of Pérusse, who remarked that "these people are very attached to their children."[118] This phrase constitutes the only testimony that seems to corroborate the notion that the French from North America loved their children who did not love them enough in return.[119] Another text nonetheless also reports "the singular attachments" that the Acadians have for one another, and more specifically in this case, the love of children for their parents.[120] Unfortunately, it is impossible to know if this was a matter of proving the commonplace adopted by French administrators of Canada and in the travel accounts of the period or rather a personal reflection on the part of the two observers.

Conclusion

If the "exotic" aspects of the Acadians are rarely mentioned, it is still difficult to explain this rarity. Is it because the Acadians were, in the end, culturally only slightly different from the French? Or was it because the administrators did not notice or were not interested in the ways of life of poorer people? We are probably not at the point of answering these questions, despite the enormous interest that they have to historians as well as to the general public. Moreover, it is easy to extract some phrases such as we have cited above from the mass of documentation consulted. But let us not be mistaken: these phrases only constitute an epiphenomenon, rarely based on direct observations, and we should not draw hasty conclusions from them about the "reality" of Acadian morals or customs of the period. The administrators only perceived the realities through the filter of the travel accounts written during the same period. For the most part, these realities remain impermeable to our observation. What is more, even if this makes them seem less exotic, the emphasis on the fine "French" characteristics of the Acadians, the references to their patriotism, their Catholicism, and so forth—which are much more frequent than references to those characteristics specific to the Acadians—should not be ignored. Even if this scenario is open to criticism, even if one could accuse this language of reflecting a biased position or of being the residue of French propaganda, it would also seem difficult to imagine that they are based on nothing at all. In other words, the refugees likely felt themselves to be subjects of the king of France like all other subjects of the kingdom, and perhaps every bit as much as they felt themselves to be "Acadians," the two feelings not being contradictory.

Chapter XI

A Group Apart?

Representations of the Acadians by Themselves

WE HAVE CONSIDERED THE WAY in which the Acadians were perceived by the French elites and how this perception was very often based on hearsay reported by intermediaries or preconceptions drawn from travel accounts instead of on personal experience acquired from contact with the Acadians themselves. The way in which the Acadians represented themselves has thus perhaps not had as large a role as one logically might think elaborating the image outlined above. Nonetheless, without a doubt the rhetoric employed by the Acadians did play a role in the shaping of this image.

To learn how the Acadians might have represented themselves to the administration and others is truly a puzzle because of the slight number of sources that might inform us on the subject. It is in the petitions addressed to the administration that the Acadians reveal themselves the most, but their statements are always conditioned by their requests: most requesting payment of overdue assistance or gratuities, or the authorization to emigrate. Furthermore, these petitions were only written by the Acadians themselves in a very slight proportion of cases, and it is always difficult to estimate what they personally brought to them and what changes the drafter made.[1] In most of the cases, from looking at the calligraphy and orthography, we may assume that the drafter of the petition was a public scribe or some other intermediary, but it is not always possible to be certain, as many of the reports are not signed.[2] We also have practically no idea of the way in which the Acadians might have represented themselves orally, except for testimony left by Lemoyne on the subject at the time of the various interviews of the Acadians in Saint-Malo. But this sole source evidently must be taken with caution, because of Lemoyne's growing irritation with the Acadians, to which we will return to shortly.

"Acadians" Above All

First of all, what did the "Acadians" call themselves? We have seen above that the inhabitants of Nova Scotia used the term "Acadian" itself very little.[3] Although my research has not been exhaustive, I have only found one occurrence of the term before the arrival of the Acadians in France in 1758.[4] On the other hand, in one of the rare documents drafted by an Acadian before the disembarkation of the refugees in France, we find the expression "neutral French." In this case, the approximate orthography and awkwardness of the phrasings leaves no doubt about the absence of an intermediary in the writing. In the document, a letter written by Joseph LeBlanc to his brother, the author salutes the "neutral French in general" and not the "Acadians."[5] Even if latter the term may have figured before 1775 in documents with which I am unfamiliar, the circumstances in which it was used, the frequency and context of its use, must be examined and compared with the use of "neutral French," which seems more common. Nonetheless, at one time in France the Acadians used the word "Acadian" generally: we find this expression in the dispensations of consanguinity, for example, on many occasions, as well as in the letters of the d'Entremont family. The exiles also sometimes represented themselves as "inhabitants of Acadia" or "of Île St. John." "Acadian" is sometimes attached to the adjective or noun "French." In France, the Acadians therefore no longer used the expression "neutral French": this denomination evidently referred to a North American context that was little known in France. Moreover, "Acadian" was recurrently used by the administrators. Even if the refugees did not use this term themselves before their arrival, they later began to copy the naval commissioners, beginning in the 1760s.

The Rhetoric

The exiles also represented themselves often as authentically "French." This is especially true of the Acadians who remained in North America and wanted to return to France.[6] Thus, some Acadians deported from Port-Royal, having succeeded in seizing the boat that carried them to the American colonies, wrote to the Abbé Daudin with the hope that he could

> Make known to the king of France, our Lord, the fidelity and inviolable attachment that we have for his sacred person. . . . Poverty, exile and all of the misfortunes of the world of trespasses nearby are incapable of making us change our feelings: we are born French and we want to die French. We have happily learned that, though many of the ships holding the Acadians have reduced them to the ultimate misery in hunger and thirst in order to force them to renounce their country; but none was so cowardly as to change his feelings. We await with patience the result of our fate, and we bless the hand of God that strikes us, fully convinced that a man faithful to his religion, and consequently to his country, could never end up badly.[7]

One finds numerous similar examples. If we believe the testimony of La Rochette of his tour through various ports of England, the Acadians represented themselves to him "as Frenchmen and as unhappy."[8] The context largely explains this insistence of the Acadians of their French allegiance, of course; since they were waiting to know their fate, they naturally tried to place themselves in the best light possible in the heart of the monarch. Subsequently, it would seem that, once in France, the Acadians no longer represented themselves in this way. Not that it was necessarily a question of a change of attitude: in fact, once repatriated, they needed to repeat that they were "French" less often, for rarely was this characteristic challenged. Thus Lemoyne stated: "I only know the Acadians as French."[9]

Beyond these considerations of vocabulary, what facets of their personality did the Acadians seek to emphasize once they reached France? As we have said, the rhetoric employed in the petitions was aimed at obtaining specific requests, and customarily worked on several levels. The refugees put forth many arguments besides the insistence on their very French character. They emphasized their patriotism, their fidelity to the king and to France and directly expressed their condition as being that of victims. Indeed, the Acadians often related their misfortunes in a way that recalls the entreaties of foreign orphans.[10] They described themselves as being poor, miserable,[11] distressed,[12] infirm,[13] and exiled, and claimed this condition in order to "recall the monarch and the faithful to doing works of charity,"[14] and they certainly always tried to obtain the fulfillment of the promises that had been made to them.

The Acadians also represented themselves as being faithful subjects of the king, sensitive to the interests of the State and thankful. They especially tried to impress the idea that, if they had suffered so much, it was because of their allegiance to the king. "We have lost everything," they wrote to the minister, "our goods, our families, rather than become enemies of as good a king as the king of France."[15] They also regretted becoming charges of the State, a roundabout way of recalling their attachment to the national interest: "we have always had at heart a desire to be useful to the State and . . . we see, on the contrary, how much money that we are uselessly costing France."[16] They later also added their gratitude: "upon arriving in France, his Majesty received us with a touching generosity . . . Filled with a just thankfulness for these benefits, there is not one amongst us who does not want to live and die under the French government" and similarly argued their preference for being under Spanish domination, "under the power of a king who is the friend, relative and ally of our monarch."[17] In all of these cases, it was obviously a question of providing words to the king or the State, in order to better ask for more, as they were always leaving France with regret. The actions or desires often contradict the statements. Nonetheless, it is worth noting that the Acadian petitions were less lyrical on the subject of patriotism than the statements drafted by the administrators or missionaries on their account, although these writers managed the emphasis more easily or projected onto the Acadians a patriotism more virulent than it was in actuality.

A Nation or a "National Body"?

In a similarly significant manner, the Acadians sometimes represented themselves as a "nation," or a "national body," or again a "people"[18] a bit apart. The Acadians thus wrote to many different people that they formed a "misfortunate people who have sacrificed everything to religion and to their love of their king,"[19] a "people who have always loved you and who will love you always,"[20] and finally "poor people who currently possess nothing but their arms and a sincere desire to settle."[21] Corollary to this progressive identification of the Acadians as a people was their use of the noun "compatriot"[22] to designate their Acadian "*confreres*."[23]

The term or expression that obtained the greatest notoriety, at least as regards Lemoyne and the contemporary historians, was the claim by the Acadians of forming a "nation" or a "national body" apart from French society. But, contrary to what the historiography would suggest, the documents in which the Acadians thus represent themselves are quite rare. All in all, I found only four documents in which the Acadians affirmed that they form a "nation" before 1775 (none before 1771), and among these four documents, only one claims that they constitute a "national body."[24] It is in fact Lemoyne, at the time of his stay at Saint-Malo in July 1773, who then takes up and widely spreads the expression, affirming that the Acadians claimed that they belonged to this nation apart. He immediately warned the ministry about this "pretention." But, rather than challenging this expression, thenceforth, the government employed it quasi-systematically to designate the exiles before their departure for Louisiana in 1785.

The use of the expression "national body" by the Acadians is thus found only once in a text coming from them, though it, once again, was written by a third party. In this document they affirm that they form a nation with particular customs in order to better request exemptions from the costs and procedures relating to the tutelage of orphans, adding that they had never been obliged to submit to such procedures before. The expressions "nation" and "national body" (used here in a sense slightly different than the then-current one designating merchant associations in a town) are repeated many times before being more detailed. The nation here seems to indicate a foreign body within the midst of a country, without an intention of settling there, and with customs apart.[25] The notion of solidarity[26] evoked in the "body" is important; it implies that the Acadians were not "in passing,"[27] or "vagabonds" [*sans aveux*], that is to say that they would remain united:

> Travelers who have died are not part of a national body; their effects would be abandoned if justice did not take charge of them to bring them to heirs or others having a claim. The position of the Acadians is very different, they are here as a national body, they are related and kind to one another; if they are about to go to another climate, they are faithful to their customs, which amount to wise precautions established by laws and fulfill their spirit. They take care of the minors, they feed them, they maintain them, they transport them and their few possessions to the place that they are to be assigned by the governor.[28]

So it is possible to understand a bit more clearly what the Acadians meant by the expression "national body." It was a question of a group, bound by family and social ties, having its own customs and usages, that had no intention of settling in the country, which is in conformity with what one might learn of the sense of this expression in old dictionaries.

A Group Apart

Uses of "Nation" and "National Body"

Let us now stop a moment to consider the way in which the administrators reacted to the presumption of the Acadians of forming a "nation," a "national body," or a "people" within the interior of France. The first statement, we have seen, is what the administrators and various other individuals like Pérusse copied from the refugees in using these terms. They, too, increasingly took on the custom of designating the regrouping of the Acadians as a particular "nation." The term—designating the Acadians—is used in a total of thirty-seven documents.[29] Again, we must state, as the graphic below demonstrates, that "nation" was very little used at the start of the period considered and does not begin to be greatly counted until after 1770. As for the phrase "national body," from the same table, in all, it was found in only ten documents of the many thousand consulted.[30] Moreover, it was written by the administrators, the ministers, or Pérusse, as well as in an unsigned document expressing requests by the Acadians of the region of Saint-Malo.[31] I have not found an occurrence of this phrase before 1773.

I have undertaken a systematic census of this phrase in the documents that I consulted and have compiled a table with the results (Figure 4).

The Material Used in Making the Table

This table analyzes the use of the term "nation" or "national body" to designate the Acadians in many thousands of documents consulted during the preparation of this work, of which nearly 1,500 have been transcribed into a database for research.[32] For the years before 1772, the table is nearly exhaustive as regards the preserved administrative correspondence.[33]

Regarding the use of the term in the Catholic registers, I only conducted systematic examinations of the marriage acts for the principal towns of Acadian residency.[34] It is possible, however, that there are occurrences of the term "nation" in the baptismal or burial acts, or in the notarial acts.[35] But it seems unlikely that it would not follow the same pronounced development that is described on the graphic below (Figure 4).

Results

On reading the texts, we may state that the number of occurrences of "nation" to designate the Acadians increases progressively. At the start of the stay of the Acadians, this designation was very rare. The increasing number of references is demonstrated in a visual way in this manner:

FIGURE 4

Number of documents in which are found at least one occurrence of the phrase "national body" or the term "nation" to designate the Acadians

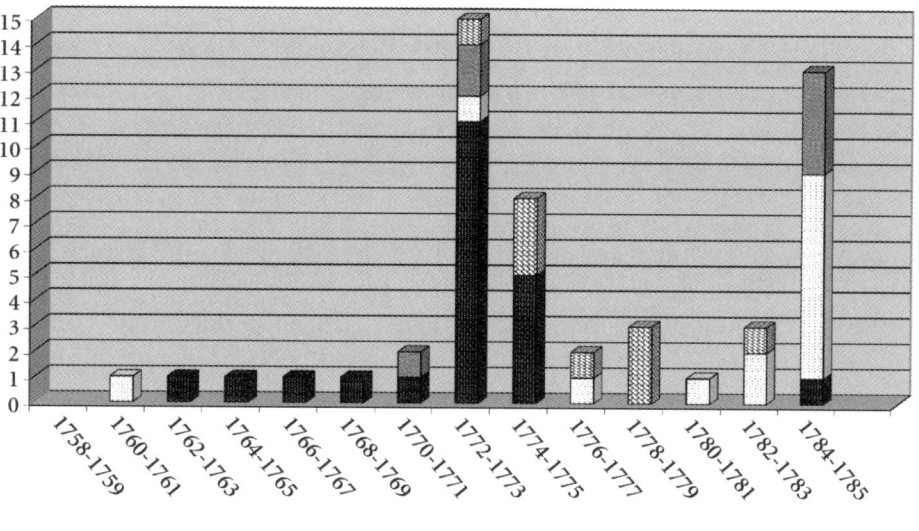

The increasing frequency of the use of the term "nation" is still more evident if we compare this first table to the number of documents transcribed in the database that serves as the source of reference for this study. In this way, we obtain the following frequencies:

FIGURE 5

Frequency of use of terms "nation" or "national body" in the documents transcribed in the database[36]

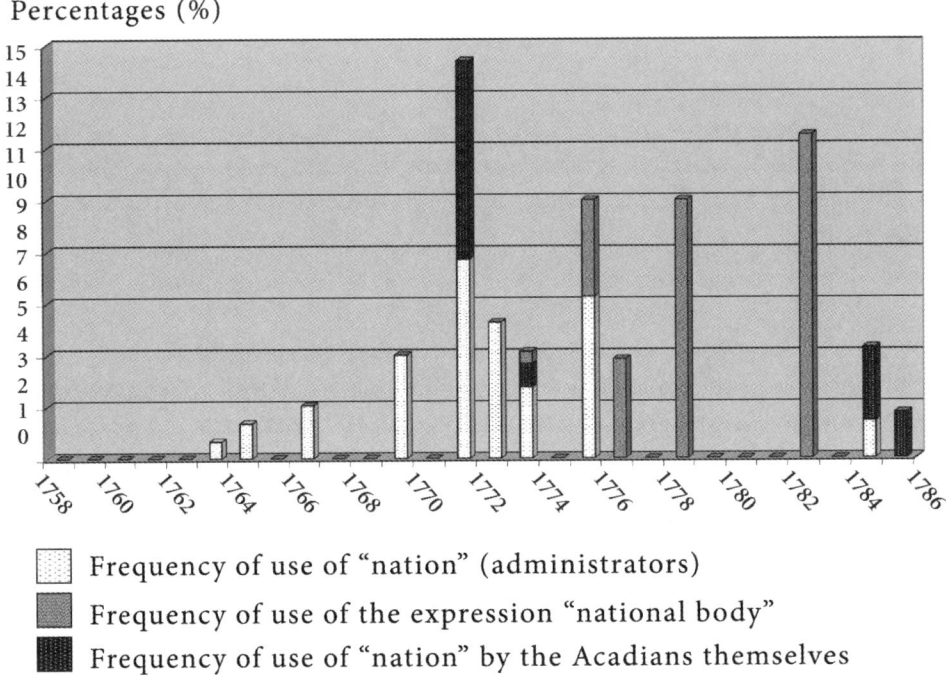

☐ Frequency of use of "nation" (administrators)
▨ Frequency of use of the expression "national body"
■ Frequency of use of "nation" by the Acadians themselves

This graph gives a good account of the infrequent use of "nation" before 1772, and all the more so as it underestimates the number of occurrences of the term after 1773. Indeed, from that year forward, the great frequency of the use of "nation" in the documents resulted in our not necessarily transcribing all of the documents that include this noun. Moreover, this word, which seems to have been used very occasionally before 1772, is almost systematically found after the middle date of 1772 in the correspondence of many observers. Thus, Pérusse d'Escars uses it in nearly half of the documents after the departure of the Acadians from Poitou, but he does not use the term at all before July 1775.

The table shows the spectacular progression of the frequency of use of "nation" by the French administration or by the Acadians themselves. For the period 1758-1770, four documents from a total of 675 (or 0.59 percent) make reference to the Acadians as a "nation;" for the period 1771-1785, 33 documents of a total of 787 use this word (or 4.19 percent) (figure 5).[37] The term "nation" therefore recurs seven times more often in the second period than in the first and we frequently find the term used many times in one document, while in the documents prior to 1770 we only find it once (figure 6).

FIGURE 6

Total proportion of documents using the word "nation" to designate the Acadians (per one hundred documents) excluding the baptismal, marriages and funerary acts

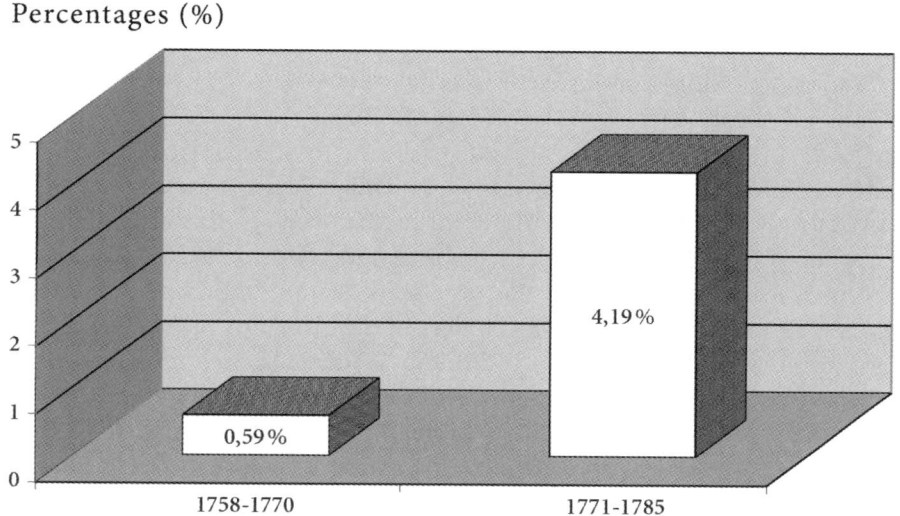

This result would be yet more surprising if we were to make a study of just the parish acts. Indeed, while at Saint-Malo we find only a single mention, in a marriage act, of the expression "of Acadian nationality," we find none in the acts of Rochefort[38] nor in the marriage acts of Poitou, though the expression did become common at Nantes.[39]

Analysis

Can we make a chronology of the use of the term "nation"? The first occurrences are within some scarce notarial acts or acts of civil status[40] signed by administrators.[41] They are clearly casual: indeed, in these first documents, the word is always used in an anecdotal manner, if not entirely by mistake and with no clear understanding of its meaning.[42] We should recall that, at that time, the term itself was not very precisely defined, and often served as a simple synonym for "group." On the other hand, after 1770, the term is knowingly and incontestably used: we find, for example, up to thirty-three uses of the word in a single document.[43]

Starting in the 1770s, we find a kind of contagion in the use of "nation." Le Loutre begins using the term towards 1770.[44] In one document, it is used four times.[45] An Acadian woman of Belle-Île uses "nation" in a letter to the intendant.[46] In 1772, Guillot, naval commissioner in Saint-Malo, uses it five times; the first in a letter addressed to Pérusse, then the following four in letters addressed to Lemoyne.[47] Guillot is also the first to use the word "body" regarding the Acadians. "They begin to form a body," he wrote, "which is a bad thing for from there come committees, reflections, etc."[48] Lemoyne first opposes the use of this term and referring to the Acadians as a "national body." In February 1773, in the margin of a report by Pérusse, he notes: "Is it suitable for the government to keep the tone of nation for this people and to give it a body?"[49] But three months later, after a petition on behalf of the Acadians of Saint-Servan,[50] (the first document in which the expression "national body" is used), Lemoyne himself repeats the word "nation" and uses it from then on at least four times, following the Acadians' lead.[51] It is from that time, as well, that we start finding the phrase in many Catholic acts, as it becomes much more common. The word is also used by Pérusse nearly ten times starting in July 1775,[52] and then came the turn of Necker,[53] Calonne,[54] and other administrators of the Contrôle Général.

What analysis can be made from these results? The problems are many. To begin with, we still do not know the origin of the sudden vogue for "nation." Christopher Hodson postulates that the appropriation of this term by the Acadians reflects their use of the political language used by opponents of the regime after the Maupeou reforms of 1770.[55] Until then, the literature about the Acadian refugees in France had preferred to find in the use of this term an affirmation of their "identity." But the intensification of the use of the term poses a problem. Is it an indication of a late awareness of the Acadians themselves as forming a group apart, or is it an indication that a reality the Acadians had felt for a long time took a while to transmit itself to the administrators, and then to the summit of the State? The Acadian origin of the expression is possible, but difficult to support, for, as we have seen, it was rarely the Acadians themselves who wrote their petitions; they were often passed through an intermediary. The same problem is posed for an interpretation of the religious acts; if it was always the priest or his vicar who drafted the act, its writing was evidently influenced by what the Acadians themselves said.[56] Moreover, if Lemoyne, at the time he interviewed the refugees in Saint-Malo, was in fact won over when they represented themselves as a "nation," it is to be presumed that the Acadians were discreet enough to not let themselves be reproached for their incorporated "communitarianism."

Perhaps the increased use of the term simply demonstrates its more general use after 1765. Should we find there a correlation with the more general use of the term "nation" in the eighteenth century? The use of the word indeed intensifies after 1765: "it is after the publication of volumes XI [in 1765] and XII of the *Encyclopédie* [volumes containing the definitions of 'nation' and of 'homeland'] that the words 'nation,' 'national' became more common and, like the word homeland, acquired a meaning that they had not had previously."[57] Nonetheless, it seems to me possible that we might deduce from the evolution of the use of the term a coming into self-awareness both by the Acadians and by the administration of their "difference" from the "French," a difference that did not necessarily surface so clearly at the start.

The parallel expansion of the use of "nation" and of "body" also very clearly implies an idea of solidarity among the members of the body. On this subject we should stress that only a portion of the Acadians seem to have claimed a strong allegiance to this group, an association which arose in order to promote their common interests. In fact, we observe the geographic displacement of the expression "national body" that follows the community, as if along its path. While the expression had its first popularity in the Saint-Malo region,[58] we then observe that it is frequently employed in conjunction with the Acadian group displaced in Poitou,[59] and then at Nantes.[60] After the departure of the large contingent of Acadians to Louisiana, "nation" only reoccurs once[61] and, as with "body," disappears entirely from the documentation, clearly showing the tie that was established between the principal group and this terminology. It is thus surely their departure in 1785 that explains the decline, and then an almost complete stop in the use of "nation." The Acadians who remained in France after 1785 no longer claimed to belong to a group apart, which certainly shows, whether from their desire for integration or from their sudden numerical weakness, that they could not still presume to represent such a body.

Finally, it is worth noting that, although it was employed relatively currently, the term "nation" initially provoked intense reactions from Lemoyne.[62] However, as we have seen, the commissioner did not hesitate to use the word himself many times in his correspondence with various people including the most important ministers of the State. Some time previously, Lemoyne had already warned the government against reassembling the Acadians, explicitly fearing that this might comfort them in their claim to form a nation apart.[63] For his part, Necker repeated the indignation of Lemoyne and recommended the dispersion of the Acadians within the French territory in order to "break" this "national body." The problems of terminology and of the definition of the Acadian group were therefore intimately bound to the troublesome reassembly or dispersion of the Acadians: to dismember the body seemed to Lemoyne, and then to Necker the only solution in order to dissolve the nation. On the other hand, the claim of the Acadians to form a "national body" little concerned the various ministers who succeeded Necker, who did not react to Lemoyne's remarks and, on the contrary, persisted in trying to reassemble the Acadians.

Foreigners in Their Homeland?

Did the growing claim by the Acadians of forming a group somewhat apart or the parallel evolution of this perception by the administration lead to a rejection of the Acadians from the category of the French? Otherwise said, were the refugees considered to be "natural Frenchmen," to use the terminology of the period, or, to the contrary, foreigners? The answer is not as clear as it might seem.

In 1756, Bougainville, in a letter well known across the Atlantic, compared the French and the Canadians, exclaiming: "It seems that we are a different nation, even an enemy."[64] Logically, Acadians might seem to be more "different" from the French than the Canadians, since they lived under the British regime since 1713 and the tie with France was only maintained by some missionaries and the regular, if rare, relations with the French of Île-Royale. If the opinion of Bougainville spread among the rest of the French colonial administration, is it possible that the Acadians, on their arrival in France, were then considered as foreigners? In fact, the frequent use of the expression "not native" to designate the Acadians leads us to seriously question their legal status.

Legal Considerations

By law, the majority of the Acadians refugees in France faced an ambiguous situation, since they were born on territories that had become British in 1713. What's more, many individuals under the government's responsibility in the years 1773-1775 had been born in England, during the captivity following the deportation. In some cases, only the grandparents or the great grandparents had been born in French territory. The Acadians in fact found themselves in a situation yet more equivocal than that in which a great many French natives were, facing the change of sovereignty of the territory in which they lived. This situation was relatively common in the seventeenth and eighteenth centuries because of the constant wars, as testified to by the requests for "declarations of citizenship" aiming to reconfirm a status whose legitimacy might seem fragile or doubtful.[65] Numerous individuals, anxious about what one might argue against them for having been born on territories lost by the kingdom (especially in preventing inheritances), requested that these doubts about their French origin be removed.

The status of the Acadians was therefore precarious since, by law, only individuals born in France of a native father and mother residing in France were considered to be "French naturals." All others were considered aliens[66] and suffered various incapabilities, notably that of inheritance. Certainly, the jurisprudence had established—since the Mabile decree in 1576—that filiation could transmit citizenship, and some cases of filiation in the second degree had been pleaded successfully.[67] But no guaranteed filiation to the third degree had been judged acceptable.

It is also true that the Acadians showed a vigorous "spirit to return," which constituted a fundamental point in the judgments of the period for assigning or recognizing citizenship. But even this point was not universally agreed upon. Those who were called neutral French had been deported in 1755. From this fact of neutrality, then, they had not shown their desire to return before deportation. They seem to have accepted the change in allegiance without major problems, and even took various oaths without manifesting a desire to return, except for those who, numerous enough, around 1750 chose to leave continental Acadia to take refuge in Louisbourg or on Île-Royale or Île Saint-Jean.[68] Then, the English barely left them the choice to stay or to leave; they thus lacked a new occasion to positively demonstrate their desire to return. Finally, the Acadians at the time of their stay in the ports on both sides of Manche seemed to be open to any proposal and could no longer hesitate between the choice of returning to English Acadia, going to Spanish Louisiana, or choosing France. At least this is what is implied from various French reports and accounts, or revealed in the fear of the administrator of Saint-Malo on seeing the Acadians flee to Jersey. Certainly, the Acadians continued to proclaim their allegiance to the king—another factor that inclines for them to be considered French—but their proclamations lacked credibility, for the same reasons as those mentioned above regarding their desire to return.

"Foreigners?"

If we now examine the administrative terminology, the Acadians were on many occasions nominally designated by the adjective or noun "foreigners," in line with what we might expect based on the above discussion. We must obviously be prudent in the interpretation of this term, which, under the *Ancien Régime*, more often signified someone that did not belong to a community rather than to a State.

In most of the cases, it is very difficult, if not impossible, to know which of the two senses is being employed by the speaker. The doubtful cases are plentiful. Thus, in a 1766 report, Germans and Acadians are designated together by Lemoyne as "foreigners."[69] Elsewhere, Lemoyne wrote, "what stops many gentlemen is the fear of entrusting their property to foreigners."[70] Even the Minister of the Navy maintained the ambiguity. Thus, at least twice, in 1766 and 1767, he inquires about "the foreign families"[71] who were waiting to be settled in different ports. From the context, we can be almost certain that in this case he was indicating the Acadians. Moreover, Mistral, commissioner at Le Havre, answered the minister, specifying: "There is not in Normandy any properly called foreign family. All of those who are there came from North America."[72] In some other cases, it is probable that the sense given the word "foreigner" as applied to the Acadians was that of being a foreigner in the community.[73] This sense is found, for example, at the time of the assigning of fee-farms at Belle-Île-en-Mer.[74] The adjutant of the governor of Belle-Île wrote: "The colonists of said parishes [Bangor and Locmaria], [were] seduced by the poor example of those of the Palais, who loudly declared to the official that they did not want to cede their villages to some foreigners, and withdrew close to their rectors while using such language."[75] Pérusse insisted on the fact that the Acadians were "true foreigners without protectors and without support."[76]

The sense of being a foreigner to the State also appeared. Thus, nationality was expressly mentioned by a noble of the province, Saint-Victour, opposing the Acadians as compared to the "nationals."[77] Other documents testify to the fact that some individuals considered the Acadians to be legally foreigners, or at least that they did not know their civil status. So, answering questions from Lemoyne about the possibility of transferring lands from the royal domain for the benefit of the Acadians, Duvonel, Master of Waters and Forests, to whom the commissioner had explained the situation of the Acadians (who were in this case to be indemnified for the losses they had sustained in Acadia by their fidelity to the king) then specified:

> If he who is deserving is a foreigner, the concession has normally as the goal not only recognizing the services that he has rendered to the State, but even establishing him in the Kingdom. This foreigner who may have children might well forbear from being expatriated to settle in a State where one could deprive him and his own of the compensations that may be granted to him.[78]

It is clear that Duvonel did not apply this description by chance, but rather because he was convinced that the Acadians were indeed aliens, or he was not sure of their status and was anticipating a question on this point. What is surprising is the evocation, further on in the same text, of the "Acadians, subjects of the king."

Non-"Natives"

Therefore, there is no doubt that, in a certain number of examples, as cited above, it was very much the sense of "foreigner to the State" that was being expressed. Moreover, the Acadians were identified in other texts as not being natives. This term does not—in theory—offer the double level of interpretation of "foreigner" since the dictionaries of the period specify that the term "is said of all natural inhabitants of a kingdom . . . and is employed, by extension, when speaking of foreigners to whom the king grants the same privileges."[79] The Acadians thus would seem to be explicitly rejected from the category of native Frenchmen.

But, in practice, "native" often was used improperly. Many correspondents seem to have not fully understood the meaning of the legal term. The first to apply it to the Acadians was Berryer, then Minister of the Navy, who in 1759 used it clearly as a simple synonym for "resident": "These inhabitants [Acadians] must not be regarded as natives in France; they are only there in passing," he wrote.[80] It is nearly certain that Berryer—or rather his agent—was only repeating the word "native" from a letter by the Abbé de l'Isle-Dieu, who had probably used the term inappropriately.[81]

The term was used ambiguously on many other occasions. Thus three other occurrences of the word are found in transcriptions of denials of consanguinity. The Acadians themselves assumed that they were not natives on two occasions and, in one file, we even find a double disavowal of the Acadians: "The banks of France [cannot] offer their services [to the Acadians], being unable to operate for *foreigners* who are not *natives*," opined the bishop of Coutances.[82]

Observers contrasted the Acadians with natives, a clear way of ascribing them as aliens, on two other occasions. An unsigned letter (probably written by one of the sub-delegates of the intendant of Caen) states that, "one assumes that these people [the Acadians] are more active and more industrious than are our natives."[83] As for Pérusse, often lyrical about the patriotism of the Acadians, he suggested in July 1773 to Terray that the king should authorize the Acadians to enjoy the "same advantages and protections that are enjoyed by the natives."[84]

Non-Domiciled, Non-Europeans

That to which the Acadians were contrasted is sometimes more revealing than that with which they were positively identified. In designating the inhabitants of France in relation to the Acadians, eighteenth-century correspondents lacked the term *"métropolitain."* The word *"métropole,"* [roughly, homeland] in its current actual sense of "the State in relation to its colonies, to exterior territories," was used for the first time by Montesquieu in *L'Esprit des lois* in 1748. This use is, however, absent from the dictionary of the Academy of 1762 and never appears in the writing of the administrators. The adjective *"métropolitain,"* in this same sense, is used in 1777, but only as a noun at a later date.[85] Because this term lacked common usage administrators resorted to paraphrases and to using a series of synonyms that show the difficulty in defining this particular group and the ambivalence surrounding them. Thus, the Acadians were distinguished simply, first of all, from the "non-Acadians,"[86] or others from North America.[87] The Acadians were again contrasted with the inhabitants of the regions where they had taken refuge, for example the Bretons and Normans,[88] as well as the "people of the same place and the customary inhabitants"[89] or the "domiciled natives."[90] Lemoyne also contrasted the "Acadians" many times with the "Europeans" or the "European families."[91]

Finally, the Acadians were contrasted with "the French,"[92] the "nationals,"[93] and "the people of the country."[94] Thus the naval commissioner of Saint-Malo wrote in 1772: "if the

[Acadians] settled in the lands, one would have to . . . put in charge of them a French cultivator."[95] The contrast, here, of "French cultivator" with "Acadian cultivator" did not suggest legal sense: in our time, too, we may encounter a contrast between the terms "French" and "Guadeloupan" or "Corsican," for example, though the latter's French nationality is not in doubt. We can certainly therefore not deduce from these examples that the Acadians were not legally considered as "French."

From this we should infer that the Acadians were unquestionably non-native foreigners in the eyes of the homeland administrators. In fact, we have seen that the term "foreigner" which is often attached to them still possessed different levels of signification in the eighteenth century. It is often difficult for us to know what exact sense the correspondents were using, whether foreigner to the region, to the community, or to the country. Undoubtedly some correspondents did not really know either and were not especially concerned about it. We have seen how the term native often referred only to the civil level and was therefore theoretically more precise, when in fact it was not in the practical writing of non-jurists. Indeed, if we study more precisely the contexts of the use of the terms "foreigners" or "non-natives," it seems that these designations served mostly to insist on the state of weakness and vulnerability of the Acadians, in order to obtain protection for them. Once again, it was most often a question of the rhetoric not referring to a legal reality, but to a strategy of entreaty. This explains, for instance, why the Acadians themselves used these terms. Furthermore, we find more frequently, and will now see, the affirmation that the Acadians were loyal and good Frenchmen, proving that their legal status was not really in question.

Or Authentic Frenchmen?

The French Character of the Acadians

Although, with what we have seen in the preceding section, it would seem to us today entirely contradictory, in some cases the French character of the Acadians was in fact positively stressed, sometimes by the same individuals who wrote that they were "foreigners." So Lemoyne, who designated the Acadians many times as foreigners, on many occasions wrote clearly[96] that the Acadians were very well and thoroughly under the jurisdiction of the country.[97] In a July 22, 1773, letter to the Controller-General transcribing a dialogue he had conducted with the Acadian leaders at Saint-Malo, Lemoyne wrote:

> I told them that I knew the Acadians as Frenchmen and not as a foreign nation, that I regarded them as subjects of the king, obedient to him and to those whom His Majesty commissioned to exercise his authority.[98]

How to interpret these apparent contradictions? First of all, the context is essential to understanding the use of the terms. As we have just explained, the Acadians represented themselves most often as foreigners or as a "foreign nation," in order to better implore compassion and assistance. In the above example, Lemoyne sought above all to express his opposition to those Acadians who resisted him; he denied their presumption of forming a nation, as well as that of representing themselves as foreigners, to better tempt them to return to their normal class. "Do these people imagine that one will take them for lords, or at least rich people?" he wrote on another occasion. "We want to provide them with work and place them at the level of other subjects of the king living in the country and earning their living by the sweat of their body. Nothing more."[99] To the Acadians, then, who requested the privilege of a particular civil status, that of being a foreign nation, he answered that he did not consider them other than ordinary Frenchmen. On other occasions or when he addressed other correspondents, on the other hand, Lemoyne himself could use the term foreigner, or the term "nation." Moreover, for the writers of the period, it does not seem that the problem of the citizenship of the Acadians was very important; consequently, it is plausible that they employed the terms "Frenchmen" and "foreigners" with a certain nonchalance.

Therefore, despite the examples detailed in the preceding section, the dominant impression that comes from these documents is that the Acadians were authentically French.[100] They were so designated by this term many times, often accompanied by a qualitative adjective: "French in origin;"[101] "Acadian French,"[102] "French who occupied Acadia and Île Saint John,"[103] "neutral French,"[104] "French originals,"[105] "French returning from Acadia."[106] The duc de Nivernais, ambassador of France in England, also explicitly included them among the "nationals,"[107] and Pérusse spoke of the "French sentiment" of the Acadians at the death of King Louis XV.[108]

Besides, even if this only had an indirect connection to their citizenship, as we saw above, the Acadians were nearly always represented as good Catholics and patriots in the highest degree, and this virtue was recalled in practically all of the documents about them. One specifies that they were "subjects of the king," "faithful, attached to the homeland," or "singularly attached to [their] religion and to [their] prince," before "regarding the other subjects of the king as their brothers."[109]

A final indication suggests that the Acadians were very much considered fully native. Peter Sahlins found no request for letters or declarations of citizenship (*naturalité*) coming from Acadians, which seems to show that they were not treated as aliens.[110] I, too, have not found in the documents I consulted any requests for the *saisie d'héritage* (proof of legal birth), procedures to which all aliens of the kingdom were obligatorily submitted. It is true, however, that, as the Acadians had few possessions, the probability that they were submitted to the alien proceedings was slight. Nonetheless, we do not find these procedures done for the rich Canadians who took refuge in Touraine, which confirms that the colonists from North America must not have encountered problems with their citizenship.[111] Finally, I conducted research in the Ministry of Foreign Affairs to determine if, for the period after 1750, certain Acadians—or Canadians—may have been considered by the services controlling foreigners as pertaining to their expertise. If some "Americans" or an "Indian" did figure as foreigners in the papers of the service, I could find no inhabitants from North America, except one Canadian mentioned briefly in a report on the ambassador from Great Britain.[112]

An Assistance Without Regard to Citizenship

The payment of assistance to the Acadians and to other refugees from North America could also lead us to think that it is because they were "French" that the Acadians received aide. In fact, the motives behind this assistance were barely if at all related to such issues.

Thus Germans, called on during the same period to populate the colonies (notably Guyana), also received assistance from the king.[113] Certainly, according to Lemoyne, the Acadians had *more* right to assistance than the Germans; but the aid was inspired, as we have seen above, by reasons other than those connected to citizenship.[114] The assistance therefore was not tied to questions of nationality, except on one point: the compensation to the Acadians for losses sustained, damages that were often assimilated into a gift of their possessions to the king of France. This fidelity to the king was, itself, well tied to the notion of allegiance.[115]

A Sensitive Subject

More often, however, there arises from reading the correspondence exchanged between various administrators and ministers responsible for the refugees the impression that they considered the Acadians as individuals with a unique civil status and whose citizenship it would have been distasteful or inappropriate to question. A kind of auto-censorship seems to pervade the texts, leaving us unable to distinguish the agreed-upon positions from the true opinions of the correspondents.

In fact, despite the theoretical problems that it might pose, the "French" citizenship of the Acadians only rarely occasioned open questioning in the administrative correspondence we have consulted. On the contrary, if they rarely approach the status of the Acadians directly, the texts frequently mention their fidelity to the king and the country and the submission of the Acadians to the sovereign. For the administrators, no doubt seems to scratch the surface of the mythic account of the deportation heard everywhere and the fine example of French loyalty of the colonists. Even those elites exasperated or aggravated by the behavior of the Acadians never questioned this basic account of the events.

Conclusion: An Ambiguity as Concerns Citizenship?

What conclusion may be drawn from the various observations made above? Examining things closely, the citizenship of the Acadians was sometimes mentioned, notably when the administrators used the expression "non-natives" to designate the refugees, or when they compared them to foreigners: we see clearly that they were fairly difficult to precisely situate. The dominant impression, however, is that the dichotomy between "French naturals" or "natives," on the one hand, and "foreigners," on the other, blurred in the minds of the elites, only a few years before the Revolution and the birth of nationalism. Above all, this question hardly concerned the correspondents, even if commissioner Lemoyne at least once openly asked the question: "[The Acadians], are they foreigners or French? I believe that it is only the latter title that they claim."[116] The conclusion he reached reinforces a series of indications that all go in the same direction: most of the time, and by most of the administrators, the Acadians seem to have been considered as true French natives.

Chapter XII

The Opinion of the Popular Classes and Matrimonial Intermingling

The Local Representations

The preceding pages contained an examination of the image of the Acadians reflected in the writings of the elites who encountered them. Now we will go further and enquire about the perception of the refugees amongst local populations.

Limitations of the Sources

In truth, we can only express some hypotheses on this subject, for no direct source informs us what the Bretons or the Poitevins might have thought of the Acadians from day to day. With just one exception, I have found no documents wherein the inhabitants of the towns or the villages where the Acadians sought refuge "spoke" directly to the subject.[1] The most illustrative sources on this question are probably the legal documents for the region of Saint-Malo, which provide some idea of the relations between the Acadians and the people of the area. These texts also inform us in an especially interesting manner about the image of the refugees among the customs officials of Saint-Malo. These people, of modest origin,[2] supplied testimony surely closer to the opinion of the humble than that of the naval functionaries, whose sentiment was often much more closely guarded.

The majority of the references to local perceptions were, however, extracted from other documents, coming most often from the local elites in more or less close contact with the "common people" in the area. It is through these that we most often find mention of popular perception. Sometimes, the source comes from administrators far removed, rarely in direct contact with the Acadians, reporting proposals of their subordinates. With such documentation, creating an interpretation is especially delicate. We must also note that, in many cases, the letters by the administrators do not presume to describe the reality, but to anticipate the attitudes or the supposedly customary movements of the "foreigners." Therefore the texts are only informative about what the upper classes imagined the "people" may have thought.

The Opinion of the Upper Classes

In this latter sort of text we find a fairly frequent mention of the hostility of the lower class towards the refugees from North America. First off, among the administrators, there was a predominant sense that the Acadians were considered to be foreigners by the local communities. Sometimes this was based on testimony. Thus, an officer reported to the governor of Belle-Île that the inhabitants had declared "loudly . . . that they did not want to cede their villages to some foreigners."[3] But, most often, the administrators only expressed a general fear, often only in anticipation. It is thus that Lemoyne considered that "this nation will form what is, so to speak, a foreign people within the center of Poitou."[4]

The administrators thus seemed convinced that the Acadians would be considered foreigners amongst the lower classes, and this conviction provoked them to express many times their fear of a general hostility towards them.[5] After having long enquired about the possibility of purchasing neighboring lands in the environs of Blaye on which to settle the Acadians, Lemoyne finally had to renounce his plan, mainly because of the problems he anticipated with the adjoining population:

> The price of acquiring [the lands of Blaye] so that we could admit the foreigners became so high that it was unsuitable . . . ; to these reflections I add that of the opposition and possible violence that the peasants might commit with regard to the acquirers . . . from which I conclude that we must no longer think of these lands in settling the Acadians.[6]

The problem, here as elsewhere, does not come from the Acadians. It results from the hostility of the neighboring population at the expropriation of "empty and wasted lands" used by the community: a classic problem, in a sense, recalling the phenomenon of resistance to the British enclosures. Le Loutre echoed the same fears regarding the settlement planned in Corsica: "The [Acadian] families who would go to settle among the Corsicans, a rustic and half-savage nation, . . . would expose themselves to being strangled by this nation, that would only view them with jealousy and reluctance."[7] These reactions have nothing to do with some kind of xenophobia at encountering the refugees themselves. Lemoyne suggests no argument of a cultural or religious nature in explaining the anticipated rejection of the Acadians by the local populations but only economic arguments about preserving their communal lands.

More specifically, Lemoyne—and he is perhaps not alone in this—feared the exploitation of the Acadians by the local populations. He very quickly draws the parallel between the situation of the former colonies of North America and those of the Germans selected to depart for Guyana, with whom he had been involved in the 1760s at Saint-Jean-d'Angély. On many occasions, Lemoyne feared that the abuses to which the Germans were subjected would be repeated with the Acadians. Thus, in 1772, he gives an account to de Boynes "of the abuses that individuals made in exploiting these foreigners."[8] If he does not specify here what individuals he is referring to, Lemoyne, convinced that the Acadians risked becoming victims, generalizes his suggestion: "all are threatened with becoming victims of the communities in which they may take up residence," he wrote a bit later.[9] Lemoyne recommended being prudent in order to avoid precisely this problem of having the local populations exploit the Acadians.

As we see, a great many texts only anticipate animosity or exploitation of the Acadians. Rarer are those sources mentioning an abuse that actually occurred.[10] We find throughout the texts some references of this kind, but they are practically always written by Lemoyne. The first comes from a meddlesome report, apparently never sent. According to this document, the most detailed that we possess on the subject, the Acadians were "considered by the people of Saint-Malo with jealousy, nearly hatred." After an initial period when the refugees were "dear," according to Lemoyne, they had progressively "become odious, and this hatred was shown in many cases: the poll tax was imposed on them, and they were obliged to conduct duty service."[11] Lemoyne clearly has a very curious idea of the "hatred" directed towards the refugees. Moreover, the decisions concerning the impositions of taxes did not arise directly from the people having begun to hate the Acadians—far from it. The arguments advanced by Lemoyne therefore do not demonstrate hostility on the part of the local population.

Later on, after a visit to the Acadians temporarily lodged in Poitou, Lemoyne reports having found tangible signs of how the local populations sought to profit from the Acadians:

> The inhabitants of Châtellerault considered the Acadians from the point of view or as a means of profiting from the needs that those entirely isolated bring along with them.... From the first point of view the unfortunate families had to pay heavily for many objects and even for all of those bare essentials of existence.... They offered to pay the women for spinning but at a price that proves what abuse they sought to take from their needs.[12]

Here again it is notable that the only example given by Lemoyne does not really come from abuses at the hands of the inhabitants of Châtellerault, but only by entrepreneurs. This should not be surprising and confirms that Lemoyne probably had only a vague notion of the relations that the Acadians maintained with the local populations.

At the same time that he mentions the hostility regarding the Acadians as foreigners or attempts at abusing them, Lemoyne presents a fair number of explanations or indicates many circumstances that brought on this hostility. We must, of course, distinguish among them depending on the place and the situation. In the ports where the refugees first stayed, the hostility was explained by the fact that the Acadians had become "the responsibility" of the local communities, which, early on, had to assist them, procure lodging for them, provide hospital beds for the sick, and offer emergency food rations, among other obligations. Moreover, the exiles were in competition with the local manpower in a marketplace of labor that was already heavily affected by unemployment. According to Lemoyne, there was no doubt that the Acadians were considered a burden.

The backlash was particularly noticeable when the Acadians were temporarily lodged, by the force of circumstances, in the homes of inhabitants of a particular place. This is what Lemoyne testifies again in the document already cited above:

> The inhabitant considers the Acadians as a burden. He is not entirely wrong; however, there were many who were prepared to lodge them and who gave them tokens of the greatest humanity. I have, with pleasure, made the acquaintance of a quantity of Acadians, but there are inhabitants by whom they were rejected and who refused them the most indispensable arrangements, water-proof coverings, broken windows lacking casements and shutters,[13] frames lacking glass to which these unfortunate people had to supply with paper that tore with the first drop of rain, doors that did not close, etc.[14]

We have also seen resistance to the arrival of the Acadians at Belle-Île-en-Mer. Other documents show the resistance of countrymen to the expropriation of their communal pastures by those foreign to the local community in a similar manner to that which developed on the encounter of the Acadians at Belle-Île-en-Mer.[15]

Beyond infringing on the lands of others, the Acadians seemed to be considered as unfair competitors in the workplace, since they benefited from the daily allowance of six *sous* per person, which presumably allowed them to be less demanding with regard to wages.[16] Furthermore, without even being such competition, the Acadians were accused of automatically making the wages lower by their presence alone unbalancing the local labor supply.[17] The Acadians, apparently aware of the impression they presented, therefore requested, through the intermediary of the commissioner general, to be employed without doing harm to the local population.[18] These problems of the competition of the Acadian manpower were aggravated by unemployment.[19]

What conclusion can we draw from these first testimonies? Many administrators gave an account of "the jealous regard" with which the Acadians were observed in the places of their stay in France. Nonetheless, we have seen that we should not have blind confidence in the opinions of these men, often barely in contact with the local populations, and who might have particular reasons to see hostility where it did not necessarily exist. It is therefore suitable for us to question the reality of this hostile regard, using other sources that we have at our disposal.

"The Jealous Regard"

It seems that some latent resentment indeed manifested itself at Belle-Île-en-Mer and perhaps in Poitou.[20] The hostility nonetheless seems less tied to the status of the Acadians as "foreigners" than to their involuntary infringement on the lands of the previous inhabitants. Other indications demonstrate a possible animosity, for example, the relatively slight number of mixed marriages, the reassembling of the Acadians into a "body," or a certain geographic regrouping in the locations of their refuge. Yet these indicators do not necessarily imply ostracism on the part of the locals. They could just as well show the voluntary regrouping of the Acadians themselves or as a result of some other less-than-evident causes.

If there was hostility in Belle-Île, nothing proves that this was also the case in Saint-Malo, Nantes, or even along the *Grand Ligne*, despite the affirmations of Lemoyne. First off, we have seen the weakness of the examples advanced by Lemoyne to support his thesis of the "malevolent eye" with which the Acadians were observed in the Corsair City. Besides that, the Acadians never complained in writing about the hostility of the communities apart from the problems of cohabitation mentioned at Poitou. In all, we are obliged to note the rarity of sources that mention this hostility, which all originate, moreover, from Lemoyne.

Furthermore, we should note that many sources emphasize the compassion of the local populations for the Acadians. Is it possible that this compassion, embodied, we have also seen, in the distribution of assistance, clothing, and such,[21] only manifested itself on the arrival of the Acadians? This is what Lemoyne[22] implied. According to him, it was only after a certain period and through contact with the local populations that the Acadians "became corrupted," became "hateful" and "odious," and that, in return, the taxes and duty service were imposed on them.[23]

The Affairs of Contraband Tobacco

Did the Acadians therefore become "odious" in the view of the local populations? If one draws on the image of the daily life of the Acadians contained in the files of tobacco fraud cases in the Saint-Malo region, we find a more nuanced perspective. First of all, the simple fact that many Acadians were implicated in the contraband trafficking might be a sign of a lack of respectability, of a certain rejection by the Saint-Malo society. This reality surely demonstrates an economic and social fragility. In Saumur, for example, 20 percent of those involved in contraband were beggars, and everywhere else in France "the day and small-time laborers, craftsmen of the boroughs dominated" the trafficking, that is, the poorer segments of the population.[24] It is possible that the Acadians were implicated in the tobacco fraud in a higher proportion than were the inhabitants of the Saint-Malo region, even if this is impossible to precisely estimate. Above all, the refugees seem to have been specifically marked by the tobacco farm as subjects especially susceptible to the crime. Their presence in troublesome groups was always specifically noted, and certain of the employees of the tobacco farm insisted on the implication of the Acadians in disruptions.

A police report against one Eugène Zerby involving rebellion is illustrative. Some customs officers, in the course of rounds at Saint-Servan, wanted to examine this individual who was "very suspicious of fraud" and who perhaps drew attention because he was accompanied by many women "as many Cadienne as inhabitants of the area." Following a refusal by Zerby to let himself be searched, a multitude of people assembled then, "as many Cadiens as others unknown to us," and insisted that the charges be drawn up immediately after the facts. One of the farm employees struck Zerby with his cane, then, "fearing a revolt," gathered with his colleagues to go to their warehouse.[25] In the subsequent complaint written by the prosecutor, reference was explicitly made to the presence of "Cadiens."[26] The Acadians were thus clearly held responsible by at least one of the witnesses for the rebellious attitude and the self-assurance of Zerby. One employee declared that "the man named Zerby, seeing many people gather, as many Acadians as others, and, becoming furious, objected to the same [crowd] and prepared to be placed in their hands." Another witness explained that "Zerby was opposed to the [crowd] of said employees. And what strengthened him in this revolt was no doubt the gathering of many Acadians who arrived at the same instant as well as many people from Saint-Servan, all of which bolstered Zerby to pronounce many invectives against the denouncer and his colleagues." A third employee again insisted: "The man called Zerby, bolstered by a multitude of people as many Acadians as others from the parish of Saint-Servan, redoubled his invectives."[27]

The tensions between the Acadians and the employees of the farm of Saint-Malo remained. So, on June 11, 1769, an indictment was drawn up by those whom the population called the "*maltotiers*" (collectors of a special, unpopular tax, the *maltôte*). Many employees described therein having been attacked, during the course of night rounds, by "many individuals . . . taken with wine." Among the crowd of their assailants, they wrote that they recognized "many Acadians whose names we do not know, among whom we recognized one or many sailors from the post of the city."[28] It is worth noting that none of the indictments drawn up following these "riots" explain how the agents of the farm recognized the "Acadians" in the crowd. Was it because of an accent, particular clothing, their above average height, or other distinctions? Perhaps, more simply, the employees knew all of the inhabitants of the small town by sight? Unfortunately, no information on this subject shows up in the documents.

If the legal sources reveal numerous conflicts between the Acadians and the customs officers, they also supply contrasting information about the relations between the refugees and the local populations. Certain indications suggest that the Acadians indeed withstood jealousy, since they were victims, on at least one occasion, of denunciations. Indeed, if we believe the criminal complaint deposed against Jean Thibaudeau, his wife, François Guillou, and other Acadians for armed rebellion and tobacco contraband, the officers were warned about Thibaudeau's trafficking by means of a secret accusation, about which, unfortunately, the proceedings provide no detail.[29] The denunciations, however, spared no one and did not concentrate only on stigmatized groups. Were the Acadians more subject to denunciations than their neighbors? Nothing allows us to affirm this. At a later interrogation into the same affair, the four witnesses brought to the trial appeared disinclined to provide details.[30] None declared to have personally seen the facts reported relative to the altercation between the group of Acadians and the employees of the farms. All said only "that they heard it said in public" that the affirmations of the customs offices were true. Two of the four were retailers of tobacco, therefore undoubtedly involved in the affair. If the first and last witness only reported the public rumors, the second witness claimed to have heard the confession by Terriot of the affair; but it is difficult to understand if he meant to charge or discharge—that is to say, if he wanted to harm Terriot or, on the contrary, absolve him from the affair.[31] As for the third witness, he declared "that he had knowledge of nothing," except only that he saw leaving his place a person fleeing who he recognized as "Paul Henry, Acadian, living in Pleudihen near the lower field." In all, therefore, the witnesses hardly took any risks in the accusation, but there again the interpretation remains difficult: Were they in solidarity with the Acadians? Did they really see nothing? Did they fear reprisals?

The employees of the farm nonetheless seem to have had difficulties in finding witnesses to the crime, since none of the four plaintiffs interrogated had visually witnessed the facts. Neighbors did not seem prepared to testify against the Acadians. The fact that this file is the sole case of supposed denunciations that we possess and that it contains the only testimonies charging the Acadians that we have found is an indication that the hostility against the refugees was undoubtedly not as widespread as Lemoyne said it was. This sense is confirmed by the impression of some social intermingling among the Acadians and the local populations. Thus, Jean Thibaudeau, in his interrogatory, tells that he spent the whole night "drinking and talking" with an inhabitant of a neighboring borough, a surgeon named Tausé, apparently a non-Acadian. In the examples mentioned above of groups attacking the employees of the farm, the Acadians were intermingled with the inhabitants of Saint-Servan or Saint-Malo.

Conclusion

If we now try to summarize, we must first note that the initial reaction of the local populations seems to have been sympathetic with the fate of the unfortunate Acadians. This commiseration is proven by the fact that the mayors or the local administrators supplied aid or organized donations. But, thereafter, the situation seems to have degenerated. Several times the administrators mentioned "the jealous regard" with which the Acadians were observed by the local populations, but it is difficult to know to what degree this jealousy was real and how it was expressed. We can only state that the Acadians barely complained directly about some hostility on the part of the people of the area with whom they were forced to cohabitate. Yet this hostility, in certain cases, like at the time of settling at Belle-Île-en-Mer, was very clearly demonstrated by other sources. It does not seem, however, that in this case the enmity of the populations was directed to the Acadians because they were foreigners, but rather because they were competing with the already settled local peasantry in obtaining the better lands. The hostility of the local populations towards the Acadians was therefore most often based on specific and real difficulties rather than cultural incompatibility or a kind of proto-racism. It was born from a conflict of interests, and it is for this reason that Lemoyne pragmatically recommended that the plan for settlement "should not be contrary to the interests of the individuals who were to be the neighbors of these people."[32]

As for the legal sources analyzed above, they do not allow us to conclude in a definitive manner about the perception of the Acadians by the popular classes, either. At the most, we may affirm that the Acadians had especially contentious relations with the employees of the Saint-Malo farm, but it was perhaps not that pronounced a case in comparison to the general hostility of the population towards the *maltotiers*. In one case, the Acadian were denounced by a source that remains anonymous and some witnesses joined the accusation, though in a modest way; the accusers seem to have had the greatest trouble in assembling witnesses for the charge against the Acadians. On many other occasions, on the contrary, the Acadians seem to have been among the agitated crowd taking a position against the unfortunate customs workers. In the absence of more abundant direct sources detailing the perception of the Acadians by the local populations who surrounded them, it would therefore be difficult to know what was in the heart of the Bretons or Poitevins in question, and we must unfortunately be content with the general impression that the Acadians did not seem to engender any particularly pronounced hostility.

A Test: The Acadian Marriages

Another way of testing hostility on the part of locals toward the Acadians consists of examining marriage records. The method most currently used by the social sciences to study the integration of a foreign group is to consider the proportion of individuals marrying within or without a group, marriage being considered as a willful sign of integration. This method can partially make up for the scarcity of more exact indicators. Before our study, the facts concerning the Acadians on this subject were fragmentary, despite some recent work.[33] It would be important to provide a balance sheet of these Acadian marriages and remarriages for the period from 1759-1785 and for all of the areas of residency.[34] Gérard-Marc Braud sought to calculate some of these proportions with his own research on Nantes, from lists edited by A.J. Robichaux and from various data provided to him by many correspondents.[35] I was able to refine a certain number of the estimates made by Braud in elaborating the figures and reproducing the tables below. Moreover, two other scholars from the association *Racines et Rameaux français d'Acadie* [French Roots and Branches from Acadia], Jacques Nerrou and Gérard Scavennec, provided me with lists of marriages that they compiled for Rochefort and for Belle-Île-en-Mer, respectively.[36]

The main stumbling block encountered in elaborating such a statistical table comes first of all from the difficulty in precisely defining the criteria by which one belonged to an Acadian group. If we use as criteria geographic origin, it is then subject to frequent omissions from the sources on this subject.

We have already mentioned in our introduction the general criteria maintained in defining who was or was not an Acadian. The practice indubitably includes some arbitrariness, and there I also specified in a general manner those I have considered as individuals clearly designated as "Acadian" or "originally from Acadia" in the texts. In the specific case of a counting of the marriages, I went beyond this rule for many reasons. First of all, a large and consequential enough number of individuals born in Acadia, descending from families called the pioneers, often married with descendants of other pioneer families but are not designated as Acadians in the acts of baptisms, marriages, and funerals.[37] Then, when we examine the marriage of an Acadian clearly identified as such to a person whose Acadian origin is not nominally specified, this does not necessarily show that the spouse was a "Frenchman" originally from the site of refuge.[38]

Let us take a specific example. Starting with a list of marriages in the region of Cherbourg, it is possible to count the number of Acadians married to compatriots or to the French, since each time we have the name of the parents and the place of origin, often Acadia, Île Saint-Jean, or Canada. On February 3, 1761, Anne Lacroix—clearly identified as an Acadian since the act specifies that she was originally from Acadia and that the name of her mother, Hébert, was one of the common Acadian surnames—married a man named Léonard Cireau (or Circaud). The latter claimed to have been born at Angoulême; his name does not figure among the Acadian surnames inventoried and is not found on any list of Acadians in France.[39] Everything would seem to indicate that he was a man of French birth, and I had originally classified this marriage among the mixed marriages, that is to say of a French man and an Acadian woman. But, in collating the list with the files of exemptions of consanguinity and affinity discussed previously, I found that this couple sought an exemption to be married on January 14, 1761, despite the degree of affinity that tied the husband to his intended.[40] This exemption tells us that in fact Léonard Cireau had lived for nine years at Louisbourg at the time of the deportation, and that he was already the widow of two deceased spouses at Cape-Breton. At Cherbourg, clearly seeking to remain within the group of Acadians,[41] he wanted to marry Anne Lacroix, an Acadian, but, "all of the Acadian women at Cherbourg [being] related to the plaintiff through the family of his deceased wife," he could not help trying to have the affinity prohibition lifted. Should we consider this Léonard Cireau to be an "Acadian"? In this case, we decided to say yes, which is entirely contestable. In a general manner, we had to simplify, and for this statistical study only, we have therefore considered in the calculations all of those individuals being indicated as inhabitants of Louisbourg, of Canada, or of Île-Royale as being Acadians.

The process could be quite confusing, as we have seen, in determining a subject's identification as "Canadian" or "coming from Canada" or those properly called Acadians.[42] Thus, for example, Guillaume Laborde and Marie-Rose Daigle who were married at Cherbourg on July 21, 1761, were both designated as coming from Canada. But in fact they both came from Île Saint-Jean, as stated in their testimony given at the time of another request for exemption from consanguinity. Thus, if it is possible that this method artificially increases the number of marriages contracted between Acadians or within the family, it is likely that, in truth, this increase only compensates for the number of individuals who—like, initially, Léonard Cireau—were classified as "French" though their ties with the Acadians were deep and longstanding, but who could not be formally identified as Acadians because of the doubt remaining about their origin. Where there was a doubt, the individuals were considered as "non-Acadian."[43] Despite all of the limitations described above, it was possible to establish a general table using all of the existing data on the subject (see below).

For better comprehension, the results of the calculations made are also put in the form of many figures below.

The first graph (Figure 7) represents the geographic division of the marriage acts counted, allowing us to see the strong bias of the Saint-Malo region, followed by the region of Nantes. Note that of the total 652 marriage acts examined, 293 were for Saint-Malo and the Rance River.

FIGURE 7

Geographic division of the marriage acts analyzed

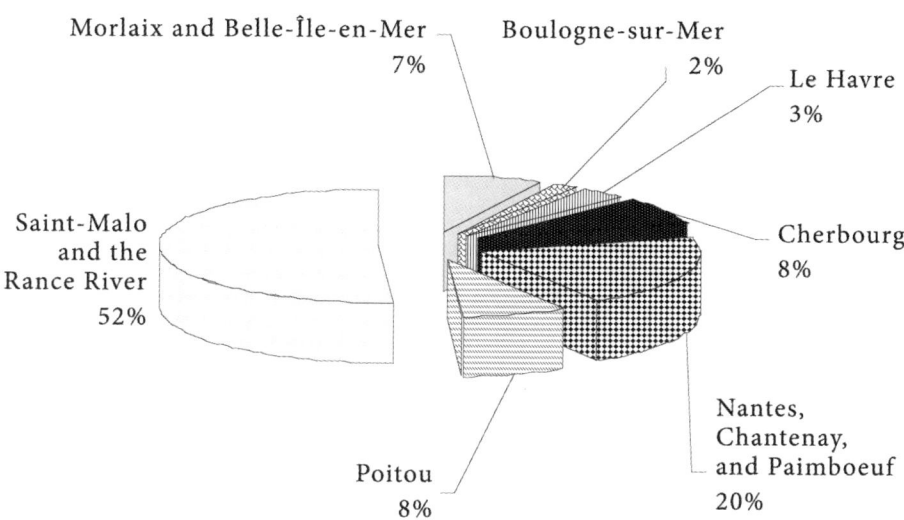

A second table—which may only be enlightening for its imperfections—demonstrates the total results that we derived (Table 4). We find a relatively higher proportion of marriages between Acadians (385, or 59 percent of the marriages) than mixed marriages (41 percent).[44] In reality, these results should be fine-tuned, for one clearly finds a strong disparity between the places where the Acadians probably had a feeling of only passing through and those places where they had more likely considered to settle. If we consider this criteria, we logically observe that the rate of mixed marriages notably changes. Thus, if we only consider the places where the Acadians were more or less stationed while waiting to be moved else-

TABLE 4
Estimates of rates of endogamous and exogamous marriages in the Acadian population staying in France between 1758-1785 and of variations by sex

Marriages	Acadians[45]		Mixed[46]				Rate[50]/Type			Total Number of Marriages	Exemptions[47]	Source	Years examined
			Number/Type										
Place	N[48]	&[49]	A[51]	B[52]	total[53]		A[54]	B[55]	total[56]				
Morlaix and Belle-Île-en-Mer	6	14%	13	23	36		36%	64%	86%	42		Jacques and Jacqueline Barré[57]	Morlaix (1763-1765) BI (1765-1785)
Boulogne-sur-Mer	6	55%	0	5	5		0%	100%	45%	11		Bruno Haffreingue	1761-1785[58]
Rochefort-sur-Mer	30	37%	36	14	50		72%	28%	63%	80		Calculations based on unpublished research by Jacques Nerrou	1759-1770
Le Havre	11	58%	6	2	8		75%	25%	42%	19		Personal research of G. M. Braud (Municipal Archives of Havre)[59]	1759-1775
Cherbourg	35	76%	2	8	10		27%	73%	24%	45		Patrice Berton and James P. Henry	1759-1781
Nantes, Chantenay, and Paimbœuf[60]	68	58%	40	9	49		82%	18%	42%	117	25	G. M. Braud, *Les Acadiens en France, Nantes et Paimbœuf, 1775-1785*. Approche Genealogique, Ouest Edition, 1999[61]	1775-1785
Poitou[62]	14	31%	28	3	31		90%	10%	69%	45	3	Calculations of G. M. Braud from A. J. Robichaux, *The Acadian Exiles in Châtellerault, 1773-1785*, Eunice, La., Hebert Publications, 1983[63]	1773-1785
Saint-Malo—River Rance[64]	215	73%	23	55	78		29%	71%	27%	293		Calculations of G. M. Braud from A. J. Robichaux, *The Acadian Exiles in Saint-Malo, 1758-1785*, Eunice, La., Hebert Publications, 1981[65]	1758-1785
TOTAL	385	59%	148	119	267		55%	45%	41%	652		Further research still possible[66]	
Place of passage	335	69%	71	79	150		47%	53%	31%	485		Only the places where the Acadians were in transit are counted[67]	
Permanent Place	20	23%	41	26	67		61%	39%	77%	87		Belle-Île and Poitou are only considered here	

where, we obtain much higher rates of endogamous marriages, to the order of 70 percent. If, on the contrary, we next consider the families settled at Belle-Île-en-Mer or in Poitou, the proportion of marriages contracted between two Acadians falls to less than 25 percent.

This illustrates in a conclusive manner that one of the determinative factors explaining the endogamous marriages was the fear, often expressed in the requests for exemptions from consanguinity analyzed above, that the husband or wife from the site would not want to follow the Acadians to the colonies in the case of another departure. The fear of abandoning the supplemental payment also played an important role. On the other hand, those of the Acadians in Poitou who married French spouses had certainly expressed reluctance to return to Acadia previously, and their matrimonial choice was probably only the logical consequence of their decision to separate from the group and to remain on the lands of Pérusse. In Poitou, other factors contributed to significantly increasing the number of mixed marriages: thus, young Acadian women were surely unable to marry within the interior of the group of Acadians, given the small population.[68] Moreover, they brought as dowry a house that clearly drew numerous suitors (often impoverished orphans from the surrounding area).[69]

Among these mixed marriages, we have also sought to discover if there was significant variation depending on sex. The results show that, in a general manner, the Acadian girls were as plentiful in joining French men as were the Acadian men in marrying French women. We will see, however, that this must be adjusted depending on the place and the time.

FIGURE 8

Division of marriages between Acadians and of mixed marriages

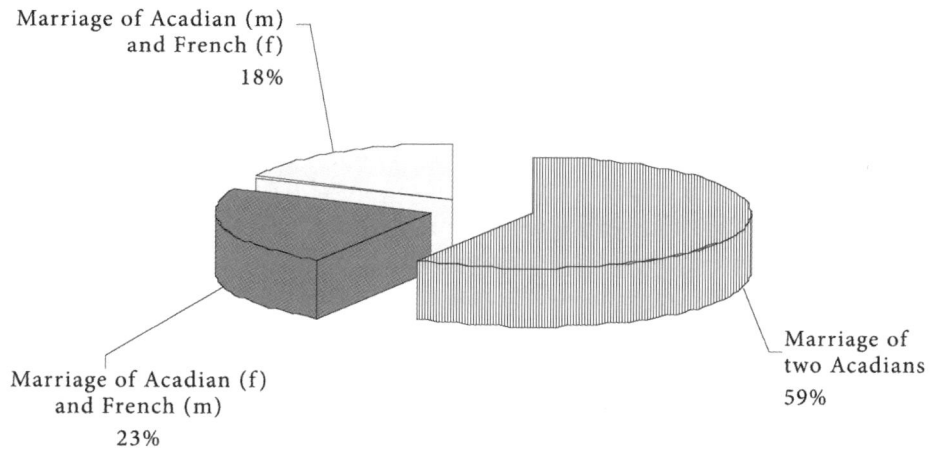

It is difficult to interpret these results in the absence of points of comparison. Did the Acadians marry more amongst themselves than did, for example, the groups of Normans or Dauphinois living in Paris? We can no doubt consider that a high proportion of endogamous marriages was the sign of a certain withdrawal into themselves and surely shows a desire to not integrate, but was there a normal standard in the matter? I also investigated if one might discern a temporal evolution in the number of marriages contracted. Here, then is the graphic made from the evolution of marriages according to the accounts made of Le Havre, Cherbourg, Saint-Malo, and Nantes (Figure 9).

FIGURE 9

Number of marriage acts featuring at least one Acadian
(Cherbourg, Le Havre, Saint-Malo and Nantes)

This table shows a strong decline in the number of marriages between around 1771 and 1780. We may pose various hypotheses to explain this. In the first place, it is likely that the Acadians—displaced many times during the period, first from the ports into which they had found refuge, then to Poitou, then from Poitou to Nantes—delayed their marriages with the expectation of a more secure situation. Moreover, we may speculate that the number of people of an age to marry was low at that time. Indeed, those children reaching twenty-five years of age in 1775 would have been born around 1750, which roughly corresponds to the start of tribulations for those Acadian families who were transferred from Île Saint-Jean. Although I have no solid facts on the matter, it would not be surprising if births were less frequent among the inhabitants of Île Saint-Jean in the 1750s, or that a large number of children born in this period died very young, because of the great vulnerability of smaller children in such dire situations. Lastly, and obviously, the Acadians were much more difficult to inventory in the documentation while they were "in transit," which would automatically lessen the number of marriages reported.[70]

Finally, I enquired if one might discern during this period any marked tendency towards more mixed marriages in the places where the Acadians knew that they were only staying in transit. Here is another way of following the main group of Acadians, by voluntarily excluding those who removed themselves from it by going to Belle-Île-en-Mer or staying in Poitou. If we now separate the types of marriages, we can construct many projections (Figure 10 and Figure 11) showing the Acadians' withdrawal amongst themselves, especially at the start of their stay in France. Thus, in Figure 11 we see that the general tendency of the intermarriages is at its lowest, with nearly 80 percent endogamous at the start of the period, going down to 60 percent at the end.

One may better perceive this entire evolution by separating the data into more representative sections. Thus, if we examine closely the Saint-Malo region (Figure 12), there does not seem to have been a notable change in the number of mixed marriages there, where a relatively low number of members of the "nation" remained throughout the period. On the other hand, we find a clear decrease in endogamous marriages among the Acadians and a clear decrease also in the total number of religious acts.

FIGURE 10

Chronological evolution of the number of endogamous or mixed marriages in Le Havre, Cherbourg, Saint-Malo, and Nantes

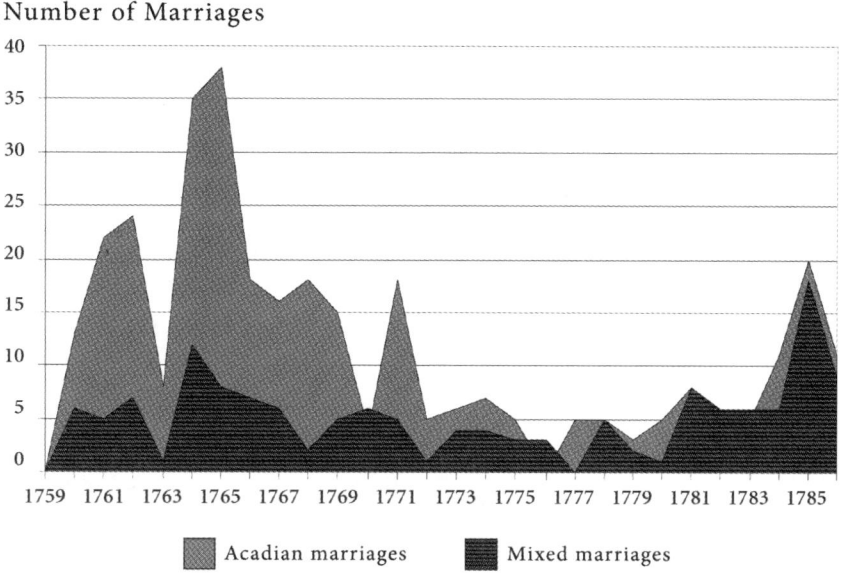

FIGURE 11

Proportion of Acadian marriages compared to the total marriages with an average curve

FIGURE 12

Marriages in the region of Saint-Malo

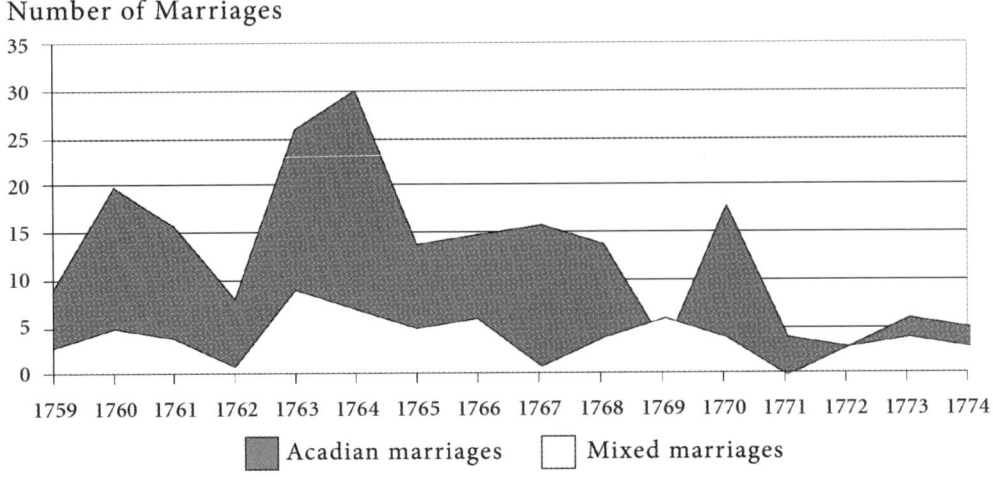

If we now compare all of the numbers from Saint-Malo and Cherbourg—where most of the marriages were celebrated before 1775—to those of Nantes after 1775, we find a significant increase in exogamous marriages. Indeed, in the first two ports the rates of inter-Acadian marriages were respectively 73 percent and 76 percent, while at Nantes the number falls to 58 percent. This acceleration is especially shown after 1780, as this table on Nantes well demonstrates (Figure 13).

FIGURE 13

Marriages at Nantes

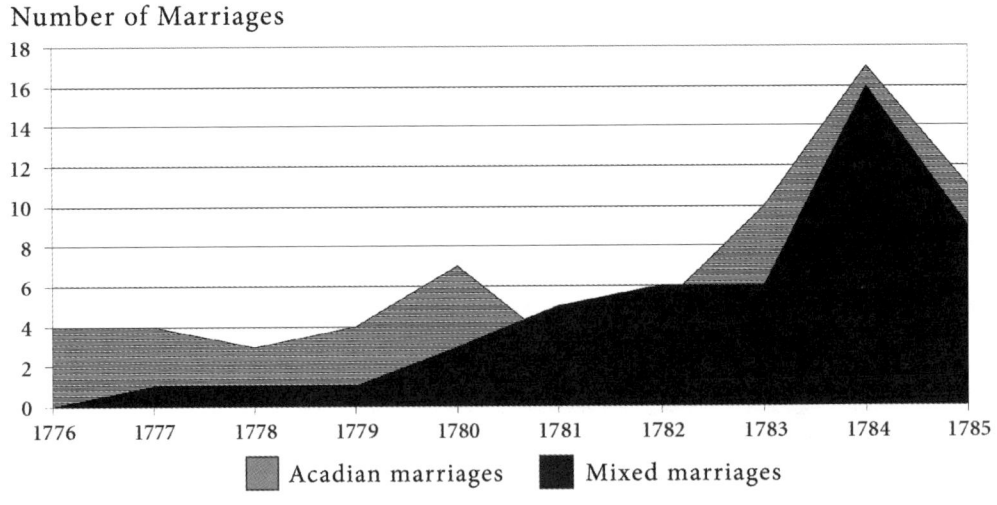

An interpretation of this graphic is clear enough. The significant increase in mixed marriages after 1780 is surely explained by the reluctance of the Acadians to marry inhabitants of Nantes at the time of their arrival in 1775, when, for the most part, they did not know what was going to happen next. Recall that, at this time, many refugees who had just left Poitou undoubtedly did not imagine that their stay at Nantes would last long. The plans then successively changed; the exiles foresaw returning to North America once the American War of Independence ended, at which point they hoped that France might regain Acadia. Moreover, we may easily imagine that some time would be needed before making ties and considering marriages with the inhabitants of the Breton port.

FIGURE 14

Proportion of inter-Acadian and mixed marriages depending on place of residence

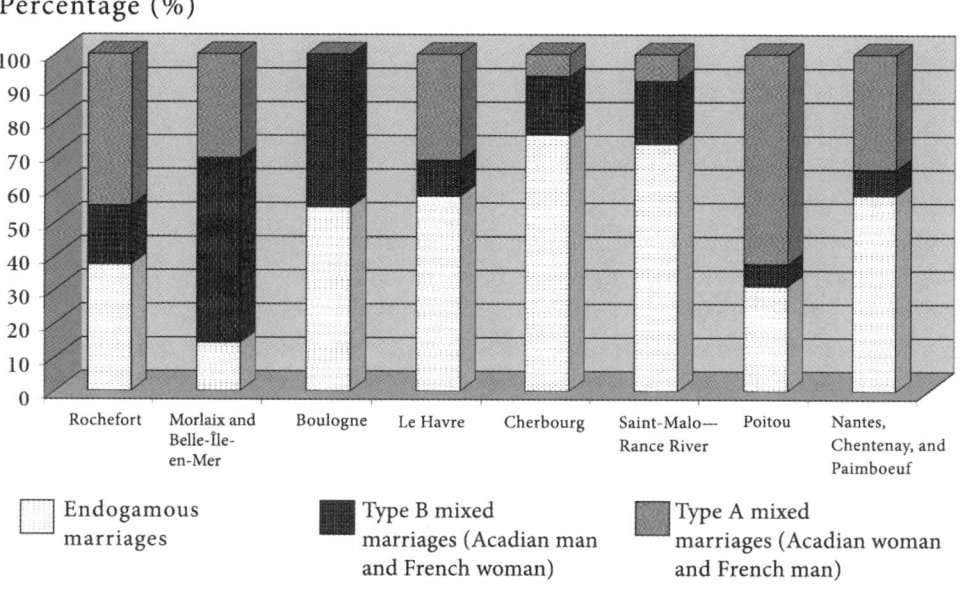

We have sought to examine a bit more the reasoning behind the Acadian matrimonial strategies by attempting to distinguish among the mixed marriages variations according to gender. On reading the summarizing table, we do not find pronounced differences where the rates were respectively 55 percent and 45 percent. If, however, we examine individually the sites of the Acadian sojourns, we find very significant local variations (Figure 14). If we eliminate the places where the numbers were too low to be representative, we nonetheless note that at Saint-Malo, of seventy-eight mixed marriages, fifty-five, or 71 percent, were contracted between a "Frenchwoman" and an Acadian. At Nantes, the proportion of this kind of marriage was entirely reversed to represent less than one mixed marriage of six in all. At Saint-Malo, it was mainly the men who married outside the group, at Nantes, therefore, the situation was clearly the reverse.

How to interpret the much higher proportion of Acadian women marrying outside the group than the men in some cases, and the reverse in others?[71] In general, the women would go to live with their husband's family and become incorporated within the community to which he belonged. Do these givens explain the more than one refusal by French women to marry Acadians, and, by extension, do they indicate that the French did not want to intermingle with the exiles? They may just as well demonstrate many other factors, such as a disparity in the matrimonial market at a given place and time. It would be quite interesting, in this regard, to have an idea of the rates of celibacy among the Acadians.

We should not, then, draw from these numbers too peremptory conclusions about the desire of the Acadians for integration. We could indeed discuss the pertinence of studying the rates of marriages in defining the integration. This method especially presupposes the mainly rational human choices, which, even in the case of a decision as important as a marriage, are far from always being such. Amorous feelings and the play of attraction and seduction were not born in our time, and we should not too hastily reject their compelling force. Neither should we neglect the chance of encounters, neighbors, and friendship, not to mention cases of marriages forced because of premarital pregnancies—marriages, even those largely arranged by the families, which have nearly always been, in French lands at least, the subject of negotiations between the actors involved.[72] Many other reasons lead us to prudence in the way we use the above numbers in trying to define the desire of the Acadians for integration or the lack thereof. We have seen how factors other than the choices involving a desire or lack thereof to assimilate with the inhabitants of the place might explain the increase of mixed marriages at the end of the period. For example, the simple fact that in a relatively restricted community like that of the Acadians in Poitou, choosing a partner from within the group, considering the parental ties among the individuals, was not necessarily made easier—if even possible—because of consanguinity.

What to conclude, then, from all of these numbers? Posing the hypothesis that the disruptive factors mentioned above were marginal with regard to the whole problem of the integration of the Acadians, the numbers obtained show a certain withdrawal into themselves among the refugees throughout the length of the period, with a clear enough majority of inter-Acadian marriages; this is especially evident if we only take into account the places where the main Acadian group sojourned. However, we find a small but perceptible decrease in the rates of these endogamous marriages through the years. When we examine each town in detail, we perceive that after a period where the proportion of inter-Acadian marriages was very high compared to mixed marriages, the proportions then tend to balance, no doubt reflecting the time necessary for the Acadians to make ties with the local communities and gain their confidence, and vice-versa.

If we examine the case of the marriages in the Nantes region, we find a strong correlation between the type of marriages and the departures to Louisiana, with a notable difference depending on gender. Thus, practically all of the Acadian women who married non-Acadians remained in France, since only three of forty-two left for Louisiana, while all of the Acadian men who married French women, or seventeen individuals in all, brought their wives to Louisiana.[73] It would be possible to verify if a similar pattern existed for the Acadians at Saint-Malo. If such was the case, could we not conclude that the marriages of type B, of an Acadian to a "Frenchwoman," were not marriages aimed on becoming integrated in France, but on the contrary, marriages integrating new feminine elements into the Acadian group? Following this logic, we could again recalculate the rates indicating a desire for integration by the Acadians by only considering the marriages of type A as being "lost" for the Acadian group. The marriages between Acadians, as well as those of type B, were then all in a sense "closed" marriages. In all, in combining these two latter types of marriages, we obtain about 77 percent of the marriages showing a desire to remain "among themselves."[74]

We could even inquire in a general way about the ability of the Acadian group to integrate within itself the French husbands of the Acadian women. Indeed, the relatively slight rates of Acadian women who followed their compatriots to Louisiana do not signify that the Acadian women marrying outside the group were entirely lost to it. On the contrary, one notes throughout the stay of the refugees in France a strong enough capacity for integration into the Acadian group of the new non-Acadian males. We can point out the example of one named Courtin (of whom we have already spoken above), a surgeon born at Blois, married to an Acadian woman, Marie Martin, who was then admitted among the Acadians of Belle-Île-en-Mer. In truth, the small number of mixed couples (including a man from the site and an Acadian woman) who followed the Acadian group is surely more easily explained by the fact that these couples were prohibited from embarking.[75]

Conclusion

What to conclude, then, about the Acadians' feelings of belonging during their sojourn in France? We have seen in our introduction how feelings of affinity of the group probably existed before deportation, articulated as a sense of being Catholic subjects of the king of France, but also how the Acadians, until their arrival in France, continued to define themselves more frequently as "neutral French" than as "Acadians." The latter word, which administrators systematically used upon their arrival in the ports of the Atlantic and of Manche, possibly contributed to reinforcing their identity and sense of belonging to a distinct group within the heart of the French entity. We have seen, however, that the administrators were hardly interested in the feelings of the Acadians or in contingent cultural differences. The refugees themselves were not given to writing on the subject, either. As for the study of the marriages made in the final section, it hardly allows us to make definitively conclusions. How might we distinguish among the factors that might have influenced the choice of a marriage? The question might be more easily resolved if the Acadians had not been convinced that they were destined to leave for the colonies or to go to other places in France. This important parameter clearly incited them to marry among the group and considerably confuses our interpretations. To find a fairly large rate of endogamous marriages does not necessarily imply that they lived withdrawn from their local communities. Even the appearance of the words and expressions "nation" and "national body" starting at the beginning of the 1770s (perhaps borrowed from the language of the opposition to the *parlements* following the Maupeou reform), hardly allows us to decide the matter. Certainly, "nation" is found in an increasing number of documents, but the Acadians themselves only used it on very few occasions. Moreover, significant dissensions permeated the group, which many refugees refused to admit themselves. In all, if it is highly plausible that a sense of belonging or of group sentiment was strengthened by the ordeal of deportation and the isolation families and individuals faced—and that it grew during the Acadians' stay in France—in truth, we are still somewhat blind on this subject.

Epilogue and Conclusion

Our story was interrupted after the orders issued by Necker to disperse the Acadians throughout the territory of France, orders that were not put into effect. We have seen how the hopes of the refugees to return to Acadia were then revived by the turn of events brought by the American War of Independence. Towards 1782-1783, it seems that a large number of Acadians sought more to emigrate or to return to Nova Scotia than to go to Louisiana. How, then, do we explain the emigration to the latter destination rather than to the former? A number of authors present the departure to the Mississippi as having been inevitable, or at least as the result of constant lobbying by the Acadians for this result. To gain a clear idea of it and to understand how the Louisiana option was finally achieved, we have conducted a detailed study of the petitions by the Acadians addressed to the administration aiming on soliciting a new emigration from France.[1] Here are the main conclusions.

The dominant impression that comes from this examination is, first of all, that of a great divide among the Acadians about the choice of a destination, a division that increased throughout the period.[2] During the first phase, corresponding to the signature of the peace treaty of 1763, the majority seemed to want to return to Acadia, but the urging by the government to go to the Southern Colonies nonetheless seems to have borne fruit. The clear decrease in references to traveling to Acadia in the later period (1764-1772), partially filled by requests for Saint-Pierre and Miquelon, is undoubtedly explained by many factors. One of these factors is surely the increase of governmental plans for settling in France itself, allied to the censuring of plans involving passage overseas. At the same time, we find the first mention of petitions for passage to Louisiana; the number of references to this destination is then maintained at a certain level almost until the end of the period, except, of course, for the years of the American War of Independence between 1776 and 1781 when the Acadians, like the government, were awaiting a result that might considerably alter the options available. Indeed, many Acadians were hopeful of a re-conquest of Acadia by the young United States, which would have allowed them an easier return to their former homeland. The rationale was that the French government would not be as hesitant to let the Acadians depart to go amongst allies as amongst enemies. As a result of the war, transfer of the sovereignty of Acadia—from London to Washington—might perhaps put an end to the discord among the Acadians. Such, at least, seems to have been the hope of a portion of the exiles. Events having been settled otherwise, dissension was again stoked after the peace. Even within the same village of residence, the refugees had trouble coming to an agreement: thus, Acadians in Nantes, Morlaix, and Saint-Malo were divided between those who wanted to go to Louisiana and those who were reluctant to do so (as we will see in more detail). Nonetheless, in some towns a majority did want to go to the same destination: those in Saint-Malo wanted to go "to Boston" for example. If the petitions to go to the Southern Colonies then completely ceased, many still sought to go to Saint-Pierre and Miquelon. The archipelago had just been regained by France after its recent conquest and devastation during the War of American Independence.

The destinations ultimately represented different stages in the break with France and Acadia. To go to the southern French colonies was to remain subjects of the king of France, to maintain certain customs of the country, to live amongst a society, speaking the same language and practicing the same religion, but it was also, according to the opinions of the time, to live in a dangerous climate that progressively would degrade the virtue of these populations more adapted to cold climates. This latter aspect especially disheartened the Acadians, who wanted to return to the aforementioned conditions and more suitable climate of Saint-Pierre and Miquelon, and, undoubtedly as a backup plan, hoped to maintain their preferred professional activities such as fishing, to rediscover some of their family, and to maintain ties with Acadia, which was relatively close and with which contacts had been reestablished. This no doubt explains the attraction of Saint-Pierre and Miquelon despite the insecurity, the limited land, and the overpopulation of the archipelago. The deportation of the inhabitants of the two islands during the War of American Independence was a serious blow that limited these requests.[3]

A return to the much missed Acadia would have undoubtedly meant a more fundamental rupture with France, for it would mean that the Acadians would lose their status as subjects of the Very Christian King, as well as culturally separating from France. Even if they had freedom to practice the Catholic religion, the impossibility of receiving French priests and life in the midst of so many Protestants represented a danger of isolation and assimilation that was surely not negligible. The hope to return "to the country" was probably the deepest anchored in the heart of the Acadians, for very understandable reasons, but it was also certainly that which became the subject of the most self-sacrifice on their part, and of the strongest veto from the government.

Concerning the other destinations proposed, Louisiana seemed to be a compromise as much for the Acadians as for the French government. As with Saint-Pierre and Miquelon , the government authorized the reassembling of the exiles with many other Acadian families expatriated from the American colonies. It also allowed them to become subjects of an allied and Catholic prince, guaranteeing the free practice of religion. Contrary to the small Miquelon archipelago, the vast Louisiana expanse—in a climate perceived as being more temperate and less dangerous than that of Guyana—assured the acquisition of lands for the settlement that was so desired. Finally, the king of Spain, wanting, like all the princes of Europe, to increase the number of his subjects, was also likely to pay for the transport of the Acadians as well as the expenses of settlement. This argument was decisive for the refugees, for most of them were indebted and incapable of paying for their transport themselves, not to mention the expenses of starting the cultivation of land in a foreign country.[4] The passage to Louisiana was finally agreed upon because it represented a compromise between the Acadian demands and those of the government.

It seems that upon their arrival in the ports of Manche and along the Atlantic, the Acadians were then deeply divided about where they wanted to go. Through the duration of the period, they clearly preferred returning to somewhere close to the former Acadia or to Saint-Pierre and Miquelon rather than going to Louisiana, which seemed attractive to only a limited number of the refugees, even up until the end of their stay in France. The departure for Louisiana, far from being inevitable or embodying a fixed idea belatedly realized, was ironically achieved, as we now will see, thanks to the mediation of a non-Acadian, Peyroux de la Coudrenière, who was motivated by his own personal profit. Peyroux was probably induced by a series of favorable factors—notably the end of the War of American Independence and the consequential diminishing of the hope of the Acadians to return to Nova Scotia—to convince a great number of the exiles who were initially reluctant. Their desire to remain grouped together also certainly played a large role. Those who did want to go to Louisiana finally won over the inertia of the others and brought a collective push for the emigration.

The Departure for Louisiana

In fact, various documents indicate the deep division of the Acadians up to the embarkation in 1785 and show that, though the solution of Louisiana finally meant a compromise acceptable to both parties, this compromise was for a long time refused as much by the French government as by the Acadians themselves.

For some of the Acadians deported into the American colonies in 1755, Louisiana came to represent hope for a new life, certainly far from the land of their childhood, but on the North American continent and within Catholic territory. We have seen that the Acadians arrived on the Mississippi directly from the Thirteen Colonies where they had initially been deported, or by way of Saint-Domingue, starting in 1763.[5] For the Acadian refugees in France, on the other hand, the idea of emigrating to Louisiana was not seriously considered immediately after the Seven Years War. It took time to build contact through correspondence between the Acadians who had been transported to the Mississippi and those who were refugees in France. Only in 1766 do we find a first letter praising the merits of the Louisiana colony and, in comparison, denigrating the conditions made for the refugees in France. Jean-Baptiste Semer, who went to Louisiana by way of Saint-Domingue in 1765, wrote his father, a refugee in Le Havre:

> They grant us six *arpents* [7.5 acres] for married couples and four and five for the young people, thus one has the advantage, my dear father, of being on his own land, and of saying "I have land of my own." The trees are very plentiful and one makes great commerce from them, for construction and for export for the building of houses at the Cape [Cap Français, in Saint-Domingue] and other islands. An individual who wants to work for goods and sacrifice will be at his ease within few years. It is an immense country, you can boldly come here with my dear mother and all of the other Acadian families. They will still be better off than in France. There are neither claims nor taxes to pay and one works more and earns more, without doing wrong to anyone.[6]

Following this letter, the father of Jean-Baptiste Semer and many Acadians from Le Havre addressed the authorities asking to go to Louisiana. In response, the minister of the Navy wrote the intendant of Le Havre that "it [would be] that much less possible to consider this request as, on the one hand, the colony of Louisiana no longer belonging to France, the considerable expenses that the transportation of so many people involved would be a total loss for His Majesty and because, on the other hand, the government is presently occupied with the means of placing all of the families from North America within the kingdom."[7] The Acadians thus saw clearly delineated a prohibition to go to this destination. However, it seems that the Acadian refugees in Louisiana had themselves not lost the hope of reuniting with their kinsmen. Thus the French governor at New Orleans gave an account to his Spanish colleague of how he had authorized the Acadians of Louisiana to urge their compatriot refugees at Saint-Pierre and Miquelon to come and join them.[8] Actually, some weeks later, the governor of the archipelago spoke of the attraction of the Mississippi for many Acadians, for which Choiseul had just encouraged them to depart Saint-Pierre and Miquelon. "Many among them would voluntarily go to Louisiana, if one wanted to transport them there," he wrote.[9]

However, the situation in Louisiana would not remain as idyllic as Jean-Baptiste Semer described it. Indeed, by November 1766, the *commissioner-ordonnateur* in New Orleans expressed the difficult situation in which the colony found itself because of the massive arrival of Acadians that he had to assist.[10] The rebellion of 1768 against the Spanish governor and the repression that followed in 1769, when several of the rebels were condemned to death, including at least one Acadian, surely put the brakes on the enthusiasm of those who wanted to emigrate to the colony. In fact, in the following years, we find hardly any references to plans of the Acadians to emigrate to New Orleans.[11] It took nearly six years for a new Acadian petition requesting passage to Louisiana to be sent to the government.[12] This petition bore the signature of Jean-Jacques LeBlanc, in the name of "110 heads of families of the department of Saint-Malo." LeBlanc, one of the Acadian delegates of the Malo region, starting at least from that date, worked in favor of the Louisiana option. As we have already written, this option was certainly the most politically acceptable for the government, therefore the one the most likely to being selected. And that is exactly what happened. While in 1766 the government could retreat behind the pretext that it sought a settlement in France for the refugees, and in the interval, the Acadian petitions to return to Acadia were denied, the petition of LeBlanc in March 1772 clearly put the ministry in a bind: Since the plans for settlement one after another had all failed, the Minister of the Navy then in charge, de Boynes, proposed to the Council of the king to accept the Acadian's suggestion. The request to go to Louisiana provoked a meeting of the council in July or September 1772, during the course of which, according to many witnesses, the king expressed his surprise that the Acadians had not yet been settled and refused any idea of emigration, suggesting on the contrary to "attach them to the soil." It was this meeting, and in particular the royal wish, that lay at the direct origin of the settlement in Poitou. The solution proposed by the government answering LeBlanc's request did not suit him, however, and he then became the principal instigator of resistance to Pérusse's plan and the first architect of the ruin of the settlement.

However, LeBlanc does not seem to have ever received the approval of all of the Acadians, and that explains his fall. First of all, we have seen, he claimed to send his petition of March 1772 in the name of 110 heads of families, representing 492 people, or less than a third of his compatriots, who comprised about 1,800 individuals in the region. But still he was the only one to sign it. No document informs us of the exact reasons for the reluctance of the other Acadians to second his request. Many factors may have played a role: the revolt of the French colonists of Louisiana and the problems with the Spanish authorities had certainly cooled their enthusiasm, if the Acadians were aware of them. The hot climate also undoubtedly discouraged them. Moreover, the first official prohibition to emigrate to Louisiana, made by the Minister of the Navy in 1766, rendered all new requests presumptuous, if not disrespectful. Perhaps some Acadians feared reprisals or reproofs, and it was no doubt for this reason that the petition was sent "against the opinion of the Abbé Le Loutre." Moreover, many Acadians probably no longer wanted to move; they feared that the departure of their compatriots might deprive them of the supplemental aid and they surely were afraid of taking to sea at the risk of their lives.

This dissension among the Acadians concerning their destination is constantly attested to in the sources. For example, in November 1772, the naval commissioner of Saint-Malo wrote to Lemoyne that certain Acadians wanted to go to Corsica, while others desired relocation to Louisiana or to Isle of France (Mauritius), and some wished to return to Canada, particularly to Acadia.[13] In July 1773, Lemoyne himself attested that the Acadians of Saint-Malo hesitated between Louisiana and Saint-Pierre and Miquelon, while their compatriots at Cherbourg wanted to return to Acadia.[14] Other documents demonstrate that this division persisted: during the period when the majority of refugees stayed in Poitou, Pérusse made many allusions to the *idée fixe* of Jean-Jacques Le Blanc of going to Louisiana, but according to what he said, LeBlanc was ready to go elsewhere if necessary, even to Acadia or to England.[15] Shortly after their arrival in Nantes, a report of a sub-delegate of the city, Ballays, again demonstrated the deep division of opinion.[16]

Towards the end of 1777, however, the government once again, although hesitantly, considered allowing the Acadians to leave for Louisiana. In fact, the Minister of the Navy did ask the ambassador of Spain about the possibility of sending two families to Louisiana.[17] The Spanish authorities were ready to accept. Soon after, perhaps following the visit of a second Acadian delegation to Versailles soliciting a new emigration, Necker approved the idea of passage to Louisiana and contacted the Spanish ambassador on this subject.[18] But, the report noted "the favorable way in which Mr. d'Aranda received it again drew the attention of the Council and they reversed themselves."[19] For the preceding five years the Council of the King had with its veto objected to any idea of emigration. It is this that pushed Necker, short on ideas, to form his plan of spreading the Acadians throughout France.

In June 1778, if we are to believe a fairly detailed report, the Acadians were still strongly divided. Curiously, the drafter of the text, undoubtedly an agent of the Contrôle Général, did not provide exactly the same version as the sub-delegate Ballays about the desires of the Acadians, although this report was written barely six months after the latter's. In fact, the 1778 report affirmed that the refugees were divided between those who wanted to return to Acadia, those who wanted to go to Louisiana, those who wished return to Poitou, or those who wanted to go to Corsica. For his part, Ballays did not mention the same destinations at all, nor had he written of any Acadian desire to return to the lands of Pérusse or to go to the Isle of Beauté or Acadia.[20] We then find little reference to what the Acadians did between June 1778 and July 1783 apart from what is said about them in a report from 1782. This report suggests that the *status quo* prevailed and that all sides awaited the end of the American War of Independence before making a decision about the Acadians. The report specifies simply that "[the French government] has stopped insisting [that the Acadians be dispersed] from the moment when the affairs in North America take a favorable turn, one considers that, with a return of peace, some combination may return the Acadians to their former country or that may provide an almost equivalent result."[21] The American War for Independence occasioned yet another deportation for the Acadians on Saint-Pierre and Miquelon, in October of 1778. On taking possession of the archipelago, after the signing of the Treaty of Versailles in September 1783, only a portion of the former inhabitants were authorized to return there.[22] Many older persons, on the other hand, were forbidden to embark from the fear that they would become the responsibility of the colonial administration.

Peyroux and Terriot

Many Acadians benefited from the interval of five years offered by the Franco-English conflict (1778 to 1783) to create a life of stability—and even profit—in Nantes. Thus we again find the traces of Basile Henry, clearly prosperous in November 1782,[23] while some other Acadians managed to open small businesses. Within this context, with the approach of peace in 1783, the first meetings between Peyroux de la Coudrenière and Olivier Terriot occurred in Nantes, with the aim of obtaining the authorization for all of the Acadians who were refugees in France to emigrate to Louisiana.

We have little biographical information about Henri-Marie Peyroux de la Coudrenière. According to the report of Olivier Terriot, he was the son of an apothecary and originally from around Nantes.[24] His marriage certificate at Nantes to Prudence Françoise Rodrigue describes him as a merchant druggist. Neither Peyroux nor his wife were Acadians.[25] If Peyroux appeared to the secretary of the Spanish ambassador at Paris as "a man of reserve, judicious and moderate" who had lived in Canada and in Louisiana, where his principal "inclination" had been natural history and who had some publications in the *Journal de physique*,[26] to the intendant of Brittany the man "was but a former spice merchant having gone bankrupt, and who had no reputation . . . and who according to all appearances only became involved in this affair for some particular self-interest."[27] His ties with Louisiana were lengthy. According to a summary provided later by Terriot, Peyroux had previously spent seven years there and "had made no fortune." Peyroux actually claimed to have passed "the finest years of [his] youth" in the Spanish colony.[28] Peyroux had a brother in Louisiana, as well as another in Nantes who proposed to transport the Acadians to New Orleans, depending, of course, on some remuneration.[29] Terriot affirmed that it was with the aim of winning back the fortune of Peyroux, who returned to Nantes in 1783, having become a recruiting agent for Spain and having formed the plan of bringing the Acadians over to their compatriots. Some years previously, de la Coudrenière had written a "report on the usefulness of a school of agriculture in every Spanish province and colony,"[30] which was sent to the authorities in Madrid, and in which were already mentioned the usefulness and talents of the Acadians for agriculture, proving his relative familiarity with the Acadians.

The aforementioned information by Terriot and the intendant's insinuations that it was from self-interest that Peyroux decided to organize the emigration of the refugees were well founded. Obviously, Peyroux himself affirmed that he was acting philanthropically to help the Acadians who were living miserably in France and to prevent their inclination to soon emigrate to the English colonies. Indeed he claimed to have motivated the Acadians in favor of his plan by explaining to them "that since they had resolved to leave France, honor and religion should oblige them to renounce returning to Acadia, and to prefer a nation friendly to France whose king was of the same blood."[31] Still, upon his arrival at Nantes, in 1783, he seems to have sought an intermediary capable of helping him reassure the Acadians. He contacted Olivier Terriot, the son of an Acadian whom we have already had the occasion to mention above: Étienne Terriot, called "Big Étienne," who was implicated many times in the affairs of contraband tobacco at Saint-Malo. Olivier Terriot, twenty-eight years old, married and the father of two children in 1785, was then presumably a master shoemaker in Nantes, but we have little information about him before the contact tying him to Peyroux de la Coudrenière, which was the main subject of a lengthy report he drafted well after the facts, in 1798.[32]

From what we can establish from the correspondence and the reports drafted relating to the emigration of the Acadians to Louisiana, the first meeting between Peyroux and Terriot occurred in June or July 1783, shortly before the signing of the peace treaty between France, the United States, and the United Kingdom. If we believe Terriot, our sole source of information on this subject, the meeting occurred in his shoemaking shop. It was Peyroux who supposedly had the idea of sending the Acadians to Louisiana and who insisted that Terriot participate in this operation. The latter affirmed that he only accepted Peyroux's offer after much reluctance and after Peyroux had promised to "share his last bit of bread with him." Terriot's first priority after this initial meeting was to try, with difficulty, to convince his compatriots of the merits of going to Louisiana, and that, this time, the operation could succeed.[33] In fact, in the first petition sent to the Spanish ambassador requesting passage to Louisiana and seconding the official request made by Peyroux to Aranda, it is noted that Terriot had succeeded in acquiring only three signatures other than his own and that of his father.[34] Terriot wrote:

> His very Christian Majesty . . . has had the generosity to grant us a very small pension until now allowing us to have lands to cultivate. But until now we have only been offered sterile land in France and unhealthy areas of the island of Corsica, which we could not accept. For many years we have asked the king and his ministers to allow us to go to Louisiana where we have a great many relatives and friends; but our plans have always been rejected because France no longer possesses any of that country.[35]

In the meantime, Peyroux had met the Spanish ambassador in Paris, and reassured the shoemaker that the ambassador was cooperative and would support the project, but that they had to await a final opinion from Madrid.[36] The negotiations between Peyroux, Terriot, and Aranda did not occur without being noticed, however. Thus Vergennes, Secretary of State for Foreign Affairs, wrote some days later that, "secret emissaries throughout Brittany . . . are working to have the subjects of the king emigrate and among whom one indicates specifically *Sieur* Peyroux de la [Coudrenière], who has been working to enlist the Acadians resident at Nantes."[37] At the end of August 1783, the sub-delegate of Nantes had Peyroux watched, but decided not to imprison him, lacking sufficient charges.[38]

The answer from the court of Spain came quickly. At the end of January 1784 Peyroux reported to his associate that King Charles III had agreed to receive the Acadians in Louisiana and to pay for their transportation. The agreement included one condition, however. Before soliciting Versailles, the Spanish ambassador wanted to be assured that the Acadians had been authorized to go to the United States, which he had heard was the case: "Once one could provide him with some certainty, he would go to see Mr. de Castries to ask that the king consent to your departure, which he cannot refuse if it is true that he had granted it to Mr. [Benjamin] Franklin."[39] Terriot was thus charged with verifying the assertion. In fact a later document mentions unfounded rumors then circulating in Nantes.[40] It is possible that Peyroux went too far in affirming that the authorization to emigrate to the United States had been given, with the aim of convincing the Spanish ambassador that the steps to obtain the Acadians would not be difficult. But the affirmation had some basis in truth: a petition from the Acadians of Saint-Malo was actually sent the following month to the Minister of the Navy, soliciting passage to Boston,[41] but it does not seem that the French government had then provided its authorization for passage to the United States. Indeed, in the month of March, after being transported to Nantes, Peyroux was obliged to warn the secretary of the Spanish ambassador, Hérédia, that the rumor was false.[42] He nonetheless requested that Spain still take the steps to claim the Acadians. The latter "beg you to ask for them from the Ministry of France," he wrote to Hérédia, "and they are convinced that you will obtain them easily."[43]

As we see, Peyroux ably manipulated the situation to force the hand of both sides. He let the Acadians believe that Spain had agreed to receive them in Louisiana, while pretending to forget that the agreement by the Spanish ambassador was conditional and that the condition had not been fulfilled. Moreover, in his reports to the Spanish ambassador, Peyroux minimized as much as possible the problems posed by the emigration: on the one hand, he let it be understood that all of the Acadians wanted to be transported to Louisiana and, on the other, he affirmed that the French authorities were disposed to allow the Acadians to leave.[44] Aranda, however, remained very hesitant, since at the end of March 1784, Peyroux asked the Spanish ambassador once again "to not further delay . . . going before the court of France" to obtain the Acadians.[45] Once again putting Hérédia and Aranda before the accomplished fact, Peyroux explained that it was now urgent to forewarn Versailles:

> Despite all of my care to keep the affair of the Acadians in a kind of dormant state until you have requested and obtained permission from the court of France, those who were in on the secret could not help but inform their compatriots; and at this moment I have learned that a great number of Acadians, unable to resist the desire of knowing something positive about their departure, have gone together as a group to see the sub-delegate to learn if the ministry has given the order to allow them to leave for Louisiana. Some letters that were written in Saint-Malo and Morlaix stirred up the same enthusiasm among the Acadians living in these two towns. . . . There is no doubt that the sub-delegate is going to write the court to inform it of all of these developments; and, the ministry having not been forewarned from other sources, it is possible that something disagreeable could consequently happen to me.[46]

If this was a deliberate strategy by Peyroux, it paid off for after only two days the Spanish ambassador finally informed the French Minister of Foreign Affairs, the comte de Vergennes, that Madrid agreed to welcome the refugees in Louisiana, on the condition that "his Very Christian Majesty allow the Acadians the freedom to go there."[47] At the same time, Hérédia suggested that they renew their request,[48] which some did days later.[49] A letter to Vergennes written by Peyroux proclaimed the Acadians' fidelity and patriotism. Recalling their misery, the refugees asked to rejoin their families in Louisiana, "under the power of a king who is the friend, relative and ally of our monarch," they wrote.[50] However, it seems that very few of the Acadians wanted to go to Louisiana, or at least stood willing to sign the petition. Peyroux had led Aranda and Hérédia to believe that all of the Acadians wanted to emigrate to Louisiana, and he was clearly embarrassed by the fact that he was only able to collect some thirty signatures on the petition addressed to Versailles. He felt obliged to justify this small number and the delay before this petition was sent, by pointing out the fact that the refugees had requested modifications to the petition he had drafted.[51] Peyroux does not elaborate about the modifications requested by the signatories, but he undoubtedly tried to force the issue. As for the small number of signatories, Peyroux explained candidly that thirty-five heads of families had signed,[52] adding, "others in greater numbers also wanted to sign, but, as the page was filled, they were told that that was enough!"[53] This excuse, leads us once again to think that Peyroux had not obtained the agreement of all of the Acadians—far from it. For good measure, Peyroux added in the same letter that the exiles were very satisfied with being "claimed by Spain" and that many cried with joy on reading Hérédia's letter.[54]

For their part, the French ministers did not hurry to ask the king for authorization to allow the Acadians to emigrate to Louisiana. After having received the official request of Hérédia, dated March 24, 1784, Vergennes, in Foreign Affairs, quickly had it sent to de Castries, Minister of the Navy. "I beg you to put this request before the eyes of the king and then allow me to instruct Mr. the *chevalier* de Hérédia of the decision of his majesty," he wrote.[55] Some days later, de Castries answered Vergennes that it was rather up to the Controller-General to ask the king for the authorization for the Acadians to go to Louisiana.[56] This back-and-forth clearly demonstrate the ministers' fear of putting this question before the monarch. It was ultimately Calonne who was charged with asking Louis XVI. A decision was prepared on April 25, 1784,[57] and on April 27 Calonne informed Vergennes that the king had finally approved the emigration to Louisiana.[58] To save appearances and to more easily obtain the consent he sought, Calonne very diplomatically presented the king a slightly different proposal than that which had always been put forth before regarding the Acadians, and which recalled the reflections of the fox on guarding the raisins in the La Fontaine's fable!

> I would ask that you please note that the departure of the Acadians is not truly an emigration of subjects of the king, Acadia having been ceded to England by the Treaty of Utrecht, the Acadian refugees in France could only become subjects of the king once one will have procured for them settlements on lands that they have been made to hope for.

The decision of the king was communicated on May 11 by Vergennes to Hérédia,[59] and some days later Calonne made various arrangements to pay the overdue assistance due to the Acadians preparing to leave for Louisiana.[60]

With authorization granted, the difficulties, however, were not all resolved. Indeed, some days before the decision was communicated to Hérédia, Peyroux informed the Spanish ambassador that the Acadians of Saint-Malo had obtained from the king authorization to go to Virginia. According to Peyroux, these Acadians said that they were unfamiliar with the Louisiana plan. This seems hardly plausible and rather reveals, once again, the deep division among the Acadians that Peyroux sought to minimize as much as he could:

> Some Acadians of Saint-Malo, not knowing what those in Nantes had asked of Spain, sent two delegates to the court some months ago to ask permission to go to Virginia. Letters from this town announce that these delegates returned and that they succeeded but that most of those who asked to go to Virginia did not want to benefit from this permission in the hope of soon going to Louisiana. If it is true that the court would allow them to settle in this English republic, it would yet more readily allow them to settle in a monarchy that is the friend and ally of France.[61]

Once again, this information is curious. In fact, I have found no other document that makes a reference to any desire of the Acadians to go to Virginia. It is difficult to imagine a reason that might have prompted Peyroux to invent such a scenario from all of the pieces, which contradicts his previous letters to Hérédia. The account is probably authentic, but it does not seem to have had a follow-up. It is nevertheless possible that Peyroux mistook Boston for Virginia.

New problems awaited Peyroux. On May 25, 1784, he was arrested by the horsemen of the constabulary on the orders of the sub-delegate, after having read the letter from Hérédia of May 11 to about 150 Acadians gathered together. Terriot himself stealthily escaped and found refuge in the home of a magistrate of the town, where he wrote to Hérédia.[62] The sub-delegate presumably acted without knowledge of Vergennes's orders allowing the refugees to leave, and no doubt in the belief that Peyroux was acting secretly and in a reprehensible manner. After the intervention of Hérédia and a clarification of the situation, Peyroux was quickly freed.[63] His difficulties did not end, however, since some days later a petition sent by "many Acadian families of Nantes . . . who pronounced themselves against the execution" of the Louisiana plan was sent to the Controller-General, who quickly sent it to the intendant of Brittany.[64] The Controller-General provided few details in this petition, only that it was signed by "thirty families of this nation pronounced against the plan to go and serve under the domination of Spain."[65] Seized with doubt, he asked for a thorough investigation of the feelings of the Acadians and their real desire to go to Louisiana.[66] The intendant answered him some weeks later that he did not know what the feelings of the Acadians were on this subject and that his sub-delegate was presently conducting an enquiry.[67] Nonetheless, the result of the enquiry has unfortunately not come down to us. Even if it may have revealed feelings mostly hostile to emigration to Louisiana, it is little likely that the government would have wanted to reverse the policy that the king had by then already requested.

The difficulties of recruiting the Acadians and the undoubtedly dubious means employed by Peyroux and Terriot to recruit volunteers reached the ears of the count de Aranda himself. In July 1784, returning from Spain, the ambassador strongly recommended that Peyroux conduct himself "without the least appearance of seduction or violence" in convincing the Acadians.[68] As a response, Peyroux addressed to Hérédia a great number of questions posed by the refugees. These questions essentially concerned various financial aspects and the delays foreseen before embarkation to Louisiana.[69] They showed clearly once again that all of the Acadians were not in agreement on the Louisiana option. Whatever the case, de la Coudrenière left Paris some days later to return to Nantes and collect signatures of volunteers for the plan of emigration.[70] Once on site, he transmitted to Terriot Aranda's instructions, according to which "the intention of the two courts is to leave the Acadians perfectly free to choose whether to remain in France or to go to Louisiana."[71]

It was at this moment that Terriot experienced yet another misadventure. As we have seen, he had been charged with informing all of the Acadians of the Nantes region of the authorization to go to Louisiana. This task does not seem to have been especially easy. Terriot thus reports that he had "to go to those of various compatriots, some of whom did not [like the idea] of leaving France: they feared that on leaving, one would suppress the assistance[72] of those who remained." One day, then, as he spread the news, he was attacked in an inn by three of his discontent compatriots who would have suffocated him without the intervention of some other Acadians present at the scene. Terriot clearly reported the hostility that his activity provoked: "At Nantes, Olivier Terriot was cursed by one, insulted by another, attacked by another, because he sought to procure subjects for his Catholic majesty."[73] These various elements again demonstrate the lack of enthusiasm of many Acadians for the idea of leaving for the Mississippi.

In fact, it seems that Peyroux also had some difficulty enlisting the Acadians. At first, he does not seem to have had too much problem in recruiting people in the region of Nantes. As of August 1784, he reported to Aranda that he had enlisted nearly 1,325 individuals from this port and Paimboeuf, and he said that he was preparing to leave for Morlaix, Saint-Malo, and other towns to enlist other volunteers.[74] At about the same time, four heads of Acadian families who had initially remained in Poitou but more recently gone to Nantes because of the poor quality of the land in the *Grand-Ligne*, also asked the Minister of Foreign Affairs to go to Louisiana.[75]

It is nonetheless likely that Peyroux once again inflated the number of volunteers because, according to a later report, only 1,160 people in Nantes actually went to Louisiana.[76] According to Terriot, one of the conditions for the embarkation was that there had to be at least 1,600 people registered.[77] The fact that there were exactly 1,600 Acadians who went to Louisiana in 1785 lends credence to the idea that a predetermined quota that had to be filled, and that therefore a portion of the refugees were probably forced to leave France. We suspect that one of the methods used to put pressure on the refugees consisted of threatening the Acadians or leading them to believe that, after the departure of their compatriots, they would no longer receive payments from the king.[78] Indeed, when Terriot reported the aggression of which he was a victim, he let it be thought that his assailants wanted to do this to him because some, wanting to remain in France, feared losing the supplement after the emigration. Moreover, Peyroux reports that only "the families rich enough to do without the generosity of the king" had not registered to leave.[79] If this new information does not allow us to positively affirm that threats were actually made to the Acadians, it clearly gives the impression that the departure was endured rather than chosen, and that it was instigated by the announced suppression of the supplemental payments.

Peyroux also reports that various Acadians doubted the promises that had been made to them:

> The absurd stories that some people told in Nantes to dissuade the Acadians from the plan they had of going to Louisiana led me to ask many questions, mainly about their future settlement. But, after having convinced them of the absurdity of these stories, I told them that the court of Spain, having welcomed their request, would undoubtedly offer them the treatment that they requested, and I assured them that they should have the greatest confidence in the beneficence of a

court that has always shown itself to be generous and magnanimous. This answer seemed to have satisfied them.[80]

Unfortunately, Peyroux was clearly little interested in expanding on the content of these "absurd stories." Would we find therein the fears of the Louisiana climate previously mentioned? Or were there suspicions that the operation was actually aimed at sending the Acadians not to Louisiana, but to Guyana? This concern, wholly unfounded as it would seem, was reported by one Louis Judice to the governor of Louisiana: "Many inhabitants here fear that these [Acadian] families were really embarked at Nantes but went to Cayenne."[81] The source of these rumors remains unknown. Perhaps the apprehension of Marguerite Landry, mentioned above, that one might be sent to "contagious islands" was not in fact a fear of being sent to Louisiana, but rather that the ships were destined for Guyana. What is certain is that the refugees defied the French government, and that they were not ready to emigrate, no matter what the condition.[82]

The Controller-General believed that a minority of the Acadians wanted to emigrate. The person in charge of the refugees within the heart of this ministry thus wrote that a "great number of those in Nantes pronounce themselves against this presumed plan of going to Louisiana. They offer to settle in Nantes and to renounce the supplemental payments on the condition that a small amount of aid might be paid to them."[83] Peyroux himself ended up frankly admitting the hesitancy of the Acadians, though he was never very explicit about the reasons for their reluctance. In a letter addressed to the count of Aranda clearly meant to justify the difficulty in recruiting the fixed "quota," he explains that the Acadians were divided and that many residents of Saint-Malo were in "negotiation with the court of France" and requested a delay before giving their response.[84] Peyroux carefully avoided specifying the subject of the rumors, but there is no doubt that, considering the other sources, the negotiations aimed to obtain authorization to emigrate to the United States—to Boston or Virginia. In Morlaix, Cherbourg, and Le Havre, the Acadians awaited the answer of those in Saint-Malo before deciding themselves, "having promised to follow them wherever they would go." Peyroux nonetheless affirmed that if these Acadians "did not obtain what they had requested, they say that they would prefer to go to Louisiana above anything else."

Peyroux is therefore clearly troubled in this document, for he could then only present 1,500 volunteers, that is to say less than the limit that the Spanish ambassador seems to have fixed. He nonetheless hoped to be able to still recruit a hundred individuals in the other regions where Acadians could be found: Bordeaux, La Rochelle, Belle-Île-en-Mer, and Brest.[85] He specified that the Acadians registered at Nantes asked that the delay requested by those at Saint-Malo would not negate their departure, for they had trouble finding lodgings and the sailors were unemployed while waiting to depart. Finally, for the first time he mentions the problem of the mixed families, hoping that one would not prevent the women from following their husbands, and vice-versa, fearing that this would only produce divorces.

Two main questions seem to have especially made the Acadians hesitate. We have some idea of the cause of this mistrust thanks to many letters that Peyroux wrote to Terriot in this period, answering the latter's questions that were clearly made in the name of his compatriots. The concern most often raised in this correspondence is the question of the payments. The Acadians were, from all evidence, anxious on this subject, and three times Peyroux tried to reassure them. On September 29, 1784, he guaranteed them that "His

C[atholic] M[ajesty] grants the Acadians up until their embarkation the payment that they have received from H[is] V[ery] C[hristian] M[ajesty] beginning from the day that the court of France would stop providing it to them. This payment will be supplied by the bankers of the court of Spain in Paris."[86] But the refugees also wanted assurance that they would receive the back payment due them from Versailles and asked for guarantees from Spain on this subject as well. Peyroux became irritated at this insistence: "It is a surprising thing that the Acadians still are insisting that the Spanish ambassador become involved with the back pay that the king of France grants them. This is none of his business and he would compromise himself if he became involved with it."[87] But Peyroux very much wanted to dispense with the problem, the issue being closely tied to that of their departure, since, according to many sources, the indebted Acadians could not leave for Louisiana before they had paid their debts, which they could not do until having been paid themselves.

This problem did not prevent the Acadians' departure for Louisiana. Indeed, according to Terriot, the question had still not been resolved on the eve of the embarkation. "On the one hand," he wrote, "the court of Spain, in its agreement with France, had agreed that no Acadian would leave without having paid his debts, and on the other hand France owes us . . . six months of our pay; an enormous overdue sum for the indigents. The Acadians, finding themselves thus so tightly squeezed between an unassailable debtor and authorized creditors, suddenly took the position of not leaving." By his own testimony, Terriot was charged with announcing the news to the Spanish consul responsible for the organization of the departure of the refugees, d'Aspres. After various negotiations, and after Aranda had written to Vergennes informing him of the problem and requesting that France pay the arrears,[88] Terriot explains that the French authorities finally paid, adding maliciously "although there was no more money, [as] the sub-delegate always said."[89]

This problem also served as a pretext for some Acadians to pressure the Spanish government into providing certain guarantees. We have previously seen how the Acadians were anxious about what would become of them in Louisiana and how they had little confidence in the promises that had been made to them. By threatening to not leave unless the arrears were paid, the refugees demanded an array of written guarantees, which were given to them shortly afterwards by d'Aspres.[90] These conditions stipulated that the Acadians would be transported to Louisiana "without it costing them anything" and that, moreover, once on site, the king of Spain would offer to provide them "lands and lodgings in proportion to the number of each family as well as tools suitable and needed for the clearing and cultivation of said lands, and, furthermore, to nourish them until every family would be in a condition to nourish itself."[91] These promises again demonstrate that the Acadians were not easily convinced to go to Louisiana.

Beyond these material aspects, the second problem that concerned a portion of the Acadians was that of authorization for the non-Acadian spouses to follow the "nation" to Louisiana. This question recurs in a large number of the letters addressed by Peyroux to Terriot. The former first announced to the latter that the "Catholic foreigners who will prove that they are not subjects of France" could go to Louisiana, on the condition of providing information about their origin and profession.[92] But the majority of the spouses of the Acadians were not foreigners, but French, and Terriot was clearly inquiring about the steps necessary for those who wanted to follow their Acadian spouses. Peyroux answered in a manner that was hardly encouraging: "Spain will accept all the Frenchmen who are married to Acadian women on the condition that they have the permission of the court of France to leave the kingdom. It is up to them to request it and not for the ambassador to be involved in it."[93] This question then led to considerable correspondence. We have seen that the proportion of mixed marriages was fairly large and the subject evidently must have preoccupied a great many of these couples. Conforming with Peyroux's recommendations, many spouses of the Acadians then directly solicited authorization to leave France from the minister.[94] Controller-General Calonne initially suggested to the Minister of Foreign Affairs that the French women married to Acadians should be allowed to leave; the women, according to the criteria of the period, took on the "naturalization" of their spouses and therefore automatically obtained the status "of Acadian women." Concerning the Frenchmen married to Acadian women, Calonne also advocated allowing them to leave. "Surely," he wrote, "the general principle prohibiting the emigration of subjects of the king is opposed to them expatriating by themselves." But Calonne considered that a very large number of petitioners comprised older people, "in little condition to be useful," often poor and dependent on their adopted families, for whom a prohibition to emigrate would perhaps leave without any resource, "if they would be abandoned to only their own strengths." He therefore advocated allowing all of those who requested doing so to leave.[95]

Calonne's proposals seem to have appeared reasonable to Vergennes, since, on May 5, 1785, just days before the departure of the Louisiana-bound *Bon Papa*, Blondel wrote the intendant of Brittany that "Mr. the Controller-General and Mr. the comte de Vergennes have agreed to grant the Frenchmen who have married Acadian women permission to go to Louisiana."[96] For an unknown reason, nonetheless, some days after the departure of this first ship for Louisiana, Blondel wrote that the two ministers had changed their minds and rather agreed to accept the "orders of the king" on this subject.[97] A week later he categorically asserted his previous orders, and indicated to the same intendant that, finally, "it has been decided that Frenchmen married to [Acadian women] grant their children the quality of subjects of the king [and] that these women must follow the fate of their husbands"; consequently these couples no longer had the authorization to go to Louisiana. Blondel added that it would be pointless for the petitioners to reiterate their demands.[98] In vain did these Frenchmen solicit the help of the bishop of Nantes; the intendant of Brittany proved inflexible.[99] The prohibition to emigrate for the mixed couples came very late for some who were well prepared to leave. This probably forced a portion of the refugees to renounce their plan to embark with their families on the ships that followed the *Bon Papa*.[100] But we also know, however, that many clandestine passengers—including fiancés having succeeded by such means to remain with the family of their engaged—were reported to have arrived in New Orleans.[101]

Winzerling suggests that the French government was "chagrined" by the departures of 1785 and that d'Aspres chartered the ships more or less secretly. He adds that the French ministry forbade any new departure of the Acadians to Louisiana once it learned of the success of the settlements on the bayous.[102] The same author also affirms that many other Acadians wanted to emigrate to Louisiana and that d'Aspres would not allow everyone to embark. These affirmations appear to me to be erroneous, regarding both the prohibition to emigrate as well as the urgency of the Acadians.[103] On the contrary, many documents show the hesitation of the Acadians until the last minute, or their determination to go to other locations. Thus, a letter by the sub-delegate of Saint-Malo, written on the very day of the departure of the *Bon Papa*, May 10, 1785, mentions Acadians, who "change their minds every day: now they say one thing and then another."[104] Moreover, shortly after the general embarkation of all of the Acadians headed for Louisiana, we can count various petitions, coming from other refugees, soliciting passage not to Louisiana but to North America, to the United States or, more specifically, to Boston. On September 4, 1785, the intendant of Brittany informed Blondel that, "most of those who remain [in Morlaix] are requesting to return to North America."[105] It is very probable that this is the petition to which the Acadian Anne-Suzanne Richard refers in a letter written in this period.[106] This request seems to have been taken into account belatedly by the French administration. Thus, it was only in May of the following year that Blondel answered it, specifying that it "was not easy to accept," for, assuming that the minister provided authorization to the refugees to go to Louisiana, it still remained true that "the Americans did not ask for them and are not proposing to bring them there, unlike the Spanish who requested the Acadians and have transported them at their expense to Louisiana."[107] The following month, the Controller-General suggested that the Minister of Foreign Affairs authorize the Acadians to emigrate at their own expense to the United States,[108] in a letter Vergennes received at the end of July 1786.[109] Many other Acadians remaining in France requested to return to Saint-Pierre and Miquelon and were allowed to some time later.[110] In reality, a substantial number of refugees migrated after 1785 to destinations other than Louisiana; so we find, for example, the passage of many Acadian families from Pleudihen, near Saint-Malo, to rejoin their relatives in Pomquet, in Nova Scotia, in the Spring of 1788.[111] Many also later went on to Louisiana.[112]

The exact number of Acadians who left for Louisiana varies slightly according to the sources, depending on if we use the lists of embarkation in France or those of disembarkation in Louisiana, if we count the clandestine passengers or not, if we include those who died during the voyage, and if we add those passengers who were not Acadians. In all, however, nearly 1,600 Acadians went to Louisiana in 1785, aboard seven ships that raised anchor in the French ports between May 10 and October 15, 1785.[113] If it does not seem that most of these Acadians were finally too upset at embarking, it is nonetheless evident that a large number of them remained defiant to the plan up until the departure and that some wanted above all to return to Acadia or to a proximity thereto rather than to emigrate to climates considered to be dangerous. For these Acadians, a new life was about to begin. Once in the colony, they would be led onto lands to be cleared, and granted a payment and tools with which to cultivate and build houses. But that, of course, is another story.[114]

The Revolution

After the 1785 departure, the French government intermittently remained preoccupied with the refugees. We have mentioned above some of the measures taken in their favor in 1786. Some also continued to receive the assistance. The survivors of the *Grand Dérangement* were, however, then dispersed in the west of France and ceased to exist as a distinctive group. Thus the government from then on only answered individual petitions and ceased to concern itself with the integration of these individuals. It is nonetheless interesting to note that, during the French Revolution, the "inhabitants of North America" were not forgotten. Following the petitions of the Acadians and Canadians of September 10, 1790, the decision was taken to continue with their assistance.[115] Their situation was debated in the Committee of Pensions and a law was voted in their favor.[116] This law made the situation of the refugees official and also foresaw making a census, in all of the departments of France, of the ensemble of the "inhabitants of North America" who previously were designated as Canadians and Acadians together. Lists were sent by the prefects from everyr of France.[117] It is difficult to evaluate if the aid was actually distributed, and if so, for how long. Martin estimates that the law probably had "no effect," but many letters requesting arrear payments testify that the aid was probably paid, even if very irregularly.[118]

The aid was continued under the Convention, which often concerned itself with refugees from various colonies and voted at least two laws in their favor.[119] Following a new petition, the Assembly allowed the Acadians and Canadians to combine the pensions from the funds of the Navy and those that were paid to them as refugees from the colonies.[120] Martin found many other decrees of the Legislative Assembly, the Convention, and the Directory relating to the same issue.[121]

Under the Directory, we find in the minutes of the Council of the Five Hundred many texts concerning aid for the "refugees from the colonies." Even then, it is not always possible to know if the Acadians were involved or not in these measures: everything suggests that they should have been involved, but, every time that their case is mentioned, it seems to be treated separately. Thus, in September 1797, the Directory declared "that various difficulties arising concerning the means of payment of the aid due to the Acadians and the Canadians have, until now, delayed payment, but it is time to reassure the beneficiaries."[122] These measures, however, did not stop the petitions. Thus on the 9th Floréal, year VII: "A member, in the name of a special commission, brings an account of a petition that the Acadian and Canadian refugees have presented, in which they request that the assistance that had been guaranteed to them by the law of February 25, 1791, be paid." The commission recommended putting up to date a table of the Acadians and Canadians who were or should have been benefiting from this assistance. In fact, the policy of the Revolutionary assemblies proved to be in continuity with that of the preceding government. The aid was founded in the force of the law, but it was still irregularly realized.[123] In any event, the payment of the assistance continued well beyond the Revolutionary period, as is shown by measures taken under the Consulate,[124] under the Restoration,[125] as well as in letters of petition written under Louis-Philippe's reign, and even a law planned in 1884.[126]

Summary

The object of this study has been to analyze three aspects of the integration of the Acadians in France during the century of the Enlightenment: the attitude of the government, that of the refugees themselves, and, finally, what we might learn about the reality of their (re)insertion into the society of the *Ancien Régime*.

What was the attitude of the government facing a situation previously unknown to the period? In the first place, it is important to note the limited and belated desire to integrate and assimilate the colonists repatriated in France. According to the preconceptions of the period, the colonists were citizens from overseas accustomed to great expanses and destined to return there. Choiseul considered them as perfect for his new projects: docile, patriotic, and, especially, French-speaking—a true windfall in a period that lacked volunteers for expatriation to far-off horizons, dreaded and cursed by the people of France. The Acadians were considered perfectly adapted to the civilizing mission that had fallen to them: populating the remains of the Empire by people of European origin. Versailles therefore initially determined to send the Acadians outside of France, and, consequently, did not foresee assimilating them in Brittany or other provinces at all. Besides, "to assimilate" was clearly anachronistic for the period. From that point the French government preferred regrouping the Acadians together: if it wanted to send them outside of France, it should avoid letting them make ties with the populations of the regions of refuge, ties that might prevent them from going where the government had need of them. Successive ministers therefore preferred marriages among the refugees themselves and let the families progressively reconstitute a community.

After the peace of 1763, however, the exiles grew despondent about going to the places Choiseul wanted to send them, to the great annoyance of the minister. After the failure of the disastrous attempt to populate Guyana, which put an end to the colonizing enthusiasm of Louis XV's principal minister, the ministries in charge of the refugees continued to formulate grand schemes for the Acadians, always considered favorably because of the period's notions about populating needs. They therefore received a new mission, in conformity with the limited horizon determined by their status as colonists and the physiocratic ideas in fashion in the second half of the century that measured wealth by numbers of men, that of cleansing a France that was always in need of new blood. This new blood would be brought by this pious and courageous people from a country where the temperate climate and bountiful nature—according to Rousseau-inspired conceptions—had profoundly sweetened the morals and reformed the hearts of the men. The king therefore formed the plan of attaching the Acadians to the land of the kingdom, while still leaving them grouped together—at that time there was still no wish to assimilate the refugees into local populations. Mingling with the French peasants risked corrupting the pure morals that the Acadians brought from America. Moreover, France consisted at the time of a mosaic of peoples living according to various customs, even speaking different languages. "To assimilate" the refugees therefore signified not transforming them into "Frenchmen," but rather into Bretons or Poitevins. In this period, we hardly find any desire of uniformity for the Acadians as we would subsequently find during the revolutionary period. Besides, the Acadians were apparently considered as authentically "French": they spoke the official language of the kingdom better than many people in France; they all practiced the Catholic religion while a minority of inhabitants of the country obstinately remained Protestant; and finally they seemed to be more patriotic than the true men of French origin at a time when France, anxious after the Seven Years War, considered itself to be in decline.[127] In sum, to assimilate the Acadians did not figure among the plans of Versailles until a later period.

On the other hand, we increasingly note the resistance and irritation of some administrators to the organization of the Acadians into a "national body," a kind of syndicate created by them in imitation of the body of merchants in the port cities where they were staying and possibly borrowing the rhetoric of the opponents of the Maupeou reforms. These administrators, with Lemoyne in the lead, strongly suggested the dismemberment of the body by the dispersion of the Acadians in order to end their resistance to orders coming from Versailles. In fact, Necker took up the proposals of Lemoyne starting in 1778, and took as his own the argument that organizing the Acadians into a national body would give them self-assurance and making them impertinent. Necker hoped that the refugees, once dispersed and swallowed within the masses, would cease to pose a problem, to seek further assistance, or ask for their own settlement. This is what his governmental directives were limited to in matters of assimilation, if one dares to use that term. Necker's program never came to fruition, lacking sufficient political will to face the resistance of the Acadians and other, minor, obstacles.

The other facet of government policy consisted of distributing aid to the refugees. Originally conceived as an emergency measure, it was later viewed as assistance meant to allow them subsist until a return to the colonies or to other lands of the kingdom and thus was not yet part of a policy of integration. However, apart from the reasons commonly advanced by the administration to justify the payments, there is no doubt that the distribution of the subsidies was also progressively thought of as allowing the Acadians to integrate themselves economically and socially in France. In fact, towards the mid-1770s the Acadians were quietly reproached by the ministries for not having benefited from the payments of six *sous* to become autonomous and cease demanding ever more assistance, although at that date some refugees were no doubt relatively well woven into the economic fiber of their habitation. These reproaches actually expressed the growing irritation of administrators confronting the problems raised by these refugees and the forlorn hope of having the situation resolve itself on its own thanks to the agreed upon modest financial effort. Moreover, they did not address or question the directive by Berryer that surely contributed to the supposed "indolence" of the refugees more than did the payments: the prohibition of combining the six *sous* per day with paid employment. This counter-productive measure cost dearly in the long term. In this area, as in that of the spatial organization of the Acadians, Necker was once again the one who acted with the most determination. He reduced the payment from six to three *sous* and objected to the fact that able-bodied men in a condition to work continued to demand aid. His action came from a noticeable evolution in awareness. While the payment was conceived, for the most part, under the reign of Louis *Le Bien-Aimé* [Louis XV], as a "charity" that would be "inhumane" to suppress, the word "charity" itself became progressively "infamous," to repeat the phrase of Voltaire. Necker, for his part, recognized the Acadians' right to aid, but could not accept that what he was the first to define as public money, "fruit of the sweat of Frenchmen," would be distributed to able-bodied men capable of working. Therefore, at the instigation of the charitable institutions, he suggested another model for assistance and integration, through working, though without providing refugees in more difficult straits with the means to achieve this estimable goal.

In sum, although at varying intervals the government was involved with the economic integration of the Acadians, it clearly seems that it was never interested enough to promote social and cultural intermingling in the kingdom, with the whims of Necker being more coercive measures than a coherent policy. On the other hand, especially because of population concerns, the State wanted to keep the refugees in France or in the extensions of the kingdom that were its colonies. From this point of view, emigration to Louisiana effectively marked an unquestionable reversal by Versailles.

Did the deportees of the *Grand Dérangement*, for their part, have a desire to be integrated in France? The arrival in France was endured rather than chosen by the Acadians. Subsequently, it is difficult to reconstitute their wishes. Did they want to remain in France or to return? From our research, the impression surfaces that all of them, at least at first, wanted to be expatriated to the destination indicated to them or that might be imposed on them. In other words, the Acadians seem to have been relatively resigned to their fate. We nonetheless observe, from the beginning of the stay in France, resistance to every whim of the government to move them, implying a desire to remain in France. This more than likely reflected an easily understandable reaction: having been physically displaced and in extremely painful and often mortal conditions, most of the refugees wanted, above all, to not again be transported, often at the peril of their lives, away from their town of refuge, if not, perhaps, to return to the site of their childhood, which was never proposed to them. Probably for the same reasons, we find among the refugees throughout the whole period of 1758-1785 deep divisions about the destination considered for new emigration. Indeed, while the majority seems to have wanted to return to Acadia or, if not, to the islands of Saint-Pierre and Miquelon, up until the very moment of embarkation to Louisiana (most of the refugees no doubt decided at the last moment, from sheer pragmatism), others, with more of a political instinct, decided in favor of the Mississippi beginning in the 1770s.

It is also tempting to interpret the regrouping of the Acadians, for instance, in the region of Saint-Malo or by means of endogamous marriages, as a refusal to integrate. These regroupings undoubtedly resulted from a deliberate desire of the refugees. For the exiles of 1755-1758, the sorrow at being removed far from home was aggravated by the dispersion of extended families, limiting the solidarity they had had before the deportation and sometimes isolating individuals far from all relatives. As a priority, the Acadians therefore sought to renew ties with members of the extended family found in exile in the same area as themselves, or at best with compatriots capable of accompanying them at the time of their hoped-for return to Acadia. But how may we isolate family ties from feelings of belonging or affinity with a community? Also, what was the relative importance of the external factors in explaining these regroupings? Even though the Acadians may have ardently wanted to live amongst themselves, did this also indicate as much a refusal to integrate or mingle with the Breton locals? Nothing is less certain. If the reassembling undoubtedly favored internal solidarity and a defense of common interests, it did not prevent contacts with the rest of the world and, ultimately, assimilation.

Finally, the refusal of the Acadians to integrate themselves does not seem to me to have been demonstrated, or, in the present state of research, even be demonstrable. "Let us assure ourselves of the fact before worrying about the cause," warned Fontenelle at the end of the seventeenth century. To seek to understand why the Acadians did not want to integrate themselves into France risks "seeking the cause of that which does not exist." Many authors are convinced of the absence of a desire of the Acadians for integration because of their departure to Louisiana, which tends to indicate that the refugees did not want to remain in France. But this departure does not definitively prove the desire of the Acadians to emigrate. As we have been able to establish from the unpublished documents, the move to Louisiana was no foregone conclusion. The idea of going to the Mississippi deeply divided the exiles and brought agreement among only a portion of them. Moreover, it is possible that the Acadians were threatened with measures of reprisal if they did not embark. Without the somewhat questionable maneuvers of Peyroux de la Coudrenière, nothing allows us to affirm if this departure might have ever occurred.

Furthermore, some interpret the departure to Louisiana as proof that the Acadians had deep feelings of "identity" that would have led them to reject France and its inhabitants because of a presumed cultural incompatibility. As we have seen above, differences between the Acadians and the local populations that observers of the contemporary period qualify as "cultural" did exist, but were they as important in their own view, and did they not appear as elements of secondary interest? The claim of an "Acadian-ness" before arrival in France does not seem to me to have been proved. No doubt such a feeling was formed or became significant during the course of the stay in France: the organization of the community into a "national body," starting in the 1770s, certainly shows an increasing awareness of common interests and of the fact of their forming a "foreign" group inside France. The fact of having shared the same traumatizing experience of deportation contributed to the solidarity of the group. But, at the same time, we should not neglect other aspects that we may assume were at least as important. The Catholic religion, notably, seems to have been especially important for the Acadians and undeniably contributed to bringing them closer to the inhabitants of the sites where they found refuge. The satisfaction of being able to practice their religion was mentioned in practically all of the Acadian petitions of the period, but this aspect is discarded by a good number of historians who prefer to insist on a poorly defined cultural or "national" identity which only rarely appeared, if even threadbare. "Let us therefore take up the party of our religion," wrote the Acadians in England to their brothers dispersed through the American colonies.[128] In many other private letters, the ability to practice the Roman religion was evoked as a positive factor, which surely does not prohibit their missing their native country.[129] To affirm that the departure for Louisiana was principally due to a cultural incompatibility seems to me, then, to be a position that has not been proven. In actuality, the Acadians were largely reluctant to the idea of emigrating to the Spanish colony and owe their departure to the dubious activities of the Frenchman, Peyroux de la Coudrenière.

What should we think, then, of the social and economic integration of the Acadians within the towns where they found refuge? Because of the uncertainty concerning the length of their stay in France, and the endemic unemployment, and perhaps the defiance of some locals, it seems that many Acadians ended up excluded or marginalized in the market for labor, at least in the early period. Indeed, many seem to have practiced precarious and not very profitable trades, a situation attributable to the absence of any corporative organization in Acadia that surely handicapped the refugees, many of whom had great difficulty obtaining access to trade associations or attaining ranks of mastery. The social denigration undoubtedly contributed to the discontent of at least a portion of the Acadians, notably those accustomed to having a valued and recognized status and better conditions of life in Acadia. However, the sources that we have examined (mainly administrative), introduce a bias into the picture we have of the conditions of life and work of the refugees, since the most problematic categories are over-represented. At the end of the period, however, many Acadians succeeded in coming out sufficiently. This is what is shown, for example, in the relative level of comfort that Basile Henry and Olivier Terriot, in Nantes—and perhaps Joseph Devau, in Paris—achieved around 1780.

On the other hand, from the point of view of the geographic apportionment, it is practically impossible to know if the Acadians intermingled with the rest of the population. Certainly, we have been able to show that they remained grouped together in the relatively limited zones around the Rance River, in Poitou, then in Nantes. But, if we take Saint-Servan as an example, a town in the region where the greatest number of Acadians were found, it does not seem that the refugees lived regrouped within one and the same area. No doubt they were dispersed among other inhabitants of the region and, besides, had little or no choice in where they were lodged. In Nantes, as well, they were clearly spread through various parts of the town, even if they were more concentrated in some areas, and there does not seem to have been any particular segregation. On the other hand, the Acadians were most often lodged in a precarious and unhealthy manner. Very few possessed their own houses and most were constrained to cohabitate with the proprietors or with many other families in the same apartment.

What were the relations between the Acadians and the local populations? Practically everything that we might learn about this subject, and that is very little, comes from studying the files of the contraband tobacco trade. What we are able to glean from this source, however, gives the impression that the contacts must have become relatively frequent and numerous and that there was no particular ostracism confronting them. On this subject, it is likely that the fact of frequenting the same churches as the people in the locality and being known and recommended by the priests of the area strongly contributed to the integration of the Acadians within the local social fabric. In any event, nothing allows us to affirm that they were victims of hostility from the populations, except in the very specific case of Belle-Île-en-Mer, where the animosity did not persist. In sum, if the integration of the Acadians who were the most harshly affected by the deportation was certainly very incomplete, many of those of the generation born in France succeeded in acquiring a certain comfort, especially by the start of the 1780s. Around this time, a large number of Acadians seem to have become relatively well integrated and on the path to assimilation.

How, then, to explain the departure of the Acadians to Louisiana? For the most part, it seems to have been unplanned. After the death of Jean-Jacques LeBlanc in Nantes in 1781, it seems that the Louisiana destination gathered fewer candidates among the Acadians than during the life of this main promoter of such emigration. Most of the refugees, at this date, were relatively little inclined to go back to sea on a perilous crossing to banks unknown, though some wanted to return to North America—to Boston or to Acadia. Without Peyroux, however, it is unlikely that so many Acadians would have chosen to leave for New Orleans in 1785. My aim here has been to not make fiction out of history, but to question the doctrine that the emigration was inevitable, and that the integration of the Acadians was necessarily doomed to failure.

APPENDICES

Glossary

Many of the expressions and terms used in this text require some explanation; we have preferred to not include them within the text so as to not overburden it. It is suitable, however, to pause here to address the problems of the vocabulary. Below we will try to define some recurrent terms and expressions.

Nation

Even the term "nation" was subject to a significant semantic ambiguity in the eighteenth century. Its use is not very easy to isolate, for the term most often recurs on two different levels, the local and the state.[1] The fourth edition of the *Dictionnaire de l'Académie française*, from 1762, provides a definition that mainly refers to the idea "of State" (the nation being "all of those inhabitants of a same State, of a same country"),[2] but also, to a lesser degree, to that of a "Province."[3] The *Dictionnaire de Trévoux*, in the edition of 1771, insists more on the notion of a country, less than a "province," but maintains the same examples of, "nation of Normandy and of Picardy" as does the Académie Française. The same goes for the definition provided by the *Encyclopédie*. If we come a few steps closer to the contemporary acceptance of "Nation state,"[4] in the current usage, the term "nation" is still sometimes used to designate the inhabitants of a particular province: thus we find expressions such as "Alsatian nationality,"[5] "Corsican nationality,"[6] or "indolent Nationality"[7] to designate the inhabitants of Limousin. Finally, nation "is also said of a certain kind of people including all of those of the same profession." (*Trévoux*) For the historian Godechot, in the eighteenth century, "the word nation, much more used then than the word country, had, on the contrary a very neutral sense, still lacking all affective weight. It indicated a people, without implying that the people so designated were installed on a given territory. Thus one would say today the 'Jewish nation.'"

An historian of the "Portuguese nation," a merchant network dispersed through the Atlantic world, provides an interesting definition of this community, which certainly might approach that which we could attribute to the Acadians dispersed after the *Grand Dérangement*, in its "merchant" character, at least:

> [The Portuguese "nation"] was an odd "nation" to the degree that it was not defined by having roots in a particular place: it was "de-territorialized." . . . By its dispersion and its mobility, this nation connects to a *diaspora*. . . . This definition brings us a second sense of the word nation, which connotes the idea of a consanguine lineage or one of common ancestors. . . . In the Portuguese case, the most suitable usage was that which was born in the European warehouses at the end of the Middle Ages: a nation was a community of foreign merchants tied by certain distinctive traits that

distinguished them from the local society or, more exactly, by a series of symbols, institutions and social ties that defined it as a living collectivity.[8]

Body [*Corps*] and "National Body" [*Corps de Nation*]

We have seen how the expression "national body" was used in one document coming directly from the Acadians themselves.[9] We have already tried to delineate what this expression might have indicated for the Acadians or at least for the Abbé de Grandclos Mêlé, who drafted the petition in their name.[10] Let us pause again for a moment on the possible sense of this expression or, at least, on its different uses.[11]

The first term, "body," was probably the most important of the two. We find it on its own at least twice in the letters of Pérusse.[12] However, the word is not defined in the *Dictionnaire de l'Académie* in the sense of "political body." On the other hand, in *Trévoux*, if the expression "national body" does not appear, we find a definition that translates its primary meaning close to the one that interests us:

> *Corps* is said again, in a figurative sense, of the union of many individuals who live under the same government and follow the same laws, the same customs.... In this acceptance, the word *corps* is said more specifically of certain companies that exist in the State under the public authority.

Numerous examples follow this definition,[13] ending thus: "*corps* is also said of all of the other communities." Here, surely, is what specifically characterizes the Acadians: they formed a united community in the eyes of the administrators. Yves Durand recalled the importance of these "bodies [*corps*]" in modern societies:[14]

> In sum, there existed, and in a universal manner, communities with interests, generally tied to a profession, that historians have grouped under the name of "*corps*."[15] In a "body" constituted by cooptation decisions were taken collectively, and it was the entire group that provided itself with rules and norms of conduct. The body most often had a public existence, a ranking in the city, and could act collectively, possess goods in common and proper privileges. They could delegate, identify themselves with a costume, traditions, and oppose themselves to others such as themselves.[16]

It seems that on a number of points, at least, this definition corresponds to the reality of the group of refugees. Evidently what bound the members of the "body" this time was not a profession, and it is without a doubt for this reason that the administrators or the Acadians added "national," to distinguish them from a professional "*corps*." But in any case, it seems that the decisions taken by the Acadian "nation" in Saint-Malo or in Nantes were made collectively as report many texts on the subject (thus the meeting of Lemoyne with a group in Saint-Malo to discuss the proposal made by the government to go to Poitou, or the meeting organized in Nantes whose minutes were written by the sub-delegate of that town).[17] It also seems that the group tried to provide for common "rules and norms of conduct." This is surely what is indicated, for instance, by the fact that the Acadians, if we believe Pérusse, were violently divided in Poitou about where to go next (some visibly reproached others for not remaining in solidarity). The public existence of the group was clearly attested to by the immense administrative correspondence devoted to them. The delegations of the Acadians were made regularly and referred to on many occasions, exactly like the existence of syndics[18] (at least after Poitou, but possibly since the stay in Saint-Malo).[19] On the other hand, we do not know if the Acadians were distinguished by any specific costume: this is unlikely and no text refers to it. As for the existence of particular customs, we have considered this question above.

The precise expression "national body [*corps de nation*]"[20] is much less frequent in the eighteenth century than the broader phrase "body of the nation [*corps de la nation*]," and should not be confused with it. It is not found as such in the *Dictionnaire de l'Académie* or in the *Furetière*.[21] On the other hand, one finds three occurrences of this exact expression in the *Encyclopédie*, in the articles "Goths," "Natchez," and "Thraces."[22] The contexts in which this expression is used allow us to form an idea of what it signifies. Thus, the article "Goths" leads the reader to distinguish clearly the Goths "who made a national body, from the Goths who were in the Empire." The article, "Natchez" specifies: "In 1630 [*sic*] the French made war on the Natchez, and killed a large number and so dispersed them that they no longer formed a national body." The third example, concerning the Thraces, reports: "Herodotus reports the names of an infinite multitude of different peoples who have inhabited Thrace. He says that if they were able, either joined under a single leader, or to be bound by interests and feelings, they would have formed a national body very superior to all of those surrounding them."

The term "national body" figures again in at least two other texts from the eighteenth century cited by David Bell.[23] In an anonymous discussion of patriotism dated 1788, we read, regarding France: "This people, formed from the assembly of a multitude of small different nations, does not present a national body."[24] Another extract comes from the work of Jean-Jacques Rousseau, *Considération sur le Gouvernement de Pologne* (1772): "Moses . . . formed and executed the surprising enterprise of establishing into a national body a swarm of miserable fugitives . . . and . . . gave them this durable institution, which, with the test of time . . . still subsists today in all of its strength."

One finds very clearly from reading these examples that this expression "national body" unquestionably implies the idea of an assembly, a grouping; in the case of dispersion, the national body does not exist or no longer exists. Moreover, and this is also very important, one notes that this "national body" implies the existence of a common leader or a binding "by interests and feelings" (the article on the Thraces) or again by a common experience (what one might call today a "communal feeling," a "culture," or a common "identity").

Finally, we should note the theory of Christopher Hodson, in which the expression "national body" is an appropriation by the Acadians of the parliamentary rhetoric that opposed the royal power after 1770.[25]

Fatherland [*Patrie*]

"The fatherland" at that time, did not have the "national" character that we grant it today. For in the *Trévoux*, the fatherland is "the country where one is born and it is said of a specific place whether province or empire, or the [S]tate where one is born. . . . One proverbially says that the fatherland is everywhere where one is comfortable." The meaning given to the term "fatherland" was the subject of fierce debates in the eighteenth century, for example between Rousseau and Voltaire, as mentioned by Godechot:[26] the fatherland for Voltaire is any place where one feels free (he adopts the sense of the *Trévoux* definition); for Rousseau, on the other hand, it is the place where one is born, and if this places does not enjoy liberty, then it must be changed, by force if necessary.

People and Country [*Peuple et pays*]

"People" is without a doubt the term most utilized to designate the Acadians in paraphrase.[27] The definition here only concerns the first meaning of people, and excludes the use of the term to designate the "populace." This word was employed by Lemoyne himself and by various correspondents: the Abbé de l'Isle-Dieu and the ministers Terray,[28] Praslin, La Rochette, and Nivernais.[29] Warren, often combined with the adjectives "poor" or "unfortunate."[30]

The use of the word "people" should not lead us to believe that the Acadians were considered by this fact automatically to be "foreigners." In fact, the word "people" (like the terms nation and foreigner described in this glossary)[31] clearly includes two levels, one "national" and the other "local," according to the distinction given by the *Dictionnaire de l'Académie*:[32]

> PEOPLE: Collective term. A multitude of men from the same country, living under the same laws. The Hebrew people.... The Roman people..... The people of Provence, of Dauphiné, etc. All of the people of the earth.
>
> It is also said of a multitude of inhabitants who live either in the same town or in the same borough or village. *There are many people in Paris. All of the people of the borough, of the village hurried to go.*
>
> It also applies sometimes to the least substantial among the inhabitants of the same town, or of the same country. *There was some emotion among the people.*

It is worth noting that at no time does this dictionary provide as an example: "French people" or the same sense combined with other adjectives of nationality (German, Italian, or Spanish, for instance).[33]

Even according to the first usage, that referring to the "country," we may remark the surprising examples of "people of Provence, of Dauphiné, etc." juxtaposed with "multitude of men of the same country." This is explained by the definition of "country,"[34] which again refers to both (1) "region, land, province," and to (2) "State":

> COUNTRY, means again Fatherland, place of birth. It is sometimes meant as the whole State in which one is born; sometimes the province, the land, or the town. *Native country. Foreign country. France is my country. To die for the salvation of his country, for the glory of his country. To love his country. The love of country. To defend his country. He never left his country. He still has the accent of his country. What country are you from? They are from the same country.*
>
> ... One says, "*A horse of the country*," of a horse born in France, to distinguish it from a horse born elsewhere, and foreign.

In most cases, therefore, it is very difficult to determine to which of these two meanings the correspondents were referring when they used this term.

Foreign (*Étranger*)

The term also most often refers to two different levels: foreign to the State and foreign to the community. This confusion is well illustrated by the definition provided by the *Dictionnaire de l'Académie française* in 1762:

> Foreign, adj. Who is from another nation.[35] . . . It is sometimes a noun. The foreigners are well treated in France.
>
> It is also used for those who are not of a family, of a company, of a community. He gave his property to foreigners to remove it from his relatives.
>
> One says proverbially, that a man is a foreigner in his country, when he does not know its customs and what is happening there.

The semantic confusion between the local level and the national level is found in most of the texts that we have consulted. The other dictionaries are hardly less ambiguous than is the definition of the Academicians. Thus, there is the article by the chevalier de Jaucourt in the *Encyclopédie*—a long tirade against those who, like the Greeks in the past, had the tendency to confuse "the word enemy with that of foreigner" and who describe the settlement of foreigners in France as "laborious and industrious." The article defines as foreigner—recalling the entry of "*aubain* [alien]"—"he who is born under another domination and in another country than the country in which he is found," but also "he who is not of the family." In *Trévoux* three meanings of the word are maintained: (a) "who is from another nation"; (b) "also said of those who are not from the same house, or family"; (c) "said again of things that are unknown to us, that are not natural." It is worth noting that one finds, in the contemporary definition of the term, the same ambiguity: the term mainly applies to one "who is from another nation," but also to one "who does not belong or who is considered as not belonging to a (familial, social) group." (*Petit Robert*)

Native (*Règnicole*)

This was the legal term of the period to designate the inhabitants of the kingdom. Here is the definition given by the *Dictionnaire de l'Académie*: "*Règnicole*. (The G is pronounced hard). Term of jurisprudence and of Chancellery, which is said of all of the natural inhabitants of a Kingdom, with regard to the privileges that they may enjoy & which is employed, by extension, in speaking of foreigners to whom the King grants the same privileges. *Alien is only used regarding those who are not natives. The Swiss are reputedly natives, having the same privileges as do the natives.*"

Alien (*Aubain*)

Here, in the legal vocabulary of the *Ancien Régime*, it designates foreigners: "Alien. Term of Chancellery & of the Court. Foreigner who is not naturalized in the country where he lives." (*Dictionnaire de l'Académie*)

Biographical References

Acadians who stayed in France and other individuals who are the subject of a biographical note in the *Dictionnaire biographique du Canada*[1]

- Nicolas Gautier, who left Saint-Pierre and Miquelon in 1766 and died in Saint-Malo around 1810.
- Joseph Bellefontaine (Godin), who resided in Cherbourg.
- Jean-Baptiste Robichaux, Acadian of Nova Scotia, who left Île Saint-Jean, was deported to Saint-Servan, then returned to North America in 1773.
- Jean-Gabriel Berbudeau, surgeon of the Acadians in Poitou.
- Joseph Dugas (Dugast), who left Saint-Pierre and Miquelon and was deported twice from the island, in 1767 and in 1778.
- Also see the case of other Acadians who experienced deportation, but did not go to France,[2] as well as the biographies of Jean-Louis Le Loutre and two Acadian priests educated in France who returned to Acadia: Jean-Baptiste Bro and Joseph-Mathurin Bourg.

Other Biographies
Some examples of the itineraries of other Acadians mentioned in this volume

- Jean Thibaudeau, accused of "rebellion and tobacco fraud." Born around 1742 in Pisiguit, Acadia, Thibaudeau was deported to England then stayed in Brittany in Pleudihen, near Saint-Malo, from 1763 to 1773. He had four âildren with Françoise Huere, or Huert, two of whom survived. The couple, at the instigation of most of the other Acadians, then went to Châtellerault, then to Nantes, where Thibaudeau then practiced the profession of sailor. His wife Françoise was buried on January 16, 1781, in Saint-Martin de Chantenay, a community located on the periphery of Nantes. Thibaudeau married again to Marie Dugast on May 10, 1785, in the same place. This family and the two living children of the latter left Nantes aboard the *Saint-Rémi* on June 27, 1785, destined for Louisiana.[3]
- Étienne Terriot [or Terrio or Terriau]. Born in 1725 in Grand-Pré, Acadia, son of Jacques Terriot and Marie Leblanc. Buried in November 1781, in Nantes. Married, around 1747, Hélène Landry, born around 1724 and buried on August 10, 1769, in Pleudihen. Étienne Terriot married again in February 1770 in Saint-Servan to

another Acadian, Marie-Madeleine Bourgeois, who was born around 1727 and was the widow of Charles Boudrot. Marie-Madeleine was buried on May 16, 1780, in Nantes. Étienne Terriot married again in Cantenay on November 14, 1780, to Margeurite Vallois, born around 1738, the widow of Olivier Dubois. Étienne Terriot must have left Grand-Pré between 1748 and 1752, since his first child was born there in 1748 and his second was baptized in Port La Joie (Île Saint-Jean); two children were then born without their place of birth being specified, but in June 1760, a child was born in Pleudihen. Terriot therefore was in all probability directly deported from Île Saint-Jean to Saint-Malo. He lived in Brittany, in Pleudihen, in Châtellerault, then in Nantes.

- Germain Semer: "Born around 1720, Petcoudiac (Acadia); buried on December 14, 1782, Nantes, Hôtel Dieu (Loire-Atl.); carpenter; resident in Nantes of the *Hôpital du Sanitat*; married to Marie Trahan, born around 1725, La Rivière-aux-Canards (Acadia); died October 25, 1776, Nantes, *Hôpital du Sanitat*; children: Semer, Madeleine, born around 1749; Semer, Marie-Claire, married to Jerôme-Dominique Doulle; Semer, Marie-Françoise, born around 1762, Le Havre de Grâce, Notre-Dame (Seine-Maritime); married on May 30, 1785, in Saint-Martin de Chantenay, to Joseph Boudreau; Semer, Grégoire-Dominique, born around 1768. This family lived in Le Havre, then in Châtellerault (Vienne) and finally in Nantes, starting in 1776. Grégoire and Marie-Françoise were announced as having departed aboard the *Amitié* but Marie-Françoise was married three months before the departure of the ship and no follow up is provided for her. As for her brother, did he leave alone? We do not know."[4]

- Pierre Haché, Acadian implicated in the trial for tobacco fraud. Born around 1725 in Île Saint-Jean. Married in 1752 in Saint-Pierre-du-Nord, Île Saint-Jean, to Marie Doiron, born around 1731 and died in February 1759 in Saint-Malo; married again in July 1759 in Dinard, to Anne Dumont, born in Saint-Pierre-du-Nord and buried in December 1765 in Saint-Servan; married a third time in September 1766 in Saint-Servan to Madeleine Daigle, born around 1734 in Louisbourg, buried on October 10, 1784, in Chanenay. Pierre Haché had four children from his first marriage, but three died during the crossing of the Atlantic to France and the fourth died in Saint-Malo on January 31, 1759. He had four more children from his second marriage and three children from his last wife. Pierre Haché was buried on June 9, 1777, in Nantes, and was designated as a sailor. Three of the children of Pierre left for Louisiana with their aunt, Françoise Doucet, the widow of Louis Haché.

- Georges Haché, brother of the preceding. Baptized in March 1744, probably in Île Saint-Jean. Married in January 1768 in Saint-Servan to Perrine Basset, a Breton woman born around 1752 in Saint-Suliac. Georges Haché died before 1785, probably in Nantes. His widow married again on November 9, 1784, in Saint-Martin de Chantenay, near Nantes, to Pierre Gentilhomme, who was not an Acadian, clearly, since he was born in Maine-et-Loire. They had six children. Perrine Basset, married name Gentilhomme, remained in Nantes with her children where many of them received aid after 1785.

It is not possible here to address the lives of all of the Acadians mentioned during the course of this study. Readers interested in the individual biographies may also use the index to find the names of other Acadians. For example, Basile Henri, Acadian "leader" and syndic, who remained in Nantes after the departure of 1785 and clearly became well integrated and more well off than most of his compatriots; Anne-Suzanne Richard, dress-maker of Morlaix, a portion of whose correspondence with a French woman has been preserved and who did not leave for Louisiana either but undoubtedly wanted to return with other Acadians to North America; Marie-Madeleine de Billy;[5] Joseph Devau; Victor Forest; and, of course, many Acadian delegates: Jean-Jacques Leblanc; Alexis Trahan; Joseph Simon Granger; Basile Boudrot; Benjamin Boudrot, and Olivier Terriot, for instance.

Administrators and Others Responsible for the Acadians

The biographical information concerning the administrators or the missionaries in charge of the Acadians has often been more difficult to gather than that concerning the Acadians themselves. The interested reader might nonetheless consult the biographies of the marquis de Pérusse[6] or of many of the ministers of Louis XV or Louis XVI, and may be able to gather some information about the administrators of lesser importance by perusing the inventories of the French Naval Archives.[7] Here follows some summary information about three of the correspondents most often cited in the text of this study.

The Abbé de l'Isle-Dieu

The Abbé de l'Isle-Dieu was a very important individual who unfortunately is not among those treated in the *Dictionnaire biographique du Canada*, mainly because he never traveled to North America.[8] This is what we may establish following the notes of Father A. David.[9] Abbé of the abbey of l'Isle-Dieu (Insula Dei), in the community of Perruel (Eure), about 25 km east of Rouen, he became vicar general for the bishop of Québec officially in 1734. Mgr. Dosquet, the bishop of Québec, returned to France around 1735, resigned from his post in 1739, and the Abbé de L'Isle-Dieu, as vicar-general, was charged with governing the diocese from France until the nomination of Mgr. De Pontbriand. "It was then agreed that the various foreign colonies (such as Louisiana, Île-Royale, Acadia, Île Saint-Jean and the St. Jean River) would address themselves directly to the Abbé de L'Isle-Dieu for presentations to be made at Court and even for spiritual direction, for which the Bishop of Québec thought to grant the Abbé de l'Isle-Dieu the most extensive powers" (Extract from a report, 1756). The Abbé, who possessed very solid general contacts, was the agent of the bishops from 1730 to 1777. He wrote in their name to the Society for the Propagation of the Faith in Rome, to the Minister of the Navy, and to others. The Abbé knew Louisiana well and, when it was ceded to Spain in 1763, "one had the resource of his services in order that the French colonists would accept the new regime in good faith."

Along with the Abbé Le Loutre, the Abbé l'Isle-Dieu especially involved himself with the Acadian refugees in France until his death. "Having come to the age of 78, the Abbé de l'Isle-Dieu offered his resignation in 1766 because of the poor state of his vision. In reply, the bishop reconfirmed his powers that he was to exercise for yet another ten years. He finally obtained permission to retire in 1776 and the king granted him a pension of 4,500 *livres* in consideration of the services that he had rendered to religion and to the State.[10] For a successor, he was provided with Mr. de Villars, the former superior of the Seminary of Québec, who received from Mgr. Briand the letters of grand vicar and, in his turn, concerned himself with the correspondence with Québec. . . . The Abbé died in April, 1779, without having ever gone to Canada."

Philippe-Antoine Lemoyne

Philippe-Antoine Lemoyne was "Squire and Counselor of the King, Commissioner-General of the Navy."[11] In the documents we consulted, he was always designated under the simple name of Mr. Lemoyne, written sometimes Le Moine or Lemoine. His Christian name is only known from the Archives of the Navy in Rochefort.[12] We have little biographical information about him apart from the document relating his various services that he sent to the Minister of the Navy, Sartine, on August 29, 1774.[13] In this document, where Lemoyne requests as compensation for his services the first intendancy that would become vacant, the commissioner stated that he took his oath as a lawyer in 1733. He would therefore probably have been born around 1710. He says that he was presented to Maurepas in 1734, then that he worked in the offices in Paris. In 1735, he was clerk at the port of Brest,[14] then, in 1737, he practiced the same job aboard the *Jason*, sailing to Canada. It is not very clear if he went to Canada or if he remained in the port of Rochefort. In 1738 he was named to the intendancy of Saint-Domingue, but he returned to France by 1740, having been relieved for illness. In 1741, he performed various tasks in Toulon: he participated in a military campaign at sea, then accompanied the ambassadors to Constantinople. In 1743 he left for Martinique, then was named *ordonnateur* in Cayenne in 1745. During the crossing to Cayenne he was wounded, captured, and sent to New England, then returned to France. He arrived in Cayenne in 1748, and remained as *ordonnateur* there until 1762. In 1764 he received a commission as commissioner-general, which had long been promised to him (he then served in Rochefort as treasurer of the colonies, according to other sources). To this end, he notably loaded the ships of Bougainville in 1766. In December 1771, de Boynes gave him orders to go to Paris to explain his views about settlement of the Acadians.[15] Lemoyne says that he arrived in Paris, following the request of de Boynes, on January 20, 1772. He then wrote many reports and assembled information about the best way of placing the Acadians. In September 1772, the "affair of the Acadians" passed before the Council of the King and left the hands of the Navy to be confided to the Controller-General and to Bertin, charged with the Bureau of Agriculture. Lemoyne then passed under the direct control of Bertin until May 1773, then that of the Controller-General. Between June and November 1773, Lemoyne undertook a tour of all of the ports where the Acadians were "regularly found," in Normandy, Brittany, Saintonge, and the area of Aunis. Starting in November 1773, Lemoyne says that he worked on the legislative portion of the settlement of Poitou. His work relating to the Acadians ended in June 1774.[16]

We have some added information concerning the end of the commissioner's life. After having been involved with the Acadians, Lemoyne pursued his career as Commissioner of the Navy, *ordonnateur* in Bordeaux.[17] The inventory of the departmental Archives of Gironde lists a farm lease signed by one Lemoyne, former Commissioner-General of the Navy, in 1785.[18] Lemoyne emigrated during the Revolution, since his library was transferred to the national repository on December 18, 1793.[19] His papers, which were probably with this library, were placed into an armoire and rediscovered at the end of the nineteenth century by Raymond Céleste, librarian at Bordeaux. They now constitute Ms. 1480 at the library of Bordeaux, one of the principal sources of documentation about the Acadians in France. In 1765, Lemoyne received 12,000 *livres* a year in salary (without counting supplemental payments that he regularly received during his mission), or about one hundred times more than the annual payment of assistance of an Acadian.[20]

Ernest Martin presents Lemoyne in an extremely favorable light. However, contrary to what this author would have us believe when referring to the functions of intendant performed by Lemoyne and his self-described status as a superior functionary,[21] it does not seem that Lemoyne had an exceptional career, and he did not receive high esteem from the ministers, who paid no more than distracted attention to his reports. The reason that de Boynes called on Lemoyne to become involved with the Acadians is not very clear. His nomination probably came more from the fact that he was the only volunteer rather than from anything else. The canon of Saint-Malo, GrandClos, had refused what Guillot referred to as an unpleasant task.[22] Another reason perhaps played a part: Lemoyne had entered into a conflict with his superior in the hierarchy,[23] and it is possible that the ministry wanted to remove him from Rochefort for some period of time. In any event, Lemoyne's mission was surely not entrusted to him, as Martin writes, because he was "the functionary the most up to date on the whole Acadian affair." Commissioner Guillot in Saint-Malo was certainly better-informed than Lemoyne about the situation of the Acadians. On the other hand, it seems that Lemoyne drew attention to himself because he sent a report in 1766 about settling the Acadians and the Germans near Saint-Jean-d'Angély,[24] and he was known by the Abbé Le Loutre and the Abbé de l'Isle-Dieu.[25] Again, contrary to what Martin suggests, the reason that Lemoyne disappears from the documentation concerning the Acadians is not his departure on retiring around 1774: Lemoyne continued his career in the Navy and clearly seems to have been removed from the administration of the Acadians. His disappearance from the documentation is surely due to the change in guardianship of the ministry, from the Navy to the Contrôle Général, in 1774, but it is also possible that his difficulties with the Acadians of Saint-Malo, his lack of tact, his authoritarianism, and the liberties he took with ministerial orders contributed to his removal from the Acadian affairs.

Frédéric Joseph Guillot, Commissioner of the Navy in Saint-Malo

"Commissioner *ordonnateur* of the Navy for the Department of Saint-Malo" around 1773, Guillot clearly belonged to a line of naval administrators: his father before him had performed the same functions.[26] Contrary to what Ernest Martin suggests,[27] Guillot was in no way subordinate to Lemoyne. He was even of a superior rank to him since he was commissioner-*ordonnateur*, a function that Lemoyne seems to have occupied in the colonies but not in the home country at the time of the settlement of the Acadians in Poitou, since he requested this rank in 1774.[28] Moreover, Guillot and Lemoyne were relatives and friends.[29] Lemoyne inquired many times about Guillot's health,[30] and they often exchanged confidences and sensitive information.

Map 4

Correspondence between Acadians during the period of exile (1757-1785)

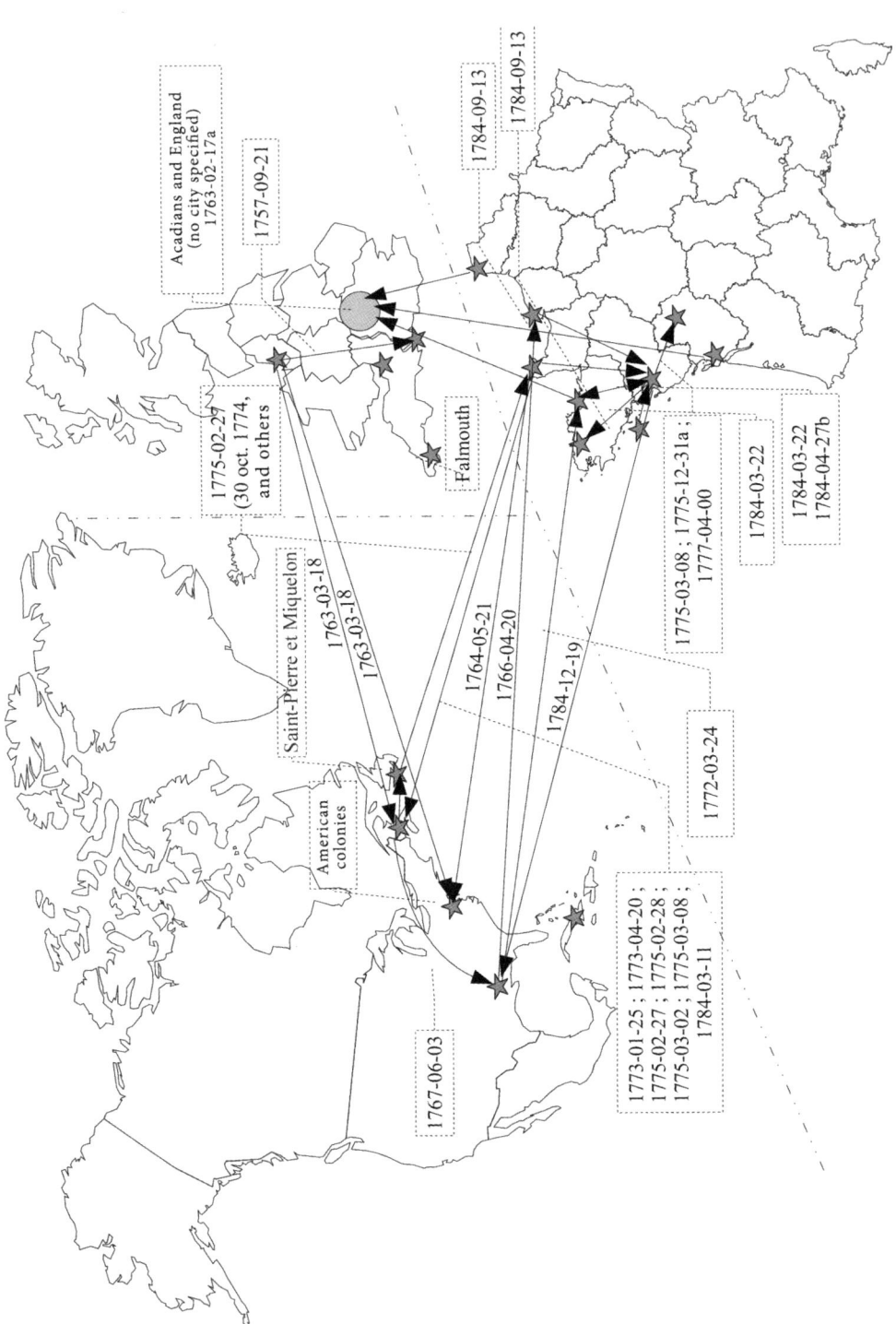

Map Of Correspondence Between Acadians

Notes on the Map

Latitudes and longitudes are inaccurate and the map is based on the States and contemporary regions.
Stars represent the places where the Acadians stayed. To not overburden the map, I have not indicated the names of the sites in France, which are, from north to south and from east to west: Boulogne, Le Havre, Cherbourg, Saint-Malo, Morlaix, Belle-Île, Nantes, Archigny near Châtellerault, and Rochefort; in England, from 1757 to 1763: Liverpool, Bristol, Southampton and Penryn, near Falmouth; in North America: Saint-Pierre and Miquelon (SPM), the region corresponding to the present Nova Scotia and New Brunswick, and, in the American colonies (not differentiated), Louisiana and Saint-Domingue.

Every arrow represents one or more letters sent that have been preserved, or those referred to by other sources. In the frame connected to every arrow, is indicated the reference of the letter corresponding to the code of the database on the Internet to assist in direct consultation of the documents of interest (www/septentrion.qc.ca/acadiens). It should be noted that many other letters must have circulated: only those documented are represented here. An example: Brasseaux[1] notes that the Acadians of Halifax must have received letters coming from Saint-Domingue around November 1764, but he does not indicate where he found this information.

Bibliography And Sources

Primary Sources

Note: What follows is only a summary presentation of the sources consulted. For more details, refer to the appendices of the thesis that is the original of this book (available on the sites www.septentrion.qc.ca/acadiens or http://jfmouhot.free.fr).

One of the difficulties in studying the Acadians or Canadians in France is the extremely scattered sources. Of the archival manuscript collections, I consulted the following sites: Centre d'études acadiennes (CEA, University of Moncton, New Brunswick, Canada); Archives and Bibliothèque nationale (Fonds des Manuscrits) of France (Paris) and the Library and Archives of Canada (Ottawa), Archives du ministère des Affaires étrangères (Paris) and the Service historique de l'Armée (Vincennes); Archivo General de Indias (Seville, Spain); Service historique de la Marine (Brest and Rochefort); Archives départementales: AD Vienne (Poitiers), AD Ille-et-Vilaine (Rennes), AD Loire-Atlantique (Nantes), AD Gironde (Bordeaux), AD Chrente-Maritime (La Rochelle), AD Indre-et-Loire (Tours), AD Loir-et-Cher (Blois), AD Côte d'or (Dijon), AD Doubs (Besançon); municipal archives: Saint-Malo, Nantes, Tours, Blois, Loches; individual collections: La Collection Baby (archives of the University of Montréal); Archives générales de la Congrégation du Saint-Esprit (Chevilly-Larue); municipal libraries (manuscript collections): Bordeaux (Manuscrit MS 1480), Tonnerre (fonds Chevalier d'Éon), and Tours.

Also, I consulted collections at the following sites:[1] Archives nationales, collection of the Colonies (Aix en Provence); Service historique de la Marine at Cherbourg; Archives municipales (AM): Cherbourg; Le Havre (extracts from the series F 1069 in the CEA); Boulogne sur Mer; Archives départementales (AD): Calvados (Caen); Finistère; Morbihan (CEA F 1040); Seine-Inférieure (today Seine-Maritime); Archives diocésaines of Coutances; Archives of the Seminary of Québec (Casgrain collection); Collection of archives of the sacred congregation of the Propagation of the Faith (*Propaganda Fidès*) (Vatican); Documents of the Public Record Office and of the Colonial Office (London); Archivo Historico Nacional (Madrid).

I also communicated by way of correspondence with the following archives researching legal documents involving the Acadians: AD Manche (Saint-Lô) and AD Côtes d'Armor (Saint-Brieux).

At my suggestion, research complementary to mine was done by the following individuals: Alain Roman (municipal archives of Saint-Malo); Jacques Nerrou (Archives départementales of La Rochelle and the Service historique de la Marine at Rochefort); Gérard-Marc Braud (registers of catholicity of Nantes and the region).

An abundant and varied documentation has been preserved. The Acadians were officially dependent upon the Ministry of the Marine (Navy) until July 1773. However, the correspondence between the successive secretaries of State, the administrators of the ports (commissioners and intendants), and the missionaries of the Acadians, preserved in series B of the Colonies (correspondence from the departure) was inventoried and summarized piece by piece by the Canadian inventories. Gaps can be completed by the corresponding collections of the ports where the Acadians stayed, as well as the large collection of series B3 (letters addressed to the Ministry of the Navy coming from the intendants, commissioners, and commanders of the ports of France and of the colonies). A very important register (Ms. 1480), sequestered during the Revolutionary period and preserved at the municipal library of Bordeaux, contains the largest portion of the correspondence relating to the refugees from the commissioner-general Antoine-Philippe Lemoyne, charged by the minister with handling the reclassification of the Acadians in the years 1772-1774. Also note that the settlement of the Acadians at Belle-Île-en-Mer whose accomplishment was the work of the States of Brittany was extraordinarily well documented in series C of the Archives of Ille-et-Vilaine.

For the period after July 1773, when the Acadians were placed directly under the responsibility of the General-Control, the documentation, more dispersed, essentially consists of some cartons[2] of paper produced by the bureaus of the General-Control of Finances, as well as the correspondence of the intendants of the provinces in which the Acadians were found[3] (series C, although a portion of the documentation that was microfilmed was more conveniently consulted at Ottawa). Concerning specifically the settlement of the Acadians in Poitou, the correspondence of Pérusse d'Escars kept at Poitiers is rich with numerous details. To this must still be added the diplomatic correspondence kept in the archives of the Ministry of Foreign Affairs, especially abundant for the period of the repatriation of the Acadians from England (in 1763) and that of the departure to Louisiana in 1785 (various contacts were then made between France and the Spanish ambassador on the subject of the Acadians). The Spanish writings corresponding to that at the Quai d'Orsay was also examined, namely the correspondence between Peyroux de la Coudrenière, Oliver Terriot, and the Spanish ambassador in Paris (Archivo Historico Nacional, Madrid) and a very interesting file compiled by Olivier Terriot reporting his activity in 1784-1785 (Archivo General de Indias, Seville). Finally, the registers of the deliberations of the municipal councils and the correspondence of the mayors of the towns in which a large contingent of Acadians stayed (Saint-Malo for the period 1758-1773 and Nantes for the period 1775-1785) were systematically examined.[4] The same goes for the administrative correspondence, forming the large portion of the documentation concerning the Acadian refugees in France.[5]

To this administrative correspondence must be added many sources used in particular by genealogists: lists of embarkation/disembarkation (most often kept in the maritime archives), registers of catholicity (that sometimes supply interesting details on the manner of designating the Acadians as well as on relational ties among individuals). Many of these sources were published in works most often indexed, saving an enormous amount of time.

The administrative correspondence that I perused was very useful for understanding and explaining the actions of the government, in a much more detailed (and critical) manner than in Martin. But one of the main problems of the works written about the Acadians in France until now is that they always have been too dependent on these administrative sources that often concern only the surface of the problems. The Canadian historians, who often also mostly depend on the same sources in compiling the history of Canada during the French regime, are aware (at least since Louise Dechêne) that one should not take the reports of the intendants or of the governors literally, and that they reflect more the wishes and desires of the government than they do the reality. To not be limited by these sources, I tried as much as possible to diversify my documentation and in this area I made discoveries that were completely unpublished, or have never been utilized within a study of the Acadians in France. Thus I was fortunate enough to find many letters (ten of which were private letters) exchanged between France and America by various Acadian exiles. I also was able to find a series of documents relating to the "dispensations of consanguinity or of affinity" that shine a previously unpublished light on the daily life of the migrants.[6] Finally, an examination of the legal archives brought to light documents that have until now remained totally unknown concerning the Acadians implicated in affairs of contraband and rebellion.

I therefore hope to have not only been able to reread with a new and critical perspective old sources partially known, but also to have made some significant archival advances allowing the conditions of the period of the stay of the Acadians in France to be seen in a new light.

Primary Printed Sources

Rapports des archives publiques du Canada (RAPC) (sometimes also quoted under the title *Rapport sur les archives canadiennes*), many years, in particular volume 2 of the year 1905 (quoted in the text as *RAPC 1905*-II).

(anon.), *Relation de ce qui s'est passé en Acadie, au sujet de 9,000 Français neuters, qui ont mieux aimé perdre leur fortune et leur liberté que de prendre les armes contre la France*, (no date, probably 1755) (BNF, 4 Lb 38699).

BUGEON, Guy and Monique HIVERT-LE FAUCHEUX. *Les Acadiens parties de France in 1785 pour la Louisiane: listes d'embarquement*. Poitiers-=Rennes (transcript), 1988.

CASGRAIN, Abbé H.R. *Collection de documents inédits sur le Canada et L'Amérique, publiés par le Canada-Français*. Québec, Demers, 1888-1891.

---. "Lettres et mémoires de l'Abbé de L'Isle-Dieu (1742-1774)," *Rapport des archives de la province de Québec*, 16, 17, 18 (1935-1938), pp. 273-410; 331-459; 147-253.

DUVAL, Louis (and the conservator of the library of Niort). *Mémoire sur les Acadiens présenté à Nosseigneurs du clergé de France assemblés à Paris au mois de juillet 1775, en vue d'obtenir une subvention annuelle de 300,000 livres pour faire face aux frais d'établissement de Monthoiron (Poitou)*, Niort, L. Clouzot, 1867.

LANCO, Joseph Marie. "Les Acadiens à Belle-Île-en-Mer. Correspondance de M. l'Abbé le Loutre, missionnaire apostolique, avec M. le baron de Warren, maréchal des camps et armées du Roy, commandant pour le Roy à Belle-Isle," *Supplément au "Lys," Bulletin mensuel de la paroisse et du pèlerinage de Notre-Dame du Roncier, Josselin,* dioceses of Vannes, Morbihan (March 1924).

RAYNAl, Abbé de. *Histoire politique et philosophique des établissements et du commerce des Européens dans les Deux Indes,* 1770.

RIEDER, Milton P. *The Crew and Passenger Registration Family Groups of the Refugee Acadians Who Migrated from France to Spanish Louisiana in 1785.* Metairie, Louisiana, 1965.

RIEDER, Milton P., and Norma GAUDET-RIEDER. *The Acadians in France, 1762-1776,* Metairie, Louisiana, 1967-1973. Vol. I, *Rolls of the Acadians living in France distributed by towns for the years 1762 to 1776,* vol. II, *Belle Isle en Mer Registers, la Rochette Papers,* vol. III, *Archives of the Port of Saint-Servan,* vii-143, vi-134, and vi-108p.

Senate/National Assembly. "Rapport fait au nom de la commission du budget chargée d'examiner les projets de loi ayant pour objet d'ouvrir au Ministre du Commerce sur l'Exercise 1884, un credit supplementaire de 10,603 francs pour les secours aux colons de Saint-Domingue, réfugiés de Saint-Pierre et Miquelon et du Canada." (1884) (BNF, 4-LE 95-3; 1884, EXTR, 163).

Secondary Sources

The Sojourn of the Acadians in France, England and in the Other Colonies

ABBAD, Fabrice, "Des Nantais au service du roi d'Espagne: l'émigration acadienne en Louisiane en 1785," in *Le Canada atlantique. Actes du Collogue de Nantes, 15-16 octobre 1982,* Nantes, Association française d'études canadiennes, 1982, pp. 95-104.

BAUDRY, J. *Étude historique et biographique sur la Bretagne à la veille de la Révolution, à propos d'une correspondence inédite (1782-1790).* Paris, H. Champion, 1905.

BOURDE DE LA ROGERIE, Henri. *Introduction. Inventaire sommaire des archives départmentales antérieures à 1790. Finistère. Archives civiles, série B. Tome III.* Quimper, A. Jouen, 1902.

BOYER-VIDAL, Yves. *Le retour des Acadiens. Errances terrestres et maritimes (1750-1850).* Éditions du Gerfaut, 2005.

BRANDILY, Daniel, "Les Acadiens à Pleudihen (exact title uncertain)," *Le Babillard (Pleudihan),* (August 1995), pp. 21-29.

BRASSEAUX, Carl A. *The Founding of New Acadia: The Beginnings of Acadian Life in Louisiana, 1765-1803.* Baton Rouge, Louisiana, Louisiana State University Press, 1987.

---. *Scattered to the Wind: Dispersal and Wanderings of the Acadians 1755-1809*. Lafayette. 1991.

BRAUD, Gérard-Marc. *Les Acadiens en France, Nantes et Paimboeuf, 1775-1785. Approche généalogique*. Ouest éditions, 1999.

---. *De Nantes à la Louisiane. L'histoire de l'Acadie, l'odyssée d'un people exile*. Ouest éditions, 1994.

---. "La déportation des Acadiens et leur descendance en France," *Centre généalogique de l'Ouest*, 66, (1991), pp. 7-14.

---. "Des patriots acadiens à Nantes pendant la Révolution française," *Bretagne-Acadie-Louisiane*, no. 44.

---. "L'odyssée acadienne à travers une famille Aucoin de Martin à Alexandre," *Cahiers de la Société historique acadienne,* vol. 31, nos. 3-4 (December 2000).

BRÉBEL, Abbé Eugène. *Essai historique sur Pleudihan sur Rance*, 1916.

BRUN, Régis Sygefroy. "Le séjour des Acadiens en Angleterre et leurs traces dans les archives britanniques, 1756-1763," *Cahiers de la Société historique acadienne*, IV, 2 (1971), pp. 62-68.

BUGEON, Guy-Charles. *Les Fermes acadiennes du Poitou et leurs occupants de 1774 à 1793*. Archigny, 1996.

CAILLEBEAU, Maurice. *Les secours aux Acadiens pendant la Révolution française et leur intérêt pour la recherché généalogique* (unpublished manuscript), CEA, Moncton, 588-1-1), 1978.

CASGRAIN, Henri Raymod. *Un pèlenirage au pays d'Evangeline*. Paris, Cerf, 1889 (1885?).

CAZAUX, Yves. *L'Acadie. Histoire des Acadiens du XVIIe siècle à nos jours*. Paris, Albin Michel, 1992.

CÉRINO, Christophe. "Les Acadiens à Belle-Île-en-Mer: une experience originale d'intégration en milieu insulaire à la fin du XVIIIe siècle," *Annales de Bretagne et des pays de l'Ouest*, 110, 1 (2003), pp. 115-124.

CHERUBINI, Bernard. "Les Acadiens en Guyane française: des colons exemplaires pour une colonization dilettante (1762-1772)," *Bulletin du Centre d'histoire des espaces atlantiques*, 5, (1990), pp. 157-196.

---. "L'odyssée des Acadiens dans la Caraïbe ou les theories humorales de la créolisation," *Cahiers de la Société historique acadienne*, 26, 1 (January-March 1995), pp. 5-22.

COLLAS, Georges. *Un cadet de Bretagne au XVIIIe siècle, René Auguste de Chateaubriand, comte de Combourg (1718-1786) d'après des documents inédits sur la vie maritime, féodale et familiale en Bretagne au XVIIIe siècle.* Paris, Librairie A.G. Nizet, 1949.

CORMIER, Isabelle. *L'Intégration des Acadiens à Belle-Île-en-Mer,* masters' thesis (history), Poitiers, May 2001.

COSTA, Fernando Solano. "La Emigración acadiana a la Luisiana española," in *Jerónimo Zurita. Cuadernos de Historia*, 1951 (published in 1954), pp. 85-125.

CURZON, Alfred de. "Les Acadiens à Liverpool," *La Grand' Goule (Poitiers),* (1930), pp. 5-6.

D'ENTREMONT, Clarence-Joseph. "Documents inédits de la famile Mius d'Entremont d'Acadie," *Mémoires de la Société généalogique canadienne-française,* IXI-XX, 97-100 (1968-1969), no. 97, pp. 143-166; no. 98, pp. 216-233; no. 99, pp. 19-46; no. 100, pp. 67-78.

---. *Histoire du Cap Sable de l'An Mil au traité de Paris, 1763,* Eunice (Louisiana), Hebert Publications, 1981.

DALIGAUT, Marguerite. "Les Acadiens prisonniers en Angleterre," *Cahiers de la Société historique acadienne,* 34, pp. 160-162.

---. "L'arrivée des Acadiens à Belle-Île," *Bulletin de l'Association pour l'histoire de Belle-Île-en-Mer,* 4, (1964).

---. "Secours aux Acadiens sous la Révolution," *Bulletin de l'Association pour l'histoire de Belle-Île-en-Mer,* 54, (1977), pp. 8-14.

DALIGAUT, René. "Les Acadiens en Bretagne (suivi de État des familles acadiennes passées dans l'Isle de B.I. en mer au 1er nov. 1765)," *Cahiers Iroise,* I, 3 (1954), pp. 24-29.

DAVID, Jean Stanislas. *Essai de comparaison du sort des réfugiés acadiens et canadiens de 1758 à 1798 dans les ports de Rochefort, La Rochelle et de Nantes,* master's thesis (history), La Rochelle, Université de La Rochelle, 1998-1999.

DEBIEN, Gabriel. "Les Exilés acadiens après leur depart du Poitou," *La Revue du Bas-Poitou et des provinces de l'Ouest,* 2 (March-April 1972).

---. "The Acadians in Santo-Domingo: 1764-1789," in Glenn R. Conrad, *The Cajuns: Essays on their History and Culture,* Lafayette, University of Southern Louisiana, 1978, pp. 21-96.

---. "Les Acadiens réfugiés aux Petites Antilles (1761-1791)," *Cahiers de la Société historique acadienne,* 15, 2-3 (June and September 1984), pp. 57-99.

DELAVAUD, L. "Documents poitevins et saintongeais. I. Les Acadiens dans les landes de Châtellerault; le marquis de Pérusse d'Ecars et M. Sarcey de Sutières," *Revue poitevine et saintongeaise*, 54 (July 15, 1888), pp. 1-4.

DEMEULENAERE-DOUYERE, Christiane. "L'État 'reparateur' des accidents de l'Histoire: l'exemple des secours aux colons spoliés," *Revue administrative*, special number "Regards croisés de l'administration sur les personnes," 2007, pp. 74-84.

---. "L'accueil en métropole des colons réfugiés d'Amérique du Nord, vue au prisme des secours de l'État (XIXe siècle)," in GUILLAUME, Pierre and TURGEON, Laurier (eds.), *Regards croisés sur le Canada et la France. Voyages et relations du XVIe au XXe siècle, actes des congers des sociétés historiques et scientifiques, 130e,* Paris, Éditions du CTHS, Québec, Presses de l'Université Laval, 2007, pp. 295-306.

DESCOTTES, Dr Edouard. "Acadie et Acadiens," *Annales de la Société d'histoire et d'archéologie de l'arrondissement de Saint-Malo. Année 1960* (1961), pp. 118-136.

DESEILLE, Ernest. "Les Canadiens (Acadiens) de l'Île Saint-Jean à Boulogne (1758-1764)," *Cahiers de la Société historique acadienne*, 4, 5 (1972[1887]), pp. 200-204.

DUHAMEL, M. "Tentative de Colonie acadienne en Corse," *Revue des Sociétés savants des departments, publiée sous les auspices du ministère de l'instruction publique des Cultes et des Beaux-Arts*, fifth series, VIII (1874- 2nd semester).

ECKENDORFF, Guillaume. *La Correspondence des classes à Cherbourg, 1756-1766*, master's thesis, Université de Caen, 1998.

---. "Les Acadiens à Cherbourg," in *Les Normands et l'Outre-Mer. Congrès des Sociétés historiques et archéologiques de Normandie,* Caen, Annales de Normandie, 2001, pp. 21-33.

---. "Les réfugiés acadiens à Cherbourg (1758-1790)," *Cahiers de la Société historique acadienne*, 32, 2 (2001), pp. 110-117.

FARAGHER, John Mack. *A Great and Noble Scheme: The Tragic Story of the Expulsion of the French Acadians from their American Homeland.* New York and London, W.W. Norton and Co., 2005.

FONTENEAU, Jean-Marie. *Les Acadiens citoyens de l'Atlantique*. Rennes, Éditions Ouest France, 2001 (1996).

FOUCQUERON, Gilles. *Saint-Malo, 2,000 ans d'histoire*. Saint-Malo, Corlet, 2001 (1999).

GALLANT, Patrice, "Les exilés acadiens en France,")," *Cahiers de la Société historique acadienne*, II, 10 (July-September 1968), pp. 266-273.

GARDA, Claude. "L'abbaye de l'Étoile et les Acadiens en Poitou au XVIIIe siècle,")," *Cahiers de la Société historique acadienne*, , 17, 3 (1986), pp. 94-102.

GODRET, Michèle. "Mariages acadiens à Cherbourg," *Racines et Rameaux français d'Acadie*, 26 (2nd semester 2002), pp. 9-17.

GOSSELIN, Auguste, "Encore le Père de Bonnécamps 1707-1790," *Mémoires de la Société royale du Canada*, second series, III (1897-1898), pp. 103-117.

GRIFFITHS, Naomi E.S., *The Acadian Deportation: Causes and development*, doctoral thesis, University of London, 1969.

---. "Acadians in Exile: the Experiences of the Acadians in the British Seaports," *Acadiensis*, IV, 1 (1974).

---. "The Acadians Who had a Problem in France" *Canadian Geographic*, 101, 4 (1981), pp. 40-45.

---. *L'Acadie de 1686 à 1784. Contexte d'une histoire*. Moncton, Éditions d'Acadie, 1997 (1992).

GUILLEMET, Dominique. "Les Acadiens de Belle-Île-en-Mer: légende noire et histoire en (re)-construction," *Acadiens, mythes et réalité. Études canadiennes*, 37 (1994), pp. 172-144.

---. "Acadie géologique et lieux de mémoire français: les exemples de Belle-Île-en-Mer et du Poitou," in *L'Acadie plurielle. Dynamiques identitaires collectives et développement au sein des réalités acadiennes*, Moncton, Centre d'études acadiennes, 2003, pp. 75-103.

GUILLEMET, Dominique and Damien ROUET. "Après la déportation, l'exil. Canadiens et Acadiens dans le Centre-Ouest," in Mickaël Augeron and Dominique Guillemet, *Champlain ou les portes du Nouveau-Monde. Cinq siècles d'échanges entre le Centre-Ouest français et l'Amérique du Nord*, Poitiers, Geste, June 2004.

HAIZE, Jules. *Saint-Servan sous la Révolution. Une commune bretonne pendant la revolution. Histoire de Saint-Servan, Ille-et-Vilain, de 1789 `1800*. Saint-Brieuc, Les Presses bretonnes et Rue des Scribes, 1989 (1907).

HEBERT, Donald J. *Acadians in exile*. Cecilia, Louisiana, Hebert Publications, 1980.

HERPIN, Julien. "Les Acadiens déportés dans la région malouine," *Nova Francia*, III, 2 (1927).

---. "Les Acadiens déportés dans la région malouine. Étude lue à la Société archéologique de Saint-Malo le 18 juin 1934," *Annales de la Société d'histoire et d'archéologique de l'arrondissement de Saint-Malo. Année 1934*, (1935), pp. 45-56.

HODSON, Christopher. *Conversations with Power: The Acadians' Atlantic, 1753-1785*. Working Paper, Atlantic Seminar, Harvard, 2003.

HOREAU, Yves. "Basile Henry, syndic des Acadiens à Nantes et sa descendance pendant la révolution française," *Bretagne-Acadie-Louisiane: la lettre*, no. 47 (December 2001), pp. 9-15.

KOREN, Henry J. *Aventuriers de la mission. Les spiritains en Acadie et en Amérique du Nord (1732-1839)*. Paris, Karthala, 2002.

LAUVRIÈRE, Émile. *La Tragédie d'un people. Histoire du peuple acadien de ses origines à nos jours*. Paris, Henry Goulet, 1924 (1st edition: Paris, Brossard, 1922).

---. *Brève histoire tragique du peuple acadien: son martyre et sa résurrection*. Paris, Librairie d'Amérique et d'Orient, 1947.

Le FAUCHEUX, Monique. "Mes ancêtres d'Acadie: les 'Hors-venus' à Saint-Suliac (Ille-et-Vilaine), 1764-74," *Cercle généalogique d'Ille-et-Vilaine*, I, 1 (1st trimester 1987), pp. 10-14.

---. "Les Patronymes des Acadiens de Saint-Malo, 1758-1785," *Cahiers de la Société historique acadienne*, 18, 3 (1987), pp. 122-139.

Le GUENNEC, Louis. *Les Barbier de Lescoët: une famille de la noblesse bretonne*. Quimper, 1991 [1935?].

Le TOQUIN-VINET, Suzanne. *Acadie Belle-Isle-en-Mer*. Vannes, 1970.

MAGORD, André (and others). *L'Acadie plurielle. Dynamiques identitaires collectives et développement au sein des réalités acadiennes*. Poitiers, 2003.

MAGORD, André, Rodrigue LANDRY and Réal ALLARD. "Identités acadiennes en Louisiane, en Poitou et à Belle-Île," *Études canadiennes/Canadian Studies*, 37 (December 1994), pp. 159-180.

MARTIN, Ernest. *Les Exilés acadiens en France au XVIIIe siècle et leur établissement en Poitou*. Paris, Hachette, 1946 (facsimile reissue, Brissaud, Poitiers, 1979).

---. "Accueil et logement des réfugiés acadiens dans le Châtelleraudais en 1773," *Bulletin des cousins acadiens du Poitou* (March 1990), pp. 5-11.

---. "La revue du commissaire general à la Marine Lemoyne," *Bulletin des cousins acadiens du Poitou*, 26 (September 1990).

MASSÉ, Claude. "Les familles acadiennes présentes à Bordeaux pendant la révolution et le prermier empire," *Cahiers de la Société historique acadienne*, 10, 1 (March 1979), pp. 12-46.

MASSÉ-DAIGLE, Claude. *Chronologie acadienne de 1604 au 20ᵉ siècle.* (no publisher, no date), 1980.

MASSÉ, Pierre. "Le syndic de la colonie acadienne du Poitou," *Revue d'histoire de l'Amérique française,* V, 1 (1951), pp. 54-68.

---. "Destinées acadiennes. La courte vie de Marie Doucet," *Mémoires de la Société généalogique canadienne-française,* V (June 1953), pp. 166-170.

---. "La Colonie acadienne du Poitou: les rapports entre Acadiens et Poitevins de 1773 à 1792," *Actualité de l'histoire,* 9 (1954), pp. 4-14.

---. "Descendances acadiennes. Les quatre filles de Marie Reine Berbudeau," *Revue d'histoire de l'Amérique française*, 8, 3 (1954), pp. 415-425.

---. "Destinées acadiennes. Anne Bras (Brau)," *Mémoires de la Société généalogique canadienne-française*, VI, 4 (October 1954), pp. 181-182.

---. Destinées acadiennes, Marie-Josèphe Guillot et sa métairie," *Revue d'histoire de l'Amérique française,* X, 1 (June 1956), pp. 105-114.

McCLOY, Shelby T. "French Charities to the Acadians, 1755-1799," *Louisiana Historical Quarterly*, 21, 3 (July 1938), pp. 656-668.

MOUHOT, Jean-François. "Des 'Revenantes?' À propos des 'Lettres fantômes' et de la correspondance entre exilés acadiens 1758-1785)," *Acadiensis. Journal of the History of the Atlantic Region—Revue d'histoire de la region atlantique,*

---. "Une ultime revenante? Lettre de Jean-Baptiste Semer de La Nouvelle-Orléans à son père au Havre, 20 avril 1766," *Acadiensis. Journal of the History of the Atlantic Region—Revue d'histoire de la région atlantique*, XXXIV, 2 (Spring 2005).

---. "Lettre d'un prisonnier: quelques observations au sujet de la constitution de l'état civil des Acadiens de Belle-Île-en-Mer et d'une lettre méconnue de Joseph LeBlanc, prisonnier en Angleterre après le 'Grand Dérangement' (1757)," *Les Amitiés acadiennes*, no. 112 (June 2005).

---. "L'invention de la nation? (Re) présentations des acadiens réfugiés en France (1758-1785)," *Études canadiennes/Canadian Studies*, 58 (Autumn 2005).

---. "Un regard sur l'historiographie du séjour des Acadiens en France après le 'Grand Dérangement' (1758-1785)," in R.G. LeBlanc, *Du Grand Dérangement à la Déportation: Nouvelles perspectives historiques*, Moncton, Chaire d'études acadiennes, 2005, pp. 391-416.

---. "La Grande Déportation des Acadiens," *L'Histoire*, 304 (December 2005).

MOURLOT, Felix. *Les Acadiens en Basse-Normandie à la fin de l'Ancien Régime*. Alençon, A. Herpin, 1901.

NÉDÉLEC, Claire. *Histoire des Bellilois acadiens*. Rennes, La Découvrance, 2001.

NERROU, Jacques. "Le Retour du 'Richemont.'" *Racines et Rameaux français d'Acadie*, 32 (December 2004), p. 17s.

OLLIÉRIC, Joseph. *Belle-Île-en-Mer: refuge des Celtes et des Acadiens*. 1987.

PAPUCHON, General A. "La colonie acadienne du Poitou," *Bulletin de la Société des antiquaries de l'Ouest* (2nd trimester 1908), pp. 311-367.

PARFOURU, Paul, A. LESORT and H. BOURDE de la ROGERIE. *Inventaire sommaire des archives départementales antérieures à 1790. Ille-et-Vilaine, archives civiles, série C. Tome III. Articles 3,797 à 5444*, Rennes, Oberthur, 1934.

PERRON, Fernand René. "Laurent Babin: assassin de grands chemins?" *Bulletin de l'Association pour l'histoire de Belle-Île-en-Mer*, no. 56 (October-December 1977), pp. 18-20.

---. "Descendants d'Acadiens en France: l'installation acadienne à Belle-Île," in Colloque international de l'Acadie, Moncton, May 1978.

---. "Un Acadien bellilois sous la revolution," *Cahiers de la Société historique acadienne*, 20, 4 (1989), pp. 169-189.

PIART, Robert, "Une Acadienne et sa fille à la maison du roi Louis XVI," *Cahiers de la Société historique acadienne*, 34, 1 (March 2003), pp. 33-41.

POIRIER, Michel. *Les Acadiens aux Îles Saint-Pierre et Miquelon, 1758-1828: 3 déportations-30 années d'exil*. Éditions d'Acadie, 1984.

PRÉVOST, Robert. *La France des Acadiens. Sur les traces des fondateurs de l'Acadie*. Moncton, Éditions d'Acadie, 1994.

QUONIAM, Cahmille Th. "Les Acadiens réfugiés à Cherbourg," *Revue de Cherbourg et de Basse-Normandie*, 6, 7, 8 (April, May, June 1907).

RAMEU de SAINT-PIERRE, Edme. *Une colonie féodale en Amérique, l'Acadie (1604-1881)*. Paris and Montréal, Librairie Plon and Granger frères, 1889.

---. "Notes explicatives sur les declarations des Acadiens conserves à Belle-Île-en-Mer, et les étblissements des premiers colons de l'Acadie, " in *Collection de documents inédits sur le Canada et l'Amérique*, 1890, pp. 135-181 and 193-204.

RIGAUD, reverend father. *Vie de la bonne soeur Elisabeth Bichier des Ages, fondatrice et première supérieure générale des Filles de la Croix dites "Soeurs de Saint-André."* Poitiers and Paris, Oudin, 1875.

ROBICHAUX, Albert J. *Acadian Marriages in France, Department of Ille-et-Vilaine, 1759-1776*. Harvey, Louisiana, Robichaux New Orleans Bicentennial Commission, 1976.

---. *The Acadian Exiles in Nantes, 1775-1785*. Harvey, Louisiana, A.J. Robichaux, 1978.

---. *The Acadian Exiles in Saint-Malo, 1758-1785*. Eunice, Louisiana, Hebert Publications, 1981.

---. *The Acadian Exiles in Châtellerault, 1773-1785*. Eunice, Louisiana, Hebert Publications, 1983.

ROGERS, N. Mc L. "Acadian Exiles in France," *The Dalhousie Review* (*Halifax*), 5, 1 (April 1925), pp. 11-21.

ROMAN, Alain. "Les registres paroissiaux des Acadiens de Saint-Pierre-du-Nord, paroisse de l'île Saint-Jean," *Annales de la Société d'histoire et d'archéologie de l'arrondissement de Saint-Malo. Année 1986* (1987), pp. 103-118.

---. *Saint-Malo et les Amériques au XVIIIe siècle*. Collection "Documents pour l'histoire de Saint-Malo," dossier no. 8, Saint-Malo, Archives municipales, 1999.

ROUET, Damien, "Les Acadiens dans le Poitou: permanence d'une identité," *Études canadiennes/Canadian Studies: Acadiens, mythes et réalité*, 37 (1994), pp. 145-157.

---. *L'insertion des Acadiens dans le Haut Poitou et la formation d'une entité agraire nouvelle, de l'ancien régime au début de la monarchie de juillet (1773-1830): etude d'histoire rurale*, doctoral thesis (history), Université de Poitiers, 1994.

---. "Diaspora et representation: le cas des réfugiés acadiens en France," Études canadiennes, vol. 58, Autumn 2005.

SCAVENNEC, Gérard, "Des Acadiens aux Malouines," *Racines et Rameaux français d'Acadie. Recherche généalogique et histoire de l'Acadie*, 30, 31, 32, 33 (April, July, December 2004 and April 2005), pp. 8-16 (1st part); pp. 16-22 (2nd part); pp. 11-16 (3rd part); pp. 11-15 (4th part).

SÉGALEN, Jean. "L'odyssée de la communauté acadienne de Morlaix," *Les Amitiés acadiennes*, 64 (1993).

SOQUES, Geneviève, "Acadie, Acadiens et Malouins," *Annales de la Société d'histoire et d'archéologie de l'arrondissement de Saint-Malo. Année* 1984 (1985), pp. 177-179.

TARRADE, Jean, "La Longue errance des Acadiens après le "Grand Dérangement" (1755-1785)," *Bulletin de la Société des antiquaries de l'Ouest*, 5, 7 (1993), trimester 1), pp. 3-19.

TURQUET de BEAUREGARD, J. "Les Acadiens à Belle-Île et le clan Le Blanc," *Bulletin et mémoires de la Société archéologique du département d'Ille-et-Vilaine*, XXXIII (83), (1981), pp. 19-38.

VINTER, Dorothy. "The Acadian Exiles in England, 1756-1763," *The Dalhousie Review (Halifax)*, 36, 4 (1957), pp. 344-353.

WHITE, Stephen A. "Les Acadiens aux îles Malouines en 1764," *Cahiers de la Société historique acadienne*, 15, 2-3 (June and September 1984), pp. 100-105.

---. "Corrections aux "Notes explicatives sur les declarations des Acadiens conserves à Belle-Île-en-Mer et les établissements des premiers colons de l'Acadie" d'Edme Rameau de Saint-Pierre," *Cahiers de la Société historique acadienne*, 15, 2-3 (1984), pp. 116-121.

WINZERLING, Oscar William. *Acadian Odyssey.* Baton Rouge, Louisiana State University Press, 1955.

Endnotes

Preface

1. The etymology of the word "Acadia" is contested. The most commonly accepted version connects the word to the Greek "Arcadia" (the mythic, bucolic country of the poets of the Middle Ages and the Renaissance, a synonym for a place of contentment). But the name could also have an Amerindian origin, either Micmac (algatig, "site of camp"), or Maleseet (quoddy, "fertile place").

2. The official language of Québec is French, while all of the other Canadian provinces are officially Anglophone. Canada itself has, as official languages, French and English. Nunavut, however, has four official languages (French, English, and two local languages).

3. This phenomenon is not limited to francophone historians. Some Anglophone authors, in sympathy with the Acadians, whether in provocation or conviction, have adopted the point of view of the victims of the *Grand Dérangement*. Thus, one of the main bards of the Acadian identity is a Canadian of British ancestry, Naomi Griffiths. Another historian, John Mack Faragher, professor at Yale University, has taken up the accusation of "ethnic cleansing" in describing the events of 1755—a label first used by the Acadian historians. On these questions, see my article "La Grande Déportation des Acadiens," *L'Histoire*, number 304, December 2005, pp. 70-74, as well as the historiography in the introduction of this volume.

4. An incomplete list of the reviews of this book, and, where possible, a link to the texts of these reviews is available on the internet site http://jfmouhot.free.fr. On the same site is a link to the podcast of the program, "2000 ans d'Histoire" on *France Inter*, a French national radio program (June 2010), where I was invited by Patrice Gélinet to talk about the book and the history of the Acadians.

5. Michel Lapierre, "Des Acadiens qui francisent la France . . . ," *Le Devoir*, May 30, 2009.

6. http://www.lafontaine.net/lesFables/afficheFable.php?id=28.

7. See the section *infra* about "identity games" for a more lengthy discussion of these matters.

8. W. Cronon, "A Place for Stories: Nature, History and Narrative," *The Journal of American History*, 78 (1992), pp. 1347-76.

9. The base is presented below, note 19, p. 257.

10. http://jfmouhot.free.fr or http://www.septentrion.qc.ca/acadiens/

Preamble

1. The charter is reproduced in *De Nantes à la Louisiane, l'histoire de l'Acadie, l'odyssée d'un people exile* by Gérard-Marc Braud, Ouest editions, 1994, p. 122.

2. Cajun or *Cadien* is a deformation of *Acadien*.

3. The region of Minas was made famous by Longfellow: the heroine of his famous poem, *Evange-*

line: a Tale of Acadia was from Grand Pré, a typical village of the region. *Cf.* map, p. xx.

4. The wanderings of Joseph LeBlanc, representative of many Acadians, are described in detail in my article, "Lettre d'un prisonnier: quelques observations au sujet de la reconstitution de l'état civil des Acadiens en Belle-Île-en-Mer et d'une letter méconnue de Joseph LeBlanc, prisonnier en Angleterre après le "Grand Dérangement" (1757)," *Les Amitiés acadiennes*, no. 112 (June 2005).

Introduction

1. In this text, for convenience, the terms "Canada" and "Canadian" refer only to the settlements in the St. Lawrence River valley and their inhabitants; "Acadia" and "Acadians" refer to the villages of the peninsula of present-day Nova Scotia, finally removed from France in 1713; insular Acadia refers to the settlements of Royal and Saint-Jean Islands (present-day Cape Breton and Prince Edward islands), composed of Acadians, some Canadians, and some Frenchmen.

2. Around four thousand Canadians went to France at the time of the conquest. *Cf.* Robert Larin, *Canadiens en Guyane, 1754-1805*, Québec, Septentrion, 2006. Most of the Canadians present in France after 1760 were officers, unlike the Acadians, who were almost exclusively day workers of "low status." I discussed the specific situation of the Canadians in "Des Pieds-blancs venus du froid? Les réfugiées canadiens à Loches et en Touraine à la fin du XVIIIe siècle," *Les Amis du pays lochois*, no. 19 (2003), pp. 129-144. The reader interested in the question might also refer to my report, *L'immigration de retour canadienne en France au XVIIIe siècle et les réfugiés canadiens en France après la chute de Québec et le traité de Paris (c1760-c1800)*, Institutut universitaire européen, 2001, available online at the address: www.septentrion.qc.ca/acadiens.

3. For more details on the development of the colony, see the recent studies: John M. Faragher, *A Great and Noble Scheme: The Tragic Story of the Expulsion of the French Acadians from their American Homeland*, New York, Norton, 2005; Nicolas Landry and Nicole Lang, *Histoire de l'Acadie*, Sillery, Septentrion, 2001; Naomi Griffiths, *From Migrant to Acadian, 1604-1755: A North American Border People*, Montréal and Kingston, McGill University Press, 2005. The work of Andrew Hill Clark, *Acadia. The Geography of Early Nova Scotia to 1760*, Madison, University of Wisconsin Press, 1968, which is still a classic, is also recommended.

4. The Treaty of Utrecht ended the War of the Spanish Succession that involved the European countries when the Spanish crown returned to a grandson of Louis XIV.

5. The means of application of the Treaty of Utrecht remained ambiguous because of this last sentence. The treaty is partially reprinted in many works, such as that of Émile Lauvrière, *La Tragédie d'un peuple. Histoire du peuple acadien de ses origins à nos jours*, Paris, Henry Goulet, 1924.

6. A.J.B. Johnston, "Borderland worries: loyalty oaths in *Acadie*/Nova Scotia, 1654-1755," *French Colonial History*, 4, (2003), pp. 31-48. This article stresses the general character of the oaths of fidelity in the period and the fact that they were undoubtedly more necessary to those governing in North America than those in Europe.

7. G. Raynal, *Histoire politique et philosophique des établissements et du commerce des Européens dans les deux Indes*, 1770, vol. VI, pp. 237-250.

8. Quoted in Jean Ségalen, *Acadie en résistance. Un abbé Breton au Canada français: Jean-Louis Le Loutre 1711-1772*, Montroules & Morlaix, Skol Vreizh, 2002, p. 37.

9. Ibid.

10. Bona Arsenault, *Histoire des Acadiens*, Montréal, Fides, 1994 (1964).

11. These Acadians were nevertheless pardoned, for it was acknowledged in the articles of capitulation of Fort Beauséjour that they had been forced to take arms against the English, under penalty of death (Faragher, *A Great and Noble Scheme, op. cit.*, p. 384).

12. The bibliography on the deportation of the Acadians, also called the *Grand Dérangement*, is very abundant (see notably the collective work *Du Grand Dérangement à la Déportation: Nouvelles perspectives historiques*, Moncton, 2005, under the direction of Ronnie-Gilles LeBlanc). Historians are divided between those seeing this deportation as having been justified by English strategy and in some way inevitable, and those considering it as a political mistake and an inhumane act. The deportation was, in fact, very harsh, sometimes leading to the separation of families and death. The very hurried conditions of transport led to many shipwrecks, and the exiles were often forced to endure lengthy wanderings.

13. Quoted in Bona Arsenault, *Histoire des Acadiens*, Montréal, Fides, 1994 (1964).

14. "A relation of the misfortunes of the French neutrals [...] by John Baptist Galerm," quoted by Ronnie-Gilles Leblanc, "Pigiguit: L'impact du Grand Dérangement sur une communauté de l'ancienne Acadie," *Du Grand Dérangement à la Déportation*, Moncton, Chaire d'études acadiennes, 2005, p. 204, note 195.

15. Quoted by Faragher, *A Great and Noble Scheme, op. cit.*

16. It is possible that another portion of the Acadians went to France by way of Saint-Domingue, even if most of these Acadians preferred to go to Louisiana, where there arrival was noted by at least 1763 (*cf.* 1763-05-14a; Émile Lauvrière, *La Tragédie, op. cit.*, p. 193).

17. The beginning of the colonization of Île Saint-Jean dates from 1720. E. Lockerby, in "The Deportation of the Acadians from Île Saint-Jean, 1758," *Acadiensis*, XXVII, 2, Spring 1998, pp. 45-94; p. 46, specifies that the island was initially populated by colonists who came directly from France, but then progressively by numerous Acadians returning to the colony under French domination who quickly became preponderant there. In this article, which also mentions the departure of the Acadians from Louisbourg to France, Lockerby questions a fair number of prejudices spread by historical works careless of sources and facts. He notably questions the idea of an idyllic existence of the Acadians at Île Saint-Jean previous to the deportation and argues that the conditions of the deportation were not as cruel as many authors have described.

18. Cape Sable corresponds to the present county of Yarmouth, at the extreme southern end of Nova Scotia. Those later imprisoned were the ones how had fled their homes to escape the proscription and lived in temporary camps in the woods. As for those deported from Gaspé, they were first brought to Halifax, then sent to Europe where they disembarked at Le Havre in January, 1759, and at Cherbourg in January, 1760.

19. The first ship transporting inhabitants of Île-Royale was noted at La Rochelle on September 16, 1758 (1758-09-16; SHM Rochefort 1 E 414, no. 498, September 16, 1758).

Important Note: In the footnotes, the references are given in the form of a dated reference of the type YYYY-MM-DD, followed by a letter (a, b, c, d). The date reference in the example above is 1758-09-16. All documents indicated in this book can be thus found via this date reference in a database available on the Internet (www.septentrion.qc.ca/acadiens). It was established for the needs of the research done during the writing of this book, according to the principles and criteria explained in detail on the internet site (in French only). An archival reference indicating the provenance of the document follows the date reference, except in the rare cases when it overburdens the text or it is a document supporting a point in detail. In some cases, when the document was transcribed from a published work, the date reference is followed not by an archival reference but the title of the work. See the detailed presentation of the database on the internet site. Most of the documents are in French. A fair number are in English, and fewer are in Spanish or Italian.

20. 84 people found refuge at Morlaix, according to a letter by Choiseul (1763-07-11b; Choiseul to Quétier, AN Col B, vol. 117, fo. 296, July 11, 1763) and 375 individuals at Saint-Malo, according to A. Robichaux (*The Acadian Exiles in Saint-Malo, 1758-1785*, Eunice, Hebert Publications, 1981), a total of 759 people. This total is slightly different in the censuses made by La Rochette in England. He states, for example, 786 people (1763-02-17d; MAE, Mem. & doc., England, 47, fo. 2-5) or 866 (1763-02-17a; "Mémoire sur les Acadiens" of Nivernais and La Rochette, AN Col C[11] D, vol. 8, fo. 242-251, February 17, 1763).

21. See Michel Poirier, *Les Acadiens aux îles Saint-Pierre et Miquelon, 1758-1828*, Éditions d'Acadie, 1984. Some Acadians found temporary refuge in the Madeleine Islands after the deportation, but the populating of this archipelago by the Acadians who had come from Prince Edward Island only began in 1765. The present Acadian population of the archipelago has at its origin about three hundred individuals who left Miquelon with their priest, having refused to swear the constitutional oath in 1793. See Poirier, *op. cit.*, p. 31 and also Chantal Naud, *Chronologie des îles de la Madeleine: assortie de quelques dates repères de l'histoire de l'Amérique*, editions Vignaud, 1993.

22. This point would later be strongly challenged by the French, who considered the Acadians from English Acadia to be authentic French subjects. On this subject see two reports from the abbé de l'Isle-Dieu written specifically to refute the British argument (1755-03-25; *RAPQ*, vol. 17, 1936-1937, p. 403s; Report "Au sujet de la prétention où sont les Anglais que les Acadiens n'appartiennent plus à la France et qu'ils sont devenus sujets de la Grande-Bretagne," attributed to the abbé de l'Isle-Dieu, published in abbé H. R. Casgrain, "Lettres et mémoires de l'abbé de L'Isle-Dieu, 1742-1774," *RAPQ*, vols. 16, 17, 18, 1935-1938, pp. 273-410; 331-459; 147-253, p. 178).

23. The former French colony, ceded to Spain in 1763, only became French again for several months in 1803 before Napoleon sold it to the United States.

24. Faragher, *A Great and Noble Scheme, op. cit.*, ch. 13.

25. D. Guillemet, "Acadie généalogique et lieux de mémoire français: les exemples de Belle-Île-en-Mer et du Poitou," in *L'Acadie plurielle. Dynamiques identitaires collectives et développement au sein des réalitéss acadiennes*, Moncton, Centre d'édutdes acadiennes, 2003, pp. 75-103; M. P. Rider and N. Gaudet-Rieder, *The Acadians in France, 1762-1776*, Metairie, Louisiana, 1967-1973, vol. 3; 1759-04-30; SHM Brest 1 P 1/8 1759 piece 68 – AN Col B, vol. 110. Guillot, commissioner of the Navy at Saint-Malo, in April, 1759, drew up a list of 1,102 inhabitants disembarked from Île-Royale and Île Saint-Jean, of whom there remained only 897 surviving. To this total, one must add those who arrived in other ports like Cherbourg, Le Havre, La Rochelle, and in the region of Saint-Malo after April, 1759. In 1758, a large part of the population of Île Saint-Jean, estimated at six thousand inhabitants, was transported to England and to France, notably to Cherbourg and Saint-Malo. Between November 1758 and March, 1759, around one thousand refugees disembarked at Saint-Malo. "Taking account of the losses at sea (more than 600) and upon arrival . . . , more than half of the Acadian contingent destined for Saint-Malo had lost their lives" (A. Roman, "Les registres paroissiaux des Acadiens de Saint-Pierre du Nord, paroisse de l'île Saint-Jean," *Annales de la Société d'histoire et d'archéologie de l'arrondissement de Saint-Malo. Année 1986* [1987], pp. 103-118, p. 104). Faragher estimates that, of the 3,100 people who embarked from Île Saint-Jean, between 1,600 and 1,700 died during the course of the crossing(*A Great and Noble Scheme, op. cit.*, p. 404).

26. Lemoyne supplied Bertin with a first estimate of 2,370, from the lists sent to him by the commissioners of the Navy of various ports. This total is mentioned many times: *RAPC* 1905-II, pp. 207-208; AN H[1] 1499[2], fo. 634; MAE, Mem. & doc., England, 47, fo. 15, piece 6. Ernest Martin (*Les Exilés Acadiens en France au XVIIIe siècle et leur établissement en Poitou*, Paris, Hachette, 1936, p. 105) speaks of 2,566 "true Acadians." Another document counts 2,510 individuals (BM Bordeaux,

Ms. 1480, fo. 539).

27. Also see the maps of LeBlanc in the appendix of Donald J. Hebert, *Acadians in Exile*, Cecilia, Louisiana, Hebert Publications, 1980.

28. 1785-10-06 (Aranda to Floridablanca, AHN (Madrid), folder 3885, no. 3, expedient 13 of the section Estado, fo. 63, October 6, 1785; this document speaks of 1,574 or 1,596 people embarked); G. Bugeon and M. Hivert-Le Faucheux, *Les Acadiens partis de France en 1785 pour la Louisiane: listes d'embarquement*, Poitiers-Rennes, 1988, p. 5. The proportion of Acadians who went to Louisiana compared to those who stayed in France is difficult to measure exactly. On this subject of the difficulties in counting see the account of Dominique Guillemet and Damien Rouet ("Après la deportation, l'exil. Canadiens et Acadiens dans le Centre-Ouest," in Mckaël Augeron and Dominique Guillemet, *Champlain ou les portes du Nouveau-Monde. Cinq sièxcles d'échanges entre le Centre-Ouest français et l'Amérique du Nord*, Poitiers, Geste, 2004).

29. There were few Acadian families at Île-Royale. Bernard Pothier, "Les Acadiens à l'île Royale (1713-1734)," *Société d'historique acadienne (Cahiers)*, 23 (1969), pp. 96-111, showed that about fifty families emigrated from Acadia to Île-Royale between 1713 and 1734, but a fair number then returned to English Acadia.

30. The Acadians of Île Saint-Jean received aid starting in 1751 (1773-05-13a; Lemoyne to Terray, BM Bordeaux, Ms. 1480, fo. 319-326). At the start of the 1750's, at Île Saint-Jean and in French Acadia, the government urged the Acadians again to flee English dominance by promising them sufficient assistance to pay for resettlement in the form of food for three years and other compensatory indemnities (Jean Ségalen, *Acadie en résistance. Un abbé Breton au Canada français: Jean-Louis Le Loutre 1711-1772*, Montroules & Morlaix, Skol Vreizh, 2002, p. 38). On January 30, 1753, the abbé de L'Isle-Dieu, vicar-general of the colonies residing in Paris, presented the minister Rouillé with a "Mémoire sur la manière d'établir les réfugiés [at Île Saint-Jean] et sur les concessions de terres à leur faire" and a "Requête de secours pour la subsistence des Acadiens réfugiés," qu'il a rédigés conjointement avec l'abbé Le Loutre (1753-01-30; CEA, Placide Gaudet resources, 1, 55-3); the abbé Girard claimed, moreover: "I have been through Canada, Acadia and Île Saint-Jean. I always saw granted to the new inhabitants of these countries three years of food, tools, clothing, and, despite all of this aid, they could not live without being assisted. They were so, both with foodstuff and seeds, for the fourth and even the fifth year at Île Saint-Jean" (document quoted in Ernest Martin, *Les Exilés acadiens en France, op. cit.*, p. 277). The Acadians installing themselves at Île-Royale also received assistance from the king. An order had in fact been given as of 1722, "to send food for the sustenance for a year to a hundred people in order to aid those [of the Acadians who left Acadia which had become English and] who went to Île-Royale to settle there" (1722-07-15; AN Col B, vol. 45, fo. 1149.

31. Dièreville uses the term "Acadian," alternating with "inhabitants of Acadia," many times in his *Relation du voyage du Port-Royal de l'Acadie ou de la Nouvelle-France*, published at Rouen in 1708.

32. A more detailed study should be made of the use of this term by the "Acadians" themselves when they were still in North America. Even where one finds some occurrences, they seem to me to be marginal compared to their insistence on the fact that they were French and neutral ("*Français neuters*"). John Johnston, in a recent study, undertakes an interesting primary semantic analysis. He notes that the French authorities frequently designated the inhabitants of Nova Scotia as "Acadians," while the British and the inhabitants of New England almost always called the colonists either "Inhabitants," French inhabitants," "French neutrals" or "Neutral French." Johnston interprets this as the recognition by the French authorities of the existence of an authority and of interests belonging to the Acadians, while the English persisted in considering the Acadians as "fundamentally and irrevocably French in their allegiance and in their orientations." The analysis that Johnston makes of the British view is very pertinent. On the other hand, I think that the appellation "*Acadiens*" by

the French officials is more clearly explained by the fact that the expression "*Français neutres*" would have no meaning to the French administration (A.J.B. Johnston, "French Attitudes towards the Acadians, *ca.* 1680-1756," in Ronnie-Gilles LeBlanc, *Du Grand Dérangement à la Déportation: nouvelles perspectives historiques*, Moncton, Chaire d'études acadiennes, 2005).

33. 1763-01-20; Choiseul to Nivernais, MAE, Pol. Corresp., England, vol. 449, fo. 148, January 20, 1763.

34. For example, the inhabitants of Île Saint-Jean called themselves such in the requests for dispensations of consanguinity (Diocesan Arch. of Coutances, microfilmed at the AD de la Manche, Saint-Lô, 6 Mi. 252 to 257).

35. On this subject, see the letters by Ruis excusing himself for the lengthy time needed in making the lists at Rochefort in 1758-1759 (1758-10-12; Ruis, intendant of the Navy at Rochefort, at SEM Massiac, SHM Rochefort, 1 E 414, no. 521, October 12, 1758).

36. Besides, this categorization was only progressively applied. The refugees were often indifferently designated by the terms "Canadians," "Acadians," or "Inhabitants of North America." It was only later that a distinction would be made between the different groups. Lemoyne often asks the administrators of the Navy to clearly distinguish those who were Acadians or those from "Île Saint-Jean counted as coming from Acadia" (1773-08-09) from the "Europeans," that is to say the colonists born in France who emigrated to Acadia and were deported with the rest of the Acadians. The latter sometimes also received assistance as "Acadians." Also see the very detailed report of 1774-09-27 (Lemoyne to an unknown correspondent, BM Bordeaux, Ms. 1480, Appendices, 1st file, September 27, 1774) that explains in detail the distinction that should be made between the individuals coming from different places.

37. For the most part, I have not made research directly from the surnames. Because of the relatively limited number of historical Acadian surnames, it is possible to make a count of the refugees in the tables of baptisms, marriages, burials, etc. This method is sometimes very useful for rediscovering certain Acadians in various sources. Nonetheless, with rare exceptions, I have not retained the documents in which one does not find the term "Acadian" or an equivalent mention.

38. This part has been published, in a more expanded form, in the collective work under the direction of R. G. LeBlanc, *Du Grand Dérangement à la Déportation, op. cit.*, pp. 391-416.

39. The final volume in the Acadian trilogy of Alain Dubos (*La Plantation de Bois-Joli*, Presses de la Cité, 2005) briefly mentions the Acadians of Belle-Île and Nantes at the moment of the departure to Louisiana in 1785.

40. Ernest Martin, *Les Exilés acadiens en France au XVIIIe siècle et leur établissement en Poitou*, Paris, Hachette, 1936 (reprinted Brissaud, Poitiers, 1979 and 1993); Oscar William Winzerling, *Acadian Odyssey*, Baton Rouge, Louisiana State University Press, 1955; Jean-Marie Fonteneau, *Les Acadiens citoyens de l'Atlantique*, Rennes, Ouest France, 2001 (1st edition 1996).

41. Edme Rameau de Saint-Père, *Un colonie féodale en Amérique, l'Acadie (1604-1881)*, Paris and Montréal, Librairie Plon and Granger frères, 1889. The first work by Rameau (*La France aux colonies. Études sur le développement de la race française hors de l'Europe. Les Français en Amérique, Acadiens et Canadiens*, Paris, A. Jouby, 1859) includes only a brief reference to the stay of the Acadians in their former home country.

42. Rameau transcribed in his work a portion of the discussions that he had made with these descendants of the Acadians who remained in Poitou (*Colonie féodale*, p. 234). Damein Rouet published a transcription of the notes of Rameau in his thesis (*L'insertion*, appendix VI; documents drawn from CEA Moncton, Fonds Rameau de Saint-Père, Acadiens du Poitou, 2, 12-4, leaflets). These notes differ on many points from the summary that Rameau made in his book.

43. Lauvrière, *La Tragédie, op. cit.*

44. Martin, *Les Exilés, op. cit.* The mistakes and assumptions made in the book are unfortunately numerous. See "Un regard sur l'historiographie," *art. cit.* in R.G. LeBlanc, *Du Grand Dérangement à la Déportation, op. cit.*, pp. 91-416. The success of the work is shown by its being republished in 1979 and 1993. The work of Winzerling, *Acadian Odyssey, op. cit.* is nonetheless more frequently quoted in North America: Faragher, in *A Great and Noble Scheme, op. cit.*, makes no reference to the work of Martin (Martin himself descended from a deported family).

45. E. Martin, *Les Exilés, op. cit.*, p. 1.

46. Martin contradicts himself on this subject.

47. Ibid. p. 109.

48. Winzerling, *Odyssey, op. cit.* The work is drawn from a doctoral thesis at the University of California, Berkeley defended in June 1949 titled: "The removal of Acadians form France to Louisiana, 1763-1785."

49. See "Un regard sur l'historiographie," *art. cit.*, in R. G. LeBLanc, *Du Grand Dérangement à la Déportation, op. cit.*, pp. 391-416.

50. Winzerling, *Odyssey, op. cit.*, p. 9 and chapter 1, note 1.

51. Naomi S. Griffiths, *The Acadian Deportation: Causes and Development*, doctoral thesis, University of London, 1969. The chapter is partially reproduced in N. Griffiths, "The Acadians Who Had a Problem in France," *Canadian Geographic*, 101, 4 (1981), pp. 40-45. The most recent work of Griffiths, *From Migrant to Acadian, op. cit.*, stops at the moment of the deportation and therefore contains no information on the refugees in France.

52. Naomi E. S. Griffiths, *L'Acadie de 1686 à 1784. Contexte d'une histoire*, Moncton, Édtions d'Acadie, 1997 (1992).

53. Carl A. Brasseaux, *The Founding of New Acadia: The Beginnings of Acadian Life in Louisiana, 1765-1803*, Baton Rouge, Louisiana State University Press, 1987.

54. Brasseaux, *Founding, op. cit.*, p. 59.

55. One could present Brasseaux with numerous contrary examples. For example, when the French government offered the Acadians settled in Saint-Pierre and Miquelon the choice of returning to France or to Acadia, two hundred of around 1,200 chose to return to Nova Scotia. The very large majority chose France (Franklin, lieutenant-governor of Nova Scotia, to the count of Shelbourne, Halifax, October 24, 1767, *RAPC* 1905-II, p. 280).

56. Brasseaux repeats the same themes, without modification, in a second book (*Scattered to the Wind: Dispersal and Wanderings of the Acadians 1755-1809*, Lafayette, 1991).

57. Jean-Marie Fonteneau, *Les Acadiens citoyens de l'Atlantique, op. cit.*

58. In this book, Faragher affirms that the expulsion of the Acadians constituted the first episode of ethnic cleansing encouraged by the State in North America. I have refuted this argument, which seems mistaken to me, in "La Grande Déportation des Acadiens," *L'Histoire*, December 2005. This work, not yet translated, is, however, much less known by the French public than are the works of Martin or Fonteneau.

59. John M. Faragher, *A Great and Noble Scheme, op. cit.*, New York, Norton, 2005, pp. 422 and 432-436.

60. Faragher nonetheless mentions the existence of an Acadian identity on other occasions, for example, pp. 253 and 306.

61. The doctoral thesis of an American historian soon to be published largely trounces this interpretation (Christopher Hodson, *Refugees: Acadians and the Social History of Empire, 1755-1785*, doctoral thesis [History], Northwestern University, Evanston, Illinois, Dec. 2004. By the same author, also see *Conversations with Power: The Acadians' Atlantic, 1755-1785*, Working Paper, Atlantic Seminar, Harvard, summer 2003). Hodson is, above all, very critical of historians using identity as an explanatory masterkey. It was not questions of identity that mainly inspired the Acadians, but rather problems of competition in the work place in context of the lack of manpower that conferred value on the Acadians, who were, according to the words of an administrator, "vassals to be desired." The colonial empires, rich in soil and lands to be cleared, on the other hand, lacked manpower. Therefore, according to this historian, it was a question of procuring the means to obtain it cheaply, wherein lie the interest in gaining the Acadian work force. Two chapters of Hodson's thesis are dedicated to the stay of the Acadians in France, and it is hopeful that this work will be published soon.

62. See the definition of these terms further along in the text (the integration and assimilation of the immigrants, p. 17).

63. For reasons that are explained below, here I have placed the word "identity" between quotation marks because of its ambiguity. Though, so as to not overburden the text, I do not always do this in this work.

64. Brasseaux, *The Founding of New Acadia, op. cit.*, p. 55.

65. "Ethnology: group of individuals who combine a certain number of civilizing characteristics, notably a community of language and of culture (while *race* depends on anatomical characteristics)" (*Petit Robert*).

66. The definition of what constitutes culture is the subject of very many debates in history and in the sciences generally. The goal here is not to examine these questions in depth or to provide a new definition of the term, but simply to state that this word is used in a very vague manner and without ever being clearly defined by the authors.

67. See, for example: Gérard Bouchard, *Genèse des nations et cultures du Nouveau Monde*, Montréal, Boréal, 2000. According to this author, the inhabitants of the country were strongly "canadianized" before 1763: "The society of New France was [...] a specific cultural entity [...] feeding a sentiment of identity" (p. 88). Also see Peter N. Moogk, *La Nouvelle France: The Making of French Canada – A Cultural History*, East Lansing, Michigan State University Press, 2000; Luca Codignola and Luigi Bruti Lierati, *Storia del Canada dale origini ai giorni nostri*, Milano, Bompiani, 1999, or Jacques Mathieur, *La Nouvelle-France. Les Français en Amérique du Nord, XVIe-XVIIIe siècle*, Paris and Sainte-Foy, Presses de l'Université Laval, 2001 (1991) which synthesizes the research of these final years. The same reasoning applies to the Acadians.

68. See Joseph-Yvon Thériault, "Vérités mythiques et vérités sociologiques sur l'Acadie," *Le Congrès mondial acadien: l'Acadie en 2004* (Moncton, Éditions d'Acadie, 1996) and J.-Y. Thériault, *L'identité à l'épreuve de la modernité*, Moncton, Éditions d'Acadie, 1995, chapter 10: "Naissance, déploiement et crise de l'idéologie national," pp. 220-244, and Christopher Hodson, *Refugees: Acadians and the Social History of Empire, 1755-1785*, doctoral thesis (history), Northwestern University, Evanston, Illinois, Dec. 2004.

69. Jean-Claude Ruano-Borbalan, *L'identité. L'individu, le groupe, la société*, Auxerre, Sciences humaines, 1998.

70. See for example Rogers Brubaker and Frederick Cooper, "Beyond Identity," *Theory and Society*, 29, 2000, pp. 1-47. I would like to thank the anonymous evaluator of the PAES for having introduced me to this article, which is translated in French under the title, "Au-delà de l'identité," *Actes de la recherché en sciences socials*, no. 139, September 2001. For a general critique of the use of the concept

of "identity," see Jean_François Bayart, *L'Illusion identitaire*, Fayard, 1996 and E. Dupin, *L'Hystérie identitaire*, Le Cherche midi, 2004.

71. Rogers Brubaker and Frederick Cooper, "Beyond Identity," *Theory and Society*, 29: 1-47, 2000, make the same remark in their article (p. 7) by distinguishing similitudes among the members of a group, which could be "similitude in and of itself" or an "experienced, felt or perceived similitude."

72. On this subject, see chapter 5 of the thesis of Christopher Hodson, *Refugees: Acadians and the Social History of Empire*, op. cit.

73. Rogers Brubaker and Frederick Cooper, "Beyond Identity," *Theory and Society*, 29: 1-47, 2000, p. 19.

74. Griffiths, *From Migrant to Acadian, op. cit.*: "local identity" (p. xi); "community identity," pp. 101, 285 and 438; "political identity," pp. 78 and 292; "social and cultural identity," pp. 106 and 312, "national identity," p. 373.

75. See, for example, the classic work of Benedict Anderson, *L'Imaginaire national. Réflexions sur l'origine et l'essor du nationalisme*, Paris, La Découverte, 1996 (1st edition 1983), as well as the work of David A. Bell, *The Cult of Nations in France: Inventing Nationalism, 1680-1800*, Harvard University Press, Cambridge, Massachusetts, 2001.

76. Griffiths, N. E. S., *From Migrant to Acadian: A North American Border People, 1604-1755*, Montréal, McGill-Queen's University Press, 2005, p. xv.

77. Joseph-Yvon Thériault, "Vérités mythiques et vérités sociologiques sur l'Acadie," *Le Congrès mondial acadien: l'Acadie en 2004* (Moncton, Éditions d'Acadie, 1996). In this article, the author convincingly denies that the Acadian community could have had a "national identity," or maybe even a "cultural" one, before the 1860s. In the eighteenth century, before the deportation, the Acadians defined themselves as Catholic, French speaking subjects of the king of France, then subjects of the king of England, but not as "Acadians." He also challenges convincingly whether there could have been any national Acadian identity before 1860. The Acadians should have been able to assimilate, in the same way as, for example, could the Scottish and Germans in the rest of Canada, or again did as those Acadians who assimilated in France, the latter retaining only a memory of the origin of their ancestors, but not a national identity.

78. For the case of Canada, similar to that of Acadia, see the criticism of Louise Dechêne in *Habitants et marchands de Montréal au XVIIe siècles*, Paris and Montréal, Plon, 1974. For a summary of the critiques of the historians of this subject, see Thomas Wien, "Habitants, marchands, historiens," in Sylvie Dépatie (editor), *Vingt ans après* Habitants et Marchands: *Lectures de l'histoire des XVIIe and XVIIIe siècles canadiens*, Montréal, Mc-Gill-Queen's University Press, 1998; Christophe Horguelin, "XVIIIe siècle des Canadiens: discours public et identitaire," *Mémoires de Nouvelle-France*, Rennes, Presses universitaires de Rennes, 2005, pp. 209-219.

79. Edme Rameau de Saint-Pierre, *Une colonie féodale en Amérique, l'Acadie (1604-1881)*, Paris and Montréal, Librairie Plon and Granger frères, 1889. Joseph-Yvon Thériault considers Rameau de Saint-Pierre, along with Longfellow, as "the principle inspiration" for the Acadian identity ("Vérités mythiques et vérités sociologiques sur l'Acadie," *op. cit.*).

80. Bona Arsenault, *Histoire des Acadiens*, Montréal, Fides, 1994 (1964).

81. This was a summary of a more lengthy study. See below for a discussion of the more recent work of Naomi Griffiths, *From Migrant to Acadian, 1604-1755: A North American Border People*, Montréal and Kingston, 2005.

82. For more detailed examples, see the introduction to my thesis.

83. *Ibid.*, pp. 117-118.

84. For more details, see R. G. LeBlanc, *Du Grand Dérangement à la Déportation, op. cit.*, pp. 391-416.

85. 1759-05-10; Ladvocat de La Crochais to Guillot, May 10, 1759, SHM, Brest 1 P1/23 piece 7.

86. In a previous article ("Lacadians in Exile: The Experiences of the Acadians in the British Seaports," *Acadiensis*, IV, 1 (1974), p. 84), Griffiths already mentions this letter. Nowhere is it written that they "refused" the cider or that they disliked the fish and vegetables.

87. The most recent work of Naomi Griffiths (*From Migrant to Acadian: A North American Border People, 1604-1755*, Montréal, McGill-Queen's University Press, 2005) stops in 1755 and therefore does not reproduce this document, which came later. It would take too long to discuss this work in depth here. See the account made by Sheila Andrew, "Exploring the Acadian Identity: a Review of Naomi Griffiths' *From Migrant to Acadian*," *Acadiensis*, XXXV, 1 (Autumn 2005), pp. 186-196. Let us nonetheless note that, besides the fact that the author never defines what she means by the word "identity," Griffiths continues to use the same arguments as in her previous work. For example, she writes that Dièreville, a Frenchman having stayed in Acadia in 1699, recognized in the Acadians "a particular identity, different from that of France" (p. 171). But what, then, was "the identity of France" at that time? As for the particular Acadian identity, Griffiths here draws from a commentary of Melvin Gallant, editor of the work of Dièreville, to affirm its existence. Gallant wrote that Dièreville spoke of the Acadians "as of a collectivity which was totally detached from France" (in Dièreville, *Relations du voyage*, Société historique acadienne, Cahiers 16, 3, 4 (1985), pp. 19-21). Faragher makes the same remark in *A Great and Noble Scheme*, writing: "Dièreville, who lived with them, and surely knew the name they used for themselves, called them *les Acadiens*." But, if Dièreville did describe the inhabitants of the area as Acadians, he also wrote that they "remained French" (original edition, p. 82); later, he spoke of their "enthusiasm for Louis." He also uses in his text the term "Acadian" appended to the names of birds or animals, for example "Acadian partridges," which implies that he used this adjective to indicate their provenance or the place where they lived. Finally, Dièreville also dedicates many more pages to speaking of the "*sauvages*" inhabiting the country, and even about the animals, food, and vegetables, than he does about the inhabitants of the colony, which probably indicates that the Acadian "culture" did not seem as exotic or unique to him as a number of subsequent authors have suggested.

88. Griffiths, N. E. S. *From Migrant to Acadian: A North American Border People, 1604-1755*, Montréal, McGill-Queen's University Press, 2005, p. xv.

89. It is true that the departures for Île Saint-Jean may also be explained by the over-filled land of former Acadia. As of the 1680s-1690s, the migrations to other regions such as Beaubassin and Petcodiac occurred, in part because of the lack of space for the new generations and in part probably in order to engage more freely in trade with New England. See Andrew Hill Clark, *Geography of Early Nova Scotia, op. cit.*, p. 139s and Jean Daigle, "L'Acadie de 1604 à 1763, synthèse historique," in *L'Acadie des Maritimes*. Études thématiques des débuts à nos jours, Chaire d'études acadiennes, Université de Moncton, 1993, p. 31s. I thank the anonymous evaluator of the PAES for these references.

90. *Petit Robert*. Though it therefore may be appropriate to keep "integration" or "assimilation" (and their variants) between quotes in this text, from convenience and to not overload the text, we have not done so.

91. *Trévoux, Dict. Acad.*

92. *Dict. Acad.*

93. "This commissioner general should visit your department in order to [...] provide a precise and detailed account of the different types of work that each [Acadian] individual may be adapted to perform." (1773-05-22c; SEM from de Boynes to Guillot, SHM Brest 1 P 1/11 (1773) piece 61, May 22, 1773).

94. This is the term used by the *Trévoux* (1771).

95. Peter Sahlins, *Unnaturally French: Foreign Citizens in the Old Regime and After*, Cornell University Press, January,2004 (p. x).

96. To avoid repetition, integration may occasionally be used instead of assimilation, where it does not lead to confusion.

97. Jean-François Dubost and Peter Sahlins, *Et si on faisait payer les étrangers? Louis XIV, les immigrés et quelques autres*, Paris, Flammarion, 1999, p. 162.

98. Necker, Controller-General of Finances, to Sartine, Minister of the Navy, April 25, 1778, AN Col F^{2}B Commerce des Colonies (ANC, MG1 18, vol. 3, carton 6, series F^{2}B (trans., Mi. C – 3056)); 1778-04-25.

Chapter 1

1. 1773-05-13a; Lemoyne to Terray, BM Bordeaux, Ms 1480, fo 319-326.

2. For example, the governor of South Carolina reported that the Acadian refugees in his colony professed "an inviolable attachment to French interests, with a determined resolve to continue the public exercise of the Roman Catholic religion, under the direction of their priests." Quoted in Faragher, *A Great and Noble Scheme, op. cit.*, p. 384.

3. In the petitions, we note the appearance of this rhetoric starting in 1772 (1772-03-24; Petitions by the Acadians to de Boynes requesting passage to Louisiana, BM, Bordeaux, Ms. 1480, fo. 89-90). It reaches a zenith after this date.

4. 1784-03-15b; ANC, MG6 A15, series C [Mi. F 849] – AD Calvados, C 1022. The case of the Entremont family is somewhat special. It demonstrates an opportunism related to the circumstances and places. In fact, at the moment of being deported and later in this period, the family asserted business contacts with the New England merchants in order to plead their cause. I thank the anonymous evaluator of the PAES for this more complete information. The phraseology of the letter by the d'Entremonts indicated above is not, however, different from almost all of the petitions written by the Acadians to the French authorities in the same period.

5. *Cf.* A.J.B. Johnston, "Borderland worries: loyalty oaths in *Acadie*/Nova Scotia, 1654-1755," *French Colonial History*, 4, (2003), pp. 31-48.

6. Moreover, many groups immediately asked to take the oath in order to avoid deportation, but they were told that an oath taken under constraint was not one freely consented to. In 1759, the inhabitants of the south of Nova Scotia asked to live in peace in their colony under the protection of the English governor. In answer, the governor had them go to Halifax and deported them to France by way of England (1760-01-14b; Henri Léandre d'Entremont, *The Baronnie of Pombcoup and the Acadians: a history of the ancient "Department of Cape Sable," now known as Yarmouth and Shelburne Counties, Nova Scotia*, Yarmouth, Nova Scotia, 1931, p. 122.).

7. 1773-05-13a; BM Bordeaux, Ms 1480, fo. 319-326. This account is universally in conformity with what the other sources of this period tell us, except in two details which are significant: for clearly strategic reasons, it seems hardly possible that the English would have asked the Acadians to explicitly take up arms against France. Furthermore, the interventions by the old men are probably a rewriting *a posteriori*.

8. This version was noted by 1756 in a printed report (1756-00-00b; Anonymous printed report on the deportation of the Acadians, BNF, 4 Lb 38 699).

9. The causes and precise circumstances of the deportation of the Acadians are the subject of controversies fed by a significant literature that it is impossible to present here. Naomi Griffiths calculated thirty years ago that already over 200 books and articles had been written on this question (*cf. Contexte, op. cit.*, p. 83).

10. 1783-07-12; MAE, Pol. Corresp., Spain, vol. 611, fo. 34.

11. At the surrender of Fort Beauséjour, on June 16, 1755, the Acadians who bore arms were spared "as they had been obliged [by the French] to take up arms under penalty of death." At least this is what one reads in one of the clauses of surrender. Apart from the Beauséjour episode, the documents provide isolated cases of collaboration of French and Canadian expeditionary forces. The Acadians notably served as guides and suppliers. Other incidents of taking up arms are better known, like those of the Broussard brothers, as well as the Acadian participation in the battle of the Plains of Abraham at Québec (Faragher, *A Great and Noble Scheme, op. cit.*, pp. 384 and 395s; Bona Arsenault, *Histoire des Acadiens, op. cit.*, p. 165). I thank the anonymous evaluator of the PAES for this information.

12. Actually, her testimony dates from 1822. She said she was then aged 70, thus she would have been born in 1752.

13. In 1822, an old Acadian woman who remained in Poitou told her story to a nun of the convent of la Puye. Her account was later transcribed (1822-00-00; reverend father Rigaud, *Vie de la bonne soeur Élisabeth Bichier des Ages, fondatrice et première supérieure générale des Filles de la Croix dites "Soeurs de Saint-André,"* Poitiers and Paris, Oudin, 1875, pp. 130-131).

14. All the more so as many Acadians feared reprisals by the Micmacs stirred up by the abbé Le Loutre if they took an unconditional oath of allegiance to England. This, at least, is what they told the English authorities. On this subject, see the article dedicated to abbé Le Loutre in the *Dictionnaire biographique du Canada en ligne* (available at http://www.biographi.ca).

15. On the stay of the Acadians in England, *cf.* N.E.S. Griffiths, "Acadians in Exile," *op. cit.*; D. Vinter, "The Acadian Exiles in England, 1756-1763," *Cahiers de la Société historique acadienne*, vol. 3, no. 10 (1970), pp. 398-407; A. de Curzon, "Les Acadiens à Liverpool," *La Grand' Goule (Poitiers)*, (1930), pp. 5-6. The articles of R. S. Brun ("Le séjour des Acadiens en Angleterre et leurs traces dans les archives britanniques, 1756-1763," *Cahiers de la Société historique acadienne*, vol. IV, no. 2, 1971, pp. 62-68) and M. Daligaut, ("Les Acadiens prisonniers en Angleterre," *Cahiers de la Société historique acadienne*, 34, p. 160s) are of interest principally for genealogists, but do sometimes supply interesting information.

16. 1763-02-17a; "Mémoire sur les Acadiens" by Nivernais and La Rochette, AN Col C11 D, vol. 8, fos. 242-251, February 17, 1763. Hereafter, referred to simply as "Report of Nivernais."

17. According to the report, the Acadians stated "We hope we shall be sent into our own countries." Extract from a letter of two reporters to the Admiralty, L.G. and J.B., to John Cleveland (?), January 4, 1763, Admiralty Records 98/9, quoted by Griffiths, "Acadians in Exile," *op. cit.*, p. 74.

18. It is perhaps excessive to write that the Acadians were "prisoners" in England. Certainly, they were not free to leave the country (although some individuals may have gone to Ireland: Marie-Josèphe Martin, born at Port-Royal in 1740, married Louis Courtin in 1760 in Cork. *Cf.* Fonteneau, *Les Acadiens citoyens de l'Atlantique, op. cit.*, p. 333). At Penryn the Acadians were relatively well integrated, even Anglicized, and did not live in an area separate from the English. Moreover, the Acadians were apparently free to circulate outside of the towns where they were quartered, since some went to London. Their situation in France would not necessarily be better on the material level or that of civil liberties than in England. In France, in fact, the government never allowed them the choice of going where they wanted to go and even forbade them from leaving the kingdom, before

the later authorization to go to Louisiana, which was perhaps not even given to all the Acadians.

19. They asked to be "under the French government again." The existence of this letter, sent by some Acadians in Liverpool, is also referred to in the report of the duc of Nivernais. Nothing allows us to know, however, if the information about the senders of the letter provided by the report of Nivernais is trustworthy (those requesting to go to Acadia would be a minority: "54 [individuals] most of whom are elderly" – since recanting – , according to La Rochette, among "170 individuals comprising 38 families" asking to return to France, of a total of 224 people).

20. Nivernais does not deny a certain reluctance by the Acadians, but tries to minimize it.

21. Griffiths tries to show that the Acadians were not truly "French" and that they did not consider themselves really as such. At the time of their detention in New England, the Acadians frequently claimed their status as British subjects. In England, they were actually treated as such.

22. 1763-02-17a; Report by Nivernais. One may add the fact that the report of the ambassador, though very expansive, does not mention one single desire of the Acadians to settle in France, when the ambassador speaks of his idea of a settlement on the island of Bouin, which belonged to him.

23. Griffiths, "Acadians in Exile," *op. cit.*, p. 79.

24. The first document is a letter by Nivernais to Praslin (1762-12-24; MAE, Pol. Corresp., England, vol. 448, fo. 355 *et seq.*). Another document is yet more troubling. In May 1763, Choiseul wrote the ambassador in London in favor of "inhabitants of Île-Royale who had returned to France [...] [and who] requested to go [to Île-Royale] to sell their land and their houses" (1763-05-16a; AN Col. B, vol. 117, p. 215). D'Éon, a secretary, therefore began procedures for these inhabitants. He met on many repeat visits an English minister, Egremont, who at first refused the authorization, then pretended to accept it but did not want to provide any written response. The *chevalier* d'Éon interpreted this refusal as a sign that the minister wanted to maintain the option of changing his mind.

25. July 11, 1764 (1764-07-11; *RAPC 1905-II*, ap. J., p. 271).

26. 1762-12-01; MAE, Pol. Corresp. England, vol. 448, fo. 203-204.

27. I am unaware of what exactly this amounted to. The *Dict. Acad.* specifies, "Amnesty, feminine singular noun. Pardon that the Sovereign grants his subjects principally for the crime of rebellion, or desertion."

28. 1763-01-20; MAE, Pol. Corresp., England, 449, fo. 148.

29. 1763-02-17c; MAE, Pol. Corresp., England, 449, fo. 336.

30. Jean-Edmond Roy, *Rapport sur les archives de France relatives à l'histoire du Canada*, Ottawa, 1991 (MAE, Pol. Corresp., England, vol. 450, fo. 2-5). It is possible that La Rochette referred to the same individuals when he wrote of Bristol (1763—05-14c; MAE, Pol. Corresp. England, Sup. 13, fo. 69).

31. 1763-03-11b; AN Col. B, vol. 117, fo. 83 (ANC, Mi. C 15665, transc.). The new colony to which Choiseul refers here was French Guyana, which he planned colonizing at this date. Nivernais had, however, specified in his report that the Acadians feared "being separated or transported to the Antilles."

32. 1763-03-14; Roy, *Rapport*; MAE, Pol. Corresp., England, vol. 450, fo. 83.

33. If one were to believe Alfred de Curzon ("les Acadiens à Liverpool," *op. cit.*), some refugees drafted a petition to go to France as of October 1762. It was possibly this petition that was transmitted by the Controller General (Bertin) to Praslin, Secretary of State for Foreign Affairs, on November 20, 1762 (1762-11-20); MAE, Pol. Corresp., England, vol. 448, fo. 67 *et seq.*). In this report, it is very clearly specified that the Acadians at Bristol asked to go to France. As for the Acadians at Exeter, they

offered "to settle anywhere that His Majesty would judge that their services might be of some utility." The other letters sent by the Acadians to the ambassador of France in London instantly demanded the protection of the king of France but not expressly passage to France.

34. In the three places (Liverpool, Bristol and Southampton) where he had the families embarked, La Rochette mentions no resistance to this embarkation (1763-05-14c; MAE, Pol. Corresp., England, sup. 13, fo. 69). At Penryn, he makes this enigmatic comment: "The Acadians here […] also the most stubborn and least candid and they have given me more trouble than I thought they would" (1763-05-26b; MAE Pol. Corresp., England, sup. 13). Were the Acadians at Penryn reluctant to go to France? It is plausible, but the documentation does not allow us to decide. La Rochette specified that at Liverpool, Jean Landry did not embark (1763-06-08, MAE Pol. Corresp. England, sup. 13, fo. 80) proving that, at least at Liverpool, the Acadians were able to choose.

35. The tone of the letters sent by the Acadian prisoners in England to their compatriots in New England leads us to think that their going to France was considered to offer a greater chance of their being rejoined with their brothers (*RAPC 1905-II*, appendix F, p. 196).

36. On this subject, see Roy (*Rapport, op. cit.*, pp. 632 and following, which contains a transcription of letters by the different deported groups).

37. For the Acadians exiled in Morlaix: "The English […] very much wanted to continue [to pay it] if we had wanted to become their subjects" (1763-10-30; AD Ille-et-Vil. C 5156).

38. *RAPC 1905-II*, app. J, p. 271.

39. See, for instance, the petitions of the Acadian prisoners in Philadelphia, Maryland, South Carolina, Boston, and Georgia reproduced in J.E. Roy, *Rapport sur les archives de France relatives à l'histoire du Canada*, Ottawa, 1911, pp. 617-648, drawn from the MAE, Pol. Corresp., England, vol. 450-451. Lists detailing the names of the volunteering emigrants are joined to these petitions.

40. The Acadians of Pennsylvania to the minister (of Foreign Affairs), June 20, 1763, MAE, Pol. Corresp., England, vol. 450, fo. 415-7.

41. The Acadians of Maryland to Nivernais, July 7, 1763; MAE, Pol. Corresp., England, vol. 450, fo. 438-9.

42. L.G. and J.B., to John Cleveland (?), January 4, 1763, Admiralty Records 98/9, quoted by Griffiths, "Acadians in Exile," *op. cit.*, p. 74.

43. Choiseul notes this desire very clearly in a later letter. According to him, the Acadian families did not want to go to hot climates, preferring France, Acadia or Canada (1763-04-04; AN Col B, vol. 117, fo. 117).

44. Nivernais promised land and assistance. The very existence of this promise supports the idea that there was a certain amount of negotiating between the Acadians, the French, and the English. Indeed, if the Acadians had all wanted to spontaneously go to France and the English government had been in agreement, Nivernais would not have had to make any sort of promises.

45. Nearly 6,000 Acadians had departed for French territories at the end of the 1750s, often under conditions of extreme misery, despite the food supplies sent by Louisbourg and Québec (Bona Arsenault, *Histoire des Acadians, op. cit.*).

46. The rumor of a deportation of the Acadians had been circulating since the beginning of the eighteenth century (*cf.* Faragher, *A Great and Noble Scheme, op. cit.*, p. 118s).

47. According to Jean Ségalen, the Acadians were promised: "new installation, nourishment for three years and indemnities for losses" (Jean Ségalen, *Acadie en résistance, op. cit.*, p. 38). See also the biography consecrated to the governor of Île Saint-Jean from 1751-1754, Bonnaventure, in the

Dictionnaire biographique du Canada which specifies that the Acadians were encouraged to settle on Île Saint-Jean with the aim of supplying Louisbourg with crops. "France promised material and provisions free to the eventual colonists, took responsibility for their transport to the island and mentioned the prospect of the freedom of religion that would be refused the Acadians under English domination." Elsewhere, Gérard Finn, biographer of Le Loutre in the *Dictionnaire biographique du Canada*, specifies that "the missionary employed dubious means – threatening them with, among other things, reprisals by the Indians – to oblige [the Acadians] to emigrate." Despite the help of the French government, the Acadians in fact found poor material conditions on arriving at Île Saint-Jean and in proximity to the fort Beauséjour where Le Loutre sent them, for they had to undertake clearing the land once again (hhttp://www.biograph.ca). See also the report of the abbé de l'Isle-Dieu in which he in so many words recognizes the questionable actions of the rather turbulent Le Loutre (*RAPQ*, volume 17, 1936-1937, p. 403s).

48. Gerard Finn, biographical note on the abbé Le Guerne in the *Dictionnaire biographique du Canada*.

49. Charles-Octave Gagnon, *Lettre de M. l'abbé Le Guerne, missionaire de l'Acadie*, Québec, s.n., 1889 (available in integral text at hhtp://www.canadiana.org). This letter, probably dating from 1757, details the conditions through which some Acadians escaped deportation. Le Guerne explains that he encouraged many people to go to Île Saint-Jean and that the commander of the island, de Villejoint, welcomed a large number of them. It was notably a question of women whose husbands were deported singly to New England (the responsibility for the separation of some Acadian exiles at the time of the exile, and the origin of the dramatic plot of the poem *Evangeline* by Longfellow, does not lie with England, but comes from the advice given by the French priests. *Cf.* on this subject Griffiths, *Context*, *op. cit.*, pp. 98-99). On many occasions in this letter, Le Guerne writes that the Acadians were attached to their country, which they did not want to leave and which they hoped that "the French" would come to reconquer.

Chapter 2

1. Nonetheless, it seems that this was not a general rule throughout the whole period. So one finds Choiseul continuing to occupy himself with the Acadian question and trying to put into effect a plan for settlement in Corsica, when he was no longer Secretary of State of the Navy and had rejoined the War Ministry (M. Duhamel, "Tentative de Colonie acadienne en Corse," *Revue des Sociétés savantes des departments, publiée sous les auspices du minisère de l'Instruction publique, des Cultes et des Beaux-Arts*, Fifth series, VIII, 1874 – 2nd semester).

2. E. Taillemite, "Administration de la Marine," in Lucien Bély, *Dictionnaire de l'Ancien Régime*, PUF, 1966.

3. Roy, *Rapport*; MAE, Pol. Corresp., England, vol. 450, fo. 205-6; Guillaume Eckendorff, *La Correspondence des classes à Cherbourg, 1756-1766*, master's thesis, University of Caen, 1998 (pp. 173 to 198); Choiseul to Guillot, 1763-07-12; SHM Brest 1 P 1/9 (1763), piece 104.

4. For convenience, in this text, the expression "Minister of the Navy" will be employed equally as that of "Secretary of State," which is the official title. The phrase "chairman of the Navy council," frequently used by various authors, is improper in the second half of the 18th century. E. Taillemite, "Administration de la Marine," Lucien Bély, *Dictionnaire biographique de l'Ancien Régime*, PUF, 1996.

5. 1763-04-16; ANC, MG6 C3 [Mi. 12881] – Arch. of the port of Cherbourg (draft of letters of the comm.. of divisions), fo. 17; 1772-07-28; BM Bordeaux, Ms 1480, fo. 117-119.

6. All of the letters sent to Rochefort, for instance, and marked "colonies" bear the same calligraphy.

7. This the case, for instance, with Le Loutre, who affirms that he met Praslin many times. Praslin directed him to the Controller-General (Lanco, "Les Acadians à Belle-Île-en-Mer," *op. cit.*).

8. 1760-11-21; AN Col B, vol. 112.

9. 1763-12-03; AD Île-et-Vil, C 5157.

10. 1772-10-23b; BM Bordeaux, Ms. 1480, fo. 180-181.

11. 1772-12-02; BM Bordeaux, Ms. 1480, fo. 225-226.

12. 1771-12-23; BM Bordeaux, Ms. 1480, fo. 8 and AN Col B, vol. 42, fo. 163.

13. This is why, starting in 1773, the documentation relating to the Acadians is no longer found in the Navy archives but in those of the General Control (in Paris) and in the series C of the intendancies (in the provinces).

14. Their names are found within the documentation: Destouches, Carvillon, and de la Croix, secretaries of the Controller-General; Coster, first agent of Finances, first secretary of Necker (1784-01-15; AD Vienne C 32); Delille; Blondel and d'Ormesson, intendants of Finances; Gojard.

15. It is possible that this La Rochette, of whom we possess little information—except for a register of personal papers held at the National Archives of Canada (MG 18-F 14)—is the "Hillaire de la Rochette" whose biography is in the *Dictionnaire biographique du Canada*. However, this dictionary does not indicate his going to Great Britain; see also Martin, *Les Exiles*, op.cit., p. 42 *et seq*.

16. Moreau seems to have been specially charged with studying the feasibility of the plan for the settlement of Brix. *Cf.* 1767-10-17 and 1767-08-01; ANC, MG6 C3 [Mi. 12881, 3rd reg., pp. 9-11]—Arch. of the port of Cherbourg.

17. 1773-01-23; BM Bordeaux, Ms. 1480, fo. 252-254. Bertin was Director of the Bureau of Agriculture, the equivalent of the Minister of Agriculture.

18. 1782-04-05; AN F15 3495.

19. The following individuals intervened, most often by means of a letter of recommendation or more informal support: the ducs de Nivernais, d'Aiguillon (then commander-in-chief of Brittany) (1763-07-31); the duchess of Duras (1769-10-25); Aiguillon again (1772-12-03); Nivernais again (1774-07-03); the count d'Artois (1777-04-00); Anne Dumouriez (1779-08-19); the duchess de Rohan (1785-04-19a); a daughter of Louix XV, madam Louise, was also interested in an Acadian Carmelite nun at Morlaix (1786-05-19b). The Acadians also solicited the protection of Marie-Antoinette (1774-07-00b), who was perhaps made aware of their situation by the intercession of madams de Neuville or de Billy (*cf.* Robert Piart, "Une Acadienne et sa fille à la maison du roi Louis XVI," *Société historique acadienne (Cahiers)*, 34, 1 (March 2003), pp. 33-41 and see below note 98, Chapter VII). However, it does not seem that the Acadians were aware that of one of their compatriots was close to the queen. They experienced many problems getting their petition to reach the queen, and the names of madams de Neuville and de Billy are never mentioned (1774-08-02a).

20. François Monnier, "Administration," in Lucien Bély, *Dictionnaire de l'Ancien Régime, op. cit.*

21. 1759-01-29; AM Saint-Malo, BB45.

22. 1760-01-16; AN Marine B^3, vol. 547, fo. 50 and fo. 121.

23. 1760-08-16; ANC MG6 – C2 (transc., Mi. C 4619) – Arch. of the Port of Saint-Servan, C8, Li 7 (C 8/7).

24. 1773-05-06; SHM Brest 1/ P 1/11 (1773) piece 56 and 1778-03-09; ANC, MG6 A15, series C [Mi. F 849] – AD Calvados, C 1021.

25. 1758-03-19b; MAE Pol. Corresp. Spain, vol. 616, fo. 269.

26. 1759-05-04c; AN Col B, vol. 110.

27. 1759-12-06; SHM Rochefort, 1 E 415, no. 726. The word *créole* in the 18th century was the "name given to a person of European origin who was born in America" (*Dictionnaire de l'Académie*).

28. 1759-12-14; SHM Rochefort 1 E 162, fo. 895.

29. 1763-02-17a (Report by Nivernais). The Acadians were perhaps more hesitant to go to France because, in England, their payment seemed to be distributed more punctually on the whole. On May 14, 1763, at Bristol, La Rochette notes that the last balance payments were dated May 1 (1763-05-14c; MAE, Pol. Corresp., England, Sup. 13, fo. 69). At Penryn, on the other hand, there were delays. (1763-02-17a; Report by Nivernais; 1763-05-26c; MAE, Pol. Corresp., England, Sup. 13, fo. 76). This situation, seemingly more favorable to the Acadians, did not prevent them from contracting many debts that were settled by the French government at the time of their embarking for France.

30. 1766-05-18; AN Marine B3, vol. 568, fo. 156.

31. It is worth noting that this "delegation" is not mentioned in any other document. The ministerial reshuffling that happened some weeks after this possible visit may explain why it is not spoken of again.

32. 1775-00-00b; AD Vienne J 64/M 7.

33. 1758-09-19; SHM Rochefort 1 E 414, no. 502.

34. 1759-02-07; N Col B, vo. 110.

35. 1759-05-04c, SHM Rochefort 1 E 161, fo. 589 and AN Col B, vol. 110.

36. In the series Marine B³ of the National Archives, reference is often made to the problems the administrative personnel themselves had being paid. An intendant of the Marine thus wrote that he had not been paid for three years.

37. 1758-12-02; SHM Rochefort, 1 E 414, no. 636. Speculation: "One so calls the usurious & excessive profit that one takes by converting into liquid currency some promise, note, or money order" according to the *Dict. Acad.* Intrigue: "Said figuratively for an group of things that are untoward, which do not fit well together," *Dict. Acad.*

38. 1759-08-17; AN Col B, vol. 110.

39. 1774-07-00b; AD Vienne 2 J dep. 2, art. 97 and Louis Duval, *Mémoire sur les Acadiens*, Niort, L. Clouzot, 1867.

40. 1774-11-29a; AD Vienne 2 J dep. 22, art. 97. Pérusse often accuses the employees of the Navy of being corrupt and enriching themselves by the aid distributed to the Acadians from which they may have taken "large withdrawals" (1774-05-18a; AD Vienne 2 J dep. 22, art. 97; 1774-09-14a; AD Vienne 2 J dep. 22, art. 97). But he then tries to sully the reputation of Lemoyne, so his accusations are not very sound. Furthermore, his addition was erroneous.

41. D. Roche, *La France des Lumières*, Paris, Librairie Antheme Fayard, 1993, p. 51.

42. 1758-11-24; SHM Brest 1 P 1/7, piece 223.

43. 1772-04-10a; BM Bordeaux, Ms. 1480, fo. 54-55.

44. 1772-07-28; BM Bordeaux, Ms. 1480, fo. 117-119.

45. 1772-08-13; BM Bordeaux, Ms. 1480, fo. 120.

46. 1773-09-17; ANC, MG6 A15, series C [Mi. F 849] – AD Calvados, C 1019.

47. 1773-06-19b; ANC, MG6 A15, series C [Mi. F 849] – AD Calvados, C 1019 and 1772-09-15; BM Bordeaux, Ms. 1480, fo. 144-146; 1773-12-05b; MB Bordeaux, Ms. 1480, fo. 523-526.

48. 1773-09-10b; BM Bordeaux, Ms. 1480, fo. 475.

49. Saint-Malo: 1758-11-00a; 1758-11-01a; 1758-11-01b; 1758-11-01d; 1758-11-15a; Rochefort; 1758-09-14 – 175809-16; SHM Rochefort 1 E 414, no. 498; La Rochelle: 1758-10-09; AN Col B, vol. 108, fo. 107; Brest: 1758-10-26a (SHM, Brest, sub-series 1 P – ANC, MG6 C4 (Mi. of originals, F-2011 and F-2102)) and 1758-11-15b (SHM Brest 1 E 155, fo. 597 – AN Col B, vol. 108); Cherbourg: Camille Th. Quoniam, "Les Acadiens réfugiés à Cherbourg," *Revue de Cherbourg et de Basse-Normandie*, 6, 7, 8 (April, May, June 1907); 1758-11-29b (AN Col B, vol. 108, fo. 328); Le Havre: 1759-03-02 (AN Col B, vol. 110), Boulogne: 1758-12-26 (AN Col B, vol. 108, fo. 348).

50. About 1,700 to 1,800 Acadians were close to the banks of the Rance River, especially the former inhabitants of Île Saint-Jean, or around 70 percent of the Acadians pensioned by the government. They left for the following parishes: Saint-Malo, Saint-Servan, Paramé, Bonnaban, La Gouesnière, Chateauneuf, Saint-Suliac, Meillac, Pleudihen, Plouër, Preslin, Trigavou, Langrolay, Pleurtuis, Saint-Enogat, Ploubalay, Saint-Briac, Saint-Cast, Lamballe, Saint-Thual, Hirel, Taden (*cf.* map 3, p. 39).

51. 1758-11-01d; ANC MG6 – C2 (transc., Mi. C 4619) – Arch. of the Port of Saint-Servan, C 8, Li 7 (C 8/7). 1,040 people from Louisbourg and from Île Saint-Jean were transported to Saint-Malo by five English ships, arriving on January 23, 1759. Of the total, 350 died during the crossing and 150 were admitted to Hôtel Dieu as soon as they arrived (Julien Herpin, "Les Acadiens déportés dans la region malouine," *Nova Francia*, III, 2, 1927). To these, we must also add the arrivals from England in 1760 and 1763.

52. 1,064 people in 1759 (1759-07-27a), 1,126 in 1762 (1762-00-00b), 1,712 in 1773 (1773-05-22b), nearly 1,800 in August 1773 (1773-08-09), 1,727 in 1774 (1774-01-00; some Acadians then left to go to Poitou).

53. *Cf.* "Liste des habitants de l'Île-Royale, de l'Île Saint-Jean et de l'Acadie qui avaient débarqué et reçu la subsistance à Rochefort, La Rochelle, et Cherbourg et qui sont venus résider à Saint-Malo avec des passeports des commissaries desdits ports (1759)" ((1759-01-16; ANC MG6 – C2 (transc., Mi. C 4619) – Arch. of the Port of Saint-Servan, C 8 Li 7 (C 8/7); the list unfortunately does not provide the reasons for the arrivals at Saint-Malo, but it was probably a question of family regroupings. "Rôle général des habitants de l'Île-Royale et de l'Île Saint-Jean distributes par paroisses pour les six derniers mois de 1759" (1758-11-00a and 1758-12-00; Arch. of the Navy, Brest, sub-series 1 P); (1759-08-10; SHM Brest 1 P 1/8 1759, piece 123 and AN Col B, vol. 110).

54. We can establish the regroupings by finding the spatial distribution of the acts of civil status involving Acadians. At Morlaix, the proportion was 86 acts in a parish, 22 acts in another, and 4 in a third; at Le Havre: 87 acts in a parish, 11 in another; at Boulogne: 100, nearly all in one of two parishes (that of the lower town). (P. Gallant, "Les exiles acadiens en France," *Les Cahiers de la Société historique acadienne*, vol. II, no. 10 (July-September 1968), pp. 266-273. The same concentration was found at Nantes after the failure of the attempt to colonize Poitou. The image of the distribution of the baptismal, marriage, and death certificates published by Gérard-Marc Braud (*Les Acadiens en France, op. cit.*, p. 8) provides a good idea of it, since one can determine that the Acadians were not harmoniously distributed and that nearly 42 percent of the acts found were registered within a single parish, Saint-Martin de Chantenay (545 of a total of 1292 acts); three other parishes of Nantes (Saint-Similien, Saint-Nicolas, Saint-Jacques), of a total of fifteen, concentrating about 36 percent of the acts found and in seven of them no act involving the Acadians was found. This is a sign that the Acadians lived in relative proximity to one another, within the same town, or at least frequented the same parishes. Surely, these concentrations, which depended on many other factors (evidently on the availability of lodgings, for instance) did not all, perhaps not even mainly, reflect a desire of the Acadians to remain close to one another. But they certainly form supplemental information on the subject.

55. Many examples are given in Faragher, *A Great and Noble Scheme, op. cit.*, chapter XIII. In particular, see the reassembly of Acadians in Georgia and in South Carolina for the purpose of sailing together to Nova Scotia, or, again, announcements placed in the newspapers seeking extended family members (pp. 385-392). Faragher also cites the very interesting journal of a pastor of Massachusetts, Ebenezer Parkman (edited by Clarence J. Entremont and Hector J. Hébert, "Parkman's Diary and the Acadian Exiles in Massachusetts," *French Canadian and Acadian Genealogical Review*, I (Winter 1968), pp. 241-293). Parkman made cordial relations with an exile, Jean-Simon Leblanc, and noted in his journal to what point the Acadians in New England frequently visited their extended families despite restrictions on movement imposed on them, .

56. 1759-09-18b; Arch. diocesan of Coutances – AD Manche, Saint-Lô, 6 Mi. 252 to 257.

57. See the letters presented in my article, "Des 'Revenntes?' A propos des "Lettres fantômes" et de la correspondance entre exiles acadiens (1758-1785)," *Acadiensis, Journal of the History of the Atlantic Region – Revue d'histoire de la region Atlantique*, XXXIV, 1 (Fall 2004), pp. 96-115. All of the letters quoted in this passage are taken from there. As an example of families separated by the deportation, see the example of Joseph LeBlanc, in the commentaries associated with the first letter presented.

58. "Des "Revenantes?", *ibid.*

59. Étienne d'Entremont, son of Joseph and Marie Josephte Moulaison, of Cherbourg, to his cousin, very probably Joseph d'Entremont, March 8, 1775. "Des 'Revenantes?'", *ibid.*

60. 1784-02-19. The Acadians of Saint-Malo to the marshall de Castries (Minister of the Navy), February 19, 1784; *RAPC 1905-II*, p. 227.

61. The reader may refer to the letters commented on available in the database. Many letters have disappeared, but their content was sometimes summarized in the surviving administrative correspondence. Interested readers may refer to the documents indicated as references in the database from the map featured in the appendix.

62. Faragher, *A Great and Noble Scheme, op. cit.*, p. 387.

63. In a period when one's network of acquaintances was determinative in deciding an individual's identity, it was also undoubtedly because the Acadians did not at any cost want to be considered as people "*sans aveux*" [vagrant, literally, having no one to vouch for him], or as "*vagabonds*," that they remained together. For, to separate from the group would be to go into an area where no one knew them, where they would risk being the victim of suspicion, if not violence.

64. 1763-03-18d; Alexis Trahan, Tranquille Prince, Joseph LeBlanc, Alexis Boudrot to the Acadians dispersed in the American colonies, March 18, 1763, *RAPC 1905-II*, appendix F, p. 196.

65. 1763-03-28b; AN Col B, vol. 117, p. 107.

66. 1767-08-24; Auguste Gosselin, "Encore le père Bonnécamps, 1707-1790," Mémoires de la Société royale de Canada, second series, III (1897-1898), pp. 103-117. The Canadians also aspired to recreate a "Little Canada," (*cf.* J.-F. Mouhot, "Des "Pieds-Blancs" venus du froid, *op. cit.*).

67. See the discussion of the meaning of this word below in the glossary.

68. The delegate in the *Ancien Régime* was "but a spokesman of the body and communities on a counseling mission with the sovereign, not exercising a decision-making power" (Lucien Jaume, "Réprésentation," in Lucien Bély, *Dictionnaire de l'Ancien Régime*).

69. "*Syndic*[advocate]. He who is elected to take care of the affairs of a Community, of a body of which he is a member," (*Dict. Acad.*). The first mention of a *syndic* is in a letter of Beauregard (1774-06-24); AD Vienne 2J dep. 22, art. 124-2). Nonetheless, Basile Henry later presumed to have been named advocate "of his country" on July 18, 1763 (1792-05-11; AN F15 3492), which is not proven

by any other source.

70. (1774-07-15; AD Vienne 2 J dep. 22, art. 124-1). The tasks of Doucet essentially consisted of taking care of the arrangement of lodgings for the Acadians, as well as supplying furniture and firewood.

71. 1782-04-05; AN F15 3495.

72. 1773-07-22a; BM Bordeaux, Ms. 1480, fo. 383-394. For instance, Lemoyne sent three Acadians to make a visit of the lands of Pérusse, adding to LeBlanc and Aucoin another Acadian favorable to the idea of going to Poitou (1773-08-19; BM Bordeaux, Ms. 1480, fo. 439-446).

73. Pérusse left detailed notes about the Acadian delegates (1775-08-27a; AD Vienne 2 J dep. 22, art. 97).

74. 1775-08-30b; AD Vienne 2 J dep. 22, art. 124-1. Pérusse repeated the same proposal the following month (1775-09-22; AD Vienne 2 J dep. 22, art. 124-1).

75. Though this surely does not constitute proof of an absence of the desire to regroup. The speech of the Acadians was not entirely free, for some of them probably did not dare ask for a reassembling that could bring disfavor.

76. 1778-01-04; AD Ille-et-Vil. C 6176.

77. See the opinions of Pérusse (1775-08-27a; AD Vienne 2 J dep. 22, art. 97) and of Lemoyne (1773-07-22a; BM Bordeaux, Ms. 1480, fo. 383-94) on this individual.

78. If the letter of Jean-Baptiste Serner convinced his father to ask to emigrate to Louisiana, it is not very reassuring on the subject, as it refers to compatriots who had died from working in the heat (reprinted in "Une ultime revenante? Lettre de Jean-Baptiste Semer de la Nouvelle Orléans à son père au Havre, 20 avril 1766," *Acadiensis, Revue d'histoire de la region atlantique*, XXXIV, 2, Spring 2005 (1766-04-20); AN Marine B3, vol. 568, fo. 31922).

Chapter 3

1. 1759-12-15; AN Col B, vol, 110, fo. 374/313. The writer had at first written, "in the colony," which was scratched through and replaced with "in America." The minister no doubt thought it more prudent to not too fully commit to the place of returning.

2. The colonies had a deplorable image in the public opinion of the period, as much among scholars as among the people. To confirm this, we need only recall the rumors that circulated in Paris in the 1750s about children being abducted and sent to the colonies (*cf.* Arlette Farge and Jacues Revel, *Logiques de la foule. L'affaire des enlèvements d'enfants, Paris, 1750*, Paris, Hachette, 1988). Jacques-Louis Ménétra also refers to these abductions in his journal (*Journal de ma vie. Jacques-Louis Ménétra, Compagnon vitrier au 18e siècle*, Paris, Montalba, 1982). This instinct of the public, associating colonies, populating, and punishment, was not without basis. We know that many salt smugglers, especially, were sent to New France in the seventeenth and eighteenth centuries. Also, Daniel Roche notes the existence of a section of Paris called "New France," owing its name to the fact that the police systematically swept through it to populate the colonies of America (*Journal de ma vie, op. cit.*, note 173, p. 168). After the Seven Years War, again, according to one source, the Council of the King thought of sending Breton peasants who had revolted to the colonies as punishment (1766-04-12; AD Ille-et-Vil. 5J 139). On the same subject, see also the excellent articles by P.N. Moogk ("Reluctant Exiles: Emigrants from France in Canada before 1760," *The William and Mary Quarterly*, XLVI, 1989, pp. 463-505) and Yves Landry ("Français passés au Canada avant 1760: le regard de l'émigrant," in Jean-Pierre Bardet, *Français et Québécois: le regard de l'autre*, Paris, Centre de cooperation interuniversitaire franco-québécoise, 2003) which both blame this deplorable image in explaining the

weakness of emigration to New France.

3. 1763-03-01c; AN Col B, vol. 117, fo. 69.

4. Concerning the Acadians repatriated to England, Choiseul soon announced that the king had ideas for them for a new colony, but that they could also stay in France if they so desired (1763-03-11b; AN Col B, vol. 117, fo. 83). Nonetheless, it was mainly to appease and reassure the hesitant Acadians that Choiseul conceded this latter point; he did not seem to at all imagine that the exiles would resist his plans and coercive methods for very long.

5. 1762-12-26a; AN Col B, vol. 115, fo. 333.

6. German women: 1762-12-26b (AN Col B, vol. 115 fo. 335); 1762-23-26d; Maltese women: 1762-12-26c (AN Col B, vol. 115); Alsatian women: 1762-12-26e (AN Col B, vol. 115).

7. See also 1763-04-25; AN Col B, vol. 117.

8. 1763-02-13a; AN Col B, vol. 117.

9. 1763-06-07b; AN Col. B, vol. 117, fo. 229. A list as exhaustive as possible of the Acadians who participated in this expedition was published by S. White, "Les Acadiens aux îles Malouines en 1764," *Société historique acadienne (Cahiers)*, 15, 2-3 (June and September 1984), pp. 100-105. However, the list is not very explicit and makes it difficult to count the names. Yet we can count about forty Acadians present in the Malouines in 1764-1765. As for Gérard Scavennac, in his article, "Des Acadiens aux Malouines," *Racines et rameaux français d'Acadie*, number 30, 31, 32, 33 (2004 and 2005), he only counts nineteen Acadians or Canadians having been sent to the present Falkland islands, of a total of 157 people. Unfortunately, this includes no indication of its sources. *Cf.* also Antoine Joseph Pernety, *Journal historique d'un voyage fait aux îles Malouines en 1763 et 1764 pour les reconnoiter et y former un établissement et de deux voyages au détroit de Magelan avec une relation sur les Patagons*, Berlin, E. de Bourdeaux, 1769, pp. 32-39.

10. 1763-05-24a; AN Col B, vol. 117, fo. 196 (Eugène Daubigny, *Choiseul et la France d'outre-mer après le traité de Paris: étude sur la politique coloniale au XVIIIe siècle, avec un appendice sur les origines de la question de Terre-Neuve*, Paris, Hachette, 1892, notes, on page 339 (note b) that the total of the embarkations for Guyana from May 16, 1763 to June 1, 1764 rose to 10,446 people, of who 3,150 were Acadians and Canadians embarked at Rochefort and Boulogne at various periods from May 1763 to June 1764). See also Robert Larin, *Canadiens en Guyane, 1754-1805*, Sillery, Septentrion, 2006.

11. 1763-05-24a; AN Col B, vol. 117, fo. 206.

12. See for example, the Acadian argument in the correspondence with Perrault, agent of the French government who sought to convince them to go to Cayenne in *RAPC 1905-II*, p. 217s.

13. AN Col C11 D vol. 8; integral text reproduced in *RAPC 1905-II*, p. 217.

14. See, for instance, the letter of Marguerite Landry of March 11, 1784 (1784-03-11; also published in Mouhot, "Des Revenantes?," *op. cit.*) mentioning the fear of going to the "contagious" islands." Peyroux de la Coudrenière also refers to the "ridiculous stories" regarding the settlement of Louisiana, allusions to rumors, some of which probably involved the climate of the colony (1784-08-16; AHN (Madrid), folder 3885, no. 3, expediente 13 of the section Estado, fo. 25). *Cf.* also note below.

15. B. Cherubini, "L'odyssée des Acadiens dans la Caraïbe ou les theories humorales de la créolisation," *Les cahiers: Société historique acadienne*, vol. 26, no. 1 (Jan.-March, 1995), pp. 5-22; Jean Meyer, *Histoire de la France coloniale, op. cit.*, vol. 1, pp. 18-20. A posthumous work of Boulainvilliers that appeared in 1756, *Les Intérêts de la France mal entendus dans les branches de l'agriculture, de la population, des Finances, du commerce, de la Marine et de l'industrie*, clearly shows the fear of his contemporaries regarding the degenerative effects of hot countries.

16. 1764-03-30; AN Col B, vo. 120, fo. 110.

17. 1764-04-14; AN Col B, vol. 120, fo. 129.

18. This is a flagrant falsehood, since we have just seen that, at least at Le Havre, the Acadians resisted. Some months later, Choiseul very hypocritically defended himself before Le Loutre regarding the use of force against those in Boulogne (1764-09-19; AN Col B, vol. 120, fo. 306).

19. 1764-05-04; AN Col B, vol. 120, fo. 153.

20. 1764-04-16b; *RAPC 1905-II*, p. 215.

21. Le Cap-Haïtien, in the north of the present state of Haïti, formerly Cap-Français, of Saint-Domingue.

22. 1765-04-02; AD Gironde C 4328.

23. On this subject, see Christopher Hodson, *Refugees: Acadians and the Social History of Empire*, op. cit., chapter III.

24. For example, eighty former inhabitants of Louisbourg emigrated collectively from Rochefort to Sainte-Lucie in 1763 (1763-08-24a; Gabriel Debien, "Les Acadiens réfugiés aux Petites Antilles, 1761-1791," *Cahiers de la Société historique acadienne*, 15, 2-3, June and September, 1984, pp. 57-99.

25. 1758-12-26; AN Col B, vol. 108, fo. 348; 1759-01-12a; AN Col B, vol. 110; 1759-01-07; *id*; 1759-01-17; ANC MG6 – C2 (transc., Mi. C 4619 – Arch. of the Port of Saint-Servan, C 8, folder 7).

26. 1759-01-12b; AN Col B, vol. 110; See also 1759-04-30; SHM Brest 1 P 1/8 1759, piece 68.

27. 1759-01-29; AM Saint-Malo, BB 45. Despite thorough examination at the Service historique de la Marine of Brest in the papers of the commissariat of the Navy at Saint-Malo and in those of the intendancy of Brittany, I was unable to find the origin of this order, nor its exact formulation nor, *a fortiori*, its objective.

28. This extract as well as those following are all drawn from many letters in the register of correspondence of the mayor of Saint-Malo (AM Saint-Malo, BB 45).

29. Perhaps the twenty-two Acadians mentioned in the later letter by Ladvocat de La Crochais (1759-05-10; SHM Brest 1 P1/23, piece 7). In this case, the destination proposed was the farms of the de La Crochais manor, near Ploubalay, some fifteen kilometers from Saint-Malo, on the other side of the Rance.

30. The Acadians were in fact especially concentrated at Saint-Servan, Saint-Enogat (on the other side of the Rance, next to Dinard), Saint-Suliac and in many parishes of the suburbs of Saint-Malo. See map 3, p. 39.

31. 1759-08-10; SHM Brest 1 P 1/8 1759, piece 123.

32. The Report of La Rochette counts 866 Acadians (1763-02-17a; MAE, Pol. Corresp., England, vol. 449, fo. 340ss.); other documents mention 753 (letter by Choiseul: 1763-04-06b) or 786 people (1763-02-17d).

33. It is very difficult to orient oneself amidst the orders and counter orders: in a first report cited below (1763-03-01a; MAE, Pol. Corresp., England, vol. 450, fo. 2-3), Choiseul recommends assembling all of the inhabitants of Île Saint-Jean who want to go to Miquelon within the same port; three weeks later (1763-03-17; AN Col B, vol. 117), he then speaks of dispersing the Acadians; on March 28, 1763, he authorizes the Acadians of Liverpool to go to Boulogne (1763-03-28b; AN Col B, vol. 117, fo. 107); on April 6, this time he orders the disembarking of the Acadians at Saint-Malo and Morlaix (1763-04-06b; Roy, *Rapport*, p. 614); on June 30, he approves lodging in barracks Acadians initially meant to go to another non-specified locale (1763-06-30b; AN Col B, vol. 117, fo. 278).

34. The Acadians indeed shared with Nivernais their fear of being separated (1763-02-17a; Report of Nivernais).

35. 1763-02-17a (Report of Nivernais).

36. 1763-02-18a and b; MAE, Pol. Corresp., England, vol. 449, fo. 353 and 355.

37. 1763-03-01a; MAE, Pol. Corresp., England, vol. 450, fo. 2-5.

38. The order of the intendant to disperse the Acadians around Saint-Malo was not final. As for that of Choiseul, it contradicts other previous and later orders and was not put into effect (1763-03-17; AN Col B, vol. 117).

39. Matrimonial dispensations similar to those granted in France were also granted to the Acadians in New England (*cf.* Mattéo Sanfilippo, "Les sources documentaries du Vatican pour l'histoire des Acadiens (1632-1922)," *Etudes canadiennes/Canadian Studies*, 37, 1994, pp. 94 to 114). The realities of the Acadian society, isolated and numerically slight, continually forced the Acadians to make this type of request of their missionaries. These requests also were continued throughout the period of resettlement in the Maritimes during the first half of the nineteenth century (I thank the anonymous evaluator of PAES for this information).

40. "REGNICOLE [Native]. Term of Jurisprudence and Chancellery, which is said of all of the natural inhabitants of a Kingdom, with regard to the privileges they have a right to enjoy and which is, by extension, employed in speaking of those foreigners to whom the King grants the same privileges. *Enfranchisement only occurs regarding those who are not native. The Swiss are considered to be native, having the same privileges as the natives*" (*Dictionnaire de l'Académie française*, 4th edition, 1762).

41. 1759-12-15; AN Col B, vol. 110, fo. 374/313. Despite thorough research, I was unfortunately unable to find the petition of the abbé de l'Isle-Dieu to which the above letter responds.

42. 1760-02-22b; AN Col B, vol. 112.

43. The bishop of Saint-Malo to the Sacred Congregation of Propaganda (1760-05-01; ANAC, MG 17 – A 25 (Vatican, Archd. de la PF, Mi. of originals.; K – 235, fo. 568, vol. 1 – Series Congressi, America Antille, 6).

44. 1767-09-16; ANC, MG 17 – A 25, PF, Mi des orig.: K – 245, fo. 288, vol. 210 (Series Lettere, 5).

45. 1769-07-01; *id.*, fo. 175-176, vol. 214 (Series Lettere, 5).

46. See the 11 files of dispensations of parental consent, consanguinity and affinity of the Acadians of the Cherbourg region (diocesan arch. of Coutances Placed at AD Manche, Saint-Lô, 6 Mi. 252 to 257 – dated between: September 18, 1759 – June 3, 1773). Photocopies of these files were kindly transmitted to me by Mrs. Michèle Godret, whom I thank. These files were partially transcribed and summarized by Michèle Godret in "Mariages acadiens à Cherbourg," *Racines et rameaux français d'Acadie*, vol. 26 (2nd semester 2002), pp. 9 to 17.

47. Requests for dispensations were made by the Acadians of the dioceses of Saint-Malo, La Rochelle and Vannes (and undoubtedly by the Acadians of other diocese) as proven by the documents sent in 1760 to 1767. But I was unable to find files of dispensations either at the departmental archives of Charente-Maritime nor those of Ille-et-Vilaine.

48. Very often the Acadians claimed exemption from the procedural fees, alleging that they were not natives in France, but the bankers of Rome refused to provide them with credit. Some bishops seem to have been reluctant to grant these general dispensations perhaps precisely because this would have reduced their usual income. (1769-08-14; ANC, MG 17 – A 25, PF, Mi. des orig.: K – 234, fo. 254, series Congressi: America Settentrionale, 6).

49. 1769-03-14; ANC, MG 17 – A 25, PF, Mi. des orig.: K – 234, fo. 243 rv, series Congressi: America

Settentrionale, 6).

50. For convenience, the extracts from these files will only be referred to by their number. The pagination is indicated when it exists in the original. The files are the following: 1) September 18, 1759: Jean-Baptiste Galherme – Cécile Aucoin (this file is separate because it is a matter of a dispensation from parental consent, the parents of J.-B. Galherme having been deported to the American colonies and thus unable to give their blessing to the union); 2) January 14, 1761: Joseph Lapierre and Rosalie Hébert; 3) January 14, 1761: Eustache Parré and Anne Mélanson; 4) January 14, 1761: Léonard Circaud and Anne Lacroix; 5) June 25, 1761: Guillot La Borde and Marie-Rose Daigle; 6) March 25, 1763: Jean Granger and Anne Landry; 7) May 15, 1763: Joseph de Mius d'Entremont and Anne Landry; 7b: May 19, 11762: Permission for the marriage of file no. 7 (May 15, 1763): Mius d'Entremont and Landry); 8) July 3, 1763: Ambroise Bourk and Modeste Moulaison; 9) August 24, 1771: Joseph Landry and Madeleine Landry; 10) April 17, 1772: Basile Chiasson and Monique Comeau; 11) June 3, 1773: Jean Broussard and Marguerite Comeau.

51. Besides, these genealogies are often erroneous. A correction was published in the journal, *Racines et rameaux français d'Amérique* (no. 27, year 2002-2003).

52. This procedure was relatively common and the Acadians were far from being the only ones to not go plead in Rome. Thus the archives of the bishopric of Coutances contain about nine thousand petitions similar to those of the Acadians mentioned above for the period of the start of the sixteenth century to the Revolution. But it still fails to justify the difficulty of having to resort to the pope. The motive invoked in this case was still that of their great poverty. Many files also mention the fact that, in Acadia, there was no need to resort to the pope for this type of dispensation, as the bishop of their area could grant it. Stephen A. White, *Dictionnaire généalogique des familles acadiennes (1636-1714)*, Centre d'études acadiennes, Université de Moncton, 1999, notes that the dispensations for third and fourth degrees (third degree refers to common great-grandparents) were granted by the missionaries who had received power to do so. The bishop of Québec had the power to grant dispensations to the second degree, in the case of someone, for instance, who wanted to marry the sister of his first wife. I also want to thank Luca Codignola for the clarifications he was able to provide. Also see the explanations of Jacques Vanderlinden (*Se marier en Acadie française XVI^{Ie} et XVII^{Ie} siècles*, Moncton, Chaire d'études acadiennes, Université de Moncton et Éditions d'Acadie, 1998) which nonetheless concern only the period prior to 1713. This study is based on the analysis of sixteen marriage contracts before the English period. The article by N. Griffiths, "Mating and Marriage in Early Acadia," *Renaissance and Modern Studies*, 35 (1992), pp. 109-122, mainly concerns marriages between Acadians and Micmacs.

53. One of the Acadians, after having mentioned a series of motivations, in conclusion adds to his statement: "The petitioner is thus found restricted to finding a woman amongst the number of Canadians who are in this said town" (file 7). Another similarly concludes, "that he can hardly marry other than an Acadian woman because if she were not Acadian he would lose the payment for her that the King provides them and which is their sole resource" (file 10).

54. Files 7, 8 and 9. It is notable that files 7 and 9 concern preventions of consanguinity of the second degree (the parties having a grandparent in common). These dispensations, in contrast to the dispensations of the 3rd or 4th degree, which were usually pleaded before a representative of the bishop, would normally be made in Rome (information from the abbé Couppey, conservator of diocesan archives of Coutances, January 2004). For these two files, then, the argument concerned more the request to not have to plead in Rome than the choice of a partner.

55. Files 7 and 8. File 9 (August 24, 1771) is the only one that has no mention of an approaching departure. The date actually corresponds to an "empty" period in the plans for settlement of the Acadians.

56. See footnote 285, above, for more on these files.

57. The reasons should rather be sought in the great difficulty that the Acadians had in providing their daughters with a dowry.

58. The geographic knowledge of the Acadians seems to have been very limited. It is likely that Guyana was thought by many of them to be an island.

59. Remember that at Cherbourg, for the period 1759-1781, of 45 marriages involving Acadians, only 10 were mixed, or less than one quarter.

60. Another witness even claims to fear the loss of his own payment. L'Anglois and Parré seem to have known each other as they figure together in numerous documents.

61. The argument is advanced in files 2, 3, 4 and 10, therefore especially at the beginning of the period.

62. Many "non-Acadians" were able to receive aid from the fact of their marriage to Acadians.

63. Inclination, friendship, and love between the two future spouses are not mentioned in file 7 alone.

64. A study of the relative proportion of the mixed marriages (French and Acadian) to those involving just Acadians is featured below.

65. Among the voluminous files transmitted by Mrs. Michèle Godret, one single positive decision is featured. On the other hand, I was able to collate the petitions for dispensations with a list of the Acadian marriages at Cherbourg compiled by Patrice Berton and James P. Henry given to me by G. M. Braud. Mention is made of all marriages for which a petition of dispensation was made, except that of Jean Broussard with Marguerite Comeau, even though they submitted a petition for dispensation on June 3, 1773. It is likely that this marriage occurred, since they both are included on one act in Poitou (Robichaux, *The Acadian Exiles in Châtellerault, 1773-1785*, p. 25, index). The marriages generally occurred between fifteen days to a month after the petition for dispensation, except in the case of Joseph de Mius d'Entremont and Anne Landry, where the marriage came nine months after the petition.

66. 1781-03-08; ANC, MG6 A15, series C [Mi. F 849] – AD Calvados, C 1022.

67. 1767-08-01-1767-10-10; ANC, MG6 C3 [Mi. 12881, 3rd reg., pp. 9-10] – Arch. of the port of Cherbourg.

Chapter 4

1. 1763-04-04; AN Col B, vol. 117, fo. 117.

2. 1763-06-23 (ANC, MG6 A15, series C [Mi. F 849] – AD Calvados, C 1019); 1765-01-31 (AN Col B, vo. 122, fo. 23); 1768-10-28b (AN Col B, vol. 131, fo. 314).

3. 1763-06-23 (ANC, MG6 A15, series C [Mi. 849] – AD Calvados, C 1019).

4. The intendants of Bordeaux and Caen, at least, had the Controller-General's letter of June 23, 1763, forwarded to all of their sub-delegates.

5. 1763-07-02; ANC, MG6 A15, series C [Mi. F 849] – AD Calvados, C 1019.

6. 173-07-03a; *id.*

7. 1763-07-05; AD Gironde (Bordeaux) C 425.

8. 1763-07-08b; ANC, MG6 A15, series C [Mi. F 849] – AD Calvados, C 1019.

9. 1763-08-21; *id.*

10. 1763-07-08a; AM Saint-Malo, BB 49, reg. Ms., fo. 12-13. One single exception: On August 15, 1763, Choiseul forwarded the letter by one Brière to Bertin suggesting that the only viable area to settle four thousand Acadians was Brittany. In any case, we do not know the exact content of this letter (1763-08-15; AN Col B, vol. 117, fo. 367).

11. 1763-07-08a; *id.*

12. Petitions by the Acadians of Morlaix to the commissioners of the States of Brittany, October 30 and 31, 1763 (1763-10-30; AD Ille-et-Vil, C 5156).

13. 1764-02-17a; letter by Jean-Louis Le Loutre to Warren, February 17, 1764, AD Morbihan, Series E, correspondence of Warren (series 1-2 E), transcribed in J.-M. Lanco, "Les Acadiens à Belle-Île-en-Mer. Correspondance de M. l'abbé Le Loutre, Missionaire apostolique, avec M. le baron de Warren, Maréchal des camps et armies du Roy, commandant pour le Roy à Belle-Île," *Supplément au "Lys," Bulletin mensuel de la paroisse et du pèlerinage de Notre-Dame du Roncier, Josselin, diocese de Vannes, Morbihan* (March, 1924).

14. *Ibid.* Two concurrent plans were proposed for the settlement of the Acadians at Belle-Île: the dispersion of the Acadians through the four parishes of the island, and (at the instigation of Le Loutre) the regrouping of all the Acadians in an area where the corners of all three parishes meet.

15. 1765-03-05; AD Ille-et-Vil. C 2691.

16. 1764-01-21; Lanco, *ibid.*

17. Rector le Sergent (1765-00-00; Jean-Marie Fonteneau, *Les Acadiens, op. cit.*, p. 287).

18. 1764-01-00; AD Ille-et-Vil. C 5157.

19. 1765-06-14; Fonteneau, *op. cit.*, p. 344.

20. 1765-10-13; *id.*, p. 299.

21. 1763-11-04a; AD Ille-et-Vil. C 5156.

22. 1764-03-20 (Lanco, *op. cit.*). The inspector of domains, Isambert, repeated the same ideas (1764—04-00; AD Ille-et-Vil. C5158).

23. 1765-09-06; Lanco, *op. cit.* Le Loutre feared seeing the Acadians assimilate with the local population, of whom he had an unflattering image (1764-04-14b; Lanco, *op. cit.*).

24. A poor population of the island comprised of day workers who also engaged in fishing.

25. 1763-10-25a; AN Col B, vol. 117.

26. 1763-12-03; AD Ille-et-Vil. C 5157.

27. 1764-0610; AN Col B, vol. 120, fo. 195 // 1765-08-26a; AN Col B, vol. 122, fo. 278 // 1765-11-02b; SHM Brest 1 P 1/20 (1765), piece 89.

28. 1765-02-11; AN Col B, vol. 122.

29. 1765-03-05; AD Ille-et-Vil. C 2691.

30. 1765-04-01; Lanco, *op. cit.*

31. 1765-03-30b; AD Ille-et-Vil. C 5157.

32. "This is said […] of the testimony that one renders of what another has said or done; It also signifies approval, consent, the agreement that a superior person gives to what an inferior has done or intends to do. […] One calls *Vagrant* [literally, un-vouched for man, *trans.*] a vagabond whom no one recognizes, a man with no use nor home" (*Dict. Acad.*). Elsewhere, Christopher Hodson, *Ref-*

ugees: Acadians and the Social History of Empire, op. cit., chapter IV, writes that this episode allowed the Acadians to negotiate a "corporate identity."

33. The statements of the Acadians are preserved in AD Morbihan (Vannes) and were published in abbé H.R. Casgrain, *Collection de documents inédits sur le Canada et l'Amérique, publiés par le Canada-Français,* Québec, Demers, 1888-1891 (3 vols.). In this same work note the commentary by Edme Rameau de Saint-Père ("Notes explicatives sur les declarations des Acadiens conserves à Belle-Île-en-Mer, et les Établissements des premiers colons de l'Acadie"). Also see the decree of the court of Brittany ordering the reestablishment of civil status (1767-01-12; MAE, Mem. & doc. (England), vol. 47, 13).

34. 1765-09-06; Lanco, *op. cit.* (extract quoted above, p. 60; Warren regretted that Le Loutre did not ultimately bring with him more families, but his insistence that they be spread around the whole island is probably one of the reasons for the small number of volunteers (1765-08-21; Lanco, *op. cit.*).

35. *Cf.* Fernand René Perron, "Larent Babin: assassin de grands chemins?," *Bulletin de l'Association pour l'histoire de Belle-Île-en-Mer,* no. 56 (October-December 1977), pp. 18-20. On the fate of the Acadian installation at Belle-Île (of a general nature) see the work of Jean-Marie Fonteneau (*Les Acadiens, citoyens de l'Atlantique*), as well as the articles that appeared in the *Bulletin de l'Association pour l'histoire de Belle-Île-en-Mer.*

36. Contrary to what Cérino indicates in his article ("Les Acadiens à Belle-Île-en-Mer," *Annales de Bretagne et desPays de l'Ouest,* 110, 1 (2003), pp. 115-124), there were few legal cases between Acadians and the islanders. *Cf.* the documents 1767-03-07 (ADIV, C-5158); 1767-08-31 (AD Morbihan, Series E, correspondence of Warren (series 1-2E); 1768-10-08 (AD Morbihan, E 1460/2); 1769-04-24 (AN Col B vol. 134; this document mentions a house that burned: an accident?).

37. We have calculated the comparative rates of mixed marriages at 85 percent. C. Cérino (*op. cit.*) indicates that, according to his calculations, only a small minority of the marriages were mixed: "15% of Acadian marriages . . . were contracted with Belle-Île residents between 1769 and 1789. Even if the majority of the exiles continued to marry among themselves, these few alliances consist of a not insignificant opening." These results are very surprising. Curiously, Laurent Babin, whom we have mentioned and who was involved in a conflict with many islanders, was one of the first to marry an islander. Was this the start of his problems?

38. Dominique Guillemet, "Les Acadiens de Belle-Île-en-Mer: légende noire et histoire en (re)construction," *Acadiens, mythes et réalités, Études canadiennes,* 37, (1994), pp. 127-144.

39. Fonteneau, *op. cit.*, appendix 2.

40. Le Loutre requested that the Acadiens not have the worst of the lots (1765-09-06; Lanco, *op. cit.*), but the previous colonists were officially given the advantage in the division of lands (1766-12-08; Fonteneau, *op. cit.*, pp. 350-351). According to F.R. Perron it is not true that the Acadians had only the poor lands ("Descendants d'Acadiens en France: l'installation acadienne à Belle-Île," in Colloque international de l'Acadie, Moncton, May 1978, tapuscript, CEA, Université de Moncton, 27-1-4). But the fact remains that the Acadians had only the second choice.

41. 1772-09-26; Lanco, *op. cit.*

42. 1772-10-31a; Fonteneau, *op. cit.*

43. 1772-12-31; SHM Brest 1 P 1/11 (1722) piece 98 and AN Col B, vol. 143, fo. 775.

44. 1773-09-06a; BM Bordeaux, Ms. 1480, fo. 469-471.

45. 1773-09-16; BM Bordeaux, Ms. 1480, fo. 446-455.

46. 1787-02-14; AD Ille-et-Vil C 2453.

47. 1901-09-17; AD Ille-et-Vil. 5J 138: Notes by Bourde de la Rogerie taken following a conversation with or letter from Le Gallen, mayor of Sauzon: "September 17, 1901, the Acadians were from the beginning mixed with the indigenous population. No memory of the latter's hostility remains. The Acadians were nicknamed crabs or sea spiders—perhaps in Breton—because of the length of their arms and legs. They were taller than the indigenous people; their descendants maintain this characteristic as well as having their bronze skin. . . . Father Le Gallen believed that it was they who introduced apples to the land. The Acadians took up the language and customs of the Belle-Île residents."

48. 1767-08-24; A. Gosselin, "Encore le Père de Bonnécamps 1707-1790," *Mémoires de la Société royale du Canada*, second series, vol. III (1897-1898), pp. 103-117, note 2, p. 113.

49. 1767-08-15a; Lanco, *op. cit.*

50. 1767-08-21; BM Bordeaux, Ms. 1480, fo. 266-267; 1768-08-26; BM Bordeaux, Ms. 1480, fo. 25-28.

51. 1767-08-01; ANC, MG6 C3 [Mi. 12881, 3rd reg., pp. 9-10] – Arch. of the port of Cherbourg. Valogne is twenty kilometers southeast of Cherbourg, and Brix is about half way between these two towns.

52. 1768-08-26; BM Bordeaux, Ms. 1480, fo. 25-28.

53. 1768-10-28b; AN Col B, vol. 131, fo. 314.

54. This is what particularly stands out regarding Brix, from the letter of 1768-08-26; BM Bordeaux, Ms. 1480, fo. 25-28.

55. 1768-11-26; Lanco, *op. cit.*

56. The first references to this plan that we have found, however, date from almost exactly a year later: 1769-08-25a, 1769-08-25b and 1769-08-25c; 1769-10-27: Service historique de l'Armée (Vincennnes), A1 3652. Alternatively, Le Loutre was perhaps again referring to the plan of Brix, which maybe was not yet abandoned at that time, or to Lemoyne's first plan, aimed at settling the Acadians in the region of Blaye (Gironde) (*cf.* 1768-00-00) with which Le Loutre was probably already familiar.

57. *Cf.* on this subject Ernest Martin, *op. cit.*, chapters III and IV; *cf.* also fiche 2004-00-00b (AD Ille-et-Vil., 5 J 140) which lists the settlement plans for the Acadians.

58. 1763-09-12; AN Col B, vol. 117, fo. 405.

59. For example, a landowner calmly contemplated "dismissing" his farmers, whom he judged weak and unproductive, to replace them with Acadians who were considered to be more productive.

60. 1773-03-31; BM Bordeaux, Ms. 1480, fo. 295-297.

61. 1767-06-26b; letter by Le Loutre to the minister of the Navy soliciting indemnities for his protégé, Paris June 26, 1767: AN Col C^{11} D, vol. 8 (ANC, Mg1-C^{11} D vol. 8 (Mi. of orig. F175, vol. 8, pp. 253 *et seq.*).

62. M. Duhamel, "Tentative de Colonie acadienne en Corse," *Revue des Sociétés savants des departements, publiée sous les auspices du minitère de l'Instruction publique, des Cultes et des Beaux-arts*, Fifth series, vol. VIII (Year 1874- 2nd semester); also see the critical report by Le Loutre after examining the plan on paper (1769-08-25a); BM Bordeax, Ms. 1480, fo. 29).

63. 1769-12-30; Chardon, intendant of Corsica, to Choiseul, December 30, 1769, AD of Corsica, series C. Letter transcribed in M. Duhamel, "Tentative de Colonie acadienne en Corse," *op. cit.*

64. *Cf.* 1763-03-07a; 1763-03-07b; 1763-06-19c.

65. 1771-10-29; AN Marine B^3 vol. 596, fo. 348 to 391.

66. 1776-09-12; AD Ille-et-Vil., 5J 139.

67. See the appendix 5 of volume II of my thesis: "La Louisiane, destination rêvée des Acadiens?," pp. 78 *et seq.*, as well as the analysis of the dispensations of consanguinity above.

68. 1767-01-10; *RAPC 1905-II*, appendix G, p. 200.

69. 1768-01-22b, *RAPC 1905-II*, p. 314.

70. 1772-03-24; BM Bordeaux, Ms. 1480, fo. 89-90.

71. 1774-00-00E; Fonteneau, *op. cit.*

Chapter 5

1. 1772-03-20; SHM Brest 1 P 1/11 (1772), piece 20. It was probably a question of a proposal to develop the fisheries of the Robins. On this subject, see R. E. Ommer, "From Outpost to Outport: the Jersey Merchant Triangle in the Nineteenth Century," doctoral thesis (history), McGill University, Montréal, 1978; David Lee, *The Robins in Gaspé, 1766-1825*, Markham, Ontario, 1984; Arthur G. Legros, "Charles Robin on the Gaspé Coast, 1776," *Revue d'histoire de la société historique de la Gaspésie*, II-IV, 1964; Christian Blais, "Pérégrinations et conquête du sol (1755-1836): l'implantation acadienne sur la rive nord de la baie des Chaleurs," *Acadiensis*, XXXV, 1 (Autumn 2005), pp. 3-23. Many Acadian families later did go to the coasts of Gaspé and Canada in the fisheries of the Robins. Terriot also alludes to the passage of a number of Acadians to "Guernesey" in order to return to Acadia at about the same time.

2. 1773-04-18a; BM Bordeaux, Ms. 1480, fo. 302-304. Lemoyne feared that the inhabitants of the colonies might be disturbed by the treatment of the refugees from the colonies in France (1773-05-13c; BM Bordeaux, Ms. 1480, fo. 329).

3. 1772-03-24; BM Bordeaux, Ms. 1480, fo. 89-90.

4. 1771-07-15; Archives du Séminaire des Missions étrangères and 1771-08-20.

5. In early 1722, Lemoyne proposed settling the Acadians near Blaye (1772-02-08a), in Limousin (1772-02-19); BM Bordeaux, Ms. 1480, fo. 9), or in the marshes near Rochefort: he returned to an old plan dating from 1765 (1765-09-15; AN Col B, vol. 122) in 1772 (1772-02-08a; BM Bordeaux, Ms. 1480, fo. 1/fo. 8).

6. 1772-06-18; BM Bordeaux, Ms. 1480, fo. 94-96.

7. For more details, see the files 1772-07-001 amd 1772-07-00b on the online database.

8. The repetition of the mistaken spelling of the name of the minister Bertin, called "Berton" by Papuchon in 1905, repeated by Lauvrière in 1924, Winzerling in 1955, and Brasseaux, in the passages where they relate these facts lead us to think that these authors simply used the initial information—itself not supported by returning to exact sources—of Papuchon. Martin is the only one to provide as reference to his information the "papers of Murard," that is to say the voluminous correspondence of Pérusse now held at the AD Vienne. For my part, I have not been able to find any source corroborating this visit. Many documents that later mention this meeting of the council never mention the visit by this delegation.

9. Because of their unavailability at the National Archives, I was unfortunately unable to consult the cartons of series E (decrees and commands) corresponding to the archives of the Council of the King for the period of the summer, 1772. Only consultation of these files would allow settling the question.

10. 1772-09-00; also see the report dating from July, 1774 (1774-07-00a; BM Bordeaux, Ms. 1480, Appendices, 1st file).

11. 1778-06-00; Mém. & doc., England, 47, fo. 18-28, piece 7.

12. The sole occurrence of this expression is found in a report by Pérusse dated January 1772, where he writes "It seems that the government should have as a goal to establish them in the kingdom by attaching them to the soil" (1772-01-09; AN H1 14992). It is quite likely that the king took up the expression of the same report of Pérusse, which must have been discussed during the course of the meeting of the council when the Acadian problem was brought up.

13. In the *Dictionnaire de l'Académie*, the *Trévoux* specifies: "Glèbe [*soil*]: spot of land... In jurisprudence, it was once used for heritage.... The serfs were attached to the soil, which is to say to the heritage. They were sold with the property [Le Gendre].

14. 1773-05-05; AN F15 3495.

15. *Dictionnaire de l'Académie*: "To naturalize. To give to a foreigner the same rights and the same privileges that the natural [citizens] of the country enjoy.

16. 1773-02-00; AN H1 14992, no. 649.

17. The "unavowed," the vagabonds, the peddlars were considered as especially subject to delinquency and dangerous. The insurrection of the Vendée during the revolutionary period, considered as one of the last French "Jacqueries" [peasant uprisings], would notably be initiated by a peddlar, Jacques Cathelineau.

18. *Dictionnaire historique de la langue française*: to hold to someone or to something indicates, since the sixteenth century (1580), "to be attached to it/them."

19. 1772-01-09; AN H^1 1499^2.

20. 1763-00-001; AD Vienne 2 J dep. 22, art. 124-2.

21. 1763-06-15; AD Vienne 2J dep. 22, art. 124-2.

22. In fact, some of these "Germans" were francophone Catholics coming from the region of Liège. However, contrary to what Ernest Martin would have us think, most of these families would experience problems of integration and did not stay in Poitou more than a few years. In 1770, only two or three families, mostly francophone, were still present. On these German families, see the article by Sébastien Jahen, "Les Allemands du Marquis. Immigration et integration dans les brandes du Châtelleraudais au XVIIIe siècle," *Bulletins du groupe de recherché d'histoire et d'archives du Châtelleraudais* (2003/2004).

23. 1770-00-00; AD Vienne 2 J dep. 22, art. 124-1.

24. 1772-01-09; AN H^1 1499^2.

25. 1774-05-20b; BN, Joly de Fleury no. 1722, Commerce and Colonies, fo. 187-191.

26. 1772-10-11a; BM Bordeaux, Ms. 1480, fo. 181-182.

27. There is no record of Saint-Victour's first name.

28. Sarcey de Sutières was director of the School of Agriculture of Compiègne in October 1772, and he stayed in Poitou from 1773 to 1776 to specially supervise the land clearings of the Acadians. *Cf.* Ernest Martin, *Les Exilés, op. cit.*, p. 193 and Guy-Charles Bugeon, *Les Fermes acadiennes du Poitou et leurs occupants de 1774 à 1793*, Archigny, 1996, p. 100.

29. 1773-02-13b; BM Bordeaux, Ms. 1480, fo. 268.

30. 1773-02-27; BM Bordeaux, Ms. 1480, fo. 269-270.

31. *Cf.* his remarks in the margin of the report of 1773-02-15a; BM Bordeaux, Ms. 1480, fo. 270-286.

32. The comte de la Marche, prince of the blood, negotiated with the Minister of the Navy at the request of the Controller-General, starting in March 1773 (1773-03-05; BM Bordeaux, Ms. 1480, fo. 289-290). He received authorization to settle eighty Acadian families in Corsica (1773-04-08; BM Bordeaux, Ms. 1480, fo. 298-299) but it was only a month later that de Boynes informed the abbé Terray (*cf.* 1773-05-11; AN Col B, vol. 144). This again demonstrates the confusion with which the affairs were treated and the frequent interferences by members of the high nobility that short-circuited the traditional hierarchy. Guillot and Lemoyne were very irritated by the behavior of the agent of the comte de la Marche, one "du Désert," but forced themselves to be accommodating as they feared the count's power. The transfer of the families to Corsica was ultimately not done, once again without us knowing exactly the reason. According to E. Martin (*op. cit.*, p. 96), Louis-François Joseph de Bourbon Conti, comte de la Marche, born in 1734, was the son of Louis-François de Bourbon, prince de Conti, grand prior of France, and he was an old friend of Madame du Barry.

33. 1773-05-05; AN F^{15} 3495.

34. 1773-05-22; BM Bordeaux, Ms. 1480, fo. 333-337.

35. 1773-05-24; BM Bordeaux, Ms. 1480, fo. 342-344.

36. 1773-06-04a; BM Bordeaux, Ms. 1480, Appendices, 1st file.

37. Le comte de Closnard, owner of vast terrains in the lands near Bordeaux, proposed receiving sixty Acadian families (1773-01-00a; BM Bordeaux, Ms. 1480, fo. 254-257), but he reneged shortly afterwards, for the reasons we have described.

38. 1772-05-09a; BM Bordeaux, Ms. 1480, fo. 71-76.

39. 1772-10-19; AN H^1 1499^2.

40. 1772-11-18b; BM Bordeaux, Ms. 1480, fo. 191-213. The opinion of Lemoyne on this subject seems to have been reinforced after an interview with a man named de La Pierre. This La Pierre estimated, according to what Lemoyne reported, that an assembly might create problems for the neighbors, and that it would be suitable to avoid it at any cost by dividing the Acadians into various communes (1773-01-15; BM Bordeaux, Ms. 1480, fo. 249-250). On the Comtau de Blaye, see Martin, *op. cit.*, pp. 80-82, in particular note 2, p. 80.

41. 1772-11-18a; BM Bordeaux, Ms. 1480, fo. 188-190.

42. It was Guillot who affirmed most decisively the inferiority of the Acadian manpower when writing to Lemoyne that the Acadians did not stand comparison with the French cultivators, that they were less assiduous and perseverant, impecunious, and that they did not know how to develop weak lands (1772-11-17; BM Bordeaux, Ms. 1480, fo. 219-223).

43. 1773-02-15a; BM Bordeaux, Ms. 1480, fo. 270-286.

44. 1773-06-04a; BM Bordeaux, Ms. 1480, Appendices, 1st file.

45. 1773-07-21b; BM Bordeaux, Ms. 1480, fo. 398-400.

46. 1773-07-26b; BM Bordeaux, Ms. 1480, fo. 402-404.

47. 1773-07-26a; BM Bordeaux, Ms. 1480, fo. 402. Lemoyne then often repeats his view of the problems engendered by the assembling of the Acadians in one place (*cf.* notably 1773-08-25; AD Vienne 2 J dep. 22, art. 124-1).

48. 1773-08-06 (BM Bordeaux, Ms. 1480, fo.430-432).

49. On this subject see all of the letters that Lemoyne wrote from Saint-Malo in July and August 1773.

50. The Controller-General disavowed the commissioner in a scathing manner (1773-08-15; BM Bordeaux, Ms. 1480, fo. 435-436). Pérusse did not want people to come against their will (1773-08-04a AD Vienne 2 J dep. 22, art. 97).

51. *Cf.*1773-08-04a and 1773-07-31.

52. *Cf.* 1773-08-16a (BM Bordeaux, Ms. 1480, fo. 423-425) and 1773-08-16b (BM Bordeaux, Ms. 1480, fo. 425-427).

53. 1773-08-23 (BM Bordeaux, Ms. 1480, fo. 438); August 16, 1773 (1773-08-16c; BM Bordeaux, Ms. 1480, fo. 427-429) he pretended, however, to have four hundred people (undoubtedly inflating the numbers).

54. 1773-10-07; ANC, MG6 A115, series C [Mi. F 849] – AD Calvados, C 1019.

55. 1773-12-14a (BM Bordeaux, Ms. 1480, fo. 529-534) and also 1773-12-24 (BM Bordeaux, Ms. 1480, fo. 541-542).

56. 1774-07-00b; AD Vienne 2 J dep. 22, art. 97.

57. An Acadian thus declared to Lemoyne: "we have friends who could better grant us what we wish. This plan is not the first that we have seen fail" (1773-08-20a; BM Bordeaux, Ms. 1480, fo. 433-434).

58. Later, however, the Acadians of Poitou requested a church for just themselves, the abbey de l'Etoile (1780-00-00; Rouet, *op. cit.*, appendice III). Fortuitously, perhaps, the commendatory abbé of this Church was a Canadian prelate, the abbé de La Corne.

59. 1773-07-31 (BM Bordeaux, Ms. 1480, fo. 415-420).

60. 1774-02-00c; AN H^1 1499^2, fo. 634.

61. 1774-09-14a; AD Vienne 2 J dep. 22, art. 97.

62. 1773-06-08b; AD Vienne 2 J dep. 22, art. 124-1.

63. The marquis de Pérusse repeats this argument in at least one other document (1773-00-00c; AN H1 14992, fo. 638).

64. 1774-02-00c; AN H1 14992, fo. 634.

65. 1773-08-04a; AD Vienne 2 J dep. 22, art. 97.

66. This was the case of the noble family Landry-d'Entremont. Joseph Landry wrote: "We told them that we were not landowners and that our ancestors had never scratched the land and that we would like as much to die here as to die there" (1775-03-02b).

67. 1774-06-24; AD Vienne 2 J dep. 22, art. 124-2.

68. In May 1776, there were only 497 people in the settlement (1776-05-01) and the number would progressively drop to become about a hundred some months later. In 1778 there were no more than 118 people in the colony (1778-01-01e) (however, one can add to this number the mixed couples and various others; the total then climbs to 180 people). *Cf.* equally 1776-12-20: 1,400 Acadians at Nantes.

69. 1775-07-18a; AD Vienne 2 J dep. 22 art. 124-2.

70. 1775-07-18b; AD Vienne 2 J 64/M 7.

71. One must, however, take the information relayed by Pérusse from this moment with much precaution, considering his efforts over many years were ruined, the marquis suffered some paranoia, accusing in turn the Acadians, the Navy in general and Lemoyne in particular, the Controller-General, the priests, and the inhabitants of the neighboring villages and others still of wanting to destroy his projects, if not his life. Moreover, he does not hesitate to considerably alter the facts in some of

his letters, if not purely and simply lying. But Pérusse is our sole source of information regarding the agitations of the Acadian "cabala."

72. 1775-08-12b; AD Vienne 2 J dep. 22 art. 124-1.

73. 1775-08-17; AD Vienne 2 J 64.

74. 1775-08-30a; AD Vienne 2 J dep. 22 art. 124-1.

75. 1775-08-30ab; AD Vienne 2 J dep. 22 art. 124-1.

76. 1775-09-22; AD Vienne 2 J dep. 22 art. 124-1.

77. In January 1777, the marquis again suggested to various families coming to settle in the colony. He promised to help as much as he could with family reunions (1777-01-10; AD Vienne 2 J dep. 22 art. 97).

78. 1775-12-24 (AD Vienne 2 J dep. 22, art. 124-1); 1776-03-09 (AD Vienne 2 J dep. 22 art. 124-2).

79. 1775-11-12; AD Vienne 2 J dep. 22 art. 124-1.

80. 1775-12-01b (AD Vienne 2 J dep. 22, art. 124-1): "Simon Aucoin, called Mazerolles, who should leave with the next convoy . . . last Sunday at the door of the church went so far as to insult those named Joseph Doucet, Jacques Bunel, Jean-Baptiste Hébert, Marin Daigle, and Jean Doucet who are part of nine families remaining at the settlement, and, after having greatly insulted them, threatened to kill them in their homes before his departure."

81. 1775-12-31a; AD Vienne 2 J dep. 22 art. 124-1.

82. 1775-12-31b; AD Vienne 2 J dep. 22 art. 124-1.

83. 1776-01-18; AD Vienne 2 J dep. 22 art. 124-1.

84. Damien Rouet, *L'insertion des Acadiens dans le Haut Poitou et la formation d'une entité agraire nouvelle, de l'ancien régime au début de la monarchie de juillet (1773-1830): etude d'histoire rurale*, doctoral thesis (History), University of Poitiers, 1994, p. 104.

85. Rouet, *ibid.*, p. 228.

86. Nearly all of the Acadian women who married young Frenchmen at the start of the colony of Poitou remained on site and started families (25 of 28).

87. Notes by Rameau de Saint-Père following a visit to Poitou in March, 1860, CEA Moncton, Fonds Rameau de Saint-Père, 2.12-4 (sheets), transcribed in Rouet, *op. cit.*, appendix VI, pp. 150 *et seq.* The remarks reported by Boudrot should be taken with much circumspection: the old man, aged 86, no longer remembered many details.

88. Summary of the remarks of Benjamin Boudrot by Rameau de Saint-Père in *Une colonie féodale en Amérique, l'Acadie (1604-1881)*, Paris and Montréal, Librairie Plon and Granger Brothers, 1889, vol. 2, p. 234.

89. 1773-10-00; AD Vienne 2 J dep. 22 art. 124-2. The report was probably written by Pérusse, who somewhat confused his desires with the realities.

90. 1773-06-04a; BM Bordeaux, Ms. 1480, fo. 345-349.

91. 1773-08-15; BM Bordeaux, Ms. 1480, fo. 435-436.

92. It should be noted that the report cited above formally forbade the Acadians from leaving the Kingdom (1773-02-00; anonymous report, possibly by Bertin, in the name of the King, AN H^1 1499^2, fo. 649).

93. Nicole Pellegrin, "Costumes régionaux," Lucien Bély, *Dictionnaire de l'Ancien Régime*, PUF, 1996.

94. On the same subject, see D. Roche, *La France des Lumières, op. cit.*, pp. 215s and 289s.

95. 1773-07-24; AD Vienne 2 J dep. 22, art. 124-1.

96. Daniel Roche, *op. cit.*, p. 216.

97. David Bell, *The Cult of the Nation of the Nation in France, Inventing Nationalism, 1680-1800*, Cambridge, Mass., Harvard University Press, 2001; Edmond Dziembowski, *Un nouveau patriotisme français 1750-1770: la France face à la puissance anglaise à l'époque de la guerre de Sept Ans*, Oxford, Voltaire foundation, 1998.

98. 1775-07-18a; AD Vienne 2 J dep. 22 art. 124-2.

99. 1782-04-05; AN F15 3495. It was possibly the plan to settle the Acadians on the island of Ouessant, a plan mentioned in the notes of H. Bourde de la Rogerie, but which I have been unable to find any trace of in the archives (2004-00-00b; AD Ille-et-Vile., 5 J 140).

100. 1778-06-00 (MAE, Mém. & doc., England, 47, fo. 18-28, piece 7) and 1782-04-05 (AN F^{13} 3495). In fact, no Acadian went to Corsica.

101. 1782-04-05; AN F13 3495.

102. 1777-11-10; AME, Mém. & doc., England, 47, fo. 18-28, piece 7.

103. 1778-01-04; AD Ille-et-Vil. C 6176.

104. It is to Guyana that Ballays refers (*cf.* 1778-04-25; AN Col F2B Commerce des Colonies).

105. The proposals of the company are perhaps those made in May 1780, by Mr. de Rosembourg, or those made a year and a half afterwards (1780-05-16b; AN Col B, vol. 172, fo. 231 and 1780-07-08; AN Col B, vol. 172, fo. 318). It is interesting to note that the latter plan specified that the Acadian families would be regrouped. Of the 12 proposals meant to lure the Acadians, only this one precisely specifies that the arrangements would be made so that the families "will live joined with one another" (1780-05-16a; "Propositions faites à Paris aux deputes acadiens de Nantes pour l'établissement des familles acadiennes à la Guyane," AN Col C^{11} D vol. 10 (ANC, MG1- C^{11} D, vol. 10, Mi. des transc. C 11362, vol. 10).

106. 1778-04-25; AN Col F2B Commerce Col. – MG1 18, vol. 3, carton 6, series F^{2}B (transc., Mi. C – 3056).

107. 1782-04-05; AN F^{15} 3495.

108. 1782-04-05; AN F^{15} 3495.

109. 1778-06-00; MAE, Mém. & doc., England, vol. 47, fo. 18-28, piece 7.

110. 1778-06-00; *id.*

111. The Amerindian tribes of North America often practiced the adoption of captured enemies, who were well treated and generally ended up mingling with the rest of the group.

112. 1756-09-05; *RAPC 1905-II*, pp. Xvii-xviii. See also on this subject Faragher, *A Great and Noble Scheme, op. cit.*, chapter XIII and notably p. 387. Faragher notes that many of the extended families were thus separated.

113. Megan Metters, "Towards a Comparative Study of Immigrant Education Policy in France and the US, 1947-1985," doctoral thesis (history), Institut universitaire européen, Florence (under preparation).

114. *Cf.* M. de Certeau, D. Julia and J. Revel, *Une politique de la langue. La Révolution française et les patois: l'enquête de Grégoire*, Paris, 1975.

115. 1783-07-12; The Acadians of Nantes to the ambassador of Spain, the comte d'Aranda, July 12,

1783 (MAE, Pol. Corresp., Spain, vol. 611, fo. 34).

116. 1784-04-04; the Acadians of Nantes to Charles de Vergennes, April 4, 1784, MAE, Pol. Corresp., Spain, vol. 612, fo. 287.

117. 1798-03-17; AGI, PPC, legjo 197, fo. 951, 960, 966, 967, 973. The plan of Peyroux was to bring the Acadians to Louisiana. Also see: 1800-09-27; AGI, PPC, legajo 217B, fo. 112-113. In the document, "Notes sur l'arrivée et séjour en Louisiane de M. Henri Peyroux de la Coudreière," after the emigration, Peyroux said that he formed the plan of organizing the emigration of the Acadians to Louisiana in 1783.

Chapter 6

1. Here we are only concerned with the Acadian "inhabitants." The officers and soldiers of Île-Royale, assembled first at Rochefort, were treated separately. The same goes for those whom the administration designated under the generic term of "inhabitants of North America," and who were mainly "Canadians" (former inhabitants of the Saint Lawrence river valley or of Gaspésie) and the inhabitants of Île-Royale (principally Louisbourg).

2. Martin, *Les Exilés acadiens en France, op. cit.* P. 261. "In 1822 and 1823, nearly 70 years after the affair of Grand-Pré, the government of the Restoration still was concerned if, among the descendants of the Acadian exiles repatriated in France in the 18th century, there were those still in need!"

3. Two reports from 1884 in the Chamber of Delegates and in the Senate foresee aid for the "Acadians expelled by the English in 1763" (Bibliothèque nationale of France (BNF), 4-LE 95-3; 1884, EXR, 163. The files for the aid distributed to the Acadians are found in the departmental archives of Charente-Maritime (La Rochelle) at least until 1880 in series 4 M 7.

4. In most summary versions, these lists only include the surnames and given names of the individuals, and the sums received or to be received.

5. 1763-10-15; AD Ille-et-Vil., 4 B 26-1 (Jurisdiction of Saint-Servan).

6. 1763-03-11b; AN Col B, vol. 117, fo. 83.

7. Jean-François Dubost considers that "the arrival of the Acadians was at first seen in a positive light as they were then persuaded that France was losing population: the influx of these refugees would help reverse this movement" ("Refuge religieux et politique en France," Lucien Bély, *Dictionnaire de l'Ancien Régime*). For a more general account of this question, see for example Carol Blum, *Strength in Numbers: Population, Reproduction and Power in Eighteenth Century France*, Baltimore, Johns Hopkins University Press, 2002).

8. Colbert to Talon, January 5, 1666, extract from *RAPQ*, 1930-1931, "Correspondance entre la cour et l'intendant Talon," p. 41.

9. Louise Dechêne, *Habitants et marchands de Montréal au XVIIe siècle*, Paris and Montréal, Plon, 1874, p. 39. Dechêne notes that the policy of encouragement produced no measurable results.

10. "Les Français passés au Canada avant 1760: le regard de l'émigrant," in Jean-Pierre Bardet, *Français et Québécois: le regard de l'autre*, Paris, Centre de cooperation interuniversitaire franco-québecoise, 2003.

11. "The idea of the depopulation of France, absurd even under Louis XIV, only gradually disappeared during the course of the second half of the 18th century" (Meyer *et al.*, *Histoire de la France coloniale, vol. I, op. cit.*, p. 18). Colin Jones notes that, starting in the 1770s, the intellectuals began to find that the population was increasing, and in a rapid way (*The Great Nation, France from Louis*

XV to the 1715-199, London, Penguin, 2002, p. 351). Population concerns were nonetheless still important at the time of the settlement of Poitou, in 1773 and 1774. For example, we find Pérusse studying scholarly calculations to show that the number of Acadians was increasing and that the Acadian women were making no voluntary limitations to giving birth (1774-02-00c; AN H^1 14992, fo. 634 and 1774-03-23b; AN H^1 1499^2, fo. 655 and 606). In 1778 again, the notices of Pérusse specify that the small Acadian colony "also offers the moving aspect of a great increase in population" (notices of Poitou, December 31, 1778 (1778-12-31; Pierre Massé, "La Colonie acadienne du Poitou: les rapports entre Acadiens et Poitevins de 1773 à 1792," *Actualité de l'histoire*, 9, 1954, pp. 4-14). On the other hand, it is quite possible, as Colin Jones notes, that the importance of these questions subsequently diminished. Indeed, most of the populating ideas about the Acadians go back to the start of the 1760s; the decline of the notion of the depopulation of the kingdom by the 1770s may also explain why the king authorized the Acadians to leave for Louisiana in 1785.

12. Denis Diderot and Jean L. R. d'Alembert, *Encyclopédie, ou dictionnaire raisonné des Sciences, des Arts et des Métiers*, Paris, 1751, volume III, p. 650, article signed V.D.F. However, the fear of the encyclopedists had no basis since, on the on hand, we find that the government constantly refused to give the Acadians the right to leave the kingdom and, on the other hand, one finds that the very large majority of the population of France had an extremely negative image of the colonies, particularly those of North America, so very few were inclined to go there.

13. 1761-00-00; abbé H, R. Casgrain, "Lettres et mémoires de l'abbé de l'Isle-Dieu (1742-1774)," *Rapport des archives de la province de Québec*, 16, 17, 18 (1935-1938), pp. 273-410; 331-459; 147-253.

14. See the many allusions to the plans for the re-conquest of Canada mentioned by Claude de Bonnault, "Le Canada perdu et abandoné," *RHAF*, vol. 2, no. 3, December 1948, pp. 331-350. These plans were, however, finally abandoned at the start of the reign of Louis XVI, according to this author.

15. Jean Meyer, *Histoire de la France coloniale, vol. I, op. cit.*, p. 17.

16. 1763-04-04; Choiseul to Bertin, April 4, 173, AN Col B, vol. 117, fo. 117.

17. 1763-07-11o; ANC, MG6 A15, series C [Mi. F 849] – AD Calvados, C 1019.

18. 1776-08-31; AD Vienne 2 J dep. 22, rt. 124-1.

19. To the contrary, very many provincial administrators did not want the Acadians on the territory of their generality, increasing unemployment and causing an overabundance of manpower.

20. Élie Alfandari, "Assistance (systèmes d')," *Encyclopédia Universalis*, Paris, 1998, 3-212a.

21. Quoted by Méthivier, *Le Siècle de Louis XV*, p. 80.

22. This is the theory defended by Camille Bloch in *L'Assistance et l'État en France à la veille de la Révolution: generalités de Paris, Rouen, Alençon, Orléans, Chalons, Soissons, Amiens (1764-1790)*, Paris (Slatkine, Reprint, Geneva, 1974, 1908, preface). The aide to the Acadians and Canadians was a precedent with which Bloch seems not to have been familiar.

23. *Cf.* the work of François Crépeau (*Droit d'asile: de l'hospitalité aux contrôles migratoires*, Bruxelles, Editions Bruylant, 1995, pp. 50-51). Also see the article by Jean-Louis Miege ("Rapatriés," *Encyclopédie Universalis*, Paris, Encyclopedia Univeralis, 1998, 19-529).

24. Emmerich de Vattel, *Le droit des gens ou principes de la loi naturelle appliqué à la conduite et aux affaires des nations et des souverains*, 1758); book I, chapter IXI, paragraph 231. Vattel was essentially a popularizer and compiler of the theories produced before him, notably by Grotius, Leibniz, and Wolff. His work had a considerable influence, especially in England and in the United States. He especially greatly modified the "right of war." His work had a very large influence on the Treaty of Paris of 1763.

25. J. F. Dubost, "Refuge religieux et politique" in Lucien Bély, *Dictionnaire de l'Ancien Régime*.

26. Vattel, *Le droit des gens, op. cit.*; book I, chapter XIX, paragraph 231. The author defines as an exile "a man chased from the place of his domicile, or forced to leave it" (paragraph 288).

27. An extract from the *Maryland Gazette* shows that certain inhabitants of New England were also sympathetic: "The deported [Acadians] arriving here today . . . have been deprived of all of the goods they possessed in Nova Scotia and were sent here in the greatest destitution. Humanity and Christian charity make it our duty to help these worthy individuals with compassion" (1755-12-00; quoted by Griffiths, *Contextes*, p. 102).

28. 1759-01-26; AM Saint-Malo, BB 45.

29. 1774-02-04b; BM Bordeaux, Ms. 1480, fo. 556.

30. 1758-09-08b; AN Col C11 B vol. 38, fo. 165-167 (http://www.archivescanadafrance.org).

31. 1758-09-30a; SHM Rochefort, 1 E 160, fo. 633.

32. 1761-11-14; SHM Brest, series 1 P 1/0 1761, piec 155.

33. 1779-08-22b; AD Gironde C 2478.

34. 1773-06-04a; BM Bordeaux, Ms. 1480, fo. 345-349.

35. 1763-02-17d; MAE, Mem & doc., England, 45, fo. 2-5.

36. 1763-05-14a; Lauvrière, *La Tragédie d'un people, op. cit.*, p. 193.

37. 1771-05-00a; BM Bordeaux, Ms. 1480, fo. 36-44; 1773-04-18a; BM Bordeaux, Ms.1480, fo. 302-304.

38. 1765-04-24; SHM Rochefort, 1 E 177, fo. 791.

39. 1772-10-29; BM Bordeaux, Ms. 1480, fo. 157-161.

40. 1773-07-02c; ANC, MG6 A15, series C [Mi. F 849] – AD Calvados, C 1019.

41. 1774-09-27; BM Bordeaux, Ms. 1480, Appendices, 1st file.

42. Martin and Lauvrière seem to strongly believe the truth of all of these accounts listing the great patriotism of the Acadians to the king, etc. For instance, Ernest Martin takes literally the propagandist reports of La Rochette that the Acadians cried "*vive le Roi de France*" to the great scandal of the English (1763-02-17a; Report of Nivernais).

43. 1763-06-13a; Jean-Edmond Roy, *Rapport sur les archives de France relatives à l'histoire de Canada*, Ottawa, 1911, pp. 615-617.

44. E. Dziembowski, *Un nouveau patriotisme français 1750-1770: la France face à la puissance anglaise à l'époque de la guerre de Sept Ans*, Oxford, Voltaire fondation, 1998, p. 9.

45. 1773-04-18a; BM Bordeaux, Ms. 1480, fo. 302-304.

46. 1773-05-13c; BM Bordeaux, Ms. 1480, fo. 329.

47. 1773-07-20b; BM Bordeaux, Ms. 1480, fo. 379-381.

48. An exception of minor significance: in 1773, the sub-delegate of the intendant of Poitiers wrote to the marquis de Pérusse shortly before the arrival of the refugees: "You would seem to desire that we place one group at Poitiers, but [...] such a number of undisciplined people in a large town would be much more difficult to supervise and control than in a smaller place" (1773-10-03; AD Vienne 2J dep. 22, art. 124-1). It was Lemoyne's letters, denouncing the reluctance of the Acadians to go to Poitou, that led this sub-delegate to fear a lack of discipline amongst the Acadians.

49. Department of Finistère, between Morlaix and Carhaix.

50. 1766-04-12; AD Ille-et-Vil. 5J 139. This letter is the only one that mentions these thoughts of the Council of the King to place the Canadians at Saint-Goazec. Despite searching thoroughly, I was unable to find the original of this document, transcribed in the file by Bourde de la Rogerie. But I was able to affirm many times the accuracy of the transcriptions by this archivist; thus there is no reason to doubt its authenticity. Raymond Delaporte, "Un sénéchal de Châteuneuf-du-Faou, Guillaume Pic de la Mirandole (1694-1778)," *Bulletin de la Société archéologique du Finistère* (1911), pp. 39-55), provides some information about the author of this letter, François Hyacinthe Pic de la Mirandole, seneschal of Châteauneuf de Faou between 1762 and 1772.

51. 1773-07-26a; BM Bordeaux, Ms. 1480, fo. 402s.

52. 1759-03-23; AN Col B, vol. 110.

53. 1764-02-13; AN Col B, vol. 120, fo. 47.

54. 1764-02-27a; ANC, Mg6 C3 [Mi. 12881] – Arch. of the port of Cherbourg (letters by Defrancy, from March 1, 1763 to April 2, 1768), fo. 79v-93.

55. The latter ultimately refused to leave at the last minute and then his payments were suspended (1764-04-13b; ANC, MG6 C3 [Mi. 12881, 23 reg., pp. 4-5] – Arch. of the port of Cherbourg (letters by Defrancy, from March 1, 1763 to April 2, 1768).

56. 1764-04-14; AN Col B, vol. 120, fo. 129: April 14, 1764.

57. 1764-00-00b; AN Col, G1 vol. 512.

58. 1765-03-04; ANC, MG6 C3 [Mi. 12881, 2nd reg., p. 10] – Arch. of the port of Cherbourg (letters of Defrancy, from March 1, 1763 to April 2, 1768).

59. When Lemoyne ordered the Acadians to go to Poitou, Joseph d'Entremont answered him that he would care as much "to die here as to die there." "And, very well, you will no longer receive payment after the 1st of January!" answered Lemoyne. But d'Entremont noted that the payments continued nonetheless, even if we do not know for how long. 1775-03-02b; Jean-François Mouhot, "Des Revenantes?," *op. cit.*

60. 177e-07-22a; BM Bordeaux, Ms. 1480, fo. 383-394. Here, Lemoyne clearly exceeds the instructions of the Controller-General who ordered the continuation of aid until January 1, 1774 (1773-06-04a; BM Bordeaux, Ms. 1480, fo. 345-349); 1773-07-17; AD Vienne 2 J dep. 22, art. 124-1.

61. 1773-08-15; BM Bordeaux, Ms. 1480, fo. 435-436.

62. 1773-07-22a; BM Bordeaux, Ms. 1480, fo. 383-394.

63. In one petition, the Acadians write that the king, through the intermediary of Nivernais, had promised "settlements in his Kingdom, which would compensate us for what we have lost" (1774-07-00b; AD Vienne 2 J dep. 22, art. 97 and 1771-05-00a; BM Bordeaux, Ms. 1480, fo. 36-44).

64. 1763-02-17a; MAE, Pol. Corresp., England, vol. 449, fo. 340ss.

65. 1778-06-00; MAE, Mem. & doc., England, 47, fo. 18-28, piece 7.

66. 1788-00-00a; AN F^{13} 3495.

67. 1775-03-02b; "Des "Revenantes?" À propos des "Lettres fantômes" et de la correspondance entre exiles acadiens (1758-1785)," *Acadiensis, Revue d'histoire de la region atlantique*, XXXIV, 1 (Fall 2004).

68. See, for example, the petition: 1772-03-24; BM Bordeaux, Ms. 1480, fo. 89-90.

69. 1772-11-18b; BM Bordeaux, Ms. 1480, fo. 191-213 and 1784-00-00a; AN Col C11 A vol. 15, fo.

535-537.

70. 1758-11-18a; SHM Brest 1P 1/7, piece 1999.

71. 1758-12-30a; SHM Rochefort 1 E 160, fo. 749.

72. 1760-08-12; SHM Brest 1 P 1/8 1760 piece 129 and SHM Rochefort, 1 E 168, fo. 595.

73. 1760-08-12; SHM Brest 1 P 1/8 1760 piece 129.

74. 1760-08-16; ANC MG6 – C2 (transc., Mi. C 4619) – Arch. of the Port of Saint-Servan, C 8, Li 7 (C 8/7).

75. This expression is featured in at least fourteen documents.

76. The expression is notably found in a letter by Lemoyne to Bertin (1772-12-28a; BM Bordeaux, Ms. 1480, fo. 246-247).

77. 1763-12-09; AN Col B, vol. 117, fo. 534. Yet Choiseul and those who expressed similar opinions did not denounce strongly enough the idleness of nobles who received immense pensions from the State and who were, in the real sense, the idlers (*e.g.,* Madam du Barry and her expenses of 300,000 *livres* per month, compared with the 300,000 annual payments for the Acadians). The Revolution would repair this oversight and with no difficulty punish the sumptuous expenses of the court or the mistresses of the king.

78. 1766-10-30; SHM Brest 1 P 1/10 (1766) piece 64 and AN Col B, vol. 125, fo. 436.

79. 1760-08-19a; SHM Brest, sub-series 1 P – ANC, MG6 C4 (Mi. of the orig., F-2101 and F-2102).

80. *Candide ou l'optmisme*, chapter XXX.

81. The first real charitable workshops that offered work to unemployed day workers appeared in the second half of the eighteenth century. It was a question of allowing the poor to earn a a salary and not receive alms (*cf.* J.-P. Gutton, "Ateliers de charité," Lucien Bély, *Dictionnaire de l'Ancien Régime*). Also see, for instance, what the administrators of the workshop of Tours wrote around 1760. 1760-00-00a; AD Indere-et-Loire, L 74.

82. 1760-08-19a; SHM Brest, sub-series 1 P – ANC, MG6 C4 (Mi. of the orig., F-2101 and F-2102).

83. 1774-12-14b; E. Martin, *Les Exilés, op. cit.*, p. 277. Remember that the majority of the Acadians then present in France came from Île Saint-Jean, where they had already benefited from the assistance of the French colonial authorities for many years before their deportation (see note 30, p. 341). The abbé Girard perhaps had other reasons to refuse Pérusse's offers: he had abandoned three hundred of his parishioners to die by saving himself from a lost ship, along with the captain and the crew, on board an Indian canoe, off of England in 1758. Perhaps he had no great desire to find himself facing the families of his former parishioners.

84. Pérusse also mentions as a main cause of the failure the promise made to them that the Acadians be lodged in groups of ten by ten within the houses constructed on the *Grand Ligne* (*cf.* 1777-01-10; AD Vienne 2 J dep. 22, art. 97).

85. 1776-03-09; AD Vienne 2 J Dep. 22 art. 124-2. These reflections were clearly motivated by Pérusse's desire to bring back the Acadians who left for Nantes and who, he thought, would surely return to his lands if one were to cut off their provisions in that port.

86. 1776-12-29c; AD Vienne 2 J dep. 22, art. 124-1. He repeats these instructions on August 22, 1779 (1779-08-22a; ANC, MG6 A15, series C [Mi. F 849] – AD Calvados, C 1021).

87. 1777-03-27; AD Vienne 2 J dep. 22, art. 124-1 and 1778-03-01; ANC, MG6 A15, series C (Mi. F 849) – AD Calvados, C 1021.

88. 1779-04-18; AD Vienne 2 J dep. 22, art. 124-1.

89. Such is the case with the Germans asked to go to populate Guyana who also received a payment of six *sous* per day (1766-12-06; BM Bordeaux, MS. 1480, fo. 260-262 and SHM Rochefort 1 R 11). They were getting more previously since Lemoyne received the order to reduce their payment to this amount. However, the Germans were not as favored as were the Acadians since their aid distributions were only paid for a very short period.

Chapter 7

1. See note 30, p. 259.

2. 1749-01-11; AN Marine B³, vol. 477, fo. 56s.

3. 1749-05-06; AN Marine B³, vol. 477.

4. 1756-03-12; AN Col B, vol. 104, fo. 44.

5. 1792-09-15a; AN F¹⁵ 3494.

6. 1758-09-21; SHM Rochefort, 1 E 160, fo. 625 and 1758-09-16; SHM Rochefort 1 E 414, no. 498.

7. The foundry was "the ancestor of the rolling mill," the place where iron was cut before being marketed or utilized. Here it was probably an unused or discarded portion from the military arsenal of La Rochelle.

8. 1758-09-19; SHM Rochefort, 1 E 414, no. 502.

9. While waiting for the precise orders from the minister, the intendant recounted what had been done at the time of the initial repatriation of the inhabitants of Louisbourg following the first siege of the town in 1749. "I am working on examining the situation of the inhabitants of Île-Royale and yet I am supplying them with subsistence because of what has been done here during their stay here after the first siege of this island," so he wrote on October 26, 1758 (1758-10-26b; SHM Rochefort, 1 E 414, no. 562).

10. 1758-09-30a; AN Col B, vol. 108, fo. 102.

11. 1758-20-09; AN Col B, vol. 108, fo. 107.

12. 1758-10-14; SHM Rochefort, 1 E 414, no. 521.

13. 1758-10-26b; SHM Rochefort, 1 E 414, no. 562. It would seem that the choice between 3 or 4 *sous* fell to the one who distributed these rations.

14. 1758-12-03; AN Col B, vol. 108, fo. 129 and SHM Rochefort, 1 E 160, fo. 713. This measure concerned the Alsatian families who were refugees at Rochefort and waiting to leave for Guyana, but it was soon applied to the Acadians.

15. 1758-12-22b; SHM Brest 1 P 1/7, piece 244 and N Col B, vol. 108, fo. 344.

16. 1759-01-07; AN Col B, vol. 110. See also: 1758-12-30 and 1759-03-02.

17. 1758-11-00a; ANC, MG6 C4 (Mi. from the orig., F-2101 and F-2102) – Arch. of the Navy, Brest, sub-series 1P.

18. 1759-01-29; AM Saint-Malo, BB 45.

19. 1763-04-07; SHM Brest 1 P 1/9 (1763) piece 38.

20. The administrators often wrote that the Acadians received six *sous* per day in England (1778-06-

00); MAE, Mem. & doc., England, 47, fo. 18-28, piece 7). In fact what was distributed to the Acadians was six pence per day (Naomi E. S. Griffiths, "Acadians in Exile: The Experience of the Acadians in the British Seaports," *op. cit.*). For, in England, it was the pound sterling and not the *livre tournois* (French pound) that was the currency. It is curious that the Acadians received nominally the same unit number of money that their compatriots in France received in the same period, which could indicate an arrangement or that this sum corresponded to a sort of minimal standard. De Curzon affirms that the aid in England was distributed by the king of France, but this is an error ("Les Acadiens à Liverpool," *La Grand' Goule [Poitiers]*, 1930). The Acadians complained to the English commissioner, Guiguier, of the "little payment that his majesty gives us" (1757-04-07; *id.*), and another petition requests more aid for faithfulness to "his Britannic majesty" (1759-06-23; *id.*). Moreover, the report of La Rochette leads us to think that the French government did not know what was paid to the Acadians, and Nivernais seems practically unaware of any such payment to them. Finally, the Acadians who were refugees at Morlaix wrote that they received the payment for seven years in England "from the English themselves who wanted us to continue receiving it if we should want to become their subjects" (1763-10-30); AD Ille-et-Vil., C 5156). The aid was distributed by the English commissioners (1763-05-14c; MAE, Pol. Corresp., England, Sup. 13, fo. 69 and 1763-05-26c; *id.*, fo. 76: – in this document, La Rochette, having learned that the suspension of aid was due to a lack of currency, himself paid what was owed to the Acadians). It is nevertheless possible that the English government only advanced these funds, and that then the French treasury paid back the accounts as with prisoners of war, according to the usages in effect in this period (A. Corvisier, "Prisonniers de Guerre," Lucien Bély, *Dictionnaire de l'Ancien* Régime). The king of France paid the English soldiers in France and vice-versa (1758-11-21; SHM Brest 1 P 1/7, piece 201). However, I did not find any traces of such a reimbursement for the Acadians. The colonies of New England similarly requested from France reimbursement for the sums employed to assist the Acadians during their captivity (1763-08-24b); CEA, Fonds Placide Gaudet, 1, 42-7).

21. 1761-07-29; AN Col. F^3, , vol. 16,

22. 1761-08-11; AN Col. B, vol. 113. See also 1761-08-28; *id.*

23. 1761-11-14; SHM Brest, 1 P 1/9 1761, piece 155.

24. 1762-12-26a; SHM Brest, 1 P 1/9 1762, piece 212.

25. 1763-04-06a; SHM Rochefort, 1 E 172.

26. For example, the seventy-eight families settled in 1765-1766 at Belle-Île-en-Mer for whom payment was suppressed at the end of December 1768. Le Loutre wrote that he had obtained the continuation of payments until the end of December 1768 (1768-11-26; Lanco, *Les Acadiens à Belle-Île-en-Mer, op. cit.*). Guillemet notes that the aid was paid until December 1769, but I have not found any references after that of Le Loutre ("Acadie genealogique et lieux de mémoire français: les exemples de Belle-Île-en-Mer et du Poitou," in *L'Acadie plurielle. Dynamiques identitaires collectives et développement au sein des réalités acadiennes*, Moncton, Centre d'études acadiennes, 2003, pp. 75-103; p. 80). Many Acadians, having left their lands at Belle-Île, asked to again receive aid at Saint-Malo in 1772, which the minister de Boynes refused (1772-12-31; SHM Brest 1 P 1/11 (1772) piece 98).

27. In some cases, even those who worked received subsistence, for example at Le Havre: 1766-06-14; AN Marine B^3, vol. 568, fo. 264. It was undoubtedly too complicated to stop payment and then to start it up again for those who worked as day-laborers.

28. 1766-10-30; SHM Brest 1 P 1/10 (1766) piece 64.

29. 1744-01-23a; BM Bordeaux, Ms. 1480, fo. 547-548.

30. 1772-10-01; BM Bordeaux, Ms. 1480, fo. 131-136.

31. 1773-05-05; AN F15 3495.

32. 1773-11-06c; BM Bordeaux, Ms. 1480, fo. 518. So, contrary to what Dominique Guillemet affirms ("Acadie genealogique," *op. cit.*, p. 78) after René and Marguerite Daligaut, Lemoyne's census was not "mistaken" about Belle-Île. It logically corresponds to the many people needing aid who, for one reason or another, were considered as being "from Belle-Île." Guillemet rightly specifies that the 103 people mentioned from Belle-Île "does not correspond to the number of Acadians remaining on the island of the 363 who settled in 1766 . . . but in fact essentially corresponds to the Acadians not in the fee-farm leases and even to some unknown people who never went to the island found at Lorient, for instance" (p. 78).

33. 1778-01-12; ANC, MG6 A15, series C [Mi. F 849] – AD Calvados, C 1021 (summarizing the various correspondence between the intendant and the Controler-General for payment of assistance to the Acadians at Cherbourg).

34. 1776-08-31; AD Vienne 2 J dep. 22, art. 124-1. The authenticity of this letter, however, is doubtful.

35. 1781-01-01; AN F^{15} 3495.

36. 1778-01-01d; AD Ille-et-Vil. C 2453: "État de ce qui est dû aux familles acadiennes résidant en Bretagne pour leur solde à raison de six sols par jour à compter du 1er juillet 1776 jusqu'au 1er janvier 1778 exclusivement." 298,959 *livres* remained due but we do not know if it was finally paid.

37. 1776-09-04; ANC, MG6 A15, series C [Mi. F 849] – Calvados, C 1021.

38. 1778-04-25; AN Col F^{2}B, Commerce of the Colonies. This document seems to contradict those cited above.

39. 1778-01-01 and 1779-08-2 (AD Gironde C 2478).

40. 1778—06-00; MAE, Mem. & doc., England, 47, fo. 18-28, piece 7.

41. 1782-04-05; 1784-06-26a; 1784-05-09.

42. 1773-06-04a; BM Bordeaux, Ms. 1480, fo. 345-349. Also see: 1773-05-24; *id.*, fo. 342-344.

43. 1773-07-22a; *id.*, fo. 383-394.

44. 1773-08-15; *id.*, fo. 435-436.

45. 1773-10-10b; *id.*, fo. 484-486.

46. The d'Entremonts could not hope for assistance after December 31, 1774 (instructions of Lemoyne from 1773-12-05a; *id.*, fo. 521-523).

47. 1773-09-06c; ANC, MG6 A15, series C [Mi. F 849] – AD Calvados, C 1019.

48. 1774-03-17a; *id.*, later, 1778-01-12 (*id.*, C 1021).

49. 1779-08-22b; AD Gironde C 2478.

50. Letter by Terray of March 17, 1774 (1774-03-17b; AD Vienne 2 J dep. 22, art. 124-1); order for continuation of aid to the Acadians in Normandy [at Le Havre] until January 1, 1776; this was the same day that Terray wrote to continue payment to the Acadians at Cherbourg until December 31, 1774 (1774-03-17a; document cited not 48).

51. 1774-03-17b; AD Vienne 2 J dep. 22, art. 124-1.

52. Four cartons of correspondence in series C between the intendant, his sub-delegates, the mayor of Cherbourg, the Acadians (mainly the d'Entremont family), and the Controller-General supply very good information about a period for which there is little documentation in the other archives.

53. *Cf.* also (1775-12-26; ANC, MG6 A15, series C [Mi. F 849] – AD Calvados, C 1020): the intendant wrote that the Acadians in his department had received payment until December 31, 1774.

54. *Cf.* 1778-03-01, 1778-03-09 and 1778-08-26 (petition by the Acadians).

55. 1775-12-26; ANC, MG6 A15, series C [Mi. F 849] – AD Calvados, C 1020. The poll tax was a "tax per head" (*Dict. Acad.*), established under Louis XIV on January 18, 1695. Mireille Touzery notes that surpluses from this capitation tax existed everywhere (the article "Capitation" in Lucien Bély, *Dictionnaire de l'Ancien* Régime). It was probably these excesses that were designated here as "free funds."

56. 1776-02-25; ANC, MG6 A15, series C [Mi. F 849] – AD Calvados, C 1020 (Turgot orders the continuation from the free funds from the capitation tax).

57. 1778-08-26; *id.*

58. 1778-08-26; *id.*

59. 1779-01-22; *id.*

60. 1779-08-22a; *id.*

61. 1782-05-10; ANC, MG6 A15, series C [Mi. F 849] – AD Calvados, C 1022.

62. 1784-03-26b; *id.*

63. 1785-08-02; *id.*: Marguerite Landry states that this means payment was withheld from them for seven years, starting in 1777 (1784-03-11).

64. The assistance for the Acadians from the government on obtaining letters of authority as well as free lodging in various municipalities will be discussed in a later chapter.

65. "Naval term. Expenses of the route paid to the sailors to take them to the military ports or to return to their quarters" (*Littré*).

66. Ex.: 1758-11-01d; ANC Mg6 – C2 (transc., Mi C 4619) – Arch. of the Port of Saint-Servan, C 8, Li 7 (C 8/7).

67. 1760-01-25b; AN Col B, vol. 112.

68. 1759-01-26e; AN Col B, vol. 110.

69. 1767-08-01; ANC, MG6 C3 [Mi. 12881], 3rd reg., pp. 9-10] – Arch. of the port of Cherbourg (minutes of letters of the commissioner of divisions). The Controller-General nonetheless refused to participate financially and rather recommended that she marry an Acadian. On the other hand, it seems that a dowry of 1,500 *livres* was indeed paid for one Miss Pouilly, born at Louisbourg in 1774, by the Minister of the Navy, on the suggestion of Lemoyne (1774-06-29; SHM Brest 1 P 1/23, 1774, piece 5-7).

70. 1786-05-19b; AN F[15] 3495.

71. 1786-09-17; AD Ille-et-Vil. C 6176. It seems that the Acadians rarely obtained the positions promised. See also the case of Êloi Thibaudeau mentioned elsewhere, who suffered the same misadventure at Lorient.

72. 1785-06-01; ANC, MG6 A15, series C [Mi. F 849] – AD Calvados, C 1022.

73. 1785-07-13, *id.*

74. We know the importance of salt in the modern era, used not only as a condiment, but also and especially for the preservation of food, particularly meat and fish. Its part in the budget of humble families of the modern period was considerable; the Acadians were sometimes obliged to go into debt to buy salt (1778-01-01g; AD Ille-et-Vil. C 2453).

75. 1773-12-00a; BM Bordeaux, Ms. 1480, fo. 536.

76. The salt tax was one of the most important and despised taxes of the *Ancien* Régime. Not only was salt taxed fairly highly, but the purchase of a minimum quantity of salt was often obligatory. As Marie-Françoise Limon points out, "the inequality of the tariff depending on the regions was the rule during the entire *Ancien* Régime" ("Gabelle," in Lucien Bély, *Dictionnaire de l'Ancien* Régime). Thus, in Brittany, the region where most of the Acadians were refugees, there was no tax on salt. Generally, all the great fishing ports were also exempted from the salt tax, since "the production of salted fish was considered as vital to the kingdom" (C. Huetz de Lemps, "Sel" in Lucien Bély, *Dictionnaire de l'Ancien* Régime). Normandy, from which some of the other Acadians sent to Poitou had come, was part of the territory called "of the great salt tax," where salt was highly taxed, but Avranches, Coutances, Bayeux, and Pont-l'Évêque benefited from a preferential tariff called the "quarter bouillon" and it is quite likely, if we believe a map by Paul Delsalle (*Vocabulaire historique de la France moderne*, p. 58) that all of Cotentin—thus Cherbourg and Granville—also benefited from this preferential tariff. Le Havre should therefore logically have been taxed on the basis of the "great salt tax" (though with an always possible local exception). In this case, the Acadians would have obtained a special privilege by paying only "on the basis of the low salt tax." But privileges under the *Ancien* Régime were legion, and M. F. Limon specifies that, "many officers or communities [...] could buy their salt, or at least some quantity, at a non-taxed price." On the other hand, curiously, according to M.F. Limon and P. Delsalle, Poitou theoretically was part of the " redeemed territory," that is to say those regions having rejected the tax in 1548 and so salt there was a bargain. The demand for salt at even better prices by the Acadians is therefore surprising.

77. 17969-03-31; AN Col C11 A, vol. 125, fo. 578. "Some tobacco pipes provided their relaxation and delight," (in Acadia) according to Guillot (1772-11-17; BM Bordeaux, Ms. 1480, fo. 219-223.

78. 1765-12-11; *RAPC 1905-I*, p. 368 – AN Col B, vol. 122.

79. 1766-12-22; AN Col F3, vol. 16.

80. 1769-03-31; AN Col C11 A, vol. 125, fo. 578. Le Loutre then complained to Praslin that the supplying of tobacco was interrupted by a special initiative of the general tax farmers.

81. 1773-05-22; BM Bordeaux, Ms. 1480, fo. 333-337.

82. 1767-07-21b; AN Col B, vol. 127, fo. 289.

83. He did not have the same opinion at all as that of his cousin regarding the behavior of the Acadians. From the reports made to him, he judged that "these complaints deserve less attention as there remain at Saint-Servan only the most corrupt of the Acadian families who only stay there from laziness, the lure of contraband and the guaranteed subsistence that they receive from the king's generosity; and that the police guard of the second battalion of the infantry regiment of Berry can barely stop the run of disorders during the time it has barracked at Saint-Servan in a place . . . populated with eighteen [thousand] inhabitants, most sea goers being given to all the most debauched excesses and in which the Acadians are nearly always involved." It is therefore that much more significant that the Acadians participated in this civil guard as they "served to supervise those of their compatriots who were implicated in the disorders" (1767-10-11c; AN Marine B3, vol. 576, fo. 42).

84. 1767-10-11a; AD Ille-et-Vil. C 892.

85. 1773-04-27a; BM Bordeaux, Ms. 1480, fo. 307-312.

86. 1773-08-06; BM Bordeaux, Ms. 1480, fo. 430-432.

87. 1758-10-14; SHM Rochefort, 1 E 414, no. 521.

88. 1759-01-s6a; AM of Saint-Malo, BB 45.

89. 1759-02-04; *id.*

90. 1759-07-27a; AM Saint-Malo, BB 45, reg. Ms. (research by Alain Roman) and 1763-07-08; AM Saint-Malo, BB 49, reg. Ms, fo. 12-13.

91. This is probably a reference to the English raid on Cancale and Paramé, within the immediate proximity of Saint-Malo, on June 18, 1758, and the alert of November 1758. After the disembarking of an English army in the north of Contentin, then the occupation of Cherbourg, on August 7, 1758, the British troops tried to take Saint-Malo, but were finally beaten at Saint-Cast (thirty kilometers from Saint-Malo) by the militia of the duc d'Aiguillon.

92. 1763-07-24; AM Saint-Malo, BB 49, fo. 23.

93. 1763-03-03; ANC, MG6 C3 [Mi. 12881] – Arch. of the port of Cherbourg (minutes of letters by the commissioner of divisions).

94. 1771-05-00a; BM Bordeaux, Ms. 1480, fo. 36-44.

95. 1773-04-27c; BM Bordeaux, Ms. 1480, Appendices, 1st file, fo. 22s.

96. 1774-09-27; BM Bordeaux, Ms. 1480, Appendices, 1st file.

97. At least most of the time. See, for example, the case of one "Madam de Montalembert, widow of a captain of the troops of Île-Royale" who initially received 12 *sous* per day for herself, as well as six *sous* per day for her son and the same sum for her servant. Berryer firmly ordered de Ruis to only pay her six *sous* per day, that is to say, to treat her like the ordinary inhabitants (1759-08-17; AN Col B, vol. 110).

98. Marie-Madeleine Buot, an Acadian woman married to a noble French officer, de Billy, received on her arrival in France a pension of 500 *livres* because of the services rendered by her husband, a former decommissioned officer, who then became a militiaman and died in 1755 (*cf.* Robert Piart, "Une Acadienne et sa fille à la maison du roi Louis XVI," *Société historique acadienne (Cahiers)*, 34, 1 (March 2003), pp. 33-41).

99. Various stipulations in the modern era ruled the conditions by which officers could reenter their country "on parole" once they had been prisoners.

100. 1758-12-11a; AN Col B, vol. 108, fo. 328.

101. The biography of Pierre Cassiet in the *Dictionnaire biographique du Canada* indicates that on his return he received gratuities of 200 then 400 *livres*, then a gratuity of 160 *livres*. Jean Manach also, thanks to the influence of the abbé de l'Isle-Dieu, received two "provisions from the court to assure his subsistence." *Idem* for the abbé Désenclaves. As for the abbé Girard, he received 400 *livres* as a pension until 1766 (1774-12-14b; E. Martin, *op. cit.*, p. 62). The case of the abbé Le Loutre is a bit unique since he was actively involved with the Acadian refugees. He also received a pension of 1,200 *livres* (court decision in May 1768, retroactive to January 1, 1767; *Dictionnaire biographique du Canada*). Besides, these missionaries had other sources of income.

102. With the exception of Marie-Madeleine de Billy (born Buot), who was chambermaid to the king (*cf.* note 98).

103. In the departmental archives of Calvados (Caen) are preserved very many petitions including requests to emigrate to Saint-Pierre and Miquelon or to receive special treatment. Many letters from this family have also been preserved.

104. Joseph Bellefontaine, the patriarch of the family, left a long memoir recounting his life in Acadia (1774-01-15a; ANC, MG6 A15, series C [Mi. F 849] – AD Calvados, C 1020). On this individual, also see the *Dictionnaire biographique du Canada*.

105. By an unfortunate stroke of chance, Cherbourg was the probable place of birth of Philippe Mius d'Entremont, baron de Pobomcoup, who left for Acadia in 1650 or 1651 and was "one of the rare Acadian lords to be involved in cultivation and land clearing" (the biography of Mius d'Entremont in the *Dictionnaire biographique du Canada*). It does not seem that the d'Entremont family kept contact with the branches of its cousins in France.

106. It was perhaps a local interpretation of the ministerial directives. What is certain is that on many occasions minister Berryer gave instructions for everyone to receive only six *sous* per day (1759-08-17; AN Col B, vol. 110).

107. 1766-06-13; ANC, MG6 C3 [Mi. 12881, 3rd reg., p. 1] – Arch. of the port of Cherbourg (minutes of letters of the commissioner of divisions).

108. 1767-01-10; *RAPC 1905-II*, appendix G, p. 200.

109. 1767-03-13b; AN Marine B3, vol. 572, fo. 148.

110. 1768-01-23; ANC, MG6 C3 [Mi. 12881, 3rd reg., pp. 13-14] –Arch. of the port of Cherbourg (minutes of the letters of the commissioner of divisions).

111. 1773-07-02c; ANC, MG6 A15, series C [Mi. F 849] – AD Calvados, C 1019.

112. 1774-05-17; BM Bordeaux, Ms. 1480, fo. 595-598. The d'Entremonts did not refer to this proposal in their letters.

113. 1773-09-06d; ANC, MG6 A15, series C [Mi. F 849] – AD Calvados, C 2019.

114. 1774-01-30; *id.*, C 1020.

115. 1778-03-01; *id.*, C 1021.

116. 1774-05-21; *id.*, C 1020.

117. 1775-10-18; *id.*

118. 1775-11-06; *id.*

119. 1775-12-26; *id.*

120. 1776-02-25; *id.*

121. 1778-08-26; ANC, MG6 A15, series C [Mi. F 849] – AD Calvados, C 1021. Some Acadians affirmed that they received nothing after 1773; 1784-05-25; ANC, MG6 A15, series C [Mi. F 849] AD Calvados, C 1022.

122. 1782-05-10; *id.*, C 1022.

123. The intendant leads us to believe that they each received 18 *sous*.

124. 1784-05-05b; *id.*

125. 1789-02-16; *id.*

126. The expression, "inhabitants and persons of the people" was employed by Berryer, for example (1758-12-30a; SM Rochefort 1 E 160, fo. 749).

127. 1758-10-09; AN Col B, vol. 108, fo. 107. Letter by Berryer; 1758-12-22b; SHM Brest 1 P 1/7, piece 244.

128. The "correspondence from the departure" of the ministry of the Navy has been entirely preserved in series B of the archives of the colonies, and there is little missing. The "correspondence from the arrival," however, series Marine B^3 in the National Archives, is quite extensive. Locally, the correspondence at Rochefort is fairly complete, but the first six months of 1759, containing the most important pieces, are lacking. As for the correspondence of the commissioner of the Navy at

Saint-Malo, it is entirely lost for the period 1733-1778. Some rare pieces were preserved at Brest in the *Service historique* of the Navy, but few involve the Acadians.

129. The "Canadians" also received assistance.

130. See for example 1773-04-01a; AN, Colonies, G1 512, as well as other documents from the same date: 1773-04-1b; 1773-04-01c, etc.

131. 1758-11-15a; AHM Brest 1 P 1/7, fo. 195. The *RAPC, 1905-I*, (p. 271) makes a misstatement of the original text. The summary states: "To Mr. Guillot. Answer to his letter on the subject of the arrival at Cancale and at Saint-Malo of the 2 truce-bearing packet-boats sent from Louisbourg to transport to France the inhabitants of Île-Royale. Lists must be made in which the distinction between those from Île-Royale, Île Saint-Jean, from Gaspé and other places will be established. What aid to be provided to them." But the text of the original specifies: "you will distinguish the status of the various inhabitants from Île-Royale and from Île Saint-Jean, from Gaspé, and other places and areas. . . . Among them, there may be some who can support themselves." Therefore it was not just a question of distinguishing between the people by their places of origin as the summary from the *RAPC* would suggest, but, on the contrary, of distinguishing them according to their social status. By this was meant not just distinguishing between the nobility, the clergy, and the third estate, but also, among the latter, those who might provide for their own subsistence, and the rest.

132. 1774-09-27; BM Bordeaux, Ms. 1480, Appendices, 1st file.

133. 1773-02-13; AN Col B, vol. 144, fo. 69. The promise of a settlement had been made only to those who had been taken from the "prisons" of England (1785-09-10; AD Ille-et-Vil, C 2453).

134. 1773-04-01c; AN Col G^1, vol. 512: "List of some families from North America resident at Rochefort to whom subsistence and lodging are being paid from the funds of the colonies" (1773-08-29b; BM Bordeaux, Ms. 1480, fo. 466-468). Lemoyne implored de Boynes to continue the aid for the families from Île-Royale who were invalid and lacked means of subsistence.

135. 1773-07-01b; BM Bordeaux, Ms. 1480, fo. 355-356.

136. *Cf.* for example: 1774-09-27; BM Bordeaux, Ms. 1480, Appendices, 1st file.

137. 1773-10-26; BM Bordeaux, Ms. 1480, fo. 493-496.

138. 1773-07-01b; BM Bordeaux, Ms. 1480, fo. 355-356.

139. 1774-09-27; BM Bordeaux, Ms. 1480, Appendices, 1st file.

140. The word "European" was frequently used in the texts. The term "metropolitan" still only indicated "Archepiscopal" in the eighteenty century (*Dict. Acad.*).

141. 1767-03-15; *RAPC 1905-II*, pp. 197, 198, 200.

142. 1759-09-18 (a, b, c, etc.); Diocesan arch. of Coutances – AD Manche, Saint-Lô, 6 Mi. 252 to 257.

143. 1765-11-24a; AN Col B, vol. 122, fo. 380.

144. 1773-10-12b; BM Bordeaux, Ms. 140, fo. 483.

145. 1784-07-16; ANC, MG6 A15, series C [Mi. F 849] – AD Calvados, C 1022.

146. This was very much in conformity with the rules in effect in the period. Patrick Weil highlights the case of a woman who lost her French nationality upon marrying a foreigner in the nineteenth century (*Qu'est-ce-qu'un Français? Histoire de la nationalité française depuis la Révolution*, Paris, Grasset, 2002).

147. 1773-08-09; BM Bordeaux, Ms. 1480, fo. 500-504.

148. "Pilot. He who conducts, who leads a vessel, a galley, & every other ocean-going structure"

(*Dict. Acad.*).

149. 1759-05-26; AN Col B, vol. 110.

150. 1766-08-00; AN Col B, vol. 124. These Germans had been recruited by the French government to populate Guyana. When the mass colonization of this colony was abandoned after the colossal number of deaths that followed in 1763-1764, a large number of Germans and Alsatians who had not yet been able to embark and who, for various reasons, could only return home with difficulty, received aid from the government, like the Acadians. Choiseul in a letter even compared the aid distributed to the Acadians to that distributed to the Germans. In a letter addressed to the commissioner at La Rochelle, he thus ordered to be distributed, "six *sous* per day to the two parents, four *sous* per day for each child less than nine years old, a dozen *livres* gratuity for each woman who has just delivered a child in order that she would have no problem caring for it. If the Germans complain of the modest treatment provided to them, have them understand that it is still more advantageous than that which the King gives to the Acadians, Canadians and Louisbourg residents in France, who are his own subjects and who rendered him considerable services in the colonies" (1764-04-13a; SHM Rochefort, 1 E 175, fo. 796-797). In this period, the Acadians in fact received a sum superior to that mentioned above, except to my knowledge the Acadian women did not receive the special benefits when they delivered a child.

151. 1758-11-00b; AN Col G1 vol. 482-488, 1763: "List of inhabitants from Canada, Île-Royale, as well as from Acadia, coming from the prisons of England to whom the King has granted payment . . . of six *sous* per day counting from the day of their arrival at Saint-Malo;" 1765: "List of payments made to the inhabitants from Île-Royale and others from North America and to their families residing at Saint-Malo and in the environs for their subsistence at six *sols* per day to each during the year 1765." Most of them received 109 *livres*, 10 *sous*, or six *sous* per day for 365 days, but some received the payment for fewer days. 1758-11-001; Arch. of the Navy, Brest, sub-series 1 P– ANC, MG6 C4 (Mi. of the orig., F-2101 and F-2102).

152. 1758-11-001; *id*. This list is perhaps the same as that of a dispatch from early December 1766. *Cf.* 1766-12-05; AN Col B, vol. 125.

153. 1759-05-04b; AN Col B, vol. 110.

154. 1759-12-14; AN Col B, vol. 110.

155. "The elderly and the invalid receive a little more, or 8 and 9 *sols* per day" (Martin, *op. cit.*, p. 33).

156. 1774-11-26; AD Vienne 2 J dep. 22, art. 124-2.

157. 1768-01-23; ANC, MG6 C3 [Mi 12881, 3rd reg., pp. 13-14] – Arch. of the port of Cherbourg (minutes of letters of the comm.. of divisions).

158. 1773-08-28; BM Bordeaux, Ms. 1480, fo. 463.

Chapter 8

1. See, for example, 1758-11-30; SHM Rochefort 1 E 160, fo. 749.

2. 1759-03-10b; AN Col B, vol. 110.

3. See, for example, 1758-12-30a; SHM Rochefort 1 E 160, fo. 749.

4. 1759-01-07; AN Col B, vol. 110.

5. 1759-05-10; SHM Brest 1 P1/23 piece 7.

6. 1772-04-10b; BM Bordeaux, Ms. 1480, fo. 56. The dry-curer was a "cod fisherman, responsible for salting the fish at the site of the catch" (*Le Petit Robert*). The evocation of the trade of dry-curer reoccurs in at least two of the reports of Lemoyne (1772-02-08a; 1772-11-18b).

7. 1759-01-12b; AN Col B, vol. 110.

8. 1759-03-10c; AN Col B, vol. 110; 1759-03-10d (*id.*) and 1759-03-23 (*id.*).

9. 1759-05-04a; AN Col B, vol. 110; 1767-06-05; ANC, MG6 C3 (Mi. 12881, 3rd reg., p. 8] – Arch. of the port of Cherbourg (minutes of letters of the commissioner of divisions).

10. 1759-03-10c; AN Col B, vol. 110; 1759-03-23 (*id.*). Sailors serving in the Royal Navy during the Seven Years War who were taken could often return home, on the condition of giving their word that they would not serve on French vessels during the remainder of the war.

11. ANC, MG6 A15, series C [Mi F 849] – AD Calvados, C 1019.

12. 1763-12-09; AN Col B, vol. 117; 1766-12-00; BM Bordeaux, Ms. 1480, fo. 264-266.

13. 1764-06-10; AN Col B, vol. 120, fo. 195.

14. We exclude here the particular case of those Acadians who were established as agricultural workers in Belle-Île-en-Mer and in Poitou.

15. Anselme Boudereau actually was trying to prove that he was not elsewhere at seven in the morning.

16. 1767-05-16; AD Ille-et-Vil. 7 B 5.

17. 1759-11-16; AN Col B, vol. 110.

18. Gilles Foucqueron, *Saint-Malo 2000 ans d'histoire*, 2001, entry, "Acadiens;" *cf.* J. L. Boithias and A. de La Vernhe, *Les Moulins à mer et les anciens meuniers du Littoral, Mouleurs, Piqueurs, Porteurs et Moulagers*, Editions Créer, 1990. The authors write: "at the levee of the "mills of Plouër," also called Les Minotais (Côtes du Nord) in the eighteenth century . . . the Acadians worked for many months in a row to repair it.

19. 1767-05-16; AD Ille-et-Vil. 7 B 5; 1759-03-02 (AN Col B, vol. 110); 1760-08-19a (Arch. of the Navy, Brest, sub-series 1 P – ANC, MG6 C4 (Mi. of the orig., F-2101 and F-2102)); 1759-11-16; AN Col B, vol. 1101786-05-19b; AN F[15] 3495; 1773-04-27a; BM Bordeaux, Ms. 1480, fo. 307-312, fo. 165-167 and AN H[1] 1499[2].

20. 1760-08-19c; AHM Brest 1 P 1/8 1760 piece 129.

21. 1765-05-24; ANC, MG6C3 [Mi. 12881, 2nd reg., p. 10] Arch. of the port of Cherbourg (minutes of letters of the commissioner of divisions).

22. Alain Roman, *Saint-Malo et les Amériques au XVIIIe siècle*, collection "Documents pour l'histoire de Saint-Malo," file no. 8, Saint-Malo, Municipal Archives, 1999. The abbé F. Robidou notes: "Many of the captains (corsairs) were direct descendants of the Acadian families deported by the English in 1755 to the Brittany coast. For example, René Rosse, Auguste Blanchard, Th. LeBlanc, Pierre Cormier. The De Bons were originally from Saint-Pierre and Miquelon" (*Les derniers corsairs malouins. La course sous la République et l'Empire 1793-1814*, Rennes, Oberthür, 1919, p. 19). Thanks to Gilles Foucqueron for having kindly communicated this information.

23. 1767-06-05; ANC, MG6C3 [Mi. 12881, 3rd reg., p. 8] – Arch. of the port of Cherbourg (minutes of letters of the commissioner of classes).

24. 1761-01-14c; Diocesan archives of Coutances – AD Manche, Saint-Lô, 6 Mi 252 to 257.

25. 1760-08-19a (Navy Archives, Brest, sub-series 1 P – ANC, MG6 C4 [Mi. of the orig., F-2101and

F-2102). These two men were not actually Acadians but they were close to them. Jean Rambourg, born in 1725 at Granville, was a resident on the Bras d'Or, a vast interior lake on Cape Breton, at the time of the census of La Roque in 1752 (*cf. Racines et rameaux françaisd'Acadie*, bulletin no. 33, April 2005, p. 4). In France he practiced the profession of boatman and vouched for the Acadian Anselme Boudereau accused of tobacco fraud, May 16, 1767 (1767-05-16; AD Ille-et Vil. 7 B 5). Paul Adam emphasized the precarious existence of the fishermen in the eighteenth century: "the fishermen, who could, like the agricultural workers, be owners of the lands that they exploited, remained poor, sometimes on the border of survival and dependant on the authorities." The coasts at the time remained very inhospitable and the fishing was essentially for resale, not for personal consumption ("Pêche," Lucien Bély, *Dictionnaire de l'Ancien Régime*).

26. Guillaume Eckendorff, "Les Acadiens à Cherbourg," in *Les Normands et l'Outre-Mer. Congrès des Sociétés historiques et archéologiques de Normandie*, Caen, Annales de Normandie, 2001, pp. 21-33 (p. 27).

27. 1767-05-22; AD Ille-et-Vil. 7 B 25-1767.

28. 1767-05-22; AD Ille-et-Vil. 7 B 25-1767.

29. The *Dictionnaire de Trévoux* specifies that one makes use of the cormorant in fishing, by means of a technique still used in our day in Asia that consists of "putting an iron ring at the base of the neck [of the cormorant] by means of which he has to surrender any large fish that remains in its esophagus." The dictionary is not clear about the geographic location of this technique. The article in the *Encyclopédie* about the cormorant says nothing of its use in France, which may suggest that it was unknown on her coasts. In his *Traité des Pesches*, section III, chapter I, p. 17 (1767), Duhamel du Monceau mentions "Fishing with the Cormorant" without mentioning a precise location. At most he mentions, "When this bird is prepared, one makes use of it for Fishing, & this is how we have seen it practiced on the Fontainbleau canal."

30. 1767-06-05; ANC, MG6 C3 [Mi. 12881, 3rd reg., p. 8] – Arch. of the port of Cherbourg (minutes of the letters of the comm.. of divisions).

31. This is also the contention of G. Eckendorff ("Les Acadiens à Cherbourg," in *Les Normands et l'Outre-Mer. Congrès des Sociétées historiques et archéologigues de Normandie*, Caen, Annales of Normandy, 2001, pp. 21-33, p. 28.

32. 1772-04-10b; BM Bordeaux, Ms. 1480, fo. 56.

33. 1766-04-20; AN Navy B^3, vol. 568, fo. 319ss.

34. Abel Pointrineau, "Métiers," Lucien Bély, *Dictionnaire de l'Ancien Régime*.

35. 1773-12-01a; BM Bordeaux, Ms. 1480, fo. 534-535.

36. 1771-08-20; Archives of the Seminary of Foreign Missions.

37. 1763-07-04; Louis Le Guennec, *Les Barbier de Lescoët: une famille de la noblesse bretonne*, Quimper, 1991. Saint-Paoul, probably a surname, was indicated as an Acadian, but this name does not surface in any other primary or secondary source.

38. 1759-04-20b; AM Saint-Malo, BB 35. Jacques Daigle, whom one does not find mentioned in any later documents, was the sole Acadian accepted as citizen of the town. I do not know the exact reasons why he asked to be admitted to citizenship or why other Acadians did not ask to be. The nature of Daigle's profession may have obliged him to request citizenship, without which he probably could not have practiced.

39. 1786-05-19b; AN F[15] 3495.

40. 1767-11-02a; AD Ille-et-Vil. 7 B 44. Jean Thibaudeau was one of the minority of Acadians who

took a wife from the area. February 28, 1764, he married Françoise Huere, native of Pleudihen, (Albert J. Robichaux, *The Acadian Exiles in Saint-Malo, 1758-1785*, Eunice, Louisiana, Hebert Publications, 1981, vol. III, p. 837). It is probable that it was Françoise Huere and not Jean Thibaudeau who owned the cabaret. See the biography of Jean Thibaudeau compiled in our appendix, p. 233.

41. 1767-03-13b; *RAPC 1905-II, pp. 197-198, 200*; G. Eckendorff indicates that the Acadian children were instructed by "schooling" ("Les Acadiens à Cherbourg," in *Les Normands et l'Outre-Mer. Congrès des Sociétés historiques et archéologiques de Normandie*, Caen, Annales of Normandy, 2001, p. 28).

42. Jean-Baptiste Brault [or Brou], Isaac Hébert, Joseph Mathurin Bourg, Pierre (or Jean-Pierre) Bourg.

43. 1766-12-22; AN Col F3, vol. 16 and 1767-06-04; H.R. Casgrain, "Lettres et mémoires de l'abbé de l'Isle-Dieu (1742-1774)," *Rapport des archives de la province de Québec*, 16, 17, 18 (1935-1938), pp. 273-410; 331-459; 147-253.

44. 1767-02-19 (H.R. Casgrain, "Lettres et mémoires," *op. cit.*).

45. 1772-07-14; Vatican Arch. of the PF – ANC, MG 17 – A 25 – Mi. (orig.) K – 235. It was a question of two half-brothers, Joseph Mathurin Bourg and Jean-Baptiste Brault (Bro). The biographies of these two priests are found in the *Dictionnaire biographique du Canada*, containing an abundant bibliography about these two Acadians who returned to North America.

46. 1772-12-28b; *id.*, K – 234.

47. 1771-08-24; Diocesan arch. of Coutances. The same expression, or an equivalent, reoccurs many times. Thus Modest Moulaison, "daily occupied at her father's with the housework" (1763-07-03b; *id.*).

48. 1767-05-16; AD Ille-et-Vil. 7 B 5. Marie LeBlanc, "without profession," testified at the trial of Anselme Boudereau.

49. 1767-05-16; AD Ille-et-Vil. 7 B 5.

50. 1760-08-19a; Navy arch., Brest, sub-series 1 P – ANC, MG6 C 4 (Mi. from orig., F-2101 and F-2102). It was probably actually a question of families exiled from Île-Royale who had to repatriate funds. However, the Acadians also practiced the profession of innkeepers.

51. 1772-04-10b; BM Bordeaux, Ms. 1480, fo. 56.

52. We will have further occasion to speak of her. Suzanne Richard is especially known from some letters that she wrote to one of her clients, Madam du Laz, which have survived and were published in J. Baudry, *Étude historique et biographique sur la Bretagne à la veille de la Révolution, à propos d'une correspondance inedited (1782-1790)*, Paris, H. Champion, 1905.

53. 1761-06-25; Diocesan arch. of Coutances.

54. 1786-05-19b; AN F^{15} 3495.

55. 1767-08-01-; 1774-06-29; 1774-03-23a, etc.

56. 1774-02-04b; BM Bordeaux, Ms. 1480, fo. 556.

57. *Cf.* Robert Piart, "Une Acadienne et sa fille à la maison du roi Louis XVI," *Cahiers de la Société historique acadienne*, 34, 1 (March 2003), pp. 33-41. The "inventor" of this story is Aegidius Fauteux; *cf.* "Les carnets d'un curieux, *La Patrie*, 23 December 1933.

58. It is possible that Marie-Madeleine's presence near Marie-Antoinette assisted with the petitions that the Acadians wrote to her in 1774, or that she at least served as an intermediary (1774-07-00b; AD Vienne 2J dep. 22, art. 97).

59. Guy Bugeon and Monique Hivert-Le Faucheux, *Les Acadiens parties en France en 1785 pour la Louisiane: listes d'embarquement*, Poitiers-Rennes (typscript), 1988. Monique Le Faucheux made significant summaries, notably at Saint-Suliac. *Cf.* Monique Le Faucheux, "Mes ancêtres d'Acadie: les "hors-venus" à Saint-Suliac (Ille-et-Vilaine), 1764-74," *Les amities acadiennes*, nos. 36 and 37, (1986). This article also appeared in the *Cercle genealogique d'Ille-et-Viliane*, 1, 1 (1st trimester 1987). This study of Saint-Malo region also allows some observation and follow-up on the fate of some individuals. The two authors note changes in the claimed professions of some. For example, Pierre Landry in 1763 at Saint-Malo, listed as carpenter and laborer, is designated as a colorist in 1785.

60. Monique Le Faucheux, "Mes ancêtres d'Acadie," *op. cit.*

61. Guy-Charles Bugeon, *Les Ferms acadiennes du Poitou et leurs occupants de 1774 à 1793*, Archigny, 1996. Nearly a fourth of the Acadians declared themselves to be sailors even while they were from 150 to 200 kilometers from the ocean.

62. Sail-maker; *Trévoux*: "Sail-maker. Also said on the sea for one who takes care of the sails, is responsible for making them, measuring them, sewing them, and putting them in a condition to be used. One otherwise called him a *Trévier*."

63. "*Indienne*. Fabric painted in the Indies. This noun became appellative and is said in reference to all kinds of painted fabrics" (*Dict. Acad.* 1762).

64. "Worker who makes arquebuses, & all kinds of portable firearms" (*Dict. Acad.*).

65. Worker charged with caulking a ship, that is to say "blocking with tarred oakum the crevices of the hull of a ship" (*Petit Robert*).

66. The letters between parentheses refer to three large categories– defined arbitrarily – as below: W = workers in wood; M = marine workers; T = workers with textiles. Some professions were listed in many categories.

67. This term does not figure in the older dictionaries that we consulted. It was probably a question of a maker of "*CATÉNIÈRE*: Fishing term. Chains bearing many drag-hooks serving to catch lines at the bottom of the sea" (*Littré*).

68. The trade of the carpenter was "one of the most esteemed in the professional hierarchy, as the durability of the construction of large buildings made of complex assemblies of girders, joists, battens and other rafters depended on their carpentry .

69. In the textile industry, notably for the preparation of *indiennes*, [Indian print fabrics] (*cf.* notes 63, 72, 74 and 75).

70. The fabrication of ropes.

71. In the eighteenth century, shoemakers were principally makers of new shoes, differing from *savetiers*, who were in principal restricted to the repair of used shoes (Poitrineau, "Trades," Lucien Bély, *Dictionnaire de l'Ancien Régime*).

72. It was probably a question of workers involved with the fabrication of Indian print fabrics. According to G. Bugeon, "the carver executes the "blocks" (in wood) or the "flat plates" (in copper) engraved either in relief or hollowed, that allow reproducing desired designs onto the tissues."

73. This term with this spelling was not found in the dictionaries (*Littré, Académie française, Petit Robert, Trévoux*). It is classed by Bugeon and Le Faucheux among the workers in wood. It could be a poor transcription from the term "*Grayer*. In some provinces, one calls *Grayers* those charged with taking care of bodies of water, pools" (*Trévoux*). It could also be a question of a word formed from the verb, "*gréer*,"[to rig].

74. The printer manipulates the "blocks" or the "flat plates," applying them to the tissues after hav-

ing them soaked with caustic or coloring material, depending on the final result desired" (notes by Bugeon and Le Faucheux).

75. Fabricator of printed Indian textiles.

76. The *pareteur* polishes the wood to make it very supple [note by Bugeon and Le Faucheux].

77. He pierces holes where pegs are inserted for the assembly of pieces of wood.

78. "A worker involved with the use of slate from Angers" (*Littré*).

79. "A worker who fabricates pulleys; a merchant who sells them" (*Littré*).

80. "One who cuts, folds, supplies, or repairs sails" (*Littré*).

81. This total is incorrect, because, unlike G. Bugeon and M. Le Faucheux, G. M. Braud does not provide a complete list of all of the trades professed by the Acadians, nor the total number of acts in which mention of the professions is made. In all, G. M. Braud affirms that he perused 1,300 civil acts from all of the parishes of Nantes, Chantenay, Rezé, Saint-Sébastien-sur-Loire, and Paimboeuf during the period from 1775 to 1785 inclusively.

82. In this same work (*De Nantes à la Louisiane, l'histoire de l'Acadie, l'odyssée d'un people exilé*, Quest editions, 1994).

83. Abel Poitrineau, "Métiers," Lucien Bély, *Dictionnaire de l'Ancien Régime.*

84. Some Acadians were undoubtedly workers in manufacturing who had "as a characteristic a position outside of the juridical frame of the regulated trades" or "communities of trades" (Poitrineau, *ibid*.). Moreover, as Poitrineau recalls in another article ("corporation ou jurande," in Lucien Bély, *Dictionnaire de l'Ancien Régime*), it is possible that membership in a "corps" of trade was difficult to reconcile with the claimed membership in the Acadian "corps of nation." Some Acadians were, however, able to obtain letters of mastery later on. Thus Olivier Terriot is indicated in an act as master shoemaker at Nantes. G. Eckendorff also notes the case of Jean Régnault, accepted as master and patron for the small coastal trade in 1771 at Cherbourg. Régnault was nonetheless not an Acadian surname, and this individual was possibly rather originally from Île-Royale ("Les Acadiens à Cherbourg," in *Les Normands et l'Outre-Mer. Congrès des Sociétés historiques et arrchéologiques de Normandie*, Caen, Annales de Normandie, 2001, pp. 21-33).

85. It is sometimes explicitly specified that the Acadians did not have letters of mastery (1786-07-07; AD Ille-et-Vil. C 6176).

86. It should be noted that they probably had the same problem at the time of their stay in England, since a French report from February 1763 "concerning the French prisoners in England among whom were Acadians," specified: "The men with trades could not establish themselves in any town of England without having paid for a mastery, whereas, in the colonies, the rank was equal for them if they went into ours. It is true that many could come to London . . . where in half of the town there was no corporation nor mastery" (1763-02-17b; MAE, Pol. Corresp., England, vol. 449, fo. 333).

87. On the price of mastery at Paris as well as more generally the conditions for becoming a master craftsman, see Daniel Roche (*Journal de ma vie. Jacques-Louis Ménétra, Compagnon vitrier au 18e siècle*, Paris, Montalba, 1982, part V, "Le Monde social").

88. On this subject, see 1766-12-14; SHM Rochefort 1 R 11 no. 482 and 1772-02-08a; BM Bordeaux, Ms. 1480, fo. 1/fo. 8.

89. 1773-08-19; *id.*, fo. 439-446.

90. 1773-06-22a; *id.*, fo. 363-365.

91. 1773-07-04; *id.*, fo. 369-373.

92. 1773-09-16; *id.*, fo. 446-455.

93. 1773-12-14; *id.*, fo. 529-534.

94. 1773-09-06c; ANC, MG6 A15, series C [Mi. F 849] – AD Calvados, C 1019.

95. 1773-11-12; *id.*

96. 1774-03-17b; AD Vienne 2 J dep. 22, art. 124-1.

97. Series F15 3495; this carton contains the papers concerning the Acadians held by the offices of General Control starting in 1773, notably that of the agents Coster and Blondel.

98. 1783-10-07; AN F^{15} 3495.

99. 1773-00-00d; AN F^{15} 3495.

100. 1784-03-07; AN F^{15} 3495; 1773-00-00d; AN F^{15} 3495; 1784-05-10; AN F^{15} 3495.

101. 1784-03-07 (AN F^{15} 3495). She wrote, regarding her husband, "The man named Joseph Devau, Acadian carpenter's companion . . . to whom the late king wanted to grant the title of gentleman." He later introduced himself as "Joseph Devau, Acadian, gentleman" (1779-03-09b;; AN F^{15} 3495).

102. 1779-03-09b; *id.*

103. 17833-10-07; *id.*

104. 1784-03-25 (*id.*); 1784-05-28 (*id.*). This widow was probably not of Acadian origin. Her surname is not Acadian and does not figure in any document nor in the secondary literature.

105. 1786-05-19a; *id.*

106. 1785-06-01; ANC, MG6 A15, series C [Mi. F 849] – AD Calvados, C 1022.

107. 1786-06-13; MAE Pol. Corresp., Spain, vol. 620, fo. 57.

108. 1786-05-19v; AN F^{15} 3495.

109. 1784-00-00b; AD Ille-et-Vil. C 2453.

110. 1784-12-22; AD Ille-et-Vil. C 6176.

111. 1786-05-19b; AN F^{15} 3495.

112. 1786-08-04; AD Ille-et-Vil. C 2453.

113. 1785-07-13; ANC, MG6 A15, series C [Mi. F 849] – AD Calvados, C 1022.

114. Zysberg, *La monarchie des Lumières, op. cit.*, p. 509.

115. If we do not find the word "*chomage*" [unemployment] as such in the documents, we do find it in the *Dictionnaire de l'Académie* of 1762 with a meaning close to the current sense.

116. 1759-05-10; SHM Brest 1 P 1/23 piece 7. Jacques-Louis Ménétra, traveling in the Saint-Malo region in 1758, does not report having had difficulties finding employment. He worked for some time as a coastal guard then embarked on a corsair (*Journal de ma vie, op. cit.*, p. 60). But no doubt his status as mate and the fact that he knew how to read and write rendered his search for employment easier.

117. 1760-08-19c; SHM Brest 1 P 1/8 1760, piece 129.

118. 1763-07-08a; AM Saint-Malo, BB 49, fo. 12-13.

119. 1760-08-17; AN Marine B^3, vol. 547, fo. 131.

120. Ambroise Bourk, 31 years old, thus declared himself "living off of payment from the King" (1763-07-03b; Diocesan arch. of Coutances).

121. 1763-04-=04; AN Col B, vol. 117, fo. 117.

122. 1763-06-23; ANC, MG6 A15, series C [Mi. 849] – AD Calvados, C 1019.

123. 1763-07-05; AD Gironde, Bordeaux, C 425.

124. 1763-07-02; ANC, MG6 A15, series C [Mi. F 849] – AD Calvados, C 1019.

125. 1763-07-03a; *id.*

126. 1763-07-08b; *id.*

127. 1763-07-17; *id.*

128. 1773-04-26; BM Bordeaux, Ms 1480, fo. 312-318.

129. 1775-07-04; AD Ille-et-Vil. C 6176.

130. 1773-10-03; AD Vienne 2 J dep. 22, art. 124-1.

131. 1773-11-30; BM Bordeaux, Ms. 1480, fo. 526-529.

132. Lemoyne – 1772-05-09b; BM Bordeaux, Ms. 1480, fo. 77-78.

133. 1773-04-27c; BM Bordeaux, Ms. 1480, Appendices, 1st file, fo. 22s. As the Acadians already were receiving a payment of six *sous* per day, in the view of the local population they were in a position to accept working for a lower salary. Note the affirmation that at the time of the arrival of the Acadians there was "more work than men" contradicts the testimony from the period, more credible, indicating endemic unemployment at the time of the arrival of the Acadians in 1758-1759.

134. 1773-1-30; BM Bordeaux, Ms. 1480, fo. 526-529.

135. 1760-08-19c; SHM Brest 1 P 1/8 1760 piece 129.

136. 1767-06-05; ANC, MG 6 C3 [Mi. 12881, 3rd reg., p. 5] – Arch. of the port of Cherbourg (minutes of the letters of the Comm. of Divisions).

137. 1773-11-30; BM Bordeaux, Ms. 1480, fo. 526-529.

138. 1772-02-08a; BM Bordeaux, Ms. 1480, fo. 1.

Chapter 9

1. E. Martin, *Les Exilés, op. cit.*, p. 258.

2. For more details on this see pp. 231 and following of my thesis.

3. In comparison, the mistress of Louis XV, Madam du Barry, spent the same amount every month on her personal expenses. Hubert Méthivier, *Le siècle de Louis XV*, Paris, PUF, 1994 (9th corrected edition), p. 121.

4. The expenses for the settling of Belle-Île amounted to 56,000 *livres* (1767-05-23; General archives of the Congregation of the Saint-Esprit, notes by A. David, box no. 430, file 7). As to the total cost of the settlement of Poitou, various numbers have been suggested. E. Martin notes an expense of 1,072,409 *livres*. A later report, however, mentions a higher sum: the expense made until then rose to 1,730,000 about a third of which had been used for the supplement to the Acadians, one tenth in supplying tools, animals, etc., and the surplus was the cost of construction of the workshops (1782-04-05; AN F^{15} 3495).

5. If the coinage of Tours was the official money of the kingdom as of 1667, it did not circulate in any definite manner. There was no piece of one *livre tournois*, for instance, but only pieces of gold, silver,

or copper. Each *livre* was worth 20 *sous* (or *sols*), which themselves were worth 12 *deniers*. The term "franc" was a simple synonym for *"livre"* (*Dictionnaire de l'Académie*). The official rate of the *livre* was fixed by the royal power (Zysberg, *La monarchie des Lumières, op. cit.*, p. 96).

6. *Cf.* Ernest Martin, *Les Exilés, op. cit.*, p. 33.

7. Daniel Roche describes the difficulty that historians have in calculating popular budgets in the eighteenth century and warns of the accuracy of these calculations (*La France des Lumières, op. cit.*, p. 554s).

8. Jean Jacquart, "Journaliers," Lucien Bély, *Dictionnaire de l'Ancien Régime*.

9. Jean-Pierre Poussou, "Crises de substance," "Salaires" and "Prix," Lucien Bély, *Dictionnaire de l'Ancien Régime*. Ernest Labrousse gives an account, at the end of his study, of the difficulty of establishing average salaries, especially because of the impossibility of isolating salaries from other forms of remuneration. Labrousse noted great variations depending on the periods and the regions. In 1793, he estimated the average salary of a non-specialized worker at 1*l*.3s.4d in the towns, and 1*l*.6d in the country (*Esquisse du mouvement des prix et des revenues en France au XVIIIe siècle*, Paris, 1932, p. 460). A more recent study by Gérard Béaur also notes that it is very difficult to posit a curve of salaries in the century of the Enlightenment. According to this author, however, the salaries were well behind the prices. While the latter increased nearly 60 percent, between 1726-1741 and 1785-1789, during the same period, the salaries only gained around 25 percent. For example, at Toulouse the average remunerations went from 12 *sols* to 15 *sols* between 1722-1726 and 1784-1789, that is to say up 25 percent, while the prices leaped in the same period some 62 percent. But the reality is less uniform. In some other areas, salaries increased 80 percent, and one observes salaries largely catch up with the prices in the final years of the Ancien Régime (*Histoire agraire de la France au XVIIIe siècle*, Paris, 2000, pp. 290 et seq.).

10. G. Frêche, *Toulouse et la region Midi-Pyrénées au siècle des Lumières vers 1670-1789*, Paris, 1974.

11. Jean-Pierre Poussou, "Salaires," Lucien Bély, *Dictionnaire de l'Ancien Régime*. According to Zysberg, in the South of France in 1725, a day laborer earned about 10 *sous* per day while, in 1780, a very qualified worker earned 1 *livre* (20 *sous*) per day in a large city (*La monarchie des Lumières, op. cit.*, pp. 63 and 411). The day workers employed by the intendant of the Navy of Rochefort earned 16*s* per day in 1759 (1759-12-06; SHM Rochefort, 1 E 415, no. 726). According to a report by the baron de l'Espérance, governor of Saint-Pierre and Miquelon in 1785, the Acadians of the archipelago earned much more by fishing: "Whatever work it is, the men earn between 4 and 5 *livres* per day and the women who bleach, iron and darn linen get never less than 20 or 30 *sols*, along with nourishment. Gardening should be considered one of the principal means of subsistence; the soil, without much cultivating, brings an abundance of potatoes that can, of necessity, supply flour and cabbage, which keep very well in the winter and that one commonly sells for 8 and 10 *sols* a piece. But as good as the fishing might be, there is not one family that can subsist without the assistance from the king" (quoted by Michel Poirier, *Les Acadiens aux îles Saint-Pierre et Miquelon, 1758-1828*, Éditions d'Acadie, 1984, p. 81). Finally, according to Lemoyne, the salary of a carpenter-mason mixer was around 3 *livres* (60 *sous*) per day in 1773 (1773-06-20b); BM Bordeaux, Ms. 1480, fo. 358-363).

12. Study cited by Daniel Roche, *France des Lumières*, p. 554. Roche reports that around 50 percent of the expenses of the day worker went to purchasing grains, but that "with two salaries, for the same period of labor, this percentage lowers to 35 percent. The available funds thus varied, doubling from 40 *livres* in the first case, to 90 in the second."

13. Jean-Pierre Poussou, "Salaires," Lucien Bély, *Dictionnaire de l'Ancien Régime*.

14. 1773-08-19; BM Bordeaux, Ms. 1480, fo. 439-446. The window maker's companion Jacques-Louis Ménétra, passing through the Saint-Malo region at exactly the time of the arrival of the Acadians

in 1758-1759, tells that he worked at the home of a bourgeois as "*sergent de bourgeoisie,*" which consisted of supervising an artillery piece and leading seven men, for a salary of 15 *sous* per day, plus nourishment. Ménétra embarked on a corsair some time later and received a salary of 27 *livres* per month and a portion of the takings (*cf.* Daniel Roche, *Journal de ma vie. Jacques-Louis Ménétra, Compagnon vitrier au 18e siècle*, Paris, Montalba, 1982, pp. 59-60).

15. See the calculations of J.-P. Gutton ("Pauvres," Lucien Bély, *Dictionnaire de l'Ancien Régime*).

16. 1759-10-12; AN Col. B, vol. 110, fo. 276.

17. 1762-04-13; AN Col. B, vol. 115, fo. 25.

18. 1766-06-14; AN Marine B^3, vol. 568, fo. 264.

19. 1767-07-21b; AN Col. B, vol. 127, fo. 289.

20. 1774-11-26; AD Vienne 2 J dep. 22, art. 124-2.

21. 1773-23-01a; BM Bordeaux, Ms. 1480, fo. 534-35.

22. 1774-02-04b; BM Bordeaux, Ms. 1480, fo. 556.

23. 1776-12-29c; AD Vienne 2 J dep. 22, art. 124-1.

24. My research at Rennes in February 2005 on this subject did not allow me to do exhaustive examination of the series for Saint-Malo and its region relating to tobacco fraud. There are actually only numerical lists for these series and one must manually examine the corresponding cartons. Nonetheless, it seems that the cases involving the Acadians were especially frequent towards 1766-1768, and it is these years on which I concentrated my research.

25. Christophe Aubert, *La contrebande du tabac devant la jurisdiction des traits de Saint-Malo au XVIIIe siècle*, thesis, University of Rennes I, 1991.

26. The recapitulative overview of the civil proceedings relating to tobacco fraud in the Saint-Malo region, elaborated by Christophe Aubert, counts for the period of the end of December 1765 to June 1769 some thirty proceedings (*ibid.*, appendix 1, p. 90). Between 1717 and 1789, about 375 condemnations for tobacco fraud were pronounced in the trade jurisdiction and the admiralty of Saint-Malo. Among the nine proceedings implicating the Acadians, three were judged by a criminal jurisdiction because of acts of resistance or rebellion. Of thirty civil procedures, then, six involved the Acadians. This proportion seems relatively high, but it is perhaps not that indicative. Aubert specifies that his overview is not exhaustive, and I have already said the same regarding my own examinations. Moreover, we must have an idea of the percentage of the Acadians in the total population in the Saint-Malo region, but facts are lacking here with which to make trustworthy calculations. It thus seems to me to be impossible to deduce from these numbers if there was a consequent overrepresentation of Acadians among the perpetrators.

27. I have said above that I did not have the time to make exhaustive examinations of the files concerning tobacco fraud at Saint-Malo during period that the Acadians were there. Furthermore, a portion of the funds does not seem to have been kept. Finally, all of the Acadians caught red handed may not have been transferred to justice. In fact, according to Aubert, "every detainee for 'tobacco fraud' or rebel apprehended by the employees of the Farm had to be transferred to justice, except if they were able to 'accommodate themselves' with the farmer. The latter played an essential role in the direction of the pursuits: either he decided to undertake a suit, or he accepted a transaction with the perpetrator, thus avoiding the expenses of a procedure. The trial occurred within the jurisdiction of duties of Saint-Malo that had civil authority over simple fraud, and criminal or 'extraordinary' authority over fraud committed by a crowd or rebellion. The agents of the Farm, dealers and military personnel were pursued according to criminal procedure, considering their quality as representatives of the king or of the Farm" (Christophe Aubert, *La contrebande du tabac devant la juridiction*

des traites de Saint-Malo au XVIIIe siècle, thesis, University of Rennes I, 1991, p. 52).

28. 1767-03-30; Criminal complaint against Jean Thibaudeau, Françoise Huere, his wife, François Guillou and other Acadians for armed rebellion against the employees of the farm and tobacco contraband, filed by Charles August Trablet (?) de la Flourie, tobacco warehouser in the town of Saint-Malo, for Provost, adjudicator of the farm of the king, March 30, 1767, AD Ille-et-Vil. 7 B 44.

29. Christophe Aubert, *La contrebande du tabac, op. cit.*, p. 8.

30. 1767-10-11c; AN Marine B3, vol. 576, fo. 42. Letter by Choiseul from October 11, 1767 to the vicomte de Barrin, who was probably the son of the former governor of New France, Barrin de la Galissonière, governor of Corsica from 1786 to 1789.

31. "*Mitouche*, Person who does not have the air of touching ground. Etymology: poor pronunciation and orthography for *sainte n'y touché*" (Littré).

32. The *traites* were duties paid on merchandise entering or leaving the kingdom, or passing from certain provinces into others" (J.P., "Traites," Lucien Bély, *Dictionnaire de l'Ancien Régime*). It was the equivalent of what today we would call customs. Aubert, *op. cit.*, p. 75. As for the penalty of 1,000 *livres*, one had to submit a sum of 300 *livres* of the penalty in the month following the sentence, under penalty of the galleys. It was this latter obligation that Victor Forest neglected. Curiously, the principle of solidarity does not seem to have functioned, since his accomplices do not seem to have been worried. The penalty of 1,000 *livres* was the "standard" penalty since 1703 (Aubert, *La contrebande de tabac, op. cit.*, p. 13). As for the corporal punishment, it was reserved for recidivists or the most serious cases. If one refers to the overview of civil proceedings for contraband tobacco elaborated by Aubert, one notices that, in very rare cases, a penalty of 3,000 *livres* was imposed on the wrongdoers. Furthermore, the penalties were combined with a confiscation of goods seized and the "expenses," or court costs.

33. 1768-07-16: Petition of the prosecutor of the farms of the king of Saint-Malo to transfer the penalty of 1,000 *livres*, not paid, of Victor Forest into serving time in the galleys, July 16, 1768, AD Ille-et-Vil. 7 B 25 – 1768. The prosecutor of the king agreed to the request (July 29 1768) (*ibid.*).

34. The secretary of State of the Navy, Praslin, to the Controller-General, Étienne Maynon d'Invault, November 11, 1768, AN Col. B, vol. 131) (summary available in *RAPC 1905-I*, p. 388). Requests for pardon were undoubtedly rare but not exceptional. Christophe Aubert notes the pardon of a weaver of Saint-Malo by a letter of discharge in 1743 (*La contrebande du tabac, op. cit.*, p. 77).

35. "List of debts of Acadian families of the department of Saint-Malo up to January 1, 1778, to be settled upon payment of their supplements, according to the reports and obligations supplied by the creditors," January 1778, Ad Ille-et-Vil. C 2453.

36. Most of the time, the wrongdoers arrested when caught transporting tobacco were acting on behalf of a well-off associate. According to Aubert, the latter, coming from "higher social classes," was practically never troubled although he often organized the fraud by supplying the funds (p. 35). In the files concerning the Acadians, the name of a certain Mr. de Guébriand or de Guay Briand is cited many times. For example, in the complaint made against Jean Thibaudeau, it is specified that the various Acadians went to find the contraband tobacco in a *rabine* (that is to say, " a grove of woods that one does not customarily cut," *Dictionnaire de Trévoux*) "near the house of Monsieur Guay Brillant," at Pleudihen (1767-03-08b; 1767-03-30; 1767-11-02a and 1767-11-02b, all from AD Ille-et-Vil., 7 B 44). Some months later, other Acadians, including Honoré Caret and Pierre Landry, affirmed that they rented the boat on which they transported 1,637 *livres* worth of contraband tobacco, from "Monsieur de Guébriand living by the bridge of Sieux in Pleudihen." No doubt this was the same person, which could not have escaped the notice of the employees. Curiously, this Guébriand was not interrogated in these two cases. Daniel Brandily did some research on this individual. He

likely was one Henry Anne Lemeur, sieur du Guébriand, born in 1703 in Tressé, died on November 16, 1779, in the same place. He was the owner of the small farm of Clos Robert, located near the bridge of Cieux. His son Philippe lived there in 1751.

37. 1769-03-31; letter by the abbé Le Loutre addressed to the secretary of State with the Navy, Praslin, AN Col. C[11] A, vol. 125, fo. 578 (available on line at http://www.archivescanadafrance.org). Also see Lemoyne to Terray, December 1773, BM Bordeaux, Ms. 1480, fo. 536.

38. Many Acadian families went to Jersey in 1773, undoubtedly to join the settlements of the Robin brothers in Gaspésie (*cf.* the letter of the Commissioner of the Navy, Antoine-Philippe Lemoyne to Bertin, Director of the Bureau of Agriculture (a branch of the General Control of Finances], April 18, 1773, AN H[1] 1499[2] and the articles on Charles Robin and on Jean-Baptiste Robichaux in the *Dictionnaire biographique du Canada*).

39. Francis Legge, governor of Nova Scotia, to count Dartmouth, Secretary of State of the American colonies, from Halifax, August 20, 1774, *RAPC 1905-II*, p. 294.

40. The statements of Honoré Caret and Pierre Landry come from the "Transcript of the arrest of Honoré Caret and Pierre Landry," July 15, 1768, AD Ille-et-Vil. 7 B 25.

41. "Hundred: . . . is also said of a certain fixed and regulated weight that one often calls *quintal*. It is composed of one hundred pounds, the pound more less strong depending on the places" (Jacques Savary de Bruslons, *Dictionnaire universel de commerce, d'histoire naturelle et des arts et métiers*, Paris, 1742).

42. In May, 1767, Anselme Boudereau declared to the employees of the farm "that his tobacco was sold at 27 *sols* a pound, as soon as payment was made" (Indictment of the prosecutor of the farm of Saint-Malo against Anselme Boudereau, Saint-Malo, May 22, 1767, AD Ille-et-Vil. 7 B 25).

43. Christophe Aubert, *La contrebande du tabac, op. cit.*, pp. 39-40.

44. Aubert provides the example of two men and two women taken while engaged in this activity. They then stated that they were paid 30 *sous* per day by a certain "La Louison" whose true name they did not know (Christophe Aubert, *La contrebande du tabac, op. cit.*, p. 37).

45. The employees of the farm had seized "three bales of codfish" on the boat of Boudereau (Account of the proceeding brought against Anselme Boudereau by the court of duties of Saint-Malo, May 16 and 23, 1767, AD Ille-et-Vil. 7 B 5). It is quite possible that it was dried or salted cod coming from North America and imported via Jersey, for example by the intermediary of the company of Charles Robin (*cf.* the biography in the *Dictionnaire biographique du Canada*) or again from Saint-Pierre and Miquelon. In the article "fishing" (in Lucien Bély, *Dictionnaire de l'Ancien Régime*), Paul Adam recalls that, "if codfish became in the 19th century the dish of the poor because fresh seafood transported by railroad was too costly, during the Ancien Régime, it was a quality product consumed by the more comfortable classes."

46. However, according to Mr. Péronnet, the prices continued to climb slowly until 1785, and then more quickly (*Le XVIIIe siècle (1740-1820). Des Lumières à Sainte-Alliance*, Paris, Hachette, 1998, p. 51).

47. J = Judgment; CP = file of criminal procedure (for "rebellion"); the criminal files contain very many pieces; I = Interrogatory(s); R = Indictment (*réquisitoire*).

48. The judgment at no time specifies any condemnation and "dismisses [the farmer's] complaints for incapacity." It therefore seems as if the Acadians were not condemned to pay a penalty.

49. Jean Thibaudeau and his wife were both condemned, but Étienne Terriot was acquitted, for lack of proof.

50. Anselme Boudereau was not, in fact, taken, and it seems that the employees of the farms were unsuccessful in proving that the merchandise belonged to him.

51. See Péronnet, *op. cit.*, p. 53, as well as Méthivier, *Le siècle de Louis XV, op. cit.*, p. 13. Many texts mention the high price of bread starting in the years 1768 (1768-01-23); ANC, MG6 C3 [Mi 12881, 3rd reg., pp. 13-14)] Arch. of the port of Cherbourg (minutes of the letters addressed by the Comm. of Divisions)); letter from Praslin to Averdy (1768-08-26; BM Bordeaux, Ms. 1480, fo. 25-28).

52. Daniel Roche gives as an example of the variance of the imposition in the election of Sens, where taxes imposed varying from 5 percent to 53 percent (*La France des Lumières*, p. 260 and following, p. 262).

53. Zysberg, *La monarchie des Lumières, op. cit.*, p. 89.

54. Zysberg, ibid., p. 296.

55. In this work, Necker demonstrated the geographic inequality of the taxes: "when the Normans paid an average of 29 *livres* per year for all of their contributions, the Bretons only paid 12.5 *livres*" (Zysberg, ibid., p. 411). The Acadians were aware of these differences. This was perhaps one reason that explains their reticence to go to Poitou or to Limousin. In answer to the proposals of settlement in Limousin, the Acadians addressed many questions all involving the taxes (1772-10-31c; "Mémoire des Acadiens pour M. de Saint-Victour," BM Bordeaux, Ms. 1480, fo. 186).

56. Morineau, "Alimentation," Lucien Bély, *Dictionnaire de l'Ancien Régime*.

57. Ibid. Another study, by Daniel Roche, indicates similar results (*France des Lumières, op. cit.*, p. 555). The Acadian Jean-Baptiste Semer wrote to his father that upon his arrival in Louisiana "one gave [the Acadians] one and a half pound of bread, and meat to pregnant women or those nursing children and to the sick" (1766-14-20; AN Marine B3, vol. 568, fo. 319ss). The quantities mentioned by Jean-Baptiste were certainly daily amounts.

58. Daniel Roche shows the difficulty in estimating the average consumption of meat and bread in Paris. The estimates of R. Philippe show that the bread supplied about 50 percent of the alimentary ration, "but only one sixth of the expense of subsistence." Daniel Roche emphasizes, moreover, the uncertainty of the calculations based on estimates of the Parisian population that were themselves uncertain (*France des Lumières*, p. 558).

59. 1759-05-10; SHM Brest 1 P1/23 piece 7.

60. Zysberg, ibid., p. 63. Lemoyne estimates that between 1767 and 1773, the price of bread tripled.

61. 1775-03-02b.

62. 1759-05-10; SHM Brest 1 P1/23 piece 7.

63. According to the *Dict. Acad.*, in Paris a pound was worth 12 ounces. Four ounces of vegetables therefore were the equivalent of a third of a pound of vegetables, or about 150 g, and 2 ounces of rice was 1/6 pound of rice (75g). (*Cf.* the article: "depot de mendicité" by Jean Imbert in Lucien Bély, *Dictionnaire de l'Ancien Régime*).

64. "Ordinance of the king bringing an injunction to the officers of the Troops serving heretofore in Canada, to withdraw in two months to the province of Touraine, there to enjoy the treatment that has been relegated to them by his Majesty," March 24, 1762, MAE, Fonds Divers, Amérique, 10, piec 354.

65. On this subject, see my article "Des "pieds-blancs" venus du froid? Les réfugiés canadiens à Loches et en Touraine à la fin du XVIIIe siècle," *Les Amis du pays lochois/Société des Amis du pays lochois*, no. 19 (2003 [January 2004], pp. 129-144).

66. 1758-11-21b; SHM Brest 1 P 1/7, piece 201.

67. 1771-05-00b; *RAPC 1905-I*, p. 395.

68. 1759-01-20; AN Col B, vol. 110.

69. 1759-03-10b; AN Col B, vol. 110.

70. 1763-08-01; Jean Ségalen, "L'odyssée de la communauté acadienne de Morlaix," *Les Amitiés acadiennes*, 64, (1993).

71. 1767-02-19; abbé H. R. Casgrain, "Lettres et mémoires de l'abbé de l'Isle-Dieu (1742-1774)," *Rapport des archives de la province de Québec*, 16, 17, 18 (1935-1938), pp. 273-410; 331-459; 147-253 (p. 229s).

72. 1768-01-23; ANC, MG6 C3 [Mi 12881, 3rd reg., pp. 13-14] – Arch. of the port of Cherbourg (minutes of the letters of the comm.. of divisions).

73. 1768-01-26; BM Bordeaux, Ms. 1480, fo. 25-28.

74. 1771-05-00; BM Bordeaux, Ms. 1480, fo. 36-44.

75. Another document from 1759, signed by the intendant of the Navy at Rochefort, affirms, however, that "the rumor is widely spread that he died of hunger" (1759-12-06; SHM Rochefort, 1 E 415, no. 726).

76. 1773-08-04a; AD Vienne 2 J dep. 22, art. 97.

77. 1773-11-30; BM Bordeaux, Ms. 1480, fo. 526-529.

78. 1773-04-20.

79. 1773-04-27; BM Bordeaux, Ms. 1480, fo. 307-312, fo. 165-167 and AN H1 14992..

80. Apart from the specific case mentioned above of the Entremont-Bellefontaine family in Cherbourg who often requested the doubling of their payment so as to not sustain "the humiliation of seeing themselves confused with al of the others [Acadians] who were their vassals or domestics" (1766-12-19b; ANC, MG6 C3 [Mi. 1288], 3rd reg., pp. 3-4] – Arch. of the port of Cherbourg (minutes of letters of the Comm. of Divisions).

81. 1783-07-12; MAE, Pol. Corresp., Spain, vol. 611, fo. 34. At the time when they wrote this petition, the Acadians received no more than 3 *sous* per day and wanted to go to Louisiana, which this "very small pension" did not allow them to do. The Acadians were not in a position to pay for their passage to Louisiana, a voyage that, in 1766, cost at the most 150 *livres* per person according to Mistral (1766-08-12a; AN Marine B^3, vol. 568, fo. 317).

82. 1798-03-17; AGI, PPC, legajo 197, fo. 951, 960, 966, 967, 973.

83. 1798-03-17; ANC, MG6 C3 [Mi. 12881, 2nd reg., p. 11] – Arch. of the port of Cherbourg (minutes of letters of the comm.. of divisions).

84. 1782-11-30; AM Nantes, BB 107 [reg. of deliberation of the municipal council of Nantes, fo. 177vo].

85. This kind of request was fairly frequent during the *Ancien Régime*. One finds many other requests for exemptions from troop lodging in the registers of the deliberations of Nantes, often on the part of individuals designated by the term "Swiss by nationality." To my knowledge, this was the only one coming from an Acadian.

86. There is no indication of the identity of this benefactor.

87. In 1772, Saint-Victour estimated at 200 *livres* a pair of cattle (1772-04-23; BM Bordeaux, Ms. 1480, fo. 109-112); Lemoyne at 250 *livres* the pair (1772-11-18b; BM Bordeaux, Ms. 1480, fo. 191-213); Pérusse at 300 *livres* (1773-02-15c); the actual price of a pair was 180 *livres* in 1764 (purchase

by Le Loutre reported by Lemoyne, 1774-05-06). *Cf.* also *La letter de Bretagne Acadie Louisiane*, no. 54, January 2004, p. 15, which indicates a price, in 1790, of 300 *livres* for two of these animals.

88. 1790-11-15: "Marriage contract of Marguerite Jeanne Boudrot," reproduced by G. M. Braud in *La lettre de Bretagne Acadie Louisiane*, no. 54, January 2004, pp. 11-15.

89. Berryer to de Ruis, 1759-12-144; AN Col B, vol. 110.

90. J.-P. Poussou, "salaries" in Lucien Bély, *Dictionnaire de l'Ancien Régime*.

91. 1759-09-18c; dispensations from Coutances.

92. 1767-05-22; AD Ille-et-Vil. 7 B 25 – 1767.

93. The Winslow order of deportation specifies: "it will be forbidden [to the Acadians] to bring whatever it may be, except portable belongings and the money that they presently possess" (cited in Bona Arsenault, *Histoire de Acadiens*, Montréal, Fides, 1994 (1964). The remarks by La Rochette about the "spoils" of the Acadians on departing from the English ports (1763-05-18; MAE Pol. Corresp. England sup. 13) or concerning signs of wealth that they ostensibly put on (1763-05-26b; MAE Po. Correp. England sup. 13) testify to this. La Rochette wrote regarding the Acadians of Penryn: "they are the most opulent [of the refugees in England]. . . . There are a dozen of them who have show large amounts of money in their pockets." Daniel Roche emphasizes the ornamental aspect of these showings, which could serve as deposits to obtain loans, or be resold for liquidities (*France des Lumières*, p. 81).

94. 1759-12-14; AN Col B, vol. 110.

95. 1773-08-09; BM Bordeaux, Ms. 1480, fo. 500-504.

96. 1774-05-20a; AN Col B, vol. 149, fo. 237.

97. 1773-10-10b; BM Bordeaux, Ms. 1480, fo. 484-486.

98. 1763-03-03; ANC, MG6 C3 [Mi. 12881] – Arch. of the port of Cherbourg (minutes of letters of the comm. of divisions).

99. Laurence Fontaine, "Crédit," in Lucien Bély, *Dictionnaire de l'Ancien Régime*.

100. 1763-07-08a; AM Saint-Malo, BB 49, reg. Ms., fo. 12-13.

101. 1773-11-30; BM Bordeaux, Ms. 1480, fo. 526-529.

102. 1774-01-23a; BM Bordeaux, Ms. 1480, fo. 347-548.

103. 1774-01-23b; BM Bordeaux, Ms. 1480, fo. 548: this is a sizeable sum. At the same period there were around 180 Acadians at Morlais, but we find no indications of the number indebted to this bread maker.

104. 1785-04-05a; AME Pol. Correp. Spain vol. 616, fo. 363.

105. 1785-00-00h; AD Ille-et-Vil. C 2453.

106. "When it was a question of leaving, the Acadians for whom I have so suffered and am so exhausted, joined among themselves to loan me what I needed to pay my debts in France" (1798-03-17; AGI, PPC, *legajo* 197, fo. 951, 960, 966, 967, 973).

107. 1798-03-17; *id.*

108. 1782-08-12; ANC, MG6 A15, series C [Mi F 849] – AD Calvados, C 1022.

109. 1773-04-27a; AN H¹ 1499².

Chapter 10

1. For more details on this portion, refer to my article, "L'invention de la nation? (Re) presentations des Acadiens réfugiés en France (1758-1785)," Études canadiennes – Canadian Studies, no. 58, Autumn 2005.

2. 1772-12-20b; BM Bordeaux, Ms. 1480, fo. 228-231.

3. 1772-12-24; BM Bordeaux, Ms. 1480, fo. 239-245.

4. Edmund and William Burke, *An Account of the European Settlements in America in Six Parts*, 1757 and abbé Raynal, *Histoire politique et philosophique des établissements et du commerce des Européens dans les Deux Indes*, 1770. The two works refer to the deportation of the Acadians and condemn it. On this subject, see J. M. Faragher, *A Great and Noble Scheme: The Tragic Story of the Expulsion of the French Acadians from their American Homeland*, New York and London, W.W. Norton and Co., 2005, p. 450s. The work of Raynal in particular was widely distributed in France. Lemoyne possessed a translation of Burke in his library (1793-12-18; BM Bordeaux, Ms. 860 and Ms. 840, fo. 225).

5. The term, quite often spelled "*Accadien*," was sometimes deformed by poorly educated administrators, like the employees of the income farms of Saint-Malo who often substituted the term "*Cadien*." The spelling of the word was haphazard. Thus one finds at Nantes in the Catholic registers "*Acadÿens*,""*Achaïens*," "*Arcadiens*."

6. See the section "Des Acadiens avant tout," pp. 231s.

7. 1759-01-20 and 1759-01-26d. The same expression was also used by a sub-delegate (1776-03-21; ANC, MG6 A15, series C [Mi. F 849] – AD Calvados, C 1021).

8. 1772-12-28a; BM Bordeaux, Ms. 1480, fo. 246-247).

9. "They are corrupted little by little, they are also as hateful ("*Mauvais*," not good, worth nothing in its field" *Dict. Acad.*) today as the people of the country."

10. 1773-01-19; BM Bordeaux, Ms. 1480, fo. 251-252. The examples above are only provided by indicative title.

11. *Dictionnaire de l'Académie*.

12. 1763-11-20; AD Ille-et-Vil. C 5156.

13. 1763-03-17; 1765-02-11; 1785-04-25.

14. 1774-05-08°; ANC, MG6 A15, series C [Mi. F 8449] – AD Calvados, C 1019.

15. The word is used by Ruis, 1759-12-06; Berryer 1759-12-14 who, repeats the term of Rus; Choiseul, but it is not definite in this case that the term applies to the Acadians, 1763-06-202; and finally by Lemoyne (1773-10-26).

16. *Dictionnaire de l'Académie*.

17. See pp. 180-81; the administrators spoke of the Acadians "domiciled" in a town or a particular region.

18. "Fugitives:" 1767-01-12; MAE, Mem. & documents, England, vol. 47, 13. This term is used, significantly, by the States of Brittany at the time of the reconstitution of the civil status of the Acadians.

19. Praslin wrote that the Acadians were "non-domiciled" and "in storage" at Saint-Malo and that for this they should not be subject to the bourgeois guard (1767-07-21b; AN Col B, vol. 127, fo. 289).

20. Lemoyne reported: "that which stops many gentlemen is the fear of entrusting their goods to strangers . . . and the little security [from?] these people having nothing to add" (1772-07-10; BM

Bordeaux, Ms. 1480, fo. 97-102).

21. 1773-02-00; AN H¹ 1499², fo. 649.

22. Between 1.57m and 1.87m, the foot varied from 30 to 35cm depending on the place and one foot was a dozen inches.

23. 1774-05-20b; BN, Joly de Fleury no. 1722, Commerce & Colonies, fo. 187-191. Also see an extract where the physicality of the Acadians was compared to the Poitevins, p. 219.

24. 1901-09-17; AD Ille-et-Vil. 5J 138. Remarks by father Le Gallen recalled by Henri Bourde de la Rogerie at Belle-Île.

25. On the question of depopulation, apart from the section above, see Carol Blum, *Strength in Numbers: Population, Reproduction and Power in Eighteenth Century France*, Baltimore, Johns Hopkins University Press, 2002.

26. The following documents, particularly, state that the Acadians were not very good workers or not very able: 1759-05-10; 1760-08-17; 1760-08-19b. The following documents call them lazy: 1760-08-19b; 1763-08-22; 1763-09-12; 1767-05-22; 1767-06-05; 1767-10-11c; 1775-04-21; 1776-00-00; 1776-03-09.

27. The following documents state that the Acadians were, on the contrary, arduous: 1763-08-24a; 1763-07-25; 1763-07-11a; able: 1759-02-04; able and arduous both: 1763-10-31b; 1763-07-04. One should add to this list the many references to "the industry" and to "the skill" of the Acadians at the time of the settlement at Belle-Île-en-Mer, as well as the many cases where the Acadians were very favorably compared to the local populations.

28. 1760-08-12; SHM Brest 1 P 1/8 1760 piece 129 and SHM Rochefort, 1 E 168 fo. 595.

29. 1760-08-17; AN Marine B³, vol. 547, fo. 131.

30. 1760-08-19b; SHM Brest 1 P 1/8 1760 piece 128.

31. 1759-02-04; AM Saint-Malo, BB 45

32. Letter by comte François Claude Barbier de Lescoët (1763-07-04); Louis Le Guennec, *Les Zbarbier de Lescoët :une famille de la noblesse bretonne*, Quimper, 1991 [1935?], p. 538.

33. 1763-10-31b; AD Ille-et-Vil. C 5156.

34. See the section herein concerning Belle-Île-en-Mer, pp. 58-62.

35. 1763-07-31; AD Ille-et Vil. C 5139. Note that the inspector based his judgment on the letters of Nivernais and the duc d'Aiguillon and not on his own observations.

36. 1772-08-15a; BM Bordeaux, Ms. 1480, fo. 136.

37. 17633-08-24a; Gabriel Debien, "Les Acadiens réfugiés aux Petites Antilles (1761-1791)," *Cahiers de la Société historique acadienne*, 15, 2-3, June and September, 1984, pp. 57-99.

38. 1763-07-11a; ANC, MG6 A15, series C [Mi. F 849] – AD Calvados, C 1019.

39. 1760-08-19b; SHM Brest 1 P 1/8 1760 piece 128.

40. Cluny de Nuis, intendant of Saint-Domingue in 1763, then of Brittany in 1765, would be Controller-General of Finances from May to October 1776. According to Pérusse, he had problems with the Acadians during his stay in Saint-Domingue. Cluny "against whom 12 or 15 Acadian families released in Saint-Domingue when he was intendant there brought serious complaints upon their arrival in France, claiming to have received the harshest treatment; he could not hear the Acadians spoken of without feeling emotion and anger" (1777-02-00; AD Vienne 2 J dep. 22, art. 97). In a later letter, the marquis did not hesitate to describe Cluny as "the most cruel enemy that the Acadians pos-

sibly had" (1777-03-15; *id.*). On the attempts to settle the Acadians in Saint-Domingue, see chapter 3 of the thesis of Christopher Hodson, *Refugees, op. cit.*

41. 1763-08-22; SHM Rochefort, 1 E 593.

42. 1763-09-12; AN Col B, vol. 117, fo. 405: Choiseul nonetheless conceded in the same letter that the Acadians were very industrious, that is to say, skillful, according to the *Dict. Acad.*

43. 1765-10-22; J.-M. Fonteneau, *Les Acadiens citoyens de l'Atlantique, op. cit.*

44. 1767-06-05; ANC, MG6 C3 [Mi. 12881, 3rd reg., p. 8] – Archives of the port of Cherbourg (letters by Defrancy, from March 1st, 1763 to April 2, 1768).

45. 1767-10-11c; AN Marine B^3, vol. 576, fo. 42.

46. Some months previously, in an indictment against an Acadian accused of tobacco fraud, the "Prosecutor of the general adjudicator of the farms of the king having a monopoly of the sale of tobacco," had already become disturbed by this (1767-05-22, AD Ille-et-Vil. 7 B 25 – 1767).

47. 1773-04-26; BM Bordeaux, Ms. 1480, fo. 312-318. Lemoyne to l'Isle-Dieu.

48. 1773-05-13a; BM Bordeaux, Ms. 14480, fo. 319-326 ("Mémoire historique," Lemoyne to Terray).

49. The *Dictionnaire de l'Académie* defines "morals" thus: 1. Natural customs acquired for good or bad, in all that regards the conduct of life […]. 2. Referring also to the manner of living, that is inclinations, customs, ways of doing things, & the particular laws of each nation," which still corresponds to two contemporary uses of the term.

50. 1759-05-10; SHM Brest 1 P1/23 piece 7.

51. The *chevalier* d'Éon writes: "Our French prisoners . . . have shown far less fidelity to France . . . than the unfortunate Acadians who have just left for France, after having surprised all of England with their probity, their morals and their inviolable attachment to the religion and to the king, despite their cruel dispersion and the frightful misery that they have endured until the end with a heroic courage that all Frenchmen should still possess" (1763-06-13a; Roy, *Rapport*, pp. 615-617 – MAE, Pol. Corresp., England, vol. 450, pp. 404-407). Also see the report by Nivernais often mentioned (1763-02-17a).

52. The bishop of Saint-Malo thus thought that the Acadians possessed the finest Catholicity: "*Posso bensi parlare più precisamente sopra la cattolicità di questi abitanti: ella è si perfetta quanto possarle fide*" (1760-05-01; Vatican Archives of the Sacred Congregation of Propaganda – ANC, MG 17 – A 25 – Mi. [orig.] K – 235).

53. We already have mentioned the "purity" of the Acadian morals in the eyes of observers, who found them "vassals to be desired" (1772-08-15a; BM Bordeaux, Ms. 1480, fo. 136). The examples are abundant. Thus, in 1763, one Daumesnil wrote: "those who are in our town especially do no want to be separated. . . . They claim that they would suffer sorrow at such a dispersion, mostly from the fear of a change to their morals the most flattering account of which is made by the duc de Nivernais" (1763-07-20b; AD Ille-et-Vil. C 5156). One finds many other similar references. See, for example: 1774-05-20b; BN, Joly de Fleury no. 1722, Commerce and Colonies, fo. 187-191; "[the Acadians] would be infinitely better off if the contagion of our morals had not spread clouds over the innocence of those who were brought from Canada" (1772-11-17; BM Bordeaux, Ms. 1480, fo. 219-223).

54. On this subject, see the section: "Émigration vers le Poitou," p. 102, in which are reproduced many reports by Pérusse explaining that he wanted to keep the Acadians together to preserve (notably) their pure morals.

55. 1770-00-00b; Abbé de Raynal, *Histoire politique et philosophique des établissements et du com-*

merce des Europeans dans les Deux Indes, 1770).

56. He seems to have drawn the large part of his information from the work of Burke, *An Account of the European Settlements in America in Six Parts*, 1757.

57. See Jean Meyer, Jean Tarrade, Annie Rey-Goldzeiguer and Jacques Thobie, *Histoire de la France coloniale, vol. I, La conquête, des origins à 1870*, Paris, Armand Colin, 1991, note 464.

58. Concerning the belief that climate shapes the character of people, see notably, David A. Bell, "The Unbearable Lightness of Being French," *op. cit.*, pp. 1226-1228.

59. 1773-06-17; BM Bordeaux, Ms. 1480, Appendices, 1st file. L'Isle-Dieu to the Acadians.

60. 1773-04-26; BM Bordeaux, Ms. 1480, fo. 312-328 (Lemoyne to l'Isle-Dieu); Pérusse also tried to defend the reputation of the Acadians on this point from the same basis (1774-03-23b, AN H[1] 14992, pieces 606 and 655).

61. 1773-05-13a; BM Bordeaux, Ms. 1480, fo. 319-326.

62. 1777-02-00; AD Vienne 2 J dep., art. 97; see also 1775-10-23, 1776-03-09, 1777-03-04.

63. *Cf.* 1772-10-29; BM Bordeaux, Ms. 1480, fo. 157-161 and 1772-09-05; *id.*, fo. 120-124.

64. It surfaced in certain letters exchanged by administrators who were friends, when they allowed themselves to say things in confidence. But these letters rarely leave the conventional frame of generalities about the Acadians, and they reflect the mood of a moment. See for example those from Guillot to Lemoyne or from Pérusse to Blossac.

65. Daniel Roche, *France des Lumières*, section "La Fin des Révoltes."

66. Ibid., p. 290.

67. One finds such an idea in the orders of Berryer, for instance, stipulating that the payment distributed to the Acadians is modest so as to make them industrious.

68. Daniel Roche, *France des Lumières*, p. 294.

69. 1772-05-14; BM Bordeaux, Ms. 1480, fo, 83,

70. 1773-04-27c; BM Bordeaux, Ms. 1480, Appendices, 1st file, fo. 22s.

71. 1772-07-18; BM Bordeaux, Ms. 1480, fo. 102-109.

72. Abbé Coyer, extract from *Dissertation sur la nature du people*, cited by D. Roche, *France des Lumières*, p. 292.

73. 1773-07-24; AD Vienne 2 J dep. 22, art. 124-1.

74. "In France, the feeling was that socially the Acadians were inferior to the native Frenchmen" (Winzerling, *op. cit.*, p. 3, note 1). "Commentateurs après commentateurs évoquent leur stupidité" (Naomi Griffiths, *The Acadian Deportation: Causes and Development*, doctoral thesis, University of London, 1969, p. 240). However, the texts do not make the slightest allusion to any stupidity or idiocy attributed to the Acadians. These words or close synonyms are never repeated in the texts.

75. 1763-07-25; the commission of the domains of the duc d'Aiguillon, July 1763, D Ille-et-Vil., C 5127, cited by Christophe Cérino, in "Les Acadiens à Belle-Île-en-Mer: une experience original d'intégration en milieu insulaire à la fin du XVIIIe siècle," *Annales de Bretagne et des Pays de l'Ouest*, 110, 1 (2003), pp. 115-124.

76. 1763-07-04; Louis Le Guennec, *Les Barbier de Lescoët, op. cit.*, p. 538.

77. 1774-03-26a; AD Vienne 2 J dep. 22, art. 124-1.

78. 1774-05-18a; AD Vienne 2 J dep. 22, art. 97.

79. 1774-05-06; BM Bordeaux, Ms. 1480, fo. 591-595. Lemoyne to Pérusse.

80. 1772-11-17; BM Bordeaux, Ms. 1480, fo. 219-223.

81. It is worth noting that in these pages I am using the term "cultural" voluntarily in its contemporary usage of "that which is related to culture," that is, "the ensemble of intellectual aspects proper to a civilization, a nation" (*Petit Robert*). The adjective "cultural" itself only dates from 1907 according to Alain Rey, *Dictionnaire historique de la langue française*, Paris, Le Robert, 1998 (1992). In order to not over burden the text, I have removed the quotation marks that should frame this word.

82. 1759-09-18a; AD Manche, Saint-Lô, 6 Mi. 252 to 257, file no. 5.

83. "The linguistic unification of France is far from being achieved at the end of the *Ancien Régime*" (Jacques Revel, "Langues et Patois," in Lucien Bély, *Dictionnaire de l'Ancien Régime*). The *Encyclopédie* emphasize that the *patois* [dialect] "was spoken in nearly all of the provinces.... One only speaks the language in the capital." The reader may refer to the map of languages spoken in France in 1789 in D. Bell, *The Cult of the Nation*, p. 16.

84. In the proper sense of "knowledge of traditions, usages and of the popular art of a country, of a region, of a human group," from the English *folklore* (1846) "knowledge (lore) of the people (folk)" (*Petit Robert*). The birth of the term, in the nineteenth century, coincides with the interest then being brought to these questions, which had received little commentary in the eighteenth century.

85. 1764-02-03; AD Ille-et-Vil. C 5156.

86. 1764-02-21; AD Ille-et-Vil. C 5140.

87. At the time of the trials, witnesses were attended by interpreters who translated their statements. Many said that they did not speak French (1764-05-03); AD Finistère [Quimper] 6 B 789, 6 B 191, 6 B 2). During the course of a dispute at Belle-Île between the Acadians and the locals, a priest played the role of mediator "in Breton and in French" (1767-03-07; Jean-Marie Fonteneaux, *Les Acadiens citoyens de l'Atlantique, op. cit.*, p. 370s). Finally, at the time of her interrogatory, Françoise Huere, wife of Jean Thibaudeau, explained that one of her co-accused, the night of the incident, "spoke a language unknown to her" (1767-11-02b; AD Ille-et-Vil. 7 B 44).

88. Jacques Revel, "Langue et patois" in Lucien Bély, *Dictionnaire de l'Ancien Régime*, quoting a study by D. Norman.

89. "These men who seem most vigorous already suffer from the heat that does not yet affect us" (1759-05-10; SHM Brest 1 P1/23, piece 7).

90. 1763-02-17a; MAE, Pol. Corresp., England, vol. 449, fo. 340*ss*.

91. 1763-04-04; AN Col B, vol. 117, fo. 117. Also see, among others examples, the same arguments repeated in an answer by the Acadians of Saint-Pierre and Miquelon to Perrault in which they mentioned the too-warm climate of Guyana (1764-09-16a; AN Col C^{11} D, vol. 8).

92. De Francy wrote regarding the d'Entremonts, who requested to go to Saint-Pierre and Miquelon, that the climate of this colony suited them better than Cayenne (1764-03-16a; ANC, MG6 C3 [Mi 12881, 2nd reg., P1-1]– Archives of the port of Cherbourg (letters by Defrancy, from March 1st, 1763 to April 22, 1768). Choiseul thought that the Acadians who went to Saint-Pierre and Miquelon, contrary to those who left for Cayenne, should not receive gratification because "they are returning to the climate from which they left" (1763-06-13d; SHM, Rochefort 1 E 172, fo. 479-480).

93. Tropical voyages, before the arrival of modern medicine, were often fatal. The Acadians risked their lives going to Guyana and they were aware of this. The attempt to colonize Guyana, undertaken by Choiseul, was more fatal than the deportation of the Acadians itself. For example, of the nearly 15,000 Europeans sent to Kourou, nearly 9,000 colonists died within some months (Luca Codignola

and Luigi Bruti Liberati, *Storia del Canada dale origini ai giorni nostri*, Milan, Bompiani, 1999, p. 227).

94. On this subject, see the article by Bernard Cherubini, "L'odyssée des Acadiens dans la Caraïbe ou les theories humorales de la créolisation," *Cahiers de la Société historique acadienne*, 26, 1 (January-March, 1995), pp. 5-22.

95. At least at the start of the stay in France, some correspondents later estimated that a certain number of refugees were perfectly well acclimated. Thus, Pérusse thought that the Acadians had more or less become Bretons when he recommended having some individuals leave who "had brought to Poitou everything bad of the Breton spirit" (1774-12-13; AD Vienne 2 J dep. 22, art. 97). According to another witness, the Acadians were acclimated at Caen. An administrator asked that they might end their days "in a country with a climate with which they were familiar and habits with which they were accustomed" (1774-01-15a; ANC, MG6 A 15, series C [Mi F 849] – AD Calvados, C 1020).

96. 1760-01-10; SHM Rochefort 1 E 164, fo. 341 and 347. The Seven Years War was then raging and the English tried to intercept all communication within the French camp. To avoid this problem, while the letters were sent by the traditional maritime route from the Gulf of St. Lawrence, Berryer thought to have duplicates sent by the St. John River to maximize the chances that one of the two copies would reach a good port. A corvette, the *Storck*, was armed for this mission, and many Acadians were recruited to participate in it. Because of the lateness of the season, the mission would be cancelled at the last minute. On the subject of the arming of the *Storck*, see series 1E in the Historical Service of the Navy at Rochefort.

97. 1785-07-13; ANC, MG6 A 15, series C [Mi. F 849] – AD Calvados, C 1022.

98. De Ruis to Berryer: 1759-12-06; SHM Rochefort, 1 E 415, no. 726.

99. 1773-04-27b; BM Bordeaux, Ms. 1480, fo. 318-319.

100. Acadia owes its name to Arcadia in Greece.

101. 1772-11-17; BM Bordeaux, Ms. 1480, fo. 219-223. In a previous letter addressed to Pérusse, Guillot had already written: "raised in a rich and fertile country, our best lands in France are for them hardly to compare to their most mediocre land in Acadia. Thus one will find them always difficult and with no good option" (1772-10-19; AN H^1 1499^2).

102. A young Acadian, who had become an orphan, needing a tutor, the fiscal prosecutor of the area wanted them to submit to going through the customary legal formalities. For various reasons explained in the report, (of which the extracts above provide a summary), the Acadians wanted to be exempted from these legal formalities. Their requests would not be granted.

103. 1773-04-27a; BM Bordeaux, Ms. 1490, fo. 307-312.

104. Warren to Le Loutre: 1764-03-20; Lanco, "Les Acadiens à Belle-Île-en-Mer," *op. cit.*

105. Jean-François Mouhot, "L'influence amérindienne sur la société en Nouvelle-France: une exploration de l'historiographie canadienne de François-Xavier Garneau à Allan Greer (1845-1997)," *Globe. Revue internationale d'études québécoises*, 5, 1 (October 2002), pp. 123-157. This theme returns in five documents: 1763-05-18; 1773-12-00a; 1773-07-22a; 1774-02-00a; 1774-05-06, all but the first of which come from Lemoyne. The Acadians had close contacts with the Micmacs before deportation. In 1758 some Acadians even exchanged English prisoners for allied Micmacs imprisoned by the British (Faragher, *A Great and Noble Scheme, op. cit.*, pp. 400-401). The refugees in France kept their memory of these contacts. The account of Benjamin Boudrot provides testimony of it, for example (1860-03-03; cited in Damien Rouet, "Les Acadiens dans le Poitou: permanence d'une identité," *Études canadiennes: Acadiens, mythes et réalité*, 37, (1994), pp. 145-157) and especially the letter by Marguerite d'Entremont that ends with these words: "Our compliments to all of

the savages that we know" (1773-01-25). Many of these "savages" came to France with the Acadians or the Canadians. Some of them even received the assistance. Thus one finds on a list of aid a certain "Sannesic," aged 39 years and domiciled in Rochefort. The administrator notes that "her quality of being a savage makes her susceptible to the kindness of the King, she is a refugee in France with the Beaubassin family. One proposes granting her 6s per day for life" (1774-03-23a; *RAPC 1905-II*, p. 220).

106. 1763-05-18; ANC, MG 18-F14 (Fonds Papiers de La Rochette), vol. 1, p. 388.

107. *Dictionnaire historique de la langue française*; "BUTIN [Booty]. Money, herds, animals, &c. when one takes enemies […]. When one speaks of wars in our day, booty is only occasionally spoken of as what the soldiers pillage from the enemies" (*Dictionnaire de l'Académie*).

108. 1773-12-00a; BM Bordeaux, Ms. 1490, fo. 536. Lemoyne to Terray: "These men, from childhood, have used tobacco like the savages with whom they lived." In another document, Le Loutre also mentions the use of tobacco from early childhood (Le Loutre to Praslin: 1769-03-31; AN Col C^{11} A, vol. 125, fo. 578).

109. 1773-07-22a; BM Bordeaux, Ms. 1490, fo. 383-394.

110. 1774-05-06; Lemoyne to Pérusse, BM Bordeaux, Ms. 1480, fo. 591-595.

111. 1759-05-10; SHM, Brest 1 P1/23, piece 7.

112. 1772-11-17; BM Bordeaux, Ms. 1490, fo. 219-223.

113. 1776-03-09; AD Vienne 2 J Dep. 22 art. 124-2: Pérusse to Blossac.

114. Transcription of the testimony of Mrs. Papuchon, born Daigle, daughter of Acadians who remained in Poitou, aged about forty years, recovered by Rameau de Saint-Père on the Acadian line, in 1860 (1860-03-03; cited in Damien Rouet, "Les Acadiens dans le Poitou," *op. cit.*, CEA Moncton, Fonds Rameau de Saint-Père, Acadians of Poitou, 2.12-14 [pages]).

115. 1763-07-20a; Report by Louis de la Vergne de Trassan, July 20, 1763, AN Col C^{11} D, vo. 8.

116. 1759-05-10; SHM Brest 1 P1/23, piece 7.

117. 1772-11-17; BM Bordeaux, Ms. 1490, fo. 219-223.

118. 1775-08-12c; AD Vienne 2 J dep. 22, art. 124-1.

119. For a good perspective on these clichés, see: Jacques Mathieu, *La Nouvelle-France. Les Français en Amérique du Nord, XVIe-XVIIIe siècle*, Paris, Sainte-Foy, Presses de l'Université Laval, 2001 (1991), in particular, chapter VII.

120. "I am aware that the singular attachment that these people have for one another makes their separation difficult and the children greatly regret seeing their fathers and mothers dispersed in hospices of charity" (1779-10-06a; ANC, MG6 A15, series C [Mi. F 849] – AD Calvados, C 1021: Sivard de Beaulieu (sub-delegate of Valognes) to intendant from Caen (Esmangart).

Chapter 11

1. The personal letters exchanged by the Acadians are the only documents that come directly from the refugees. But the Acadians only rarely mention the conditions of their life in France. Note that some of the less literate used the intermediary of public writers to draft their personal letters, as demonstrated for example by the letter of Jean-Baptiste Semer (*cf.* the introductory commentaries to this letter in my article, "Une ultime revenante," *Acadiensis. Revue d'histoire de la region atlantique*,

XXXIV, 2 (Spring 2005), pp. 124-129).

2. These intermediaries were most often anonymous. We may they were naval functionaries or benevolent priests. It is very probable that they utilized manuals containing model forms for these letters (the *Secrétaires*).

3. See note 32, pp. 259-60.

4. *Cf.* 1756-07-31; AN Col C^{11}A, vol. 987, fo. 405-406. This was a letter written by the Acadians to their priest. This document was, however, possibly considerably "retouched" by the abbé de l'Isle-Dieu.

5. 1757-09-21; CEA A 6 – 1 – 1.

6. One finds the claim to be "French" in practically all of the letters written by these Acadians (see the transcriptions of these letters in Roy, *Rapport*, p. 617s).

7. 1756-07-31; AN Col C^{11} A, vol. 87, fo. 405-406. Daudin had by then already died.

8. 1763-02-17a; MAE, Pol. Corresp., England, vol. 449, fo. 340ss.

9. 1773-07-22a; BM Bordeaux, Ms. 1480, fo. 383-394.

10. Peter Sahlins, "La Nationalité avant la lettre. Les pratiques de natrualisation en France sous l'Ancien Régime," *Annales. Histoire, sciences socials* (September-October 2000), pp. 1081-1108.

11. 1773-04-27a; BM Bordeaux, Ms. 1480, fo. 307-312.

12. 1772-03-24; BM Bordeaux, Ms. 1480, fo. 89-90.

13. 1774-01-23a; BM Bordeaux, Ms. 1480, fo. 547-548.

14. Daniel Roche, *France des Lumières*, p. 291.

15. 1772-03-24; BM Bordeaux, Ms. 1480, fo. 89-90.

16. 1772-03-24; *id.*

17. 1784-04-04; AGI, PPC, legjo 197, fo. 954.

18. "People" is repeated in all in fifteen documents written by the Acadians.

19. 1783-07-12; MAE, Pol. Corresp., Spain, vol. 611, fo. 34.

20. 1772-03-24; BM Bordeaux, Ms. 1480, fo. 89-90.

21. 1763-10-30; AD Ille-et-Vil. C 5156. The use of the plural in this instance, as above by Alexis Trahan with "Acadian nations" also in the plural, is probably not significant. On the difference to be made between the people and the peoples, see D. Roche, *France des Lumières*, pp. 292 and 287.

22. We find this term in about a dozen documents written by the Acadians, starting in 1763.

23. This word figures in two documents: 1772-10-11a; BM Bordeaux, Ms. 1480, fo. 181-182 and 1773-05-16; SHM Brst 1 P 1/11 (1773), piece 4.

24. The first use, by a refugee, of "nation" to designate the Acadian group is in a petition by Marguerite Granger to an intendant: "It is with the most complete trust that I take the liberty to address myself to your highness, being informed of your justice and your generosity to my nation" (1771-07-20; CEA A9 – 2 – 7 AD Morbihan Series E, Correspondence of Warren). Two years later, a petition written by the abbé de Grandclos Mêlé in the name of the Acadians of Saint-Malo uses this word many times as well as the phrase "national body" (*cf.* 1773-04-27a). Shortly afterwards, it was the turn of a refugee from Morlaix, Alexis Trahan, to use this term curiously in the plural. He wrote to Lemoyne that he regretted to have suffered "misery for having attempted to be useful to the Acadian nations" (1773-05-16; SHM Brest 1 P 1/11 (1773), piece 4). The final occurrence before 1775 comes

from the document wherein Lemoyne wrote that the Acadians had presented themselves to him saying: "you have left it to the leaders of the nation" (1773-07-22a). Of the four occurrences before 1775, two come thus unquestionably from the Acadians, and two were reported by third parties.

25. 1773-04-27a; BM Bordeaux, Ms. 1480, fo. 307-312. All of the extracts hereafter are drawn from this same report.

26. This idea of solidarity and family ties is expressed in other documents: "We recently received a list which has come from *our fathers, our brothers, our first cousins*" (1772-03-24; BM Bordeaux, Ms. 1480, fo. 89-90).

27. The abbé Grandclos perhaps was repeating the usage by Berryer in a letter to the abbé de l'Isle-Dieu, of which he probably possessed a copy: "these inhabitants should not be regarded as natives in France; they are only here in passing" (1759-12-15; AN Col B, vol. 110, fo. 374/313).

28. 1773-04-27a; BM Bordeaux, Ms. 1480, fo. 307-312.

29. Including in the count the expression "national body," but not counting those occurrences in the religious acts. We find "nation" in sixty documents for the period before 1790, but the term is also used to designate other groups than the Acadians, in particular the French and English national groups. Many correspondents often use "English" and "French nation." In the texts consulted, nation sometimes, though rarely, indicates the inhabitants of a province, like those of Limousin (1772-11-03), the Corsicans (1769-08-25b), or even a Canadian (*cf.* "Déposition et rapports faits par un Canadien de nation nommé François Mercier," from 155-12-01). When we eliminate these various uses of the word, there remain thirty-seven documents in which "nation" is used to indicate the Acadians. Of the total of sixty occurrences, twenty documents are previous to 1770, or 33 percent. Of the occurrences just designating the Acadians, we find a total of four documents before 1770 and thirty-three after, or a proportion of about 10 percent of the occurrences before 1770. But we can hardly draw a conclusion from these results as I have selected a certain number of documents precisely because of their use of the term.

30. Or one fourth of those bearing the word "nation."

31. 1773-04-27a; AN H[1] 1499[2].

32. In fact I consulted many more documents than those transcribed in the database, which is only a selection of documents related to my various specific queries (www.septentrion.qc.ca/adaiens). A presentation of the main characteristics is available on the site.

33. With the exception of the abundant documentation regarding Belle-Île in which I was only able to make preliminary searches (AD Ille-et-Vil., Rennes, Series C). The term almost never appears in this series and it is not used with at all the same frequency as in the texts after 1772, where it is repeated much more.

34. Saint-Malo (293 acts), Nantes (80), and Châtellerault (45). The majority of the matrimonial acts of the Acadians have been published by Robichaux in *The Acadian Exiles in Saint-Malo, op. cit.*; *The Acadian Exiles in Nan tes, op. cit.*; *The Acadian Exiles in Châtellerault, op. cit.* Braud found about forty acts supplementary to those collected by Robichaux for Nantes. The acts transcribed by Robichaux are translated into English literally. I have retained the use of the term "of Acadian nationality." I have no information about the use of the term "nation" for the marriages at Boulogne-sur-Mer, Morlaix, and Belle-Île. Regarding Cherbourg, the requests for dispensation of consanguinity never use this term. Finally, at Rochefort-sur-Mer, Jacques Nerrou found no use of the term "of Acadian nationality" in his research (from personal interview).

35. Damien Rouet, "Diaspora et representations, le cas des réfugiés acadiens en France," Études canadiennes, no. 58, Fall 2005) notes the mention in 1754 at Montréal of a man named Dominique

Gallant, "Acadien de nation," in a contract of employment as *voyageur* [commercial traveler]. Rouet adds that he found this term in the parish registers and the notarial acts in Poitou. In one act there is a reference to *Sr.* Charles Hébert and his wife, of "Acadian nationality" (October 1, 1773, the notary De Montigny to Monthoiron; private archives – Vouneuil).

36. Here I have excluded the matrimonial acts from the calculation.

37. Here I add occurrences of "nation" and of "national body," and I do not include baptismal, matrimonial, or burial acts.

38. Information supplied by Jacques Nerrou, to whom I am thankful.

39. The term is repeated twelve times in Albert J. Robichaux, *The Acadian Exiles in Nantes 1775-1785*, Harvey, Louisiana, A. J. Robichaux, 1978. Moreover, G. M. Braud, at my request, undertook research in acts of all kinds (baptisms, marriages and burials) at Nantes. Of around four hundred acts for the parish of Saint-Martin, he found some thirty acts bearing mention of "of Acadian nationality" (email correspondence of April 5, 2005).

40. In a contract of employment of an Acadian at Montréal in 1755, indicated in note 35, as well as in the matrimonial act of Charles Guedry and Agnes Bourg, Saint-Suliac, January 13, 171, "the newly married were of Acadian nationality."

41. The phrase was used by Lescoêt Barbier, administrator working for the States of Brittany (1763-10-31b), by Choiseul (1764-08-10) then by the commission of the States of Brittany (1766-00-00d).

42. Choiseul, in 1764, wrote, for instance: "I would approve if the pregnant Acadian women that you had embark on the ship *Le Postillon* for Cayenne absolutely wanted to remain in France, that you have them along with their husbands replaced by a number of persons from the same nation that you would select from among those who have remained in Morlaix" (1764-08-10; AN Col B, vol. 120, fo. 278).

43. 1778-06-00; Anonymous report, June 1778, MAE, Mem. & doc., England, 47, fo. 18-28, piece 7.

44. 1769-08-25c and 1771-05-00a; BM Bordeaux, Ms. 1480, fo. 36-44.

45. 1771-05-00a; BM Bordeaux, Ms. 1480, fo. 36-44/26.

46. "I am taking the liberty to address your highness, being informed of your justice and your generosity for my nation" (1771-07-20; CEA A9 – 2 – 7 – AD Morbihan Series E, Correspondence of Warren).

47. 1772-10-23b; 1772-10-31b; 1772-11-17.

48. 1772-10-19; AN H^1 1499^2. Ménétra uses practically the same expression (*Journal de ma vie, op. cit.*, p. 197).

49. 1773-02-15a; BM Bordeaux, Ms. 1480, fo. 270-286.

50. 1773-04-27a; BM Bordeaux, Ms. 1480, fo. 307-312.

51. 1773-05-13a; 1773-07-21c; 1773-10-12b; 1773-05-16. Moreover, if one believes the testimony of Lemoyne, it is as a "nation" that the Acadians presented themselves to him at Saint-Malo (1773-07-22a).

52. 1775-05-13a; AD Vienne 2J dep. 22, art. 124-1.

53. 1778-03-01; ANC, MG6, A15, series C [Mi. F 849] – AD Calvados, C 1021 and 1778-04-25; AN Col F^{2}B Commerce of the colonies – MG1 18, vol. 3, carton 6, series F2B (transc., Mi. C – 3056).

54. 1784-06-26a; MAE Pol. Corresp., Spain, vol. 613, fo. 108.

55. Christopher Hodson, *Refugees: Acadians and the Social History of Empire, 1755-1785*, doctoral

thesis (history), Northwestern University, 2004, chapter 5; Gail Bossenga, "Status, Corps and Monarchy: Roots of Modern citizenship in the Old Regime," in Robert Schwartz and Robert Schneider, ed., *Tocqueville and Beyond: Essays on the Old Regime in Honor of David D. Bien*, Newark, Univesity of Delaware Press, 2003; David Bell, *The Cult of the Nation in France, op. cit.*

56. G. M. Braud notes that the role of the priests was important, since practically all of the acts using the term "of Acadian nationality" were drafted by the same parish priest, "principal propagandist" of the phrase according to Braud (email of April 5, 2005). Of thirty occurrences of "Acadian nationality," twenty-four are from this parish priest and three from his vicar. In the other parishes, the phrase is practically unused.

57. Jacques Godechaut, "Nation, patrie, nationalisme et patriotisme en France au XVIIIe siècle," *Annales historiques de la Révolution française*, 43 (1971), pp. 481-501 (p. 491).

58. One finds it first in a petition (1773-04-27a; BM Bordeaux, Ms. 1480, fo. 307-312), then in many letters by Guillot and Lemoyne.

59. Pérusse uses the word "nation" or the expression "national body" in ten of his letters, and we find at least one use in a notarial act (cited above in note 35, pp. 325-26.

60. One finds many mentions in the acts of baptisms, marriages, and burials and in the correspondence of the Controller-General relating to the Acadians staying in this town. G. M. Braud, *De Nantes à la Louisiane, l'histoire de l'Acadie, l'odyssée d'un people exile*, Ouest editions, 1994, p. 59.

61. 1786-01-10; AD Ille-et-Vil. C 2453.

62. 1773-07-22a; Lemoyne to the Controller-General Terray, July 22, 1773, BM Bordeaux, Ms. 1480, fo. 383-394: Lemoyne wrote that the Acadians came before him saying, "You have transferred to the leaders of our nation…," but that he interrupted them immediately: "[I] told them that I only knew the Acadians as Frenchmen and not as of a foreign nation, that I regarded them as subjects of the king, submitting to his obedience, and to those that His Majesty commissioned to exercise his authority."

63. 1773-02-15a; Commentaries by Lemoyne in the margin of a report by Pérusse, "Idée de l'établissement propose pour 2000 Acadiens sur ses terres" from February 15, 1773, BM Bordeaux, Ms. 1480, fo. 270-286 and *id*, appendices, 1st file.

64. Bougainville to his brother, November 7, 1756 (transc.), Musée de la civilization, dep. of the Seminary of Québec, Henri-Raymond Casgrain collection, P14/0-0415, p. 13.

65. Peter Sahlins, *Unnaturally French: Foreign citizens in the Old Regime and After*, Cornell University Press, January 2004; Jean-François Dubost and Peter Sahlins, *Et si on fasait payer les étrangers? Louis XIV, les immigrés et quelques autres*, Paris, Flammarion, 1999.

66. The alien is "the foreigner who lives in a country where he has not become a citizen," according to the *Dictionnaire de l'Académie,* 4th edition, 1762.

67. See Peter Sahlins in "La Nationalité avant la lettre. Le spratiques de naturalization en France sous l'Ancien Régime," *Annales: Histoire, sciences socials* (September-October 2000), pp. 1081-1108.

68. The Acadians who chose to leave Acadia before 1755 showed the greatest desire to return. Some were refugees at Île-Royale, but the deportees from this island were indemnified in France less generously than the properly called Acadians. There was thus a certain paradox, that does not seem to have struck the contemporaries, that it was *a priori* the most faithful subjects of the king – those, at least, who chose to freely leave Acadia before deportation – who were the least compensated.

69. 1788-00-00; AN Col b, vol. 124. Note also that Lemoyne did not entirely place the two groups on the same level since he made a distinction between the Germans and the Acadians because of the

Protestant religion of some of the former.

70. 1772-07-10; BM Bordeaux, Ms. 1480, fo. 319-326.

71. 1767-10-22; SHM Brest 1 P 1/10 (1767), piece 70 and 1766-11-25; SHM Brest 1 P 1/10 (1766), piece 72.

72. 1767-10-26; AN Marine B³, vol. 572, fo. 138.

73. See for example 1772-04-11b; BM Bordeaux, Ms. 1480, fo. 49-53 and 1773-08-06; *id.*, Appendices, 1st file: Report and letters from 1766 to 1774, fo. 22s.

74. 1763-07-31; 1764-01-27; 1764-02-21; 1764-04-07…, and others. It was also the case of the parish priest of Bangor, Le Sergent (1766-05-00a).

75. Lamy to Warren (1765-03-30a; Lanco, "Les Acadiens à Belle-Île-en-Mer," *op. cit.*).

76. 1774-07-20; AD Vienne 2 J dep. 22, art. 97.

77. 1772-07-01; BM Bordeaux, Ms. 1480, fo. 112-116; "National," as a noun, is not in the *Dictionniare de l'Académie* of 1762 nor in *Trévoux*. The *Dictionnaire historique de la langue française* (DHLF) notes "those in the jurisdiction of a nation receive the name of "national" […] in *1769.*" The text of Saint-Victour dates from 1772, or only three years after the first example of the word in the DHLF.

78. 1772-11-00a; BM Bordeaux, Ms. 1480, fo. 168-172.

79. *Dictionnaire de l'Académie*, 4th edition, 1762.

80. 1759-12-15; Berryer to the abbé de l'Isle-Dieu, December 15, 1759, AN Col B, vol. 110, fo. 374/313.

81. See, for example, his exchanges with Ruis (1759-12-14; AN Col B, vol. 110). which repeat many phrases from the original letter of Ruis (1759-12-06; SHM Rochefort, 1 E 415, no. 726). It is also to be noted that the abbé de l'Isle-Dieu considered that the Acadians were not "of French origin" in a later letter since he mentions "the impossibility in which [the Acadians] would find themselves … in joining … with those of French origin." 1769-03-14; Vatican Archives of the Sacred Congregation of Propaganda, Congressi Series: America Settentrionale, 6 – ANC, MG 17 – A 25 (Mi orig. K – 234).

82. 1763-05-19; Diocesan archives of coutances, May 19, 1763 (AD Manche, Saint-Lô, 6 Mi 252 to 257).

83. 1763-07-11a; ANC, MG6 A15, series C [Mi F 849] – AD Calvados, C 1019.

84. 1773-07-00a; AD Vienne 2 J dep. 22, art. 97.

85. Alain Rey, *Dictionnaire historique de la langue française*, Paris, Le Robert, 1998, 3 vols.

86. 1772-12-00; BM Bordeaux, Ms. 1480, fo. 257-258; 1772-06-01; BM Bordeaux, Ms. 1480, fo. 84-88.

87. 1772-12-00; BM Bordeaux, Ms. 1480, fo. 257-258; 1773-07-20b; BM Bordeaux, Ms. 1480, fo. 379-381. The Families from North America were families coming from Île-Royale and from Canada. The term is very poorly chosen, as the Acadians were also themselves families originally from North America.

88. 1772-11-09; BM Bordeaux, Ms. 1480, fo. 174-177.

89. 1773-04-26; BM Bordeaux, Ms. 1480, fo. 312-318.

90. Lemoyne explains the difficulty that the Acadians had working because of the preference given "to domiciled natives who in this quality should have preference and do in fact have it" (1772-05-09b; BM Bordeaux, Ms. 1480, fo. 77-78).

91. See for example: 1774-05-06; BM Bordeaux, Ms. 1480, fo. 591-595; 1773-06-20a; 1773-09-30a, etc.

92. "This latter arrangement . . . would smooth the way for all the isolated French widows and even for men from Europe who may have married Acadians" (1773-06-20d; Lemoyne to de Boynes). Also see the following letters: 1775-12-26 by the intendant of Caen; 1785-05-03 by Blondel; 174-06-08b by Pérusse).

93. Opposition to "national families," 1772-04-23; then to "national leasing farmers" (1772-07-01).

94. 1768-08-26; BM Bordeaux, Ms. 1480, fo. 25-28.

95. 1772-11-17; BM Bordeaux, Ms. 1480, fo. 219-223.

96. He successively refers to the Acadians as "French" (1773-05-13a), "Acadian French" (1773-05-13a), or "of French origin" (1774-03-00).

97. *Ressortissant* [nationals; those under jurisdiction of a nation] is only used as a noun and in the modern sense in the twentieth century (DHLF).

98. 1773-07-22a; BM Bordeaux, Ms. 1480, fo. 383-394.

99. 1773-01-19; BM Bordeaux, Ms. 1480, fo. 251-252.

100. See for example what the marquis d'Argenson wrote: "Deplorable image of 9,000 Frenchmen who inhabit the portions of Acadian claimed by the English and that they took from us. . . . They want to return to us" (1756-02-18; Marquis d'Argenson, *Journal et Mémoires*, Rathéry, 1864). See also 1773-05-13a; BM Bordeaux, Ms. 1480, fo. 319-326.

101. "The Acadians, of French origin, are only in France because they never wanted to deny the fidelity that they have sworn to hold to the king" (1774-03-00; BM Bordeaux, Ms. 1480, fo. 573-590).

102. 1773-05-13a; BM Bordeaux, Ms. 1480, fo. 319-326.

103. 1772-12-s4; BM Bordeaux, Ms. 1480, fo. 239-245.

104. 1763-02-17a (report by Nivernais).

105. Bureaus of General Control – 1782-04-05; AN F15 3495.

106. 1760-05-11; AN Marine B^3, vol. 547, fo. 121 – Ranché, intendant [of the Navy] at Le Havre, to the minister.

107. 1763-02-17c; MAE, Pol. Corresp., England, vol. 449, fo. 336: Nivernais uses the term "nationals" to designate the French born in France or in the colonies.

108. 1774-05-22a; AN H1 14992: Pérusse to Bertin.

109. 1772-11-00a; BM Bordeaux, Ms. 2480, fo. 168-172; fo. 239-245 and fo. 174-177. The reality of the patriotism of the Acadians is very difficult to evaluate. This desire to be more royalist than the king or more French than the French was perhaps transmitted through the exceptional character—according to various observers—of the devotion of the Acadians to the sovereign. This fervor was observed in particular at the time of the death of Louis XV, while the rest of France welcomed the news with nearly general indifference. The Acadians on this occasion showed a "French sentiment" that was remarked by many witnesses (Pérusse to Bertin, Departmental archives of Vienne J dep. 22, art. 124-1, May 22, 1774; Affiches of Poitou, July 7, 1774, Municipal Library of Poitiers, B.P. 403, 6 vols. In 4, cited by Ernest Martin, *Les Exilés, op. cit.*, p. 186, note 1).

110. Peter Sahlins, professor at the University of California, Berkeley. From a personal communication (March 2004) following the research in the sources that served him to write his book *Unnaturally French* (*op. cit.*), including around six thousand letters of naturalization (delivered between

1660 and 1789) preserved at the National Archives in series 01. *Idem* for the file AN M 1031 of the ministry of the Navy that contains about eighty letters of naturalization of colonists (practically all from the Antilles).

111. Nonetheless, if the Acadians were considered to be under British jurisdiction, which nothing indicates, the *Encyclopédie* specifies that "the English are exempt from the law of aliens, at least for what involves movable property, by virtue of article 13 of the treaty of Utrecht" (*Encyclopédie, ou dictionnaire raisonné des sciences, des arts et des métiers*, Paris, 1751; article "Aubain" [alien]).

112. 1778-03-13; MAE, Control of foreigners, 21.

113. *Cf.* 1766-08-00; AN Col B, vol. 124.

114. 1774-03-00; BM Bordeaux, Ms. 1480, fo. 573-590 and 1773-01-15; BM Bordeaux, Ms. 1480, fo. 249-250. *Cf.*, Chapter VI, p. 125.

115. In fact, even in this case. according to Lemoyne's explanations, what prompted the aid was less the allegiance or fidelity to the king in itself, as it being compensation for losses sustained. This is what explains, for example, the compensation and the more lengthy and thorough pursuits by the Acadians as compared to the Canadians and the refugees from Île-Royale who, according to Lemoyne, were included in the surrender and therefore were able to keep their property (but in the case of Louisbourg, the place having been leveled, the inhabitants evidently were unable to save their homes).

116. 1772-09-05; Lemoyne to Guillot, September 5, 1772, BM Bordeaux, Ms. 1480, fo. 120-124.

Chapter 12

1. 1767-11-09a; AD Ille-et-Vil. 7B44, November 9, 1767: examinations of witnesses in the affair of Jean Thibaudeau, appearing for contraband in tobacco and rebellion against the agents of the farm.

2. The modest origin of these employees is unquestionable: the written reports are often filled with spelling errors and more or less phonetic transcriptions that demonstrate a rudimentary education. They are the only ones, for example, to write "Cadiens" instead of "Acadiens" or "Accadiens," the term used by the "literate" members of the Navy. Also see Christophe Aubert, *La contrebande du tabac devant la juridiction des traites de Saint-Malo au XVIIIe siècle*, report for DEA (diploma in advanced studies), Université de Rennes I, 1991, which provides information on the social origin of the employees of the tobacco farm.

3. 1765-03-30a; Lanco, "Les Acadiens à Belle-Île-en-Mer, *op. cit.*, (Lamy to Warren).

4. 1773-07-26a; BM Bordeaux, Ms. 1480, fo. 402 (Lemoyne to the Controller-General).

5. The elites were indeed convinced that a general hostility against the foreigners prevailed (1763-00-001; AD Vienne 2 J Dep. 22 art. 124-2). Pérusse also explained that the inhabitants of Poitou neighboring his properties did not view his plans for clearing the land favorably, since this would put an end to their use of the communal lands that they had in effect "appropriated."

6. 1772-04-11b; BM Bordeaux, Ms. 1480, fo. 49-53 (Lemoyne to Nardot).

7. 1769-08-25b; BM Bordeaux, Ms. 1480, fo. 33 (Le Loutre to Praslin).

8. 1772-02-08b; BM Bordeaux, Ms. 1480, fo. 80-82.

9. 1773-04-27c; BM Bordeaux, Ms. 1480, Appendices, 1st file, fo. 22s, and 1773-08-06; BM Bordeaux, Ms. 1480, fo. 430-432: Lemoyne to Carvillon.

10. More specifically, the Acadians had received bad press among the Belliois "who did not view them in a good way" (1765-09-06); Lanco, "Les Acadiens à Belle-Île-en-Mer," *op. cit.*, Le Loutre to Warren).

11. 1773-04-27c; BM Bordeaux, Ms. 1480, Appendices, 1st file, fo. 22s. Some time later, Lemoyne repeated almost the same words in another letter (1773-08-06; BM Bordeaux, Ms. 1480, fo. 430-432).

12. 1773-11-30; BM Bordeaux, Ms. 1480, 526-529: Lemoyne to Blossac.

13. Casements: windowed sashes, ordinarily closing, that close a window. Wind shutter: large exterior shutter.

14. 1773-11-30; BM Bordeaux, Ms. 1480, fo. 526-529: Lemoyne to Blossac.

15. 1768-00-00; BM Bordeaux, Ms. 1480, Appendices, 1st file.

16. 1773-04-27c; BM Bordeaux, Ms. 1480, Appendices, 1st file, fo. 22s.

17. 1773-11-30; BM Bordeaux, Ms. 1480, fo. 526-529, Lemooyne to Blossac.

18. 1773-11-30, *id.*

19. 173-07-08a; AM Saint-Malo, BB 49, reg. Ms., fo. 12-13; 1773-04-26; BM Bordeaux, Ms. 1480, fo. 312-318.

20. *Cf.* a document claiming that there were altercations between the Acadians and the locals in 1780 (Rouet, *L'insertion des Acadiens, op. cit.*, appendix III). At the moment of the arrival of the Acadians, Pérusse affirmed that relations were going wonderfully, but it was in his interest to claim that everything was going well (1774-06-04a; AD Vienne 2 J dep. 22, art. 97).

21. 1763-07-24; AM Saint-Malo, BB 49, reg. Ms., fo. 12-13; 1773-04-26; BM Bordeaux, Ms. 1480, fo. 312-318.

22. 1773-04-27c; BM Bordeaux, Ms. 1480, Appendices, 1st file, fo. 22s.

23. 1773-04-27c, *id.*

24. Daniel Roche, *La France des Lumières, op. cit.*

25. 1767-11-05a; AD Ille-et-Vil. 7B44

26. 1767-12-29b; AD Ille-et-Vil. 7B44.

27. 1767-12-30; AD Ille-et-Vil. 7B44

28. 1769-06-11; AD Ille-et-Vil. 7B25-1769.

29. 1767-03-30; AD Ille-et-Vile. 7B44.

30. 1767-11-09a; AD Ille-et-Vil. 7B44 (all quotes below come from this document).

31. This second witness is one Joseph Le Roy sieur de Bourbonnier, "squire, aged 50 years, living in the suburb of Pleudihen, retailing tobacco," probably "Bourbonnier Le Roy," witness to three Acadian marriages at Pleudihen in 1760, 1761, and 1764 according to Robichaux (*The Acadian Exiles in Saint-Malo, 1758-1785*, Eunice, Louisiana, Hebert Publications, 1981). Bourbonnier does not seem to have been an Acadian himself. He testified "that he was unaware of the facts brought by the complaint, but that he had heard it said by individuals whose names he did not know that Etienne Thériault [Terriot], Acadian, had received the money for the tobacco in question when the employees arrived there." As for the mention of money that Terriot had dropped and which was then gathered up by the employees, was this a clever attempt to accuse the employees of embezzling the funds and of blaming Terriot, with whom Bourbonnier seems to have maintained friendly relations? The mention of Terriot's remorse perhaps follows the same logic. But we could also interpret the same document in exactly the opposite sense. The denunciations could also have come from the Acadians.

Caret and Landry, taken in the act of contraband the following year, denounced as an accomplice one "big guy, Acadian" who had once again succeeded in fleeing. It was in fact the same Étienne Terriot (called "Le Gros," the big), who was certainly very busy (1768-07-26; AD Ille-et-Vil. 7B25-1768). On the same subject, we may note as a sign of solidarity among the refugees that none of the witnesses charged in the affairs were Acadian (except for Caret and Landry). To the contrary, the Acadians clearly closed their ranks and kept together. For example, all of the witnesses cited by Anselme Boudereau in his defense in another affair were Acadians. Similarly, when an Acadian was arrested, he was systematically accompanied by other Acadians, and sometimes exclusively by Acadians. Jean Thibaudeau, for example, was said to be accompanied by eight or nine of his compatriots. Moreover, the Acadians seem to have been physically "solid" and were reputed to act as a "band." The wife of Jean Thibaudeau, who was not herself an Acadian, thus threatened the employees of the farm with an attack by a "band of Acadians and people who would be going to the first mass" (1767-03-30; AD Ille-et-Vil. 7B44).

32. 1772-02-08a; BM Bordeaux, Ms. 1480, fo. 1 (Lemoyne to de Boynes).

33. D. Rouet made calculations of the group remaining in Poitou after the departure of the majority of the Acadians to Nantes. In the first part of his work, Rouet presents estimates of the proportion of mixed marriages in the population of the refugees during the stay of the Acadians in France (*L'insertion des Acdiens dans le Haut Poitou, op. cit.*, pp. 40-43). But Rouet provides mistaken estimates coming from the transcriptions of the lists of embarkation to Louisiana. He writes that "the study of the lists of the Acadians who left France for Louisiana in 1785 . . . indicates that nearly 10% were composed of mixed couples" (p. 43). But, it is hard to see how he could arrive at such a number, since, after having let the Frenchmen married to Acadian women leave on the first three ships, the government then prohibited such couples from emigrating. In these circumstances the calculations from the aforementioned lists could not be representative since there was an exclusion of a portion of the mixed families. Braud, too, was specifically interested in the question in his last work (*Les Acadiens en France, op. cit.*). With the exception of these two books, the genealogists who have published the lists of Acadian marriages in France have never made statistical calculations of this subject.

34. In many cases, the marriages were actually remarriages. G. M. Braud has stated that a good proportion of the unions at Saint-Malo and at Nantes were in fact remarriages (e-mail from G.M. Braud of January 16, 2004). Thus, at Saint-Malo and the region, 100 marriages of 293, or practically 1 in 3, involved widows or widowers. Of the 100 marriages involving widows or widowers, 84 were intermarriages among Acadians, and only 16 were with persons on site. In this case, widows and widowers were therefore more susceptible to remarrying within the interior of the group, perhaps because of their more advanced age than the average of the other marriages. At Nantes, the respective proportion of remarriages was a bit more balanced.

35. Gérard Marc Braud, *Les Acadiens en France, Nantes et Paimboeuf, 1775-1785*, Ouest Edition, 1999. It would also be possible to go further in the analysis of these marriage acts, for example, by closely examining the names of the witnesses. This was the sort of analysis done, for example, by Monique Le Faucheux in an article dedicated to the Acadians of Saint-Suliac, a parish some kilometers to the south of Saint-Malo ("Mes ancêtres d'Acadie: les "hors-venus" à Saint-Suliac [Ille-et-Vilaine], 1764-74," *Cercle genealogique d'Ille-et-Vilaine*, 1, 1 [1st trimester of 1987], pp. 10-14). In this parish, she shows that, not only were there no mixed marriage between Acadians and Bretons between 1759 and 1774, but that, "in the religious ceremonies, the witnesses were Bretons for the Breton ceremonies and Acadians for the Acadian ceremonies."

36. One finds at Rochefort mainly the inhabitants and soldiers from Louisbourg. A great number of these individuals were not originally from Acadia and did not descend from the pioneer families, "frequenters in Acadia," as they said then. It is said that a large number of former inhabitants of Cape Breton contracted marriages with the soldiers, often born in France but many of whom no doubt

had to serve defending the fortress of Louisbourg or were assigned to the service in other colonies. This is why the calculation that I have done for this port is undoubtedly the most arbitrary and least representative and to be taken with the greatest precaution. In the other places, the mixture between Acadians and Louisbourg residents was much less.

37. Braud conducted a survey of the 467 marriage certificates in the three parishes of Nantes for the period 1775-1785. Of the total, 324 individuals, or 70 percent, were clearly identified as Acadians. On the other hand, in 143 certificates, or 30 percent, there is no mention of their origin, but one may be certain, from various verifications, that that they were indeed Acadians. The inscriptions mentioning "Acadian," "Canadian," "Cayun," etc., evidently depend on the judgment of the priest. Thus, for example, certain families were explicitly designated as "Acadian" on the birth certificate of a child. But some months later, at the time of the burial of the same child, the same family is no longer designated by this adjective. It seems that there was some decrease in the frequency of the mention of "Acadians" in the documents of the 1780s (e-mail of March 26, 2005).

38. We should note that, often, when the partners were not Acadians, they were soldiers, frequently Swiss or Alsatians and generally came from far away. See Jacques Nerrou and the embarkation lists to Louisiana of Bugeon and Le Faucheux, *Les Acadians parties de France en 1785, op. cit.*

39. Those of Braud, *Les Acadiens en France*, those of Robichaux for Saint-Malo and Poitou, and the embarkation lists to Louisiana of Bugeon and Le Faucheux, *Les Acadians parits en France en 1785, op. cit.*

40. 1761-01-14c, Diocesan archives of Coutances – AD Manche, Saint-Lô, 6 Mi 252 to 257.

41. However, we do not rediscover this couple either in Poitou, in Nantes, nor on the lists of embarkation to Louisiana.

42. Recall that Acadia was unofficially dependant on the bishopric of Québec and that, consequently, the Acadians often said they were from "Île Saint-Jean, [diocese] of Québec."

43. Concerning the calculations made for Nantes, G. M. Braud changed the percentages of marriages that he had calculated for his work that appeared in 1999 (*Les Acadiens en France*). Indeed, this researcher included among the "Acadians" those individuals having only an Acadian mother or father. In his work, he indicated that 59 of the 117 marriages from this community and Paimboeuf were mixed (p. 9). But, in examining these documents more closely, he affirmed that, of the 59 "non-Acadian" spouses of these mixed marriages, ten were in fact themselves children of an Acadian. This is what led him to increase the number of marriages between Acadians and to decrease the number of mixed marriages. No doubt, the proportion of mixed marriages counted in the table reproduced below would decrease to the degree that new information might be collected on the Acadians in France, and as it may be possible to multiply the confirmations of the sources.

44. If we examine more precisely by geographic site, there were only two places where exogamous marriages exceeded endogamous ones, namely Morlaix and Poitou. The exception of Poitou is surely explained by the fact that the marriages celebrated after the departure of the majority of Acadians to Nantes were included in the calculation of data. The small group that remained had an attitude quite different from that of the other Acadians. The "matrimonial market" was probably strongly reduced in the group and many perhaps had no other choice but to marry spouses from Poitou. Between 1776 and the end of 1781, 18 Acadian women were married or remarried in Poitou, and only three selected a spouse from among their compatriots. At the same time, four Acadians took a Poitou wife. Damien Rouet writes: "we notice there a deliberate choice to meld with the local population. From 1776 to 1800, we count in all only 43 marriages, more than half of which were concluded between 1776 and 1781. 90% of these marriages were mixed . . . and, of the whole, 71% joined an Acadian woman and a Poitou man" (*L'insertion des Acadiens dans le Haut Poitou, op. cit.*, pp. 121-122). But to

try to extrapolate on the quantity of Acadian marriages in Poitou after 1776 makes little sense: necessity became the law and the Acadians hardly had the choice of marrying within the group because of the numeric scarcity remaining and the prohibitions of consanguinity.

45. Endogamous marriages: between two Acadians.

46. Exogamous marriages: one of the partners was not Acadian.

47. Number of dispensations of consanguinity or of affinity granted of the total of the marriages. Calculations come from the works of Robichaux.

48. Number of marriages among Acadians.

49. Proportion of marriages between Acadians with relation to the total marriages (percentages rounded off).

50. Proportion of mixed marriages.

51. Number of marriages of type A (an Acadian woman and a Frenchman).

52. Number of marriages of type B (an Acadian man and a French woman).

53. Total number of mixed marriages (sum of types A + B).

54. Proportion of marriages of type A in relation to the total of mixed marriages.

55. Proportion of marriages of type B in relation to the total of mixed marriages.

56. Proportion of mixed marriages in relation to the whole group of marriages (mixed + non-mixed).

57. Other data was sent to me by Gérard Scavennec (February 23, 2004). After discounting the marriages, we obtain nearly the same results as those given above by another source; of a total of 33 marriages counted at Belle-Île-en-Mer between 1765 and 1786, I count 6 inter-Acadian marriages and 27 mixed marriages. On the other hand, Christophe Cérino estimates at only 15 percent the ratio of mixed marriages for the period 1769-1789. This is probably a mistake ("Les Acadiens à Belle-Île-en-Mer: une experience originale d'intégration en milieu insulaire à la fin du XVIIIe siècle," *Annales de Bretagne et des Pays de l'Ouest*, 110, 1, 2003, pp. 115-124).

58. Eleven marriages between 1761 and 1785, but 9 of the 11 were contracted between 1761 and 1764.

59. Partial data. Braud only researched up to the letter M.

60. Note by G.M. Braud: "Of the 42 Acadian women who married Frenchmen or foreigners, only 3 went to Louisiana. While the 17 Acadian men who married French women all brought their wives to Louisiana and followed their people to this new exile. Moreover, of the 58 wholly Acadian couples, married at Nantes/Chantenay, 11 remained in that town, some of whom after the death of their spouse (or 20 percent). It was only starting in 1781/82 that mixed marriages became common, while before this date, the Acadians married amongst themselves.

61. Data from the book corrected by the author, G.M. Braud (January 2004); personal communication. Variation from the period: 1775-1781: majority of Acadian marriages. 1781-1785: majority of mixed marriages (note by Braud).

62. Practically all of the Acadian women who married young Frenchmen at the start of the colony of Poitou remained on site and founded families (25 of 28). Damien Rouet notes—for the period after the departure for Poitou: "From 1776 to 1800, we count in all 43 marriages, most of which were contracted between 1776 and 1781; 90% of these marriages were mixed . . . and, of the whole, 71% joined an Acadian woman to a man from Poitou" (Rouet, *op. cit.*, pp. 121-122).

63. 24 of these marriages (of 45) occurred between the summer of 1776 and 1785, thus after the

departure of the majority of the group to Nantes.

64. Monique Le Faucheux ("Mes ancêtres d'Acadie: les 'hors-venus' à Saint-Suliac (Ille—et-Vilaine), 1764-74," *Cercle généalogique d'Ille-et-Vilaine*, vol. 1, no. 1 (1st trimester 1987), pp. 10 to 14) notes that she found no mixed marriage at Saint-Suliac for the period 1764-1774, in contrast to other villages of la Rance.

65. Included in the total are thirty marriages of "non-Acadian" inhabitants of Louisbourg.

66. There were probably other marriages among the Acadians dispersed in other ports, but their number could hardly be sizeable. For La Rochelle, it is possible to make an estimate from documents produced by the Cercle généalogique of Aunis-Saintonge and reprinted in the appendix of J.S. David, *Essai de comparaison du sort des réfugiés acadiens et canadiens de 1758 à 1798 dans les ports de Rochefort, La Rochelle et de Nantes*, master's thesis (history, Université de La Rochelle, 1999 (List of descendants of the colonists who married at Saint-Louis-de-Rochefort (1999) and Canadians and Acadians married at La Rochelle (1997). There must have been some marriages between Acadians, since dispensations of consanguinity were granted to the bishop of La Rochelle (1769-07-01; MG 17-A25, Vatican, Arch. de la PF, Mi. of orig., K-245.

67. Therefore here I only am considering Boulogne, Le Havre, Cherbourg, Nantes and its region, and Saint-Malo and its region. I am eliminating Belle-Île-en-Mer and Poitou where the Acadians were soon in a minority and probably adopted different matrimonial strategies, for they undoubtedly wanted to remain on site. If we only consider Belle-Île-en-Mer and Poitou, we note that the rate of Acadian marriages was very small (23 percent to 77% percent of mixed marriages). Rochefort being something of a special case, with many inhabitants of Louisbourg who were often not properly speaking Acadians, has also been eliminated.

68. In 1784, there remained only 91 Acadians in Poitou, according to Damien Rouet (*L'insertion des Acadiens dans le Haut Poitou*, p. 121). Practically all of the marriages between Acadians represented in the table following the text were contracted during the two short years of the Acadians' stay at Poitou (1773-1775). Afterwards, practically all of the marriages were mixed. Rouet notes that, between 1776 and 1784, there were 26 marriages of Acadians with spouses from Poitou compared to only two intermarriages (Rouet, *ibid.*, p. 101).

69. Poitou men marrying Acadian women were in the majority orphaned by at least one parent (80 percent of the cases), according to Damien Rouet (ibid., pp. 100-101).

70. Nonetheless, the determinative coefficient (R2 – 0.2153) is slight, indicating that the tendency reflected is barely reliable.

71. The ratios of 45/55 are a flagrant example of a mistaken statistic that falsely gives the impression of uniformity and completely omits the extreme disparity of the ratios depending on the sites.

72. Jean Gaudemet, *Le Mariage en Occident*, Paris, Cerf, 1987; Patricia Seed, *To Love, Honor and Obey in Colonial Mexico: conflicts over Marriage Choice, 1574-1821*, Stanford, 1988. On the rationality of human selections, see for example Jon Elster, *Ulysses Unbound: Studies in Rationality, Precommitment, and Constraints*, Cambridge, 2002).

73. G. M. Braud (*Les Acadiens en France*, p. 9). It is impossible to know, however, if the Acadian women remaining at Nantes were unable to embark because their French husbands did not want to join the Acadian group, or if, on the contrary, the reason that they stayed in France was a prohibition by the French government.

74. If we add the two categories, we find 504 "closed" marriages (385+119), for a total of 652, or a proportion of 77%.

75. *Cf.* 1785-05-20 (AD Ille-et-Vil. C 2453) and 1785-06-05 (AD Ille-et-Vil. C6176).

Epilogue and Conclusion

1. The results of this study are presented in the appendix of volume II of my thesis.

2. So we find at one point those among the Acadians of Nantes who wanted to leave for Acadia or Louisiana, ally themselves against those who wanted to accept being settled in Corsica (according to a report of June 1778 already mentioned: 1778-06-00; MAE, Mem. & doc., England, 47, fo. 18-28, piece 7).

3. The majority of the Acadians were already re-embarked from St. Pierre in October 1767, on the orders of Choiseul, because of the presumed overpopulation of the island. Some of them then went back to Acadia, while a majority would increase the number of refugees in the ports of the kingdom. About three hundred Acadians returned to the archipelago starting in the next year but were again deported in 1778 on the occasion of the new French-English war. About the history of this tormented archipelago, see Michel Poirier, *Les Acadiens aux îles Saint-Pierre et Miquelon, op. cit.*

4. The Acadians at Saint-Malo finally obtained permission from the king to go to Boston in 1786 (1786-07-28; AD Ille-et-Vil. C 2453). But, as the French government refused to pay the expense of their transport, it seems that a limited number of Acadians then went to America. Paul Delaney, "Chronologie des deportations et migrations en Acadie, (1755-1816)," *Cahiers de la Société historique acadienne*, 36, 2-3, summer 2005, pp. 51-136.

5. C. Hodson, *Refugees, op. cit.*; Émile Lauvrière, *La Tragédie d'un peuple, op. cit.*; M.A. Menier, E. Taillemite, G. de Forges, *Inventaire des Archives coloniales. Correspondance à l'arrivée en provenance de la Louisiane*, vol. II, Paris, Archives nationals, 1983; 1765-02-25, 1765-04-30a, 1765-04-30b; 1766-04-20 (AN Marine B^3, vol. 568, fo. 319ss); 1766-08-12a (AN Marine B^3, vol. 568, fo. 317).

6. 1766-04-20; AN Marine B^3, vol. 568, fo. 319ss.

7. 1766-09-13; AN Col. B, vol. 125, fo. 450vo.

8. Carl. A. Brasseaux, "Phantom Letters: Acadian Correspondence, 1776-1784," *op. cit.*

9. Émile Lauvrière, *La Tragédie d'un peuple, op. cit.*, 1924, vol. II, p. 209.

10. M. A. Menier and others, *Inventaire des Archives coloniales, Correspondance à l'arrivée en provenance de la Louisiana*, vol. II, *op. cit.*, p. 593.

11. Just before the revolt of 1768, Le Loutre made reference to his approach to the Minister of the Navy and the Controller-General to obtain either a settlement in France, or the authorization to allow the Acadians to leave to go to Spain, probably implying Louisiana (Joseph-Marie Lanco, "Les Acadiens à Belle-Île-en-Mer," *op. cit.*). Le Loutre later explained that the minister always refused the authorization that the Acadians requested (1771-05-00a; BM Bordeaux, Ms. 1480, fo. 36-44).

12. 1772-03-24; BM Bordeaux, Ms. 1480, fo. 89-90.

13. 1772-11-22; *id.*, fo. 217-219.

14. 1773-07-22a; *id.*, fo. 383-394. A month later, Lemoyne wrote that the Acadians wanted to leave in large numbers to Saint-Domingue, Miquelon, and to the Mississippi (1773-08-16a; *id.*, fo. 423-425).

15. 1775-08-30b; AD Vienne 2J dep. 22, art. 124-1; 1775-11-26b; AD Vienne 2J dep. 22, art. 124-1. Pérusse especially sought to create problems for the Acadian.

16. 1778-01-04; AD Ille-et-Vil. C6176. The instructions of Necker were then to disperse the Acadians within the kingdom. LeBlanc and twenty families opposed the plan and asked to go to Louisiana;

ninety families (450 individuals) wanted to remain at Nantes, forty families (200 individuals) to go to Saint-Pierre and Miquelon, thirty-five families (160 individuals) wanted to return to Saint-Malo, ninety families wanted to go to Guyana, and, finally, some families requested to go to Le Havre, to remain at Paimboeuf, or to await the return of a husband gone to sea before deciding.

17. 1777-10-17; AN Col B, vol. 161, fo. 429.

18. 1778-01-00; MAE, Mem. & doc., England, 47, fo. 18-28, piece 7.

19. 1782-04-05; AN F^{15} 3495.

20. 1778-06-00; MAE, Mem. & doc., England, 47, fo. 18-28, piece 7.

21. 1782-04-05; AN f^{15} 3495.

22. Poirier, *Les Acadiens aux îles Saint-Pierre et Miquelon, 1758-1828*, Editions d'Acadie, 1984.

23. 1782-11-30; AM Nantes, BB107 (deliberation registers of the municipal council of Nantes, fo. 177°).

24. 1798-03-17; Report of Olivier Terriot, AGI.

25. Marriage certificate of July 22, 1777, found by G.M. Braud at Nantes (personal communication). In this certificate Peyroux declares himself aged thirty-four and affirms his noble origin. The act attests that Peyroux was born at Mortagne sur Sèvre. The intendant of Brittany told the Controller-General that Peyroux "is not Acadian" and that his wife, Prudence Rodrique, was a native of Nantes (1764-07-05; MAE; Pol. Corresp., Spain, vol. 613, fo. 232).

26. Fabrice Abbad, "Des Nantais au service du roi d'Espagne: l'émigration acadienne en Louisiane en 1788," *Le Canada atlantique. Actes du Colloque de Nantes, 15-16 octobre 1982*, Nantes, Association française d'études canadiennes, 1982, pp. 95-104.

27. 1784-07-05; MAE, Pol. Corresp., Spain, vol. 613, fo. 232.

28. 1784-03-07b; *id.*

29. 1784-07-05; MAE Pol. Correp., Spain, vol 613, fo. 232; 1784-09-13; AHN (Madrid), folder 3885, no. 3, resource 13 of the section Estado, fo. 34.

30. 1782-00-00; AHN (Madrid), folder 3885, no. 3, resource 13 of the section Estado

31. 1800-09-27; AGI, PPC, legajo 217B, fo. 112-113.

32. 1784-07-18; AGI, PPC, legajo 197, fo. 958; Olivier Terriot and Marie Aucoin were married after having obtained a dispensation of consanguinity given by the bishop of Nantes in 1777 (Robichaux, *The Acadian Exiles in Nantes 1774-1785*, Harvey, Louisiana, self-published, 1978); 1798-03-17; Report of Olivier Terriot, AGI. According to information from G.M. Braud, it is possible that Olivier Terriot had been partially educated in a Breton seminary, which would no doubt explain why he was literate and of a higher social status than most of his compatriots.

33. 1798-03-17; Report by Olivier Terriot, AGI.

34. 1783-07-12; MAE, Pol. Corresp., Spain, vol. 611, fo. 34.

35. 1783-07-12; *id.*.

36. 1783-08-08; AGI, PPC, legajo 197, fo. 952.

37. 1783-08-11; MAE Pol. Corresp., Spain, vol. 613, fo. 232.

38. 1783-08-22; *id.*

39. 1784-01-24; AGI, PPC, legajo 197, fo. 953. It was in all likelihood a reference to Benjamin Franklin, who was then on a mission as ambassador to France. This letter is the only document that refers

to negotiations between the Acadians and Franklin.

40. 1784-03-07b; AHN (Madrid), folder 3885, no. 3, resource 13 of the section Estado, fo. 11.

41. *RAPC 1905-II*, pp. 227-228. This petition is very curious because the Acadians were making it understood that the government had offered them the choice of going to Louisiana, to the Mississippi, to Spanish Florida, or to "a country of the continent of Boston." If the authenticity of the petition is not in question, it still remains very unlikely that the French government proposed that the Acadians go to Boston; at the least the Acadians were giving credence to one of the similar rumors that circulated in Nantes whose origin we have said we do not know but that also have proven to be false (*cf.* the letter from Peyroux to Herédia of 1784-03-07b; AHN (Madrid), folder 3885, no. 3, resource 13 of the section Estado, fo. 11). The request by the Acadians of Saint-Malo to go to Boston or to Acadia is also shown in a private letter by Marguerite Landry).

42. 1784-03-07b;; AHN (Madrid), folder 3885, no. 3, resource 13 of the section Estado, fo. 11.

43. 1784-03-07b; *id.*

44. 1784-03-07b; *id.*

45. 1784-03-22; MAE, Pol. Corresp., Spain, vol. 612, fo. 240.

46. 1784-03-22; *id.*

47. 1784-03-24 and 1784-03-26c.

48. 1784-03-26c; AHN (Madrid), folder 3885, no. 3, resource 13 of the section Estado, fo. 11.

49. 1784-04-04; MAE, Pol. Corresp., Spain, vol. 612, fo. 287.

50. 1784-04-04; *id.*

51. 1784-04-08; AHN (Madrid), folder 3885, no. 3, source 13 of the section Estado, fo. 13.

52. In fact, only 31 if we count the names on the petition.

53. 1784-04-08; AHN (Madrid), folder 3885, no. 3, source 13 of the section Estado, fo. 13.

54. 1784-04-08; *id.*

55. 1784-03031b; MAE, Pol. Corresp., Spain, vol. 612, fo. 270.

56. 1784-04-04a and b (*RAPC 1905-II*, p. 228 and MAE, Pol. Corresp., Spain, vol. 612, fo. 286).

57. 1784-04-25; AN F[15] 3495. This decision also authorized payment of the back due supplement for a total of 300,000 *livres*, 180,000 of which was just for the Acadians at Nantes.

58. 1784-04-27; MAE, Pol. Corresp., Spain, vol. 612 (1784), fo. 367.

59. 1784-05-11; *id.*, fo. 21.

60. 1784-05-16; AN F[15] 3495.

61. 1784-04-27b; AHN (Madrid), folder 3885, no. 3, source 13 of the section Estado, fo. 16.

62. 1784-05-27; MAE, Pol. Corresp., Spain, vol. 613 (1784), fo. 88 and 1784-05-27b; AGI, PPC, legajo 197, fo. 956 (letters from Mme. De la Coudrenière and Olivier Terriot).

63. Peyroux violently charged the sub-delegate in a subsequent letter (1784-06-01; MAE, Pol. Corresp., Spain, vol. 613 (1784), fo. 107). The intendant of Brittany, brought into the issue, took up the defense of Ballays in a letter to the Controller-General (1784-07-05; MAE, Pol. Corresp., Spain, vol. 613, fo. 232)_.

64. 1784-06-26c; MAE, Pol. Corresp., Spain, vol. 613, fo. 109.

65. This actual petition was not found.

66. 1784-06-26a; *id.*, fo. 118.

67. 1784-07-05; *id.*, fo. 232.

68. 1784-07-17; AGI, PPC, legajo 197, fo. 957.

69. 1784-07-17 AHN (Madrid), folder 3885, no. 3, source 13 of the section Estado, fo. 21.

70. 1784-07-18; AGI, PPC, legajo 197, fo. 958.

71. 1784-08-01; *id.*, fo. 959.

72. Amounting to a payment of 3 or 6 *sous* per day.

73. 1784-08-00 (extract from the report by Olivier Terriot). The exact date of this misadventure is not known. Two documents mention the episode (1798-03-17; Report of Olivier Terriot, AGI and 1792-04-02; AGI, PPC, legajo 197, fo. 968). The facts probably go back to the summer of 1784, after August 1.

74. 1784-08-10; AHN (Madrid), folder 3885, no. 3, source 13 of the section Estado, fo. 23.

75. François Daigle, Nicolas Albert, François Arebout, Charles Naquin (1784-07-27;; MAE, Pol. Corresp., Spain, vol. 613, fo. 334).

76. 1785-09-04b; AD Ille-et-Vil. C 2453.

77. 1798-03-17; Report by Olivier Terriot, AGI. The official number of Acadians going to Louisiana is estimated in the Spanish documents at 1,574, then 1,596 (1785-10-06; AHN (Madrid), folder 3885, no. 3, source 13 of the section Estado, fo. 63). The real number of persons embarked was different, however, because of added stowaway travelers.

78. See, for example, the authorization of emigration of 1784-05-11b; AGI, PPC, legajo 197, fo. 955. Moreover, Calonne, the Controller-General, expressly wrote after the first departure of the Acadians, that "the Acadians remaining in Brittany . . . continue to receive the supplement of three *sols*" (1785-06-10b; AD Ille-et-Vil. C 2453).

79. 1784-08-16; AHN (Madrid), folder 3885, no. 3, source 13 of the section Estado, fo. 25.

80. 1784-08-16; *id.*

81. 1784-12-19; AGI, PPC, legajo 197, fo. 359-360.

82. Rumors circulated according to which the food rations in Louisiana were insufficient, the local rain and hurricanes had made many people sick, and many refugees had been sold as slaves. The Acadians also wanted to know if the supplemental aid would be continued in Louisiana, and if it would be possible to leave in the summer rather than in the midst of winter (Winzerling, *op. cit.*, p. 122).

83. We read further on in the same report: "those of Nantes, . . . seem divided in two groups, one of which still trusts the views of the government, and the other is still very unsettled in its resolutions" (Ernest Martin, *Les Exilés acadiens, op. cit.*, p. 278).

84. 1784-09-13; AHN (Madrid), folder 3885, no. 3, source 13 of the section Estado, fo. 34. Also see the letter written three days later to Olivier Terriot, and which contains similar information (1784-09-16; AGI, PPC, legajo 197, fo. 963). Peyroux began by explaining that there were only 2,300 Acadians in France instead of 3,000 and that many had gone to Saint-Pierre and Miquelon or "have quickly left this kingdom."

85. Indeed, some days later, Peyroux followed with a "list of Acadian families from the department of Bel-Isle [*sic*]," listing five families (35 individuals) from the island who wanted to emigrate to Louisiana (1784-09-17; AHN (Madrid), folder 3885, no. 3, source 13 of the section Estado, fo. 36).

86. 1784-09-27; AGI, PPC, legajo 197, fo. 961.

87. 1784-10-09; *id.*, fo. 962.

88. 1785-04-05a; MAE, Pol. Corresp., Spain, vol. 616, fo. 363.

89. 1798-03-17; Report by Olivier Terriot, AGI.

90. 1785-03-23; AGI, PPC, legajo 197, fo. 965.

91. 1785-03-23; *id.*

92. 1784-09-27; *id.*, fo. 961.

93. 1784-10-09; *id.*, fo. 962.

94. 1785-04-19b; 1785-03-23; MAE, Pol. Corresp., Spain, vol. 616, fo. 403 and 1785-04-19c; *id.*, fo. 407.

95. 1785-04-19a1785-03-23; MAE, Pol. Corresp., Spain, vol. 616, fo. 403.

96. 1785-05-12; *id.*

97. 1785-05-12; *id.*

98. 1785-05-20; *id.*, C 2353.

99. 1785-06-05; *id.*, C 6176.

100. This was notably the case of a refugee from Morlaix whose sad story is summed up in a later document: "Magdeleine Granger, 50 years old, female. This woman was one of the number of Acadians meant to go to Louisiana with her sister, wife of a very poor man of this town with three children. The latter having disembarked with her family by order of the government. motivated by the fact that her husband was French and could not be part of the settlements that Spain was granting, Magdeleine Granger returned with her sister and, unable to find any resources at her age, was alone and isolated in a foreign country. Today as she has lost this sister she is responsible for the three children whose father is in no condition to provide the necessary help. She strongly requests the supplement of 3[?]s. having for herself and her three wards only her work, and being unable to leave them to once again take up the position of chambermaid that she had previously performed" (1786-08-04; AD Ille-et-Vil. C 2453).

101. Maurice Caillebeau, *Les secours aux Acadiens pendant la Révolution française et leur intérêt pour la recherché genealogique* (unpublished manuscript, CEA, Moncton, 588-1-1, 1978).

102. Oscar William Winzerling, *Acadian Odyssey, op. cit.*, chapter X, p. 152.

103. Concerning the prohibition to emigrate, Winzerling only substantiates his statement with a letter by d'Asprès of December 24, 1785 (d'Asprès to Aranda, Paris, December 24, 1785, Estado-Legajo 3885 [13], carta 70, AHN). In this letter the Spanish consul at Saint-Malo asserts that, among nearly 250 Acadians returning after a short time from Miquelon, all wanted to go to Louisiana, but that the court of France would have refused them permission to do so. In the extract cited by Winzerling, however, d'Asprès only mentions seventy Acadians having made efforts to emigrate, efforts that led to a refusal. I have found no mention of this prohibition to embark to Louisiana made by Versailles during this period, and it seems all the more curious as many groups of Acadians received such authorization, at nearly the same time, to emigrate to the United States at their expense. On the other hand, it is possible that it is a question of a local prohibition made by the naval commissioner of La Rochelle, who was perhaps unaware of the official orders.

104. 1785-05-10b; AD Ille-et-Vil. C 6176.

105. 1785-09-04b; *id.*, C 2453.

106. 1785-09-16; J. Baudry, Étude historique et biographique sur la Bretagne à la velle de la Révolution, à propos d'une correspondance inedité (1782-1790), Paris, H. Champion, 1905.

107. 1786-05-06; AD Ille-et-Vil. C 2453.

108. 1786-06-13; MAE Pol. Corresp., Spain, vol. 620, fo. 57.

109. 1786-07-28; AD Ille-et-Vil. C 2453.

110. In the same file (AD Ille-et-Vil. C 2453), we find mention, in 1787, of Acadians asking to go at the king's expense to Saint-Pierre and Miquelon. The authorization to go at their own expense was granted, but free passage was refused, for all the more reason that there was no more room on that island for supplemental population. The permission to go to this archipelago, requested many times during this period by various Acadians, was first refused to those at Cherbourg under the pretext that there was no work for them there (1785-08-013; AN Col B, vol. 189, fo. 421). It is stated that this request was made at the very moment of the embarkations to Louisiana. We find other requests for passage to Saint-Pierre and Miquelon through the course of these years (1785-07-13; 1787-02-14).

111. Paul Delaney, "Chronologie des deportations et migrations des Acadiens (1755-1816)," *Cahiers de la Société historique acadienne*, 36, 2-3 (September 2005), pp. 51-136.

112. Delaney thus notes the arrival of some forty Acadians in Louisiana coming from France in 1788, as well as the authorization granted, the same year, to twenty Acadians living at Saint-Pierre and Miquelon, to go to the Spanish colony.

113. According to the census made by the intendant of Brittany, the exact number of Acadians who emigrated rose to 1,599 individuals, whose specifics he provides by "departments" as follows: Nantes (1,160), Paimbeouf (55), Morlaix (52), Belle-Île-en-Mer (16), Saint-Malo (316) (1785-09-04b; AD Ille-et-Vil. C 2453). According to the Spanish authorities, the number rose to 1,574 or 1,596 people (1785-10-06; AHN (Madrid), folder 3885, no. 3, source 13 of the section Estado, fo. 63).

114. On the subject of the arrival of the Acadians in Louisiana, see C.A. Brasseaux, *The Foundng of New Acadia, op. cit.*

115. Ernest Martin notes, "on January 10, 1790, the 23 Acadians living in Cherbourg brought their complaints to the local section of 'the Society of Friends of the Constitution,' which featured among its adherents Le Tourneur, the future member of the Directory. These complaints were transmitted to the National Assembly. Following an intervention by La Révellière-Lépeaux, another future member of the Directory, then reporter of the Committee of Pensions, the National Assembly decreed, on September 10, 1790, "that the assistance until then granted to the Acadians would be continued, and that the most efficient and prompt means would be undertaken to assure them work and subsistence" (1936, p. 259). Numerous petitions, reports and other claims have been preserved in the National Archives in series F^{15}; see in particular F^{15} 3492-3494: "Secours aux Acadiens, aux Canadiens et aux Mayençais." 1789-an VI and *Table des matières (index) des noms et lieux et des noms de personnes contenus dans les Procès-verbaux des séances de l'Assemblée constituante, depuis le 5 mai 1789 jusqu'au 3 septembre 1791 inclusivement.*

116. 1791-02-21 (AN printed archives, AD XVIII B/52 and various other places).

117. These lists are sometimes accompanied by interesting commentaries. For example, this letter from series F^{15} (3494), coming from the directory of the department of l'Ariège and dated from Foix, October 17, 1792, the first year of the French Republic: "No Acadian nor Canadian has come . . . to request the assistance that the law of February 21, 1791 has granted to this special class of individuals who have become French."

118. Martin, *op. cit.*, p. 260.

119. 1795-04-04-; AN printed archives, AD XVIII B/138 & 139 and 1794-12-27; *id.*

120. Some Acadians and Canadians from La Rochelle sent a petition that was forwarded to the Committee of Assistance (1795-02-23; *id.*); 1795-04-04; *id.*

121. Notably those of November 26, 1792 (6 Frimaire an I), November 28, 1793 (8 Frimaire an II), October 18, 1794 (27 Vendémaire an III), November 16, 1794 (26 Brumaire an III), October 8, 1796 (17 Vendémaire an V), December 7, 1796 (17 Frimaire an V) (Martin, *op cit.*, p. 260).

122. Cited by Martin, *op. cit.*, p. 260. According to Martin, "the 2 nivôse an VI (December 22, 1797), the Acadians received an account of 12,000 francs, and on the following 26 thermidor (August 13, 1798), a credit of 900,000 *livres* was opened under the title of 'aid for the refugees and deportees from the colonies,' from which the Acadians would be the first to benefit. Finally, the law of 28 germinal an VII (April 17, 1799) assigned, counting from the 1st Vendémiaire of that year, an aid of 30 *fr.* 'to the refugees or deportees from the colonies' of both sexes aged over 21 [...etc.], upon the presentation of a certificate of poverty renewable each semester" (p. 261).

123. In 1797, the major part of the Canadians had no longer received assistance for three or four years (Maurice Caillebeau, *Les secours aux Acadiens pendant la Révolution française*, Poitiers, 1978).

124. Section AF IV, vol. 1330-1332.

125. "In 1822 and 1823, nearly 70 years after the affair of Grand-Pré, the government of the Restoration was still concerned to know if, among the descendants of the exiled Acadians repatriated in France in the 18th century, there were still some in need!" (Martin, *op. cit.*, p. 261).

126. 1884-00-00; BNF 4-LE 95-3; 1884, EXTR, 163 and 1884-12-18a and b (*id.*).

127. David A. Bell, "The Unbearable Lightness of Being French," *op. cit.*, pp. 1232-1235; Belle, *The Cult of the Nation, op. cit.*; E. Dziembowski, *Un nouveau patriotisme, op. cit.*

128. *RAPC 1905-II*, appendix F, p. 196.

129. 1775-03-02b. Joseph Landry, a refugee in France, wrote to his cousin Joseph d'Entremont who had returned to Nova Scotia. In this letter, Landry surmises that their situation is more enviable than that of their cousins, but that, in practice, because of the irreligion in France, it was ultimately not better. This letter shows the importance that religion played for certain Acadians.

Glossary

1. For a more thorough discussion of the definitions of "*nation*" and "*patrie*," see especially the following: David A. Bell, "The Unbearable Lightness of Being French," *op. cit.*, pp. 1221 and 1225. Bell notes that the provinces were nations by the same rights as was France. The Seven Years War was considered for the first time as a war of nations and the term became a central concept in France starting in the 1770s. Also see Jacques Godechot, "Nation, patrie, nationalisme et patriotisme en France au XVIIIe siècle," *Annales historiques de la Révolution française*, 43 (1971), pp. 481-501; Werner Kraus, "'Patriote,' 'patriotique,' 'patriotisme' à la fin de l'Ancien Régime," in *The Age of the Enlightenment: studies presented to Theodore Besterman*, London, 1967, pp. 387-394; Edmond Dziembowski, *Un nouveau patriotisme français 1750-1770: La France face à la puissance anglaise à l'époque de la guerre de Sept Ans*, Oxford, Voltaire Foundation, 1998.

2. The definition continues thus: "who live under the same laws and speak the same language."

3. It is indeed remarkable that the terms "country," "people," or even "foreigner," like "nation," always refer to two levels, one local and the other "national" or on a "state" level.

4. It is already the modern usage that Turgot employs in his "mémoire du Roi sur les municipalities:"

"The cause of the difficulty, Sire, comes from the fact that your Nation has no constitution. It is a society composed of different Orders poorly united and of a People whose members have only scant social ties between them.... There is no public spirit, because there is no visible and known common interest" (quoted by E. Marti, *Les Exilés, op. cit.*, p. 203).

5. Jacques Nerrou found many occurrences of this expression in the registers of baptisms, marriages, and burials in the region of Rochefort and La Rochelle (for example in the registers of the parish of Saint-Louis de Rochefort, microfilms 5 Mi. 209 and 209, ADLA, marriage of Antoine Morland and Apolinne Vandelle; two witnesses are designated as "Alsatians of nationality." Other documents use the same expression (*cf.* Jacques Nerrou, "Mariages acadiens de Rochefort-sur-Mer)," in the revue of the association *Racines et Rameaux français d'Acadie*, supplement to no. 34 of July 2005).

6. 1769-08-25b; BM Bordeaux, Ms. 1480, fo. 33: "some [Acadian] families who went to settle among the Corsicans, a rustic and semi-savage nation,... were threatened with murder by this nation which only saw them with jealousy and regret." Commentaries by Le Loutre on the plan of de L'Isle.

7. 1772-11-03; BM Bordeaux, Ms. 1480, fo. 186-188: Saint-Victour: "This country can certainly nourish its inhabitants but not without work, and it is mainly because the nation is lazy that I have wanted to show you some hardworking, sober and intelligent men because of what you have had the honor to tell me."

8. Daviken Studnicki-Gizbert, "La Nation portugaise," *Annales. Histoire, sciences socials*, 58, 3 (May-June 2003), pp. 627-648.

9. 1773-04-27a; BM Bordeaux, Ms. 1480, fo. 307-312 and AN, H1 1499 2.

10. See volume I, chapter XI.

11. Linguists consider that words do not have meanings, but only employments. *Cf.* Jacques Godechot, "Nation, patrie, nationalisme et patriotisme en France au XVIIIe siècle," *op. cit.*, p. 483.

12. A primary letter mentions the necessity of reuniting the Acadians "in order that, as a body, they might better preserve their morals" (1773-06-08b; ADV J Dep. 22, art. 124-1). Another letter speaks of some "representatives of the body" (1774-12-14a; ADV J dep. 22, art. 97).

13. "The States are composed of the body of the Clergy, of the body of the Nobility, of the body of the Third Estate. The *parlement*, the sovereign courts act as a body of the Court. One generally says of the assembled companies that they are political bodies. One also says the body of the town when speaking of the officers of the town, who are the Provost of the merchants, the municipal magistrates and the councilors of the town and the prosecutor of the king. The six bodies of merchants in Paris are the Haberdashers, the Grocers, the Drapers, the Hosiers and the Silversmiths. The wine merchants presumably make the seventh body.

14. *Les Solidarités dans les sociétés humaines*, PUF, 1987. An article by Yves Durand in *L'Histoire aujourd'hui*, Editions Sciences humaines, 1999, repeats the main themes of his work.

15. Not to be confused with the "corporations" that, according to Yves Durand, "formed trade societies united by an oath and placed under the protection of a saint."

16. Yvres Durand, "Solidarités d'autrefois," in *L'Histoire aujourd'hui, op. cit.*, p. 34.

17. 1778-01-04; ADIV C 6176.

18. This term, which means "one who is elected to take care of the affairs of a community, of a body of which he is a member" according to the *DA*, is used many times.

19. Beginning in 1767, Choiseul spoke of a syndic (1767-10-11c; AN, Marine B3 vol. 576, fo. 42), but the text is not specific enough for us to be certain that it involved the Acadians.

20. We can say this from having done some investigation of integral texts in the old dictionaries and the *Encyclopédie*. We find, for example, twenty-seven uses of the phrase "body of the nation" in the *Encyclopédie* for only three of "national body."

21. Research done in the integral text of these two dictionaries thanks to the advanced research functions of the CDROM "Atelier historique de la langue française," Redon editions.

22. Research done once again in integral text thanks to the tools of the electronic edition of this work (project ARTFL; this project is only accessible by subscription, for example, through the library of the Institut universitaire européen).

23. *The Cult of the Nation, op. cit.*

24. Quoted by Bell, *The Cult*, p. 14.

25. Christopher Hodson, *Refugees: Acadians and the Social History of Empire, 1755-1785*, doctoral thesis (history), Northwestern University, 2004.

26. Jacques Godechot, "Nation, patrie, nationlisme et patriotisme," *op cit.*

27. "People" figues in 184 documents of the database (but it is also largely used in the sense of "poor"); "nation" in 123, but in only 55 involving the Acadians themselves (details below).

28. 1773-08-15; BM Bordeaux, Ms. 1480, fo. 435-436: Terray to Lemoyne: "the attachment that you have to this people will undoubtedly bring you to enlighten them about their real interests."

29. 1763-02-17a (Report by Nivernais); many uses of the term in this text.

30. 1772-12-30: "this poor people;" 1773-05-13a: "at the time of the expedition of M. the duc Danville, this people enjoyed the use of . . . immense terrains;" 1773-01-19: "How should one place this people:" 1772-09-14: Lemoyne to Bertin: "unfortunate people" (used many times). 1772-11-05b; Lemoyne to Duvonel: "unfortunate people;" 1773-04-26: "a people who deserve the generosity [of the king] by so many rights;" also examples above, such as 1772-12-24: "people attached to their prince," etc.

31. We have seen this above, the contemporary dictionaries of the eighteenth century note that this term "nation" covered both a "national" dimension (in the modern sense of the word, as opposed to "regional" or "provincial") *and* a provincial one (nation of Normandy and of Picardy).

32. The *Encyclopédie* describes people as "a collective noun difficult to define, because one has different ideas of it in various places, times and depending on the nature of governments." The definition of the *Trévoux* is much closer to that of the *Dictionnaire de l'Académie* from which its Jesuit authors were clearly inspired. The only notable difference involves the addition of the example "French people": "The French people loves their sovereign and their sovereign is concerned with the happiness of his people, of his peoples." The addition of "his" (plural) before people in this example shows clearly the ambiguity and difficulty of defining if "one" or "some" "French peoples" exist; on the distinction to be made on this subject, see D. Roche, *La France des Lumières*, pp. 292 and 287.

33. Research done in integral text in the Historical Studio. On the other hand, the *Trévoux*, some years later, provides as an example "French people" (see the previous note).

34. The *Encyclopédie* again admits the difficulty in defining this term: "this word designates an undetermined space; it is said of different, more or less large portions of the surface of the earth." As for the *Trévoux*, it also returns to the State and to the province: "The word country expresses a more or less considerable portion of the terrestrial globe inhabited by a people, or by many different nations, but considered as being under the same nation. Africa is a country burned by the heat of the sun. Holland is a country cut through by canals. One also calls country the small cantons, many of which together make a province."

35. See the definition of "nation" above. The term nation is also ambiguous and includes the two distinct levels (local and national), specifically in the *Dictionnaire de l'Académie* (the *Trévoux* is more precise).

Biographical References

1. The *Dictionnaire biographique du Canada* is available at no charge online (http://www.biographi.ca).

2. Biographies of Michel Bastarache, who undertook a lengthy trip to rejoin his wife on Île Saint-Jean via South Carolina and Québec; Étienne Hébert, who tried to reassemble the exiles of the village he was from in Québec; Benoni d'Entremont; Joseph Brossard (or Broussard), called Beausoleil, who went to Louisiana in 1764 by way of Saint-Domingue, accompanied by J. B. Semer.

3. Gérard-Marc Braud, *Les Acadiens en France, Nantes et Paimboeuf, 1775-1785. Approche généalogique*, Quest Éditions, 1999, p. 241. The information about the other individuals cited in this part also comes mainly from this work.

4. Gérard-Marc Braud, *Les Acadiens en France, Nantes et Paimboeuf, 1775-1785. Approche généalogique*, Quest Éditions, 1999, p. 241.

5. See Robert Piart, "Une Acadienne et sa fille à la maison du roi Louis XVI," *Cahiers de la Société historique acadienne*, 34, 1 (March 2003), pp. 33-41.

6. Jacqueline Gagnaire and Claudine Pauly, *Pérusse des Cars. Un seigneur en Poitou au siècle des Lumières*, June 2004.

7. For example, Henri Buche, Jean Mallon, and Etienne Taillemite, *Inventaire des archives de la marine, sous-série B3 (fin), tome VIII (B3 561-803)*, Paris, Imprimerie nationale, 1963.

8. One finds biographical information about this individual in abbé H. R. Casgrain, "Lettres et mémoires de l'abbé de L'Isle-Dieu (1742-1774)," *Rapport des archives de la province de Québec*, 16, 17, 18 (1935-1938), pp. 273-410; 331-459; 147-253; Auguste Gosselin, "Encore le Père de Bonnécamps 1707-1790," *Mémoires de la Société royale du Canada*, second series, III (1897-1898), pp. 103-117; Louis-Marie Le Jeune, *Dictionnaire général de biographie, histoire, literature, agriculture, commerce, industrie et des arts, sciences, moeurs, coutumes, institutions politiques et religieuses du Canada*, Ottawa, 1931. One probably very interesting report, a master's thesis (history) was not available to be studied in the framework of this study (Isabella Santini, *Le relazoni tra il Canada e la Santa Sede nella corrispondenza di Pierre de La Rue, abbe de L'Isle-Dieu, vicario generale della diocesi di Quebec (1760-1776)*, Universita di Pisa, June 21, 1984).

9. General Archives of the Congrégation du Saint-Esprit, Chevilly-Larue, resource 2D19.1. The passages between quotations are by A. David, but the entirety of this biographical article comes from his notes.

10. *RAPC 1905-I,* p. 413.

11. The overwhelming majority of the superior officers such as the commissioners-general of the navy were members of the nobility. This was particularly the case with Lemoyne, according to many documents found in the Archives nationals (AN, series T, vol. 1087-1088). In 1780, Lemoyne was designated as Squire and Counselor to the King, Commissioner-General of the Navy. He had a brother, Sieur Joachim Félix Léon Blanchard, Squire, lord of Changey. According to the *Dictionnaire de l'Académie*, "Once is prohibited from taking the rank of Squire, if he is not noble." The son of Lemoyne, embarked on the Étoile with Bougainville, bore the title de Montchevry (Gérard Scavennec,

"Des Acadiens aux Malouines," *op. cit.*).

12. Dick Lemoine, *Répertoire numérique des Archives de l'arrondissement maritime de Rochefort, série R (Colonies-Pays étrangers) et série E (services administratifs)*, Paris, 1925).

13. *Cf.* 1774-08-29; BM Bordeaux, Ms. 1480, Appendices, 1st file.

14. Clerk was the first rank of officers of the navy (Michel Vergé-Franceschi, "Officiers de la marine," in Lucien Bély, *Dictionnaire de l'Ancien Régime, op. cit.*).

15. Contrary to what E. Martin has written, Lemoyne was not responsible for the Acadians in France from 1766 to 1774, but only from the start of 1773 to the end of 1774 (*Les Exilés, op. cit.*, note 2, p. 67). Lemoyne then was over sixty years old. He previously had the responsibility for some Acadians at Rochefort and for 2,000 to 3,000 Germans at Saint-Jean d'Angely.

16. The last letters that we have from Lemoyne on the subject of the Acadians date from September 1774 (1774-09-27); BM Bordeaux, Ms. 1480, Appendices, 1st file).

17. Starting in 1777, he appears in the inventory of series AN Marine B3 643 as Lemoyne, Commissioner of the Navy, *ordonnateur* at Bordeaux (Henri Buche, Jean Mallon and Étienne Taillemite, *Inventaire des archives de la marine, sous-série B3 (fin), tome VIII (B3 561-803)*, Paris, Imprimerie nationale, 1963). Lemoyne was also assigned as *ordonnateur* at Toulon for the same year in 1777 (inventory AN Marine B3 645). The commissioner was probably transferred that year from Toulon to Bordeaux, since he was in the latter city in 1785 and at the start of the Revolution, where his papers were seized.

18. AD Gironde, C 1520.

19. Ms. 840 and Ms. 860, BM Bordeaux.

20. Marine B3 vol. 566, fo. 245.

21. Ernest Martin, *Les Exilés, op. cit.*, note 2, pp. 79 and 325.

22. 1772-10-23b; BM Bordeaux, Ms. 1480, fo. 180-181.

23. *Cf.* inventory of series B3 608 (1773), "Daubenton, intendant of the Navy at Rochefort: conflict with Mr. Lemoine on the subject of the nomination of a clerk," fo. 18 to 35.

24. 1766-08-00; BM Bordeaux, Ms.. 1480, appendices, 1st file.

25. *Cf.* 1773-08-00; BM Bordeaux, Ms. 1480, appendices, 1st file and 1773-07-20a; BM Bordeaux, Ms. 1480, fo. 404-407. Also see AN series F5 A, vol. 1: in a letter dated from 1775, the abbé de l'Isle-Dieu recommends Lemoyne.

26. A document from the SHM Brest, 1 P 1/9 designates him as "Jean-Joseph Guillot, Councilor of the King in his councils, Commissioner-General of the Navy, *ordonnateur* in the department of Saint-Malo."

27. Martin, *Les Exilés*, p. 85.

28. *Cf.* 1774-07-00a; BM Bordeaux, Ms. 1480, appendices, 1st file.

29. In a letter from 1772010-19 (AN H1 1499 2), the Saint-Malo commissioner speaks of a certain Mr. L'Anglois, master of accounts, who was both the nephew of Lemoyne and the cousin of Guillot.

30. See, for example: 1773-12-05b; BM Bordeaux, Ms. 1480, fo. 523-526.

Notes on Map

1. Carl Brasseaux, "Phantom Letters: Acadian Correspondence, 176-1784," *Acadiensis*, XXIII, 2 (Spring 1994), pp. 124-132.

Bibliography And Sources

1. These sources were consulted either (a) by obtaining copies of documents by contacting the services of the archives involved (I obtained photocopies from the Archivo Historico Nacional (Madrid), from the Municipal Archives of Boulogne-sur-Mer, and the Archives of the dept. of Finstère), or (b) from microfilms consulted at the Library and Archives of Canada (Ottawa), at the AN Québec (Montréal), the CEA of Moncton, and the AN, or (c) from transcriptions of documents that have been published, and, finally, (d) from photocopies of documents sent by various correspondents (the documents from the diocesan archives of Coutances were sent to me be Mrs. Michèle Godret).

2. Notably, cartons H^1 1499^2 (for the period of the settlement of the Acadians in Poitou); F^{15} 3495 (mainly for problems other than those of the settling of Poitou for the period 1773-1790). These two sources were, however, unfortunately, very deficient.

3. Indeed, the intendants reported directly to the Controller-General of Finances. After July 1773, it was thus they who were charged with taking care of the Acadians. Series C of the intendancy of Caen is especially rich for the period after 1773, as is that of the intendancy of Brittany (preserved at Rennes in the corresponding series C).

4. Alain Roman, professor of history emeritus and author of many books about Saint-Malo, at my suggestion made a complete examination of the registers of Saint-Malo that an all too short visit to the archives in that city did not allow me to complete. For this he is very gratefully thanked.

5. Ernest Martin effectively only made use of this administrative correspondence (as he was unaware of the other sources mentioned below). Regarding the documentation consulted by Martin (who has the most thoroughly examined the most sources for the whole of France), many new documents have been found. Notably: (1) Martin did not conduct research at Rennes, nor, curiously, at Rochefort and La Rochelle; he found nothing at Nantes; and he was unaware of the existence of Spanish sources; also unaware of series H^1 1499^2 in the Archives nationals and he did not consult the important series of older resources of the navy (Marine series B3); (b) unlike Martin, I was not content with summaries of the inventory of series B of the Colonies and systematically examined the originals, allowing me to discover important documents hidden behind the seemingly infertile summaries, and to correct a number of errors.

6. I also thank Michèle Godret for having sent me a copy of eleven files of testimony by the Acadians requesting various expenses, forming an exceptional group of documents.

INDEX

A

Aiguillon, duc d' (governor of Brittany), 60, 270, 299, 318 n35, 320 n75
Aranda, Pedro Pablo Abarca de Bolea, count de, 36, 207, 209-15
Archigny, France, 41, 70, 73, 76, 78, 239
Arebout, François, 239, 339 n75
Argenson Marquis d', 329 n100
Arsenault, Bona, 14-15, 316 n93
Artois, count d', 270 n19
Asprès, d' (Spanish Consul in Brittany, in charge of the expedition of Acadians for Louisiana), 215-16, 340 n103
Aucoin, Joseph, 140-41
Aucoin, Marie, 337 n32
Aucoin, Simon (Mazerolles), 73, 76, 274 n72, 287

B

Babin, Laurent, 61
Ballays (subdelegate of Nantes), 79-81, 207, 338 n63
Barbier de Lescoët, François Claude, comte, 318 n32
Bardet, Jean-Pierre, 274 n2
Barrin, vicomte de, 312 n30
Barry, Madame du, 285 n32, 293 n77, 309 n3
Bazer, Marguerite, 106
Beaubassin, Acadie, 24, 121, 264 n89, 323 n103
Béaur, Gérard, 310 n9
Beausejour, Fort, 3, 24-25, 257 n11, 266 n11, 269 n47
Bellefontaine family, 105, 109-10, 135, 315 n80

Bellefontaine, Joseph, 233, 299n 104
Bellefontaine, Michel, 119
Belle-Île (-en-Mer), 11, 70, 73, 179, 214, 239; Acadian community at, 106, 156-158, 160, 163, 165, 281 n35, 282 n47, 296 n32, 318 n27, 321 n87; marriages, 195-96, 201, 281 n37, 334 n57, 335 n67; resistance towards Acadians, 81, 97-98, 186-88, 191, 223; settlement of, 6, 32, 55, 58-64, 66, 69, 71-72, 93, 135, 309 n4
Berryer, Nicolas-René, 142, 147, 164, 180, 220; and Acadian refugees, 36-37, 44, 47-49, 54, 97, 103, 111, 115; payment distribution, 94, 96, 105-106, 109, 113, 299 n97, 300 n106, 320 n67; work programs, 116, 137, 156
Bertin, Henri Léonard Jean Baptiste (minister of agriculture), 33-35, 57, 68-70, 72, 89, 116, 236, 270 n17, 283 n8
Blaye, France, 186, 282 n56, 283 n5
Blois, France, 201
Blossac (intendant of Poitou), 33, 37, 97-98, 132
Bon Papa (ship), xix, 216-17
Bordeaux, France, 91, 104, 112, 136, 214, 279 n4, 285 n37, 346 n17; library of, xiii, 241-42
Bouctouche (Acadian village), 127
Boudereau, Anselme, 117, 120, 140-41, 303 n15, 304 n25, 305 n48, 313 n42, n45, 314 n50, 332 n31
Boudiche, Pierre, 140-41
Boudrot, Alexis, 273 n64
Boudrot, Basile, 118, 235
Boudrot, Benjamin, 77, 235, 287 n88, 322 n105

Boudrot, Charles, 234,
Bougainville, Louis-Antoine de, 45, 164, 177, 236, 345 n11
Bouin (island), 57, 65, 267 n22
Boulogne, France, 6, 36, 38, 40, 46, 48, 111, 113, 116-17, 154, 194, 239, 272 n54, 275 n10, 276 n18, 33, 325 n34, 335 n67
Bourbonnier, Joseph Le Roy, sieur de, 331 n31
Bourg, Agnes, 326 n40
Bourg, Alexandre, 70
Bourg, Joseph Mathurin, 120, 233, 305 n42, n45
Bourg, Pierre (or Jean-Pierre), 305 n42
Boynes, Pierre-Etienne Bourgeois de (minister of the Navy), 37, 62, 67-68, 72, 111, 142, 186, 206, 236-37, 265 n3, 285 n32, 295 n26, 301 n134
Brandily, Daniel, 312 n36
Brasseaux, Carl, 11, 239, 283 n8
Braud, Gérard-Marc, 124-25, 191, 194, 241, 307 n81, 325 n34, 327 n56, 333 n37
Brest, France, 38, 119, 128, 139, 214, 236, 241
Bristol, England, 25-26, 39, 239, 267 n33, 268 n34, 271 n29
Brittany, France, 32, 58-62, 70, 72, 79, 93, 97-98, 104, 128-29, 131, 142, 160, 209, 219, 233, 234, 236, 242, 280 n10, 298 n76, 341 n113
Brix (forest of), 63-64, 270 n10, 282 n56
Broussard family, 266 n11
Broussard, Jean, 278 n50, 279 n65
Broussard, Joseph (Beausoleil), 345 n2
Bugeon, Guy, 121-22, 124-25
Buot, Marie-Madeleine, 121, 299 n98

C

Caen, France, 58, 104-105, 109-10, 127-28, 138, 180, 322 n95
Calonne, Charles-Alexandre de, 128, 176, 211, 216, 339 n78
Cancale, France, 129, 299 n91
Cape Breton, Nova Scotia, 2, 163, 192, 199, 221, 274 n2, 282 n47

Caret, Honoré, 139-41, 312 n36, 332 n31
Cassiet, Pierre, 299 n101
Castries, de, (minister of the Navy), 210-11, 273
Cayenne, 44, 46, 57, 94, 214, 236, 321 n92, 326 n42. See also Guyana
Chanteloup, Pierre Le Fer de, 47, 58, 148, 156
Chantenay. See Saint-Martin de Chantenay
Chateaubriand, Comte de, 65
Châtellerault, France, 132, 143, 187, 194, 233-34, 239, 325 n34
Cherbourg, France, 6, 31, 38, 46, 65, 73, 77, 94-95, 104, 111-19, 121, 127, 142-43, 145, 164, 192, 207, 214, 239, 257 n18, 258 n25, 298 n76, 299 n91; aid to Acadians, 105-13, 129-30, 137, 147; marriages, 50-54, 194-98, 279 n65
Chignectou, New Brunswick, 2
Choiseul, Etienne-François de: aid to Acadians, 94, 97, 102-103, 112-13, 137, 293 n77, 302 n150; colonization efforts, 27, 44-46, 57-58, 63-65, 89; Guyana colony, 44-46, 218-19, 267 n31, 321 n93; French settlements, 60, 66, 280; tobacco, 106, 157-58
Cireau [Circaud], Léonard, 192-93, 278 n50
Closnard, comte de, 67, 71, 285 n37
Cluny de Nuis (intendant of Saint-Domingue), 157, 318 n40
Colbert, Jean-Baptiste, 31, 44, 57, 88
Comeau, Marguerite, 278 n50, 279 n65
Comeau, Monique, 278 n50
Compiègne, France, 36, 67
Copeguit (Acadian village in Canada), 8
Corsica, 64-65, 67-68, 70, 79, 97-98, 186, 207, 209
Courtin, Louis, 201, 266 n18
Coutances, France, 50, 112, 130, 147, 180
Coyer, abbé, 160

D

Daigle, François, 94
Daigle, Jacques, 119, 304 n38
Daigle, Madeleine, 234

Daigle, Marie-Rose, 53, 121, 162, 192, 278 n50
Daigle, Marin, 287 n80
Daigre, Paul, 106
Daudin, abbé, 170
Destouches (secretary of the Controller-General), 71
Devau, Joseph, 126-29, 222, 235, 308 n101
Doucet, Augustin, 40
Doucet, Françoise, 234
Doucet, Jean, 287 n80
Doucet, Joseph, 287 n80
Dunkirk, France, 116
Duon, Pierre, 141
Duvonel (master of waters and forests), 179
Dziembowski, Edmond, 92

E

Egremont (English minister), 267 n24
Entremont, d', Charles, 110, 148
Entremont, d', Étienne, 273 n59
Entremont, d', family, 23, 54, 105, 109-10, 118, 135, 170, 265 n4
Entremont, d', Joseph de Mius, 273 n59, 278 n50, 279 n65
Entremont, d', Philippe Mius, 300 n105
Evangeline (poem), 249 n 69

F

Falmouth, England, 26, 39, 239
Faragher, John Mack, 11-12, 41, 261 n58, 264 n87
Flanders, 69, 137
Fontaine, Jean de La, xvi-xvii, 211
Fonteneau, Jean-Marie, 11
Fontette, François-Jean Orceau de, 58
Forest, Victor "Mitouche," 138-39, 141, 149, 235, 312 n32

G

Galherme, Jean-Baptiste, 278 n50
Galissonière, de la (governor of Corsica), 312 n30

Gallant, Dominique, 326 n35
Gallant, Melvin, 264 n87
Gallen (mayor of Sauzon), 282 n47
Gaspé, Quebec, 6, 8, 102, 111, 257 n18, 283 n1
Georgia, xv, 7, 268 n39, 273 n55
Gilbert, Louis, 97
Girard, abbé Jacques, 97, 259 n30, 293 n83, 299 n101
Grandclos Mêlé, abbé de, 32, 96, 228, 324 n24
Granger, Jean, 278 n50
Granger, Joseph Simon, 235
Granger, Magdeleine, 340 n100
Granger, Marguerite, 324 n24
Granville, France, 105, 298 n76
Gravier, Charles, 36
Greenville, George, 26
Griffiths, Naomi E. S., xiii, 11, 14-16, 25-28, 160
Guadeloupe, 44, 57
Guébriand (or Guay Briand), 312-13 n 36
Guegot (custom officer), 118
Guerne, abbé Le, 29, 269 n49
Guillemet, Dominique, xiv, 61
Guillot, Jean-Joseph, 31
Guillot, Frédéric Joseph: and Acadians, 71-72, 161, 164-65, 167, 176; payment distribution, 35, 101-102, 147; Saint-Malo, 31, 35, 48, 237
Guillot, Marie-Josèphe, 250
Guyana: Acadians in, xv, 6, 19, 204, 214, 275 n10; Choiseul, Etienne-François de: resettlement idea, 45-46, 57, 219; Company of, 79; German settlers, 183, 186

H

Haché, Georges, 141, 234
Haché, Louis, 234
Haché, Pierre, 141, 234
Haffreingue, Bruno, xiv, 194
Halifax, Nova Scotia, 3, 24, 239, 257 n18
Hébert, Dominique, 112
Hébert, Étienne, 345 n2
Hébert, Isaac, 305 n42

Hébert, Jean-Baptiste, 287 n80
Hébert, Rosalie, 278 n50
Henry, Aimable, 117
Henry, Basile, 32, 76, 144, 208, 222, 273 n69
Henry, James P., 194
Henry, Paul, 190
Henry, Pierre, 70
Herédia, chevalier de (secretary to Aranda), 210-212
Hirel (community near Saint-Malo), 272 n50
Hodson, Christopher, 176
Huere, Françoise, 233, 312 n28, 321 n87

I

Île-Royale, 113, 154-55, 192; Acadian deportation, 4, 6, 23, 92, 259 n30; aid to Acadians, 35, 49, 101-3, 107, 111, 299 n97, 301 n134; French territory, 2, 29-30, 178; refugees in France, 5, 8-9, 57, 91, 111, 177, 301 n131, 327 n68
Île Saint-Jean, 47, 108, 112, 118, 196; Acadian deportation, 4, 6, 23-24, 178, 258 n25; aid to Acadians, 35-36, 49, 91, 101-3, 106, 111, 137, 259 n30; French territory, 2, 16, 29-30, 269 n47; refugees in France, 5, 8-9, 91, 111, 154, 293 n83, 301 n131, 327 n68
Invault, Étienne Maynon d', 47
Isambert (Belle-Île-en-Mer inspector), 59
Isarn (commissioner of divisions at Saint-Malo), 31, 96, 157
Isle-Dieu, abbé de l', 32, 34, 40, 49, 63-64, 71, 74, 119, 127, 135, 143, 158, 180, 230, 235, 237

J

Jersey, England, 67, 92, 139, 178, 313 n38
Judice, Louis, 214

L

La Borde, Chevalier de, 70, 154
Laborde, Guillaume, 192
La Corne, abbé de, 286 n58
Ladvocat de La Crochais, 115-16, 129-31, 156, 158, 163, 166-67
La Gouesnière (community near Saint-Malo), 272 n50
la Marche, Louis-François Joseph de Bourbon Conti, comte de, 64, 70, 285 n 32
Lamballe (community near Saint-Malo), 272 n50
Landry, Anne, 278 n50, 279 n65
Landry, Jean, 268 n34
Landry, Joseph, 95, 278 n50, 342 n129
Landry, Madeleine, 278 n50
Landry, Marguerite, 275, 338
Landry, Pierre, 140-41, 306 n39, 312 n36
L'Anglois, 53, 279 n60, 346 n29
Langrolay (community in Côtes d'Armor), 272 n50
Lapierre, Joseph, 51, 278 n50
Lauvrière, Émile, 10, 43, 87, 114
Le Havre, France: Acadian workers, 130, 156; Île Saint-Jean refugees, 6, 38, 137, 179; marriages, 194-97; payments to Acadians at, 35, 104; resettling efforts, 46, 65, 77, 79, 205, 214; salt tax, 106, 298 n76
LeBlanc, Jean-Jacques, 40-41, 73, 76, 94, 166, 206, 223
LeBlanc, Jean-Simon, 273 n55
LeBlanc, Joseph, xix, 170
LeBlanc, Marie, 305 n48
Le Blanc, Pierre, 139, 141
Le Faucheux, Monique, 121-22, 124-25
Legge, Francis, 313 n39
Lemoyne, Antoine-Philippe (Commissioner of the Navy): 67-68, 219, 236-37, 242, 345 n11; Acadian census, 7, 103; Acadians' connection to France, 23-24, 154, 170-71; Acadian "nation," 74-75, 176-81; Acadians resettlement to Poitou, 62, 73, 77, 94-95, 103-4, 106, 133, 292n59; and Acadian workers, 120-21, 126-27, 130-32, 136-37; aid to Acadians, 92-93, 106, 109, 111-13, 183, 294 n89, 301 n134, 330 n115; as

intermediary for Acadians, 32-35, 37, 157-61, 166, 186-88, 190-91; and Pérusse's plan, 71-72, 74-75, 77
Lescoët, Barbier, 160
Liverpool, England, 25-26, 28-29, 39-40, 239, 268 n34
Locmaria Parish, 179
London, England, 266 n18, 307 n87
Longfellow, Henry Wadsworth, 255 n3, 263 n79, 269 n49
Lorient, France, 106, 129
Louisbourg, Canada: Acadians, 9, 103; aid to displaced, 111-12, 269 n48; English capture, 4, 92, 101; fortress, 2, 4, 333 n36; refugees, 5, 27, 30, 47, 157, 178, 257 n17,
Louisiana: Acadians in, 28, 36, 45, 65, 92, 177, 206, 216-17; aid for Acadians, 148, 339 n82; Leblanc group, 41, 79, 207; and Nantes Acadians, 7, 144, 200, 213; and Peyroux, 208-12, 214-15, 222, 289 n117; professions of Acadian emigrants, 121, 123-24; reluctance to go to, 203-5; requests to go to, 67-68, 70, 76, 81, 203
Louis XV, 3, 6, 10, 27, 68, 127, 160, 182, 219-20, 235
Louis XVI, 81, 121, 140, 211, 235
Loutre, abbé Le, 74, 92, 119, 207, 233, 237; aid for Acadians, 142-43, 235, 295 n26; Acadian nation, 58-61, 63, 175, 186; Acadian resettlement, 16, 29, 32, 70, 108, 336 n11; Micmacs, 3, 266 n14

M

Mabile decree, 178
Malouine (Falkland) Islands, 6, 45, 275 n9
Maltese (families), 45
Manach, Jean, 299 n101
Marche, comte de la, 70
Martin, Ernest, 10, 12, 29, 35, 43, 70, 87, 101, 105, 113, 136, 142, 291 n42, 347 n5
Martinique, 44, 46, 57

Martin, Marie, 201
Maryland, 28, 268 n41
Mazerolles. *See* Aucoin, Simon
Meillac (community near Combourg), 272 n50
Mélanson, Anne, 53, 278 n50
Ménétra, Jacques-Louis, 308 n2
Metters, Megan, 82
Minas Basin, xix, 8, 24
Mississippi: River, 83, 166, 203, 205-6, 221; Territory, 203, 213, 221; Valley, xix, 7, 41, 203
Mistral (commissioner of the Navy at Le Havre), 36, 46, 132, 137, 179
Mitouche. *See* Forest, Victor
Moncton, General, 24
Monthoiron, France, 41, 70, 73
Moreau (director-general of garden nurseries), 33
Morineau, Michel, 136
Morlaix: Acadian arrival in, 6, 38, 46, 48; aid to Acadians in, 103, 107, 143, 148, 295 n20; employment, 106, 117, 119, 121, 129; marriages, 194, 333 n44; refugees to Louisiana, 203, 210, 213-14, 217
Moulaison, Joseph, 273 n59
Moulaison, Marie Josephte, 273 n59
Moulaison, Modest, 305 n50

N

Nantes, France: Acadians in, 7, 38, 40-41, 75-76, 79, 228; aid for Acadians, 32, 81, 104, 144, 177, 338 n57; employment, 122-25, 128, 208-9; marriages, 175, 191, 193-200, 332 n34, 333 n 37; refugees to Louisiana, 210, 212-14, 216, 223, 337 n16
Necker, Jacques (Controller-General), 18, 33, 54, 55, 60; aid to Acadians, 91, 98, 104-5, 135, 138, 220; division and assimilation of Acadians, 78-82, 176-77, 203, 220, 336 n16; refugees to Louisiana, 207

Nerrou, Jacques, 191, 194, 343 n5
Neuder, Yves Le, 141
Neuville, Madame de, 270 n19
New Brunswick, Canada, 2-3, 5-8, 28, 239, 241
New England, 6, 92, 236, 267 n21, 269 n49, 273 n55, 295 n20
Nivernais, duc de (French Ambassador in London), 25-30, 33, 48, 57, 65, 74, 78, 80, 95, 156, 163, 182, 230, 295 n20, 268 n44
Nova Scotia: Acadians, 8, 11, 159, 161, 167, 169, 259 n32; Acadian plans to return to, 26, 29, 81-82, 203, 261 n55; British hold, 2, 4, 6, 24; deportations, 4, 23, 30; smuggling, 139

P

Paramé, France, 129, 272 n50, 299 n91
Parré, Eustache, 278 n50
Pellegrin, Nicole, 78
Penryn, England, 26, 29, 239, 266 n18, 268 n34, 316 n93
Pérusse d'Escars, marquis de, 6, 127, 135, 143; Acadian "nation," 172, 174, 176, 179, 228; aid to Acadians, 37, 271 n40; opinion of Acadians, 159-161, 167, 180, 182; Poitou settlement, 33, 40-41, 74, 97, 195; project proposals, 34, 69-78, 104, 206-207, 286 n71, 293
Peyroux de la Coudrenière, 337 n25; and Louisiana, 41, 205, 208-16, 121-23, 275 n14, 289 n117
Pleudihen, France, 117, 119, 138, 190, 217
Pleurtuis, France, 272 n50
Plouër, France, 117, 272 n50, 303 n18
Pobomcoup, baron de, 300 n105
Poitiers, France, 131
Poitou, France: Acadians in, 7, 40-41, 68, 103, 158, 160, 186-88, 206-7, 213, 286 n58, 290 n11, 309 n4; aid for Acadians, 36, 98, 104-7, 109, 135-36, 143, 148; employment, 113, 122, 126, 145, 155; failed settlement, 81, 90, 272 n54; and Lemoyne, 62, 72-74, 77, 94, 133, 292 n52; marriages, 194-96, 199-200, 175, 333 n44, 334 n62, 335 n68; and Pérusse d'Escars, 33, 69-70, 74-79, 97, 242, 322 n94, 330 n5
Prince Edward Island. *See* Île Saint-Jean

Q

Québec, Canada: Acadian refugees, 4, 7, 62, 268 n45; British conflicts, 2; founding, 1; battle of the Plains of Abraham, 266 n11; seminary, 236, 241

R

Rambourg, François, 118
Rambourg, Jean, 118, 304 n25
Rameau de Saint-Père, Edme, 10, 15, 77
Rance River, France, 47, 76, 193, 222, 272 n50, 276 n29, 335 n64
Ranché (naval intendant at Le Havre), 35, 329 n106
Raynal, abbé, 2, 154, 158
Régnault, Jean, 307 n84
Richard, (Anne-) Suzanne, 121, 129, 217, 235
Richard, Margeurite Rosalie, 129
Richard, Marie Esther, 129
River, Jean, 6, 119, 164, 235
Robichaux, A.J., 191
Robichaux, Jean-Baptiste, 233
Rochefort, France: Acadians in, 38, 91, 102, 111; aid to Acadians, 104, 107-9, 113, 136-37, 147; employment, 106; Louisbourg refugees, 5, 332 n36, 335 n67; marriages, 175, 191, 194
Rochelle, France: Acadians in, 38, 47, 111, 214; aid to Acadians, 36, 104, 107, 136, 147; dispensations, 50; Louisbourg refugees, 5; marriages, 335 n60
Rochette (emissary to the duc de Nivernais), 25-26, 28, 33, 36, 91-92, 165-66, 170, 230, 244
Roque (first agent of the Navy), 31, 304 n25
Rouet, Damien, 70, 76

Rozière (bureau chief of court funds), 33
Ruis-Embito, Charles Claude de, 113, 164, 260 n35

S

Sahlins, Peter, 17-18, 182
Saint-Briac, France, 272 n50
Saint-Domingue, 6, 28, 44, 46, 57, 157, 205, 236, 239, 257 n16, 276 n21, 318 n40
Saint-Enogat, France, 272 n50, 276 n30
Saint-Goazec, France, 93, 292 n50
Saint-Jean-d'Angély, France, 133, 186, 237
Saint-Malo, France: Acadians in, 6-7, 58, 79, 165, 258 n25, 272 n50; Acadians to Louisiana, 203, 206-7, 210-17; Acadian "nation," 38-41, 46-48, 71-72, 169-72, 175-78, 228-29; aid to Acadians, 31, 35-37, 62, 91, 94, 96, 102, 107, 113, 136-37, 145-49; employment, 117, 121-22, 129-31; and Lemoyne 77, 104, 237; marriages, 193-200, 332 n34; opinion of Acadians, 156-62, 187-88, 191; religion, 32, 53; tobacco, 138-41, 147, 189-90, 311 n26
Saint-Martin de Chantenay, 194, 233-34, 272 n54
Saint-Pierre and Miquelon islands (North America): Acadians in, 6-7, 27, 52, 62, 64-65, 208, 261 n55; Acadian requests to go to, 79, 94, 95, 163-64, 203-204, 217; Acadians to Louisiana, 206-207; aid to Acadians, 63, 341 n10; Choiseul plans, 45-46, 276 n33, 321 n92; smuggling, 139
Saint-Servan, France, 7, 112, 117, 119, 138, 157, 176, 189-90, 222, 233-34, 272 n52, 276 n30, 298 n83
Saint-Similien, France, 272 n54
Saint-Suliac, France, 234, 272 n50, 276 n30, 332, 335
Saint-Thual, France, 272 n50
Saint-Victour (no known first name), 160, 179
Saquet, Julien, 141

Sartine, Antoine de, 18, 80, 236
Scavennec, Gérard, 191
Semer, Germain, 234
Semer, Jean-Baptiste, 119, 205-206, 250, 274 n78, 314 n57, 323 n1
Southampton, England, 26, 39, 239, 268 n34
Storck (ship), 322 n96
Sutières, Sarcey de, 70

T

Terray (controller-general), 62, 68, 71, 77, 104, 127, 155, 180, 230
Terriot [Thériault, Terriau, Terrio], Étienne, 140-41, 209, 233-34, 313 n49, 331-32 n31
Terriot, Jacques, 139, 141
Terriot, Olivier, 144, 148, 190, 208-15, 222, 235, 307 n84, 337 n32, 339 n84
Théfruit [Tefruit], Marie Michelle, 128
Thibaudeau, Eloi, 128-29, 141
Thibaudeau, Jean, 119, 138, 140-41, 190, 233, 304-5 n40, 312 n28, 313 n49, 330 n1, 332 n31
Touraine, France, 182, 314 n64
Tours, France, 241, 309 n5
Trahan, Alexandre, 70
Trahan, Alexis, 235, 273 n64, 324 n24
Trahan, Marie, 234
Treaty of Paris, 130, 290 n24
Treaty of Utrecht, 2
Trigavou, France, 272 n50
Turgot, Anne Robert Jacques, 75, 78, 127, 157

V

Vergennes, Charles Gravier, comte de, 36, 209-12, 215-17
Versailles, 32, 36, 40, 72, 78, 80, 82, 88, 90, 207-11, 215, 219-20, 340n103
Viard, Marguerite, 112
Villejoint, Gabriel Rousseau, sieur de, 91, 269n49
Virginia, xix, 4, 6, 8, 25, 211-12, 214

W

Warren, Richard, Baron de, 58-63, 73, 157, 165, 230, 281n34
Winzerling, Oscar, 11, 160

Y

Yarmouth, Nova Scotia, Canada, 257 n18

Z

Zerby, Eugène, 141, 189